KT-225-827

MasterCard
The Future of Money

Published by
Johansens, 175-179 St John Street, London EC1V 4RP
Tel: 0171-490 3090 Fax: 0171-490 2538
Find Johansens on the Internet at: http://www.johansen.com

Editor:	Rodney Exton
Publisher:	Jolyon Harris
European Executive Inspectorate:	Sarah Berry Stephanie Court Charlotte Evans Carol Blench Pierre–Jérôme Degy Anne-Sourice Garrett
Production Manager:	Daniel Barnett
Production Controller:	Kevin Bradbrook
Designer:	Michael Tompsett
Map Illustrations:	Linda Clark
Copywriter:	Sally Sutton
Style Editor:	Sarah Tucker
Sales and Marketing Manager:	Laurent Martinez
Marketing Executive:	Samantha Lhoas
Sales Executive:	Babita Sareen
P.A. to Managing Director:	Angela Franks
Managing Director:	Andrew Warren

Johansens is a member company of Harmsworth Publishing Ltd,
a subsidiary of the Daily Mail & General Trust plc

ISBN 1 86017 504X

Printed in England by St Ives plc
Colour origination by Graphic Facilities

Distributed in the UK and Europe by Johnsons International Media Services Ltd, London (direct sales) & Biblios PDS Ltd, West Sussex (bookstores). In North America by general sales agent: ETL Group, New York, NY (direct sales) and The Cimino Publishing Group, INC. New York (bookstores). In Australia and New Zealand by Bookwise International, Findon, South Australia.

HOW TO USE THIS GUIDE

If you want to identify a Hotel whose name you already know, look for it in the indexes on page 297.

These indexes are arranged by Country.

If you want to find a Hotel in a particular area,

- Turn to the map of Europe on page 2, which will show you the Countries in which there are Johansens Recommended Hotels.
- Turn to the title page of the Country that you want, where you will find a Map. The location of each Hotel appears in red on the Map with a number corresponding to the page on which the Hotel entry is published.

The Countries and place names appear in alphabetical order throughout the guide.

Mini Listings pages 298–301: The names, locations and telephone numbers of all Johansens recommendations in the British Isles and North America are listed. A display of the Johansens guides in which these recommendations appear is on the outside back cover. Copies of these guides are obtainable direct from Johansens by calling +44 990 269397 or by using the order coupons on page 304.

The prices, in most cases, are a guide to the cost of one night's accommodation with breakfast, for two people. Prices are also shown for single occupancy. These rates are correct at the time of going to press but they should always be checked with the hotel.

CONTENTS

Cover Picture: Burghotel auf Schönburg, Germany (see page 160).

FOREWORD BY THE EDITOR

People who use Johansens guides often ask why we never say anything critical about a hotel, an inn, a country house or a business meetings venue which we recommend. The answer is easy. If we knew anything bad to say about one of our selections we would not recommend it

We visit all establishments regularly and irregularly, overtly and covertly – our professional inspectors non-stop, the rest of us ad hoc; but the many thousands of you who use our guides are really the best guardians of quality. Our recommendations must be reliable, so keep sending us those freepost Guest Surveys which you find among the back-pages of our guides. They provide our inspectors with the first hint of any fall in standards, though, as you will be glad to read, the majority of Guest Surveys are entirely complimentary. In 'The Caterer & Hotelkeeper' a regular columnist recently wrote that a characteristic of Johansens guests is that "they come to enjoy themselves". Keep helping us to help you do just that – to have a good time!

Rodney Exton, Editor

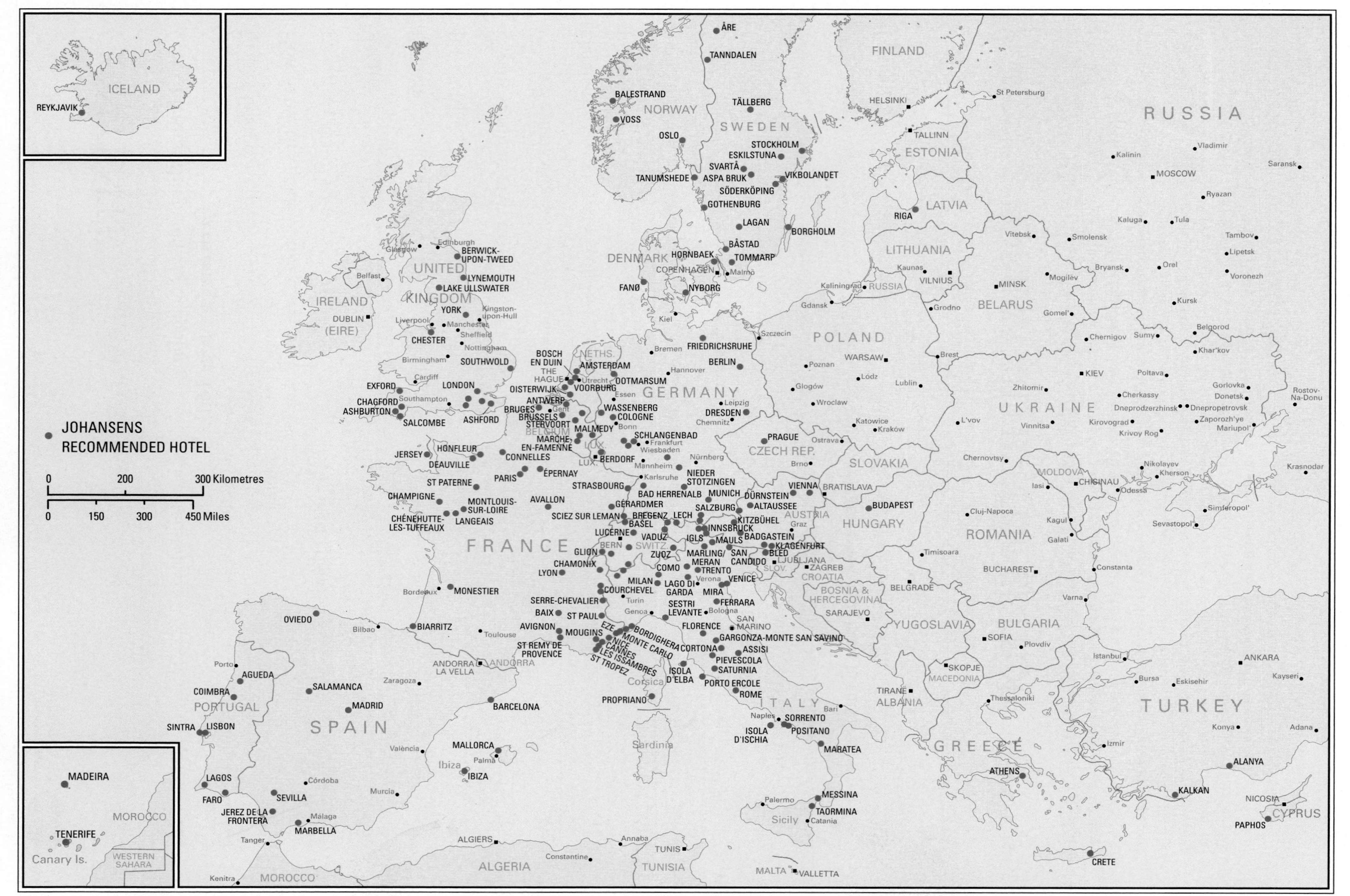

JOHANSENS RECOMMENDED HOTEL
0 200 300 Kilometres
0 150 300 450 Miles
REYKJAVIK
ICELAND
MADEIRA
TENERIFE
Canary Is.
MOROCCO
WESTERN SAHARA
IRELAND (EIRE)
DUBLIN
UNITED KINGDOM
BERWICK-UPON-TWEED
LYNEMOUTH
LAKE ULLSWATER
YORK
CHESTER
SOUTHWOLD
LONDON
ASHFORD
EXFORD
CHAGFORD
ASHBURTON
SALCOMBE
JERSEY
HONFLEUR
DEAUVILLE
ST PATERNE
CHAMPIGNE
CHÊNEHUTTE-LES-TUFFEAUX
MONTLOUIS-SUR-LOIRE
LANGEAIS
PARIS
CONNELLES
EPERNAY
AVALLON
FRANCE
MONESTIER
BIARRITZ
LYON
CHAMONIX
GLION
COURCHEVEL
SERRE-CHEVALIER
BAIX
ST PAUL
AVIGNON
MOUGINS
ST REMY DE PROVENCE
EZE
NICE
CANNES
LES ISSAMBRES
ST TROPEZ
MONTE CARLO
BORDIGHERA
PROPRIANO
Corsica
SPAIN
OVIEDO
SALAMANCA
MADRID
BARCELONA
MALLORCA
IBIZA
SEVILLA
MARBELLA
JEREZ DE LA FRONTERA
PORTUGAL
AGUEDA
COIMBRA
SINTRA
LISBON
LAGOS
FARO
ALGERIA
TUNISIA
BRUGES
BRUSSELS
ANTWERP
OISTERWIJK
BOSCH EN DUIN
THE HAGUE
AMSTERDAM
VOORBURG
STERVOORT
MARCHE-EN-FAMENNE
MALMEDY
BERDORF
WASSENBERG
COLOGNE
OOTMARSUM
SCHLANGENBAD
STRASBOURG
GERARDMER
BAD HERRENALB
GERMANY
FRIEDRICHSRUHE
BERLIN
DRESDEN
NIEDER STOTZINGEN
MUNICH
SALZBURG
LUCERNE
BASEL
SCIEZ SUR LEMAN
VADUZ
ZUOZ
BREGENZ
LECH
IGLS
INNSBRUCK
MAULS
KITZBÜHEL
BADGASTEIN
ALTAUSSEE
DÜRNSTEIN
VIENNA
KLAGENFURT
BLED
MARLING/MERAN
SAN CANDIDO
MILAN
COMO
LAGO DI GARDA
VENICE
TRENTO
MIRA
FERRARA
SESTRI LEVANTE
FLORENCE
CORTONA
GARGONZA-MONTE SAN SAVINO
ASSISI
ISOLA D'ELBA
PIEVESCOLA
SATURNIA
PORTO ERCOLE
ROME
ISOLA D'ISCHIA
SORRENTO
POSITANO
MARATEA
ITALY
TAORMINA
MESSINA
VALLETTA
PRAGUE
CZECH REP.
AUSTRIA
HUNGARY
BUDAPEST
SLOVAKIA
POLAND
WARSAW
DENMARK
FANØ
NYBORG
HORNBAEK
COPENHAGEN
NORWAY
OSLO
VOSS
BALESTRAND
SWEDEN
TANUMSHEDE
ASPA BRUK
SVARTÅ
ESKILSTUNA
GOTHENBURG
SÖDERKÖPING
BÅSTAD
TOMMARP
LAGAN
BORGHOLM
VIKBOLANDET
STOCKHOLM
TÄLLBERG
TANNDALEN
ÅRE
FINLAND
ESTONIA
LATVIA
RIGA
LITHUANIA
BELARUS
UKRAINE
RUSSIA
MOSCOW
ROMANIA
BULGARIA
YUGOSLAVIA
CROATIA
BOSNIA & HERCEGOVINA
ALBANIA
GREECE
ATHENS
CRETE
TURKEY
KALKAN
ALANYA
PAPHOS
CYPRUS

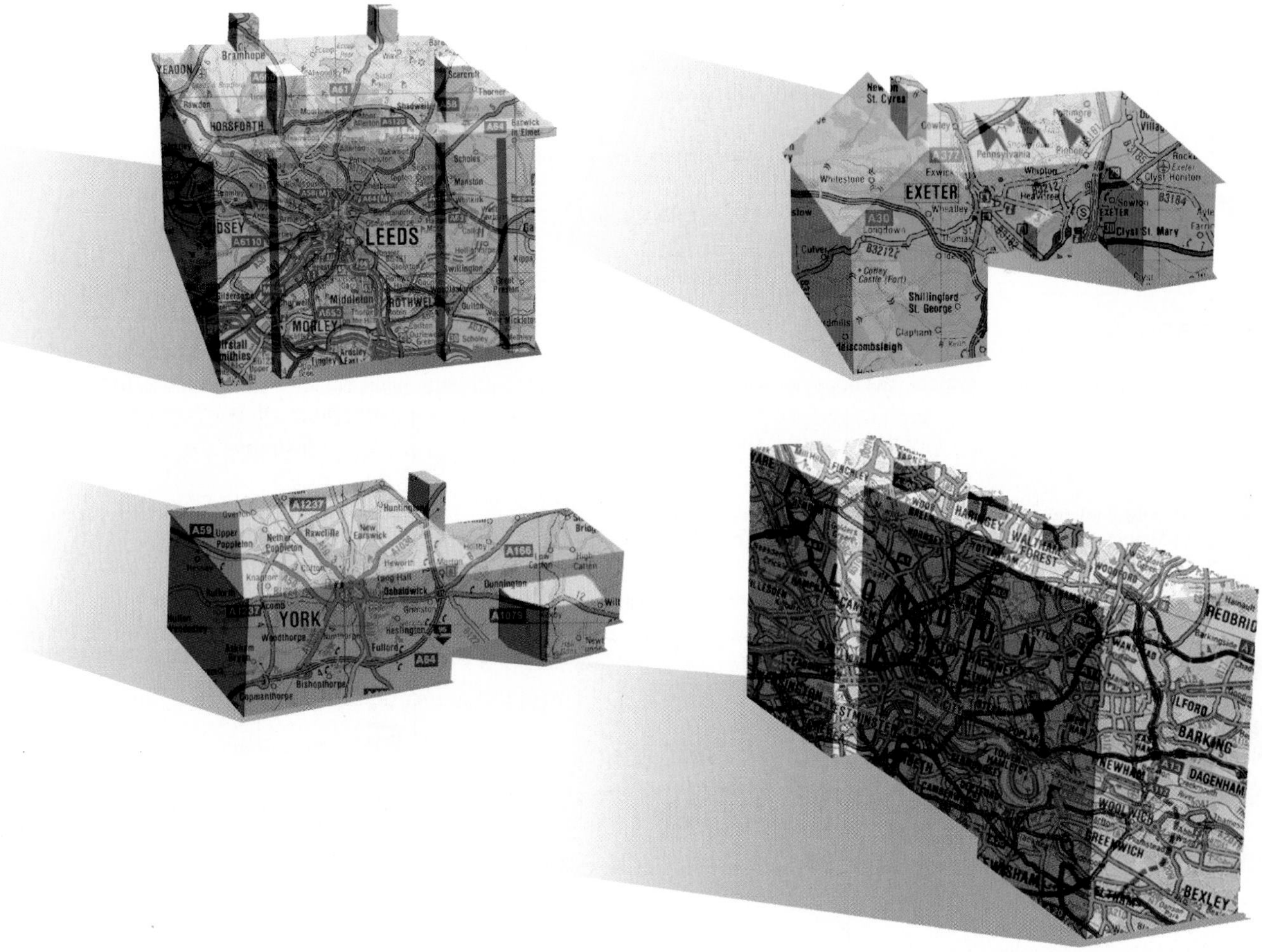

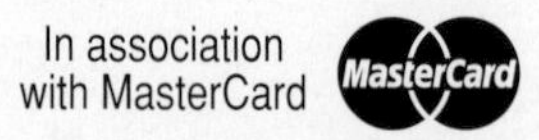

KEY TO SYMBOLS

Total number of rooms	Nombre de chambres	Anzahl der Zimmer
MasterCard accepted	MasterCard accepté	MasterCard akzeptiert
EuroCard accepted	EuroCard accepté	EuroCard akzeptiert
Visa accepted	Visa accepté	Visa akzeptiert
American Express accepted	American Express accepté	American Express akzeptiert
Diners Club accepted	Diners Club accepté	Diners Club akzeptiert
Quiet location	Un lieu tranquille	Ruhige Lage
Access for wheelchairs to at least one	Accès handicapé	Zugang für Behinderte

(The 'Access for wheelchairs' symbol (♿) does not necessarily indicate that the property fulfils National Accessible Scheme grading)

Chef-patron	Chef-patron	Chef-patron
Meeting/conference facilities with maximum number of delegates	Salle de conférences – capacité maximale	Konferenzraum-Höchstkapazität
Children welcome, with minimum age where applicable	Enfants bienvenus	Kinder willkommen
Dogs accommodated in rooms or kennels	Chiens autorisés	Hunde erlaubt
At least one room has a four-poster bed	Lit à baldaquin	Himmelbett
Cable/satellite TV in all bedrooms	TV câblée/satellite dans les chambres	Satellit-und Kabelfernsehen in allen Zimmern
Direct-dial telephone in all bedrooms	Téléphone dans les chambres	Telefon in allen Zimmern
No-smoking rooms (at least one no-smoking bedroom)	Chambres non-fumeurs	Zimmer für Nichtraucher
Lift available for guests' use	Ascenseur	Fahrstuhl
Air Conditioning	Climatisée	Klimatisiert
Indoor swimming pool	Piscine couverte	Hallenbad
Outdoor swimming pool	Piscine de plein air	Freibad
Tennis court at hotel	Tennis à l'hôtel	Hoteleigener Tennisplatz
Croquet lawn at hotel	Croquet à l'hôtel	Krocketrasen
Fishing can be arranged	Pêche	Angeln
Golf course on site or nearby, which has an arrangement with hotel allowing guests to play	Golf	Golfplatz
Shooting can be arranged	Chasse	Jagd
Riding can be arranged	Équitation	Reitpferd
Hotel has a helicopter landing pad	Piste pour hélicoptère	Hubschrauberlandplatz
Licensed for wedding ceremonies	Cérémonies de noces	Konzession für Eheschliessungen

BRUT IMPÉRIAL
MOËT & CHANDON
Turning nature into art
MOËT & CH

Austria

You will notice an awe inspiring grace in the rural and urban landscapes of Austria. The countryside is consistently dramatic and spectacular. The major cities overwhelm the visitor with grandeur. A walk through their streets transcends into a walk through centuries chronicling the lives of those who have shaped the world of the arts – nowhere more emphatically than in Vienna.

This city for all seasons galvanises the visitor with its history. This capital of capitals is one of the few which during the coldest and most forbidding of winters, glows brightest through the grey. The imposing Baroque and Gothic architecture compete

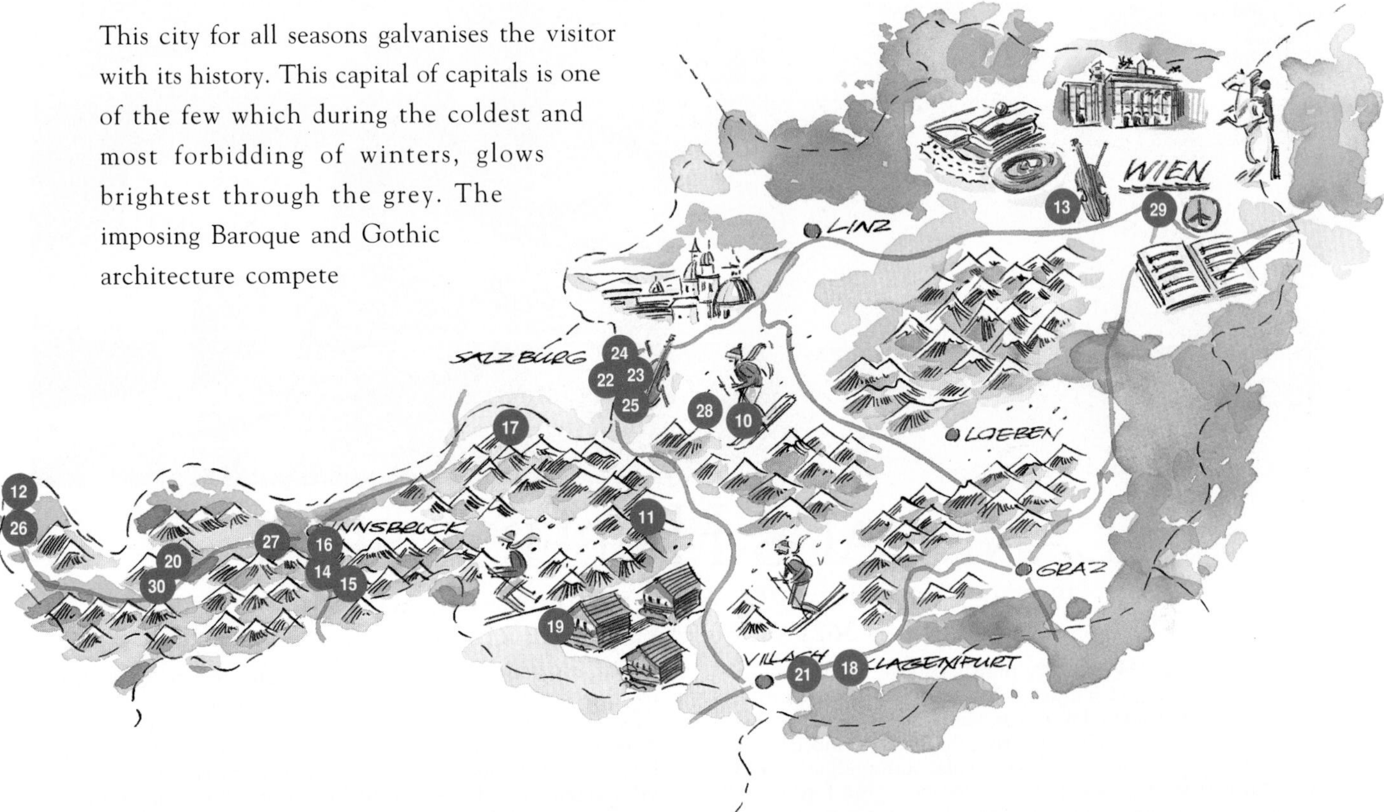

with the ornate Summer Palaces for your attention. Go to the enchanting Lippizaner Riding School where snorting, glistening stallions leap through the air as though suspended by some invisible wire – inspired by the waltz and the magnificent chandeliers which hang high above their heads. . Visit the Belvedere Galleries where huge picture windows allow views stretching out to graceful ornate gardens.

A disciplined mind and strong pair of shoes are pre-requisites to a successful tour of a city in love with its past. Inspiration for Haydn, Mozart, Beethoven, Schubert, Brahms, Strauss, Mahler – you hear their music playing from every restaurant, supermarket, corner and ubiquitous coffee shop.

Small, but perfectly formed – the old centre of Salzburg overflows with antiquity – from remnants of the Roman city, Juvavum, to the churches, palaces and squares constructed during Salzburg's thousand years under the powerful prince-archbishops. Towering over the city is the medieval fortress, symbol of the power politics and religion which ruled the town. The sound of music shapes this city – in the churches, palaces, castles and concert halls.

At every season of the year there are beautiful sights everywhere in Austria: flowers in summer, snow in winter. Cities, rivers, mountains, lakes. Austria has everything.

LANDHAUS HUBERTUSHOF

PUCHEN 86 – 8992 ALTAUSSEE, STEIERMARK, AUSTRIA
TEL: 43 3622 71280 FAX: 43 3622 71280 80

This enchanting 19th century hunting lodge has a wonderful display of authentic memorabilia of the chase. Countess Strasoldo has transformed it into an elite hotel, welcoming guests into her private home. The attractive chalet-style Hubertshof has its own verdant parkland, and spectacular surrounding scenery – mountains, the Altaussee, the village and pine forests. It is wonderfully peaceful, a sanctuary from the fast stream of city life. Pine panelling, a carved staircase and rustic furniture. colourful rugs and wooden floors enhance the idyllic country life ambience. There is also an exquisite south-facing suite. Guests awake to spectacular views of the lake and mountains. The Countess prepares breakfast herself, and this is enjoyed in the morning room or on the sunny terrace. No other meals are offered, but there are many local inns and restaurants serving delicious dinners, beers and local wines. Altaussee is a cultural centre, home of artists and literary cognoscenti. It also offers sporting visitors tennis, golf, hiking, climbing, trout fishing and boat trips in summer, and skiing in winter. It is convenient for the Salzburg Festival and the thermal spas nearby. Directions: A1, exit Gmunden. Follow directions to Bad Ischl, then Bad Aussee. At Altaussee, take second left and watch for signs to the Landhaus. Price guide: Double/twin550–650öS; suite700–850öS.

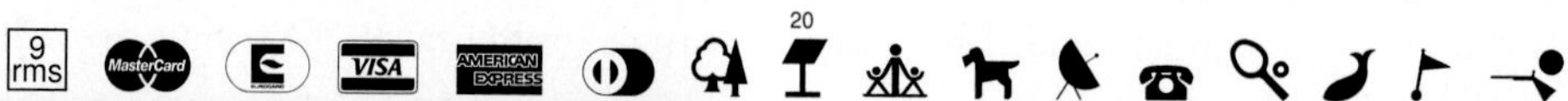

HOTEL & SPA HAUS HIRT

KAISERHOFSTRASSE 14, BAD GASTEIN, AUSTRIA
TEL: 43 64 34 27 97 FAX: 43 64 34 27 97 48

The Haus Hirt is ten minutes walk from the centre of the spa resort of Bad Gastein. It is in a lovely park, one of the sunniest places in the area, peaceful and verdant, with breathtaking views over the Gastein valley to the mountains. There are pleasant rooms in which to relax, and a superb terrace frequented by sunbathers. Al fresco eating is also encouraged and many of the delightful bedrooms have balconies. A whole floor is dedicated to building up health and reducing stress. Guests indulge themselves with thermal cures, mud-baths, hydrotherapy, aromatherapy, sauna and steam bath, massage, the solarium and beauty salon with Maria Galland Cosmetics. The energetic take exercise classes or dive into the large, scenic indoor pool. The versatile restaurant, with attractive rustic furniture and overlooking the valley, prepares delicious, imaginative meals, both for those who are hungry and those on special diets. Fine wine is listed, and there is a cocktail party once a week. The hotel is well situated for first-class skiing, with many lifts and cablecars, and spectacular pistes. Après-ski includes a visit to the Casino. In summer, golf and riding are popular. **Directions:** From Salzburg, exit at Bischofshofen to Schwarzach and the Gastein Valley. On reaching the town centre, follow the Kaiserhofstrasse to the Haus Hirt. Price guide: Single öS490–1040; double/twin öS990–2780.

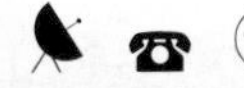

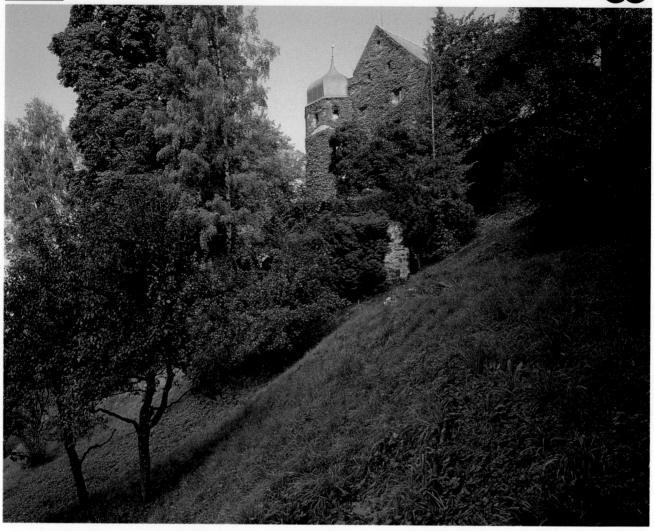

DEURING SCHLÖSSLE

EHRE-GUTA-PLATZ 4, A-6900 BREGENZ, AUSTRIA
TEL: 43 55 74 47800 FAX: 43 55 74 47800-80 E-MAIL: DEURING@SCHLOESSLE.VOL.AT

Covered in Virginia creeper, with its onion domed tower, this spectacular hotel is high on a hill above the Bodensee, Lake Constance, surrounded by a beautiful park full of flowers. The interior of the 'little castle' is magnificent, the salons filled with exquisite inlaid 18th century furniture. Brilliant rugs cover the polished floors and the lighting is discreet. The Armoury houses a superb collection of swords and sabres. The delightful bedrooms overlook either the Bodensee or Bregenz, while the opulent suites in the octagonal tower have views in all directions. The pride of this hotel is its restaurant and its wine cellar. Panelled walls, candle-light and graceful furniture are the setting for delectable meals. Fish from the lake, game from the hills, mushrooms from the forests, fruits from the gardens and other delicacies are presented in great style and Bernadette, the sommelier, advises on the selection of the best of French and Austrian wines. There is a marvellous timbered hall which is ideal for seminars and private functions. Concerts take place here occasionally. Sailing on the lake, relaxing in the hotel grounds, enjoying music festivals or feasting during one of the gourmet weekends are pleasant occupations. **Directions:** Leave A14 Bregenz exit, take Bahnhof Strasse, Kirchstrasse, then Thalbach Strasse towards the Old City. Price guide: Single ATS1100–1470; double/twin ATS1800–2540; suites ATS2800–3850

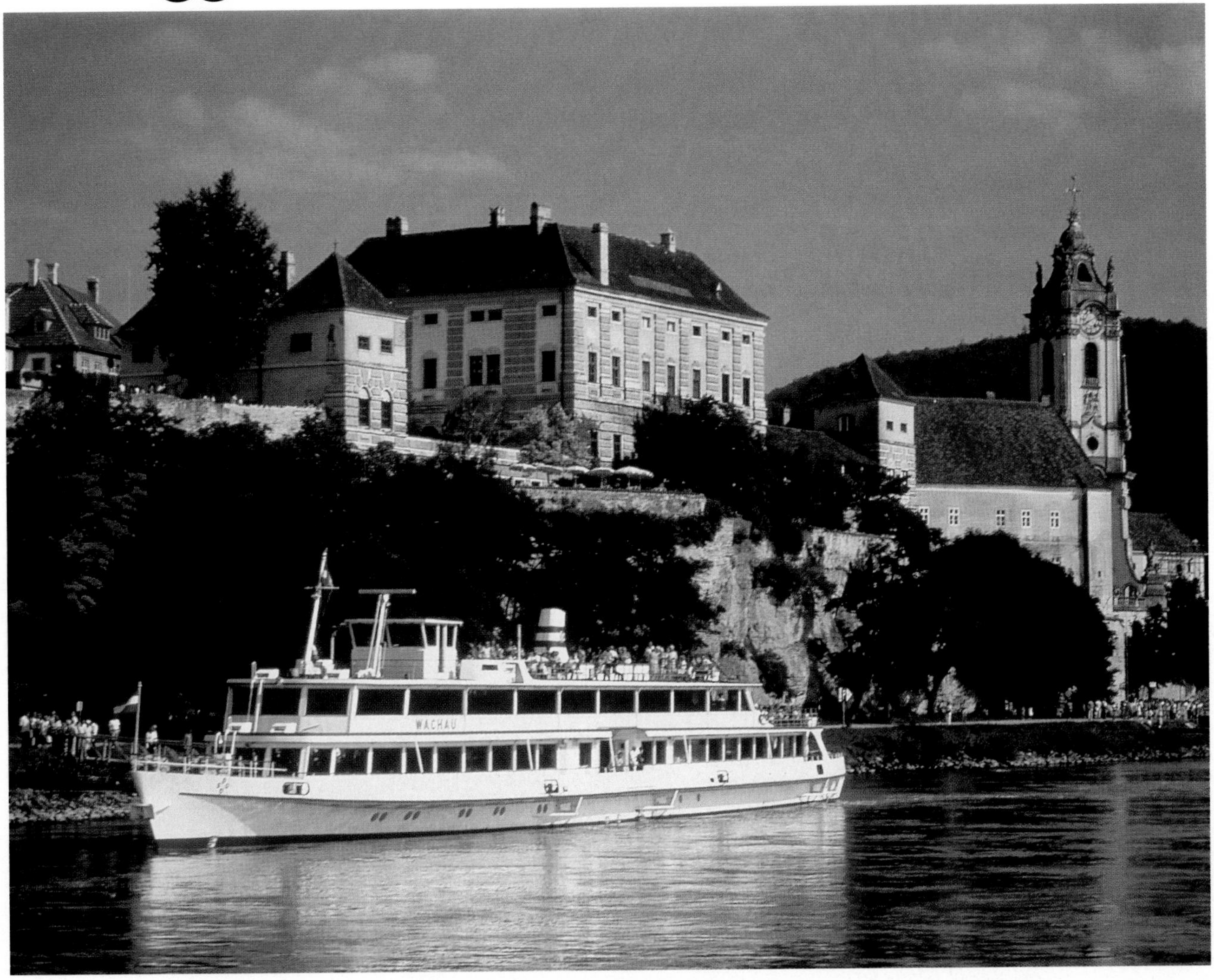

HOTEL SCHLOSS DÜRNSTEIN

3601 DÜRNSTEIN, AUSTRIA
TEL: 43 2711 212 FAX: 43 2711 351

A fairytale castle built for royalty in the 17th century, standing on the banks of the Danube, today an exclusive hotel. It has an enviable position, with the river to the fore and the verdant Wachau Valley in the background. The guest rooms all differ yet are equally charming, reflecting the history of the castle through the Baroque, Biedermeier and Empire periods. The furnishings are magnificent, with elaborate drapes, and the bathrooms opulent. The salons are filled with antiques. The impeccable staff will bring superb coffee and irresistible Austrian patisseries. The intimate bar is an ideal rendezvous before entering the grand dining room with its lofty arches. The menu recommends regional and international dishes and the wine list includes a wide choice of wines, among them superb dessert wines. In summer meals are served on the enchanting Danube Terrace. There are two pools, one in the flower-filled patio and the other indoors, part of the fitness centre. Tennis and golf are nearby, the hotel has bikes for exploring the Wachau valley, while the Danube offers waterskiing, fishing and boat trips. Vienna is just 1 hour away, with its galleries and concerts. **Directions:** A1 from Vienna, exit Melk, cross the Danube taking Road A3 towards Krems, following the Danube to Dürnstein. Price guide: Single öS1650–1850; double/twin öS1950–2100; suites öS2200.

SCHLOSSHOTEL IGLS

VILLER STEIG 2, A-6080 IGLS, TIROL, AUSTRIA
TEL: 43 512 37 72 17 FAX: 43 512 37 86 79 E-MAIL: schlosshotel.igls@tyrol.at

Igls, on a sunny terrace above Innsbruck, is the beautiful tree-lined site for the Schlosshotel, an enchanting Tyrolean castle with turrets and spires. Glistening white with snow in the winter, in summer the hotel parkland becomes flower-filled gardens leading out to brilliant green pastures. The Schloss has deserved its award of five stars. The interior of the hotel is exquisite, with the most lovely festooned curtains and co-ordinating wallpapers, graceful period furniture, clever use of colour and discreet lighting. The bedrooms and suites are charming, with views across the countryside to the Patscherkofel Mountains. The spacious reception area is welcoming and the bar, with its baroque fireplace, very convivial. Guests linger in the elegant dining room, appreciating the fine food and wines served by attentive staff. The hotel has an indoor/outdoor swimming pool, steam room, saunas and solarium. Skiing is for Olympians, families, beginners and those who enjoy cross-country. Bobsleigh, skating and curling are alternative winter sports. In summer, tennis, walking in the 'old park' and golf on nearby courses are the principal activities. Nearby Innsbruck has theatres, concerts, exhibitions and museums. Internet: http://www.schlosshotel .igls.tyrol.at**Directions:** Leave Innsbruck on the Inntal highway, following signs to Igls. Price guide: Single öS1,850–2,350; Double/twin öS3,400–öS4,400; suites öS4,000–öS5,000.

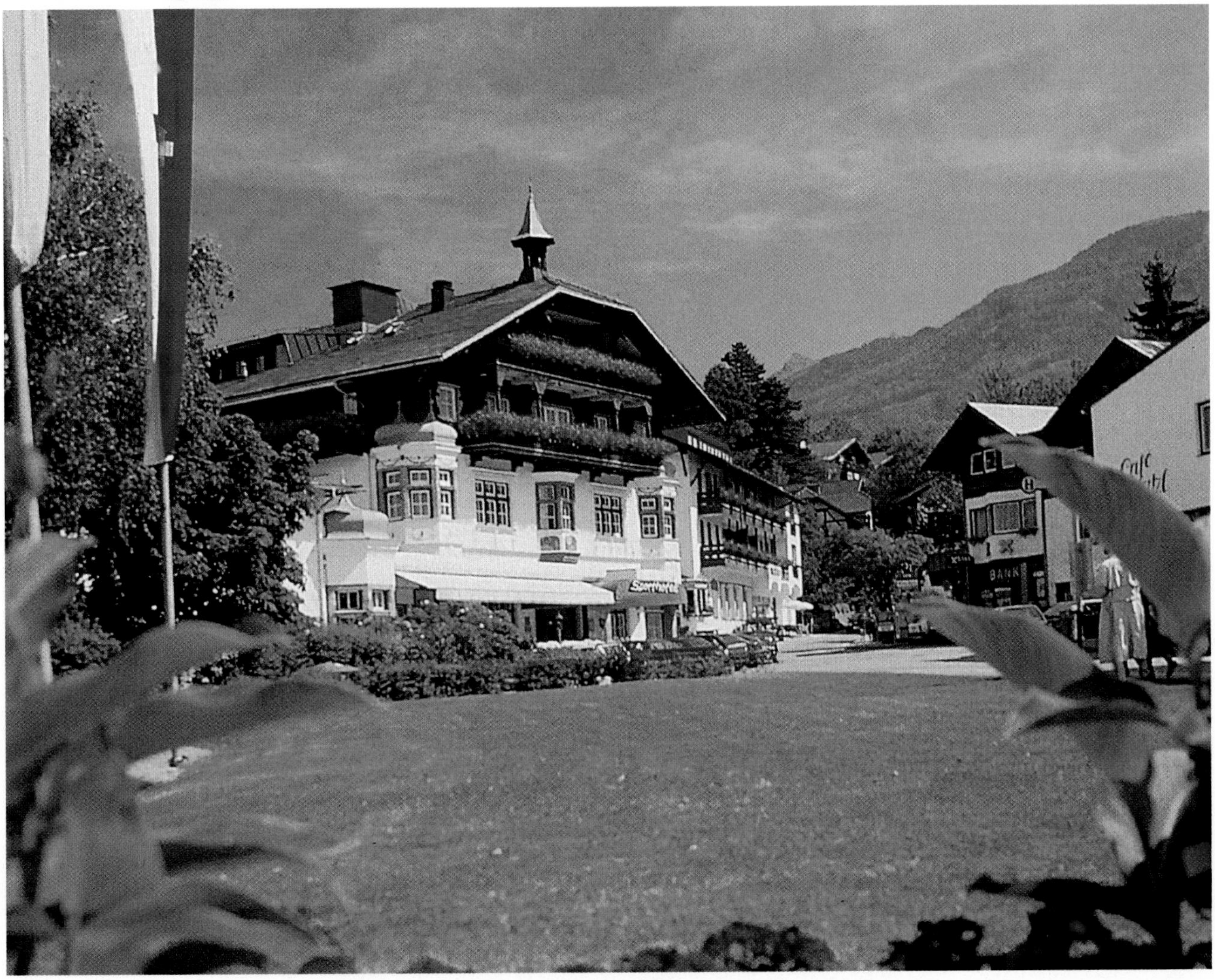

SPORTHOTEL IGLS

HILBERSTRASSE 17, A-6080 IGLS, TIROL, AUSTRIA

TEL: 43 512 37 72 41 FAX:43 512 37 86 79 E-MAIL: sporthotel.igls@tyrol.at

In Igls, on its sunny terrace above Innsbruck, stands this élite chalet-style hotel offering traditional Austrian hospitalilty all the year – in winter when Igls is a premier ski resort and in summer when visitors enjoy the many sporting activities and walking through the scenic countryside. It is also an exceptional venue for conferences. Fine pieces of Austrian period furniture can be found in the hall and the spacious elegant salon. The bedrooms, suites and apartments are very comfortable. Guests relax in the winter garden, take apéritifs in the lounge or join friends in the Tyrolean dance-bar. Dinner is by candelight in the handsome restaurant, a feast of new Austrian cuisine which has won many awards. Marvellous buffets appear for occasions and conference guests enjoy superb banquets in the private dining hall. The excellent wine list is cosmopolitan. The leisure centre is magnificent – a large indoor/outdoor pool with a poolside bar, saunas, solariums, gymnasium, whirl-pools and a beauty parlour. Winter sports include skiing, skating, curling and tobogganing. In summer guests play golf, tennis and bowls, explore the countryside on bikes or on foot and climb the mountains. Innsbruck offers theatres, music, and museums. **Directions:** Leaving Innsbruck on the Inntal highway, follow signs to Igls. Price guide: Single öS1,000–öS1,350; double/twin öS1,740–2,400; suites öS2,480–3,160.

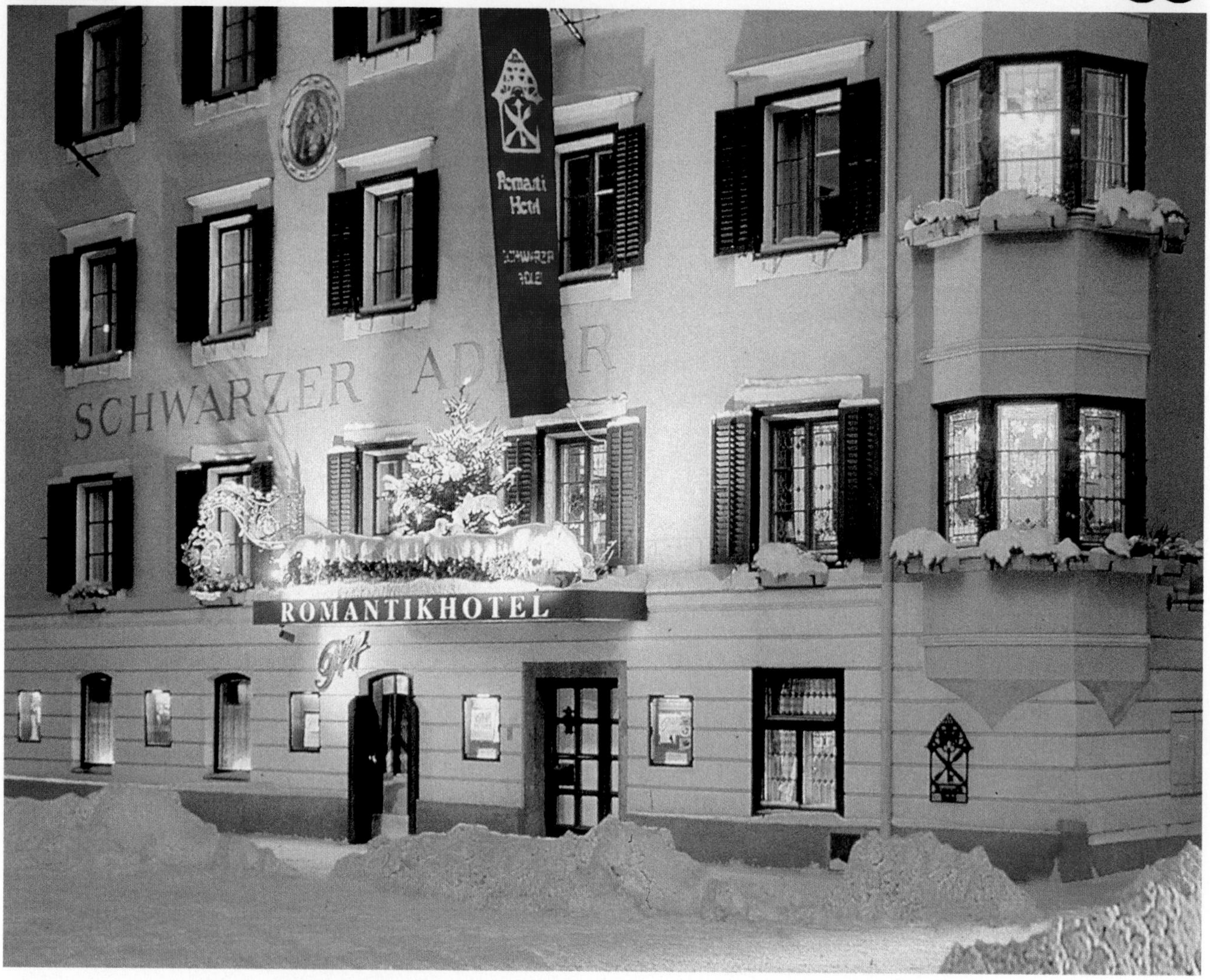

ROMANTIK HOTEL SCHWARZER ADLER

KAISERJÄGERSTRASSE 2, 6020 INNSBRUCK, AUSTRIA
TEL: 43 512 58 71 09 FAX: 43 512 56 16 97

Surrounded by lofty mountains and over 1000 years old, Innsbruck is one of the most fascinating places in Austria, and close to the romantic Old Town is the successful Hotel Schwarzer Adler, which has been in the hands of the Ultsch family for four generations. Careful modernisation of the 16th century building has preserved its Tyrolean charm, and the panelled walls, beamed ceilings and staff in national dress enchance the atmosphere. The bedrooms, decorated in soft relaxing colours, have simple period furniture from the region, and many have balconies. The bar is very convivial, open to the locals. In fine weather drinks are served in the courtyard. Diners choose between two restaurants, one elegant with a sophisticated menu, the other rustic, offering succulent local specialities. Fine wines are listed. Breakfast is a fabulous buffet. This is a popular base for winter sports enthusiasts, in summer walkers enjoy the countryside, maybe visiting the Alpine Zoo. Those exploring the town will find many historic buildings and museums. Nightlife includes theatres, clubs and the casino. **Directions:** From Salzburg leave A12 at Innsbruck Ost exit. Follow signs to the main station, turn left into Museumstrasse then right into Sillgasse, finding the hotel on the right. Price guide: Single öS900–1250; double/twin öS1600–2300; suites öS2700–2900.

25 rms

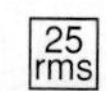

120

ROMANTIK HOTEL TENNERHOF

6370 KITZBÜHEL, GRIESENAUWEG 26, AUSTRIA
TEL: 43 5356 6 3181 FAX: 43 5356 6 318170

Once a farmhouse, now a first-class hotel, the Tennerhof is a most attractive chalet-style building, with flower bedecked balconies, standing in beautifully kept grounds – snow-covered in winter and much enjoyed by summer guests. The reception rooms are charming, the spacious lounge with its elegant furnishings and the more traditional stone-floored sitting-room with its fireplace. Bridge players have their own corner and there is a smart, well-stocked bar. The bedrooms, many with panelled walls, beamed ceilings and traditonal painted furniture include highly romantic suites. There are two restaurants, one slightly more formal where jackets are requested, and a popular terrace for alfresco dining. The chefs prepare gourmet international specialities, using home-grown vegetables. Well-chosen wines are listed. Other facilities within the hotel are a well-equipped conference room, and a leisure complex with a palatial pool surrounded by plants and spectacular murals, a sauna and steam-room. A second, outdoor pool is a focal point in summer. In winter Kitzbühel is a famous ski-resort, and when the snows go there are three golf courses. The hotel also arranges excursions with wonderful picnics. **Directions:** Take A12 from Innsbruck, exit at Wörgl, take the B312, then B161 to Kitzbühel. Price guide: öS1470–öS2190; double/twin öS2290–öS4160; suites öS2860–öS6480.

42 rms         40     

HOTEL PALAIS PORCIA

NEUER PLATZ 13, 9020 KLAGENFURT, AUSTRIA
TEL: 43 463 51 15 90 FAX: 43 463 51 15 90 30

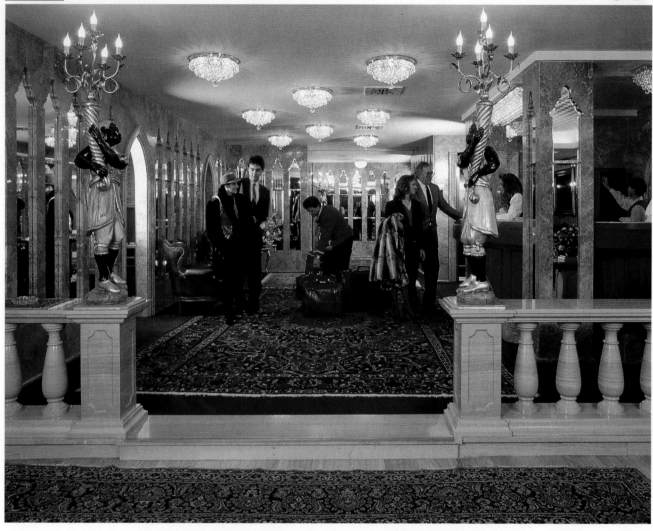

A unique townhouse in the very heart of Klagenfurt, Hotel Palais Porcia has great style. Immediately on entering the hotel, guests are aware they have come to somewhere very special, far from the ultra-modern large hotels of the 20th century. The house was built in the 17th century and has been decorated appropriately. The reception area is glamorous, with its marble, mirrors and blackamoor lamps. The salon, which has the bar at one end, is very handsome, with wonderful big period chairs, magnificent wall-covering and rich Persian rugs. A superb meeting place! The guest rooms are stunning, the furnishings baroque and the colour schemes glorious. The beds are ornately carved - they are also extremely comfortable. The opulent marble bathrooms, by contrast, are modern in design. The hotel has no restaurant, but it has a magnificent breakfastroom, again with mirrors used to great effect. The walls are hung in red and gold, the chairs elegant, and there is fine porcelain on the table. In summer residents appreciate the hotel's private beach on the Wörthersee. Golf is 20 kms distant, tennis closeby. The museums and castle are fascinating and there is a vibrant nightlife in the town. **Directions:** From A2 take Viktringer Ring, turning left into Oktoberstrasse, finding the hotel on the Neuer Platz. Valet car-parking is available. Price guide: Single öS950; double/twin öS1,350–öS4,800; suites öS2,500–öS4,800.

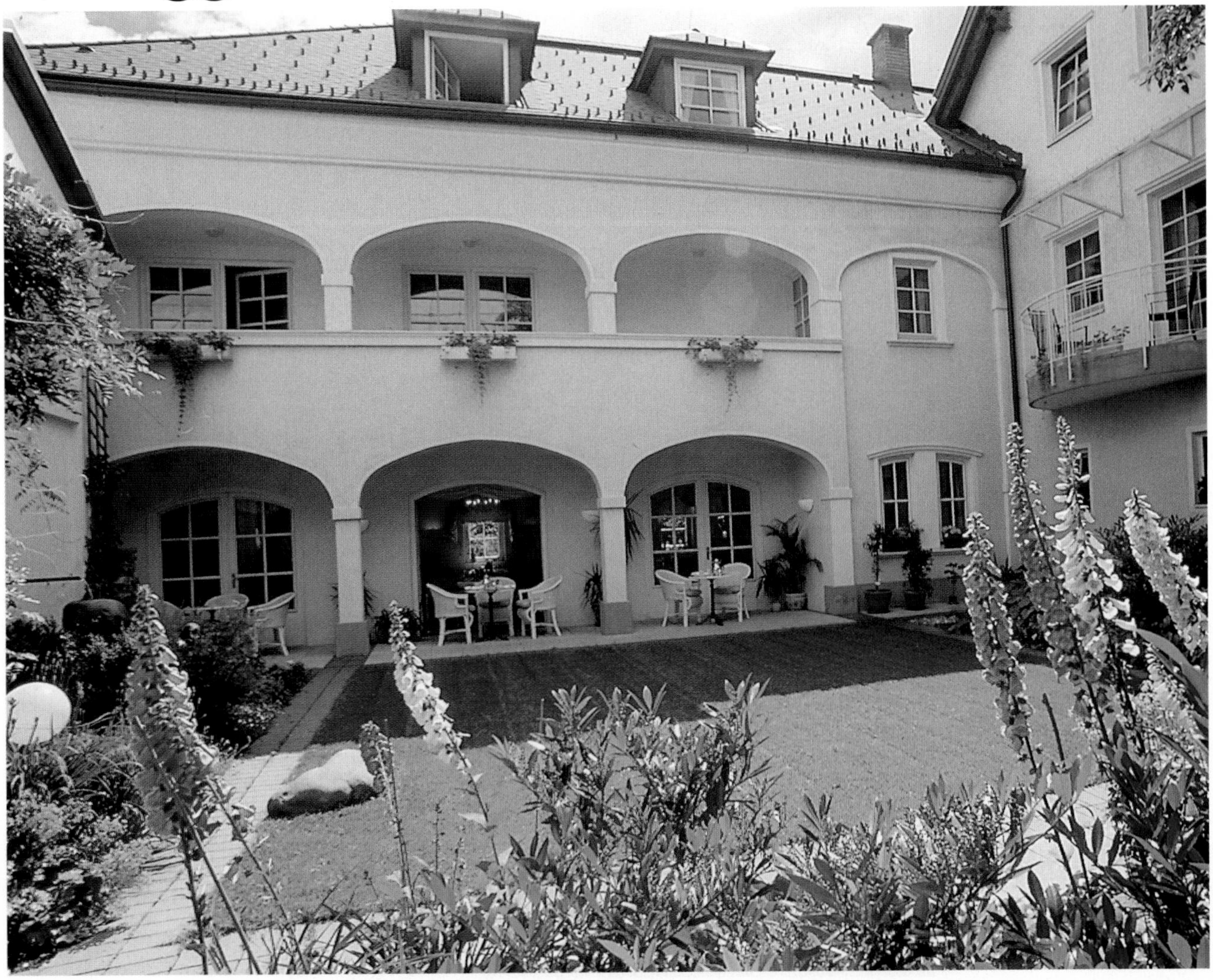

LANDHAUS KELLERWAND

MAUTHEN 24, 9640 KÖTSCHACH – MAUTHEN, AUSTRIA
TEL: 43 4715 269 / 378 FAX: 43 4715 37816

To visit here is to stay in the private home of Sissy Sonnleitner, one of Austria's most famous chefs, such is the ambience of the Landhaus Kellerwand – a restaurant where connoisseurs of fine food and good wines may reside in great comfort! The hotel's architecture is typical of the neighbourhood, with its little turret, tall windows and colourful windowboxes. There are pleasant gardens behind the house. The drawing room is delightful, big chairs covered in rose chintz, where guests relax by the fireside, with a drink and canapés, perhaps listening to the piano. The apartments and suites are luxurious, with whirlpool baths and separate living rooms, and the bedrooms are charming, with their rustic furnishings. There is also a fitness room and spa with its own waterfall! The pièce de résistance is the restaurant, an elegant and sophisticated setting for the magnificent dishes prepared by Sissy, accompanied by superb wines. On warm days visitors enjoy aperitifs on the terrace. The hotel offers several special packages – one includes Cookery Seminars; others are for golfers, wild flower and nature lovers or include the local cheese festsival and Advent ceremonies. Directions: A10 motorway, following signs to Seeboden, then take E66 at Oberdrauburg and follow signs to Kötschach-Mauthen. Price guide: Single öS735–öS890; double/twin öS850–öS1005; suites öS1000–öS1155.

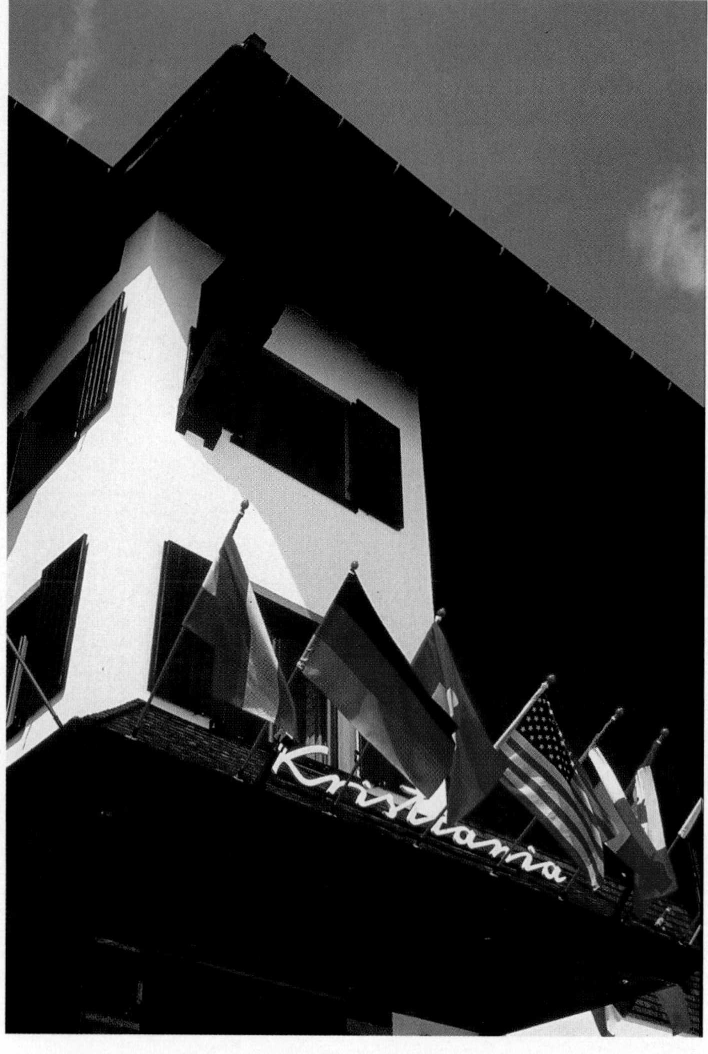

SPORTHOTEL KRISTIANIA

OMESBERG 331, 6764 LECH AM ARLBERG
TEL: 43 5583 25 610 FAX: 43 5583 3550

This enchanting chalet hotel on the outskirts of Lech is only open in the winter-sports season. It is owned by Olympic slalom champion Othmar Schneider, who has named it after the Kristiania ski turn. The surrounding scenery is magical – snowclad mountains, pine forests and the picturesque village. The Schneider family have created a warm and colourful ambience. The bedrooms are delightful, furnished with comfortable modern chairs, fine old rugs and local antiques. Some have balconies opening onto spectacular views. All amenities are provided. Après-ski guests relax in the cheerful bar before indulging in delicious dishes listed in the sophisticated buffet and dinner menus, presented with appropriate wine suggestions. The restaurant is charming and part of the Schneider's fine modern art collection is exhibited on its pineclad walls. Another showpiece which fascinates visitors is the impressive display of trophies won by their host. The Kristiania is ideally situated, five minutes from the slopes, next to the cross country run. Non-skiers sunbathe on the terrace. Lech offers skating, curling, tobogganing, sleigh rides and ski kindergarten. It has a lively night life. Directions: First right after Arlberg tunnel, following signs to Lech, finding the hotel on left just before entering the village. Price guide: Single öS1450–öS2700; double/twin öS2900–öS5600; suites öS3400–öS6100.

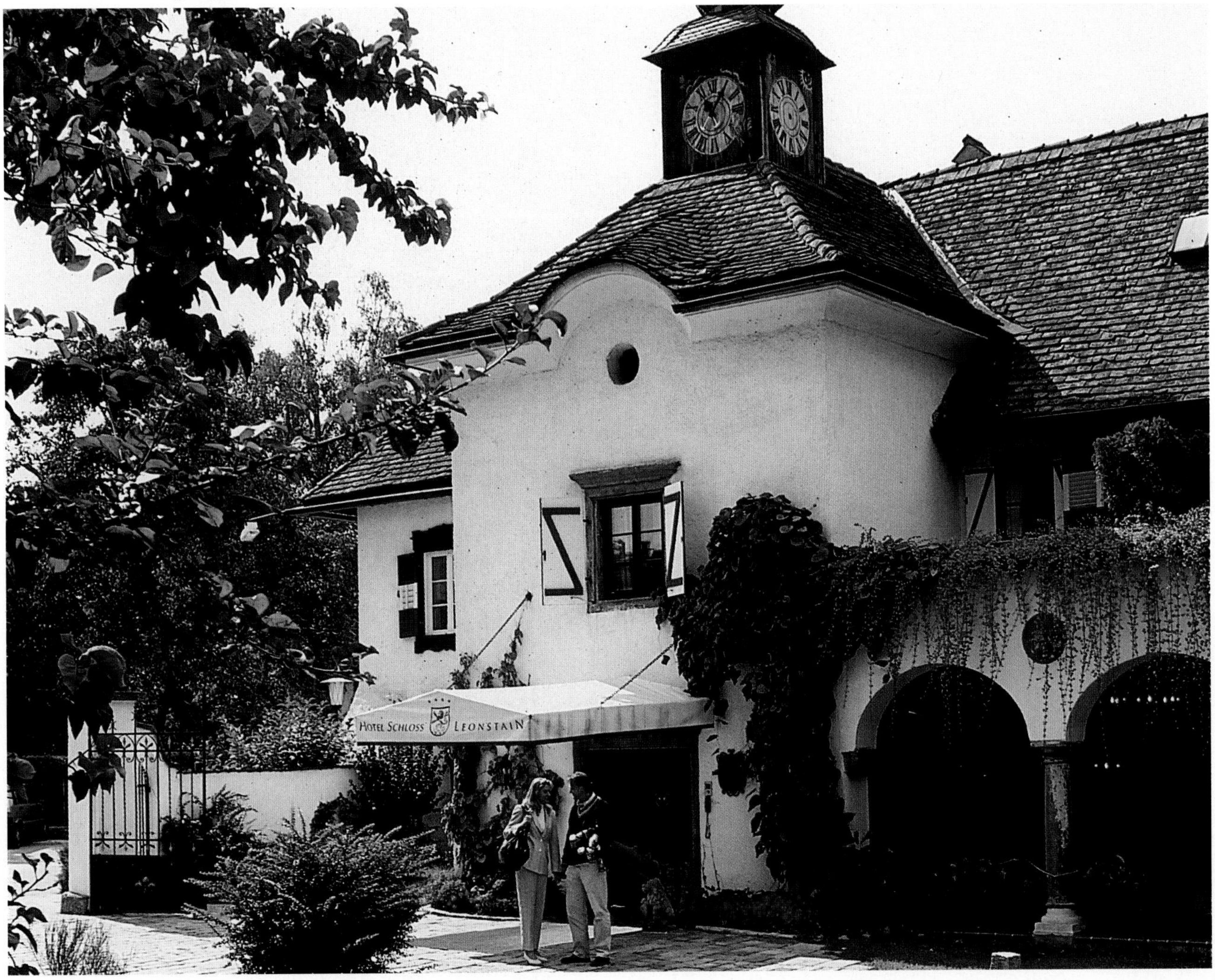

Hotel Schloss Leonstain

LEONSTEINSTR 1, PÖRTSCHACH AM WÖRTHER SEE, AUSTRIA
TEL: 43 4272 28160 FAX: 43 4272 2823

A sophisticated hotel in a 14th century castle near a sparkling lake! The charming village of Portschach is on the Wörther See, one of Austria's larger lakes, surrounded by mountains and forests. The castle has been imaginatively restored, and the focal point is the central courtyard. The gardens are pretty, with fountains, pools, statues and fine old trees. Many original features of the castle have been retained, carved doors, painted ceilings, graceful archways, tiled floors – a background for the many fine antiques. The guest rooms are pleasant, decorated in soft colours, furnished with period pieces and having all modern comforts. The spacious salons are elegant and the smart bar is well stocked. The Leonstain is proud of its kitchen, and guests feast on Austrian specialities in the splendid dining hall which opens onto the courtyard on sunny days. The Leonstain has a private beach on the lake, just minutes away, rowing boats, table tennis and children's playground. Water-sking, wind surfing, sailing, tennis and golf can be arranged. Boat trips are fun and Klagenfurt should be explored. Directions: Leave motorway between Villach and Klagenfurt at Pörtschach exit, follow signs to the lake, and on leaving town centre find the Schloss behind white walls on the right. Price guide (including breakfast and dinner, per person per day): Single öS1100–1510; double/twin öS850–1500; suites öS1250–1940.

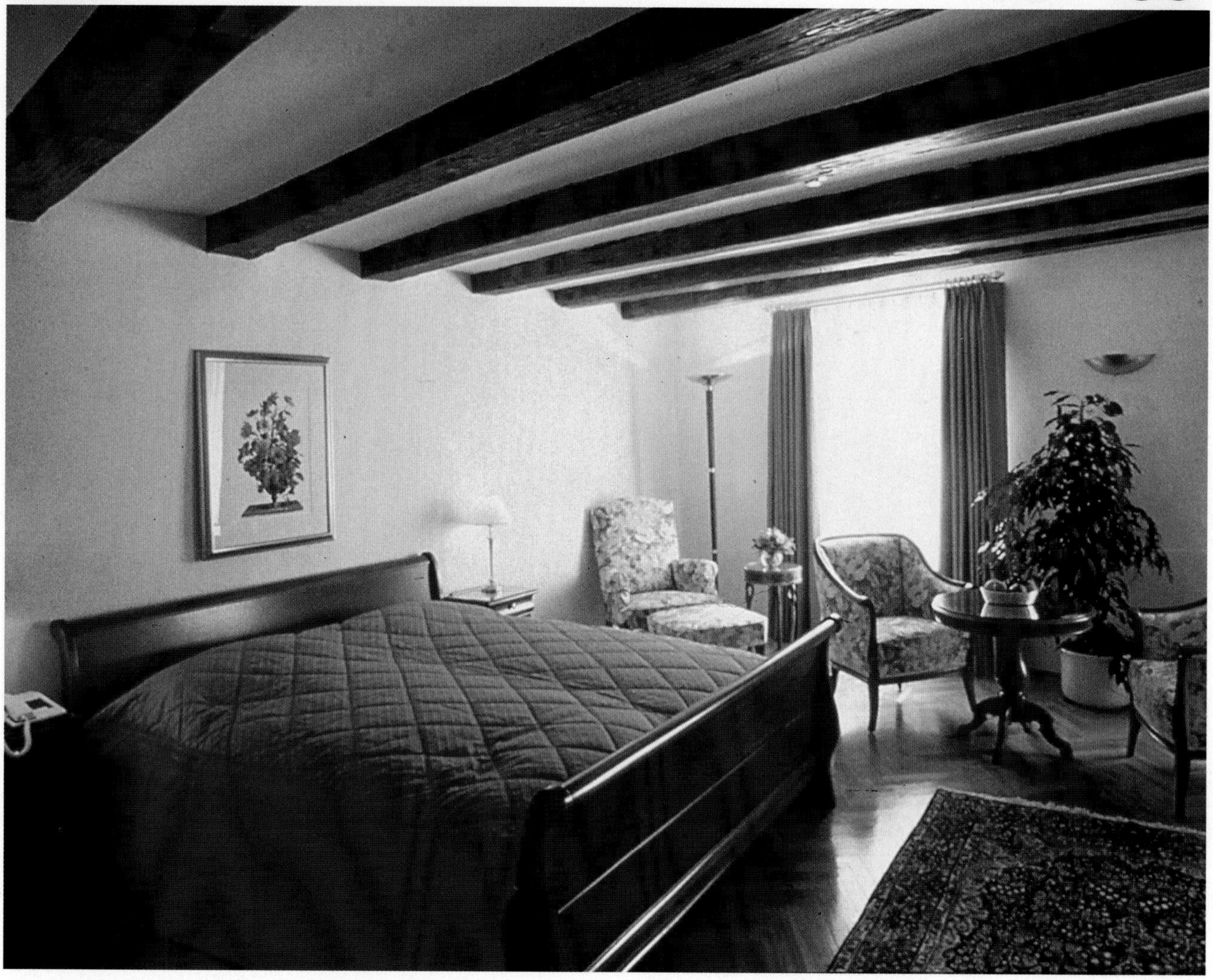

Hotel Altstadt Radisson SAS

RUDOLFSKAI 28 / JUDENGASSE 15, A-5020 SALZBURG, AUSTRIA
TEL: 43 662 84 85 71 0 FAX: 43 662 84 85 71 6

This hotel, with its graceful architecture, has a long history which can be traced back to 1377. Originally an inn, one of the oldest in historic Salzburg, it is now an elite and luxurious hotel offering immaculate and personal service. The elegant facade tells new arrivals that the Hotel Altstadt is very special; once inside, the enchanting interior rooms with low stone archways, fine antiques, and the fascinating glass atrium confirm this impression. The bedrooms are individual, some large and some small. They offer a choice of views over the Salzach River with the Kapuzner Monastery on the far bank, the Fortress or the old town. The bar is a popular rendezvous. The enchanting Restaurant Symphonie with its verandah-style wall providing a spectacular view across the river serves the finest food and wine, while special occasions in the beamed Renaissance Saal are memorable. Small conferences can also be accommodated. Salzburg, the birth place of Mozart, is famous for its music festivals. It has many places of historic interest to explore, theatres and opera. River trips are possible and leaving the city, the famous White Horse Inn on the Wolfgangsee is not too far away. **Directions:** Follow signs to the centre of Salzburg, The hotel is adjacent to the river, opposite the monastery. Garage service can be arranged. Price guide: Single öS1850–öS3900; double/twin öS2700–öS6500; suites öS4950–öS9700.

50

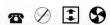

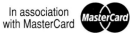

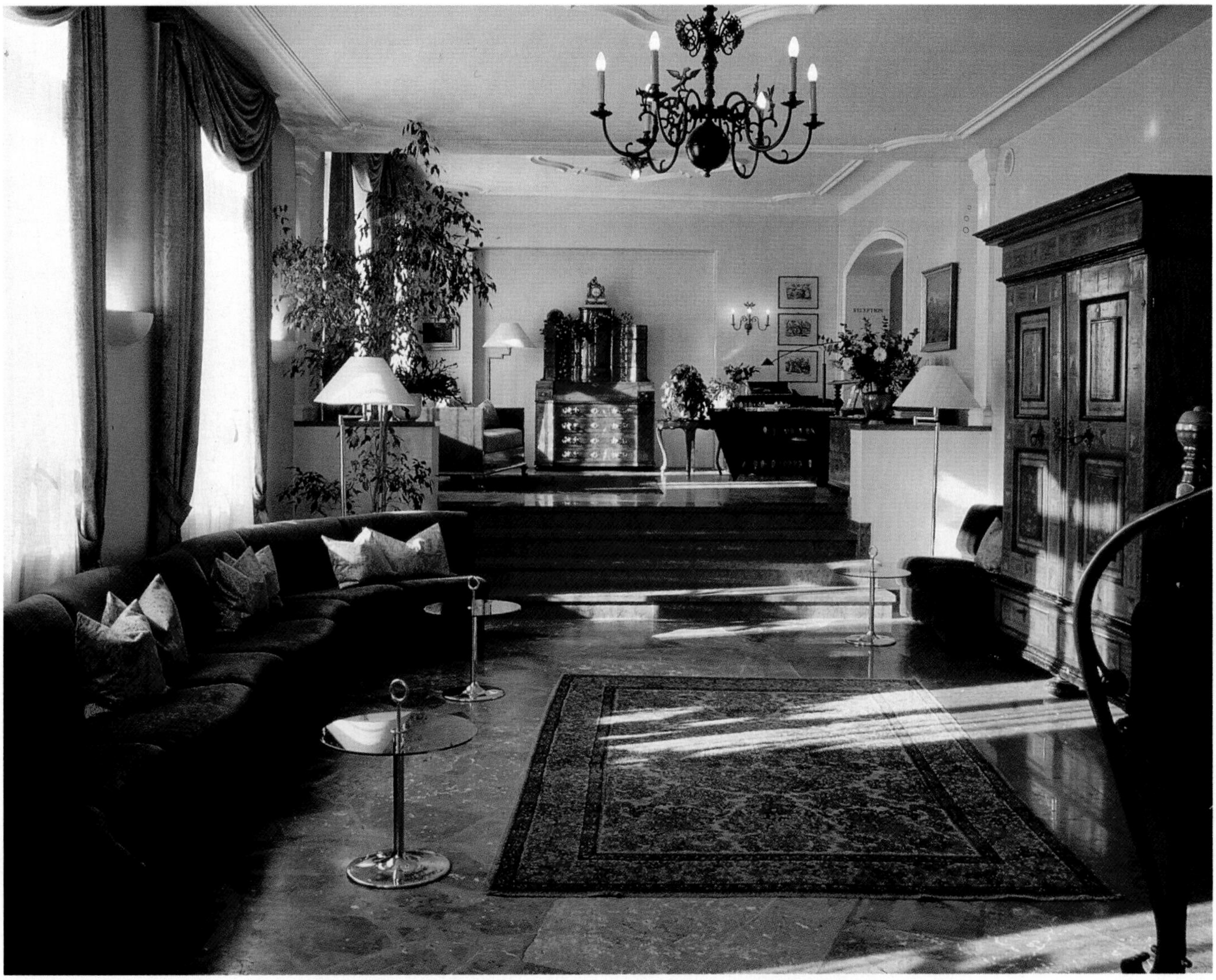

Hotel Auersperg

AUERSPERGSTRASSE 61, A-5027 SALZBURG, AUSTRIA
TEL: 43 662 88 944 FAX: 43 662 88 944 55

The Hotel Auersperg is a traditional family run hotel near the right bank of the River Salzach. Just five minutes walk from the fascinating Old City in which Mozart was born. The hotel has beautiful green and sunny gardens, a wonderful place to relax after a long day's sightseeing. The guest rooms and suites are delightful, with comfortable modern furniture, big windows and chintz covers – each individually decorated in harmonious colours. A fitness centre with a sauna and steam-bath occupies the top floor, together with a roof-terrace which has spectacular views. The welcoming spacious reception hall, with its marble floor and 19th century moulded ceiling, leads into the drawing room, filled with antiques and period furniture. The smart library-bar is convivial, informal meals being available in the dining area. International dishes and local specialities are served in the restaurant, and some of the wine is from the region. Salzburg is famous for its music, major festivals taking place regularly. Many historic old buildings, museums and the castles wait to be explored. Pleasant days can be spent driving to the mountains and lakes, including the famous Wolfgangsee. **Directions.** Take the Salzburg North exit from the Autobahn. Auerspergstrasse runs east off Schwarzstrasse by Kongress Haus. The hotel has car parking. Price guide: Single öS960–öS1250; double/twin öS1380–öS2120; suites öS2090–öS2980.

57 rms · MasterCard · Eurocard · VISA · American Express · Diners · 30

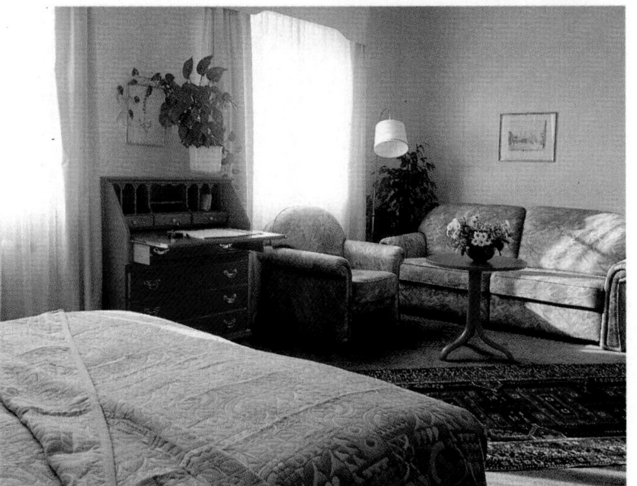

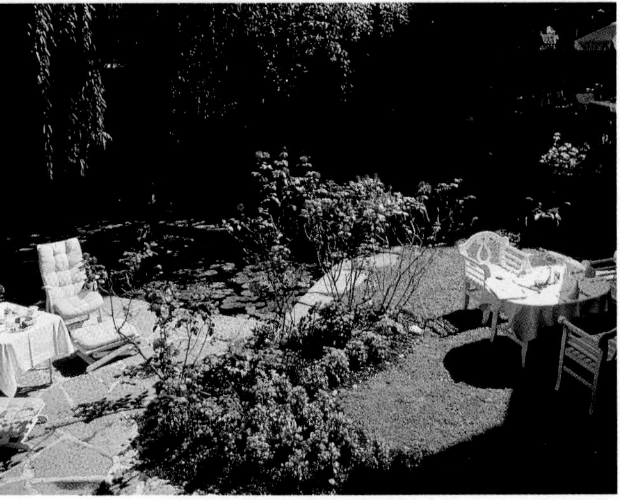

HOTEL SCHLOSS MÖNCHSTEIN

MÖNCHSBERG PARK 26–JOH, A-5020 SALZBURG–CITY CENTER, AUSTRIA
TEL: 43 662 84 85 55 0 FAX: 43 662 84 85 59 E-MAIL: moenchstein@salzburginfo.or.at

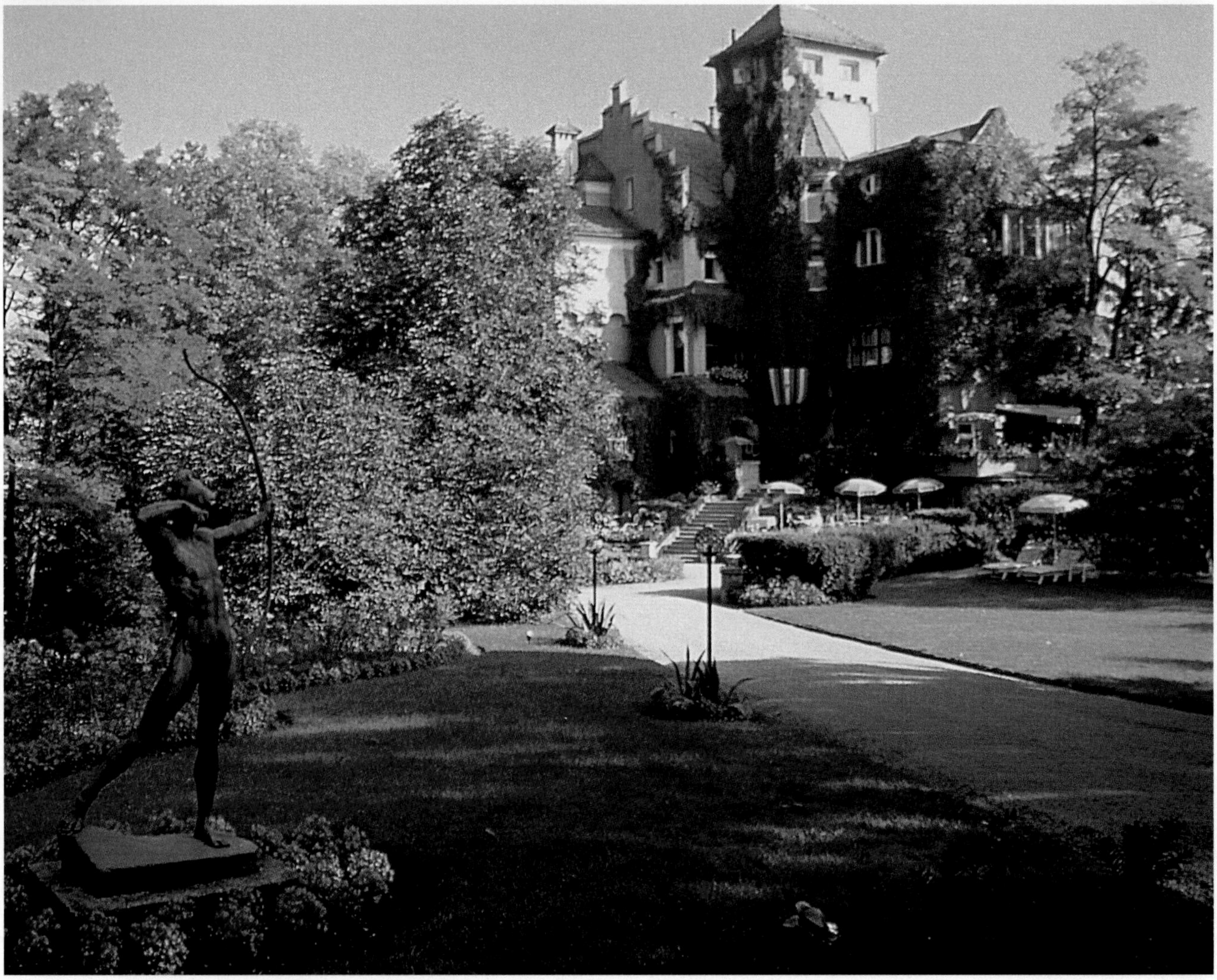

This enchanting castle, described as 'The urban sanctuary of the world' by Hideaway Report, has offered hospitality since the 14th century. It stands on the Mönchsberg, a hill in the heart of Salzburg, surrounded by the most beautiful gardens, an ivy-clad haven far above the city and yet part of it. The intimate Paris Lodron Restaurant, "Restaurant of the year 1995" – CLL-D, has the finest reputation in Salzburg, founded on the exquisite table settings with the view over the old city, impeccable staff and, above all, the imaginative presentation of Austrian dishes and a connoisseurs' wine list. Guests meet in the friendly Cocktail Bar, divine pastries in the Schloss café "Maria Theresia" or on the garden terrace "Apollo". Romantics exchange vows in the Wedding Chapel followed by a banquet. A sign on the "Salzburger Wedding Wall" keeps this special event in the memory forever. Music is very important in Salzburg and there is a rich programme throughout the year. The castle itself holds harp concerts every Saturday and Sunday. Conference facilities in unique atmosphere; Royal and Princely suite. Internet: http://www.salzburginfo.or.it/hot_rest/werbes/moenchst/hotel.htm **Directions:** On reaching Salzburg, take the Müllner Hauptstrasse, the Augustiner Gasse and follow the signs for the Hotel Schloss Mönchstein. Price guide: Single ATS2000–3400; double/twin ATS2400–6500; suite ATS4900– 28000.

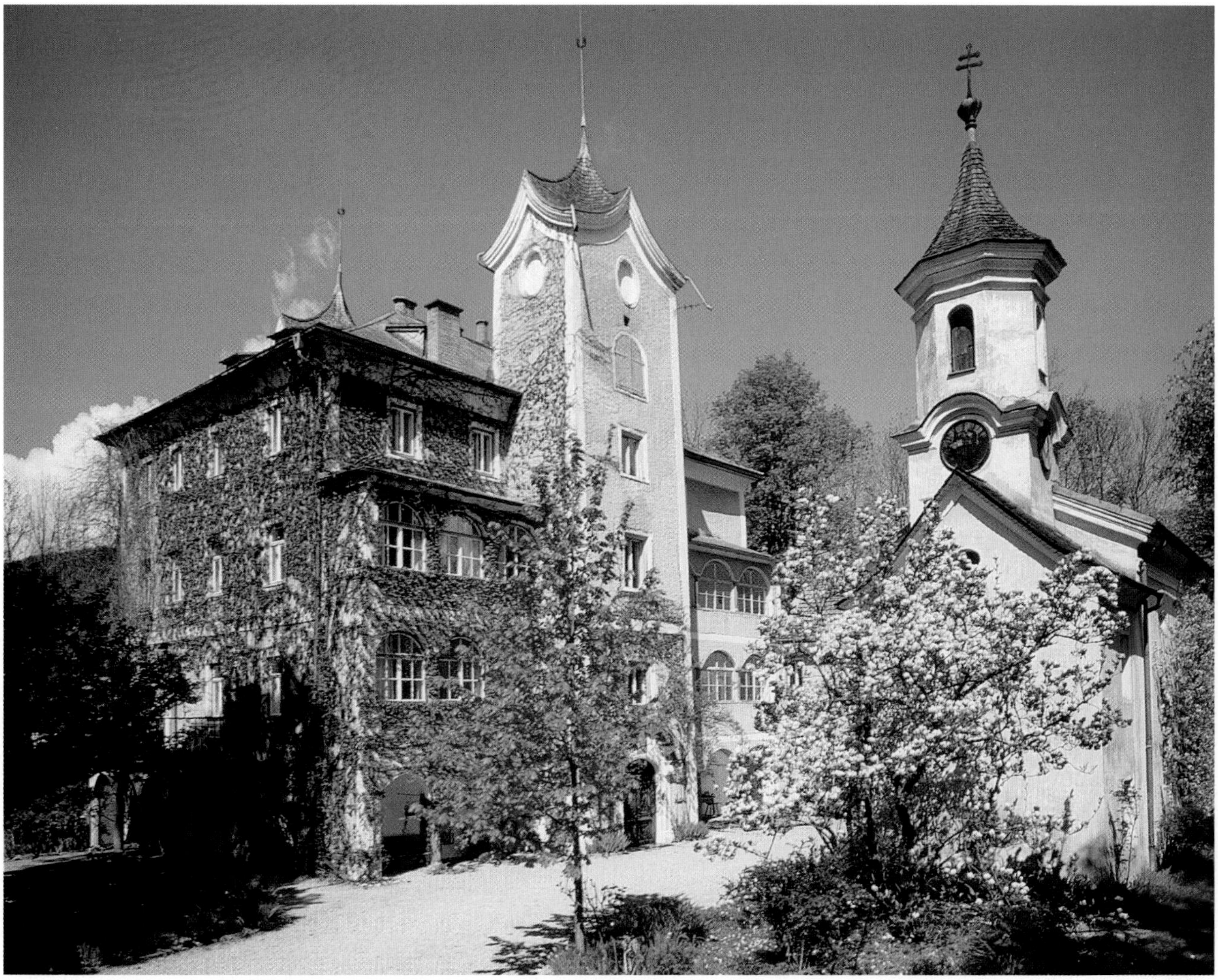

SCHLOSS HAUNSPERG

A–5411 OBERALM BEI HALLEIN (SALZBURG), AUSTRIA
TEL: 43 6245 80 662 FAX: 43 6245 85 680

To stay at this bewitching castle, just fifteen minutes drive from Salzburg, is a unique and unforgettable experience. Built in the 14th century, it has the most lovely architecture – a graceful ivyclad mansion with wrought iron balconies and a splendid tall tower. Its own Baroque chapel has painted ceilings and an ornate gold altar. Eike and Georg von Gernerth are splendid hosts. Both multilingual, they welcome guests into their magnificent home with great enthusiasm. The salons are treasure-troves, filled with priceless antiques, fine Persian rugs, brilliant chandeliers, yet comfortable and lived-in. There is a strong emphasis on music and a Black Bosendorfer grand piano is in the dramatic music room. The guest rooms, some enormous, are filled with period furniture and objets d'art – it is a privilege to stay here. Breakfast – fruit, eggs, cheese, meat and breads, is a joy; starched linen, gleaming silver, fresh flowers completing the picture. At dusk the Gernerths invite guests to join them for glasses of Austrian wine in the parlour. They will prepare light meals on request, but there is an excellent restaurant nearby. Sporting guests play tennis, golf or squash, others enjoy Salzburg and its music festivals, visit nearby lakes or wander in the castle grounds. Directions: A10 exit 16 Hallein, follow directions to Oberalm then signs to the hotel. Price guide: Single ATS 950–1300; double/twin ATS 1530–1900; suite ATS 2100–2500.

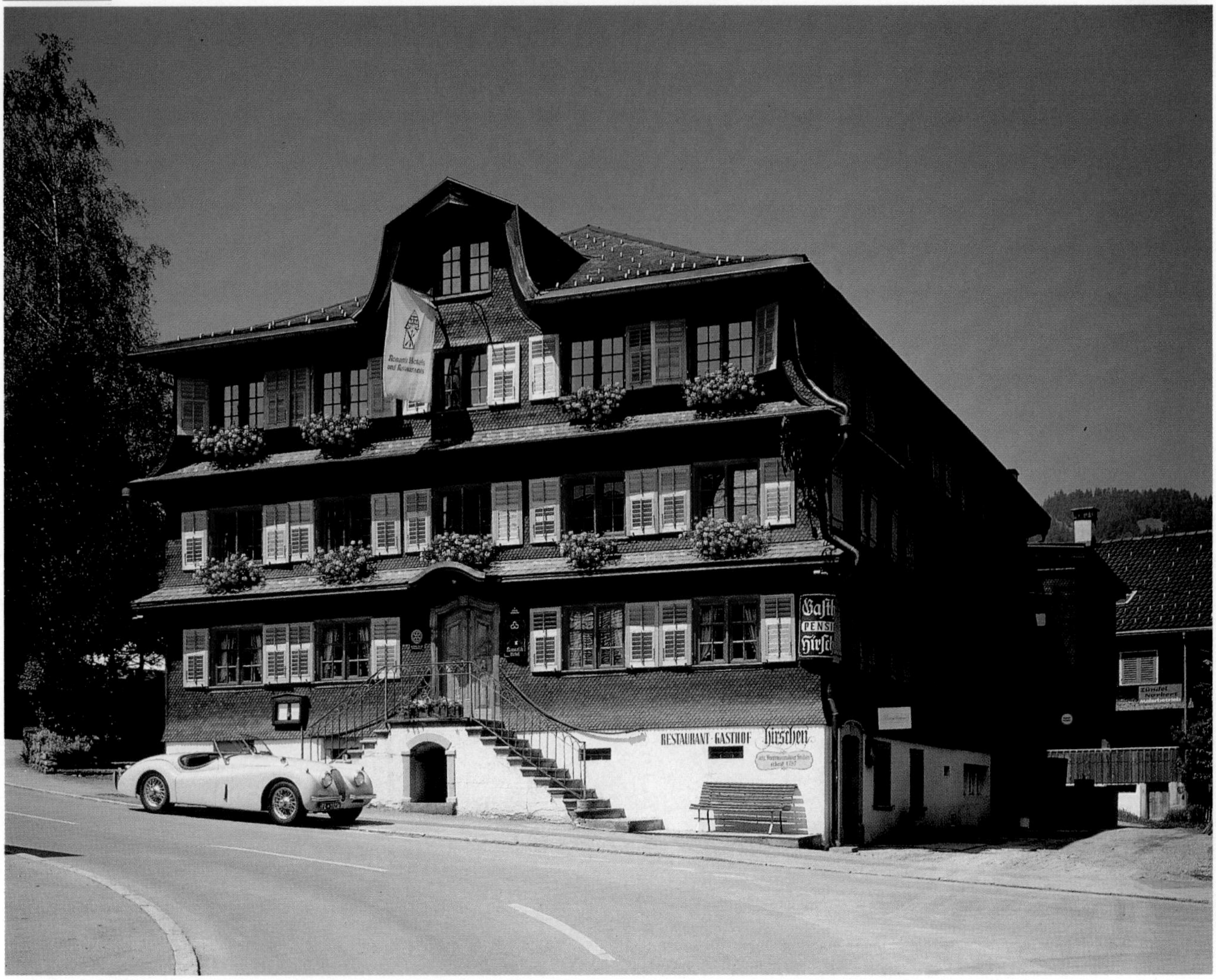

ROMANTIK HOTEL GASTHOF HIRSCHEN

HOF 14, A–6867 SCHWARZENBERG, AUSTRIA
TEL: 43 55 12 29 44 0 FAX: 43 55 12 29 44 20

The Gasthof Hirschen, in Schwarzenberg, one of the prettiest villages in the Vorarlberg, has offered hospitality since 1757. Still with baroque detail, it is now a delightful hotel in surroundings that are snowclad in winter and verdant in summer. The spacious and elegant lounge, with its big fireplace, is also the bar. The restaurant, with its carved ceiling, stone floors and traditional furniture, faces an attractive courtyard with a fountain. The menu is Austrian /cosmopolitan, and the wine list extensive. Bedrooms in the Gasthaus are cosy and rustic, with fabulous views across to the Arlberg. A second house, once the old farmhouse, just 30 metres from the hotel, has been converted into a contemporary annex. Other facilities include a sauna, steam room and underground parking. In winter this is a skiers' hotel, with superb skiing made especially pleasant by the many ski huts along the pistes. Summer is the time for walkers and climbers to explore the Bregenzerwald. Nearby Bregenz has many attractions, the old town with historic buildings and the new with its shops and casinos, boat trips on Lake Constance and superb music at festival time and during the Schubertiade festival in Feldkirch and Schwarzenberg. **Directions:** Leave the A14 at the Dornbirn Nord exit, driving through Dornbirn to Bödele and Schwarzenberg, the Gasthof is in the square. Price guide: Double/twin SFrS1080–SFrS1500; suites SFrS1800–SFrS2850.

HOTEL KLOSTERBRÄU

6100 SEEFELD, TIROL, AUSTRIA
TEL: 43 5212 26210 FAX: 43 5212 3885

Seefeld is a superb holiday resort all the year round. In its centre there is an enchanting castle – the 5 star Hotel Klosterbräu – with its fairy-tale architecture and background of mountains in the quiet pedestrian area, Once a monastery, today the hotel is vibrant yet traditional. Friendly staff in national costume, historic rooms with stone walls, magnificent wooden ceilings and panelled walls, all contribute to the superb ambience. The spacious bedrooms are charming and the bathrooms efficient. The Klosterbräu has four restaurants offering gourmet food and regional specialities. The old Kapuziner Keller hosts small gatherings – in summer dine in the old monastery courtyard. Breakfasts in the dining room are served late for all night revellers! Inspecting the incredible wine cellar in the vaults is a must. High life includes the piano bar, the night club (après ski tea dances in winter), Tyrolean Braükeller, the live music Siglu-Bar and disco. Additionally the hotel has conference rooms and a pool area in the extensive leisure and beauty centre. Hotel Klosterbräu is an ideal point of departure for many sports activities: the hotel has it's own tennis courts and putting-green with a championship golf course nearby and only a few minutes away from the skiing pistes. **Directions:** Leaving Innsbruck on A12, take Seefeld exit then follow signs to the Zentrum. Hotel has valet parking. Price guide: Single öS1,380–1,840; double/twin öS1,380–1,840; suites öS1,950–3,500.

100 rms 180

Romantik Hotels & Restaurants

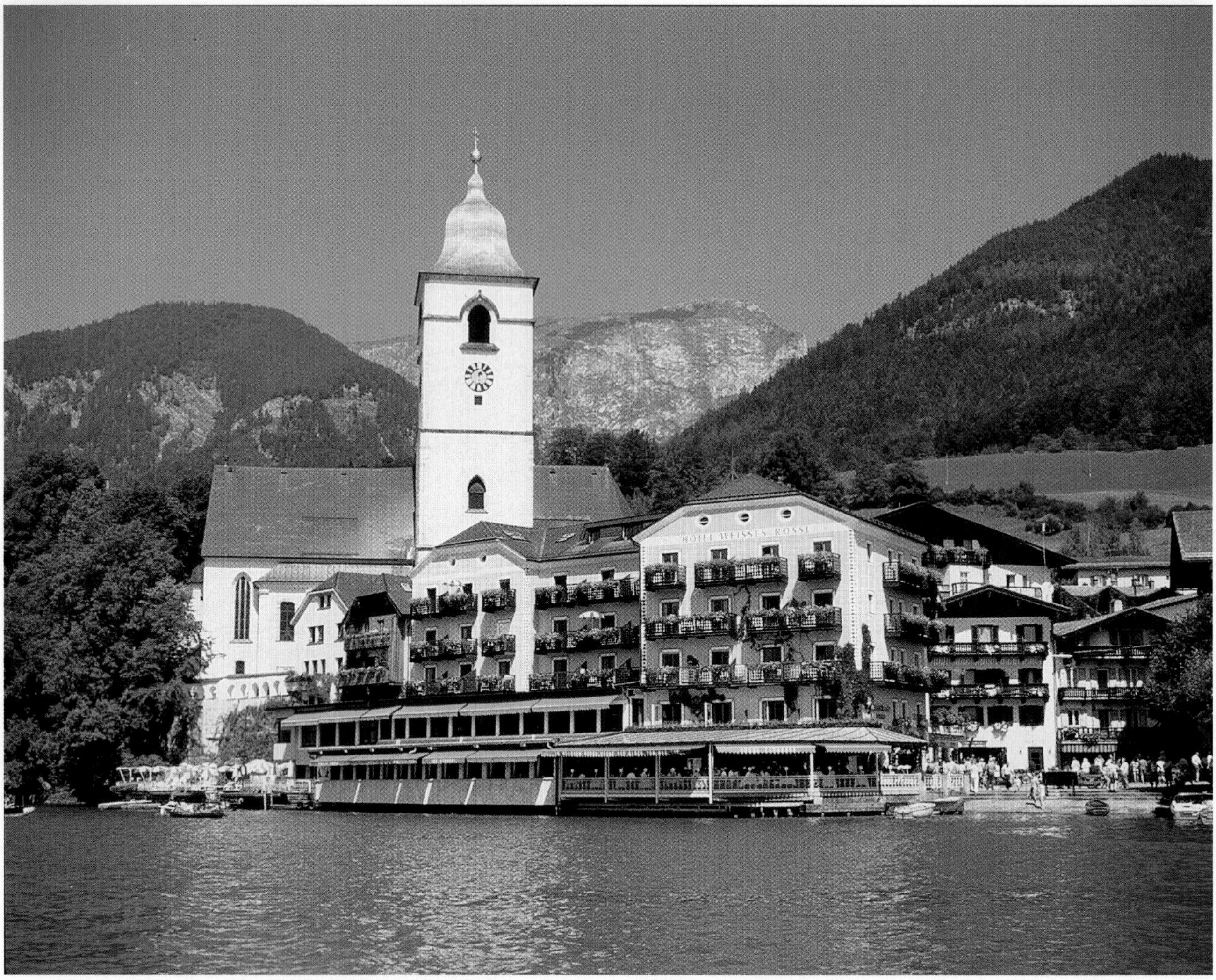

ROMANTIK HOTEL IM WEISSEN RÖSSL

5360 ST WOLFGANG AM SEE, SALZKAMMERGUT, AUSTRIA
TEL: 43 6138 23060 FAX: 43 6138 2306 41

This magical hotel became legendary through "The White Horse Inn" operetta, and has retained its refreshing Austrian charm. It stands on the edge of Lake St Wolfgang, a delightful building with its terraces and flower-filled window boxes, overlooking the waterfront, adjacent to the church spire and set against a background of the village, mountains and pine forests. It has benefited from being in the hands of the Peter family for three generations. The bedrooms are pleasant and comfortable and both they and the bathrooms are pristine. The reception rooms are delightful and there are sunny terraces for warm weather. Guests soon relax in the inviting bar. The restaurant serves gorgeous Salzkammergut dishes and delicious Austrian wines. Leisure activities abound: swimming in the pool or lake, windsurfing and other water sports, boat trips, tennis, golf, fishing and in winter downhill or cross country ski-ing or sledging. There are also activities for children. At night there is dancing, occasionally operettas or marvellous music in Salzburg. **Directions:** From Salzburg City Centre take A-Road 158 for St Gilgen, the follow signs to St Wolfgang. The Weissen Rossl is in ST Wolfgang See. Price guide: Single öS950–1400; double/twin öS1400–2800; apts öS2100–2800.

HOTEL IM PALAIS SCHWARZENBERG

SCHWARZENBERGPLATZ 9, A–1030 VIENNA, AUSTRIA
TEL: 43 1 798 4515 FAX: 43 1 798 4714 E-MAIL: palais@schwarzenberg.via.at

This grand hotel, built for the "noble knight" Prince Eugen in the centre of Vienna, is palatial and nostalgic of imperial Austria when baroque architecture was in fashion. It stands in enchanting gardens with famous roses, ornamental ponds and acclaimed sculptures. The guest rooms are spacious and luxurious, with their graceful period furniture, harmonious colour schemes and views over the courtyard. The bathrooms are in marble. The reception rooms, several of which are ideal for conferences and meetings, are sumptuous – the Kuppelsaal (entrance hall) has a superb domed ceiling, there is a circular gilded lounge and the spectacular Marble Hall with its exquisite frescoes transforms into the most spectacular private dining hall. The Palais Bar is perfect for cocktails and the Viennese rendezvous in the elegant Terrace Restaurant looking out over the park, while enjoying classical French or Austrian cuisine and superb wines. Lighter, more informal meals can be found in the Kaminzimmer or on the coffee terrace. Guests play croquet on the lawns or follow the jogging trail. The nearby tennis club is available and golf is just 5km away. Vienna is renowned for its music and art galleries. It also has an exciting night life. **Directions:** From the airport, follow A4 to the centre of Vienna. There is a large private car park. Price guide: Double/twin öS3400–öS5600; suites öS5600–öS7200

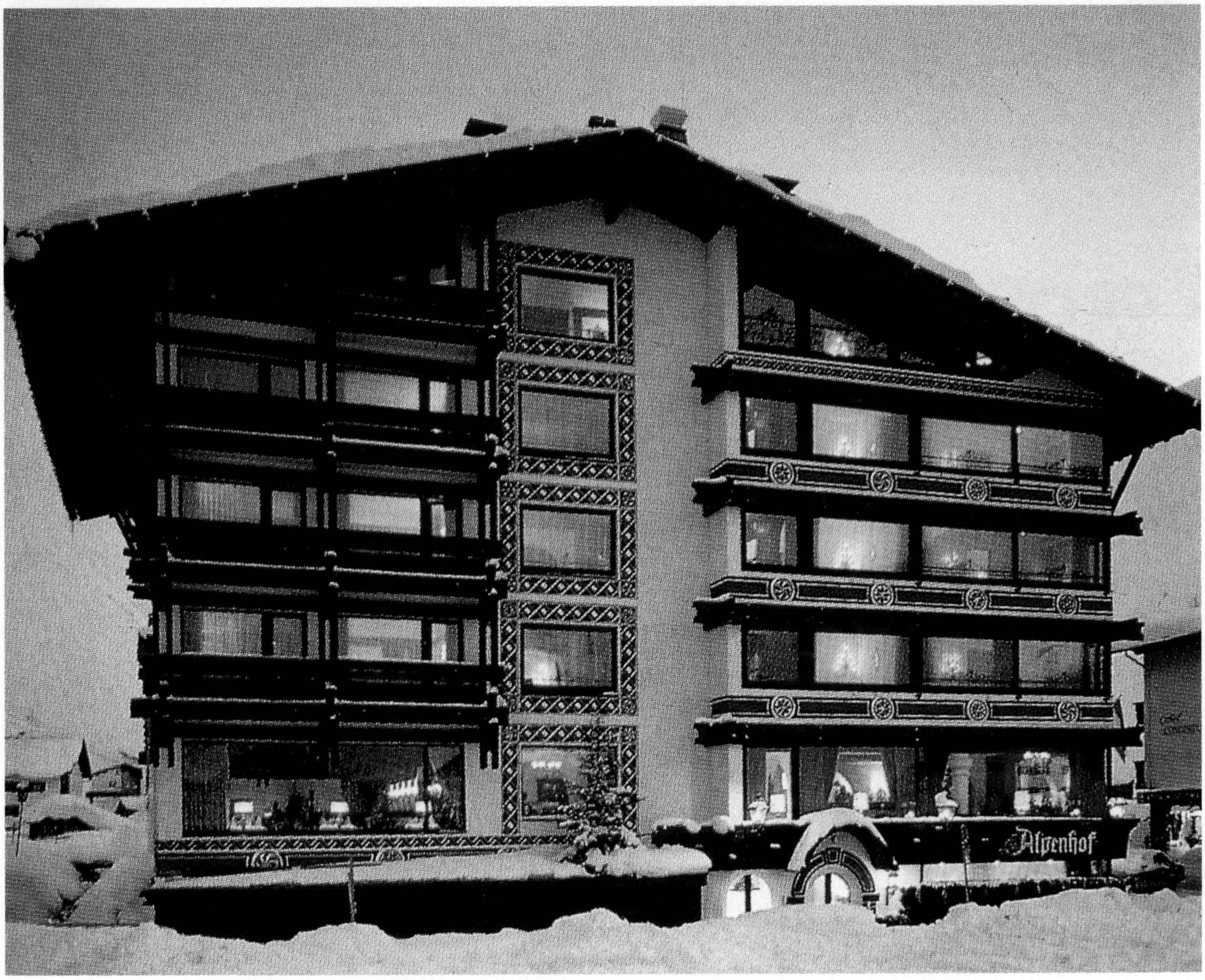

Prima Hotels

THURNHERS ALPENHOF

A–6763, ZÜRS/ARLBERG, AUSTRIA
TEL: 43 5583 2191 FAX: 43 5583 3330

The Thurnhers Alpenhof is an attractive family-owned chalet hotel, high up in the Alps. Dedicated to winter sports enthusiasts of all ages, it is only open in the Season. New arrivals are instantly aware of the professionalism of the staff and the warmth projected by the owners' interest in antiques and other delightful memorabilia. The roomy bedrooms are light and very pretty, floral fabrics covering the comfortable chairs by the window, looking out over the snow. The bathrooms are sophisticated! Guests mingle in the piano bar throughout the evening, and dine well by candlelight in the Alpine Restaurant – the gourmet menu includes local specialities and most weeks there are a Gala Dinner, Fondue Evening and Bauern Buffet. The cellar is impressive, with wines for all budgets. The skiing is marvellous, with direct access from the hotel to the graded pistes for novices and experts, cross country or downhill. Après-ski is important and exotic cocktails or warming gluhwein are always waiting at the end of the day. Guests relax in the pool or in the exotic solarium or have weary muscles massaged. Children have their own ski school and programme. **Directions:** The nearest international airport is Zürich. Leave the motorway at Bludenz, following signs to Zürs/Arlberg. Price guide (per person): Single ATS1760–3080; double/twin ATS1760–3040; suites ATS2700–4050.

41 rms 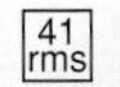     50    

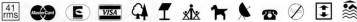

Belgium

Belgium is the uncut diamond of Europe. Thankfully the Channel Tunnel is gradually revealing this undiscovered gem to a wider audience than those who travel only to its capital for parliamentary purposes.

Throughout this country there flourishes an unapologetically bourgeois culture. Dukes, counts, and lesser lords have built many a feudal castle on Belgian land, and abbots and cardinals have constructed towering religious edifices, but it was the merchants who built the cities and commissioned the works of art we admire today.

Brussels stands in the very centre of the country. A booming city which has established itself as the capital of Europe. Here the European Community has its headquarters.

The south of the country is a wild, wooded area, with mountains rising to more than 2000 feet. In contrast, in the north, the land is flat and heavily cultivated, much as it is in neighbouring Holland. Here stand the medieval Flemish cities of Ghent and Bruges, with their celebrated carillons and canals – not to mention the 42 miles of sandy beaches that make up the country's northern coastline. Due north of Brussels lies Antwerp, the country's dynamic seaport. The city, where the painter Rubens lived, is now the world's leading diamond cutting centre.

Despite the city being famed for its moules – the mussels in Brussels originate from Holland not Belgium. Belgian chocolate is most definitely authentic. If chocolate be the food of the Gods, then Belgium is their dining place. Especially in the cobbled cobweb of streets in Brussels leading from the illustrious Grande Place, shop windows artistically display edibles with such care as though they be precious diamonds. Decorated in florid satin ribbons, bows and the finest Belgian lace – they look too good to eat. Well, almost.

FIREAN HOTEL

KAREL OOMSSTRAAT 6, B–2018, ANTWERPEN, BELGIUM
TEL: 32 3 237 02 60 FAX: 32 3 238 11 68

This exclusive and prestigious townhouse hotel in a quiet residential street close to the centre of Antwerp was built in preparation for the 1930 World Exhibition. Today its exquisite Art Deco style ensures an appreciative clientele, who travel worldwide and are weary of large standardised chain hotels. The Art Deco theme is evident throughout The Firean, from its stunning entrance, through the unique doors leading into the salon, with authentic Tiffany enamel and glass, and in the furnishings of the comfortable bedrooms (the bathrooms are modern and efficient). The high standards of courtesy of that era are maintained by the proprietors who like to welcome guests personally, ascertaining any special needs. While breakfast is served and drinks are available in the small, friendly bar – enjoyed on the patio in good weather – there is no restaurant but Antwerp is famous for its choice of places to eat so this is no problem. It also has museums, and excellent shopping. **Directions:** From Brussels, (A1-E19) Antwerp exit through tunnel, over bridge, following signs for Antwerpen Centrum; 3rd traffic light find hotel on left. From UK/Paris/Bruges(A14–E.17) 2nd exit after Kennedy Tunnel, left over bridge into Karel Oomsstraat. The hotel has a private garage. Price guide: Single Bf4250–4700; double/twin Bf5150–5900; suites Bf7800.

Hotel Rubens

OUDE BEURS 29, 2000 ANTWERP, BELGIUM
TEL: 32 3 222 48 48 FAX: 32 3 225 19 40 E-MAIL: hotel.rubens@glo.be

Antwerp – a busy port and the centre of the diamond market over many centuries – has a fascinating Old Town, and this is where business people and tourists alike are delighted to find the Hotel Rubens, close to the Grande Place. The Rubens dates back to the sixteenth century but inside its graceful old exterior it has been completely renovated. The reception hall, with the bar at one end, is smart, but on fine days guests tend to congregate in the attractive plant-filled inner courtyard. There is also a secluded flower garden at the rear of the hotel. The colourful bedrooms are beautifully decorated and quiet, many overlooking picturesque old houses. The luxurious Rubens Suite, with a lovely view of the cathedral, has a spacious sitting room, perfect for meetings. The hotel has no formal restaurant, although a substantial breakfast buffet and room service are available. However there are many good restaurants and interesting bistros in walking distance. The Cathedral, Rubens' House and the Diamond Museum should be visited, and boat trips are a pleasant way to sightsee. **Directions:** Available on request when making reservation. Parking facilities available. Price guide: Single Bfr4500–5500; double/twin Bfr4500–7500; suites Bfr7000–18,000.

36
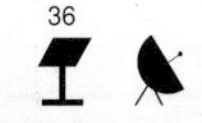

Die Swaene

STEENHOUWERSDIJK, B–8000 BRUGES, BELGIUM
TEL: 32 50 34 27 98 FAX: 32 50 33 66 74

Swans are legendary symbols in Bruges. Die Swaene, dating back to the 15th century, once the home of city elders, has been brilliantly transformed into the most magnificent hotel, romantically situated by a pretty canal and surrounded by historic buildings. Guests enter into luxury on a grand scale – lovely antiques, gleaming chandeliers, large mirrors, baskets of fruit and bowls of fresh flowers, indoor plants and statuary abound. The drawingroom is reminiscent of Louis XV. There is a terraced garden where guests enjoy apéritifs on fine evenings and gracious dining areas where spectacular candlelit dinners and champagne lunches take place. The menu offers classical and contemporary dishes and the large cellar houses some rare vintage wines. The bedrooms are opulent, with exotic festoons over ornately carved beds, although there are some simpler rooms available. Facilities include a well equipped conference room, fitness centre, indoor pool and private car park. Guests enjoy exploring Bruges, taking the canal tours arranged by the hotel. **Directions:** Enter Bruges from Katelijnepoort, taking Katelijnestraat, turn right along Gruuthusestraat, and follow the canal, keeping it on the left, along Dyver and then left at Vismarkt into Steenhouversdijk. Price guide: Single Bf4500; double/twin Bf5500–Bf6800; suite Bf8950–Bf10950.

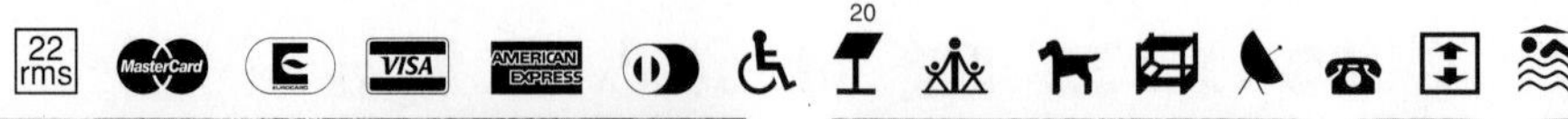

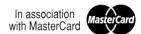

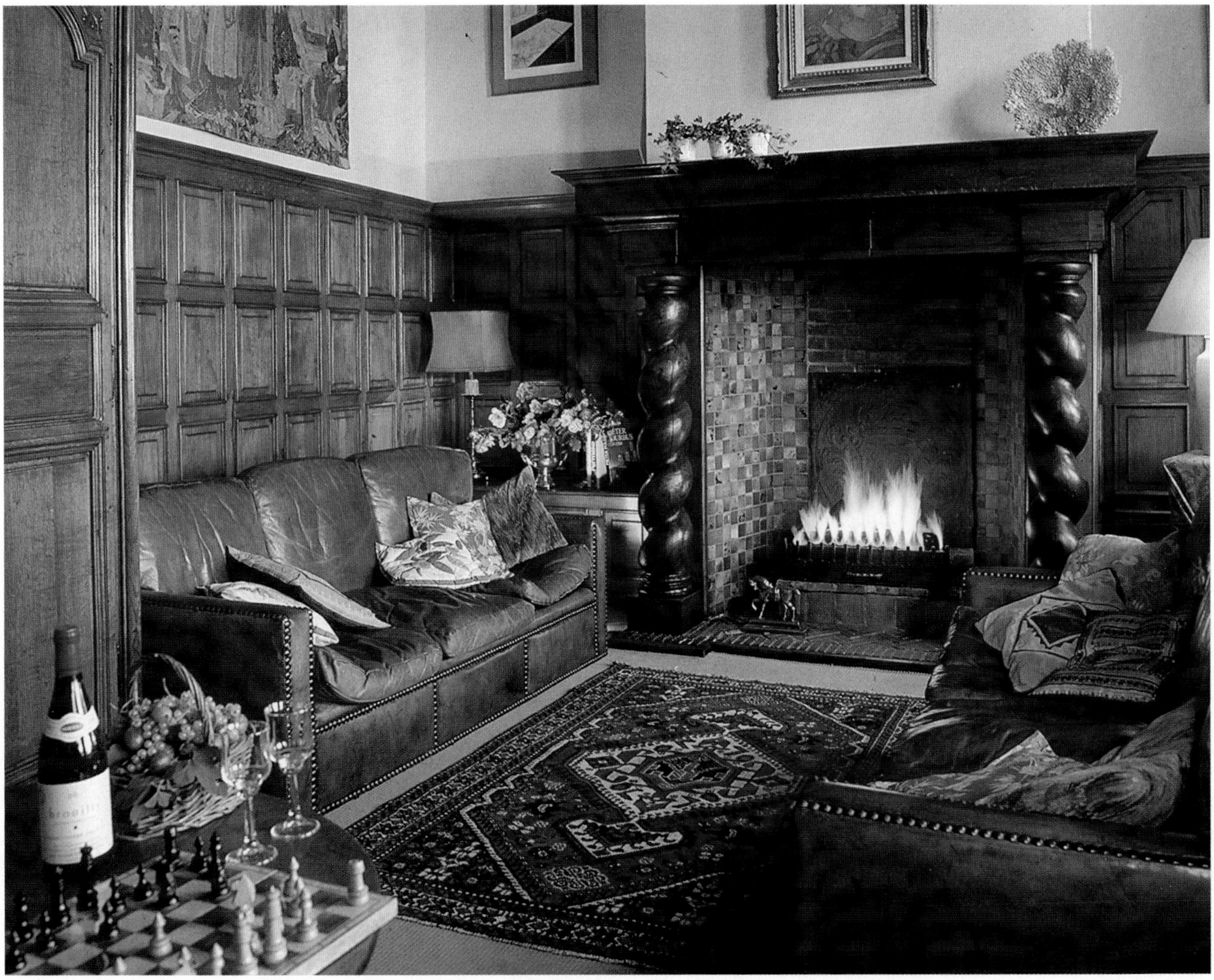

HOTEL DE ORANGERIE

KARTUIZERINNENSTRAAT 10, B-8000, BRUGES, BELGIUM
TEL: 0032 50 34 16 49 FAX: 0032 50 33 30 16

The nuns who lived in this 15th century convent would envy today's residents; today it is a small, attractive hotel with a big sunny terrace overlooking the canal, on the other side of which is its bigger and elegant sister, Hotel De Tuilerien. Both are owned by vivacious Madame Beatrice Geeraert, legendary for her hospitality. The exterior is delightful, with long tall windows at the front, and at the back flower bedecked balconies. Guests relax in the generous sized bedrooms, appreciating the warm, welcoming colour schemes, the comfortable furnishings, and the marble bathrooms. A pleasant lounge awaits guests and there is an inviting small bar but only breakfast (very substantial) is served in the dining room, with its pretty china and flowers on every table. Residents, however, enjoy eating in the neighbouring bistros and restaurants. The Tuilerien hosts many conferences and the Orangerie is often used to accommodate delegates. The fitness facilities are shared by visitors from both hotels. Bruges is a marvellous city to explore, with its many historic buildings and fascinating waterways – special walks have been identified for the benefit of tourists. Directions:E40/Exit 8 (St Michaels), take Koning Albertlaan, 't Zand, Zuidzandstraat, Steenstraat, Markt, Wollestraat, then turn into Kartuizererinnenstraat Price guide: Single Bf6950; double/twin Bf7950; suites Bf8950.

19 rms — 120

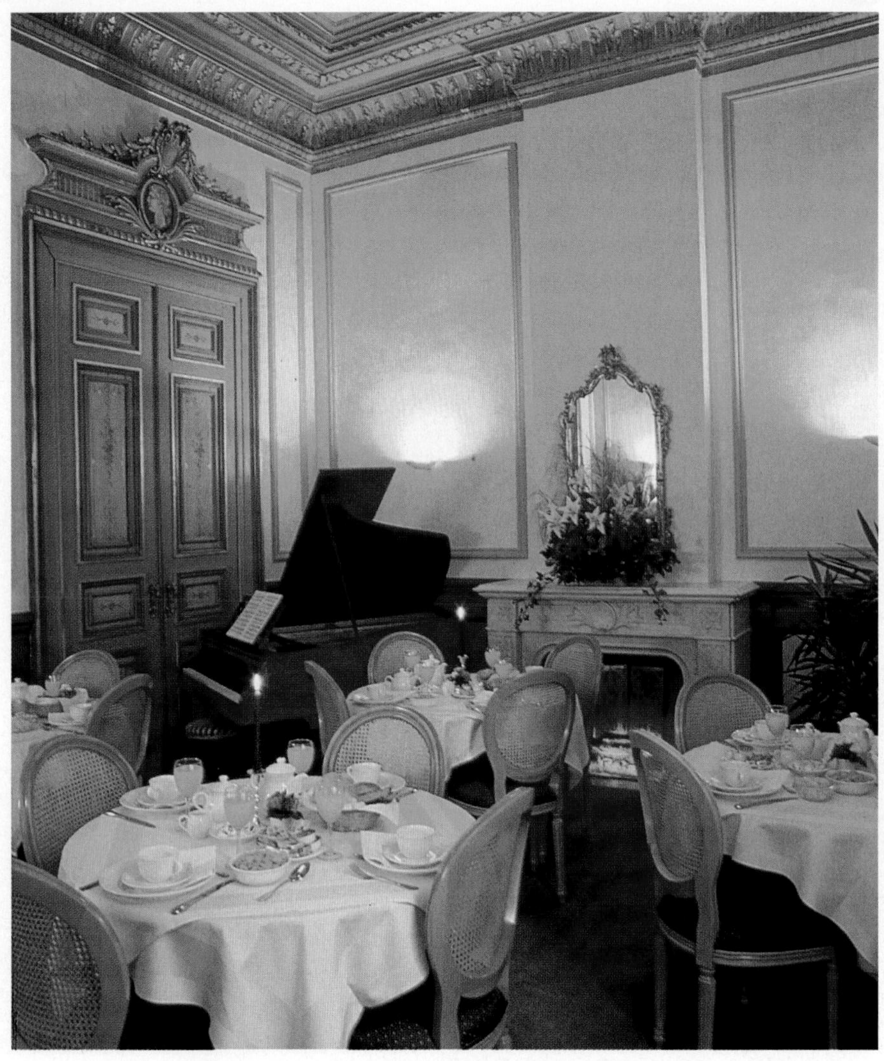

HOTEL HANSA

N. DESPARSSTRAAT, NO.11, 8000 BRUGES, BELGIUM
TEL: 32 50 33 84 44 FAX: 32 50 33 42 05

Bruges is so easy to get to, especially by rail, being linked to the Eurostar, and it has some mid-19th century mansions, one of which has now been meticulously renovated, and is now an excellent value hotel close to the Market Square in the very centre of the city. The Hansa has a fine facade and the talents of a skilled interior decorator are evident in the decorations and furnishings throughout the hotel. It is a small hotel, with just twenty bedrooms, all in soft colours and extremely comfortable and equipped with all modern amenities. The bathrooms are efficient. A small bar in the reception area is adjacent to a pleasant, welcoming lounge, which in turn leads through attractive glass doors into the charming breakfast room which reflects the Hansa's elegant past – it has an ornate ceiling and gilded cornice, marble fireplace and gilderd mirrors. The hotel does not have a restaurant, but there are many places to dine in the locality, to suit all tastes and budgets. Small seminars can be held in the conference room. Audio-visual systems can be arranged. Bruges is fascinating, and canal trips are a favourite way to explore the historic city. Internet: url:http://www.hansa.be **Directions:** E40, exit 8, head for Brugge Centrum, through Ezelstraat and St Jacobstraat to Eiermarkt. At junction left into Niklaas Desparsstraat. Price guide: Single BEF 2700–5200; double/twin BEF 2950–5500.

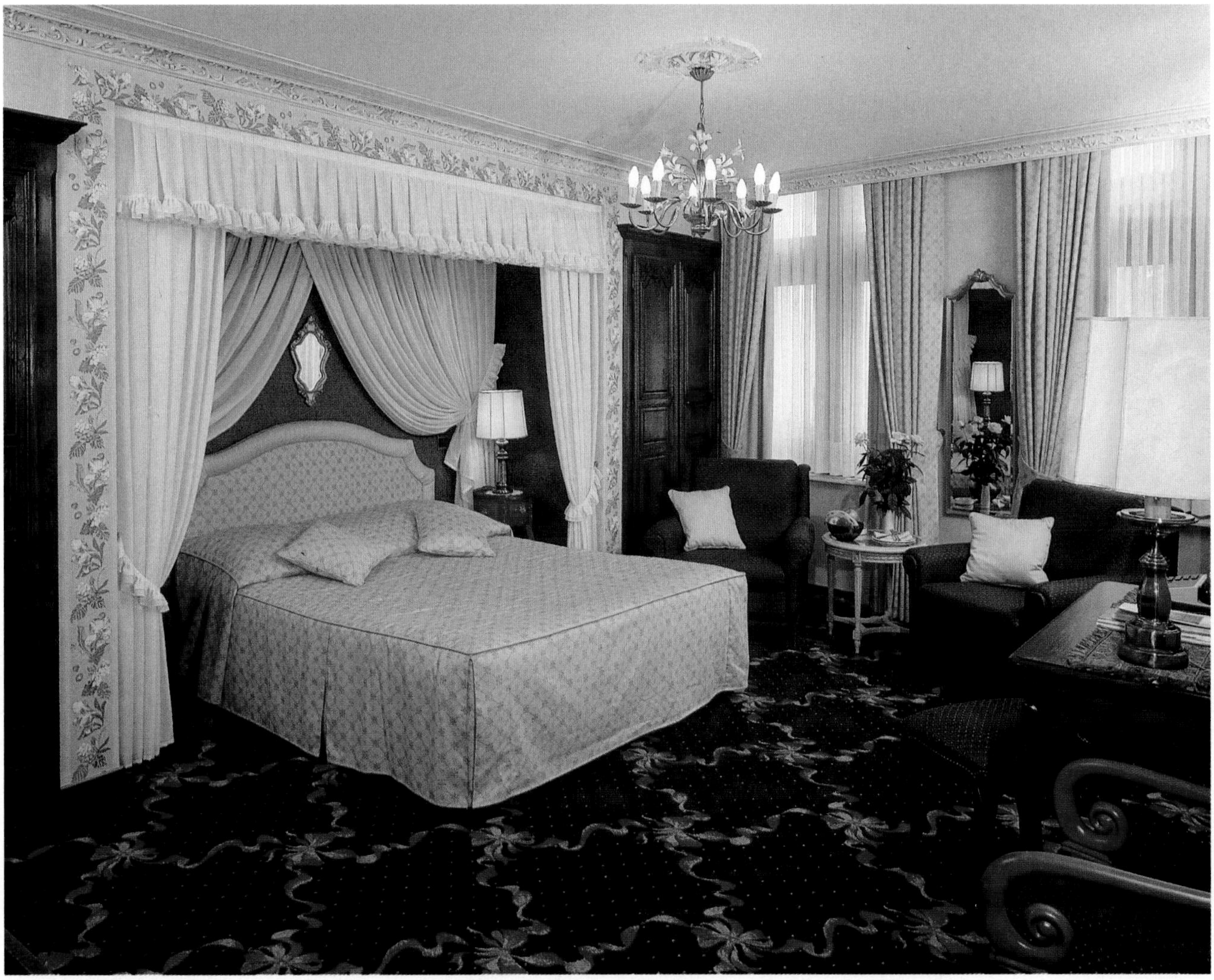

HOTEL PRINSENHOF

ONTVANGERSSTRAAT 9, B–8000 BRUGES, BELGIUM

TEL: 32-50-34 26 90 FAX: 32-50-34 23 21 E-MAIL: prinsenhof@unicall.be

This 20th century Flemish mansion, in the very heart of Bruges, having been renovated with great flair, is now a superb small hotel hidden down a side street. A member of Relais du Silence, it is family run, the ambience is warm, with a feeling that guests are all-important. The interior decoration, in the style of Burgundy, is rich with chandeliers, moulded ceilings and antiques, polished floors and marvellous rugs. The breakfast room is charming, where an excellent buffet is served in the mornings, but there is no restaurant, although drinks are available from the licensed bar. Many interesting places to dine can be found nearby. The bedrooms are peaceful, double glazing keeping out noise, beautifully furnished in traditional style and having particulary elegant drapery. A discreet mini-bar completes the many comforts provided. Businessmen find the central location ideal, and tourists enjoy wandering through the maze of small streets, along the canal banks and exploring the many museums and fascinating shops. **Directions:** Approaching Bruges from Zeebrugge or Ostend, leave the ring road at Ezelpoort, taking Ezelstraat, forking left into St Jakobstraat, right into Geldmunstraat to Noordzandstraat, with a right turn into Ontvangersstraat. Internet: http://www.prinsenhof.be Price guide: Single 3100Bf–3500Bf; double/twin 3975–4975Bf; suite 6800Bf.

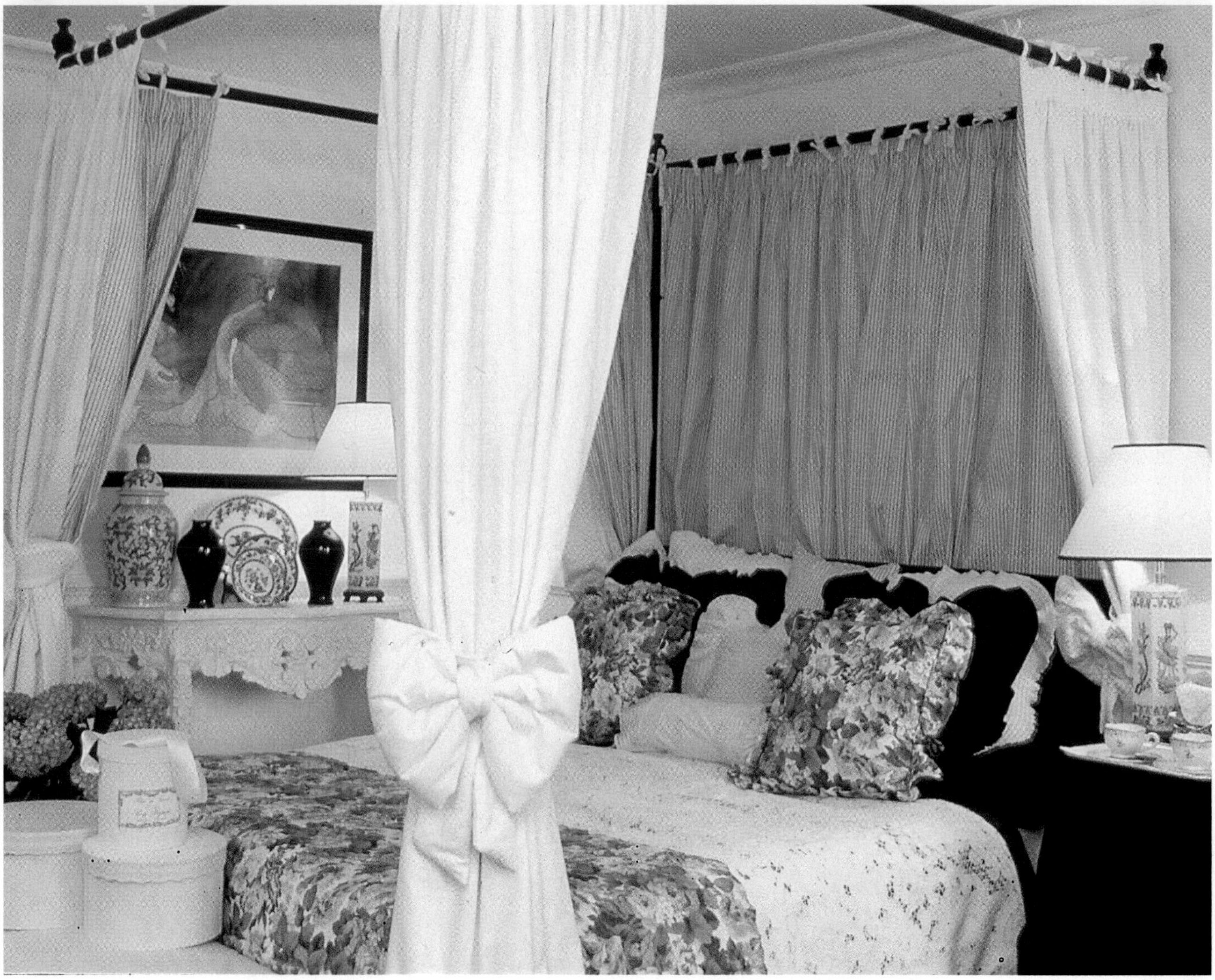

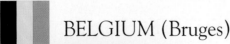

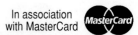

Romantik Pandhotel

PANDREITJE 16, B–8000 BRUGES, BELGIUM
TEL: 32 50 34 06 66 FAX: 32 50 34 05 56

Once an 18th century mansion, the Pandhotel has been thoughtfully restored and transformed into an elegant small hotel. It stands in a leafy square, within sight and sound of the famous Belfry. Many charming features of the original house remain, and the original carriage house is now the reception hall. The suites and bedrooms are delightful, lovely antiques vying with fabrics that harmonise with the wallhangings. The two sitting rooms reflect the care with which the renovation has been carried out, and guests enjoy relaxing in front of the old chimney piece, in comfortable chairs and sofas surrounded by fresh flowers. A delicious breakfast is served, and although there is no dining room, the hotel has good relationships with the best restaurants in the area.Themed visits are a speciality – these include wonderful dinners, boat trips on canals, sightseeing in a horse-drawn carriage, golf, cycling. The personal attention of Mrs Vanhaecke Dewaele, who is an Official Guide of Bruges, her son Frederik and daughter Lyne, ensures a memorable stay. **Directions:** The hotel supplies a map with detailed instructions, and will recommend car-parking nearby. Price guide: Single Bf3890–Bf6290; double/twin Bf4890–Bf6290; suites Bf7290.

L'AMIGO

1-3 RUE L'AMIGO, B–1000 BRUXELLES
TEL: 32 2 547 47 47 FAX: 32 2 513 52 77 E-MAIL: hotelamigo@compuserve.com

Just off the Grand'Place, visitors to Brussels will be delighted to find this friendly hotel. A corner building, enlivened by colourful flowers and shrubs in window boxes on the many balconies, the reception rooms are charming, very light, spacious and comfortably furnished. Handsome paintings hang on the walls, and big bowls of flowers add to the welcoming ambience. The bedrooms are enchanting, with small chandeliers, wonderful brocades used to create harmonious colour schemes, tall windows letting in the morning sun, and luxurious marble bathrooms. The suites are particularly splendid, some having terraces looking out across the city. The small well-stocked bar is congenial, an ideal meeting place before dining in the excellent restaurant, which has a fine wine list including a 1986 Grand Cru Bordeaux! The hotel has superb meeting rooms and an elegant banqueting hall, where corporate functions can be hosted in great style. The Bourse is nearby, also the Theatre Royal and the Palais Royal. Prestigious boutiques and cafés help pass the day and the hotel arranges tours around Brussels and to Bruges. **Directions:** Leave Autoroute E42 at Exit 6, following signs to the Grand'Place (Grote Markt). The hotel has parking for 50 cars. Price Guide: Single BEF6.200–BEF7.300; double BEF6.950–BEF9.000; suite BEF16.500–BEF21.300; executive BEF12.450.

200

STANHOPE HOTEL

9, RUE DU COMMERCE, B-1000, BRUSSELS, BELGIUM
TEL: 32 2 506 91 11 FAX: 32 2 512 17 08

This recherché hotel, retreat of the cognocenti in this busy city, has maintained its aura of a fin-de-siècle private residence. It was built round a courtyard, today laid out as an attractive garden where guests can relax. The many salons, intercommunciating and varying in size, are exquisite, furnished with fine antiques, traditional chairs, brilliant chandeliers, handsome portraits, silk curtains and Oriental rugs. Bowls of fruit and tall vases of flowers add to its charisma – there is no ordinary bar but a table of cut crystal decanters and elegant glasses, where guests can enjoy their favourite drink. The Library is a quiet refuge after a stressful day. The guest rooms are enticing, with their lovely period pieces, gilt mirrors, beautiful fabrics and wall hangings and the luxurious suites in the old annex open out onto the private garden. The bathrooms are lavish, having many indulgent accessories. The restaurant is enchanting, with murals, columns and candelabra. The tables are laid with crisp linen, fine porcelain and sparkling silver. The chef creates Ambrosian dishes which should be accompanied by vintage French wines. The superb fitness centre is much frequented by guests as tennis, golf and swimming are all some distance away. **Directions:** The Stanhope is in the centre of the business quarter, close to the Palais Royal. Garage parking. Price guide: Single Bf9,900; double/twin Bf12,900; junior suite Bf17,500; suite Bf22,500.

50 rms 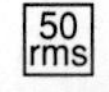     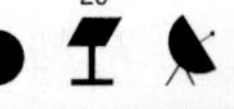 20  

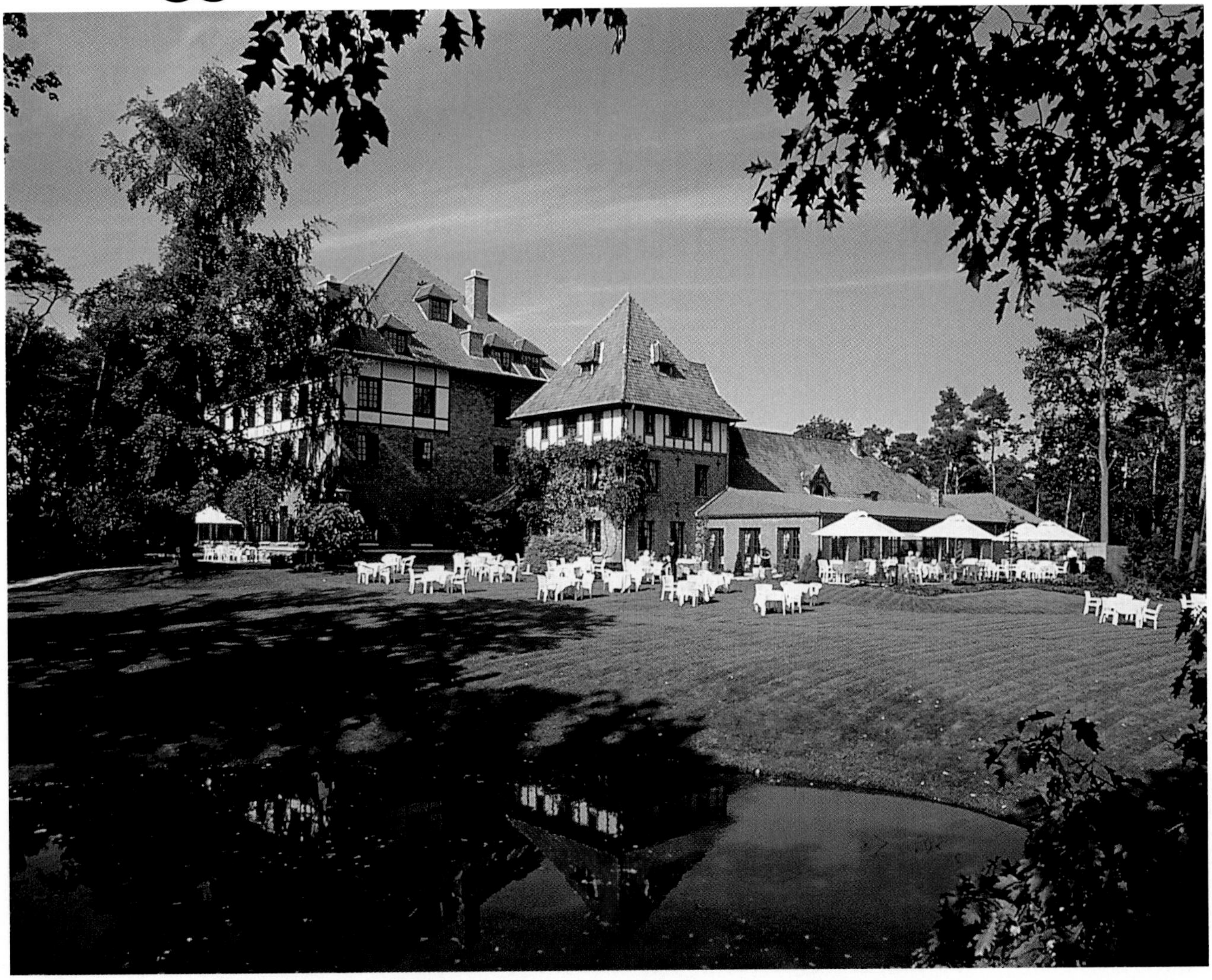

LA BUTTE AUX BOIS

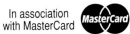

PAALSTEENLAAN 90, 3620 LANAKEN, BELGIUM

TEL: 32 89 72 12 86 FAX: 32 89 72 16 47

This twentieth century château, built in 1924, only became a hotel in 1986. Much work has taken place since then, and today it is sophisticated, with extensive conference and exhibition facilities. Geographically it is well situated, in the Euroregion of Maastricht, Hasselt, Liège and Aachen. A verdant estate surrounds La Butte aux Bois, providing the peace and privacy sought by weary executives. The terraces and pools are floodlit at night, to spectacular effect. The ambience is English country house. The salons are spacious and comfortable, with fires in winter and tasteful flower decorations. The bedrooms are roomy, with harmonious colour schemes, thoughtfully furnished and equipped to meet the demands of today's traveller. Guests gather in the lounge or on the terrace for drinks before adjourning to the palatial restaurant. The Chef prepares inspired interpretations of traditional dishes and the cellar holds fine wines. Corporate functions are frequently hosted in private rooms or in the grounds. The hotel has a pool, beauty spa and cycles for exploring the countryside. Tennis and golf can be arranged. Cultural activities abound. **Directions:** Leave E25 for Antwerp (E314). Cross border, take first turning,N78 towards Lanaken. After 5 km, right into Paalsteenlaan, finding the hotel 1km later. Three car parks. Price guide: Single Bfr3400–Bfr5500; double/twin Bfr4100–Bfr6400.

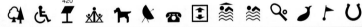

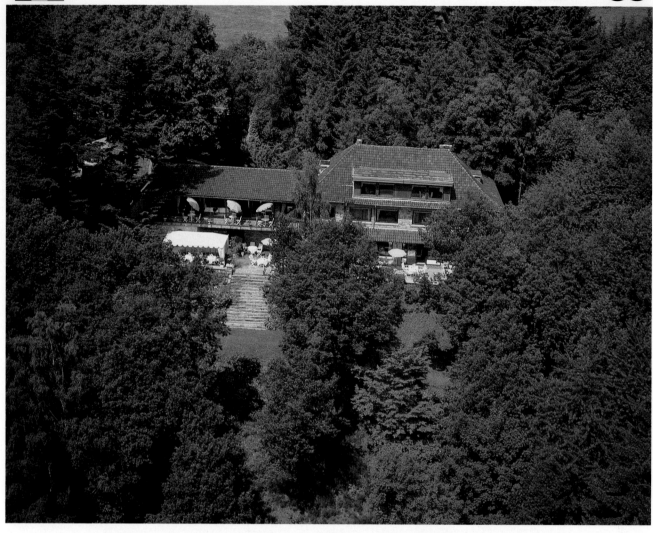

HOSTELLERIE TRÔS MARETS

ROUTE DES TRÔS MARETS, B-4960 MALMÉDY, BELGIUM
TEL: 32 80 33 79 17 FAX: 32 80 33 79 10

This delightful hotel, surrounded by forest, atop a small mountain, is close to Germany, Luxembourg and Holland. In winter the snow-clad terrain attracts skiers and in summer visitors enjoy the sunshine and fresh air. The Trôs Marets has modern comfort and style. The lounge and dining room have spectacular views. The furnishings are elegant while creating a relaxing ambience, and the same theme has been applied in the bedrooms, well-equipped for today's traveller. The annex houses four superb suites, with balconies off the drawing rooms and luxurious bedrooms – the bathrooms have sunbeds! There is a small conference room. The pretty indoor swimming pool is in this part of the hotel and opens onto the garden in fine weather. There is an attractive terrace for alfresco dining, but serious eating is in the outstanding restaurant where succulent meals are served, including many fish dishes. Perfectly cooked vegetables, immaculate service and wine served at the correct temperature complete a memorable occasion. Nearby are the Ardennes and Bastogne, where the Americans victoriously battled in 1944. Energetic guests explore the forest but others unwind in the tranquil atmosphere. **Directions:** From Liège follow the E40 over the scenic viaduct to the Malmédy exit, then follow the N68 uphill for 5 kilometres. Price guide: Double/twin Bf3900–Bf8500; suite Bf9000–Bf18,000.

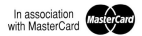

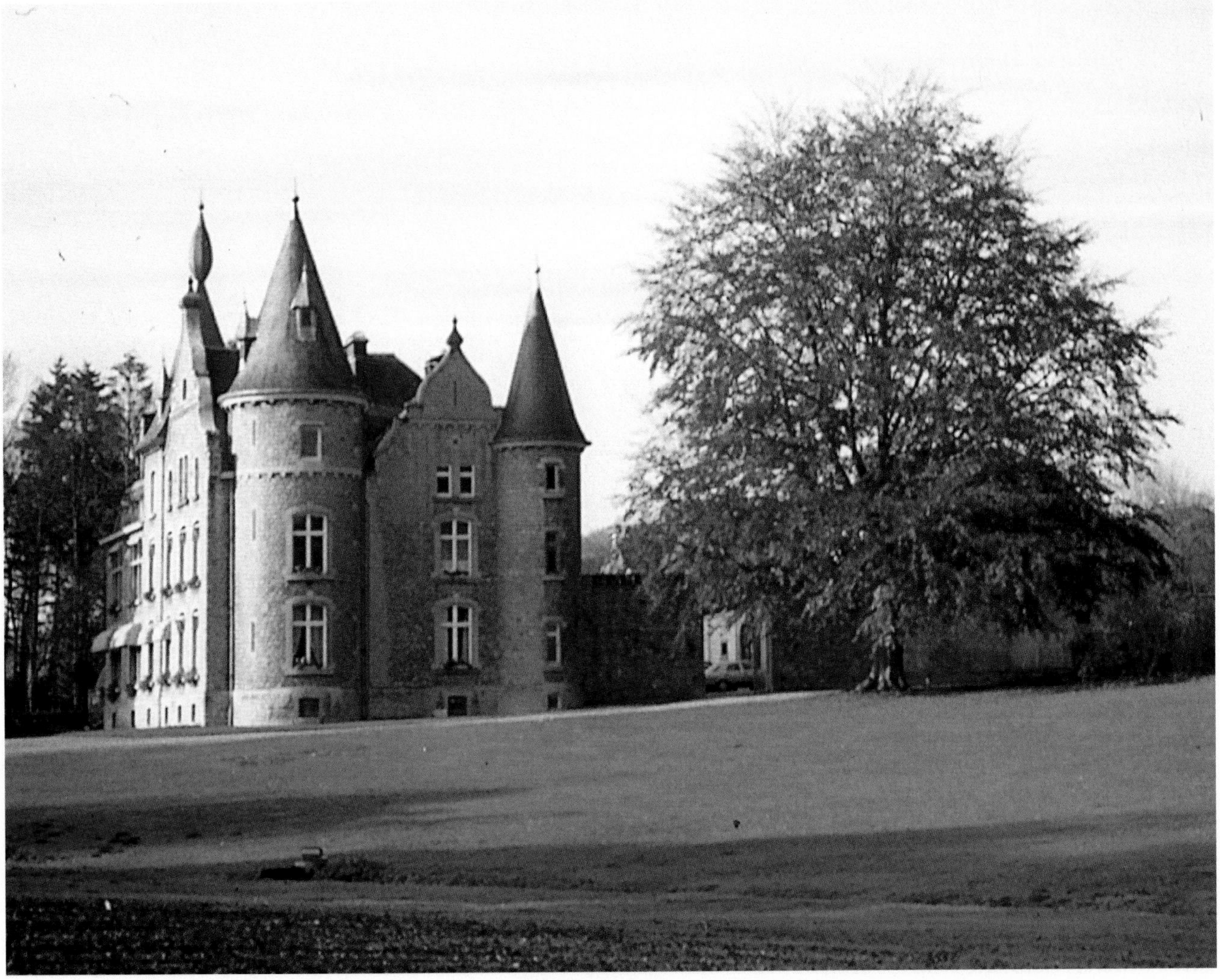

CHÂTEAU D'HASSONVILLE

MARCHE-EN-FAMENNE, B-6900, BELGIUM
TEL: 32 84 31 10 25 FAX: 32 84 31 60 27

This is a fairy-tale 17th century château, with turrets, spires and pinnacles and peacocks strutting on the lawns. It is owned by the Rodrigues family, ideal for a long stay of for an overnight stop when travelling. The interior is sumptuous and the decoration very grand – brilliant chandeliers, swagged silk curtains in jewel colours and exquisite antiques. The bedrooms facing the park have wonderful views, furnished for a sybaritic lifestyle, the bathrooms are contemporary appointed. Guests start their day taking breakfast in the graceful conservatory, filled with exotic plants. Later in the day, after relaxing with apéritifs in the bar, they feast in the elegant restaurant amidst candles, sparkling crystal and gleaming silver. The menu is sophisticated, and the award winning sommelier advises on the choice of wine. There are museums and caves nearby or residents explore the countryside on the house bicycles or in hot air balloons. Others fish, take boats out on the river, play snooker, try clay pigeon shooting and watch falconry displays, while golfers use the hotel's practice ground before playing the three local courses. **Directions:** From Brussels take the outway No: 18 (Marche) on the E 411 Bruxelles–Namur. On the N4 go out on Km 98 (Aye) and follow 6Km the castle indications. Price guide: Single Bf4500; double/twin Bf5200–Bf7200.

20 rms · MasterCard · VISA · AMERICAN EXPRESS · 20

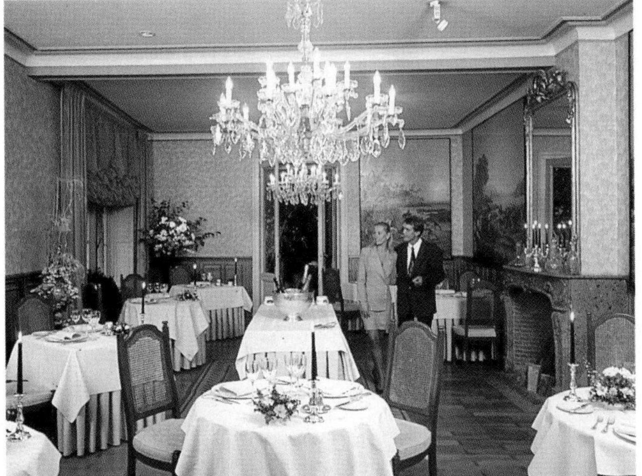

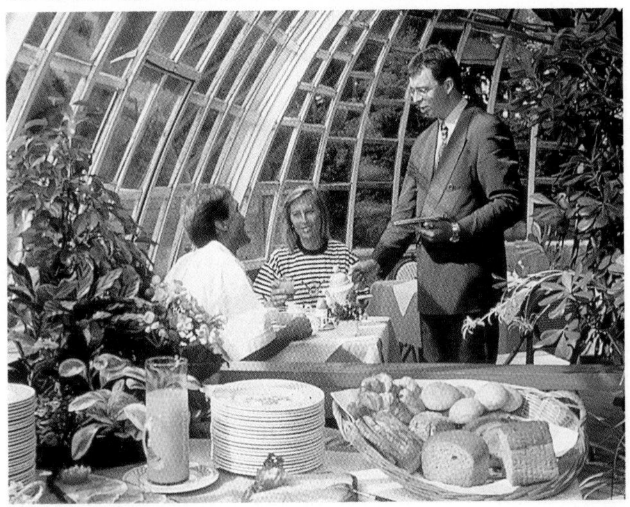

SCHOLTESHOF

KERMTSTRAAT 130, B-3512 STEVOORT, HASSELT, BELGIUM
TEL: 32 11 25 02 02 FAX: 32 11 25 43 28

Roger Souvereyns is a famous chef who has been awarded two Michelin stars, his other talents include landscape gardening, antique collecting, writing about culinary myths, and a flair for renovating old houses. All this is immediately apparent on arriving at the Scholteshof. This restaurant-hotel stands in eleven hectares, having its own vineyards, the grounds planted for colour the year round, pools, fruit trees and a prolific herb garden. The interior has polished slate and tiled floors, fine panelling, and the salons are appropriate settings for the many beautiful antiques and paintings. Fragrant flowers, freshly picked, add to the welcoming ambience. The guest rooms differ delightfully, each as charming as the next, with individual colour schemes and characteristics, great attention having been given to detail and modern comforts. Having studied Roger Souvereyns inspired menu, guests should next visit his awe-inspiring wine cellar to select a mellow wine to accompany his legendary cooking. A special arrangement with the Limburg Golf & Country Club has led to privileged Golf & Gastronomy packages. The Midweek Spring Flings are reasonable. Impressive corporate meetings can be organised. **Directions:** From Brussels take E314 towards Louvain, then exit 25 towards Hasselt(N2), watching for signs to Stevoort. Price guide: Double/twin BEF2900–5000; suites BEF8500; apartments BEF14000

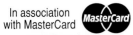

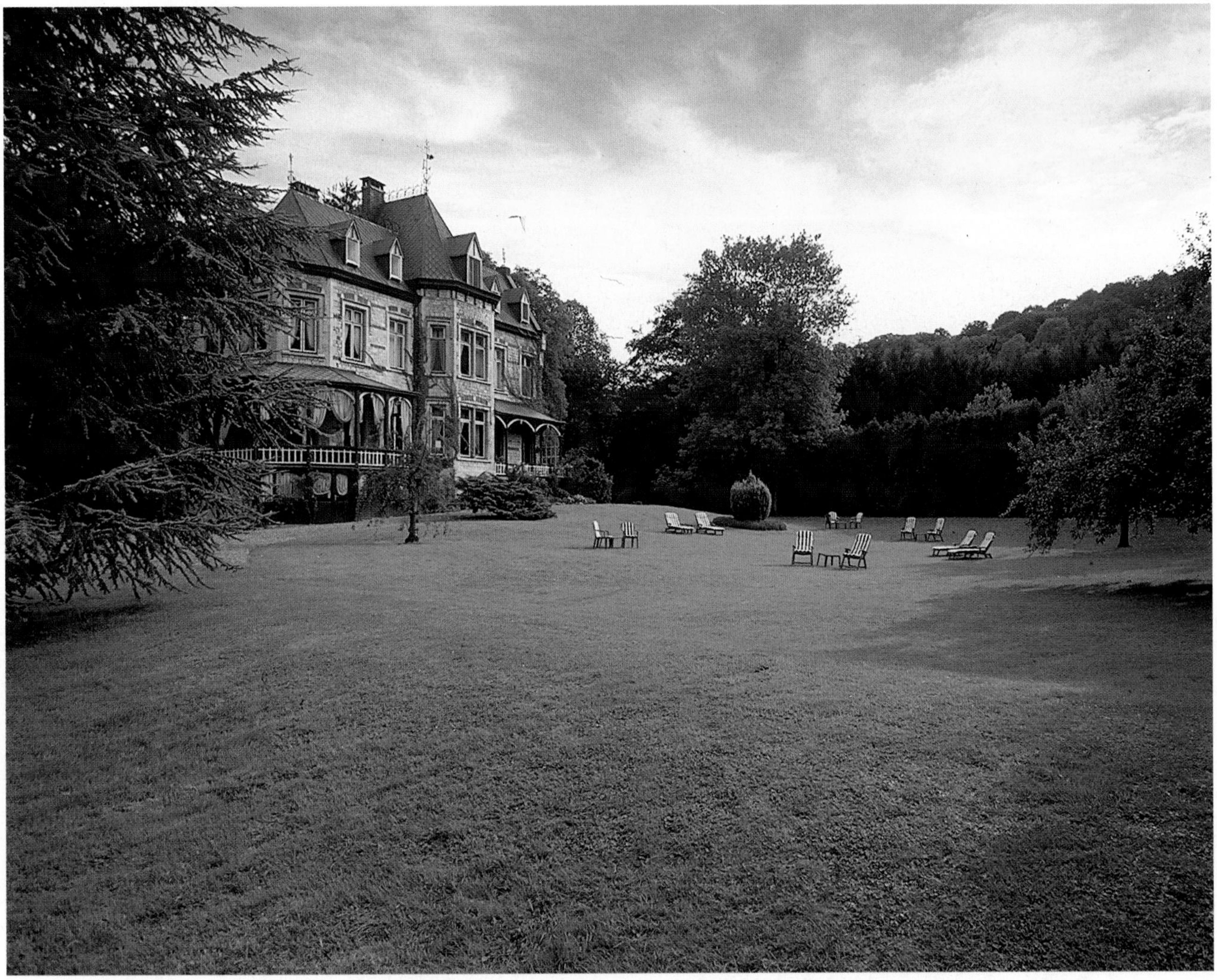

HOTEL CHÂTEAU DE PALOGNE

ROUTE DU PALOGNE, 3, 4190 VIEUXVILLE, BELGIUM

TEL: 32 86 21 38 74 FAX: 32 86 21 38 76

The Château de Palogne was built in the last century – its beauty is magical – and the surrounding parkland filled with centuries' old trees is bordered by two rivers, the Lambree and the Ourthe. It is on the outskirts of the attractive village of Vieuxville, not far from Lieges. It is an elite hotel, with just eleven guest rooms – each named after a different flower and having its own appropriate colour scheme. The period furniture is handsome and all have fine views over estate. They have been thoughtfully equipped to meet the demands of today's travellers. Breakfast always includes a delicious platter of fruit. Guests relax in the elegant salon, filled with fine antiques and big bowls of flowers, or enjoy aperitifs in the bar, or in warm weather on the terrace, while waiting for the car service which will take them just 1 km distant to the Restaurant au Vieux Logis where they can dine in splendour and drink the finest wines. Daniel and Dely Pauwels are superb hosts and have created a tranquil and welcoming ambience. They will arrange golf, tennis, cycle hire, riding and canoeing for energetic guests and recommend lovely walks. **Directions:** From Brussels take Highway E411 towards Namur and N4 through Durbury after which follow signs to Barvaux, Bamal and Vieuxville. Price guide: Double/twin Bf2500–5500.

The British Isles 

William Blake was right. England is a green and pleasant land. You will also find soaring medieval cathedrals, tributes to the faith of the churchmen and craftsmen who built them, grand country mansions of the aristocracy, filled with treasures, amongst them paintings, furniture, and tapesteries, and set in elegantly landscaped grounds; grim fortified castles, their grey stone walls still fronting a bygone hostile world; and endless gardens, rich with lilies and roses, tended by generations of dedicated gardeners.

All these can be visited by everyone, either free or for only a small entrance fee. Equip yourself with as many membership tickets as you can get from English Heritage, British Tourist Authority and the National Trust.*But Great Britain and the islands around it are more than one vast historical theme park. Many of its most profound pleasures are to be found in wandering through the changing countryside, at any season of the year.

A short ride, for instance, from York, will take you through long stretches of wild, heather-covered moorland, ablaze with colour in the Autumn, or past the steep, sheep covered mountainsides of the Dales.

Venture further afield and the images will haunt you. Ireland for example which has a countryside and seaside of amazing beauty and wonderful golf courses.

The hillside of the Cairngorms in Scotland, where bright purple heather casts swathes of colour on hills where only game birds and deer are hardy enough to survive. The dramatic mountain peak of Snowdon, the tallest mountain in Wales – a dramatic backdrop to the Snowdonia National Park –with its thickly wooded valleys, mountain lakes, moors and estuaries, or the country lanes of the Lake District – a combination of superb peaks, tumbling rivers, waterfalls and shimmering lakes.

*find out more in Johansens Guide to Historic Houses, Castles and Gardens.

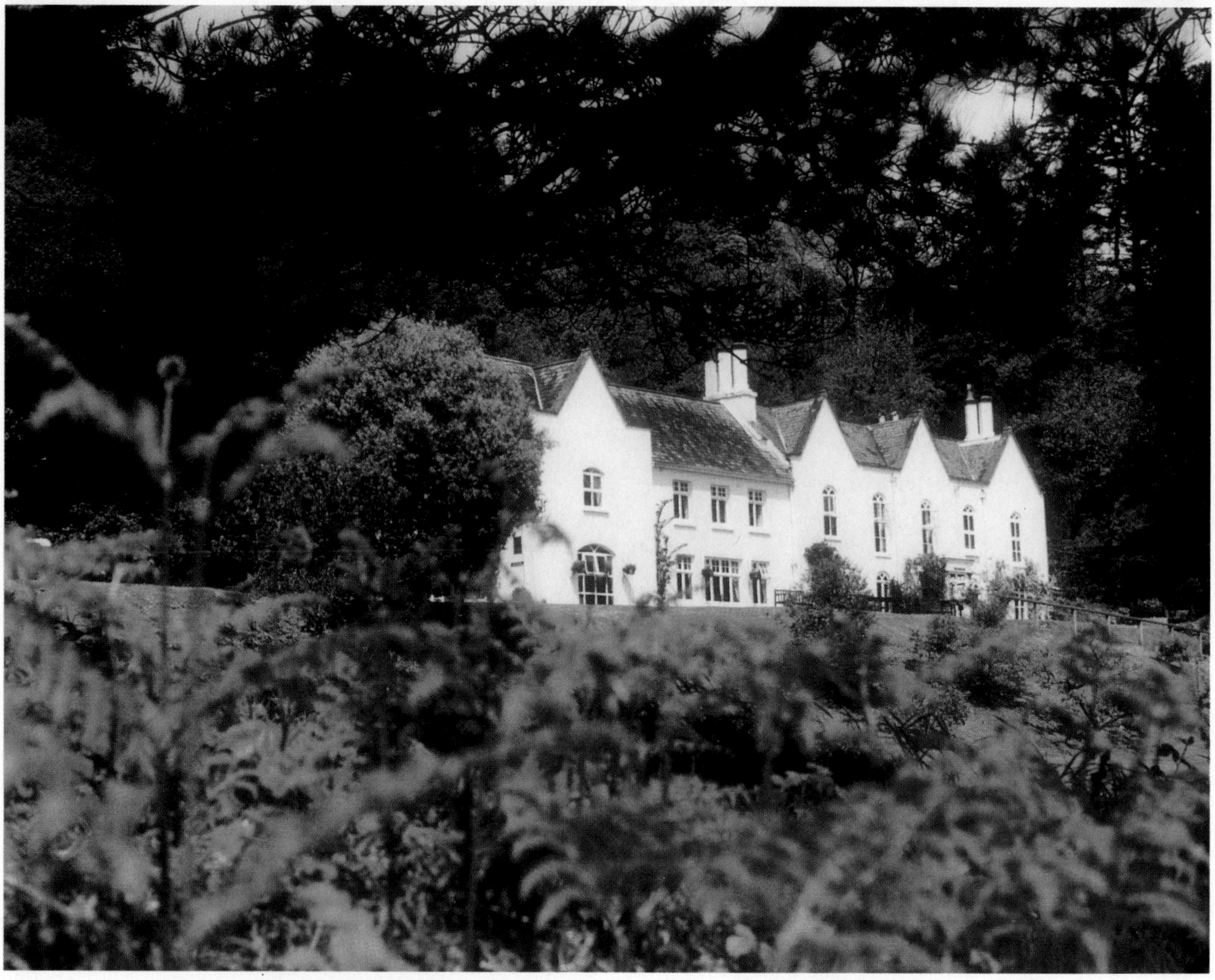

HOLNE CHASE HOTEL AND RESTAURANT

NR ASHBURTON, DEVON TQ13 7NS

TEL: 44 1364 631471 FAX: 44 1364 631453 E-MAIL: info@holne.chase.co.uk

With sweeping lawns, and an outstanding position in over 70 acres of park and woodland inside Dartmoor National Park, Holne Chase is dedicated to relaxation. Its previous role as a 11th-century hunting lodge has become the hotel's theme for attracting visitors to traditional pursuits in a break from the bustle of everyday life. Fly-fishermen can enjoy the hotel's mile-long beat on the River Dart and driven shoots can be arranged in season. The hotel's stables have been converted to provide "Sporting Lodges" with sitting room and fire downstairs and bedroom suite upstairs. All the hotel's en suite bedrooms are individually furnished and many command spectacular views over the Dart Valley. A walled garden supplies the inviting restaurant, where Master Chef Wayne Pearson provides imaginative cuisine. Holne Chase is a good base for exploring Dartmoor's open moorland and wooded valleys. Picturesque villages and sandy beaches are within reach while Exeter, Plymouth and the English Riviera are just a short drive away. Canoeing, golf and riding can all be arranged. A member of Relais Du Silence, AA 3 Star, 3 Rosettes. **Directions:** Take the Ashburton turning off the A38 and follow the signs for Two Bridges. Holne Chase is on the right after the road crosses the River Dart. Price guide: Single £75; double/twin £115; suite £150.

EASTWELL MANOR

BOUGHTON LEES, ASHFORD, KENT TN25 4HR
TEL: 44 1233 219955 FAX: 44 1233 635530

In the midst of a 3,000-acre estate, set in 62 acres of lovely grounds, lies Eastwell Manor. It was once the home of Queen Victoria's second son, Prince Alfred, and his wife. The Queen and her elder son, later to become Edward VII, were frequent visitors here. The elegant bedrooms are named after past owners, lords, ladies and gentlemen, bearing witness to the hotel's rich history. Each room is individually and gracefully furnished and offers every modern comfort. Huge open fireplaces with stone mantles, carved panelling, leather Chesterfield sofas and fine antique furniture are features of the lounges, billiard room and bar. Modern British cuisine is served in the handsome wood panelled dining room, matched by an excellent cellar of carefully chosen wines. Guests are invited to take advantage of the hotel's tennis court and croquet lawn, while a variety of other leisure pursuits are available locally. The Manor is conveniently located for visiting the historic cathedral city of Canterbury, Leeds Castle and a number of charming market towns. It is also sited near to the Ashford stop for Eurostar. **Directions:** M20 junction 9. A28 towards Canterbury, then A251 signed Faversham. Hotel is three miles north of Ashford in the village of Boughton Lees. Price guide: Single £120–£160; double/twin £160–£210; suites £280–£300.

80

TILLMOUTH PARK

CORNHILL-ON-TWEED, NEAR BERWICK-UPON-TWEED, NORTHUMBERLAND TD12 4UU
TEL: 44 1890 882255 FAX: 44 1890 882540

Designed by Charles Barry, the son of the famous Victorian architect of the Houses of Parliament in Westminster, Tillmouth Park offers the same warm welcome today as it did when it was an exclusive private country house. It is situated in a rich countryside farmland of deciduous woodland and moor. The generously sized bedrooms have been recently refurbished in a distinctive old fashioned style with period furniture, although all offer modern day amenities. The kitchen prides itself on traditional country fare, with the chef using fresh local produce to create imaginative and well presented dishes. The restaurant serves a fine table d'hôte menu, while the Bistro is less formal. Fresh salmon and game are always available with 24 hours' notice. A well chosen wine list and a vast selection of malt whiskies complement the cuisine. Tillmouth Park is an ideal centre for country pursuits including field sports, fishing, hill walking, shooting, riding, birdwatching and golf. For the spectator there is rugby, curling and horse racing during the season. Places of interest nearby include stately homes such as Floors, Manderston and Paxton. Flodden Field, Lindisfarne and Holy Island are all within easy reach and the coast is just 15 minutes away. **Directions:** Tillmouth Park is on the A698 Cornhill-on-Tweed to Berwick-on-Tweed road. Price guide: Single £80–£95; twin/double £115–£150.

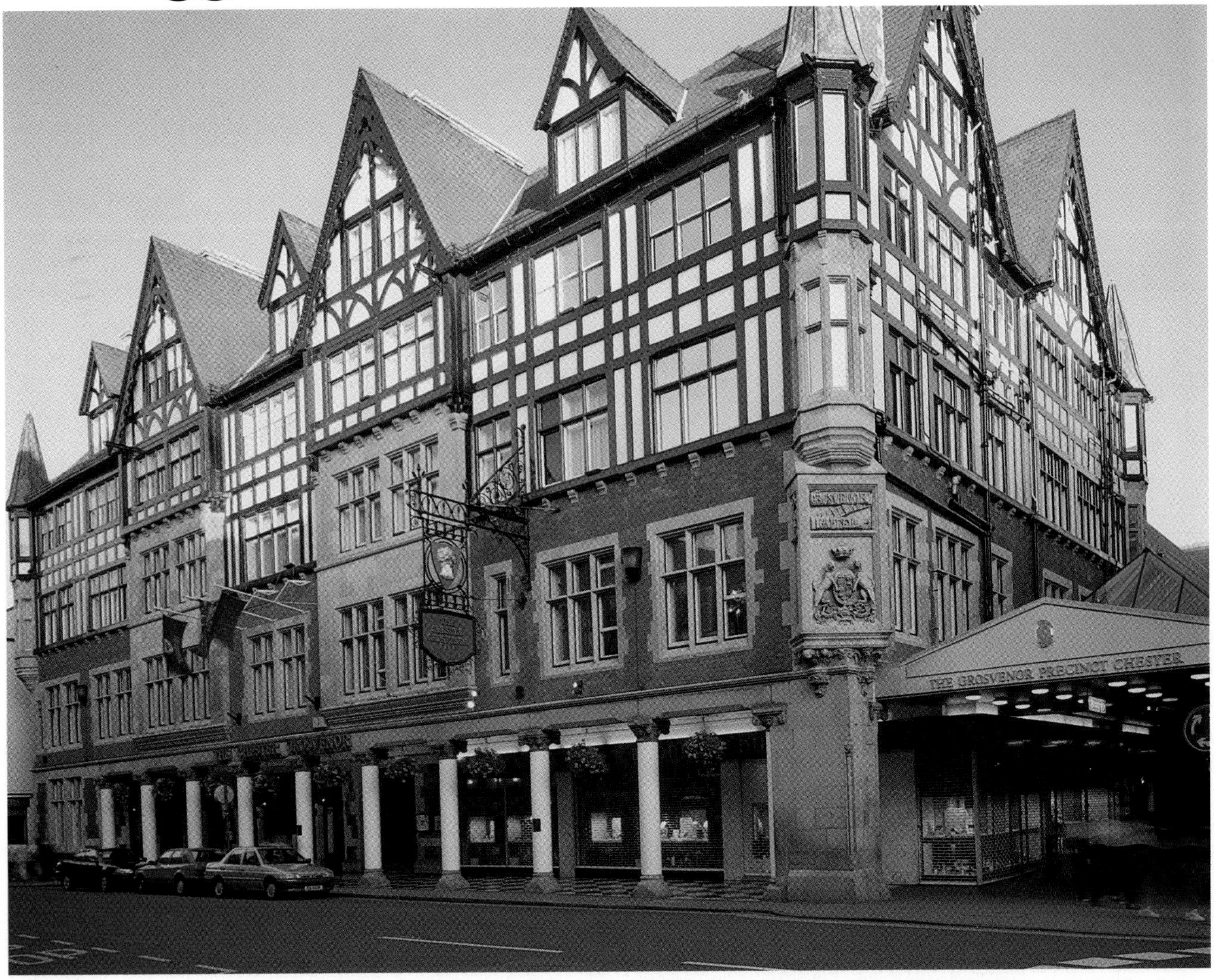

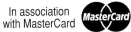

THE CHESTER GROSVENOR

EASTGATE, CHESTER CH1 1LT

TEL: 44 1244 324024 FAX: 44 1244 313246

The Chester Grosvenor is in the heart of the historic city of Chester beneath the famous Queen Victoria Clock. The hotel is owned by the Duke of Westminster's Grosvenor Estate. It is renowned for its fabulous cuisine and has two restaurants – the Arkle and La Brasserie. The Arkle is an award winning gourmet restaurant, named after the famous racehorse Arkle. La Brasserie is an informal Parisian style restaurant which is open all day every day. The Chester Grosvenor has an extensive cellar with over 600 bins of fine wine. There are 85 bedrooms of which 11 are suites. All are beautifully appointed, fully air-conditioned with 24 hour room service provided and each room is equipped with all the amenities expected in a de luxe hotel awarded 5 AA Stars. The hotel has its own leisure suite with a multi-gymnasium, sauna and solarium and membership of an exclusive local country club which has indoor and outdoor swimming pools, tennis and squash. Adjacent are the famous Roman Walls and the Chester Rows with their boutiques and exclusive shops. A short stroll away is Chester Cathedral, Chester race course and the River Dee. **Directions:** In the centre of Chester on Eastgate. 24-hour NCP car parking – follow signs to Grosvenor Precinct Car Park. Price guide: Weekend break rate from £150 per double room per night. Single from £160; double/twin from £250; suites £400.

      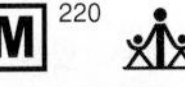      

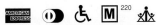

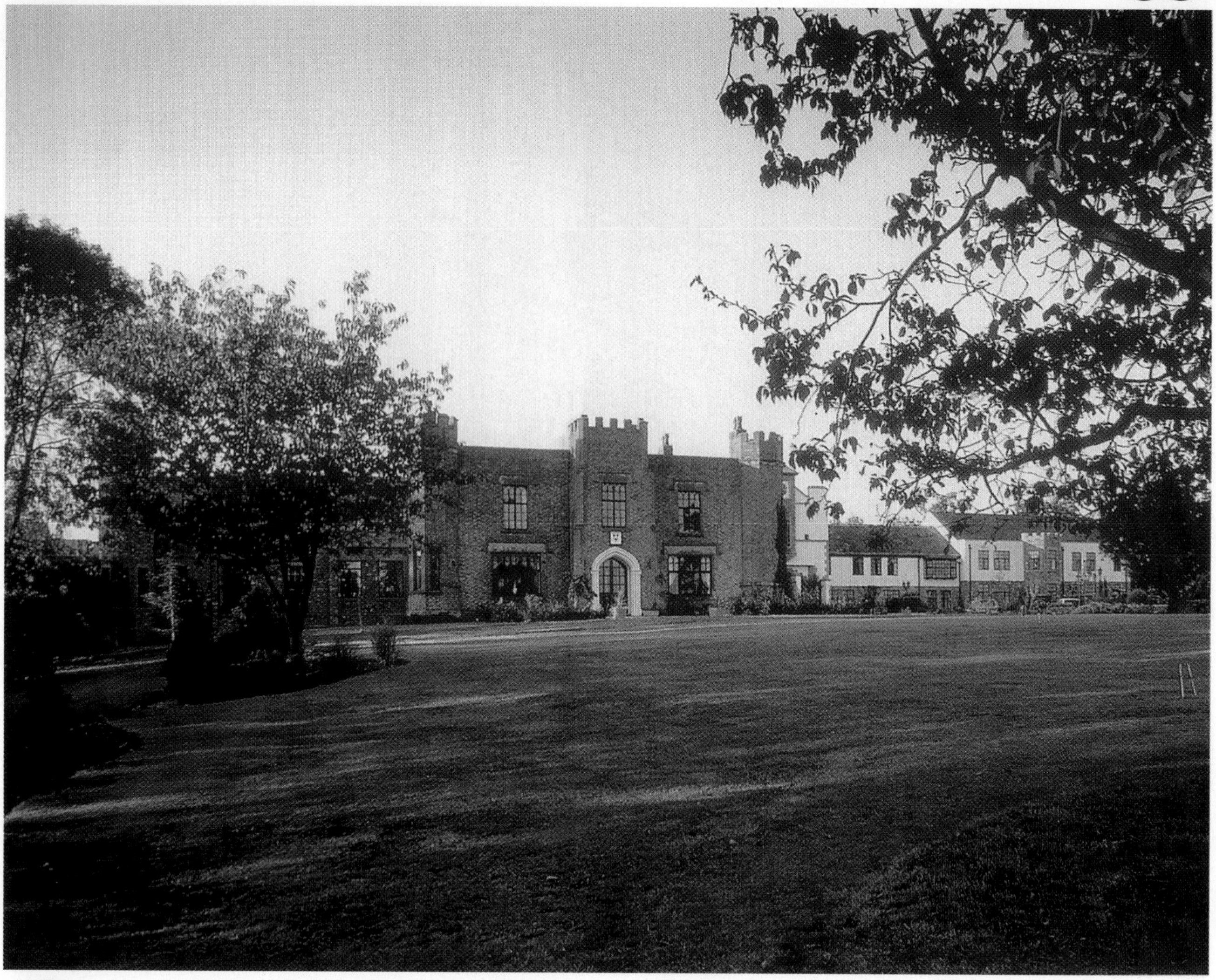

CRABWALL MANOR

PARKGATE ROAD, MOLLINGTON, CHESTER, CHESHIRE CH1 6NE
TEL: 44 1244 851666 FAX: 44 1244 851400 E-MAIL: SALES@CRABWALL.U-NET.COM

Crabwall Manor can be traced back to Saxon England, prior to the Norman Conquest. The present Grade II listed manor at the heart of the hotel is believed to have originated from a Tudor farmhouse. Set in 11 acres of wooded parkland on the outer reaches of Chester, the hotel has achieved a fine reputation under the ownership of Carl Lewis. A relaxed ambience is enhanced by staff who combine attentive service with friendliness and care. Bathrobes and sherry are among the many extras to be found in the bedrooms and luxury suites. Brightly printed drapes and pastel shades lend a freshness to the décor of the spacious lounge and reception areas, while a log fire crackling away in the inglenook fireplace adds warmth. Chef Michael Truelove, formerly of The Box Tree Restaurant in Ilkley, introduces a classic French influence to traditional English dishes. Manchester and Liverpool Airports are 30 minutes away by road. Chester, the Wirral and North Wales are all easily accessible. **Directions:** Go to end of M56, ignoring signs to Chester. Follow signs to Queensferry and North Wales, taking the A5117 to the next roundabout. Left onto the A540, towards Chester for 2 miles. Crabwall Manor is on the right. Price guide: Single £90–£120; double/twin £105–£160; suite £190–£250. Weekend rates available. Internet: http://www.hotelnet.co.uk/crabwall

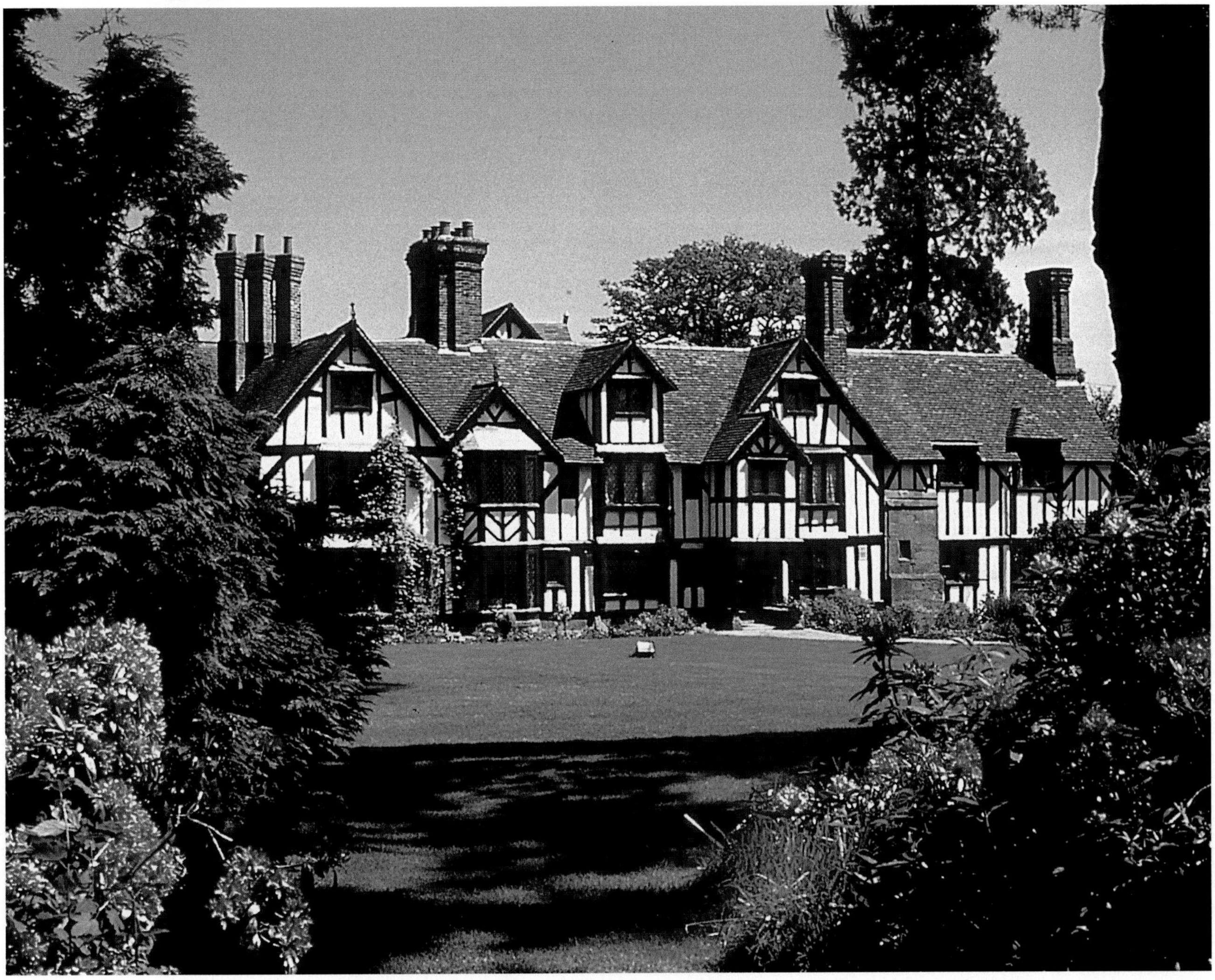

NAILCOTE HALL

NAILCOTE LANE, BERKSWELL, NR COVENTRY, WARWICKSHIRE CV7 7DE
TEL: 44 1203 466174 FAX: 44 1203 470720

Nailcote Hall is a charming Elizabethan country house hotel set in 15 acres of gardens and surrounded by Warwickshire countryside. Built in 1640, the house was used by Cromwell during the Civil War and was damaged by his troops prior to the assault on Kenilworth Castle. Ideally located in the heart of England, Nailcote Hall is within 15 minutes' drive of the castle towns of Kenilworth and Warwick, Coventry Cathedral, Birmingham International Airport/Station and the NEC. Situated at the centre of the Midlands motorway network, Birmingham city centre, the ICC and Stratford-upon-Avon are less than 30 minutes away. Leisure facilities include indoor swimming pool, gymnasium, solarium and sauna. Outside there are all-weather tennis courts, petanque, croquet, a challenging 9-hole par-3 golf course and putting green (host to the Midland Professional Short Course Championship). In the intimate Tudor surroundings of the Oak Room restaurant, the chef will delight you with superb cuisine, while the cellar boasts an extensive choice of international wines. En suite bedrooms offer luxury accommodation, and elegant facilities are available for conferences, private dining and corporate hospitality. **Directions:** Situated 6 miles south of Birmingham International Airport/ NEC on the B4101 Balsall Common–Coventry road. Price guide: Single £125; double/twin £135; suite £155–£195.

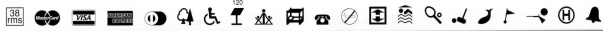

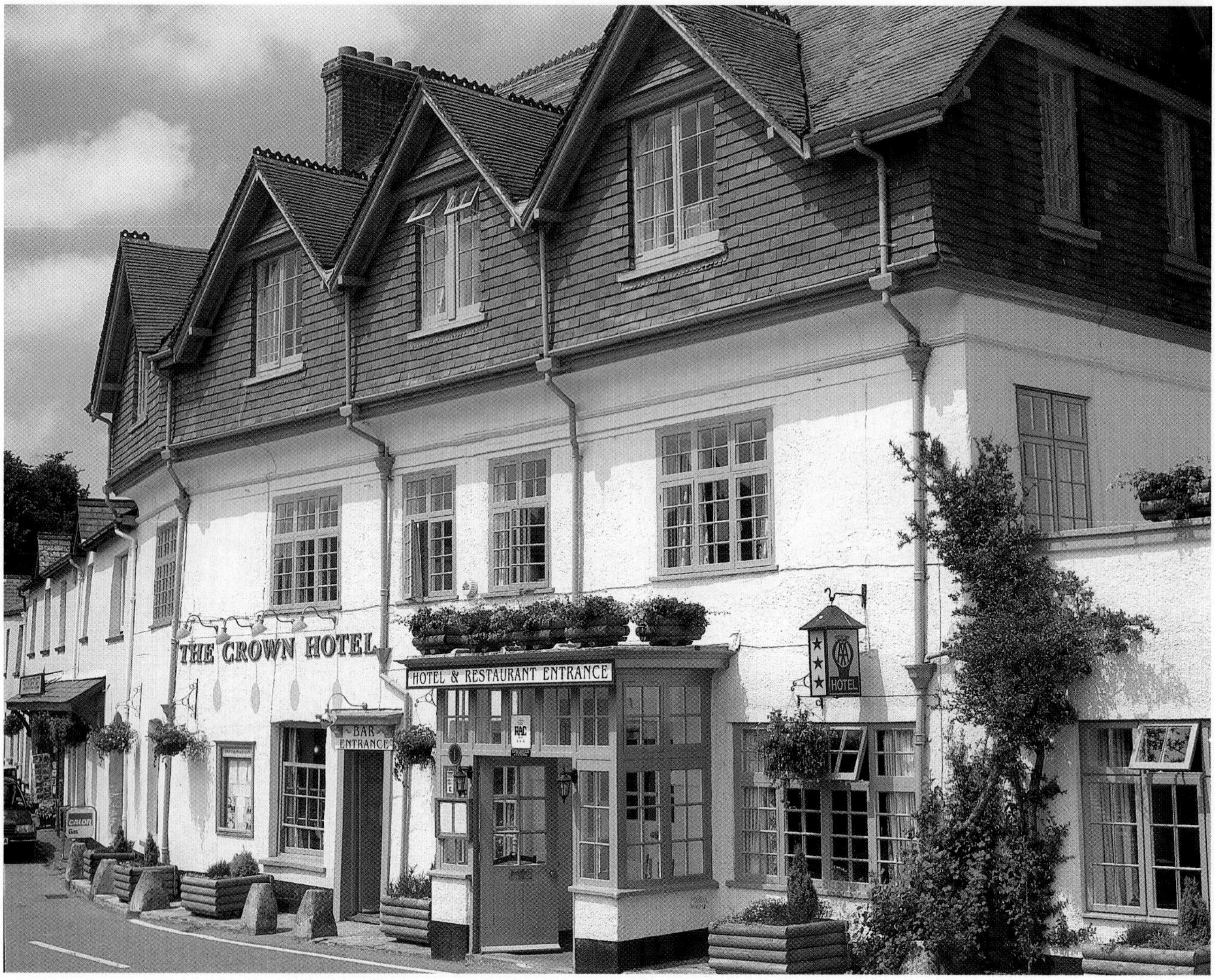

THE CROWN HOTEL

EXFORD, EXMOOR NATIONAL PARK, SOMERSET TA24 7PP
TEL: 441643 831554/5 FAX: 441643 831665 E-MAIL: bradleyhotelsexmoor@easynet.co.uk

This coaching inn, almost three hundred years old, in the Exmoor National Park is surrounded by wonderful countryside, from coastline to valleys, streams and moorland, populated with red deer, ponies, amazing birdlife and salmon. The hotel has been completely refurbished, to the highest standards of elegance and comfort. Guests can enjoy its comfort in every season – its coolness in summer, its warmth in winter.The bedrooms, all en suite, have been beautifully decorated and are well-equipped with modern necessities.There is a lively bar, patronised by the locals, for drinks or informal meals ordered from the extensive menu, or guests may prefer an apéritif in the lounge before entering the delightful dining room for a beautifully presented evening meal from the seasonal menu. Good wines complement the meal. After dinner guests may wish to sroll in the water garden. Nearby, fly fishing (and tuition) in local rivers, riding over the moor and clay pigeon shooting can be arranged. Order a packed lunch and walk the moor or visit Lynmouth and Porlock. **Directions:** Exit M5, junction 27. Drive eight miles down the A361, then take the A396 to Wheddon Cross, where Exford is signposted. Price guide: Single £42–£57; double/twin £84–£100

SOUTH LODGE HOTEL

LOWER BEEDING, NR HORSHAM, WEST SUSSEX RH13 6PS

TEL: 44 1403 891711 FAX: 44 1403 891766 E-MAIL: inquiries@southlodgehotel.dial.iql.co.uk

South Lodge is a magnificent country house hotel, which has successfully captured the essence of Victorian elegance. With one of the most beautiful settings in rural Sussex, unrivalled views may be enjoyed over the South Downs from the hotel's elevated position. The mansion was originally built by Frederick Ducane Godman, a 19th century botanist and explorer, and the hotel's wonderful 90 acre grounds are evidence of his dedication. Many original features have been preserved, wood panelling throughout the hotel and open fires in the reception rooms. The 39 individually designed bedrooms are luxuriously equipped with every modern day requirement. The Camillia Restaurant has menus which change with the seasons and are complemented by a wine list from many countries. The private rooms are perfect for both social and business functions. A variety of leisure facilities, including croquet, tennis and clay pigeon shooting, are available on site (shooting and archery by prior arrangement), also golf at South Lodge's two spectacular 18 hole championship courses just minutes from the hotel. Nearby attractions include Glyndebourne, Chartwell and the Royal Pavilion in Brighton. **Directions:** On A281 at Lower Beeding, south of Horsham. Gatwick airport 12 miles. Nearest motorway M23 junction 11. Price guide: Single from £120; double/twin from £145; suite from £265.

LYTHE HILL HOTEL

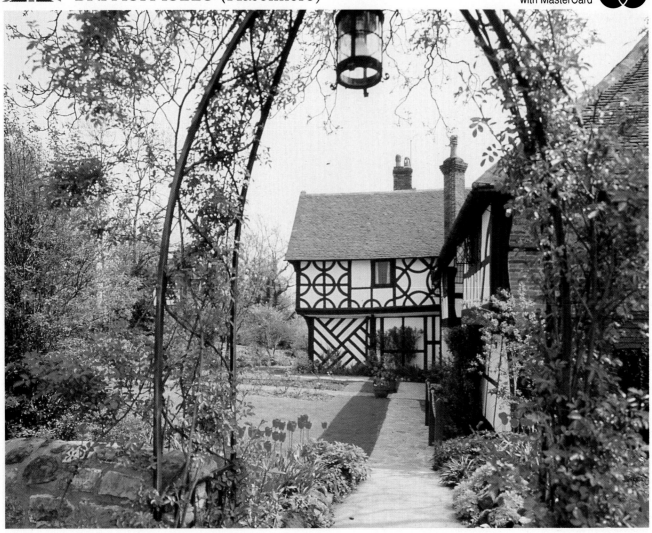

PETWORTH ROAD, HASLEMERE, SURREY GU27 3BQ

TEL: 44 1428 651251 FAX: 44 1428 644131 E-MAIL: lythehill@grayswood.co.uk

Cradled by the Surrey foothills in a tranquil setting is the enchanting Lythe Hill Hotel. It is an unusual cluster of ancient buildings – parts of which date from the 14th century. While most of the beautifully appointed accommodation is in the more recently converted part of the hotel, there are five charming bedrooms in the Tudor House, including the Henry VIII room with a four-poster bed dated 1614! There are two delightful restaurants, the Auberge de France offers classic French cuisine in the oak-panelled room which overlooks the lake and parklands, and the 'Dining Room' has the choice of imaginative English fare. An exceptional wine list offers over 200 wines from more than a dozen countries. Its situation, easily accessible from London, Gatwick and Heathrow. An excellent train service at Haslemere makes both central London and Portsmouth less than one hour away. National Trust hillside adjoining the hotel grounds provides interesting walking and views over the surrounding countryside. The area is steeped in history, with the country houses of Petworth, Clandon and Uppark to visit as well as racing at Goodwood and polo at Cowdray Park. Brighton and the south coast are only a few miles away. **Directions:** Lythe Hill lies about 1½ miles from the centre of Haslemere, east on the B2131. Price guide: Single from £99; double/twin from £115; suite from £138.

SHARROW BAY COUNTRY HOUSE HOTEL

HOWTOWN, LAKE ULLSWATER, PENRITH, CUMBRIA CA10 2LZ
TEL: 44 17684 86301/86483 FAX: 44 17684 86349

Now in its 50th year, Sharrow Bay is known to discerning travellers the world over, who return again and again to this magnificent lakeside hotel. It wasn't always so. Francis Coulson arrived in 1948. He was joined by Brian Sack in 1952 and the partnership flourished, to make Sharrow Bay what it is today. Recently they have been joined by Nigel Lawrence and Nigel Lightburn who carry on the tradition. All the bedrooms are elegantly furnished and guests are guaranteed the utmost comfort. In addition to the main hotel, there are four cottages nearby which offer similarly luxurious accommodation. All the reception rooms are delightfully decorated. Sharrow Bay is universally renowned for its wonderful cuisine. The team of chefs led by Johnnie Martin and Colin Akrigg ensure that each meal is a special occasion, a mouthwatering adventure! With its private jetty and 12 acres of lakeside gardens Sharrow Bay offers guests boating, swimming, and fishing. Fell-walking is a challenge for the upwardly mobile. Sharrow Bay is the oldest British member of Relais et Châteaux. Closed in December and January. **Directions:** M6 junction 40, A592 to Lake Ullswater, into Pooley Bridge, then take Howtown road for 2 miles. Price guide: (including 7 course Dinner and full English Breakfast) Single £110–£260; double/twin £220–£350; suite £340–£350.

London

London is the flavour of the year. Everyone who is anyone is talking about this city as though they have single handedly unearthed a buried treasure. Londoners are happy to be associated with a capital thought of as the style capital, the fashion capital, the music capital, the film capital and today even the restaurant capital of Europe.

But what is different? What has changed? This city has always been great.

The Tower of London, Buckingham Palace, the resonant grandeur of our Royal parks have not changed. St Paul's Cathedral has always inspired and been spectacular during the day and night – as the spotlight falls gracefully on its dome and the white collar workers of the City dash to their next meeting, or wine bar, or home – nothing has altered.

The turnaround in London restaurants is incredible – in part due to the hard work and inspiration of people like Terence Conran. Our London chefs now have worldwide recognition as being some of the best in the world. Marco Pierre White, Brian Turner, Gary Rhodes and Co have helped to establish flair and a sense of fun in eating out. The variety of cuisine on offer to the visitor is comparable with that offered in the other restaurant capitals of the world.

Traditionally London has been divided between the City to the east, where its banking and commercial interests lie, and Westminster to the west, the seat of the royal court and of government. In these two areas stand the Tower of London and St Paul's Cathedral, Westminster Abbey and the Houses of Parliament, Buckingham Palace, and the older palace of St James's.

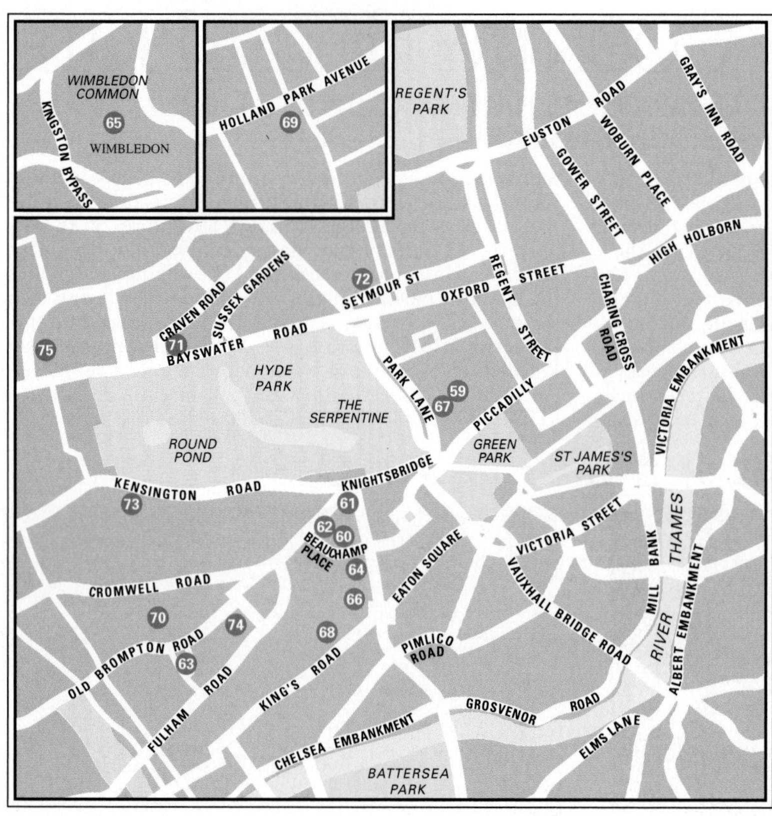

Other parts of London worth exploring include Covent Garden, where the former fruit and flower market has been converted into a lively modern bazaar; Hyde Park, Green Park, St James's Park and Kensington Gardens; the museum district of South Kensington; the South Bank Arts Complex; and Hayward Gallery where you can view the very best and latest in performing arts. The views from the gallery are stunning – to the west Parliament and Big Ben, to the east the dome of St Paul's on London's changing skyline.

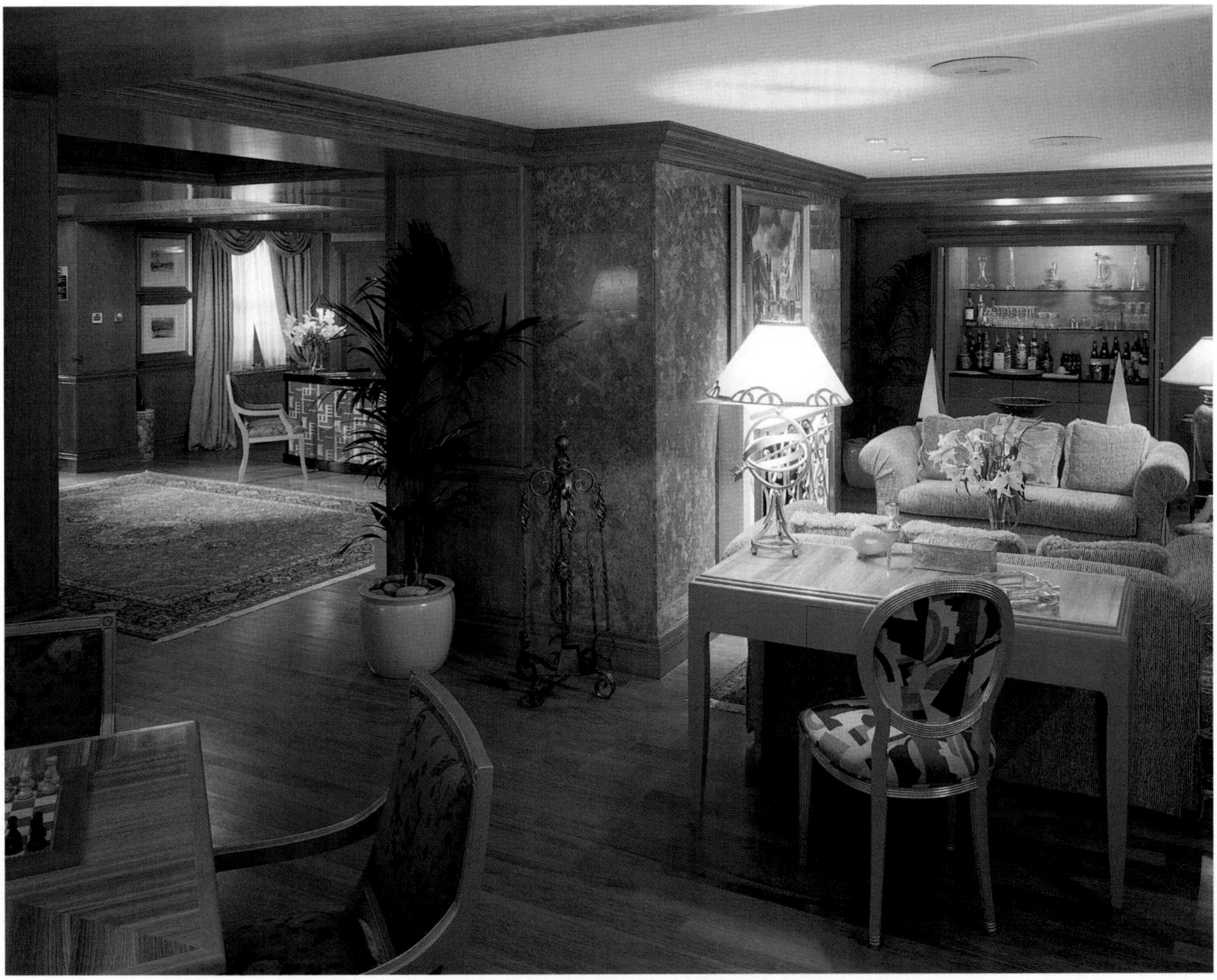

THE ASCOTT MAYFAIR

49 HILL STREET, LONDON W1
TEL: 44 171 499 6868 FAX: 44 171 499 0705

This, the latest concept in city centre accommodation, offers all the benefits of a hotel and yet also privacy and space in what the brochure describes as "residences", with one, two or three bedrooms, in a spectacular art deco building. The apartments have a 24 hour concierge for security and assistance. A maid will be assigned to you for the full duration of your stay. There is no restaurant; however, a complimentary Continental breakfast is served on weekdays in The Terrace, overlooking the private gardens. There is an Honour Bar in The Club where guests can mingle or entertain. The Hothouse offers a gym, sauna, steamroom and solarium. The Business Service includes the use of a private boardroom. A marvellous kitchen is provided in each apartment with everything necessary for entertaining in the versatile lounge. The study area has fax and computer links. The sitting room is extremely comfortable and beautifully decorated. It has satellite television, a music system and video. The luxurious bedrooms have amazing en suite bathrooms, full of soft white towels. The Ascott is in the heart of London – Mayfair being close to all the major shopping centres and best restaurants, theatre-land and sightseeing. **Directions:** Hill Street is off Berkeley Square, near Green Park Underground Station. Price guide: 1 bed £164–£247 daily, £1,040–£1,565 weekly; 2 beds from £375daily–£2,365 weekly. (All rates are subject to VAT).

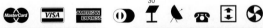

THE BEAUFORT

33 BEAUFORT GARDENS, KNIGHTSBRIDGE, LONDON SW3 1PP
TEL: 44 171 584 5252 FAX: 44 171 589 2834 E–MAIL: thebeaufort@nol.co.uk.

The Beaufort offers the sophisticated traveller all the style and comfort of home – combining warm contempory colourings with the highest possible personal attention. The owner Diana Wallis (pictured below) believes that much of the success of the hotel is due to the charming, attentive staff – a feeling happily endorsed by guests. The Beaufort is situated in a quiet tree-lined square only 100 yards from Harrods and as guests arrive they are all greeted at the front door and given their own door key to come and go as they please. The closed front door gives added security and completes that feeling of home. All the bedrooms are individually decorated, with air conditioning and a great many extras such as shortbread, Swiss chocolates and brandy. The hotel owns a video and cassette library and is home to a magnificent collection of original English floral watercolours. Breakfast is brought to the bedroom – hot rolls and croissants, freshly squeezed orange juice and home-made preserves, tea and coffee. In the drawing room there is a 24-hour honour bar with complimentary champagne and between 4-5pm every day a free cream tea is served with scones, clotted cream and jam. The hotel is proud of its no tipping policy and is open all year. **Directions:** From the Harrods exit at Knightsbridge underground station take the third turning on the left. Price guide: Single £130; double/twin from £150; suites £240.

28 rms

BASIL STREET HOTEL

BASIL STREET, LONDON SW3 1AH

TEL: 44 171-581 3311 FAX: 44 171-581 3693 – FROM USA CALL FREE: UTELL 1 800 448 8355

The Basil feels more like an English home than a hotel. Privately owned by the same family for three generations, this traditional Edwardian hotel is situated in a quiet corner of Knightsbridge, on the threshold of London's most exclusive residential and shopping area. Harrods, Harvey Nichols and other famous stores are only minutes away. It is close to museums and theatres. The spacious public rooms are furnished with antiques, paintings, mirrors and *objets d'art*. The lounge, bar and dining room are on the first floor, reached by the distinctive staircase that dominates the front hall. Bedrooms, all individually furnished, vary in size, style and décor. The Hotel's Dining Room is an ideal venue either for unhurried, civilised lunch or dinner by candlelight with piano music. The Parrot Club, a lounge for the exclusive use of ladies, is a haven of rest in delightful surroundings. The Basil combines tradition and caring individual service with the comfort of a modern, cosmopolitan hotel. There is a discount scheme for regular guests, for weekends and stays of five nights or more. E-Mail: thebasil@aol.com **Directions:** Close to Pavilion Road car park. Basil Street runs off Sloane Street in the direction of Harrods. Near Knightsbridge underground and bus routes. Price guide: Single from £115; double/twin from £145; family room from £230. (Excluding VAT).

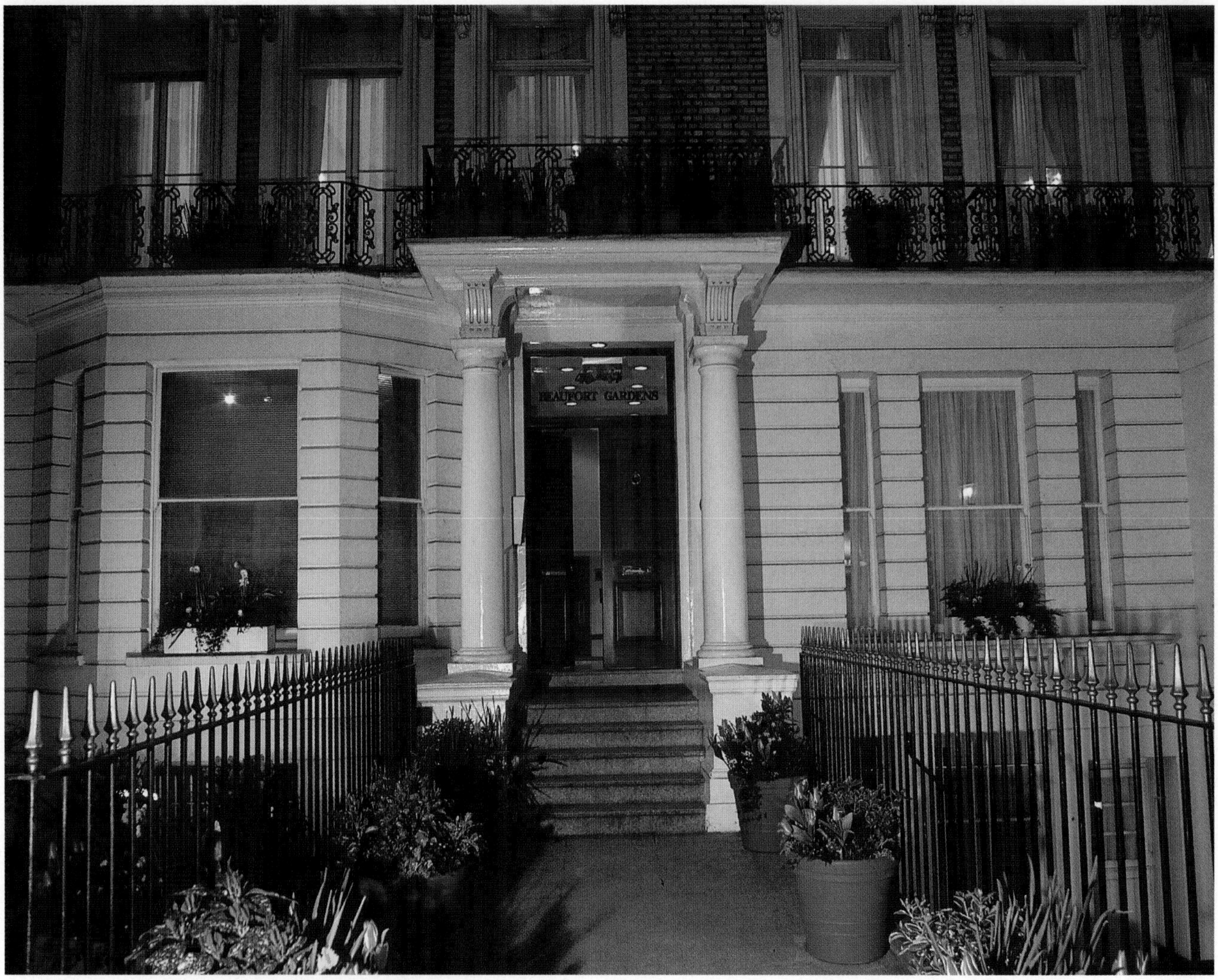

BEAUFORT HOUSE APARTMENTS

45 BEAUFORT GARDENS, KNIGHTSBRIDGE, LONDON SW3 1PN
TEL: 44 171 584 2600 FAX: 44 171 584 6532 – USA CALL FREE: 1-800- 23-5463

Situated in Beaufort Gardens, a quiet tree-lined Regency cul-de-sac in the heart of Knightsbridge, 250 yards from Harrods, Beaufort House is an exclusive establishment comprising 22 self-contained fully serviced luxury apartments. All the comforts of a first-class hotel are combined with the privacy and discretion and the relaxed atmosphere of home. Accommodation ranges in size from an intimate one-bedroomed suite to a spacious, four-bedroomed apartment. Each apartment has been individually decorated in a contemporary style to a standard which is rigourously maintained. All apartments have direct dial telephones, personal safes, satellite TV and video systems. Most bedrooms benefit from en suite bathrooms and several have west facing balconies. The fully fitted and equipped kitchens include washers/dryers; many have dishwashers. A daily maid service is included at no additional charge. Full laundry/dry cleaning services are available. For your added security, a concierge is on call 24 hours a day, through whom taxis, theatre tickets, restaurant reservations and other services are also available. Executive support services are provided with confidentiality assured at all times. Complimentary membership to health and leisure facilities at Champney's Piccadilly is offered to all guests during their stay. **Directions:** Beaufort Gardens leads off Brompton road. Near Harrods and Knightsbridge Tube. Price Guide: £160–£408 per night (+VAT).

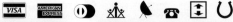

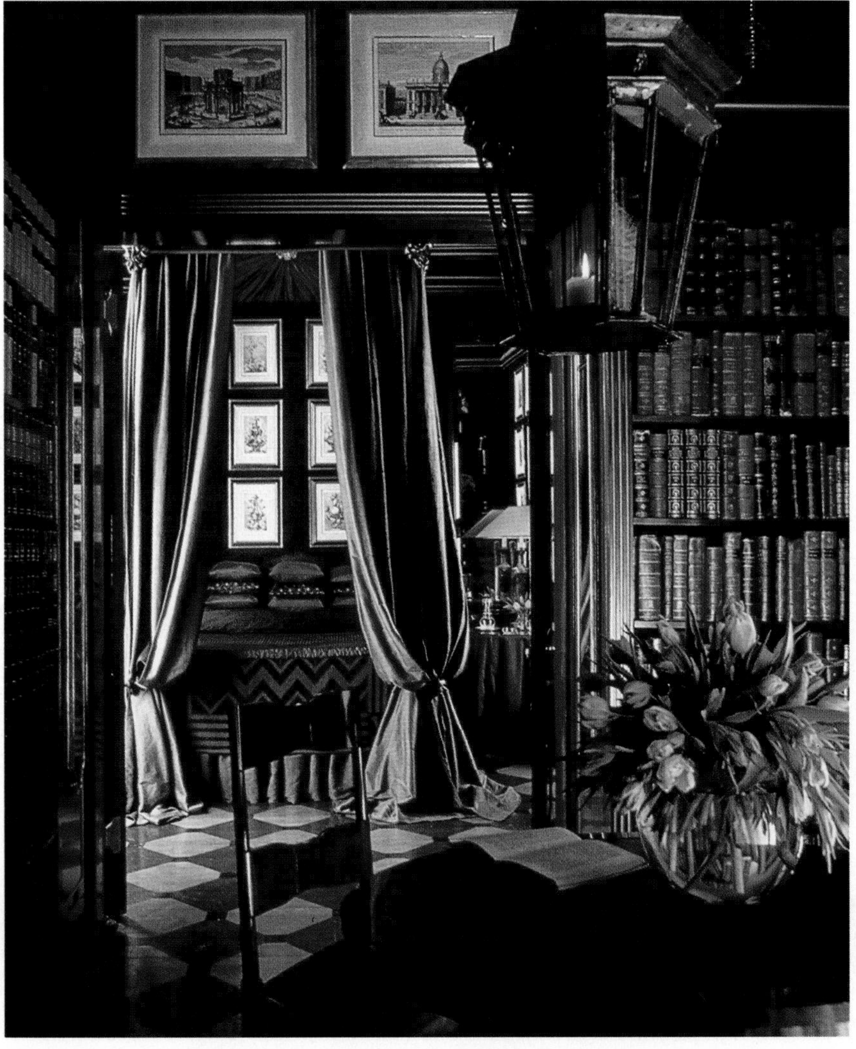

BLAKES HOTEL

33 ROLAND GARDENS, LONDON SW7 3PF
TEL: 44 171 370 6701 FAX: 44 171 373 0442 FROM USA CALL FREE: 1 800 926 3173

Created by Anouska Hempel, designer, hotelier and couturiere, Blakes is unique – a connoisseur's refuge. Each room has been individually designed, the colour schemes are daring, stunning and dramatic – black and mustard, rich cardinal reds, lavender, vanilla washes of tea rose and a room that is white on white on white offering style and elegance to the discerning traveller. "If ever dreams can become reality, then Blakes is where it will happen". The bedrooms and suites have been described as each being a fantasy. A full 24 hour room service is provided and if a guest is travelling on business the hotel will provide a room fax machine, full secretarial services and a courier service if required. Blakes intimate restaurant is recognised as one of the finest in the capital and is open until midnight. Breakfast, summer lunches and candlelit dinners can be enjoyed on the Garden Terrace which overlooks the private and secluded courtyard – an explosion of greenery all year round. The smart, fashionable shops of Brompton Cross are only a short stroll away through the leafy streets of South Kensington and Harrods can be reached by taxi in five minutes. **Directions:** Roland Gardens is a turning off Old Brompton Road. The nearest underground tube station is South Kensington. Price guide: Single £155; double/twin £190–£350; suite £540–£780.

50 rms MasterCard VISA AMERICAN EXPRESS 22

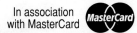

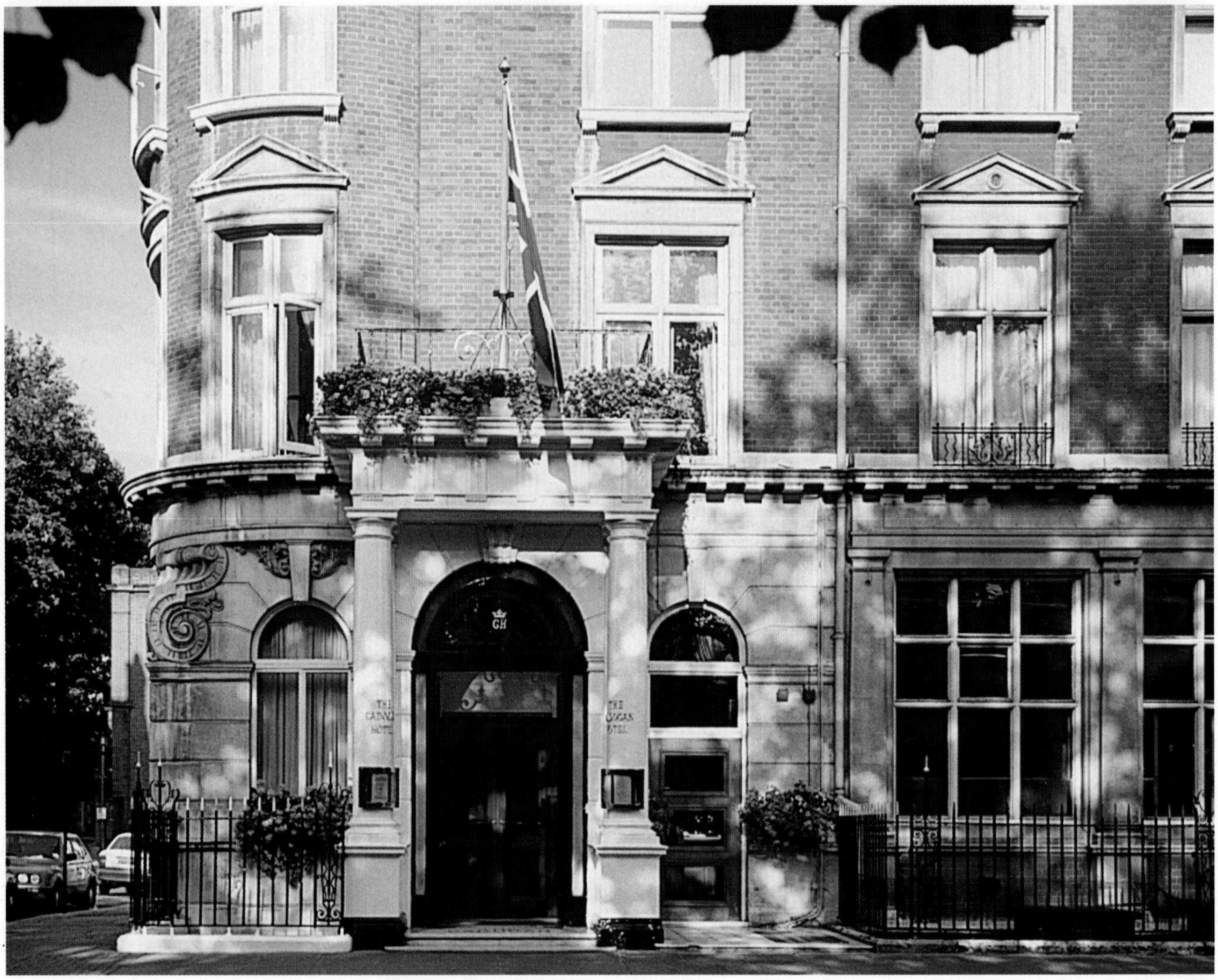

The Cadogan

SLOANE STREET, LONDON SW1X 9SG

TEL: 44 171-235 7141 FAX: 44 171-245 0994 E-MAIL: www.cadogan–hotel.com

FROM USA FAX TOLL FREE ON: 800 260 8338 CALL TOLL FREE Prima Hotels: 800 447 7462; Utell International 1800 44 UTELL

The Cadogan is an imposing late-Victorian building in warm terracotta brick situated in a most desirable location in Sloane Street, Knightsbridge. It is well known for its association with Lillie Langtry, the 'Jersey Lily', actress and friend of King Edward VII, and her house in Pont Street now forms part of the hotel. Playwright and wit Oscar Wilde was a regular guest at The Cadogan. The Cadogan's elegant drawing room is popular for afternoon tea and the meals served in the air conditioned restaurant, which has 2 AA rosettes, combine imaginatively prepared food with value for money. The hotel has 65 comfortable bedrooms and suites equipped to the highest standards; several are air conditioned. The Langtry Rooms on the ground floor, once the famous actress's drawing room, make a delightful setting for private parties, wedding receptions and small meetings. The hotel is an excellent base for shopping trips being close to Harrods, Harvey Nichols and Peter Jones. Business visitors will find its central position and easy access make it a most acceptable place to stay when visiting London. **Directions:** The hotel is halfway along Sloane Street at the junction with Pont Street. Close to Knightsbridge and Sloane Square tubes. Price guide: Single £140–£190; double/twin £185–£215; studio/suite £265–£290.

CANNIZARO HOUSE

WEST SIDE, WIMBLEDON COMMON, LONDON SW19 4UE
TEL: 44 181 879 1464 FAX: 44 181 879 7338

Cannizaro House, an elegant Georgian Country House, occupies a tranquil position on the edge of Wimbledon Common, yet is only 20 minutes by train from central London. Cannizaro House has, throughout its history, welcomed royalty and celebrities such as George III, Oscar Wilde and William Pitt, and is now restored as a hotel which offers the very highest standards of hospitality. Winner of the AA's Courtesy and Care Award for London 1997. The 18th century is reflected in the ornate fireplaces and mouldings, gilded mirrors and many antiques. All the hotel's 46 bedrooms are individually designed, with many overlooking beautiful Cannizaro Park. Several intimate rooms are available for meetings and private dining, including the elegant Queen Elizabeth Room – a popular venue for Wedding Ceremonies. The newly refurbished Viscount Melville Room offers air-conditioned comfort for up to 100 guests. Ray Slade, General Manager of Cannizaro House for many years, ensures the high standards of excellence for which the hotel is renowned, are consistently met. The award-winning kitchen produces the finest modern and classical cuisine, complemented by an impressive list of wines. **Directions:** The nearest tube and British Rail station is Wimbledon. Price guide: Single £135–£145; double/twin from £155–£175; suite from £280–£395. Special weekend rates and celebratory packages available.

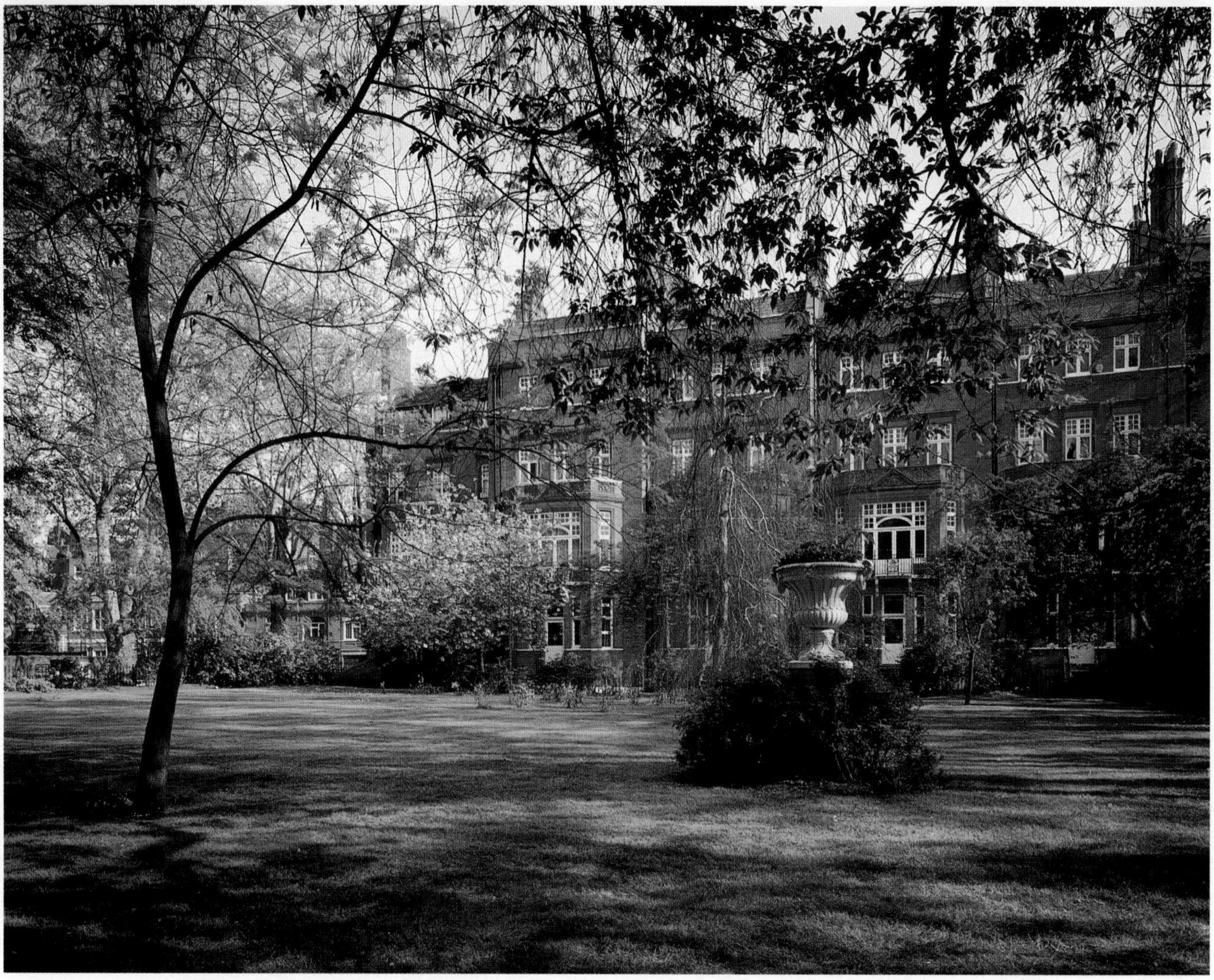

THE CLIVEDEN TOWN HOUSE

26 CADOGAN GARDENS, LONDON SW3 2RP

TEL: 44 171 730 6466 FAX: 44 171 730 0263 FROM USA TOLL FREE 1 800 747 4942

The Cliveden Town House offers the perfect balance of luxury, service, privacy and location. Tucked discreetly away in a tranquil, tree-lined garden square between Harrods and Kings Road it is at the very centre of fashionable London and is the epitome of stylish good taste and elegance. Like its gracious country cousin at Cliveden, one of England's most famous stately homes, The Cliveden Town House combines the grandeur of the past with the luxuries and conveniences of today, offering the sophisticated traveller all the exclusive comforts and ambience of a grand private residence. The Town House has enhanced its assured charm with the addition of nine more suites. Spacious, splendidly decorated rooms reminiscent of the Edwardian period combine with the highest possible 24-hour service and personal attention. The rooms and suites all have air conditioning, satellite television, stereo video, CD players, dedicated fax lines and voice mail. Nanny and baby sitting services can be arranged. Cliveden's standards of luxury can also be enjoyed at The Royal Crescent in Bath. The fashionable shops and first-class restaurants of Knightsbridge, Chelsea and Belgravia are within walking distance. West End theatres and the City are within easy reach. **Directions:** Nearest tube station is Sloane Square. Price guide: Single From £120; double/twin £210–£250; suite £310–£620.

THE DORCHESTER

PARK LANE, MAYFAIR, LONDON W1A 2HJ
TEL: 44 171 629 8888 FAX: 44 171 409 0114 TELEX: 887704

The Dorchester first opened its doors in 1931, offering a unique experience which almost instantly became legendary. Its reopening in November 1990 after an extensive refurbishment marked the renaissance of one of the world's grand hotels. Its history has been consistently glamorous; from the early days a host of outstanding figures has been welcomed, including monarchs, statesmen and celebrities. The architectural features have been restored to their original splendour and remain at the heart of The Dorchester's heritage. The 192 bedrooms and 52 suites have been luxuriously designed in a variety of materials, furnishings and lay-outs. All bedrooms are fully air-conditioned and have spectacular Italian marble bathrooms. There are rooms for non-smokers and some equipped for the disabled. In addition to The Grill Room, there is The Oriental Restaurant where the accent is on Cantonese cuisine. Specialised health and beauty treatments are offered in The Dorchester Spa with its statues, Lalique-style glass and water fountain. A series of meeting rooms, with full supporting services, is available for business clientèle. As ever, personalised care is a pillar of The Dorchester's fine reputation. **Directions:** Toward the Hyde Park Corner/Piccadilly end of Park Lane. Price guide excluding VAT: Single £240–£270; double/twin £270–£300; suite £400–£1,675.

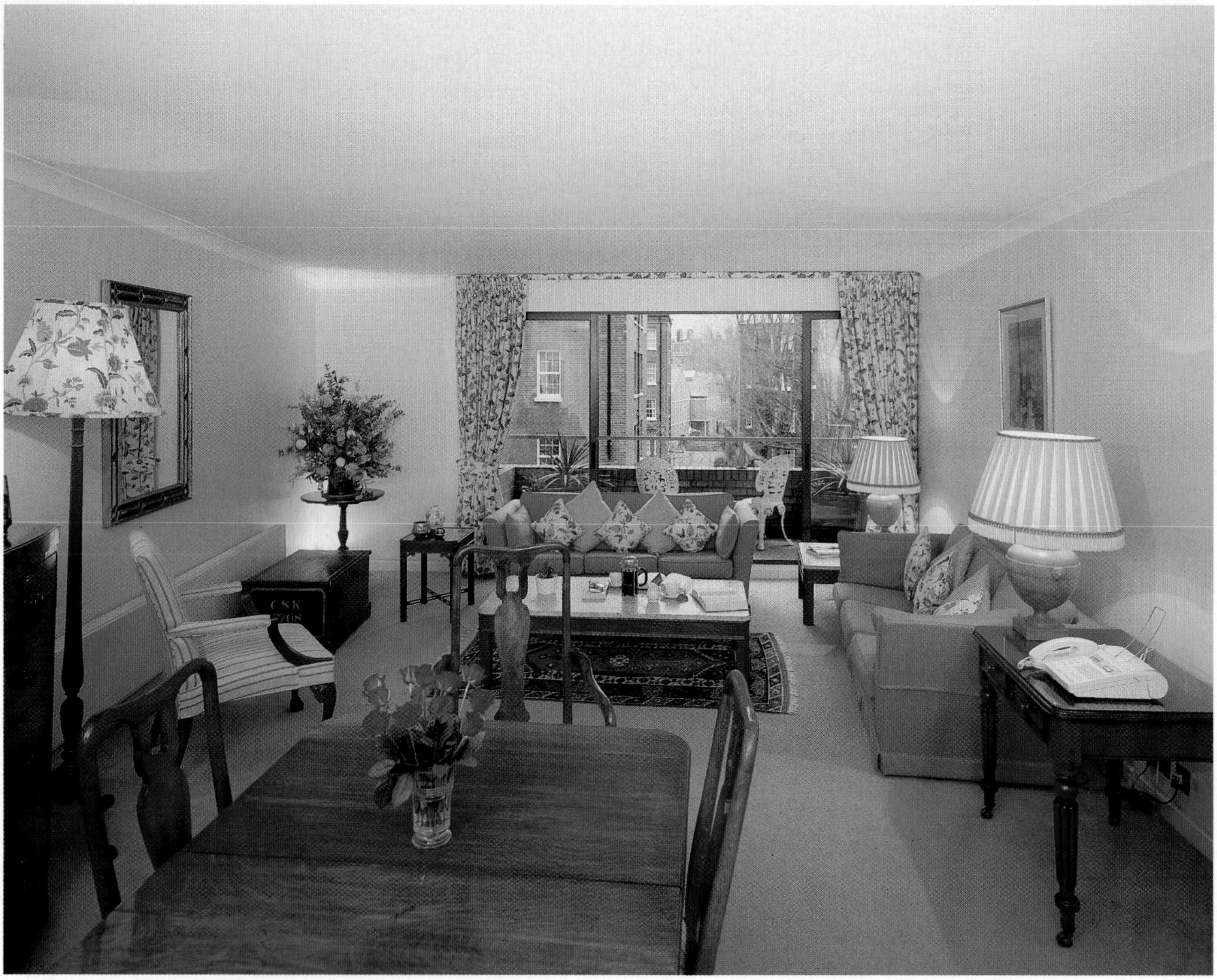

DRAYCOTT HOUSE APARTMENTS

10 DRAYCOTT AVENUE, CHELSEA, LONDON SW3 3AA

TEL: 44 171-584 4659 FAX: 44 171-225 3694 E-MAIL: sales@draycotthouse.co.uk

Draycott House stands in a quiet, tree-lined avenue in the heart of Chelsea. Housed in an attractive period building, the apartments have been designed in individual styles to provide the ideal surroundings for a private or business visit, combining comfort, privacy and security with a convenient location. All are spacious, luxury, serviced apartments, with three, two or one bedrooms. Some have private balconies, a roof terrace and overlook the private courtyard garden. Each apartment is fully equipped with all home comforts; cable television, video, radio/cassette, a private direct line for telephone/fax/answer machine. Complimentary provisions on arrival, milk and newspapers delivered. Daily maid service Monday to Friday. In-house laundry room and covered garage parking. Additional services, laundry and dry cleaning services. On request cars, airport transfers, catering, travel and theatre arrangements, child minders and an introduction to an exclusive health club. The West End is within easy reach. Knightsbridge within walking distance.Internet: http:/ www.Draycotthouse.co.uk **Directions:** Draycott House is situated on the corner of Draycott Avenue and Draycott Place, close to Sloane Square. Price guide: from £1037–£2522 +VAT per week: £164-£396 +VAT per night. Long term reservations may attract preferential terms. Contact: Jane Renton, General Manager.

THE HALCYON

81 HOLLAND PARK, LONDON W11 3RZ

TEL: 44 171 727 7288 FAX: 44 171 229 8516 E-MAIL: 101712.2063@CompuServe.COM

This small, exclusive hotel in Holland Park, winner of Johansens Most Excellent London Hotel Award 1996, offers an exceptional standard of accommodation and service. Essentially a large Town House, its architecture has been meticulously restored to the splendour of the Belle Epoque to take its place amongst the many imposing residences in the area. The generous proportions of the rooms, along with the striking individuality of their furnishings, creates the atmosphere of a fine country house. Each of the bedrooms and suites has been beautifully furnished and has every modern amenity. All have marble bathrooms and several boast a Jacuzzi. A splendid restaurant, opening onto a ornamental garden and patio, serves distinctive international cuisine complemented by a well chosen wine list. The adjoining bar provides a relaxing environment to enjoy a cocktail and meet with friends. The Halcyon prides itself on offering a superb service and ensuring guests' absolute comfort, privacy and security. Secretarial, Internet and fax facilities are all available. London's most fashionable shopping areas, restaurants and West End theatres are all easily accessible from The Halcyon. Directions: From Holland Park tube station, turn right. The Halcyon is on the left after the second set of traffic lights. Price guide: Single from £175; double/twin from £260; suite from £295.

43 rms 12

HARRINGTON HALL

5-25 HARRINGTON GARDENS, LONDON SW7 4JW
TEL: 44 171 396 9696 FAX: 44 171 396 9090 E-MAIL: 101752.2030@compuserve.com

The original façade of late Victorian houses cleverly conceals a privately owned hotel of substantial proportions and contempory comfort. Harrington Hall offers 200 air-conditioned luxury bedrooms which have been most pleasantly furnished and equipped with an extensive array of facilities. A marble fireplace dominates the comfortable and relaxing Lounge Bar, where guests can enjoy a drink in pleasant surroundings. The restaurant's mixture of classical decoration and dramatic colour creates a delightful setting for the appreciation of fine cuisine. A choice of buffet or à la carte menu is available, both offering a tempting selection of dishes. Nine fully air conditioned conference and banqueting suites, with walls panelled in rich lacewood and solid cherry, provide a sophisicated venue for conferences, exhibitions or corporate hospitality. Harrington Hall also has a Business Centre for the exclusive use of its guests, along with a private Fitness Centre with multigym, saunas and showers. **Directions:** Harrington Hall is situated in the Royal Borough of Kensington and Chelsea, in Harrington Gardens south of the Cromwell Road, close to Gloucester Road underground station, two stops from Knightsbridge and Harrods. Price guide: Single £160; double £160; suites £195 (including VAT & service).

THE HEMPEL

HEMPEL GARDEN SQUARE, 31-35 CRAVEN HILL GARDENS, LONDON W2 3EA
TEL: 44 171 298 9000; FAX: 44 171 402 4666

Designer Anouska Hempel has created The Hempel to be elegant, re-defining space for the traveller. Situated within easy reach of London's many attractions, the hotel with its immaculately preserved Georgian facade houses 47 individually designed rooms and fully serviced apartments. Influenced by the peace and simplicity of the Orient, the structure of Ancient Egypt with up to the minute technology from the Western World for the business connoisseur. The Hempel is innovative, monochromatic and full of surprises – tapwater that is lit at night, an open fire place that appears to float, a mix of light and shadow that can keep guests guessing how and pondering on just how this can all be real. The huge atrium within the lobby is astounding. A delicious mix of Italian-Thai and Japanese food, devised by Anouska Hempel is presented with style and flair in the I-Thai restaurant. Guests enjoying a pre-dinner drink in The Shadow Bar are surrounded by illusion and fantasy as The Hempel aims to take them out of this world and make their dreams a reality. **Directions:** The Hempel is situated in Lancaster gate with a short walk to Kensington Gardens and Hyde Park. Paddington railway station with Lancaster Gate and Queensway underground railway stations nearby. Price guide: Room/suite/apartment: from £220–£775 (excluding VAT)

48 rms 30

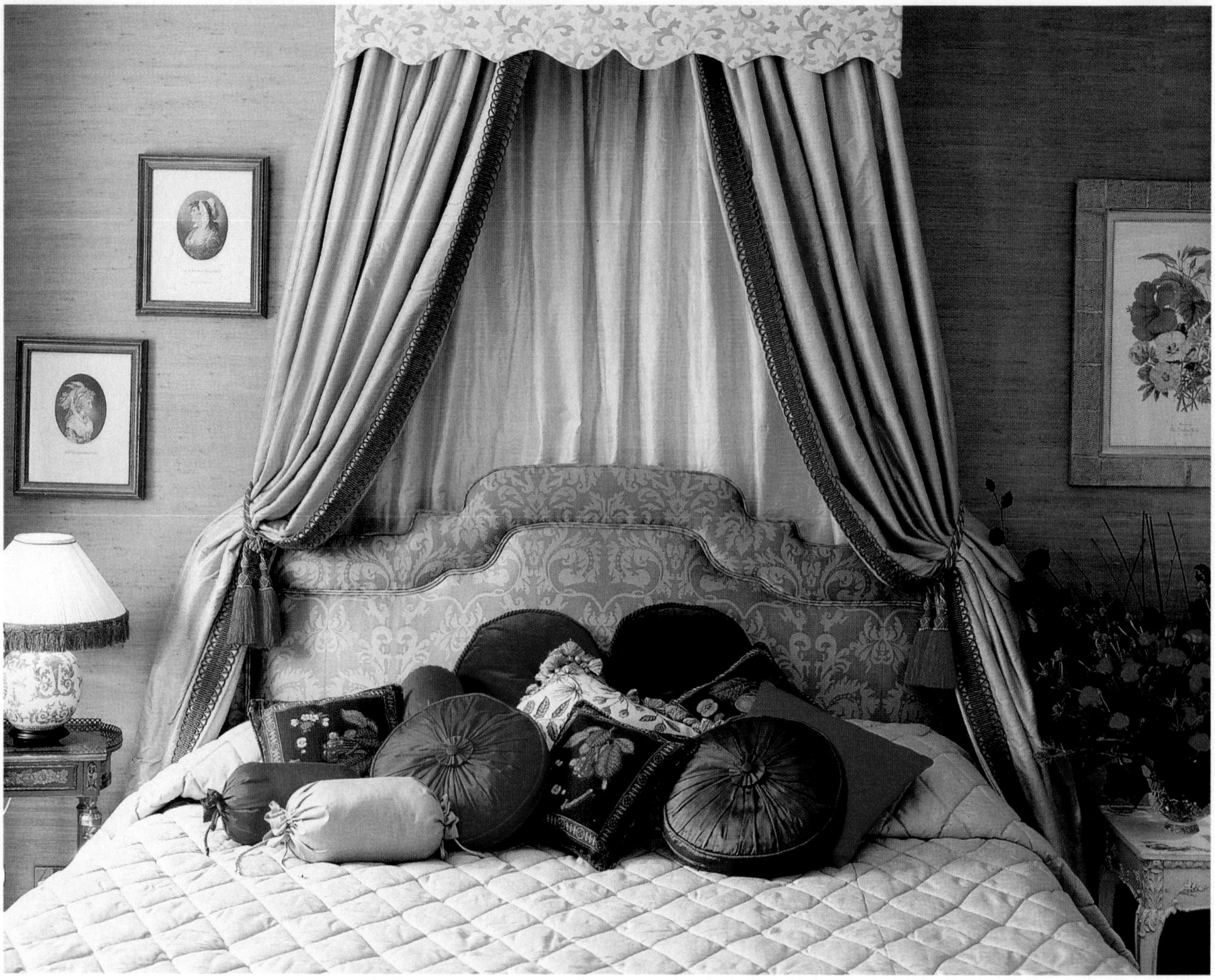

THE LEONARD

15 SEYMOUR STREET, LONDON W1H 5AA

TEL: 44 171 935 2010 FAX: 44 171 935 6700 E-MAIL: the.leonard@dial.pipex.com

Four late 18th century Georgian town houses set the character of this exciting new property which opened in 1995 and has already proved to be extremely popular with Johansens guests, being winner of the Johansens Recommended London Hotel of the Year Award 1997. Imaginative reconstruction has created six rooms and twenty suites decorated individually to a very high standard. Wall coverings present striking colours, complemented by exquisite French furnishing fabrics creating a warm luxurious atmosphere. All rooms are fully air-conditioned and include a private safe, mini-bar, hi-fi system and provision for a modem/fax. Bathrooms are finished in marble and some of the larger suites have a butler's pantry or fully-equipped kitchen. For physical fitness and stress reductions there is a compact exercise room. "Can do" staff ensure that guests can enjoy the highest level of attention and service. Breakfast is available in the café bar and light meals are served throughout the day. 24-hour room service is also available. There are, of course, many good restaurants nearby. The Wallace Collection is just a short walk away and one of London's premier department stores, Selfridges, is round the corner in Oxford Street. **Directions:** The Leonard is on the south side of Seymour Street which is just north of Marble Arch and runs west off Portman Square. Car parking in Bryanston Street. Price guide: Double £170–£190; suites £230–£375.

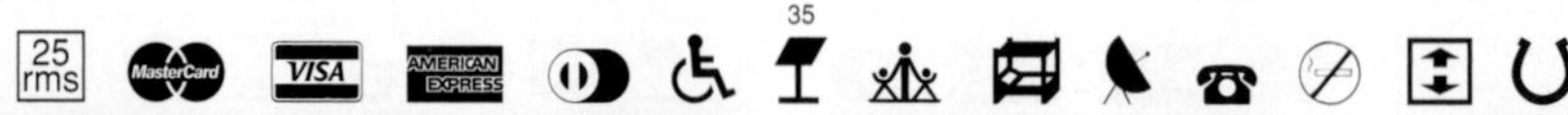

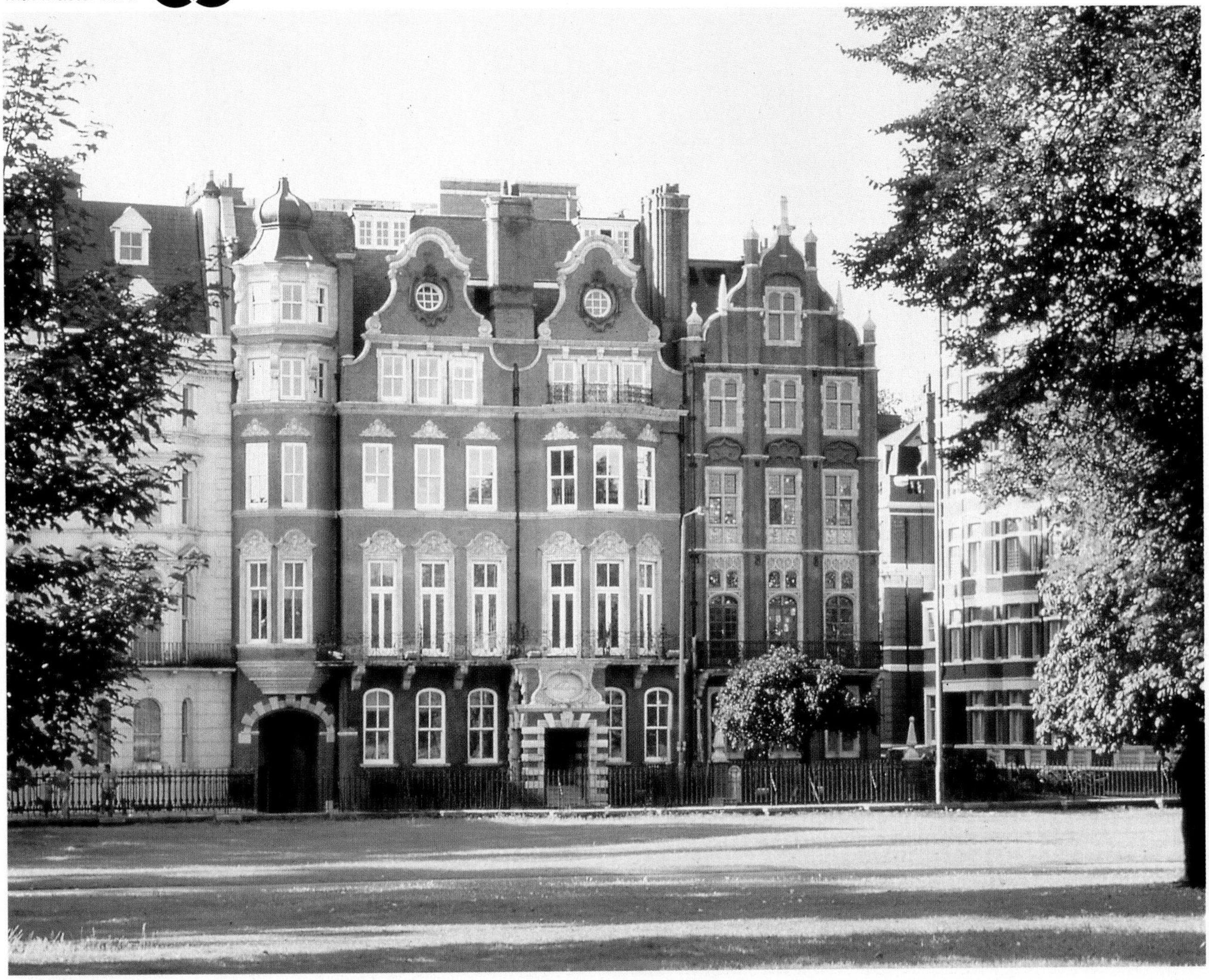

THE MILESTONE

1–2 KENSINGTON COURT, LONDON W8 5DL
TEL: 44 171 917 1000 FAX: 44 171 917 1010 FROM USA TOLL FREE 1 800 854 7092

The beautifully appointed Milestone Hotel is situated opposite Kensington Palace with uninterrupted views over Kensington Gardens and the remarkable Royal parklands. A Victorian showpiece, this unique hotel has been carefully restored to its original splendour whilst incorporating every modern facility. The 53 bedrooms including 12 suites are all individually designed with antiques, elegant furnishings and some have private balconies. Guests may relax in the comfortable, panelled Park Lounge which, in company with all other rooms, provides a 24-hour service. The hotel's original Dining Room has an elaborately carved ceiling, original fireplace, ornate windows and an oratory, which can now be used for small private parties. The health and fitness centre offers guests the use of a solarium, spa bath, sauna and gymnasium. The traditional bar on the ground floor is an ideal place for meeting and entertaining friends. The Milestone is within walking distance of some of the finest shopping in Kensington and a little further away in Knightsbridge and is a short taxi ride to the West End, the heart of London's Theatreland. The Albert Hall and all the museums in Exhibition Road are nearby. **Directions:** At the end of Kensington High Street, at the junction with Princes Gate. Price guide: Single from £220; double/twin £270; suites from £330.

NUMBER SIXTEEN

16 SUMNER PLACE, LONDON SW7 3EG

TEL: 44 171 589 5232 US TOLL FREE: 1800 592 5387 FAX: 44 171 584 8615

On entering Number Sixteen with its immaculate pillared façade visitors find themselves in an atmosphere of seclusion and comfort which has remained virtually unaltered in style since its early Victorian origins. The staff are friendly and attentive, regarding each visitor as a guest in a private home. The relaxed atmosphere of the library is the perfect place to pour a drink from the honour bar and meet friends or business associates. A fire blazing in the drawing room in cooler months creates an inviting warmth, whilst the conservatory opens on to a beautiful secluded walled garden which once again has won many accolades and awards for its floral displays. Each spacious bedroom is decorated with a discreet combination of antiques and traditional furnishings. The rooms are fully appointed with every facility that the discerning traveller would expect. A light breakfast is served in the privacy of guests' rooms and a tea and coffee service is available throughout the day. Although there is no dining room at Number Sixteen, some of London's finest restaurants are just round the corner. The hotel has membership of Aquilla Health and Fitness Club, 5 minutes away. The hotel is close to the West End, Knightsbridge and Hyde Park. **Directions:** Sumner Place is off Old Brompton Road near Onslow Square. South Kensington Tube Station is a 2 minute walk. Price guide: Single £80–£115; double/twin £150–£180; junior suite £190.

36 rms · MasterCard · VISA · AMERICAN EXPRESS · 12

PEMBRIDGE COURT HOTEL

34 PEMBRIDGE GARDENS, LONDON W2 4DX
TEL: 44 171 229 9977 FAX: 44 171 727 4982

This gracious Victorian town house has been lovingly restored to its former glory whilst providing all the modern facilities demanded by today's discerning traveller. The 20 rooms are individually decorated with pretty fabrics and the walls adorned with an unusual collection of framed fans and Victoriana. The Pembridge Court is renowned for the devotion and humour with which it is run. Its long serving staff and its two famous cats "Spencer" and "Churchill" assure you of an immensely warm welcome and the very best in friendly, personal service. Over the years the hotel has built up a loyal following amongst its guests, many of whom regard it as their genuine 'home from home' in London. Winner of the 1994 RAC Award for Best Small Hotel in the South East of England, the Hotel is situated in quiet tree-lined gardens just off Notting Hill Gate, an area described by Travel & Leisure magazine as 'one of the liveliest, most prosperous corners of the city. "The Gate" as is affectionately known, is certainly lively, colourful and full of life with lots of great pubs and restaurants and the biggest antiques market in the world at nearby Portobello Road. **Directions:** Pembridge Gardens is a small turning off Notting Hill Gate/Bayswater Road, just 2 minutes from Portobello Road Antiques Market. Price guide: Single £110–£140; double/twin £160–£170 (inclusive of both English breakfast & VAT)

20 rms

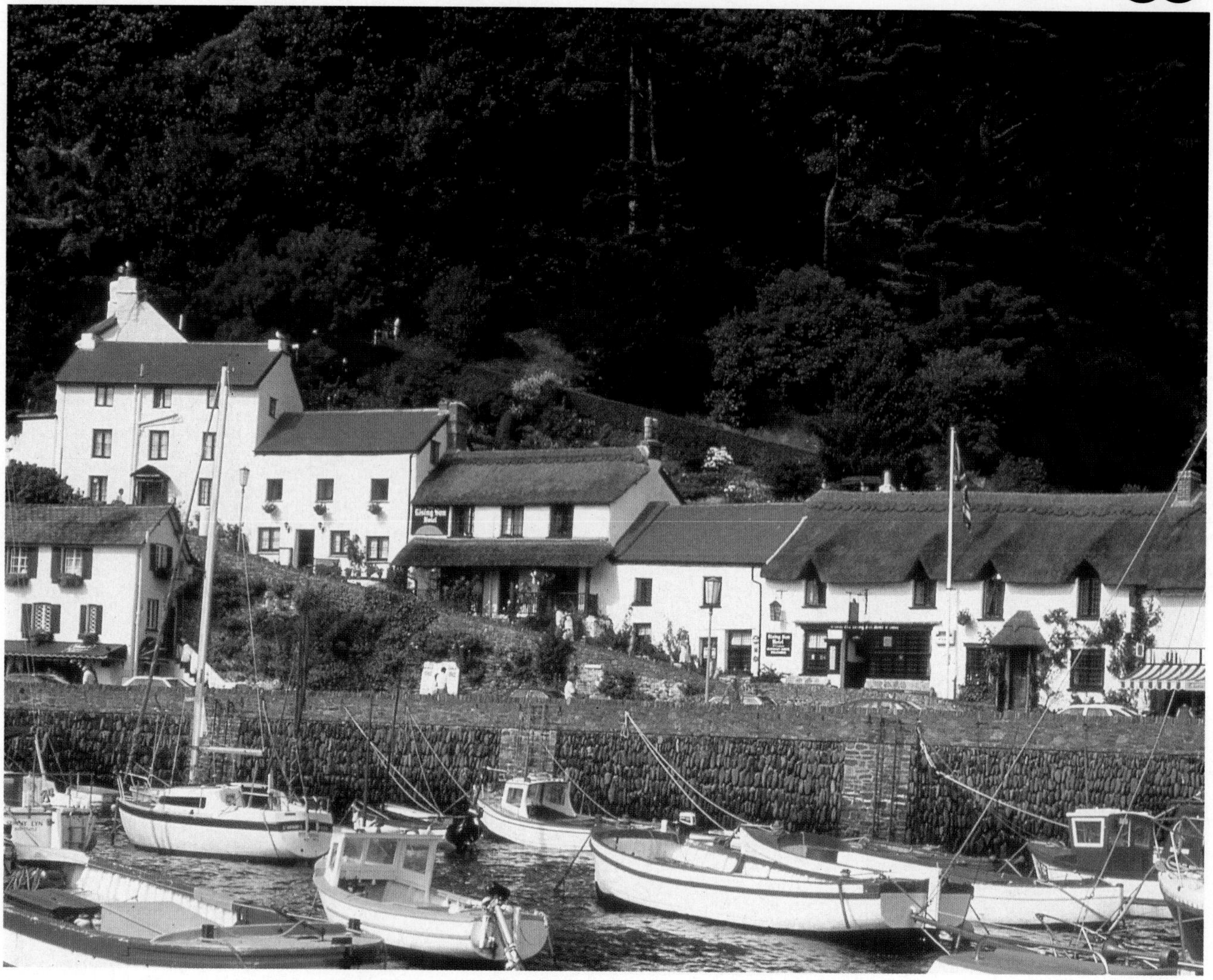

THE RISING SUN

HARBOURSIDE, LYNMOUTH, DEVON EX35 6EQ

TEL: 44 1598 753223 FAX: 44 1598 753480 E-MAIL: risingsunlynmouth@easynet.co.uk

Recommended in every way, this award-winning 14th century thatched smugglers' inn is perfectly positioned on the picturesque harbour overlooking East Lyn River. The building is steeped in history: Lorna Doone was partly written here and the inn's adjacent cottage – now luxuriously equipped for guests' use and pictured below – was once the honeymoon retreat for the poet Shelley. The best of the inn's medieval character has been preserved: oak panelling, uneven floors, open fires and crooked ceilings, all enhanced by tasteful furnishings and modern comforts. The bedrooms lack nothing and, like the terraced gardens, have splendid views. Parking in Lynmouth can be difficult at the height of the season. The food served is of excellent quality. Classic modern English and French cuisine is provided on an à la carte menu, which also features local specialities such as freshly caught lobster and salmon. All this is accompanied by a superb wine list. Good value bar meals are also available. The inn owns a ½ mile stretch of river for salmon fishing and there are opportunities for sea angling. The hills and combes of Exmoor National Park, the North Devon coastline and the hunting country of Doone Valley are also near. Directions: Leave the M5 at junction 23 (signposted Minehead) and follow the A39 to Lynmouth. Price guide: Single £55; double/twin £79–£130

12 rms       

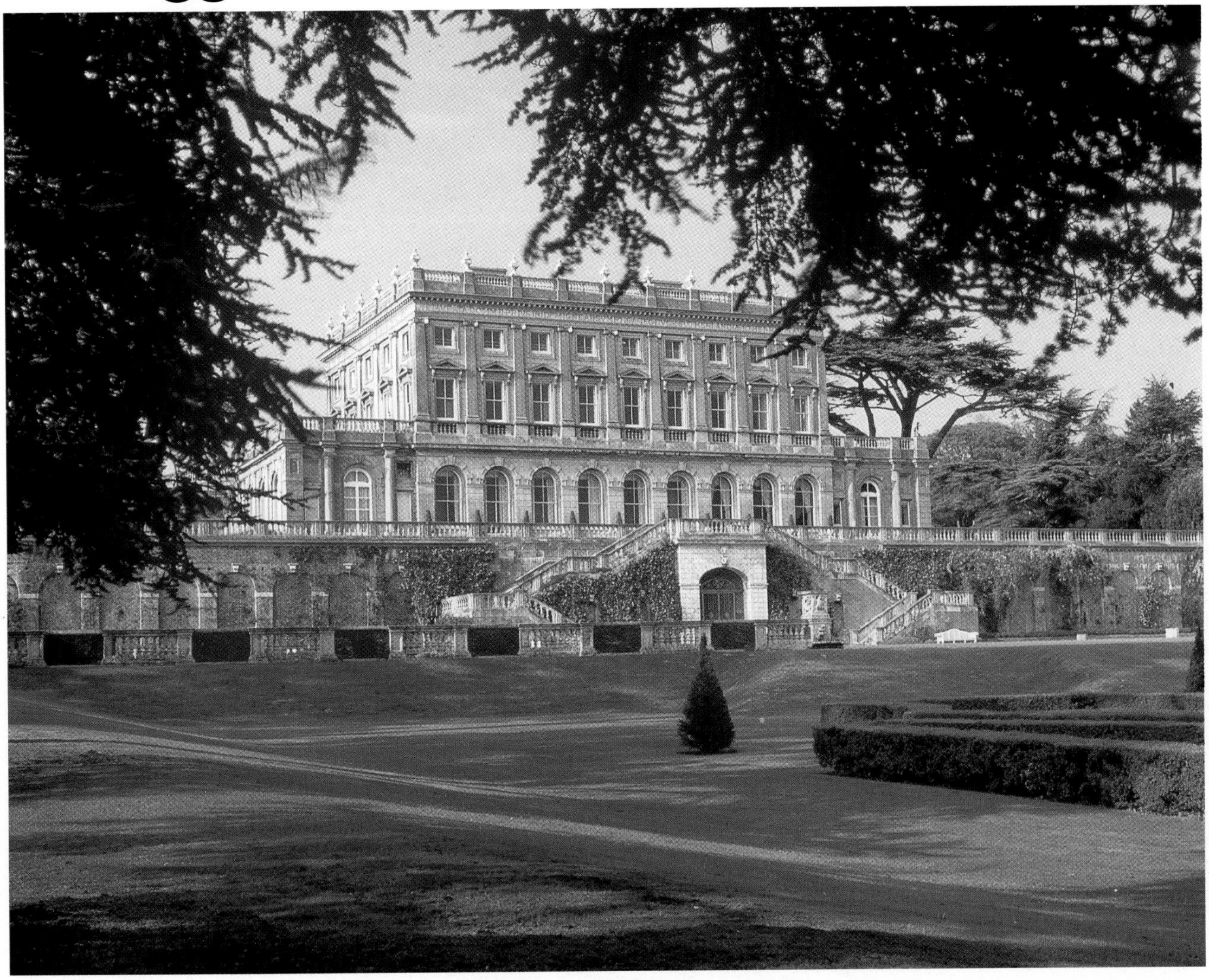

CLIVEDEN

TAPLOW, BERKSHIRE SL6 0JF

TEL: 44 1628 668561 FAX: 44 1628 661837

Cliveden, Britain's only 5 Red AA star hotel that is also a stately home, is set in 376 acres of gardens and parkland, overlooking the Thames. As the former home of Frederick, Prince of Wales, three Dukes and the Astor family, Cliveden has been at the centre of Britain's social and political life for over 300 years. It is exquisitely furnished in a classically English style, with a multitude of oil paintings, antiques and *objets d'art*. The spacious guest rooms and suites are appointed to the most luxurious standards. One of the greatest pleasures of eating at Cliveden is in the choice of dining rooms and the scope of the menus. The French Dining Room, with its original Madame de Pompadour rococo decoration, is the finest 18th-century *boiserie* outside France. Alternatively, relish the Michelin-starred cuisine of chef Ron Maxfield in Waldo's Restaurant. The Pavilion offers a full range of health and fitness facilities and beauty therapies. Guests can ride Cliveden's horses over the estate or enjoy a leisurely river cruise on an Edwardian launch. Comprehensively equipped, the two secure private boardrooms provide self-contained business meeting facilities. Exclusive use of the hotel can be arranged. Cliveden's style may also be enjoyed at the Cliveden Town House, London and the Royal Crescent, Bath. **Directions:** Situated on B476, 2 miles north of Taplow. Price guide: Single £220; double/twin £245; suites from £398.

Soar Mill Cove Hotel

SOAR MILL COVE, SALCOMBE, SOUTH DEVON TQ7 3DS
TEL: 44 1548 561566 FAX: 44 1548 561223

Owned and loved by the Makepeace family who for nearly 20 years, have provided a special blend of friendly yet professional service. The hotel's spectacular setting is a flower-filled combe, facing its own sheltered sandy bay and entirely surrounded by 2000 acres of dramatic National Trust coastline. While it is perhaps one of the last truly unspoiled corners of South Devon, Soar Mill Cove is only 15 miles from the motorway system (A38). All the bedrooms are at ground level, each with a private patio opening onto the gardens, which in Spring or Summer provides wonderful alfresco opportunities. In winter, crackling log fires and efficient double glazing keeps cooler weather at bay. A strict "no conference policy" guarantees that the peace of guests shall not be compromised. Both the indoor and outdoor pools are spring-water fed, the former being maintained all year at a constant 88°F. Here is Keith Stephen Makepeace's award winning cuisine, imaginative and innovative, reflecting the very best of the West of England; fresh crabs and lobster caught in the bay are a speciality. Soar Mill Cove is situated midway between the old ports of Plymouth and Dartmouth. Closed 1 November to 9 February. Open for Christmas and New Year House Parties. **Directions:** A384 to Totnes, then A381 to Soar Mill Cove. Price guide: Single £65–£114; double/twin £130–£172.

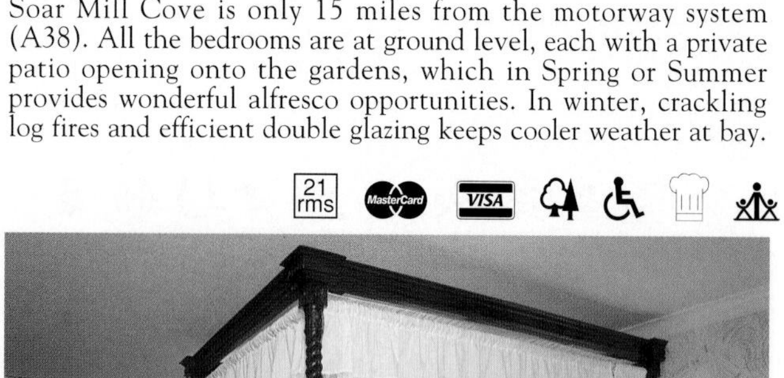

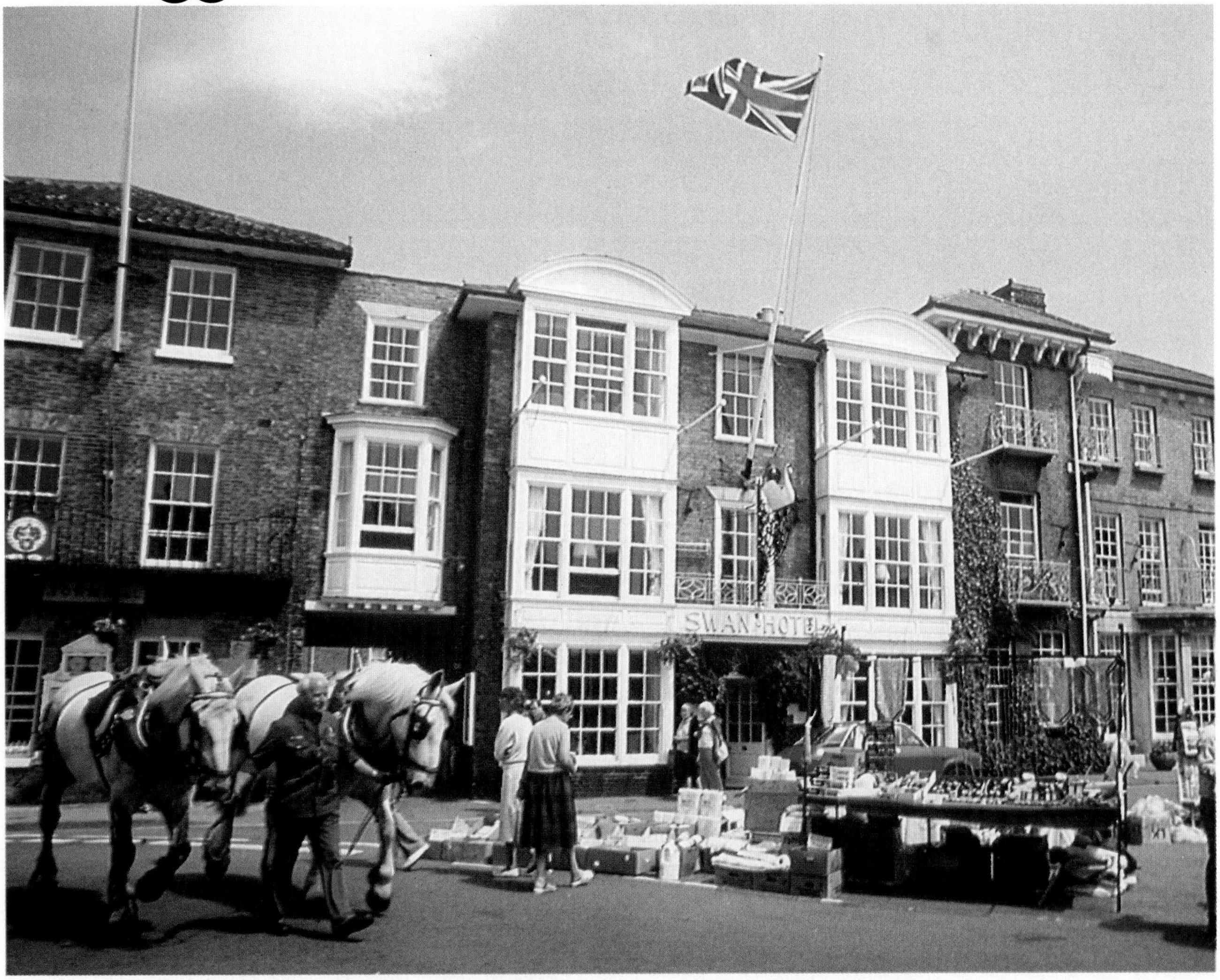

THE SWAN HOTEL

MARKET PLACE, SOUTHWOLD, SUFFOLK IP18 6EG

TEL: 44 1502 722186 FAX: 44 1502 724800

Rebuilt in 1659, following the disastrous fire which destroyed most of the town, The Swan was remodelled in the 1820s, with further additions in 1938. The hotel provides all modern services while retaining its classical dignity and elegance. Many of the antique-furnished bedrooms in the main hotel offer a glimpse of the sea, while the garden rooms – decorated in a more contemporary style – are clustered around the old bowling green. The Drawing Room has the traditional character of an English country house and the Reading Room upstairs is perfect for quiet relaxation or as the venue for a private party. The daily menu offers dishes ranging from simple, traditional fare through the English classics to the chef's personal specialities. An exciting selection of wines is offered. Almost an island, Southwold is bounded on three sides by creeks, marshes and the River Blyth – making it a paradise for birdwatchers and nature lovers. Hardly changed for a century, the town, built around a series of greens, has a fine church, lighthouse and golf course. Music lovers flock to nearby Snape Maltings for the Aldeburgh Festival. Winner of Country Living Gold Award for the Best Hotel 1993/94. **Directions:** Southwold is off the A12 Ipswich–Lowestoft road. The Swan Hotel is in the town centre. Price guide: Single £40–£58; double/twin £86–£125; suite £145–£155.

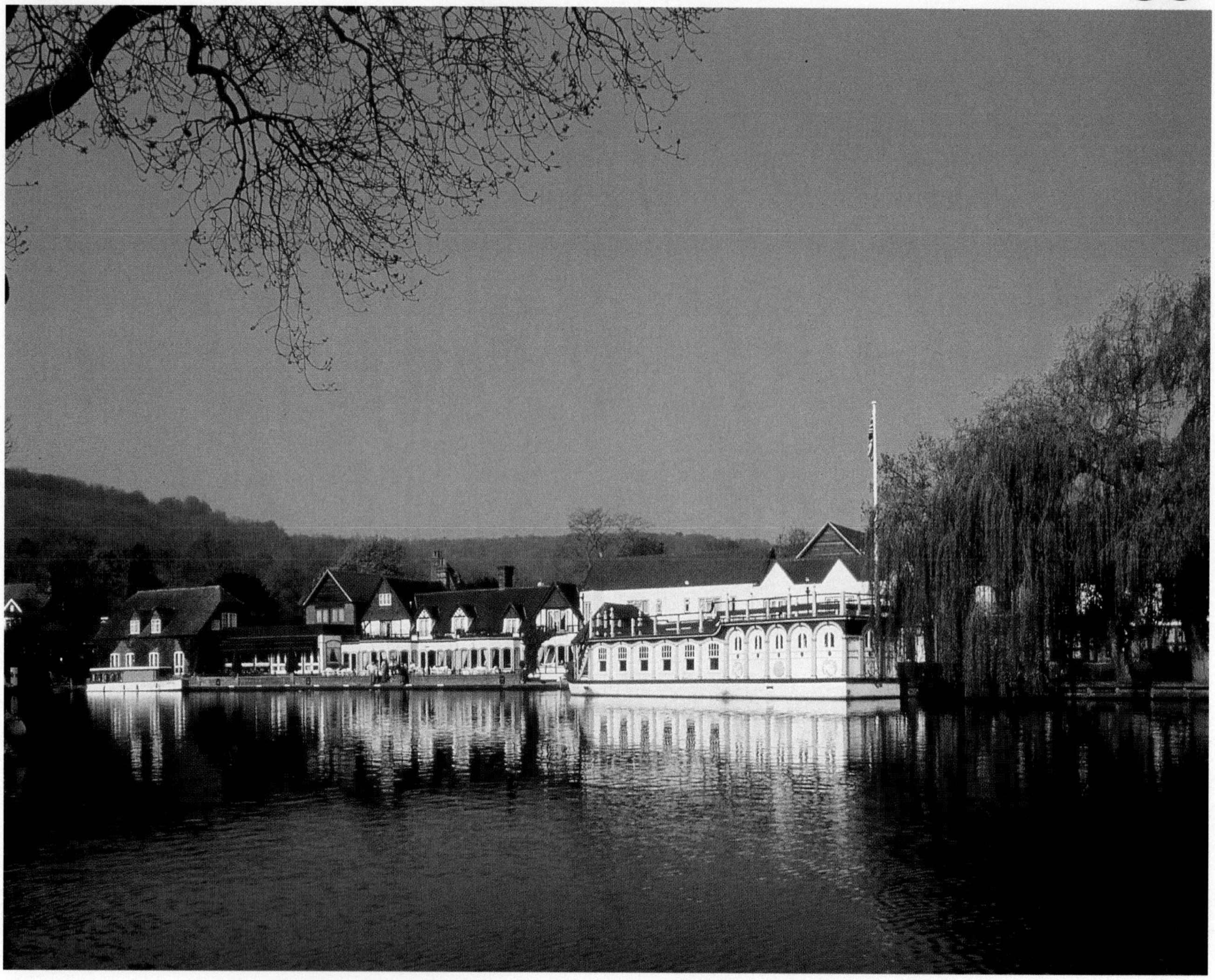

THE SWAN DIPLOMAT

STREATLEY-ON-THAMES, BERKSHIRE RG8 9HR
TEL: 44 1491 873737 FAX: 44 1491 872554

In a beautiful setting on the bank of the River Thames, this hotel offers visitors comfortable accommodation. All of the 46 bedrooms, many of which have balconies overlooking the river, are appointed to high standards with individual décor and furnishings. The elegant Dining Room, with its relaxing waterside views, serves fine food complemented by a good choice of wines. Guests may also choose to dine in the informal Bar. Moored alongside the restaurant is the Magdalen College Barge, which is a stylish venue for meetings and cocktail parties. Business guests are well catered for – the hotel has six attractive conference suites. Reflexions Leisure Club is superbly equipped for fitness programmes and beauty treatments, with facilities that include a heated 'fit' pool; rowing boats and bicycles may be hired. Squash, riding and clay pigeon shooting can all be arranged. Special theme weekends are offered, such as bridge weekends. Events in the locality include Henley Regatta, Ascot and Newbury races, while Windsor Castle, Blenheim Palace, Oxford and London's airports are easily accessible. **Directions:** The hotel lies just off the A329 in Streatley village. Price guide: Single £57–£110; double/twin £87–£140.

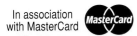

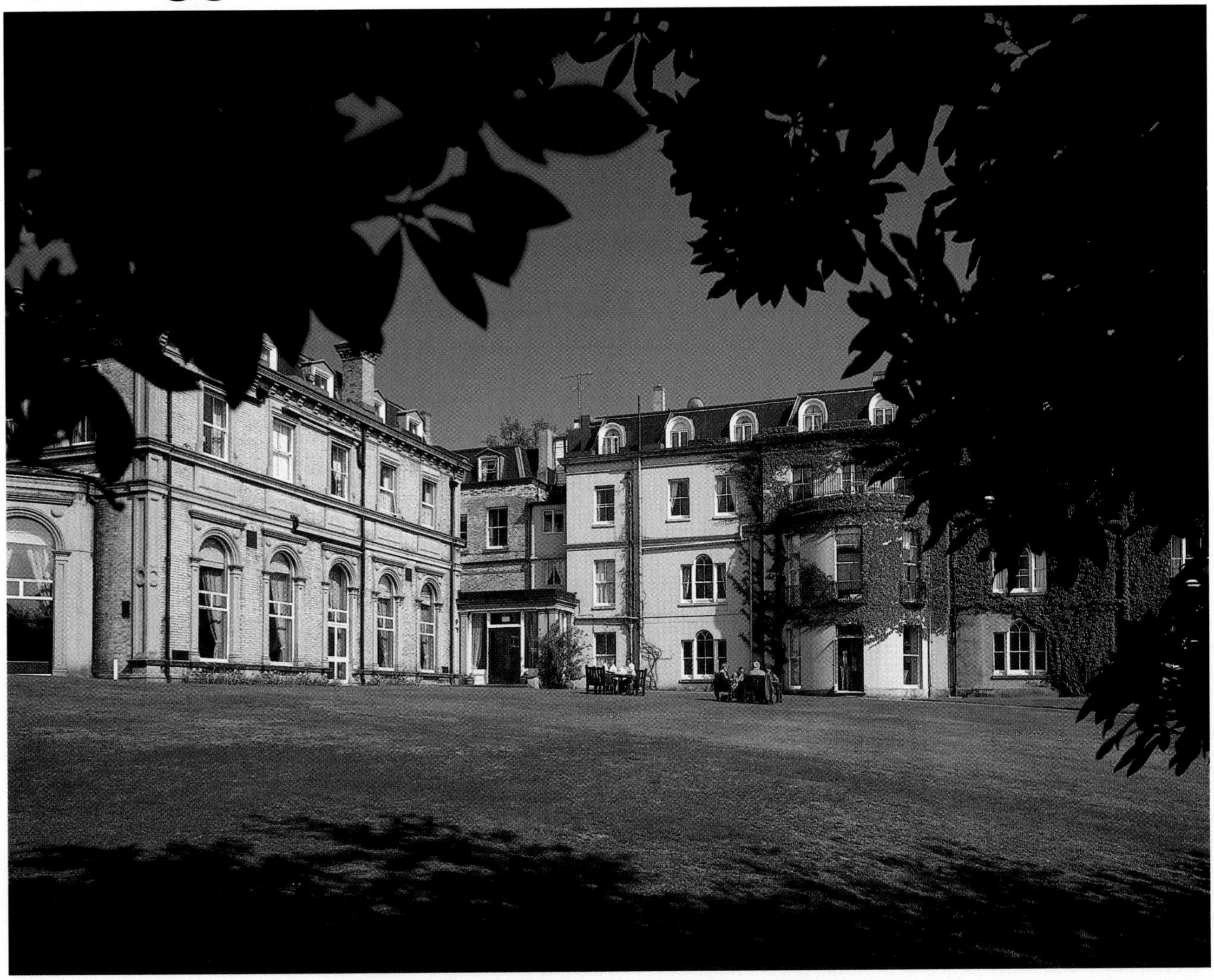

THE SPA HOTEL

MOUNT EPHRAIM, ROYAL TUNBRIDGE WELLS, KENT TN4 8XJ

TEL: 44 1892 520331 FAX: 44 1892 510575

The Spa was originally built in 1766 as a country mansion, with its own parkland, landscaped gardens and two beautiful lakes. A hotel for over a century now, it retains standards of service reminiscent of life in Georgian and Regency England. All the bedrooms are individually furnished and many offer spectacular views. Above all else, The Spa Hotel prides itself on the excellence of its cuisine. The grand, Regency-style restaurant features the freshest produce from Kentish farms and London markets, complemented by a carefully selected wine list. Within the hotel is Sparkling Health, a magnificent health and leisure centre which is equipped to the highest standards. Leisure facilities include an indoor heated swimming pool, a fully equipped state-of-the-art gymnasium, cardiovascular gymnasium, aerobics dance studio, steam room, saunas, sunbeds, beauty clinic, hairdressing salon, flood-lit hard tennis court and 1/2 mile jogging track. The hotel is perfectly positioned for exploring the castles, houses and gardens of Kent and Sussex. Special weekend breaks are offered, with rates from £70 per person per night – full details available on request. **Directions:** Facing the common on the A264 in Tunbridge Wells. Price guide (excluding breakfast): Single £79–£84; double/twin £94–£105; suites £115– £140.

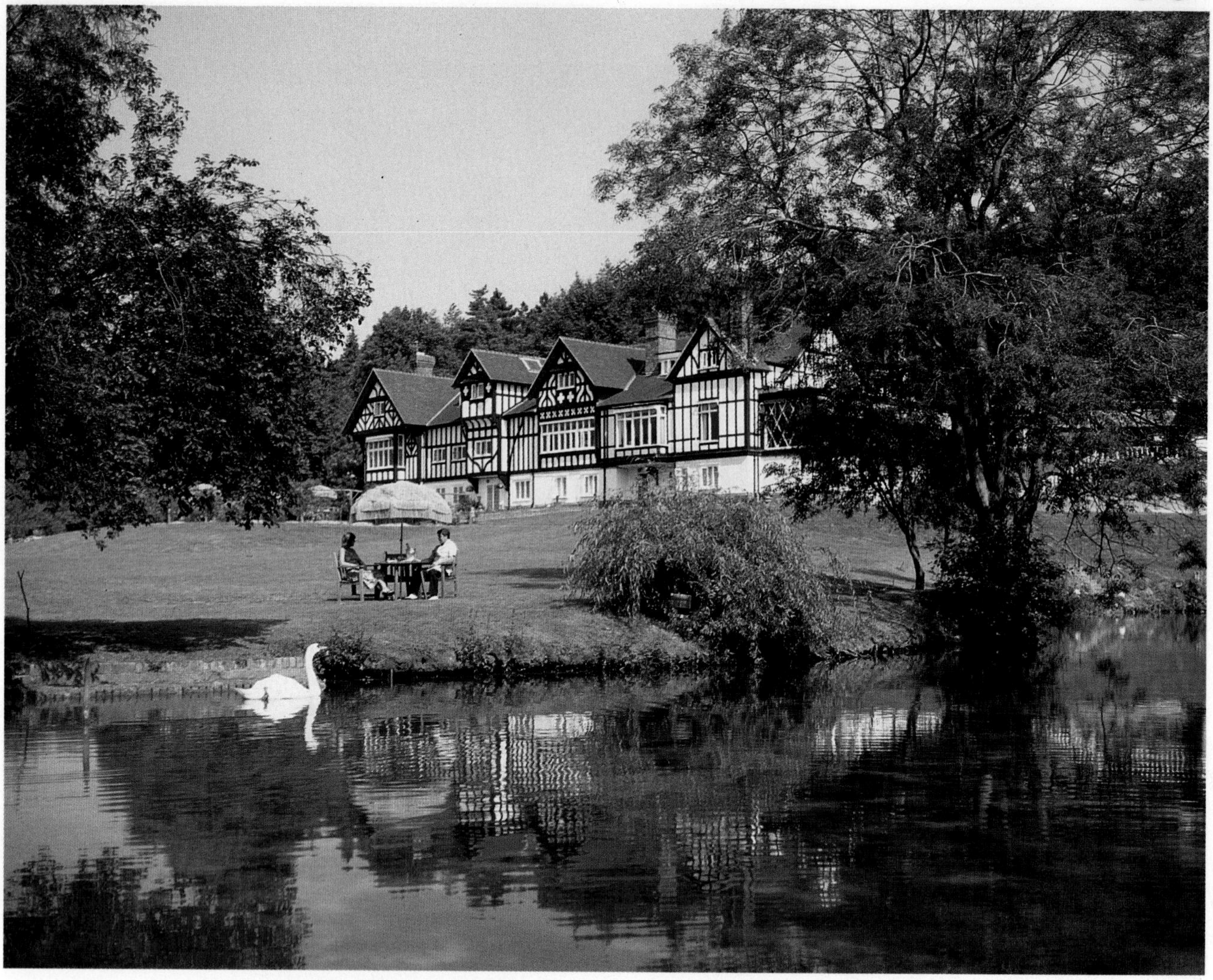

THE SPRINGS HOTEL

NORTH STOKE, WALLINGFORD, OXFORDSHIRE OX10 6BE
TEL: 44 1491 836687 FAX: 44 1491 836877

The Springs is a grand old country house which dates from 1874 and is set deep in the heart of the beautiful Thames valley. One of the first houses in England to be built in the Mock Tudor style, it stands in six acres of grounds. The hotel's large south windows overlook a spring fed lake from which it takes its name. Many of the luxurious bedrooms and suites offer beautiful views over the lake and lawns, while others overlook the quiet woodland that surrounds the hotel. Private balconies provide patios for summer relaxation. The Lakeside restaurant has an intimate atmosphere inspired by its gentle décor and the lovely view of the lake. The restaurant's menu is changed regularly to take advantage of fresh local produce and seasonal tastes. A well stocked cellar of carefully selected international wines provides the perfect accompaniment to a splendid meal. Leisure facilities include the swimming pool, a putting green, sauna and touring bicycles. A new 18 hole golf course is due to open April '98. Oxford, Blenheim Palace and Windsor are nearby and the hotel is convenient for racing at Newbury and Ascot and the Royal Henley Regatta. Directions: From the M40, take exit 6 onto the B4009, through Watlington to Benson; turn left onto A4074 towards Reading. After ½ mile go right onto B4009. The hotel is ½ mile further, on the right. Price guide: Single from £82; double/twin £115–£150; suite from £155.

30 rms · MasterCard · VISA · AMERICAN EXPRESS · 50

SECKFORD HALL

WOODBRIDGE, SUFFOLK IP13 6NU
TEL: 44 1394 385678 FAX: 44 1394 380610

Seckford Hall dates from 1530 and it is said that Elizabeth I once held court there. The hall has lost none of its Tudor grandeur. Furnished as a private house with many fine period pieces, the panelled rooms, beamed ceilings, carved doors and great stone fireplaces are displayed against the splendour of English oak. Local delicacies such as the house speciality, lobster, feature on the à la carte menu. The original minstrels gallery can be viewed in the banqueting hall, which is now a conference and function suite designed in keeping with the general style. The Courtyard area was converted from a giant Tudor tithe barn, dairy and coach house. It now incorporates ten charming cottage-style suites and a modern leisure complex, which includes a heated swimming pool, exercise machines, solarium and spa bath. The hotel is set in 34 acres of tranquil parkland with sweeping lawns and a willow-fringed lake, and guests may stroll about the grounds or simply relax in the attractive terrace garden. There is a 18-hole golf course, where equipment can be hired, and a gentle walk along the riverside to picturesque Woodbridge, with its tide mill, antiques shops, yacht harbours and the rose-planted grave of Edward Fitzgerald. Constable country and the Suffolk coast are nearby. **Directions:** Remain on the A12 Woodbridge bypass until the blue-and-white hotel sign. Price guide: Single £79–£115; double/twin £110–£135; suite £125–£150.

32 rms · 100

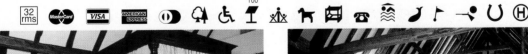

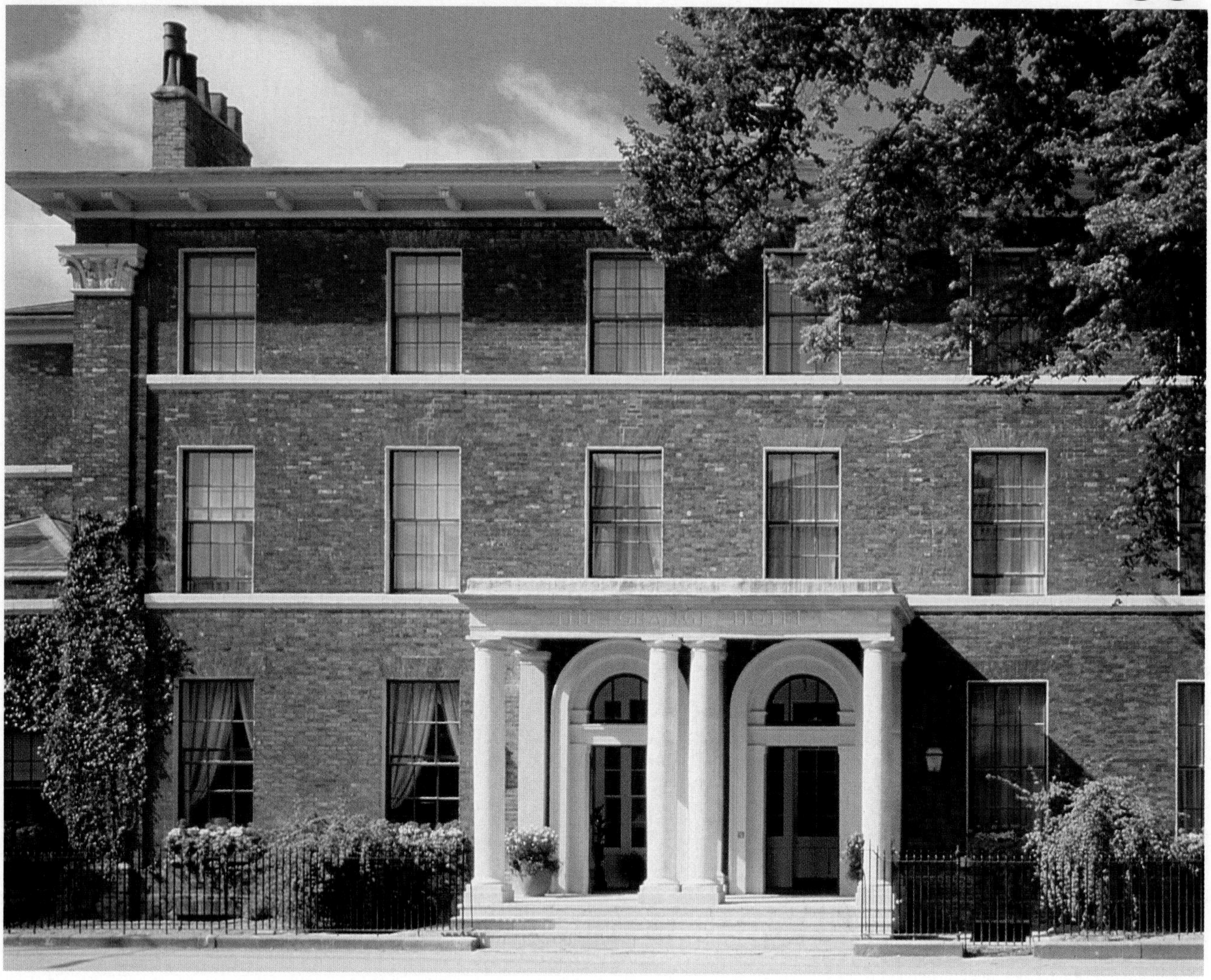

THE GRANGE HOTEL

1 CLIFTON, YORK, NORTH YORKSHIRE YO3 6AA
TEL: 44 1904 644744 FAX: 44 1904 612453

Set near the ancient city walls, 4 minutes' walk from the famous Minster, this sophisticated Regency town house has been carefully restored and its spacious rooms richly decorated. Beautiful stone-flagged floors in the corridors of The Grange lead to the classically styled reception rooms. The flower-filled Morning Room is welcoming, with its blazing log fire and deep sofas. Double doors between the panelled library and drawing room can be opened up to create a dignified venue for parties, wedding receptions or business entertaining. Prints, flowers and English chintz in the bedrooms reflect the proprietor's careful attention to detail. The Ivy Restaurant has an established reputation for first-class gastronomy, incorporating the best in French and country house cooking. The Dom Ruinart Seafood bar has two murals depicting racing scenes. The Brasserie is open for lunch and dinner until after the theatre closes in the evening. For conferences, a computer and fax are available as well as secretarial services. Brimming with history, York's list of attractions includes the National Railway Museum, the Jorvik Viking Centre and the medieval Shambles. **Directions:** The Grange Hotel is on the A19 York–Thirsk road, 1/2 mile from the centre on the left. Price guide: Single £99; double/twin £108–£160; suites £190.

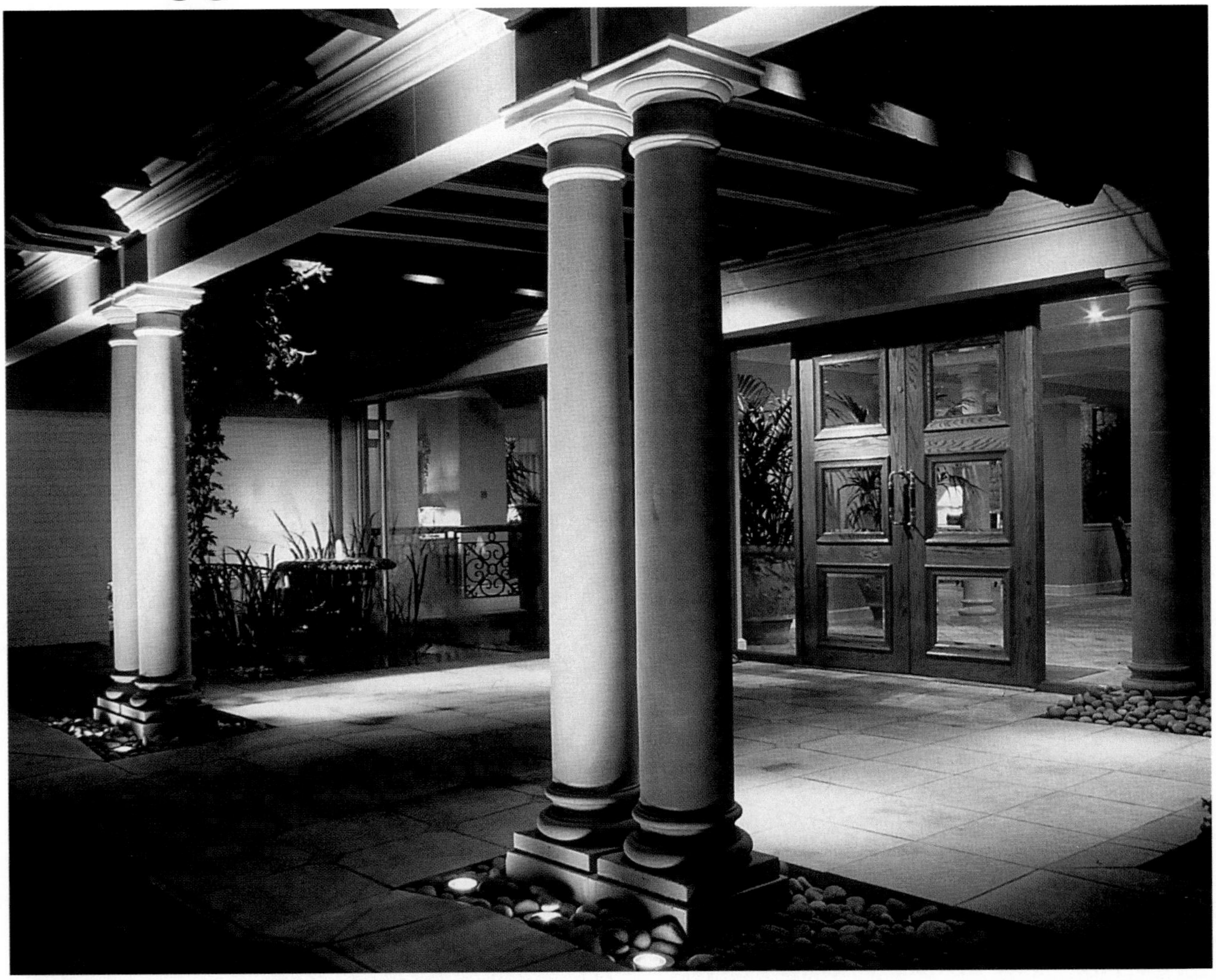

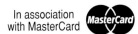

THE ATLANTIC HOTEL

LA MOYE, ST BRELADE, JERSEY JE3 8HE

TEL: 44 1534 44101 FAX: 44 1534 44102 E–MAIL: atlantic@itl.net

A major refurbishment programme in 1994 has transformed this modern building into one with classical warmth and style internally. Privately owned and supervised, every aspect of the four-star service matches its location overlooking the five-mile sweep of St Ouen's Bay. Situated in three acres of private grounds alongside La Moye Golf Course, there is something here for everyone. General Manager, Simon Dufty and his team provide the highest standards of welcome and service. The 50 bedrooms are furnished in the style of the 18th century and like the public rooms, all have co-ordinated colours and fabrics. All have picture windows with views of the sea or the golf course. There are luxury suites and garden studios within the hotel as well. The award-winning restaurant, beautifully situated overlooking the open air pool and terrace, specialises in modern British cooking created by Head Chef, Tom Sleigh. For the more energetic guest, or those wishing to lose excess calories, The Atlantic has extensive indoor health and leisure facilities in The Palm Club including an indoor ozone treated pool. The hotel is an ideal spot from which to walk on the beach or coast paths, to play golf, go riding or just relax. There are comprehensive meeting facilities. **Directions:** Off a private drive off the A13 at La Pulente, two miles from the airport. Price guide: Single £95; double/twin £120; suite £190.

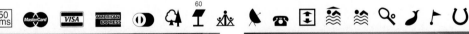

Cyprus

Leave the main roads of Cyprus, and discover for yourself another world and time. A few miles from the westernised modern towns, with their luxury hotels, you will stumble across crumbling hamlets and isolated farms smudged in the heat haze of the day on this most enchanted and enchanting of islands.

Along these dusty roads you'll meet shepherds and labourers whose knowing faces tell tales and who seem to belong to times long gone by. English is one of the languages spoken on Cyprus, so you may be lucky and get the locals to tell you a few stories.

In the plains of the interior, villages nestle silently among olive groves and citrus orchards. The old and young of these small communities congregate in neat village squares to debate, to philosophise, to shelter and "people watch" in the shade of Cyprus trees. Goats and sheep weave among ruins of ancient Greek temples and Roman markets. The small bells hang carelessly about their necks – swaying in an endless breeze – gently awakening spirits which seem to linger still in these ancient monuments.

Vineyards precariously climb the sunny hillsides and – higher up still – cyprus trees frame a somnolent abbey or the skeleton of an abandoned fortress.

This landscape is almost too enchanting a picture to paint – although you will find many an amateur attempting to capture this wild beauty on your travels. But reality surpasses the artist's touch.

Every community in Cyprus thrives on any excuse to celebrate. Festivals are celebrated with flamboyance and enthusiasm. You will see Cyprus at its best in the Spring and Autumn, when the air is sweet and warm, and if total peace and tranquillity is what you seek, or alternatively the frenetic colour and energy of carnival, you will find both on this island – in abundance.

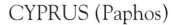

THE ANNABELLE

P.O. BOX 401, PAPHOS, CYPRUS
TEL: 357 62 38 333 FAX: 357 62 45 502

Paphos, the birthplace of Aphrodite who rose there from the sea, is a fitting setting for this luxurious hotel with elaborate tropical gardens stretching right down to the water's edge. Almost every room in the hotel overlooks the sea. The bedrooms and suites all have roomy balconies and the private bungalows have large terraces and lawns. They are beautifully decorated in cool colours and extremely comfortable, provided with every amenity demanded by today's 'five-star' travellers. A sybaritic lifestyle is offered, with a wide choice of bars, the Grotto, the Lobby, the Pool Bar and the Byzantine Bar which has live music and dancing into the night. In addition there are four restaurants from the sophisticated Fontana Amorosa through to the Mediterraneo serving local dishes, especially seafood. The Andromeda Health & Beauty Centre pampers guests who are not taking advantage of the tennis courts and swimming pools, attending the diving school or out fishing with the locals. Paphos Village, full of mythology with several archaeological sites and a fishing harbour dating back to 1600BC is only minutes walk away. **Directions:** Ten minutes by taxi from Paphos airport. The hotel is in the resort of Paphos right on the beach. Price guide: Single CY£82.50–CY£108.50; double/twin CY£123–CY£185; suites CY£225–CY£695.

Czech Republic

Bohemia and Moravia together make up the Czech Republic – a Scotland sized nation on the edge of the Germanic and Slavic worlds. It's one of Europe's most historical countries, full of fairytale castles, châteaux, manors and museums. The medieval core of several dozen towns has been carefuly preserved and there's so much to see that you could make endless visits and discover something new each time.

Ninety per cent of visitors limit themselves to Prague, but the clever few soon experience just how helpful the Czech people can be – as almost everything outside this city is still off the beaten tourist track.

Visit the historical castles and châteaux which rise out of the forests in central Bohemia, or the famous spa town of Karlsbad in West Bohemia, where Brahms, Tolstoy, Chopin, Beethoven and Bismarck came to take the waters – albeit not at the same time.

The many quaint little towns of South Bohemia have a Bavarian or an Austrian flavour, enhanced by some 5000 medieval carp ponds in the surrounding countryside, many of them dating from the Middle Ages. The Bohemian countryside is a restful world of gentle hills and thick woods. It is especially beautiful during the Autumn or in May, when the fruit trees that line the roads are in blossom.

Moravia, the other historical land of the Czech Republic, is usually neglected by travellers visiting Bohemia – but has a wealth of history and natural beauty all its own. The theatres and art galleries of Brno, the capital are excellent and quaint towns like Znojmo and Mikulov await discovery.

Prague is like a history lesson come true. As you walk among the long stone palaces or across the Charles Bridge with the Vltava river flowing below and pointed towers all around, you'll feel as if history had stopped somewhere back in the 18th century.

HOTEL SIEBER

SLEZSKÁ 55, 130 00 PRAGUE 3, CZECH REPUBLIC

TEL: 422 2 24 25 00 25 FAX: 422 2 24 25 00 27

This intimate townhouse hotel is in a quiet one-way street close to Wenceslas Square in the centre of Prague. Its nearest landmark is the impressive National Museum. It is ideal for those visiting the city on business, immaculate and very civilised, yet having a warm ambience achieved by an understanding host. Modern lines have been softened by clever use of wood panelling and Alfons Mucha prints. The bedrooms are spacious and comfortable, thoughtfully designed and supplied with today's requisite amenities. There is one floor dedicated to non-smoking. The three duplex suites are luxurious, with handsome open staircases connecting the living area with the sleeping quarters, perfect for those making a long stay, as the Sieber has no sitting-room nor patio. The small bar leads into the restaurant, an attractively lit room where diners can indulge in Czech specialities or familiar international dishes prepared by the well-known chef. An excellent selection of wines is available. The hotel will arrange tours of Prague with its famous castle, river and museums, organise tickets for concerts and direct guests to the nearby fitness centre, tennis and city night life. **Directions:** The hotel is close to Jirio Z Podebrad Metro. For those driving, from Wenceslas Square, follow Vinohradska, turning right down Perunova, then right again into Slezska. Overnight parking is 500m away. Price guide: Single £83; double/twin £88; suites £104.

12 rms 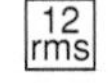        

Denmark

Denmark is the only Scandinavian country without wild tracts of forest and lake. This is a land of well groomed agriculture, where every acre is rich in orchard and field. Nowhere are you far from water, as you drive on and off the ferries and bridges linking the three regions of Jutland, Funen, and Zealand.

Denmark is a series of over 400 islands, about 60 of them inhabited and four accessible by car. The scenery is a mix of rolling hills, heather-clad moors and fertile farmland, dotted with windmills, white-washed churches, thatched farmhouses and story-book villages. The towns are compact and easy to explore – many have a historic centre which has been lovingly restored, and probably a museum proudly displaying local antiquities.

Copenhagen and the bigger cities boast excellent museums and galleries which compare brilliantly with any in Western Europe, and many towns have summer music festivals. When Denmark ruled Norway and Sweden in the 15th century, Copenhagen was the capital of all three countries. Today, the city is still the liveliest Scandinavian capital, with about 1 million inhabitants. It's a city meant for walking, the first in Europe to recognise the value of pedestrian streets in fostering community spirit. If there's such a thing as a cosy metropolis, you'll find it here.

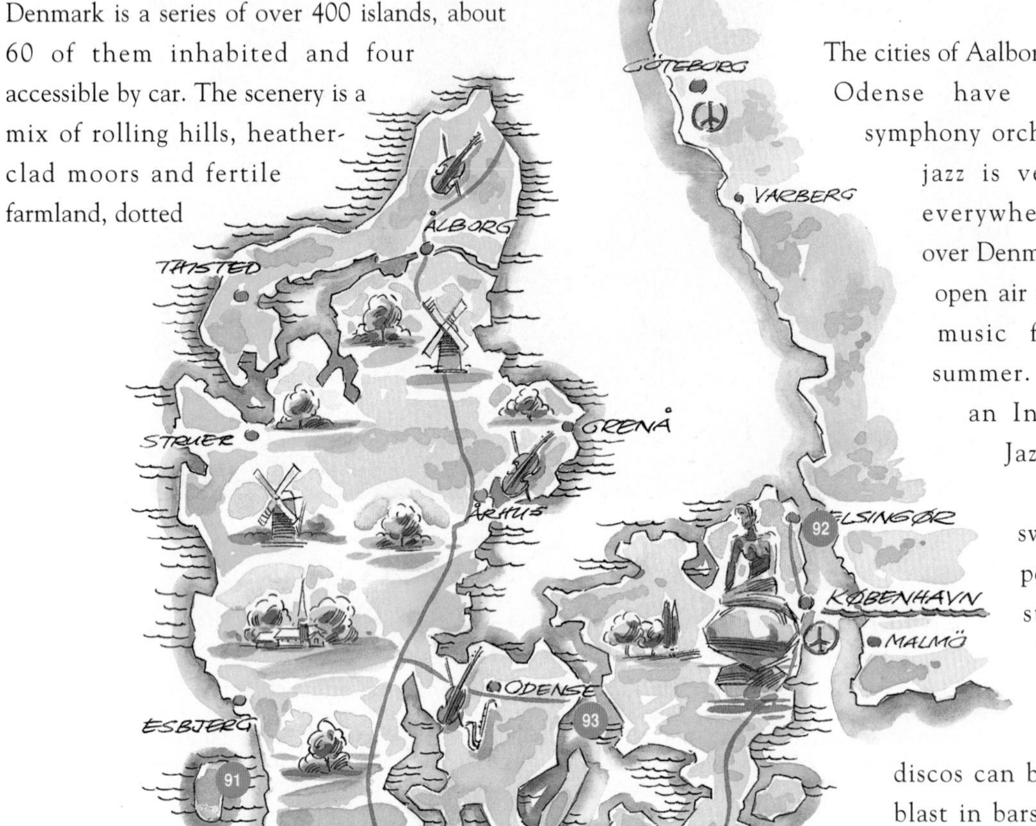

The cities of Aalborg, Arhus and Odense have their own symphony orchestras. Live jazz is very popular everywhere, and all over Denmark there are open air concerts and music festivals in summer. Odense has an International Jazzhus. Street musicians swarm around pedestrianised streets, live bands play nightly in cafés, and discos can be heard full blast in bars throughout the city.

The Danes are a very friendly and uninhibited nation – and a nation of sun worshippers, who have organised their school and working hours to run from 8 am to 4 pm to take full advantage of the long summer days. Many families own or rent a summer house in the country or by the sea. Watersports especially sailing and wind surfing, are very popular. Fitness is rated highly, as is cycling – Danes have the greatest number of bikes per capita in the world, and indeed, with its flat landscape and uncrowded roads, Denmark is a cyclist's paradise.

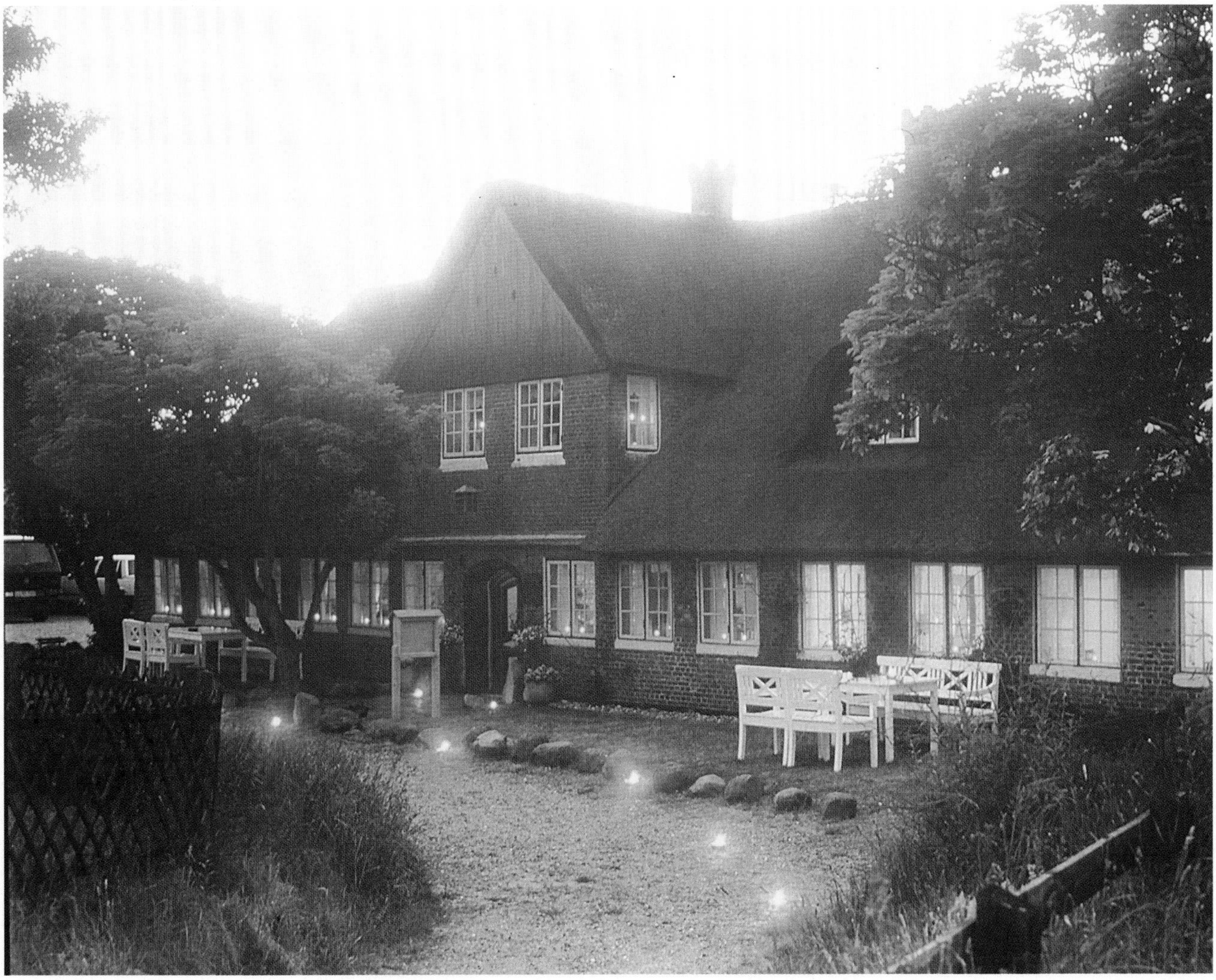

SØNDERHO KRO

KROPLADSEN 11, SØNDERHO, DK-6720 FANØ, DENMARK
TEL: 45 75 16 40 09 FAX: 45 75 16 43 85

Birgit and Niels Sørensen are very proud of their unique and historic hotel – a listed building going back to 1722, it is Denmark's oldest inn. It stands on the southern tip of the enchanting island of Farø, off the south west coast of the mainland, in the delightful village of Sønderho which has only 325 inhabitants and some 50% of their homes are also protected buildings. The 12 bedrooms are unusual, all in a charming quiet building in the garden and each one is named after a ship – "Sophie", "Vennerne", etc. They have individual, attractive styles and are comfortably furnished. Four of the efficient bathrooms have showers only . Guests can drink an aquavit in front of the fire in the lounge before enjoying a delicious three-course dinner, based on local produce including smoked specialities, wonderful fish and gorgeous desserts. Fanø has its own sunny climate, ideal for walking along the lovely stone free beaches or exploring the island on bicycles. Fine golf is just 12km away, tennis is nearer. In summer several music festivals take place. **Directions:** A twelve minute ferry crossing from Esbjerg to Nordby (reservations are recommended as the ferry only takes 25 cars), then drive 12km south to Sønderho. There is also a ferry from Harwich to Esbjerg. Price guide: Single 675kr–980kr; double/twin 780kr–1190kr.

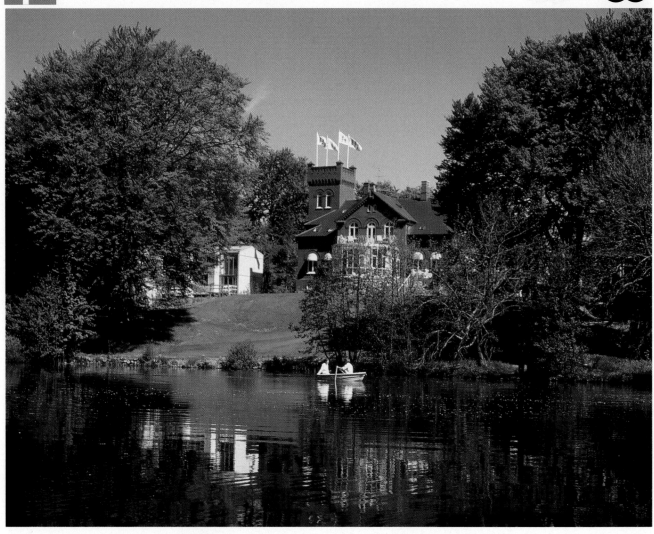

Havreholm Slot

4 KLOSTERRISVEJ, HAVREHOLM, DK–3100 HORNBÆK
TEL: 45 4975 8600 FAX: 45 4975 8023

This splendid mansion standing high above the River Gurre was built in 1872. Early this century the Danish artist, Joakim Skovgard, decorated the Paradise Hall with paintings of The Garden of Eden. This is the magnificent background to the main diningroom. The bedrooms are situated in 16 comfortable guest houses in the surrounding parkland which has its own lake and waterfall. Seven of these houses have their own kitchenettes. The reception rooms are splendid – a handsome library for reading or a game of chess. In the summer the terrace is a popular rendezvous for drinks and al fresco eating and guests enjoy the elegant restaurant with its immaculate service, wonderful food and superb wines. There are also excellent facilites for conferences and receptions, able to accommodate meetings from 4 to 45 people, while the Pavilion overlooking the lake can host 200 visitors. Active delegates appreciate the fitness centre, indoor and outdoor pools, tennis, squash, golf, billiards, boules, riding, rowing boats and explore the countryside on bicycles. Others enjoy the park, watching the wild birds. Directions: Leave Helsingor Highway from Copenhagen at Exit 4 (Hornbaek) to Tikob, 5km later turn left signed Havreholm. The hotel is on the left. Price guide: Single 950kr–1200kr; double/twin 1350kr–1500kr; Suite 1800kr.

HOTEL HESSELET

CHRISTIANSLUNDSVEJ 119, DK–5800 NYBORG, DENMARK
TEL: 45 65 31 30 29 FAX: 45 65 31 29 58

Situated on the garden Island of Funen, surrounded by woods and adjacent to the beach, is the renowned Hotel Hesselet, a member of Small Luxury Hotels of the World. The distinctive Japanese – Scandinavian architecture, combined with the tasteful decor of the interior and the panoramic views, gives the hotel a special atmosphere. Antiques and beautiful paintings contribute to the "home away from home" feeling that makes the hotel a favourite country retreat. Spacious well-decorated rooms and suites with well-fitted ensuite granite bathrooms together with beautiful reception rooms and the candle-lit Tranquebar Restaurant offer a restful stay. Active guests will appreciate the indoor pool with fitness equipment or may prefer to swim from the hotel jetty, play tennis on artificial grass, see the countryside on the hotel's bikes, play golf on the 8 nearby courses or visit Odense, the town of Hans Christian Andersen. Driving in Denmark on the excellent roads is easy and pleasant. You can travel by Scandinavian Seaways from Harwich to Esbjerg (distance to hotel approx. 100 miles) or by air to Billund in Jutland (approx. 75miles) or to Copenhagen (approx. 70 miles plus ferry 50 mins.). **Directions:** Leave the E20 at Exit 45 and the hotel is 3 minutes away, just north of Nyborg. Price guide: Single DKK 890–990; double/twin DKK 1.250–1.450; Suite DKK 1.800–2.800.

France

The essence of French savoir vivre is simplicity. Everyday things count – eating, drinking, talking, dressing, shopping. Get in the mood – daily rituals are meant to be enjoyed. Food is the best example. The French don't like rushing meals. They plan them in advance, painstakingly prepare them, look forward to them over an apéritif admire the loving presentation of each dish, savour each mouthful. The pace is unhurried, and the wine flows.

Make the most of the simple pleasure to be had from basking in the sunshine outside a café. Admire the casual elegance of the passers-by or the old men in their time honoured berets. Even the most mundane things can become objects of beauty in French eyes. The daily market is a festival of colours and textures, with fruit and vegetable stalls artistically and imaginatively composed. Shop windows are works of art.

Encompassing Brittany with its Celtic martime heritage the Meditteranean sunbelt, Germanic Alsace-Lorraine, and the rugged mountain regions of the Auvergne and the Pyrenees, Paris remains the fulcrum – but not the heart of France – with its urbane citizens and intense pace of life.

Most French towns and villages are quietly attracive and historic. Chances are that the ornate town hall has been there since the Revolution, and the church or cathedral since the Middle Ages. The main streets tend to be lined with sturdy trees planted before living memory. The 20th century is kept firmly at bay.

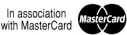

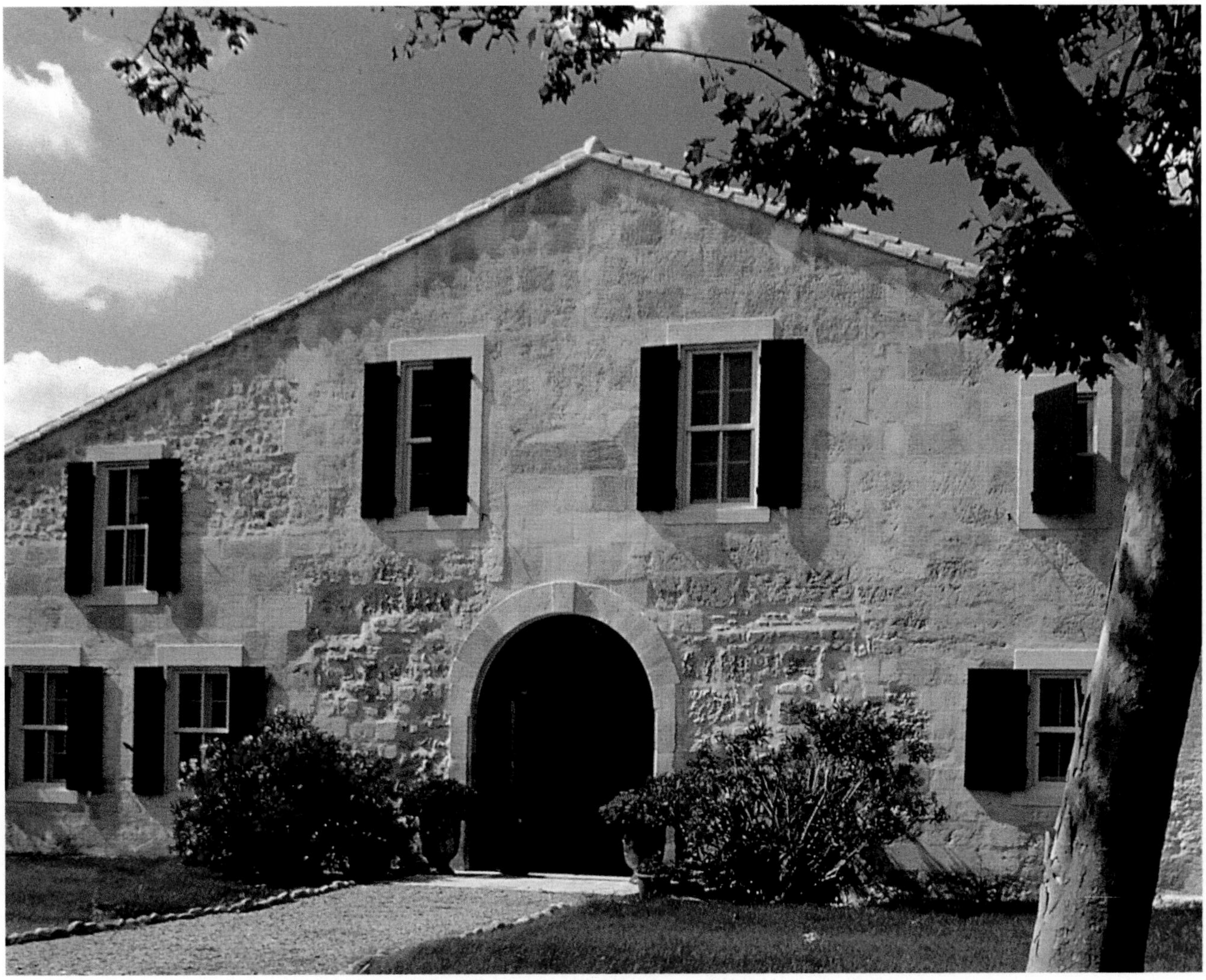

LE MAS DE PEINT

LE SAMBUC, 13200 ARLES, FRANCE

TEL: 33 4 90 97 20 62 FAX: 33 4 90 97 22 20 E-MAIL: peint@avignon.pacwan.net

To be in the Camargue is to commune with nature, and Le Mas de Peint, dating back to the 17th century, stands in its own extensive manade (estate) in one of the most verdant areas of France. It is still a working farm, quite remote, and therefore this small, intimate hotel could almost be designated 'chambre d'hôte' as guests live in the proprietor's home. The salons are elegant and relaxing, with antique furniture from the region, low beams and stone floors. The bedrooms are charming, the bathrooms are modern. Meals are taken in a delightful Provençal room, once the kitchen. Dinner, a set menu, is superb. Recipes handed down by the Grandmère and now beautifully prepared in refined Provençal style – feature with delicious local specialities. Breakfast and lunch can be taken on the terrace or by the pool, which has its own poolhouse to change in. A guide from the farm takes guests out to see the famous wild horses and his magnificent Camargue bulls. Nearby are a nature reserve, museum, bird park and walkers can follow the river running down to the coast. Internet: http//www.ila.chateau.com/monade **Directions:** Leave Arles on D570 towards Saintes- Maries-de-la-Mer. Take D36 to Salin-de-Giraud, finding Le Mas de Peint soon after Le Sambuc. Price guide: Single Ff1050–1500; double/twin Ff1750–1980; suites Ff1700–1900.

Château De Vault De Lugny

11 RUE DU CHÂTEAU, F-89200 AVALLON, FRANCE
TEL: 33 3 86 34 07 86 FAX: 33 3 86 34 16 36 E-MAIL: lugny@transco.fr

First sight of this magnificent domaine is magical – there is an authentic moat encircling the verdant estate, a 13th century watch tower – the château itself is 16th century – and there are proud peacocks and gaggles of geese in front of the historic farm buildings. This elite hotel is run by two marvellous hostesses, Madame Audan and her daughter, who have created a unique blend of sophistication and history. The interior is dramatic – marvellous panelling, superb antiques, big elaborate fireplaces and ornate ceilings. The luxurious guest rooms have romantic four poster beds. There is one large family suite. All the amenities of the hotel and the restaurant are exclusively for resident guests. On Saturday evenings residents are invited to aperitifs. Three interesting menus, Seasonal, Burgundian and Gourmet, ensure that dining is memorable, whether al fresco or seated amiably round the kitchen table. The wines are exquisite Picnics can be arranged for those exploring the countryside, although it is fascinating to see the estate from an air balloon! Tennis, trout fishing, riding, exploring medieval Vézelay and wine-tasting are suggested recreations – gently strolling in the gardens is idyllic. There is a special games area for children. Intenet: http://www.transee.fr/lugny/home.html **Directions:** N6, exit Avallon, taking road for Vézelay until Pontaubert. Turn right, watching for signs to the Château. Price guide: Double/twin Ff750–2400.

LA CARDINALE ET SA RESIDENCE

QUAI DU RHONE, 07 210 BAIX, FRANCE
TEL: 33 4 75 85 80 40 FAX: 33 4 75 85 82 07

The Rhône valley, famed for its many prestigious vineyards, is exceptionally beautiful, and it is here, in Baix village, standing against a background of the Ardèche mountains, that a glorious French mansion has been skillfully transformed into an elite hotel. The Hostellerie was built four centuries ago. Old world charm and courtesy are pervasive and modernisation has been discreet. The original facade has been restored and the old stonework is in evidence in the gardens too. The private salon is exquisite. The romantic guest rooms, reminiscent of the Louis XIV era and evocative of Provence, are inviting and the bathrooms are splendid, in marble with historic overtones. La Cardinale also has 'Sa Residence', some 3.5 kms away which is surrounded by 24 hectares of verdant parkland and is another distinguished old house with an outdoor pool. It is enchanting and very comfortable. Breakfast is served al fresco on the balcony or indoors. Lunch and dinner are in La Cardinale with drinks beforehand on the terrace. Wines of distinction accompany the gourmet menu. The short ride to and from the residence can always be chauffeur driven. Wine tasting, trips down the river, whatever you wish to do, the management will assist with the arrangements. **Directions** A7, exit Loriol, towards Le Pouzin, then N86 south to Baix. Price guide: Single Ff700–1100; double/twin Ff800–1800; suites Ff1500–2000.

        35     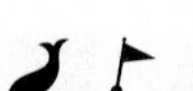 

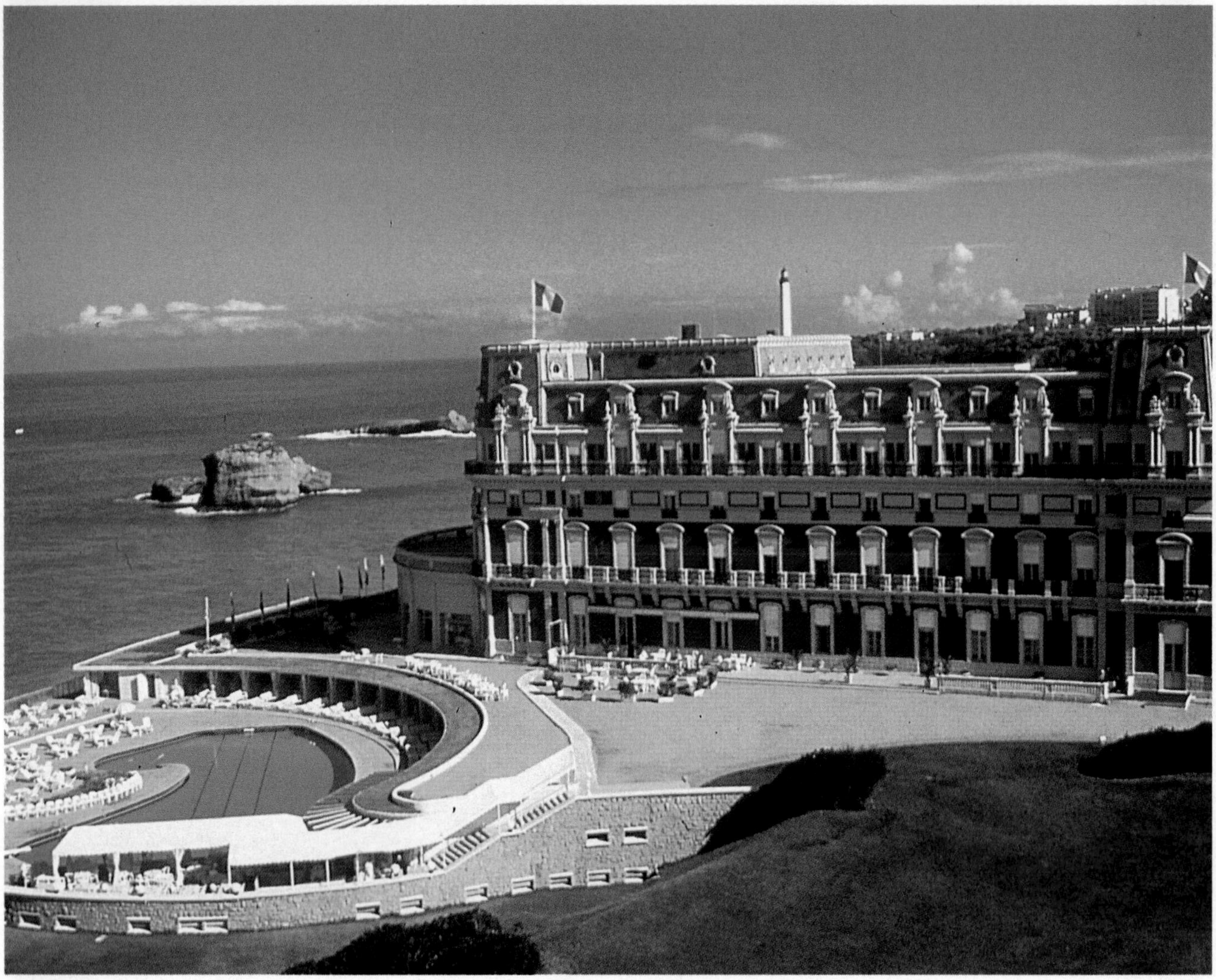

Hôtel Du Palais

F–64200 BIARRITZ,AVENUE DE L'IMPÉRATRICE, FRANCE
TEL: 33 5 59 41 64 00 FAX: 33 5 59 41 67 99 E-MAIL: palais@cotebasque.tm.fr

This is a true palace, having been the summer haunt of royalty since 1855 – balls, receptions, charades, picnics and fireworks were the programme then (as they are now!). It became a hotel in the fabulous Belle Epoque, the 1880s, when the guest list included Queen Victoria. In 1950 a famous decorator undertook the complete renovation of the Palais, maintaining its grand style and today it is a sumptuous residence overlooking the waterfront. The richly furnished foyer has marble pillars, glistening chandeliers, superb antiques and a dramatic staircase. The bedrooms are luxurious, many with balconies facing the sea, and access is easy for those with mobility problems. Sophisticated bars, cool in the hotel or on the terraces, are appreciated by guests before feasting in the elegant Michelin star restaurant, with a spectacular view across the sea. Lighter meals in an informal ambience are also served, including a buffet beside the pool. Families use the private beach huts between the pool and the sand. Sporting guests enjoy tennis, squash, 10 golf-courses, scuba-diving, riding or watching pelota, the Basque national game. Others explore the countryside, right up into the Pyrenees. At night the casino is a great attraction. **Directions:** Biarritz is signed from the A63 and N10. Price guide: Single Ff1200–Ff2100; double/twin Ff1500–Ff 2850; suites Ff 2000–Ff6350. Internet: http://www.cotebasque.tm.fr/palais

Hôtel Savoy

5 RUE FRANÇOIS EINESY, F–06400 CANNES, FRANCE
TEL: 33 4 92 99 72 00 FAX: 33 4 93 68 25 59

This modern hotel with elegant balconies and terraces, is just off the famous Boulevard de la Croisette, giving easy access to the beach and to the town centre. Bedrooms provide modern comfort for the business or pleasure guest. The barman mixes cocktails in the intimate bar before diners enter La Roseraie, the terraced restaurant in front of the hotel with its own waterfall. The menu offers good choices from the region including grilled seabass and rack of lamb, provençal style. A more modest menu reflects the best local market produce. Many of the wines listed are from the region. The Blue Beach on the 6th floor has a wonderful terrace alongside the swimming pool, serving drinks and buffet lunches to sun-worshippers. A private beach is ready for those who prefer sea and sand. Not far from the Palais des Congrès, The Savoy has its own well equipped conference suites, ideal for receptions and banquets. Exploring old Cannes and the modern shops is fascinating, as is the delightful countryside behind the coast. Museum of Perfumery at Grasse, tennis and watersports are available, and golf is not far away. **Directions:** 24km from the Nice Airport, driving take the N7 or leave the A8 motorway at the Cannes exit. There is parking under the hotel. Price guide: Single Ff600–1305; double/twin Ff730–1455; suites Ff1800–5000.

Star Clippers

FRED OLSEN TRAVEL, FRED OLSEN HOUSE, WHITE HOUSE ROAD, IPSWICH IP1 5LL
TEL: 44 1473 292200

The Tall Ships race is always a spectacular and emotive occasion and Star Clippers are offering this exciting opportunity to emulate those who take part – albeit in far greater comfort and without doing any of the work! What better way to approach many fascinating Mediterranean ports than on a graceful ship, under 36,000 sq ft. of white sails. These vessels are designed so that passengers do not feel crowded, as although there are many active areas, there are retreats such as the Edwardian library and quiet corners on deck. The cabins are opulent, with marble bathrooms, thick carpets, ample mirrors and a dedicated steward to attend to guests' needs. Grade 1 have Jacuzzis, Grade 6 bunk beds for children. On deck there are pools and the Tropical Bar, where dancing under the stars is part of the programme. The Piano Bar is perfect for champagne before dining in grand style (casual elegance is the uniform and there is no rigid table plan) Informal buffet lunches are served on deck. The voyage starts in Cannes. The ports of call – with long enough ashore to explore – are Corsica, Sardinia, Elba and Giglio off the Tuscan Coast, the Italian Riviera and St Tropez on the return to France. Another cruise in Europe heads for the Aegean waters. Further away other Star Clippers yachts head for exotic islands off the Malaysian coast, Bahamas and West Indies. Price guide(per person/for 7 nights): Single £1230; twin £995 (Category 6 – upper/lower berths). Port Charges £95.

190

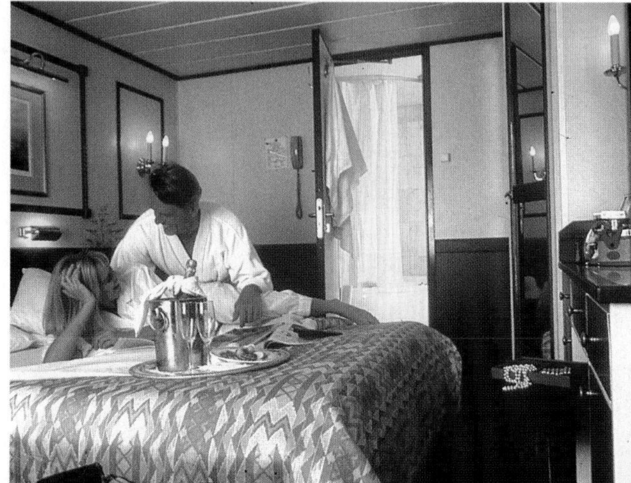

CHÂTEAU DE CANDIE

RUE DU BOIS DE CANDIE, 73000 CHAMBÉRY-LE-VIEUX, FRANCE
TEL: 33 4 79 966300 FAX: 33 4 79 966310

The history of this magical château dates back to the 14th century when it was built as a fortress by Knights returning from the Crusades. Almost at the Millennium, it is a comfortable and friendly hotel, its fine Savoyard architecture undiminished by the years. The Château reflects the talents and passions of its distinguished owner, Didier Lhostis. It is a connoisseur's paradise, filled with priceless antiques and collections of paintings; trompe l'oeil enhances the salons. To visit here is to stay in a magnificent private mansion with echoes of each past generation. Statues lurk in corridors, intriguing bibelots are on display. The meeting rooms are pleasant. The gorgeous bedrooms and suites are named after historical personalities and furnished accordingly. The bathrooms are opulent – one bath is carved out of a block of 19th century marble! The kitchen is in the hands of Chef Gilles Hérard who, having trained under famous Parisian chefs, has returned home to Chambéry, where his impeccable presentation and innovative cooking of Savoyan dishes excite the most discerning guests in the three exquisite dining rooms. The wines are superlative. Stroll through the idyllic park, relax on the terrace, explore the region, play golf or tennis and enjoy marvellous winter sports resorts nearby. **Directions:** Leave A43 Exit 15 for Chambéry Le Haut. Price guide: double/twin Ff500–Ff950; duplex Ff1200.

LE HAMEAU HOTEL ALBERT 1ER

119, IMPASSE DU MONTENVERS, F–74402 CHAMONIX – MONT BLANC
TEL: 33 4 50 53 05 09 FAX: 33 4 50 55 95 48 INTERNET: http://www.silicone.fr/hotalber

Since 1903 the Hotel Albert 1er has been a popular hotel in Chamonix. This year it has changed its name to Le Hameau Albert 1er, for it has grown into a small hamlet! Owned by the Carrier family, whose inspired use of wood, local stone and terracotta has made the hotel so attractive, the complex includes enchanting small chalets and luxurious farmhouses – just 50 metres from the Albert 1er. Martine and Pierre's decorating skills have created the same warm ambience in the new houses The bedrooms and suites are charming, many having balconies looking across to mountains, not least of which is Mont Blanc. In summer the view is parkland and flower-filled gardens. The inviting bar and lounge encourage guests to relax and socialise. In addition to the hotel restaurant, where Pierre's inspired cooking has won a Michelin star, guests can enjoy Savoyard specialities in "La Maison Carrier", a rustic bistro in one of the farms. Fabulous French wines are listed. The Hameau has indoor and outdoor pools, a gymnasium and sauna for visitors returning from an exhilarating day's skiing and skating. In summer, mountaineering, glacier skiing, tennis, golf and paragliding are among the sports available. Chamonix has a lively night-life. Directions: Follow Route Blanche past the station, finding Impasse du Montenvers on the right. Price guide: Double/standard Ff660–Ff760; double/deluxe Ff1100–Ff2800.

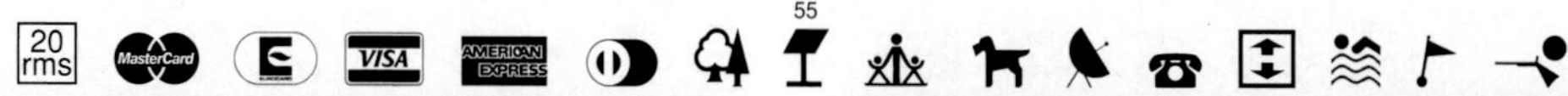

CHÂTEAU DES BRIOTTIÈRES

49330 CHAMPIGNÉ, FRANCE

TEL: 33 2 41 42 00 02 FAX: 33 2 41 42 01 55

This enchanting château, surrounded by well-kept lawns and 360 acres of parkland 'à l'anglaise', has been in the same family for over 200 years.Indeed this is not a hotel, but a stately home in which guests are graciously received. It is in Anjou, an unspoilt corner of France. The interior is lovely, filled with Louis XV antiques and memorabilia, family portraits and a pervading air of serenity. This château was used as the setting for the film "Impromptu" starring Emma Thompson and Hugh Grant. The bedrooms have windows looking out over the estate, letting in the fragrant perfumes of herbs and flowers. It is a joy to awake here in the mornings. Breakfast may be taken in the bedrooms or at separate tables downstairs. Lunch is not available and everyone meets again for apéritifs with the owner of the property, François de Valbray, before a convivial dinner (served at 8.30pm) in the impressive dining room – traditional family recipes accompanied by delicious Anjou wines. The château offers swimming in summer, fishing in the lake and billiards in the evenings; golf and riding are nearby. Not far away are the Loire châteaux and the Anjou wine trail, further west Brittany fishing ports. **Directions:** From Paris, take A11 towards Nantes, exit no.11 Durtal, then Daumeray on D859 then Châteauneuf s/Sarthe to Champigné, then follow the signs for 4 kms. Price guide: Double/twin Ff600–Ff750; suites Ff900–Ff1100.

9 rms      200     

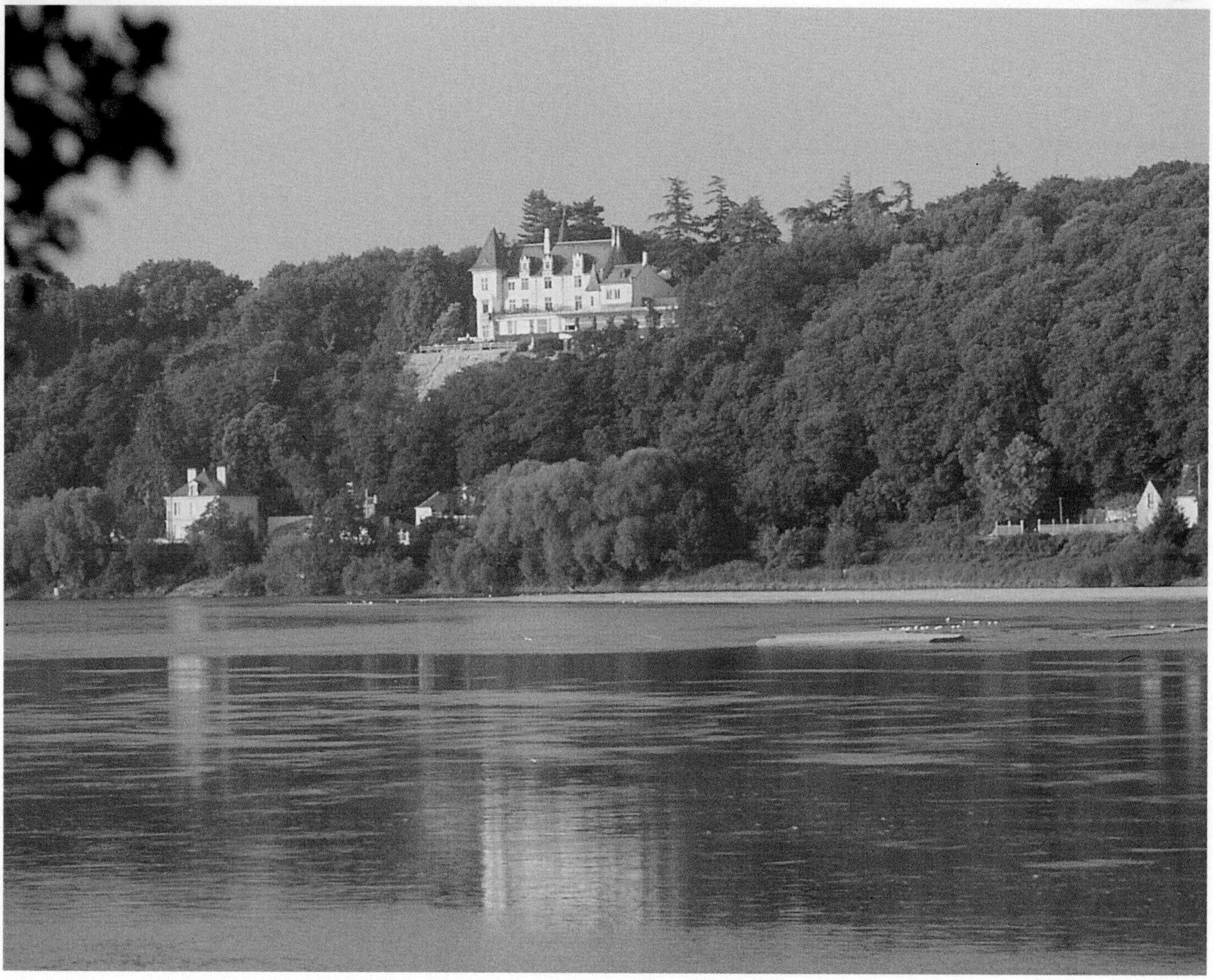

Le Prieuré

F–49350 CHÊNEHUTTE-LES-TUFFEAUX, SAUMUR, FRANCE
TEL: 33 2 41 67 90 14 FAX: 33 2 41 67 92 24

This magnificent Renaissance manor house stands on history – firstly the site was an important Roman camp and, in the 12th century, a famous abbey here overlooked the Loire. 15th and 16th century architecture brought turrets and cherubs to enhance this slate-roofed palace – inside, the spiral staircase has a vaulted ceiling with medieval gargoyles. The salons are regal, with tall fireplaces and Louis XV furniture, chandeliers and wonderful paintings. The bedrooms are spacious, beautifully decorated, many having canopy beds. Consideration has been given to visitors with mobility problems. Those on a budget might prefer one of the cottages among the trees. Apéritifs on the terrace, watching the sunset over the river is the perfect start to the evening. Guests dine by candle-light in the baronial restaurant, enjoying superb dishes reflecting the chef's generous use of local wines, fresh herbs, fruit and vegetables. All the Anjou vineyards are represented in the cellar. Active guests appreciate the pool, tennis courts and jogging trail, others relax in the well tended gardens. Fishing and golf are nearby. The area abounds with vineyards and châteaux to visit. Watching the famous Cadre Noir in Saumur training their horses is fascinating. **Directions:** From Paris A10. N152 over the Loire. Pass through Saumur towards Gennes on the D751. Price guide: Ff500–Ff1500.

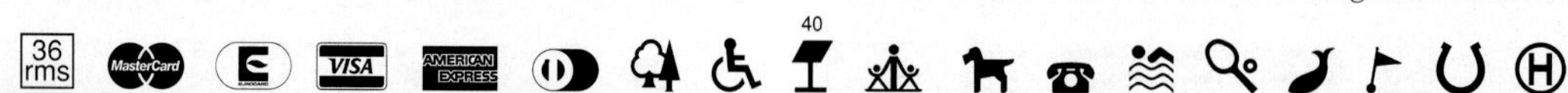

LE MOULIN DE CONNELLES

40 ROUTE D'AMFREVILLE-SOUS-LES-MONTS, 27430 CONNELLES, FRANCE
TEL: 33 2 32 59 53 33 FAX: 33 2 32 59 21 83

On an island of its own in a by-water of the Seine a few miles above Rouen stands Le Moulin de Connelles, a fabulously beautiful old manor house and water mill. This is the part of the river that so appealed to Monet and his fellow impressionists. There are six luxurious suites and seven luxurious bedrooms. Antiques and fine décor perpetuate the ambience of charming seclusion – the latest modern equipment provides, if audio-visual is required, immediate contacts with the outer world. Comfort is similarly assured by the up-to-date amenities. The manor's lounge and bar welcome guests with furnishings that induce that sense of well-being that can be heightened only by a glass of calvados. The restaurant poised above the water is famed for the skill of its young chef. As early guide books might have said: Le Moulin is worth more than a détour. The manor's swimming pool, pool house and tennis courts, nearby international golf courses, riding school and sailing or water skiing on the lake are the breath-taking choice of sporting pursuits. **Directions:** 110Km from Paris motorway A13 exit 18; 28Km from Rouen motorway A13 exit 19; 15Km from Louviers. Price guide: Single Ff550–Ff700; double/twin Ff650–Ff800; suites Ff800–Ff950.

HÔTEL ANNAPURNA

F–73120 COURCHEVEL (1850), FRANCE
TEL: 33 4 79 08 04 60 FAX: 33 4 79 08 15 31

Hotel Annapurna is a sophisticated hotel in the midst of the Alps. Built this century, it has recognised the needs of its sporting guests when they leave the pistes. The interior is spacious and elegant, reflecting the designer's savoir-faire. There are relaxing lounges, with comfortable modern furnishings. The bedrooms are luxurious, with panelled walls and ceilings, all with a south-facing balcony. The piano bar is an ideal après-ski rendezvous, perhaps after taking advantage of the leisure centre. This has a magnificent pool, looking out to the snowfields, a Jacuzzi, sauna, gymnasium, UVA, turkish bath masseur, table-tennis and billiards. After an exotic cocktail or two, studying the menu of the handsome restaurant, with its spectacular view of the mountains, the superb French food, beautifully served, is greatly appreciated, especially when accompanied by connoisseur wines. An orchestra plays on Thursday evenings. The Annapurna is a fantastic place for small seminars and conferences, and all appropriate facilities are available. Every form of winter sports is possible in Courchevel, 600 Kms wonderful runs, Langlauf, skating, curling and tobogganing. At night there are discothèques, cinemas, clubs. **Directions:** A41 to Montmelian, then A43 to Albertville, then N90 to Moutiers, after which Courchevel is signed. Price guide per person: Single Ff980–2165; double/twin Ff980–1620; suites Ff2690–3200.

90

HÔTEL DES TROIS VALLÉES

BP 22, F-73122 COURCHEVEL CEDEX, FRANCE
TEL: 33 4 79 08 00 12 FAX: 33 4 79 08 17 98

This hotel is the ultimate skiers' paradise, at Courchevel, the Olympic sports complex high in the Savoie mountains, located on the slopes (in and out skiing) close to the ski-lifts. Only open in the winter months, it promises marvellous snow conditions. After the rigours of the day, skiers appreciate the luxury of this elegant chalet-style residence just a two minute walk from the centre of town. The ambience of a sybaritic lifestyle is created by music, silk curtains, luxurious, classical modern furnishings, gleaming crystal and attentive staff. Those wanting total peace retreat to the contemporary and extremely comfortable bedrooms, with opulent bathrooms. The piano bar has large leather armchairs in which guests relax, enjoying a drink while listening to the music. The menu in the delightful and spacious restaurant concentrates on haute cuisine supported by a wine list of the highest calibre. Fine days bring a barbecue on the terrace. Après-ski activities include benefiting from hydromassage, saunas, Turkish baths, the solarium, gymnasium and beauty salon. **Directions:** Daily direct flights from Paris in the Twin Otter and at weekends faster journeys in the Dash Seven; alternatively the TGV Paris–Moutiers where the hotel will meet you. Driving from Lyon, A43, A430 and N90. Price guide: double/twin Ff900–1420; suites Ff1500–2400. Per person per day half board.

LE BYBLOS DES NEIGES

BP 98 - F–73122 COURCHEVEL, FRANCE
TEL: 33 4 79 00 98 00 FAX: 33 4 79 00 98 01

Courchevel is a prestigious ski resort, made more so by hosting the Olympic Games in 1992, and Le Byblos Des Neiges has an unparalleled situation in the Jardin Alpin, in the midst of the pistes, close to ski-lifts and cable cars. From the exterior it looks a modern hotel, inside new arrivals find the immaculate service and luxurious furnishings of the great chalets of earlier this century. The reception rooms are splendid, with tall larch pillars and big, comfortable chairs. Wonderful glowing fabrics give the spacious bedrooms a special warmth. Rustic yet contemporary furniture, balconies with spectacular views over the snow and lavish modern bathrooms add to the pleasure of staying here. La Clairière Restaurant is famous for its buffets and regional dishes; skiers enjoy lunch on its sunny terrace. At night guests can also dine in the L'Écailler, an elegant venue renowned for its in fabulous fish specialities. Aldo Bar is the meeting place in Courchevel, soft piano music and a big fire adding to its charm. Backgammon is played in the games room. Children have their own territory. After the day's exertions, the large pool and health centre are ideal, a wide range of treatments being offered. **Directions:** From Lyons A43, then A90 to Moutiers, follow signs to Courchevel. The hotel has a heated garage. Price guide (half-board per person): Single Ff1750–Ff2340; double/twin Ff1450–Ff2470; suites Ff2530–Ff5000.

HÔTEL ROYAL

BOULEVARD CORNUCHÉ, 14800 DEAUVILLE, CALVADOS, FRANCE
TEL: 33 2 31 98 66 33 FAX: 33 2 31 98 66 34

A 20th century grand hotel, right on the waterfront in Deauville, immortalised in the paintings of Duty, the Royal has maintained its traditions of impeccable service in magnificent surroundings. It is part of the Lucien Barrière Group, who also own the nearby Hôtel Normandy, the famous casino and the delightful Hôtel du Golf, built on the edge of the course at Mont Canisy. Special packages enable guests to take advantage of all these facilities. The spacious salons are very impressive, with huge sofas and magnificent flower displays. The bedrooms are enormous and beautifully appointed to meet the needs of the most demanding guests. Those with mobility problems will appreciate specially adapted accommodation. The hotel has two restaurants, one for gourmets for which fabulous dishes are prepared and the dining room where lighter meals are served. The cellar is extensive. The Bayeux Tapestries are of great interest to tourists, and Deauville, famous for its race-course and film festival, itself is fascinating to explore. Excellent golf, with a choice of courses in the vicinity, is popular. The hotel has a splendid fitness centre, and outside in the grounds are tennis courts and swimming pool with a terrace bar. **Directions:** Following the coast road, the hotel is a landmark midway along the seafront. Price guide: Single/double/twin from Ff1150–Ff2300; suites Ff2200–Ff10,000.

LE GRAND HOTEL DU DOMAINE DE DIVONNE

AVENUE DES THERMES, 01220 DIVONNE LES BAINS, FRANCE
TEL: 33 4 50 40 34 34 FAX: 33 4 50 40 34 24

The Domaine de Divonne ia a vast estate in sight of Mont Blanc, close to the Swiss border, just fifteen minutes drive from Geneva The Domaine has Le Grand Hotel, Le Golf and Le Casino. The Grand Hotel is a dramatic Art Deco residence – decorated mirrors, exotic fireplaces, tasselled lampshades, stained glass, vibrant colours and a pianist playing Duke Ellington! The bedrooms are inviting, and guests should laze on the balcony gazing at the Jura mountains. The marble bathrooms have gold fittings! Informal meals are enjoyed in La Brasserie de Léman. The pièce de résistance is La Terrace, an romantic restaurant which stretches into the enchanting gardens. The chef is legendary, the cuisine cosmopolitan. Le Golf has Le Pavillon restaurant in the Clubhouse, with 1930s decor and views of Mont Blanc. The challenging course is immaculate. At night guests seek Le Casino, with its magnificent collection of early slot machines. Traditional gambling tables are busy. Its Four Seasons Restaurant serves French and Lebanese specialities. Dancing through the night at Le Club Oxygène is fantastic. The countryside offers mountains, lakes, rivers – explore them by bike, otherwise relax after tennis and sunbathe by the pool. **Directions:** N1 from Geneva, exit Coppet/Divonne. Surveillance car parking. Price guide: Single Ff750–1200; double/twin Ff1150–1650; suites Ff2700–9000.

Chateau De Bellinglise

60 157 ELINCOURT SAINTE-MARGUERITE, FRANCE
TEL: 33 3 44 96 00 33 FAX: 33 3 44 96 03 00

It takes just one hour from Paris to reach this very beautiful château, and to leave city life far behind. Surrounded by verdant parkland and dramatic lakes mirroring its elegant facade, this legendary sixteenth century manor house overlooking the Matz Valley has been transformed into an elite and luxurious hotel. The interior is breath-taking: graceful arches and pillars, priceless antiques, handsome paintings, brilliant chandeliers, a spiral staircase, gorgeous flowers – and the immaculate, attentive staff add a hospitable ambience. The exquisite guest rooms are adorned with rich drapery, period furniture and softly tinted marble bathrooms. Some bedrooms are in the Valois annex. The salons are peaceful and timeless, there is a sunny conservatory overlooking the courtyard, a stylish smoking room, and guests sip aperitifs in the friendly bar or on the terrace with its heavenly views across the estate. The Chef is an artist, creating magnificent dishes, matched by fine wines from the cellar. The hotel also has six state-of-the-art meeting rooms. Residents enjoy walking, riding, cycling and tennis in the grounds, excellent golf in the vicinity or neighbouring châteaux and museums. Families head for the nearby pleasure parks. **Directions:** A1, Exit 11, then D15 watching for signs to the Château de Bellinglise. Price guide: Single Ff645–Ff1335; double/twin Ff845–1435; suites Ff1130–1680; annex Ff435–560.

HOSTELLERIE LA BRIQUETERIE

4 ROUTE DE SÉZANNE, F–51530, VINAY – ÉPERNAY, FRANCE
TEL: 33 3 26 59 99 99 FAX: 33 3 26 59 92 10

La Briqueterie, standing at the foot of the Côte des Blancs, is surrounded by beautiful flower-filled grounds in the heart of the champagne country. It is owned by the Trouillard family, whose interest in vintage cars is evident from the distinctive works of art in the informal reception area. The salons are elegant, and the quiet countryside even pervades the enchanting bedrooms and suites, identified by floral panels on the doors, the colours of which are echoed in the decor inside. The bathrooms are large and luxurious. The family have their own Champagne House, and their vintages are among the prestigious champagnes imbibed in the attractive conservatory bar in the garden summerhouse. A wonderful buffet is served in the Breakfast Room, overlooking the pool. At night in the handsome beamed restaurant diners have a choice of Regional and Dégustation menus or they select succulent dishes from the à la carte suggestions. The wines are superb. A splendid private dining room and conference facilities are also available. Visitors explore Reims Cathedral, tour champagne cellars or cruise on the Marne. Others relax at the hotel, in the gorgeous pool or the gymnasium. **Directions:** Drive 6km along the Route de Sézanne, signposted from the centre of Épernay, or land on the helipad. Price guide: Single Ff620–Ff750; double/twin Ff730–Ff870; suites Ff1150.

CHÂTEAU EZA

RUE DE LA PISE, 06360 EZE VILLAGE, FRANCE
TEL: 33 4 93 41 12 24 FAX: 33 4 93 41 16 64

Eze Village is medieval, a total contrast to the sophisticated towns along the Côte d'Azur. The Château Eza is 1300 feet high on the great rock above the Mediterranean and was the residence of Prince William of Sweden from 1927 to 1957. Several 13th century houses have been transformed into this élite hotel, with its incredible view over the coast. The original stone walls and ancient oak beams are still evident in the graceful salons and magnificent suites. Log fires, unexpected alcoves, tapestries, superb rugs on tiled floors and fine antiques are part of the unique ambience of this historic hotel. Guests approach the château along a cobbled path, while their cars when unloaded are driven by hotel staff to a parking area at the foot of the village. Lunch and dinner is served on the elegant terrace, weather permitting, with its fantastic outlook over the sea to the horizon. It is a charming place for guests to watch a brilliant sunset, and at dusk the scenery becomes a mass of flickering lights. Dinner is also served in the lovely panoramic restaurant which is renowned for its unique ambience and superb dishes created by the Chef de Cuisine. 400 great wines are listed. Guests explore Eze Village, visit perfume houses and wine caves, or tour the exotic Riviera with its beaches and casinos. **Directions:** Eze village is on the Moyenne Corniche between Nice and Monaco. Price guide: Single Ff1600–Ff2400; double/twin Ff2000–Ff3200; suites Ff3200–Ff3700.

HOSTELLERIE LES BAS RUPTS

88400 GÉRARDMER, VOSGES, FRANCE
TEL: 33 3 2963 0925 FAX: 33 3 2963 0040

The Vosges Mountains region is enchanting and Lake Gérardmer, just off the Routes des Vins, has its own magical retreat, the Hostellerie Les Bas Rupts with its adjacent Le Chalet Fleuri – appropriately named, for flowers are the theme of this pretty building with its exquisitely painted doors and friezes along the walls and colourful window boxes along the balconies. The Hostellerie is idyllic and welcoming, surrounded by lovingly tended gardens. The bedrooms are charming, peaceful and comfortable, with elegant period furniture. Delightful small salons provide a romantic ambience. Michel Philippe is a Maître Cuisinier de France, supported by a talented team – and connoisseurs of good food will be in heaven. A superb breakfast starts the day, on the terrace in summer, and it ends with a feast of inspirational interpretations of local specialities, accompanied by carefully selected wines. The view from the restaurant adds to the joy. In winter guests work up their appetites skiing, and in summer they cycle, explore the countryside, go boating or play tennis – and in the evenings share their experiences in the bar, perhaps before visiting the village casino! **Directions:** From Paris, take the Nancy, Epinal road, N57 to Remiremont, left onto D417 to Gérardmer and right for 3km towards Bresse. Price guide: Double/twin Ff 780–900.

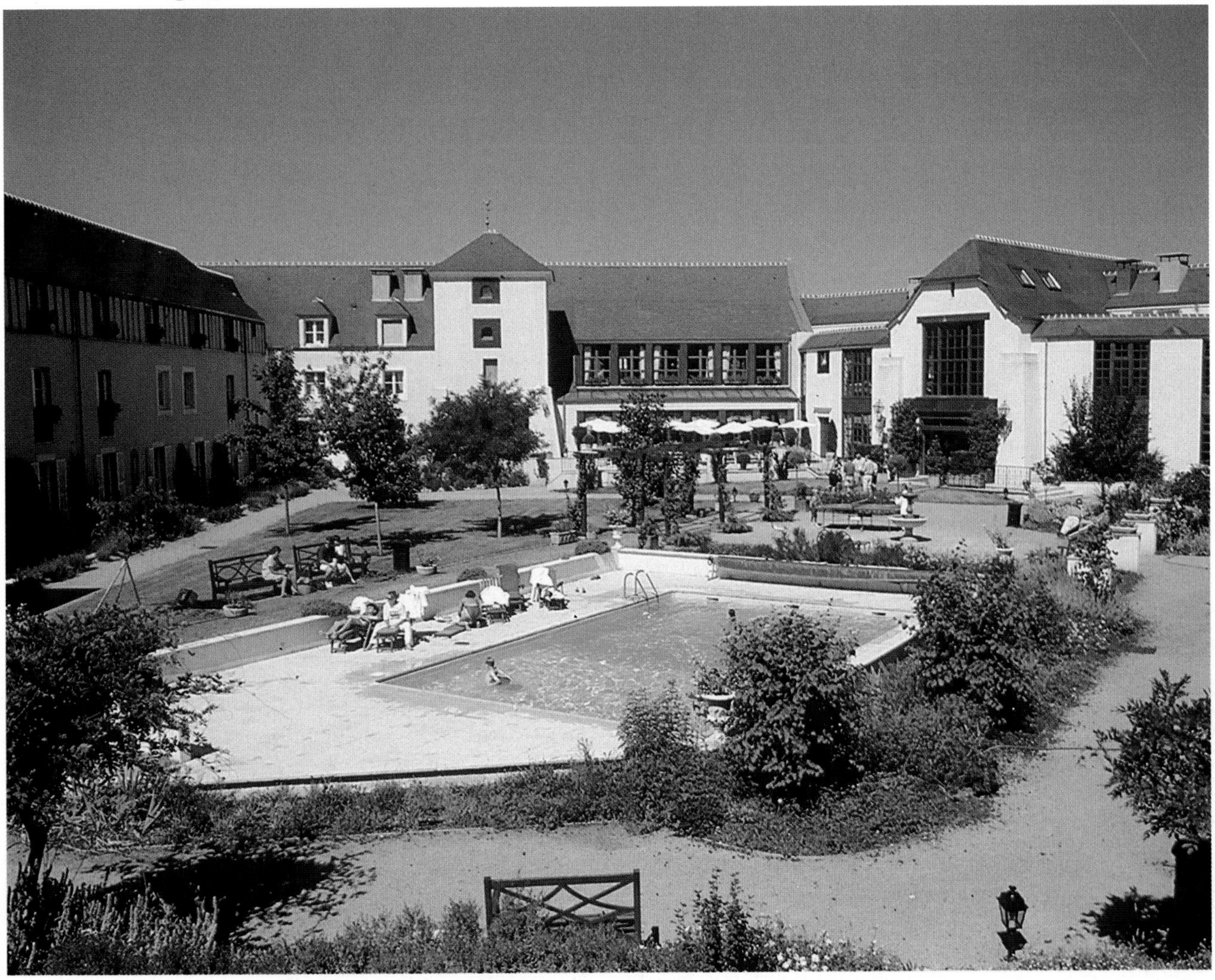

LE MANOIR DE GRESSY

F–77410 GRESSY EN FRANCE, SEINE ET MARNE, NR PARIS, FRANCE
TEL: 33 1 60 26 68 00 FAX: 33 1 60 26 45 46

Once upon a time a graceful 17th century manor house stood in this quiet village just ten minutes from Charles de Gaulle Airport and Villepinte Exhibition Centre – today a delightful hotel built in 1993 in the style of a traditional manor house around a courtyard awaits travellers to this superb centre for visiting Paris and the Ile de France. It is also an ideal venue for business meetings. A handsome staircase leads from the welcoming reception area. The salons are enchanting, with period furniture and harmonising colour schemes. The bedrooms (some non-smoking) echo this warm country house ambience. Several rooms are suitable for those with mobility problems. Dining is in splendid Le Cellier du Manoir where the cuisine and fine wines reflect the very best of French culinary tradition. In summer guests often eat on the terrace overlooking the pool. Apart from swimming, tennis, or cycling along the Canal de l'Ourcq, golf, boating and riding are nearby. While families decide to visit Disneyland and Parc Asterix, others may prefer exploring the many sights and forests of the Seine et Marne region, special packages are offered. An Arcadian Hotel. **Directions:** A1 or A3 from Central Paris, then A104 and N2 towards Soissons, then right onto D212 towards Claye-Souilly and Gressy en France. Free shuttle service to and from the airport and nearby subway station to Paris. Price Guide: Single Ff950–Ff1250; double Ff950–Ff1250. Contact hotel for details about monthly promotions.

La Chaumière

ROUTE DU LITTORAL, 14600 HONFLEUR, FRANCE
TEL: 33 2 31 81 63 20 FAX: 33 2 31 89 59 23

A historic Norman house has been transformed into this intimate hotel with spectacular views of the coast. It is wonderfully peaceful, surrounded by verdant gardens. Today it is difficult to remember that the D-day landings were not far from here and envisage the turmoil of those days. The sitting room is authentic old Normandy country house style, with its tiled floor, enormous fireplace, elegant chairs and fine antiques. The quiet guest rooms are delightful, with pretty drapes and wallpapers, period furniture and scented with lavender. The modern marble bathrooms are well designed. Sipping apéritifs on the terrace watching the yachts approaching Honfleur and bigger ships heading for Le Havre is a pleasant recreation. Dining in the small but lively restaurant is memorable, from the tasty amusettes to the petits fours. Being close to the sea the Prix Fixe menu usually includes delicious fish and puddings. The wine list is excellent. Strolling in the fragrant hotel gardens is therapeutic. Challenging golf courses are nearby. Itself fascinating, Honfleur offers sailing, tennis, museums and boat trips. Bikes are available for exploring the countryside. Those wanting a casino or other more sophisticated activities drive to Deauville, 15km away. **Directions:** A13, exit 28 taking D180 for Honfleur, then D513 along coast road towards Trouville. Price guide: Double/twin Ff990–2400.

La Ferme Saint-Siméon

RUE ADOLPHE–MARAIS, 14600 HONFLEUR, FRANCE

TEL: 33 2 31 89 23 61 FAX: 33 2 31 89 48 48

Honfleur is an enchanting small port, much loved by the great impressionist painters, Monet and Boudin especially. Its yacht basin is always busy with boats flying flags from all parts of the globe. It is surrounded by magnificent countryside and just a mile away the Boelen family have created this elite and beautiful hotel. The half-timbered traditional Normandy farmhouse is most attractive, flanked by delightful cottages with decorative brickwork and colourful window boxes. The gardens are glorious. The salon has a beamed ceiling, a big fireplace filled with flowers in summer, fine antiques and comfortable sofas, with fascinating bibelots adding to its charm. The smart meeting room is well equipped. The bedrooms and apartments, some in Le Pressoir, are luxurious, with wonderful wall coverings, warm colour schemes and graceful furniture. The marble bathrooms combine elegance with opulence. The semi-circular bar has great style, and the terrace with its pretty striped parasols and chairs and spectacular view over the estuary has joie de vivre. The exquisite restaurant is another gem with artistic menus listing sophisticated dishes. The cellar holds over 1000 items. The dramatic fitness area resembles a Roman temple, with murals, pillars, exotic plants, statues and an azure blue pool. **Directions:** D180 to Honfleur, then D513 along the coast. Price guide: Double/twin Ff790–3510; suites Ff4400–5100.

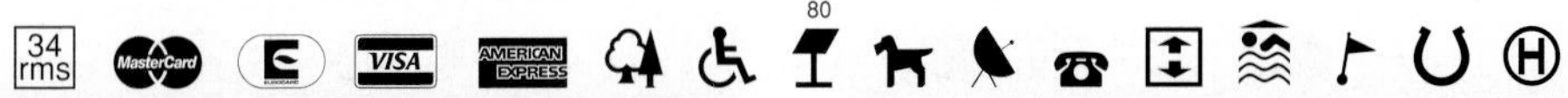

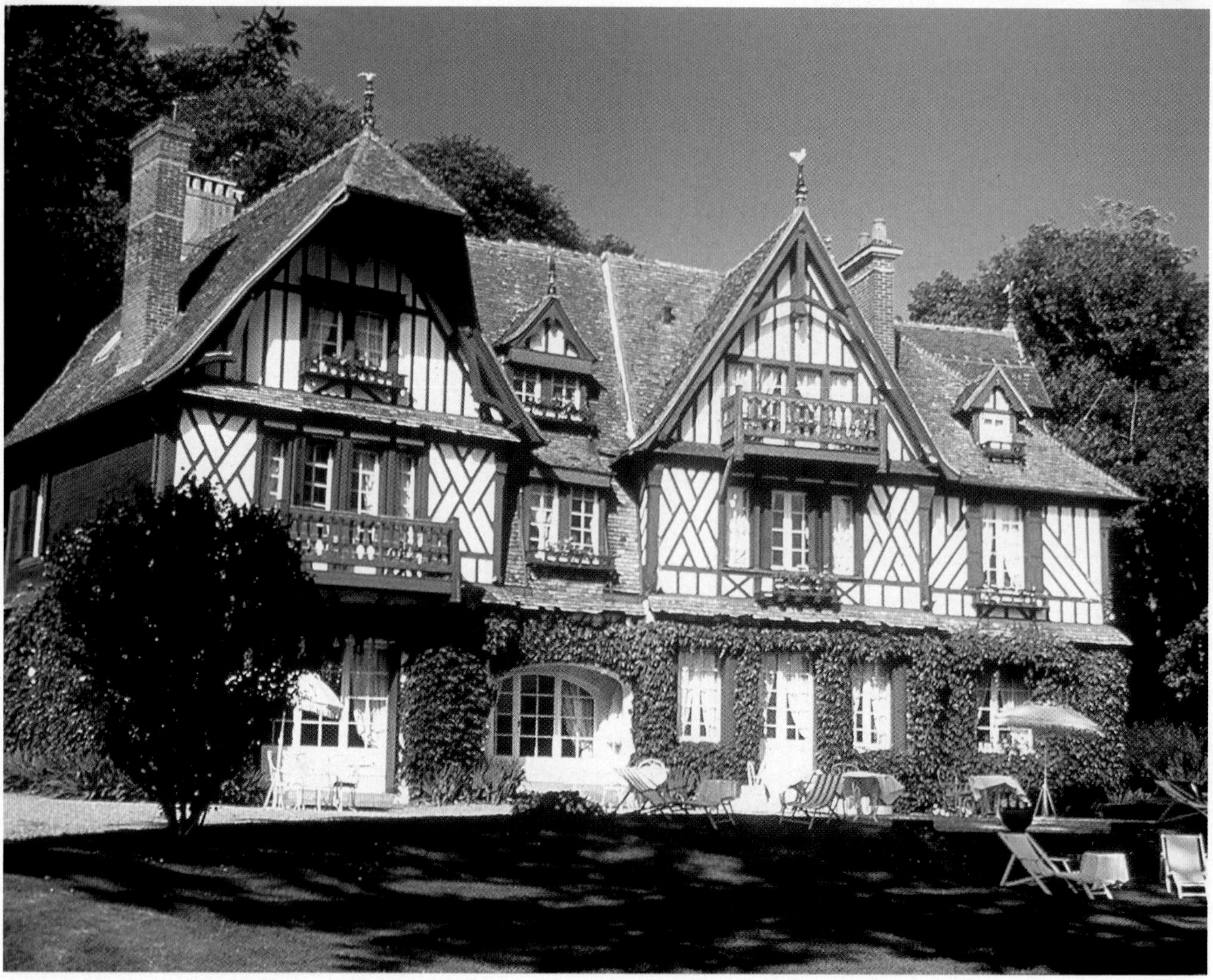

Le Manoir Du Butin

PHARE DU BUTIN, 14600 HONFLEUR, FRANCE
TEL: 33 2 31 81 63 00 FAX: 33 2 31 89 59 23

Honfleur, on the estuary of the Seine, is a fascinating and historic port, with many narrow streets that have changed little over the centuries. Impressionist painters gathered here in the 19th century, friends and pupils of Eugène Boudin – Monet among them. A short drive from the centre, Le Manoir du Butin – a magnificent example of 18th century architecture with its distinctive halftimbering and graceful eaves – is now an idyllic retreat for those seeking tranquillity. It is surrounded by formal gardens and parkland. The guest rooms, just nine, are exquisite, with delicate fabrics on the walls and at the windows, and local period furniture. Luxurious accoutrements add to guests' pleasure and the marble bathrooms are lavishly equipped. At night dinner is served in the romantic dining room, which has unique frescoes over its Palladiun fireplace. Intriguing ornaments and small statues add to its charm and the traditional bar has a fine array of bottles, surely including good Calvados. Normandy cooking is fabulous and fish caught that day by local trawlers is superb. Visitors wander along the quay, drink with the yachtsmen, play golf, tennis, take boat trips, explore the D-Day beaches or just relax in the hotel gardens. **Directions:** A13, exit 28 to Honfleur, follow D513 along the coast and turn left at Phare du Butin. Price guide: Double/twin Ff640–1970

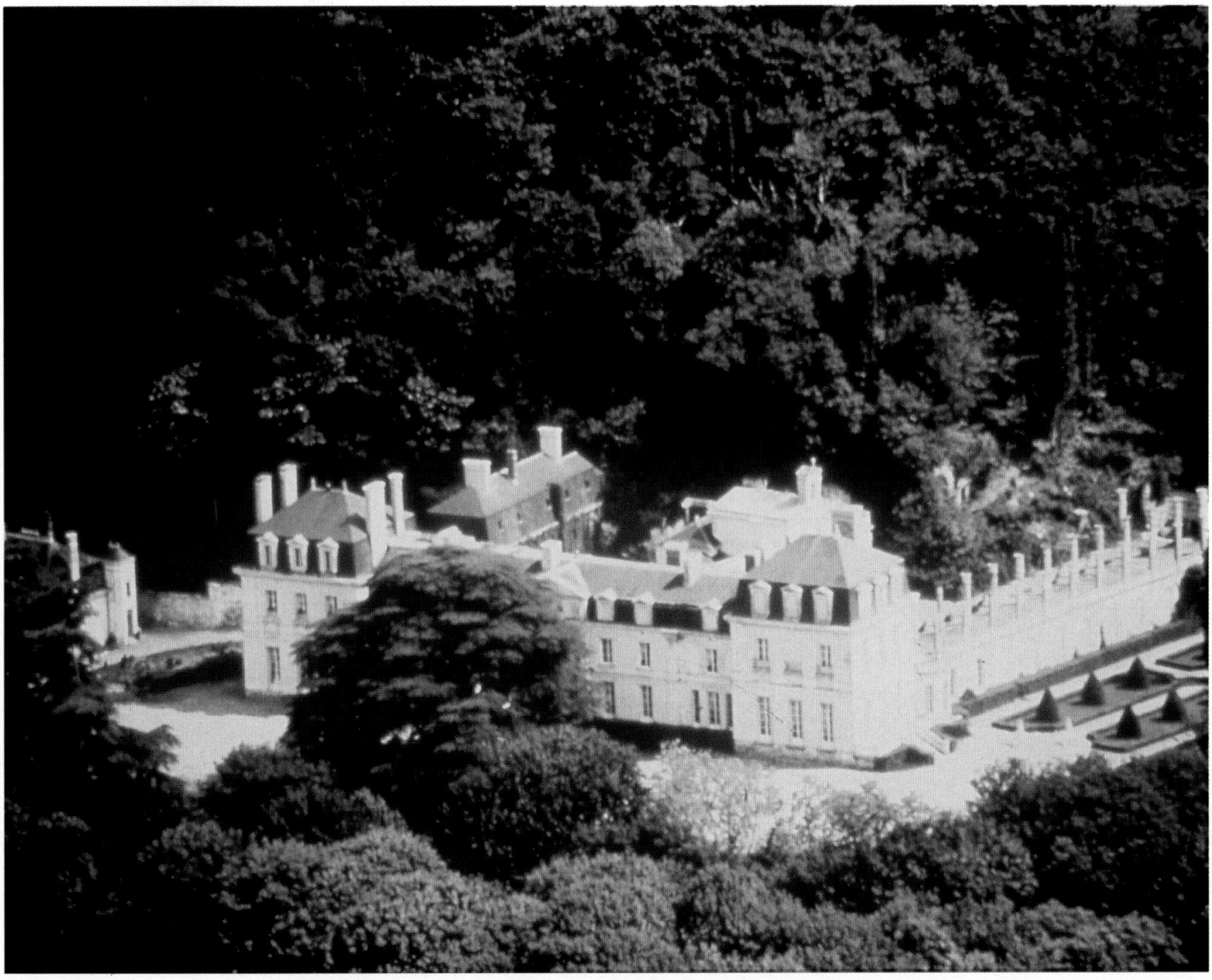

Château De Rochecotte

SAINT-PATRICE, 37130 LANGEAIS, FRANCE
TEL: 33 2 47 96 16 16 FAX: 33 2 47 96 90 59

It is a privilege to stay at this exquisite château, once the home of Prince Talleyrand. It is a minature palace and the original facade is immaculate. Extensive parkland ensures peace and privacy. This is an aristocratic hotel, yet the ambience is warm. The salons are spacious and inviting, and it has a exceptionally beautiful Italianate terrace overlooking the formal French gardens, complete with topiary – ideal for apéritifs. The guest rooms and suites are ethereal, with delicately patterned chintz, eclectically furnished with antiques, Aubusson rugs and modern comfortable armchairs. The bathrooms are well-equipped. A few rooms are in the delightful 17th century annex. The dining room has great panache, with tall terracotta columns, palm trees, contemporary candlesticks and splendid views over the park, an appropriate setting for the distinguished Loire wines and the perfection of every dish prepared by a great chef. Seminars held in the 3 meeting rooms will surely be memorable. The château has a pool, and residents relax on sunbeds or stroll through the cool grounds. Golf and fishing are nearby, as are splendid castles, fascinating Tours and the vineyards of Chinon and Saumur, all well worth a visit. **Directions:** A10, exit Tours, follow N152 through Langeais, then take D35 towards Bourgueil, quickly coming to signs for the château in the village of St. Patrice. Price guide: Double/twin Ff580–950; suites Ff1250.

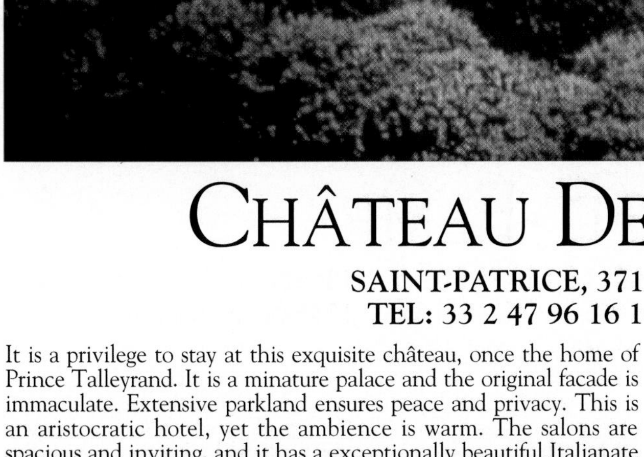

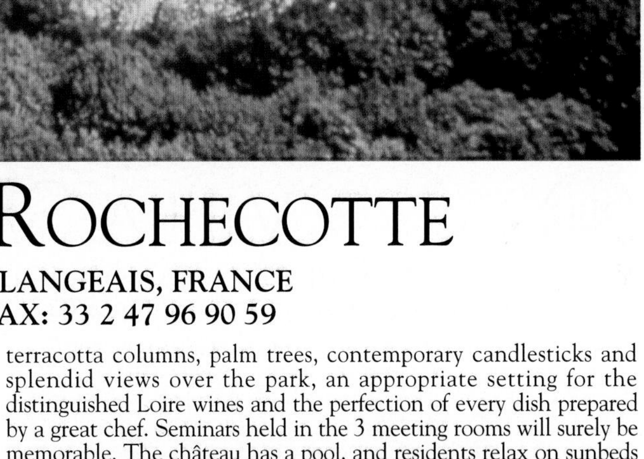

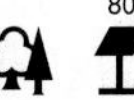

VILLA SAINT-ELME

CORNICHE DES ISSAMBRES, 83380 LES ISSAMBRES, FRANCE
TEL: 33 4 94 49 52 52 FAX: 33 4 94 49 63 18 E-MAIL: 101603,12558@compuserve

This gorgeous 1930s villa is in an enviable and secluded position just off the Corniche between Saint-Tropez and Saint-Raphael. It is evocative of the past, when the guest list included Maurice Chevalier and Edith Piaf. The hotel is on the sea front, the garden filled with exotic trees and the air fragrant with jasmine. The luxurious bedrooms are pristine, beautifully decorated, air-conditioned and have well-equipped bathrooms. Suites with a definite Provençal influence are in the Bastide, across the road on the waters edge. There is a pleasant ground floor room for those with mobility problems. The Art Deco salons are joyous. Guests enjoy the 'Cocktail Maison' on the terrace. Painters exhibit in the bar, and a pianist plays at weekends. The summer restaurant is al fresco, serving aromatic Mediterranean dishes and regional wines; in winter the dining room, overlooking the sea, has an unusual glass dome, the light creating a unique atmosphere. The Villa has a pool, private beach, and fitness facility. Nearby are tennis, excellent golf, and water sports. Visit the markets, perfumeries at Grasse, Saint Paul de Vence and the many islands. Excellent Provençal wines can be found at local Châteaux and Domaines. **Directions:** 45 minutes from Nice International Airport. Autoroute 8, exit Fréjus, take N98 towards St Tropez reaching Les Issambres. Security parking is available. Price guide: Single/double/twin Ff850–2900; suites Ff1700–3100.

LA TOUR ROSE

22 RUE DE BOEUF, F–69005 LYON, FRANCE
TEL: 33 4 78 37 25 90 FAX: 33 4 78 42 26 02

Lyon is famous for its silks and for its gastronomy, the latter a legacy from the talented chefs who cooked for the famous banking and silk houses. Philippe Chavent has created a Tuscan garden with terraces, waterfalls and ornamental pools as the setting for La Tour Rose. Each of the twelve suites has been named after and decorated by a different Lyon manufacturer, often using the silks quite unexpectedly so that a variety of eras and styles gives individual character to every room. La Tour Rose is, in fact, three Renaissance buildings. Guests walk through their courtyards perhaps to the Jeu de Paume bar and or relax in the sunlit gardens. Silk aficianados move from the restoration rooms to the textile designers' salons where magnificent exhibitions are staged. The restaurant is unique, a former chapel leading onto a terrace. Philippe Chavent's avant-garde talents transform classic dishes into nouvelle cuisine. Close by he has opened Le Comptoir du Bœuf where guests can taste vintage wine selected from the 35,000 bottles in his cellar. Lyon deserves exploring, with its musuems and historical buildings. Guests can attend the cookery school above the hotel kitchen, and enjoy jazz concerts in the evening. **Directions:** Vieux-Lyon. Detailed directions and a map will be sent following reservations. Price guide: Single Ff950–1650; double/twin Ff1200–1650; suites Ff1650–2800.

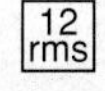

L'ANTARÈS

LE BELVÉDÈRE, 73550 MÉRIBEL LES ALLUES, FRANCE
TEL: 33 4 7923 2823 FAX: 33 4 79 23 2818

Méribel first became a ski resort in 1939, with just one lift. Today it reigns supreme, having hosted the Winter Olympics in 1992. High up in the Belvédère area the Hotel l'Antarès is a sophisticated dome shaped chalet, encircled by balconies, thus ensuring every room has spectacular views of the Alps. L'Antarès has a dramatic atrium, and eclectically furnished salons. The guest rooms have every imaginable modern comfort. Lunch is a joyous occasion, on the sunny terrace. Later guests meet in the intimate Piano Bar, while deciding whether to feast on brilliant gourmet dishes in the gastronomique restaurant Cassiopée, decorated with amusing murals, or relax over Savoyard specialities in the Altair. Two state-of-the-art conference rooms are much in demand, as is the excellent fitness centre. Winter sports are for all ages, Les Petits Loups free for skiers under 5 years old. Snowshoe tours, snowbikes and special passes for the gondolier lifts ensure non-skiers enjoy themselves. There is a ski-shop in the hotel. In summer and winter the hotel has a great pool. Méribel has a fabulous golf course, tennis, rafting and fishing can be arranged; it also has a vibrant night-life. Children have their own programmes. **Directions:** From Moutiers follow signs Méribel les Allues, then to Le Belvédère, finding the hotel indicated. Price guide: Single Ff1410–2020; double/twin Ff1560–2280; suites Ff2210–4140.

CHÂTEAU DES VIGIERS

24240 MONESTIER, FRANCE
TEL: 33 5 53 61 50 00 FAX: 33 5 53 61 50 20

A "Petit Versailles" offering golf and its own fine wines is near to paradise for its guests! This beautiful 400 year old château on a 425 acre estate with its own vineyards, in the heart of the Bordeaux country, is now a luxurious hotel. The well-known golf architect and writer Donald Steel has added Château des Vigiers to the list of élite courses which he has designed or improved, including St Andrews, and it is now a prestigious golf and country club. Michel Roux created the fantastic kitchen and gourmet restaurant. The bridge and tea salons, the library and billiard room are regal, with handsome antiques, rich rugs and fine paintings. The guest rooms are equally impressive, with French country house furniture. Perigordian suites in the adjacent Dépendences have their own terraces. Additionally excellent conference facilities are available. At night a sophisticated restaurant, Les Fresques,serves Périgord specialities such as home made foie gras with wines from the estate. Alternatively, the Club House/Brasserie serves simpler food both at lunch time and in the evening. The estate also offers swimming, tennis, cycling, fishing and fitness centre. The hotel staff are pleased to organise wine tasting excursions to St. Emillion, Pomerol and the Médoc. **Directions:** From Bordeaux N89 to Libourne, D936 towards Bergerac, at Sainte-Foy-la-Grande D18 towards Eymet. Price guide: Single Ff750–1350; double/twin Ff750–1350; suites Ff900–1550.

CHÂTEAU DE LA BOURDAISIÈRE

37270 MONTLOUIS-SUR-LOIRE, FRANCE
TEL: 33 2 47 45 16 31 **FAX:** 33 2 47 45 09 11

In the Loire Valley, between the River Cher and the River Loire there is a magnificent Renaissance château, built for a King's mistress. Today it belongs to the de Broglie family whose motto is appropriate for this elite hotel – For the Future Generations. The Château has been modernised with great care, its history evident in the splendid black and white tiled 14th century entrance, the salons with graceful Louis XIV furniture and the formal gardens, resplendent with topiary and terraces. Deer roam in the surrrounding parkland. The guest room walls are covered with romantic toiles or fine wallpaper, antiques abound and the fabrics are gorgeous. Some are in the towers or 'annexes' of the Château. The hotel has an 'honour bar', guests serving themselves to aperitifs, or maybe digestifs after returning from a gourmet expedition to one of the excellent restaurants in the neighbourhood. Private or corporate entertaining can be arranged in the great vaulted XIVth century hall and there are good facilities for seminars. The park has an outdoor pool and tennis court; windsurfing and golf are nearby. There are wines to be tasted at famous vineyards, fascinating museums and the famous Cadre Noir Riding School to visit. **Directions:** A10, exit Tours centre towards Amboise (D751), after 10km watching for signs to the Château. Parking. Price guide: Double/twin Ff 550–1200.

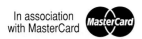

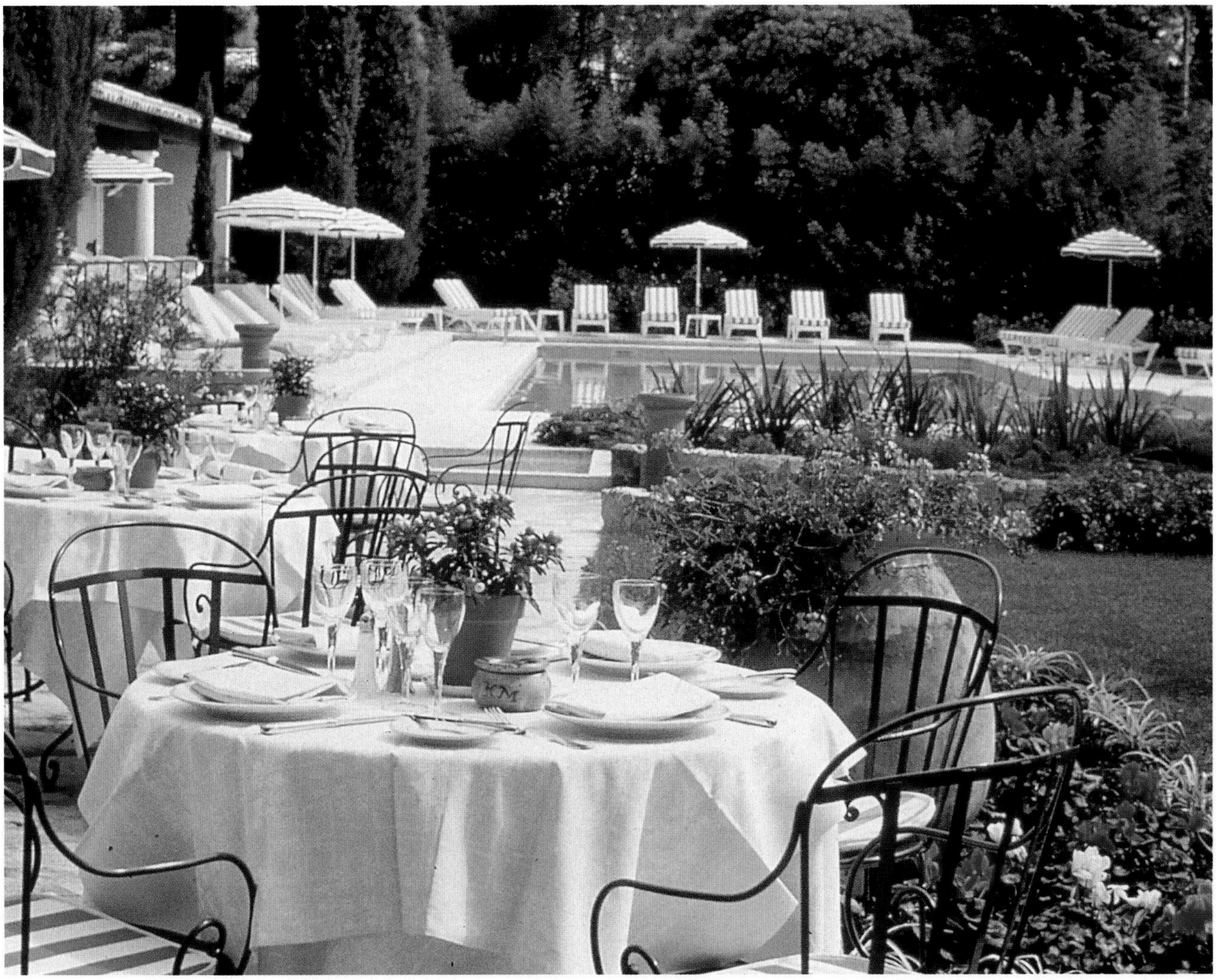

HOTEL DE MOUGINS

205, AVENUE DU GOLF, 06250 MOUGINS, FRANCE
TEL: 33 4 92 92 17 07 FAX: 33 4 92 92 17 08

Mougins is an enchanting town, about 5 miles from Cannes, high up above the Côte d'Azur, with intriguing artists' ateliers off its narrow winding streets. A fine hotel has been created by carefully restoring a lovely old farmhouse, adding four delightful villas, and transforming the immediate surroundings into gardens, scented by lavender, mimosa and rosemary. The cool salons are elegant, contemporary Provençal style, opening onto an attractive terrace, and the charmingly decorated bedrooms are mostly in the 'Bastides', all having a balcony or patio. They are air-conditioned and provided with many 'extras'; the bathrooms are well designed. The hotel has two bars, a convivial one by the pool terrace, adjacent to the 'summer grill' where informal meals are prepared, and the other an inviting room next to the superb La Figuière Restaurant, which serves gourmet interpretations of local specialities, either in the delightful dining room or in the shade of an old ash tree, accompanied by good wines. Golf is the dominating sport, with nine excellent clubs nearby. Other activities are tennis, boules and swimming. Expeditions should be made to the perfumeries of Grasse, the Picasso Museum in Antibes, the glass-blowers at Biot and exciting shops in Cannes. **Directions:** Autoroute 8, then Voie Rapide second exit, for Antibes. Price guide: Single/double/twin Ff800–1100; suites Ff1600.

HOTEL WESTMINSTER CONCORDE

27, PROMENADE DES ANGLAIS, 06000 NICE, FRANCE
TEL: 33 4 92 14 86 86 FAX: 33 4 93 82 45 35

La Promenade des Anglais is surely famous throughout the world, stretching along the seafront at Nice, lined with palm trees. This splendid hotel, once two grand villas, dating back to 1880 is in the centre of this elite road, with spectacular views of the beach and the sunsets over the Mediterranean Ocean. The Westminster is a hotel with great panache. Many of its delightful Art Nouveau features have been retained – the ornate pillars and ceiling in the Hall, the gilt and glass stair balustrade and the stained glass windows. The salons are magnificent – simultaneously joyful and elegant. The spacious guest rooms are charming, with delicate fabrics framing the tall windows, the furniture upholstered in harmonizing colours. "Le Westminster" Bar is a sophisticated rendezvous, but the most popular venue for wining and dining is the chic terrace in front of the hotel, facing the Promenade des Anglais. In house, Le Farniente is a celebrated restaurant, serving Mediterranean dishes with great eclat; the cellar holds superb wines. The beach, the casino and the shops play an important part of life here. Golf, tennis and watersports can be arranged. The hotel has its own private beach. Directions: A8, Exit 8, follow signs to Nice and the Promenade des Anglais. Price guide: Standard Ff750–950; supreme Ff1300; junior suite Ff1500.

Paris

Thanks to the Eurotunnel, visitors to France are taking time to explore this capital: staying a little longer, discovering the quiet, leafy, ornate courtyards in the most unexpected places in the centre of town, daring to travel le métro which is fun and fascinating, detouring from the tourist track and finding out more about the major landmarks of this most romantic of cities. Did you, for example, know that Gustave Eiffel – the great designer in metal, not only created the Eiffel Tower but also the framework of the Statue of Liberty in New York?

Paris is full of many other wonderful surprises if you take time to look and tour. With the possible exception of the Bois de Boulogne and Montmartre, you can easily walk from one sight to the next. Divided in two by the River Seine, with two islands – Ile de la Cité and Ile St Louis – in the middle. The south – or Left – Bank has a more intimate, Bohemian flavour . The east – west axis from Chatelet to the Arc de Triomphe, via the Rue de Rivoli and the Champs-Elysées, is the principal thoroughfare for sightseeing and shopping on the Right Bank.

The most enduring symbol of Paris, and its historical and geographical heart is Notre Dame Cathedral, on the Ile de la Cité, one of the two islands in the middle of the Seine, where Paris's first inhabitants settled around 250BC.

Paris is also the home of fashion and perfume. The top shops are along both sides of the Champs-Elysées, along the Avenue Montaigne and the Rue du Faubourg St Honoré.

A city where some of the world's best fashion designers live and work, undisturbed – Paris never fails to inspire with its unique atmosphere

Poets, philosophers, writers, artists and radical thinkers have all adorned the pavement cafés, the ethnic shops and avant garde theatre of the Latin Quarter.

Only in Paris could you find such a modern building as the Forum des Halles and Pompidou Centre – in the heart of the Beaubourg. In Paris, the seemingly inappropriate and unexpected – works – and works brilliantly

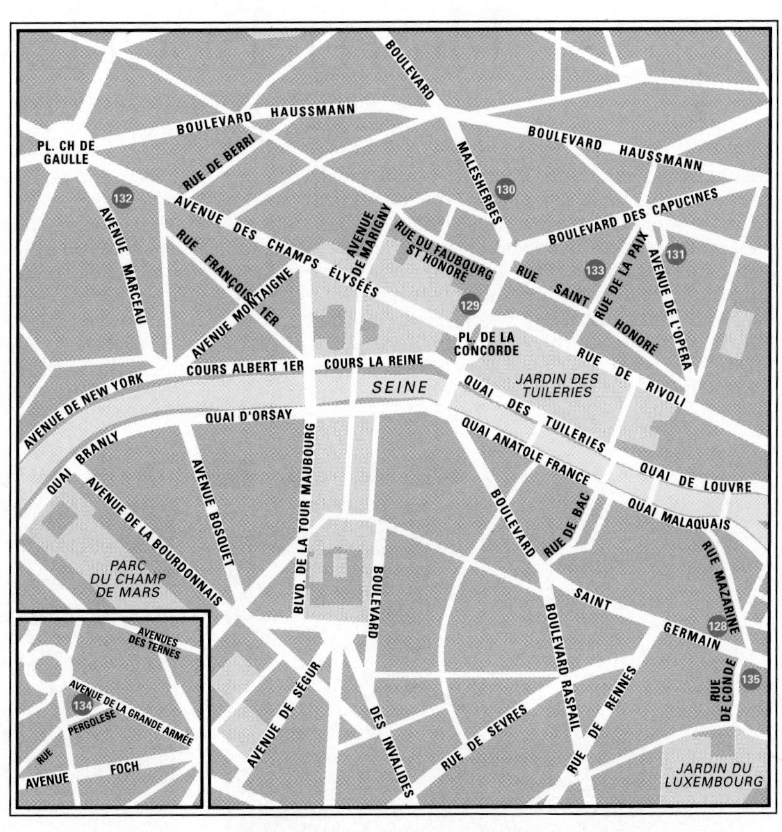

DESIGN HOTELS

HOTEL BUCI LATIN

34, RUE DE BUCI, F–75006 PARIS

TEL: 33 1 43 29 07 20 FAX: 33 1 43 29 67 44

This intriguing small hotel is for francophiles who are determined to find the Latin Quarter as described by the literati. It is close to St. Germain, in a maze of narrow streets where market stalls vie for business with luxurious boutiques. The atmosphere is vibrant. Hotel Buci Latin has no restaurant, but there are many exciting bistros and clubs nearby. It does, however, have an excellent coffee bar, with water cascading into a small plant-filled pond. The interior is unique, 20th century art deco perhaps, with unusual lights, much wrought iron and eclectic furnishings to add to its charm. The doors have all been painted by different artists and grafitti are all along the stairwell. The bedrooms are spotlessly clean and equipped with all modern amenities – and the door knobs are made from boules! In one of the suites there is a little terrace where drinks can be enjoyed on fine evenings.There is so much to do in Paris – watch the Left Bank artists at work, ascend the Eiffel Tower, explore Notre Dame or cross the Seine to visit the Louvre, drink the traditional onion soup in Les Halles, stroll down the Champs Élysées, go shopping or make an expedition to Versailles. At night take a boat down the river or find good jazz near the hotel. **Directions:** Saint Germain Des Prés is the nearest Metro Station, the hotel has no parking facilities. Price guide: Double/twin Ff970–1250; Suite Ff1650–1750

27 rms MasterCard VISA AMERICAN EXPRESS

Hôtel de Crillon

10, PLACE DE LA CONCORDE, 75008 PARIS, FRANCE
TEL: 33 1 44 71 15 00 FAX: 33 1 44 71 15 02

Built during the reign of Louis XV, the Hôtel de Crillon was one of two magnificent buildings designed by the famous architect Jacques-Ange Gabriel on the north side of the Place de la Concorde, one of the most beautiful squares in the world. This prestigious hotel enjoys a premier location and has attracted a distinguished list of guests including statesmen, royalty and many of the world's elite dating back to 1909. The interior has remained quintessentially French, elegant and sophisticated. Parquet floors, Aubusson carpets, harmonious grey and gold colour schemes, magnificent tapestries, Louis XV furniture, terraces with Corinthian columns all contribute to the unique ambience of the Crillon. The luxurious bedrooms are sumptuously decorated with exquisite silks and furnished with antiques. All have opulent marble bathrooms. Tea is taken in the delightful Jardin d'Hiver, and the striking bar stocks 80 different whiskies. The original ballroom is now the legendary restaurant Les Ambassadeurs overlooking the square. An inspired chef creates imaginative dishes based on traditional recipes, the sommelier presents an extensive wine list. L'Obélisque serves lighter meals. There is no better place from which to explore Paris, whether to visit the exclusive boutiques nearby or cross the Seine to the Latin Quarter. **Directions:** The Champs-Élysées leads to the hotel. Price guide: Single FF2600–3250; double/twin FF3250–4200; suites FF4900–33,450.

163 rms · MasterCard · VISA · AMERICAN EXPRESS · 120

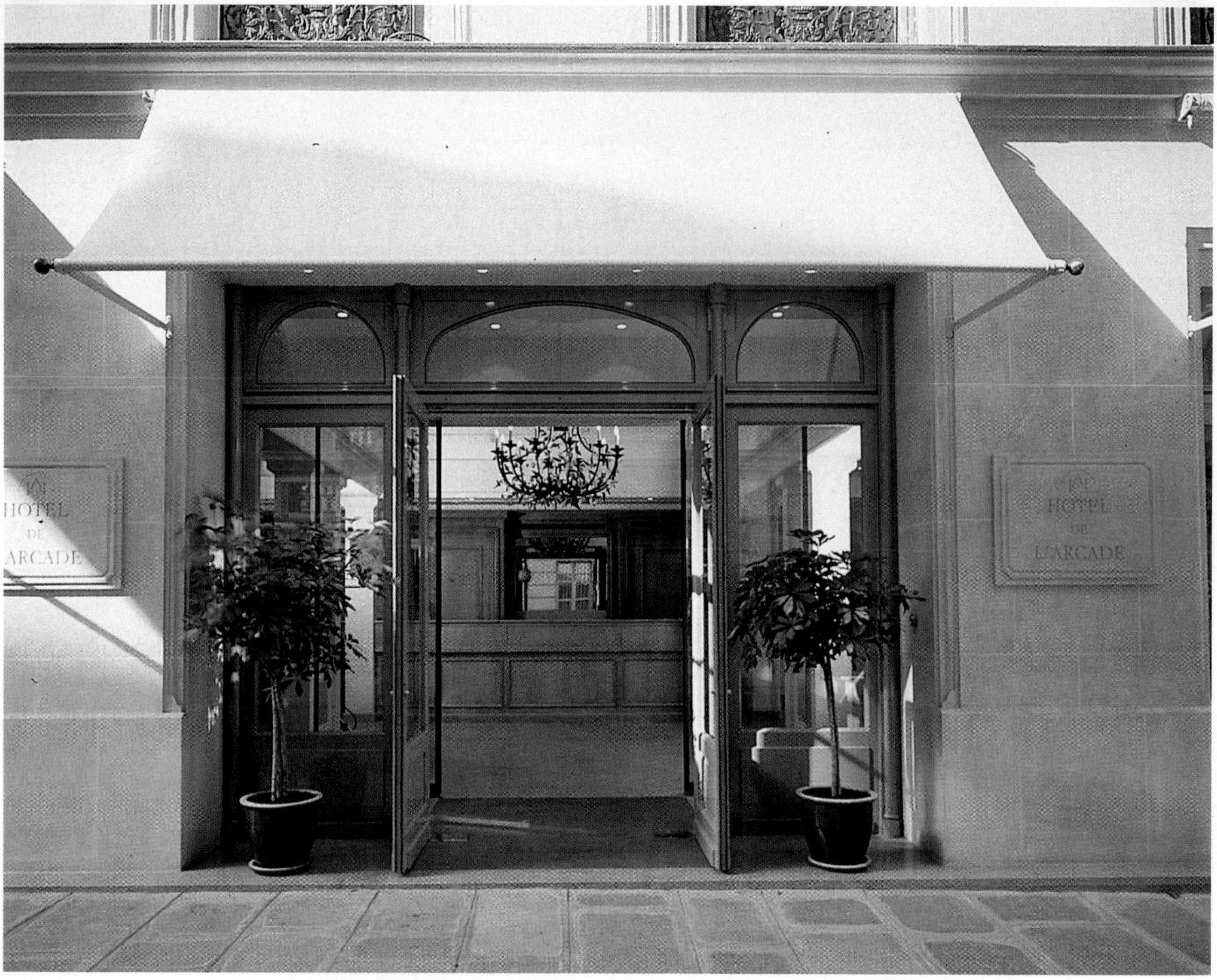

HÔTEL DE L'ARCADE

9 RUE DE L'ARCADE, F–75008 PARIS
TEL: 33 1 53 30 60 00 FAX: 33 1 40 07 03 07

This graceful 19th century townhouse, the renovations clearly carried out with love as well as skill, is now a haven in the heart of the business district of Paris, close to the Madeleine, the Opera and the Place de la Concorde. The facade and the interior have been brought back to their original elegance, reflecting the talents of the well known designer, Gerard Gallet. The salons are decorated in muted colours creating an ambience of tranquillity away from the busy world outside. Stone fireplaces, Louis XVI pieces, lovely paintings on the walls, comfortable chairs, discreet lighting and big bowls of flowers add to the pleasure of staying in this elite hotel. The sound-proofed bedrooms are equally delightful, with white bedspreads and softly coloured linen drapes. Thoughtful planning is evident in the furnishings and accessories and the marble bathrooms have amusing windows opening onto the bedroom to catch daylight. Only breakfast is served in the restaurant but the area abounds with bars, cafés and a wide choice of excellent places to dine. Guests enjoy wandering past famous boutiques and couture houses, exploring the Louvre, or heading for the Tuileries Gardens. **Directions:** Rue de l'Arcade is just off Place de la Madeleine, and cars can be parked opposite by prior arrangement. Price guide: Single Ff780–Ff880; double/twin Ff960; duplex (apartment) Ff1150.

HÔTEL L'HORSET OPÉRA

18 RUE D'ANTIN, F–75002 PARIS, FRANCE
TEL: 33 1 44 71 87 00 FAX: 33 1 42 66 55 54

This is a delightful small hotel in the Opéra Garnier area, where many important events in the history of France have taken place. The surrounding streets are now a fascinating mélange of important monuments and sophisticated boutiques. On arrival guests first notice the elegant façade of L'Horset Opéra and once inside they are impressed by the spacious, attractive reception area and the efficient, friendly staff. The bedrooms are charming and comfortable. Downstairs in the bar, which has panelled walls and handsome furniture, the barman will mix wonderful cocktails and discuss the excellent wines listed. Breakfast is a superb buffet. This is a wonderful base for exploring Paris. The hotel will make reservations for a memorable night at the opera and recommend restaurants and bistros close by. Minutes away are the spectacular Place Vendôme, the Louvre, the Palais Royal, the Jardin des Tuileries and enticing antique shops. Excellent department stores can be found in the Rue de la Paix, just round the corner. **Directions:** Rue d'Antin is off Avenue de l'Opéra. The hotel does not have car parking, but business people will appreciate its accessibility by Métro. Price guide: Single Ff1220; double/twin Ff1350; suite Ff2800.

Prima Hotels

HÔTEL VERNET

25 RUE VERNET, F–75008 PARIS, FRANCE
TEL: 33 1 44 31 98 00 FAX: 33 1 44 31 85 69

This prestigious and intimate hotel in the centre of Paris has a joyous facade, with its pretty fin de siècle wrought iron balconies, scarlet sun blinds and smart brass canopy at the entrance. The foyer is impressive, with marble floors, graceful archways, lovely rugs and plants on tall pedestals. This leads into the elegant salon with its graceful drapes, chandeliers and fine period furniture. The bedrooms are charming, decorated in restful colours, and they are well equipped with all the accessories expected by today's travellers. The bathrooms are luxurious, with much marble in evidence and many have Jacuzzis. The small traditional bar is very inviting. The Michelin two star restaurant, Les Élysées, is dramatic with its art deco glass domed roof and unusual chandeliers. A pianist plays softly in the background and a large team of impeccable staff ensure that guests dine well from the intriguing menu with its Provençal flavour. The sommelier has selected magnificent wines. Hotel Vernet has no leisure facilities but guests have courtesy access to the Thermes of Royal Monceau, just 5 minutes walk away. This has a fine pool, squash, gymnasium and other spa features including a beauty centre. Residents are ideally placed to explore Paris or attend meetings at La Défense. **Directions.** Rue Vernet is off the Étoile – Place Charles de Gaulle. Price guide: Single Ff1700–Ff1900; double/twin Ff2100–Ff2500; suites Ff3900.

57 rms 15

Hôtel Westminster

13, RUE DE LA PAIX, 75002 PARIS, FRANCE
TEL: 33 1 4261 5746 FAX: 33 1 4260 3066 US TOLL FREE: 1 800 203 3202

Once a convent this historic building became a coaching house when Baron Haussmann redesigned Paris with its wonderful boulevards in the 1840s. The hotel, celebrating its 150th anniversary, is named after the Duke of Westminster who often stayed there. In a select part of Paris between the Place Vendôme and the Opéra, its architecture is baroque, its style impeccable. The marble lobby is spectacular, with its antiques, massive flower arrangements and glittering chandeliers. It is a popular rendezvous, with thoughtful seating arrangements. The delightful bedrooms, smart suites and sumptuous bathrooms all reflect renovations recommended by an accomplished French interior designer, including double glazing to eliminate street noise. The barman of "Les Chenets" piano bar mixes some exotic cocktails! A Michelin star has been awarded to Le Céladon restaurant, an elegant setting for the chef's magnificent dishes. Superb wines are listed. The Westminster is in walking distance of the Louvre, the Tuileries Gardens, the Champs Élysées and other historic landmarks. Discerning shoppers will enjoy the exclusive boutiques and jewellers in the nearby Rue du Faubourg Saint-Honoré. Owned by Warwick International Hotels. **Directions:** From Place de la Madeleine, drive up Boulevard des Capucines, finding Rue de la Paix on the right. Valet parking. Price guide: Single Ff2300; double/twin Ff2600; suites Ff4300–9000.

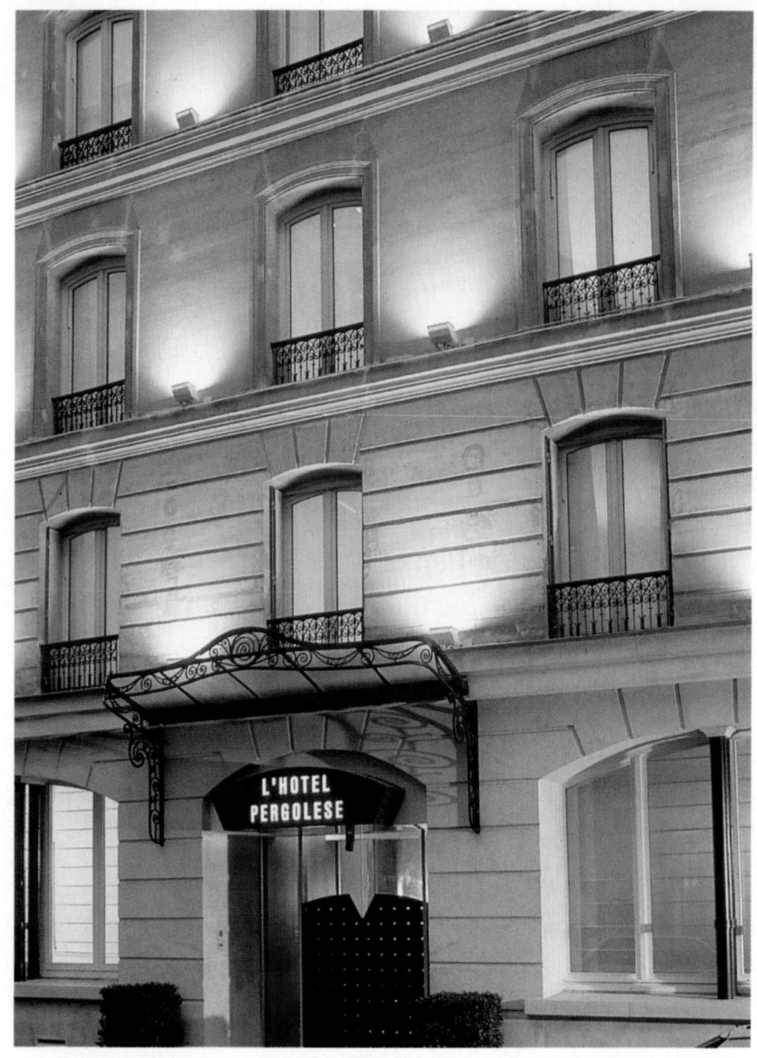

L'Hôtel Pergolèse

3 RUE PERGOLÈSE, 75116 PARIS, FRANCE
TEL: 33 1 40 67 96 77 FAX: 33 1 45 00 12 11

The vibrant L'Hôtel Pergolèse, close to the Étoile and the Champs-Élysées. The hotel has a subdued exterior, a 19th century bourgeois townhouse. but the interior is very chic, for it has been designed throughout by the brilliant futuristic Rena Dumas. Light, warmth and colour make an instant impact on new arrivals: parquet floor, stylish leather chairs, gorgeous rugs and inspired use of the five house colours – blue, golden yellow, apricot, deep red and garden green – create a charismatic ambience. The bedrooms have old fashioned comfort and exciting contemporary furnishings in restful, interesting colour co-ordinations. The television and bar are secreted in a unique mahogany 'tower'. Soundproofing eliminates street sounds. By contrast the bathrooms are sparkling white: marble, glass and chrome, with amusing stainless steel basins. Breakfast and drinks are served in the foyer, curved glass walls opening onto the plant-filled courtyard. The Pergolèse has no restaurant but all Paris is on the doorstep, offering a choice of informal bistros and smart restaurants. Guests enjoy the proximity of exclusive boutiques and historical buildings, stroll through the Bois de Boulogne and later enjoy the city's fascinating night-life. **Directions:** No 1 line from La Défense, close to the Porte Maillot terminal. Parking nearby. Price guide: Single Ff1150–1250; double/twin Ff1250–1400; deluxe Ff1550–1700.

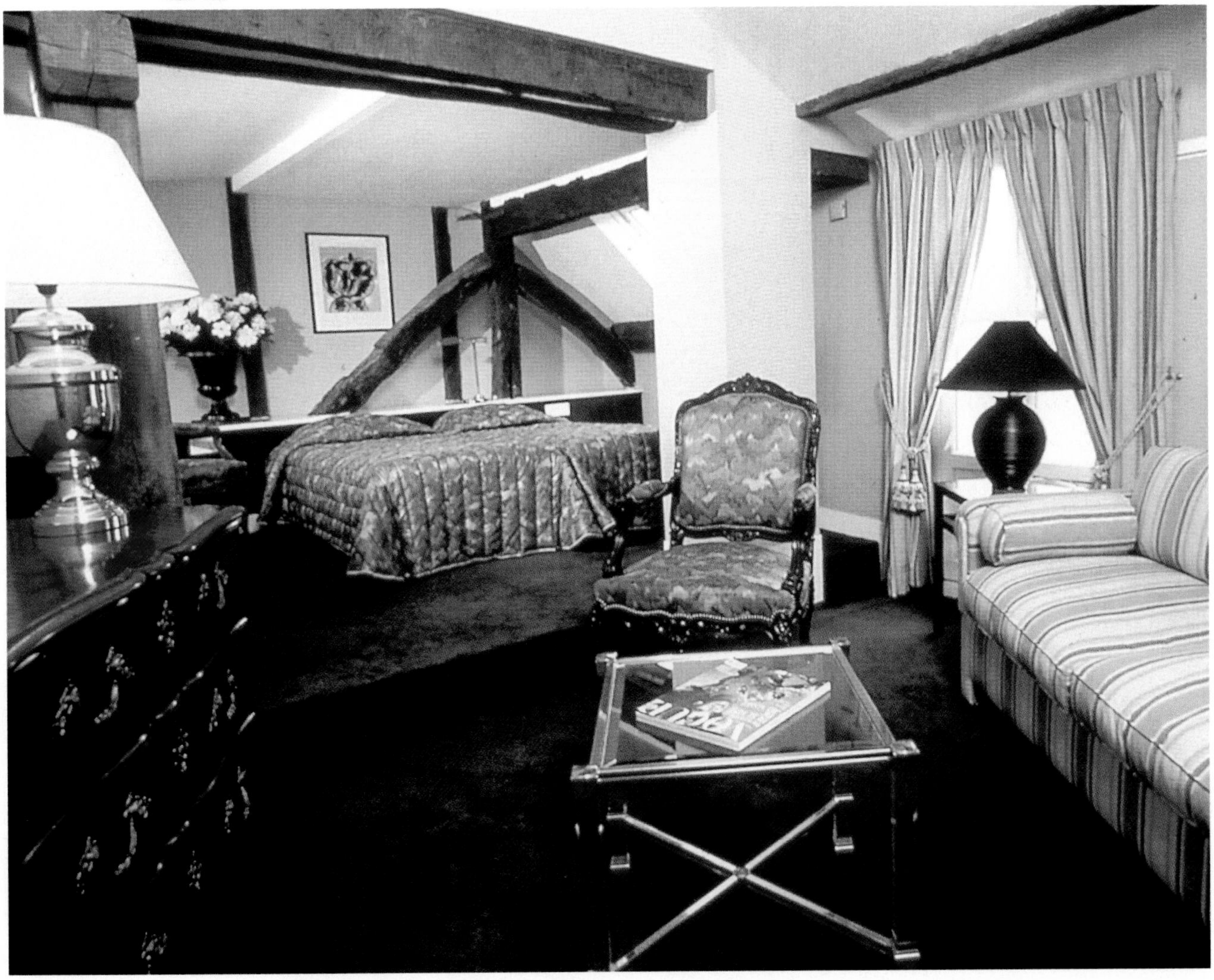

Relais St Germain

9 CARREFOUR DE L'ODÉON, 75006 PARIS, FRANCE
TEL: 33 1 43 29 12 05 FAX: 33 1 46 33 45 30

Le Relais Saint-Germain is an attractive small hotel in the heart of the Left Bank area, famous for its culture and association with the arts. Restoration has not detracted from the charm of this 17th century townhouse, where old and new have been carefully blended – warm tiled floors, handsome oil paintings and beautiful antiques unexpectedly harmonising easily with modern cupboards, mirrors and a fax machine. The character of this hotel is evident in that the bedrooms are named after famous French authors. They also have superb period furniture and enchanting chintz curtains and all still have their original beamed ceillings. They are peaceful and cool, being sound-proofed and air-conditioned. The bathrooms are luxurious, all in marble. A delicious breakfast is served and there is an efficient room service available. The hotel wine bar has an excellent selection of French wines. This lively part of Paris offers a choice of restaurants and cafés where guests can mingle with artists, poets, musicians and the cognoscenti. The Relais Saint-Germain is within walking distance of the Louvre, Orsay and Notre-Dame Cathedral, the sophisticated boutiques and the Pompidou Centre. **Directions:** The hotel is just off Boulevard Saint Germain, close to Métro Odéon. Three public car parks are nearby. Price guide: Single Ff1290; double/twin Ff1550–1750; suites Ff2000.

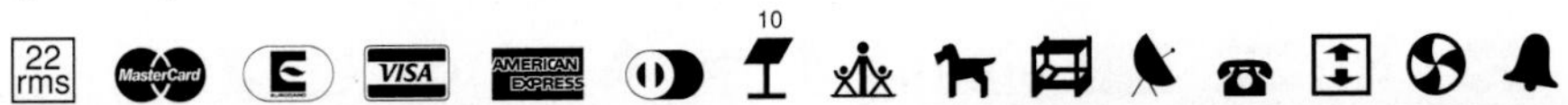

Grand Hotel Miramar

ROUTE DE LA CORNICHE, 20110 PROPRIANO, CORSICA, FRANCE
TEL: 33 4 95 76 06 13 FAX: 33 4 95 76 13 14

Southern Corsica has a wonderful balmy climate, and Propriano is a fascinating small port. It has splendid golden beaches – and this is the setting for this enchanting hotel, surrounded by lush gardens. The interior has cool tiled floors and the salons are elegantly furnished The charming bedrooms are spacious, each having a terrace or balcony overlooking the blue sea. There are also three beautifully designed apartments in an adjacent house, with romantic private gardens. The life style is al fresco; a delicious breakfast is served in the grounds or in the attractive loggia, while lunch and dinner are usually enjoyed on the shady terrace by the grand swimming pool (magical when floodlit at night), with spectacular views of the Gulf of Valinco. The restaurant is famous for its aromatic specialities, including fish caught just hours earlier by the Propriano fishermen, and the excellent local wines should be sampled. There are two pleasant, well-stocked bars, one outside. There is a well-equipped conference room. Guests can borrow mountain bikes to explore the rugged terrain inland. Most water sports are possible. More relaxing are excusions along the coast in a gorgeous 14 metre yacht belonging to the hotel. Golf and tennis can be arranged. **Directions:** The nearest airports are Figari and Ajaccio. Ferries from Toulon. Price guide: Single Ff850–1150; double/twin Ff1200–2250.

32 rms        40     

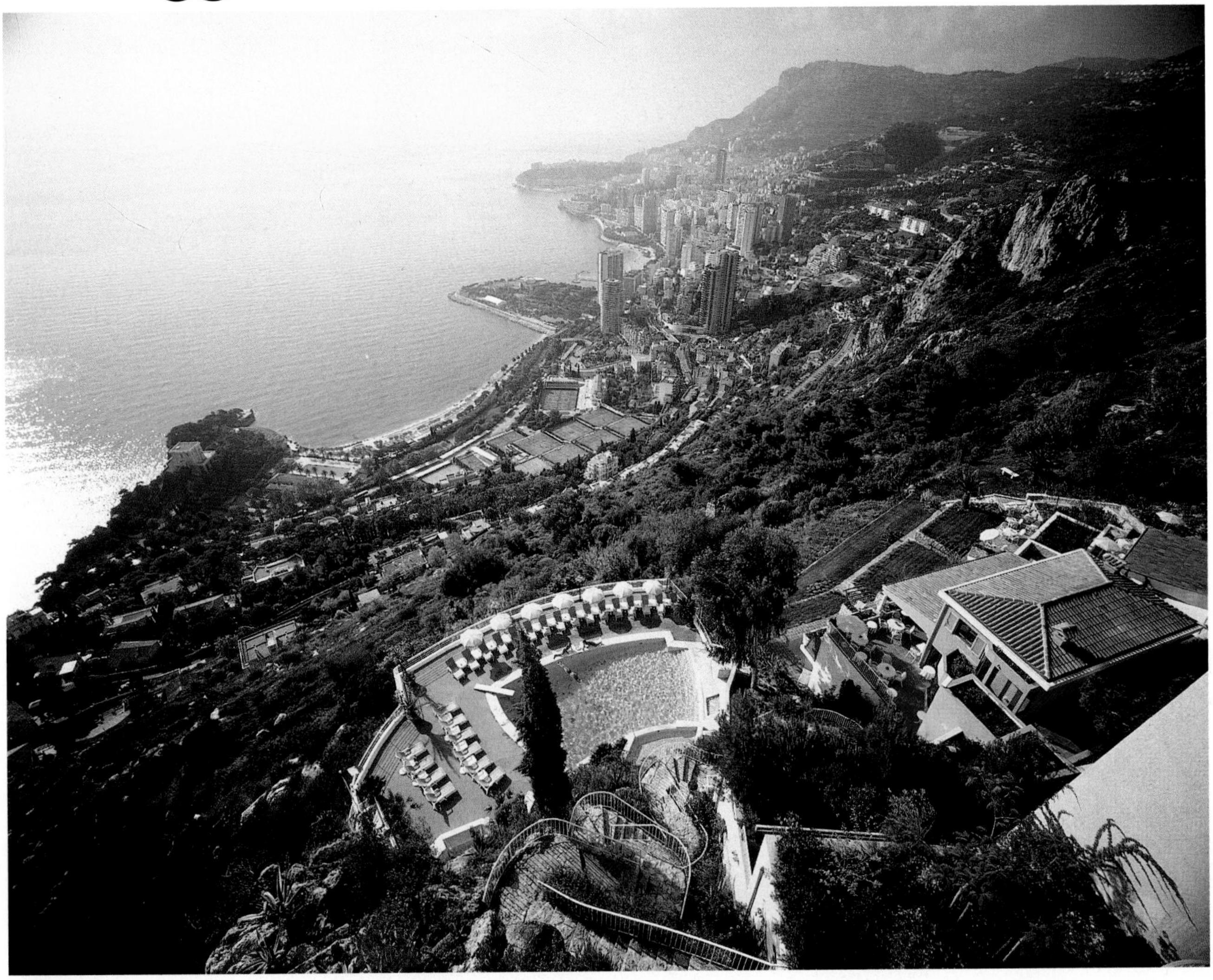

The Leading Hotels of the World®

Grand Hotel Vista Palace

ROUTE DE LA GRANDE CORNICHE, F-06190 ROQUEBRUNE/CAP MARTIN, FRANCE
TEL: 33 4 92 10 40 00 FAX: 33 4 93 35 18 94

This ultra-modern hotel, having been built into the rocks high above Monaco, commands spectacular views of Monte Carlo, its harbour and Cap Martin. Exotic gardens and terraces are interspersed with blue swimming pools and colourful sunshades. Indoors contemporary furnishings offer efficent, relaxed modern comfort. The well-equipped bedrooms all have sea views while four of the suites have private swimming pools. Most rooms are in the main building, but a few are in the excellent conference complex which is connected to the hotel. The Presidential Suite is a true paradise, a superb penthouse high up in the sky! Breakfast and lunch are often taken on the terraces. At night guests enjoy cocktails in the spacious Lounge Icare which shares panoramic views of the lights of Monte Carlo and the waterfront with the fabulous Vistaero Restaurant and with La Corniche, famous for its Mediterranean specialities. The winelist is huge and includes a good selection of Provençal rosés. Historical tours of the Eze region can be arranged, while other visitors explore the town, or workout in the hotel's Fitness Centre. After dinner the Casino of Monte Carlo is the major attraction. **Directions:** Arrivals use the helipad or leave Motorway A8 at Exit 57 to Turbie, following signs to Roquebrune then the Grand Hotel Vista Palace. Price guide: Single Ff1050–Ff1550; double/twin Ff1250–Ff1850; suites Ff1750–Ff6000.

CHÂTEAU DE COUDRÉE

DOMAINE DE COUDRÉE, BONNATRAIT, F-74140 SCIEZ-SUR-LÉMAN, FRANCE
TEL: 33 4 50 72 62 33 **FAX:** 33 4 50 72 57 28

Those seeking an idyllic summer holiday on the edge of Lake Geneva should stay at this enchanting 12th century château, with its fairytale turrets and pinnacles, surrounded by a vast private estate. The gardens are immaculate. This is an elite hotel, with just nineteen guest rooms, all furnished with fine antiques, beautifully decorated with the drapes in lovely fabrics. The smart bathrooms are well designed. Some bedrooms are in the oldest parts of the château. Guests to fall asleep lulled by the lapping of the water against the shore. Exquisite salons, an inviting bar and big terrace overlooking the pool and gardens down to the water's edge add to guests' pleasure. Dining is a memorable gastronomic experience – classic dishes presented with great flair, using the best local ingredients, in a superb setting, with immaculate linen, candles, gleaming silver and sparkling crystal. The wines are magnificent. There is also a handsome banqueting hall and the Château has several well-equipped meeting rooms. Residents relax by the pool, enjoy the private beach on Lake Geneva, play tennis in the grounds. Golf and riding are nearby and there is a casino at Evian. **Directions:** From Paris A40, exit Annemasse/ Thonon/Evian then follow signs to Sciez Bonnatrait. Price guide: Single from Ff680; double/twin from Ff780–1480; apartments for families from Ff1280–1980.

Romantik Hotels & Restaurants

L'AUBERGE DU CHOUCAS

05220 MONETIER-LES-BAINS, SERRE-CHEVALIER, HAUTES-ALPES, FRANCE

TEL: 33 4 92 24 42 73 FAX: 33 4 92 24 51 60

In the centre of an enchanting Alpine village, next to the XVth century church with its fine steeple, there is a small hotel, L'Auberge du Choucas. This lovely old building is characteristic of the region with a pretty garden in front. The ambience is marvellous, created by the friendly greeting, big log fires in the winter and the aroma of good living – herbs, flowers, wines, cooking. The bedrooms are cosy, many with balconies, light and airy, with attractive oak furniture in alpine style. After a long day's ski-ing, the dining room is a delight. relecting the age of the Auberge, with its vaulted archways and walls in the original stone, its tiled floor, candelight and sparkling crystal. Exquisite creative specialities of the house are served and enjoyed with wines chosen from among the best in France. There is magnificent ski-ing close by at Serre-Chevalier, a famous winter sports resort (400m from the Auberge). In summer Monêtier-les-Bains is a joy for walkers who appreciate the old stones, the wild flowers and the superb mountain air. Athletic climbers tackle the peaks. A day spent in Briançon (14 km from the Hotel) would be fascinating: a historic old town with 17th century fortifications. **Directions:** Leave Grenoble on the N91 towards Briançon, reaching Monêtier-les-Bains shortly after the Lautaret pass. Hotel is behind the church. Price guide: Single Ff500–Ff600; double/twin Ff700; suites Ff1080–Ff1180 (for 2 people).

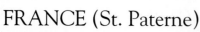

CHÂTEAU DE SAINT PATERNE

F-72610 SAINT PATERNE, FRANCE
TEL: 33 2 33 27 54 71 **FAX:** 33 2 33 29 16 71

This enchanting small château is the home of Charles Henri de Valbray, whose family have lived here since the 17th century, and he is delighted to welcome guests into his home. Careful modernisation has not intruded into the historical and aristocratic ambience of the château, which reflects the authentic furnishings and decorations of the past centuries. The salons are pleasant with the patina of age. The guest rooms are beautiful and individual: the one called Canards has 17th century panelling, Henry VI a painted ceiling, Terrace an 18th century pierglass, Oiseaux its own entrance, Tour is Provençal and Pigeonnier is in a medieval tower. The excellent dinner featuring vegetables from the kitchen garden is served in the traditional dining room, the table set with fine crystal, hand-painted porcelain and the finest silver. Wines are well-chosen. Cookery courses are scheduled for the Autumn. Guests can explore the area on bicycles, play tennis, croquet and ping-pong and visit local wine caves. Other nearby activities include golf, swimming and motor racing at Le Mans and the Musée de l'Automobile. The Bayeux Tapestries, Chartres Cathedral and the port of Honfleur are alternative attractions. **Directions:** N12 from Paris, at Alençon take A28 towards Le Mans, after 1.5 km watch for signs to St Paterne village. Price guide: Double/twin Ff550–Ff800.

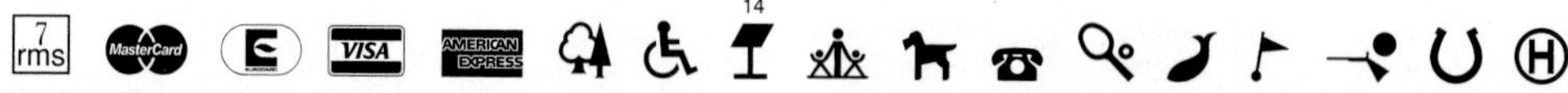

MAS d'ARTIGNY

ROUTE DE LA COLLE, F–06570 SAINT-PAUL, FRANCE

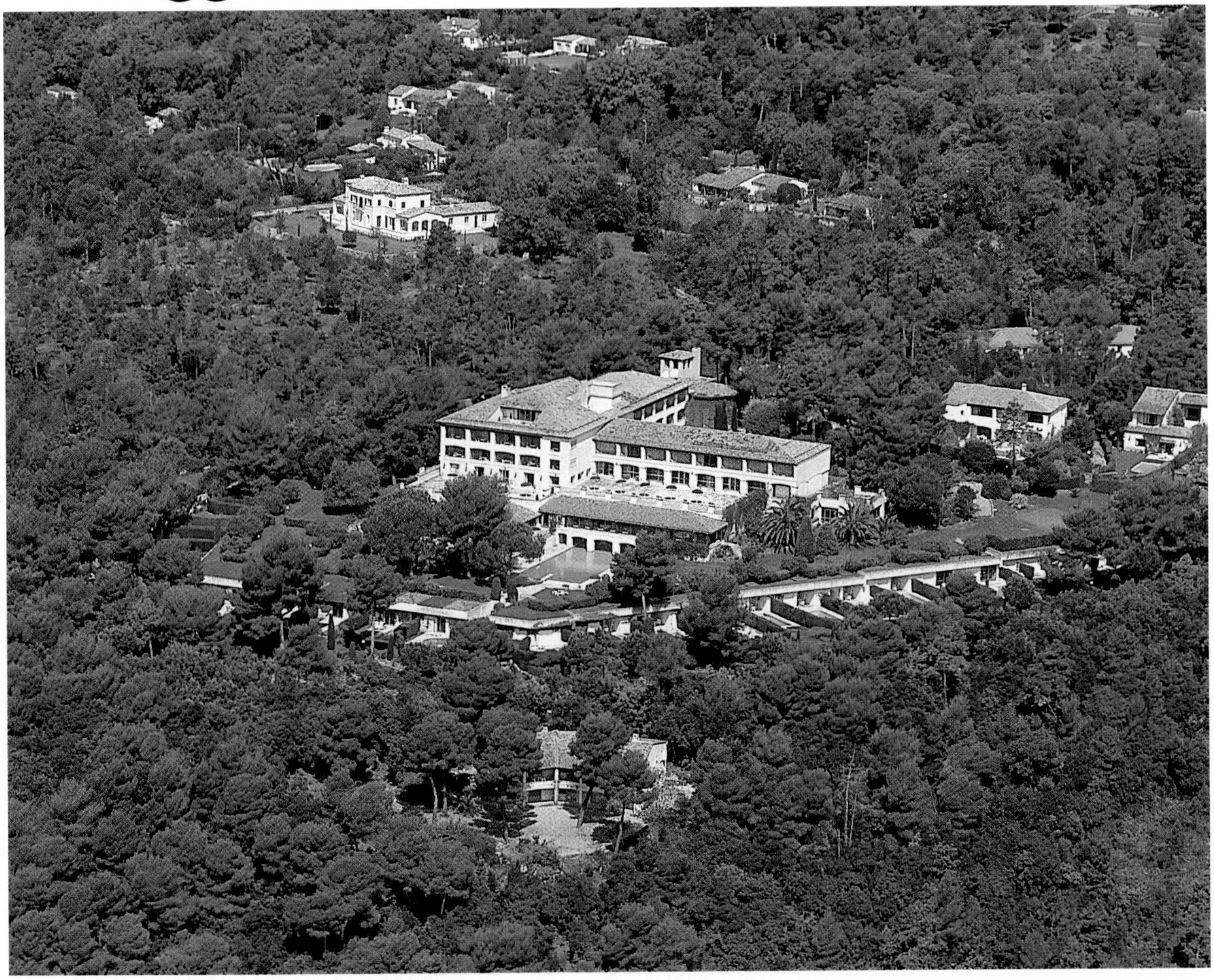

TEL: 33 4 93 32 84 54 FAX: 33 4 93 32 95 36 E-MAIL: Mas D'artigny@wanadoo.fr

A unique hotel set in the hills high above Antibes with uninterrupted views of the Côte d'Azur, has 25 individual swimming pools and superb conference facilities. The striking white marble entrance immediately alerts arrivals that their stay at Mas d'Artigny will be memorable. The interior is sophisticated, spacious and uncluttered, with wide archways and graceful furniture, while the magnificent pool is the central focus point. The accommodation offered is superb, the bedrooms, all with luxurious bathrooms, have their own balconies, while the apartments lead onto private patios with their own pool. Additionally there are three villas, ideal for families, with their own pools and gardens. Six meeting rooms have state-of-the-art conference equipment. The fabulous dining room extends onto the Terrace, with a glorious outlook right across to the coastline. Guests linger here while studying the delicious regional and classical dishes that have won a Michelin star. Wines are from the reasonable to the sublime. Mas d'Artigny has its own golf practice ground and tennis courts and the beaches are not far away. **Directions:** Leave A8 at Cagnes-sur-Mer exit taking Route de Grasse, turning left after La Colle sur Loup, before reaching St-Paul-de-Vence on the right. There is a helipad. Price guide: Single Ff525–1670; double/twin Ff640–1850; suites Ff1760–2700.

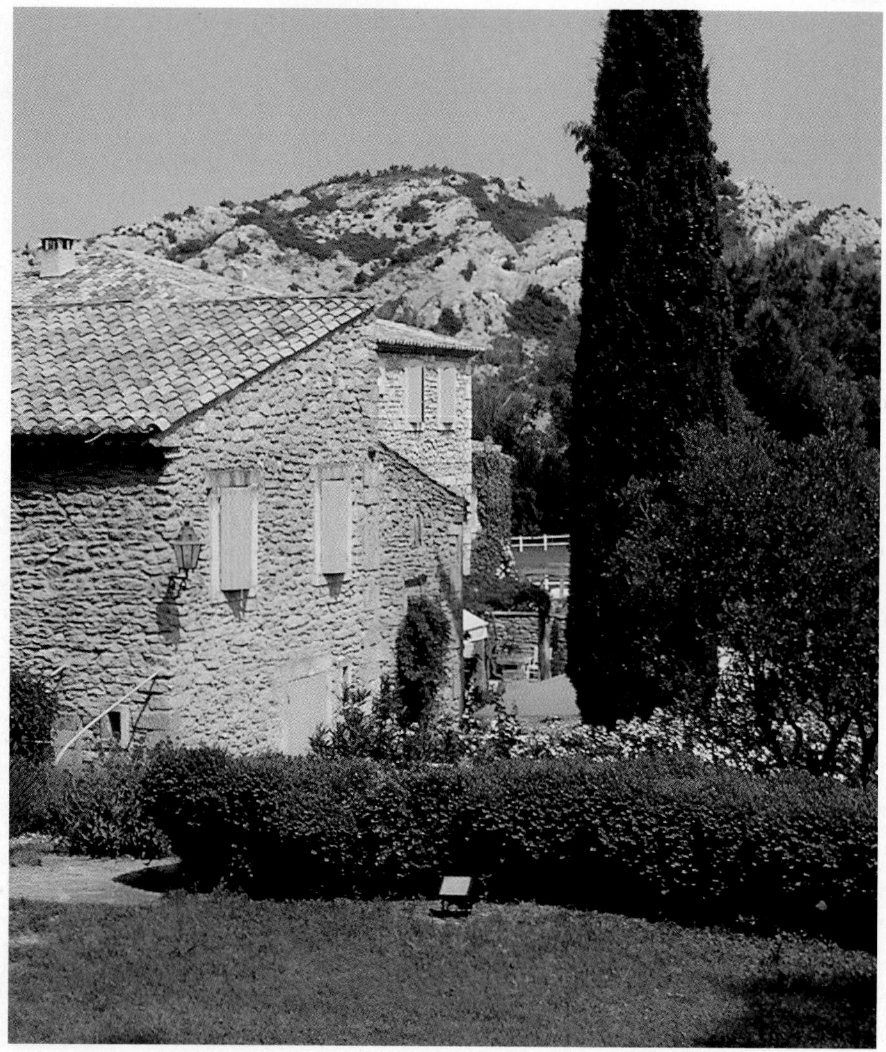

DOMAINE DE VALMOURIANE

PETITE ROUTE DES BAUX, F–13210 SAINT RÉMY DE PROVENCE, FRANCE

TEL: 33 4 90 92 44 62 **FAX:** 33 4 90 92 37 32

This delightful farmhouse in the hills known as La Chaîne des Alpilles, built in the attractive stone familiar to this area, is now an intimate and luxurious family-run hotel, which stands in flower filled grounds with a background of vineyards and olive trees, the air redolent of lavender and herbs. The salon is elegant, cool and comfortable and the spacious bedrooms are charming, decorated in traditional Provençal fabrics. The attractive terrace is where guests often gather for apéritifs before dinner and light informal meals are served. Memories of dining in the handsome restaurant will linger for a long time – the exquisite interpretation of regional dishes, fish from the Mediterranean, salads dressed in interesting oils, lamb cooked with herbs from the garden, gorgeous puddings and fine French wines, including local rosés. Guests enjoy the swimming pool with its Jacuzzi or tennis on the hotel courts and strolling in the park, visiting local markets and antique shops, exploring the countryside, tasting wine, going to see Nimes or Avignon, or playing golf close by. At night a gentle game of billiards is very pleasant. **Directions:** Leave the A7 at Avignon South exit, taking D571. At the centre of Saint-Rémy-de-Provence, take the D99 towards Tarascon then the D27 signed Les Baux de Provence. Price guide: Double/twin Ff590–Ff1140; suite Ff1160–Ff1550.

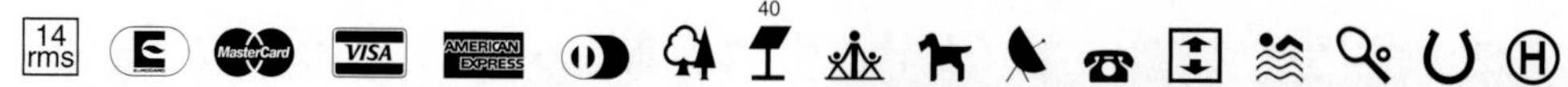

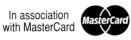

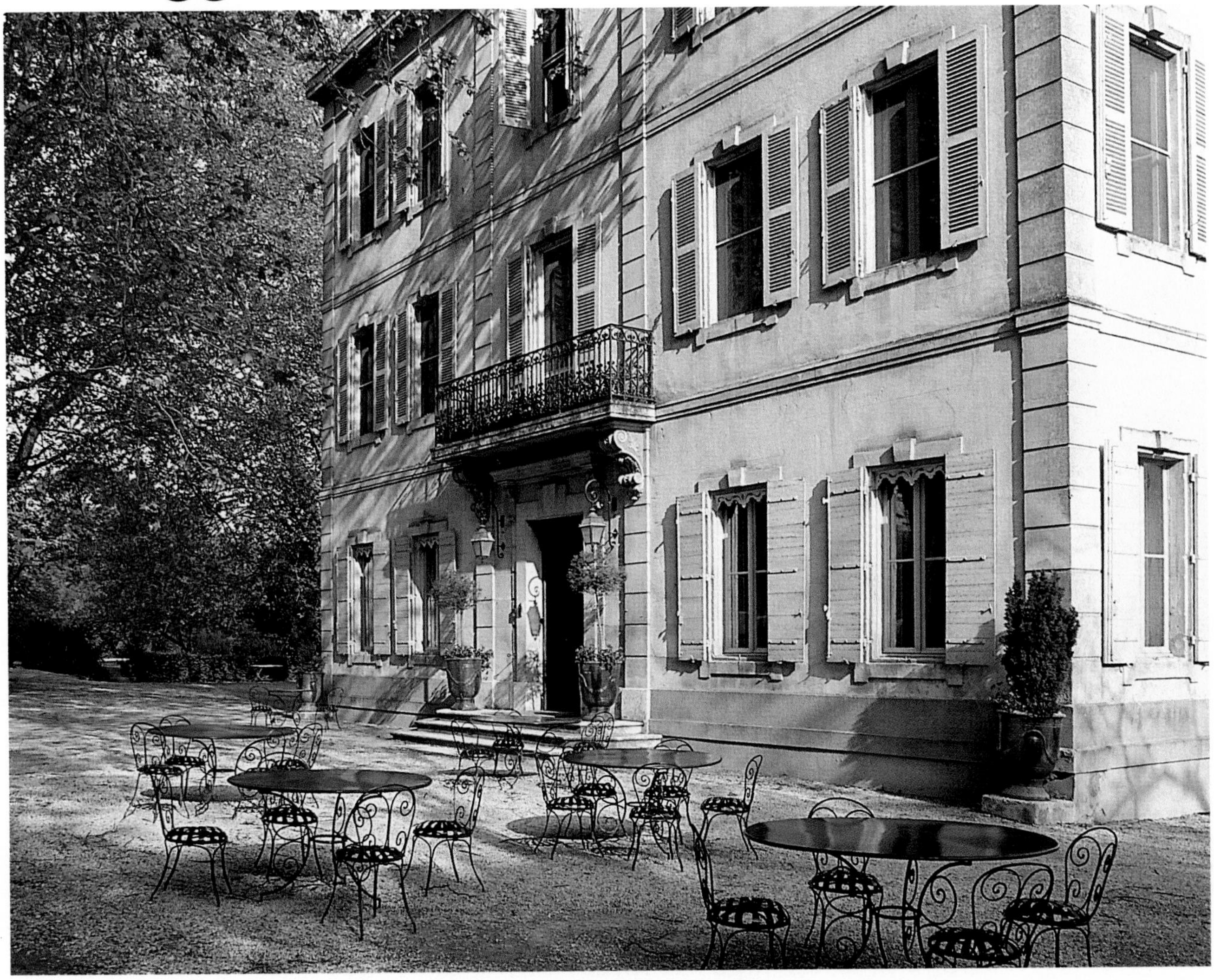

CHÂTEAU DES ALPILLES

ROUTE DÉPARTEMENTALE 31, ANCIENNE ROUTE DU GRÈS, F-13210 SAINT RÉMY DE PROVENCE, FRANCE
TEL: 33 4 90 92 03 33 FAX: 33 4 90 92 45 17

This very elegant 19th century château, just a short distance from St. Rémy, is wonderfully secluded. Rare old trees provide avenues, shade and add a touch of the exotic to the verdant surroundings. There are two other buildings, the original 'Mas', now known as 'la ferme', rebuilt to provide modern suites and apartments, and the original 'Chapelle', now available to guests as a lovely private villa. The salons in the château reflect its age-old grandeur, with moulded ceilings, mosaic floors, tapestries on the walls, enormous gilded mirrors, antique furniture and rich festooned curtains. Some of the bedrooms repeat this splendour, others are more contemporary with pretty Provençal fabrics. All are air-conditioned. Rooms equipped for seminars are also available. Guests mingle in the intimate bar, and those not dining out can enjoy simple regional dishes in the dining area adjoining the reception lounge. Exploring the countryside on foot or on bicycles is a popular pastime, going down the "Old Sandstone Road" to Les Baux. Others stay close to the Château, lazing in the cool gardens, playing tennis or sunbathing by the swimming pool. **Directions:** Leave St. Rémy on the D31 towards Tarascon. Price guide: Single Ff900; double/twin FF980–Ff1130; suites Ff1320–Ff1690; chapelle Ff1490–Ff2000.

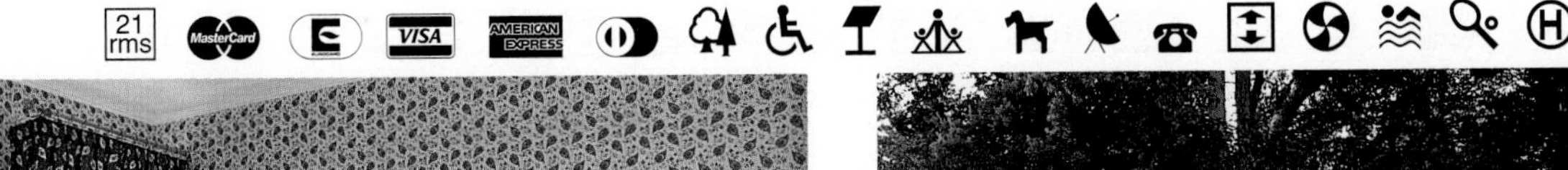

The Leading Hotels of the World®

HÔTEL BYBLOS

AVENUE PAUL SIGNAC, F–83990 SAINT-TROPEZ, FRANCE
TEL: 33 4 94 56 68 00 FAX: 33 4 94 56 68 01

This unique hotel, with its elite clientele, has the ambience of a Provençal village – it is a succession of delightful houses interlinked with flower filled small courtyards, the air scented by the lavender and olive trees. It is just a few minutes from the famous beaches of St. Tropez, close to the fascinating small port. The salons are cool and elegantly decorated; the Lebanese room being particularly splendid. The bedrooms and suites are luxurious, each individually styled with Provençal prints much in evidence. Many of the opulent bathrooms have their own Jacuzzi. Caviar and foie gras can be found in the minibars! Breakfast is served in the proximity of the pool, and room service will bring a superb brunch to late risers. Les Arcades is presided over by the well known chef, Philippe Audibert, who suggests light lunches by the pool, while dinner is a glorious feast of provençal and local fish dishes. The bistro 'Le Relais des Caves' is open until late at night. A complete fitness centre with sauna, hammam, massage and body care is available. Golf and tennis are nearby. 'Les Caves du Roy' is the vibrant and famous discotheque of Saint-Tropez. L'Annonciade's Museum exhibiting famous artists' work, the exclusive boutiques and local market should all be visited. **Directions:** A8, then N.98. Price guide: Single Ff1080–1790; double/twin Ff1450–2570; suites Ff2140–6500.

HÔTEL SUBE

15 QUAI SUFFREN, 83990 ST TROPEZ, FRANCE
TEL: 33 4 94 97 30 04 FAX: 33 4 94 54 89 08

Many people are unaware that St Tropez is not just a 20th century beach resort for beautiful people, and they are delighted to discover its fascinating old port, filled with graceful yachts mingling with the fishing fleet. Overlooking the activity of the waterfront there is a small, bright hotel – the Hotel Sube. A warm welcome awaits guests, who instantly appreciate the appropriate nautical ambience – models and paintings of old sailing ships in the reception area – and the small balcony facing the marina is the perfect place to have a cool drink while absorbing the colourful atmosphere. The bedrooms are charming and some have a balcony or terrace – at the back they open out onto a attractive patio, shaded by olive trees, scenting the air. Breakfast is croissants in the sun, watching the multi-national flags on the tall masted boats. In the evening the English bar is a popular rendezvous for both visitors and locals. There is no restaurant but an endless choice of bistros and restaurants to explore nearby. Swim in the sea, go fishing or drive inland to the Provencal wine caves and the perfumeries at Grasse. **Directions:** A8/A7 Le Muy exit, signed St. Tropez. Reaching the centre, follow signs to the port, finding the hotel on the quay. Price guide: Single from Ff390; double/twin Ff590–Ff1200; suites Ff990–Ff1500.

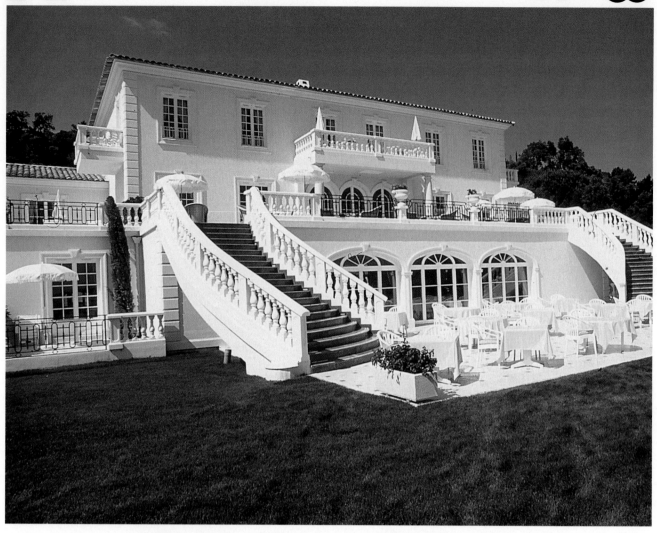

Hôtel Villa Belrose

BOULEVARD DES CRÊTES, LA GRANDE BASTIDE, F-83580 GASSIN, FRANCE
TEL: 33 4 94 55 97 97 FAX: 33 4 94 55 97 98

An elite hotel standing in a large estate in Gassin, a quiet part of the Cap de St Tropez, where the inspired architect created a Provencal palace with echoes of California, built into the hillside. The Villa has grand sweeping steps leading up to the terrace, from which visitors have spectacular views of the Riviera coastline. The hotel is immaculate, and the staff impeccable. The cool salons are the epitome of elegance. Every guest room has a private balcony, and all are exquisite, very light, with classical furnishings and wonderful flowery fabrics. The lavish marble bathrooms have been thoughtfully equipped. The Belrose has been designed for al fresco living, with its many large terraces, one outside the bar, where exotic cocktails and champagne vie with fine old Cognacs and Armagnacs. The sophisticated restaurant also extends outside. The menu is Mediterranean, more Italian than French; the cellar holds the best French wines. Residents relax round the enormous pool. Tennis and golf are nearby and the hotel hires out small mopeds or scooters for trips to the beach or into St Tropez, which has good shopping and a colourful nightlife. Other attractions are local vineyards and markets. **Directions:** From A8, exit Le Muy, then N98, 800m before reaching St Tropez take Avenue des Mesanges for Gassin. Excellent parking. Price guide: Single Ff1250–2700; double/twin Ff1900–3750; suites Ff5750–12,000.

HÔTEL REGENT PETITE FRANCE

5, RUE DES MOULINS, 67000 STRASBOURG, FRANCE
TEL: 33 3 88 76 43 43 FAX: 33 3 88 76 43 76

Strasbourg is a fascinating city with its waterways and the Regent has a prime position on the banks of the River Ill in the intriguing Petite France, part of the Old Town. Close to one of the splendid bridges, the facade of this elite hotel is traditional, three centuries old houses joined together, but going through the doors is to step into another era, for the interior is late twentieth century, designed for the Millennium. The brilliantly lit reception hall's seating is a pastiche of colour, and vivid contemporary paintings fill the walls. The bedrooms are relaxing, the furnishings extremely modern and comfortable. The views over the canals and Old Town are spectacular. High technology has been discreetly installed and many luxurious extras are provided. The Bar des Glacières is ritzy and amusing. The Coffee Shop is ideal for those wanting light meals, and the Pont Tournant Restaurant has a unique elegance. Fabulous regional specialities are on the menu and some wonderful Alsace wines are listed. The hotel also has state-of-the-art conference facilities. Reflecting its industrial past, the Regent has created a Museum of Ice-Making. Boat trips down the canals are entertaining. Sporting guests will find golf and tennis nearby. **Directions:** Leave A35 at Porte Blanche exit, following signs to the town centre. Valet parking. Price guide: Double/twin Ff1090–1490; suites Ff1850–2300.

Germany

Time stands still in much of Germany. you notice this in much of the architecture to be seen in the towns throughout this enchanting land, and in the number of castles which beautify its rural landscape. Germany has castles of all periods and styles.

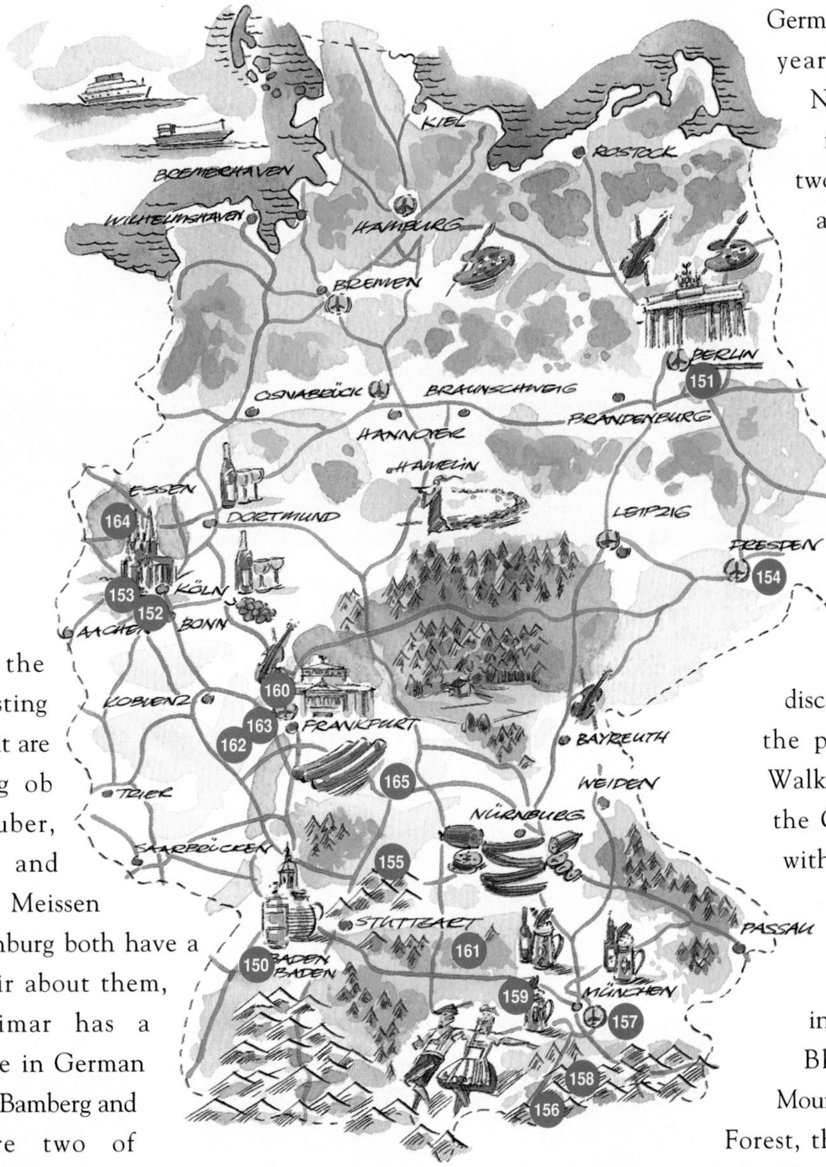

Some of the most interesting places to visit are Rothenburg ob der Tauber, Goslar and Regensburg. Meissen and Quedlinburg both have a fairy-tale air about them, while Weimar has a special place in German culture, and Bamberg and Lübeck are two of Europe's half hidden gems.

Perhaps no other country is Western Europe has such a complex past as well as modern history. Much of this history can be viewed by visitors today, in a country of sheer beauty where outdoor activity is a way of life. There is a huge variety of museums, architecture from most periods and a heavy emphasis on cultural interests. Road and rail transport is extremely well organised, and there is plenty of excellent beer, wine and food – and accommodation as you will discover.

Now as of old one country, the cultural , social and economic differences of the recently separate Germanys will take many years to disappear. Nevertheless the integration of the two is well advanced, and first time visitors to Germany may not notice too many big difference between them.

As in most countries in Europe, the best way to discover the places and the people is on foot. Walking trails crisscross the German landscape with more than 80,000 miles of marked paths. Popular areas for hiking include the wonderful Black Forest, Harz Mountains, the Bavarian Forest, the so-called Saxon Switzerland area and the Thuringian Forest. The Bavarian Alps offer the most inspiring scenery, however and are the centre of mountaineering in Germany if you are admirably energetic. A picturesque river voyage on the Rhine accompanied by the local wines may be more suitable for the rest of us.

MÖNCHS POSTHOTEL

D-76328 BAD HERRENALB, GERMANY
TEL: 49 70 83 74 40 FAX: 49 70 83 74 41 22

Bad Herrenalb is an attractive small town in the Black Forest, and the Posthotel, with its traditional half-timbered façade enlivened by green and white shutters, has extensive shady parkland at the back, much appreciated by guests in hot weather. The interior is beautifully decorated in harmony with the wooden beams that remain from the original building, flowers and plants in every corner, fine paintings and lovely antiques completing the picture. The bedrooms and suites have delightful colour schemes, comfortable furniture and opulent bathrooms. The intimate piano bar is an elegant meeting place. The two restaurants are very different – the sophisticated Klosterschänke has fine panelled walls, a reputation for superb cooking and an extensive selection of Bordeaux and Italian wines. The Locanda specialises in Mediterranean dishes, including a variety of pastas. A smart meeting room, with full presentation equipment, is available for seminars. Guests enjoy strolling in the park and relaxing by the heated swimming pool. They can play tennis and golf, walk in the Black Forest and ski in winter. Baden Baden, half an hour away, is full of history. Its casino is a famous inheritance from the 19th century. **Directions:** On the A5 from Basel exit at Rastatt, following signs to Gernsbach or from Frankfurt exit for Bad Herrenalb. Price guide: Single 180–195Dm; double/twin 270–360Dm; suites 470–520Dm.

The Leading Hotels of the World® GRAND HOTEL ESPLANADE BERLIN

LÜTZOWUFER, 15, D-10785 BERLIN
TEL: 49 30 254780 FAX: 49 30 265 1171

The Grand Hotel Esplanade, rated the most popular hotel in Berlin, is the epitome of modern luxury, in a superb situation just near the city centre overlooking the river and an inner city park, and close to the Kulturforum. A monument to modern Bauhaus architecture, the dramatic interiors are filled with space and light, one wall is a fountain and famous contemporary Berlin artists have contributed sculptures, paintings and other forms of modern art. The bedrooms are peaceful, with sound insulation, decorated in relaxing fabrics. The suites with business areas and other amenities, each more opulent than the next, have accommodated an impressive guest list. The day starts with breakfast in the enchanting Orangerie. Later in the day visitors rendezvous in the sophisticated Harry's New-York Bar or enjoy a beer in the typical Berlin-Pub before wining and dining superbly in the brilliant Harlekin. The Esplanade, an exciting conference/restaurant ship, is moored on the river bank. The hotel pool, spa facilities and Beauty Salon are on site; joggers might try bikes in the Tiergarten. Visitors should explore Berlin's galleries, museums, shops and fabulous nightlife. **Directions:** From Kurfürstendamm head towards Lützowplatz via the Europa-Center. Extensive parking available. Price guide: Double/twin 380Dm–530Dm; suite 680Dm–2,600Dm.

400 rms · 350

DES IGN HOT ELS

Hotel Cristall

URSULAPLATZ 9–11, 50668 COLOGNE, GERMANY
TEL: 49 221 16300 FAX: 49 221 1630 333

In the centre of Cologne, and very convenient for the convention centre, is the Hotel Cristall, a fin-de-siècle Art Deco building which has moved into the 20th century. The decor of this 'design' hotel is stunning – minimalist geometric lines, strong contrasting colours, unique light patterns. The bedrooms continue the same theme,simplistic and pristine, uncluttered and with surprising touches that add warmth to the austere yet striking furnishings. The bathrooms are contemporary, and very efficient, showers taking preference to baths. Some bedrooms are designated non-smoking. The bar is very trendy, with sculptured green leather chairs, the chrome and marble fittings a curious blend of nostalgia for the Art Nouveau era and moving towards the Millennium. While The Cristall has an excellent coffee shop, it does not have a restaurant – however the concierge will recommend good restaurants in the locality. The hotel exhibits modern art – outside there is the magnificent cathedral, fascinating museums and galleries showing fine collections of paintings. Theatres, opera and river trips to see the Rhine castles will please traditionalists, younger visitors will probably prefer pop art and the city's vibrant night life. Directions On reaching Cologne, follow signs to the Cathedral and city centre. The hotel is adjacent to the railway station. Price guide: Single 190–270Dm; double/twin 250–390Dm.

84 rms          

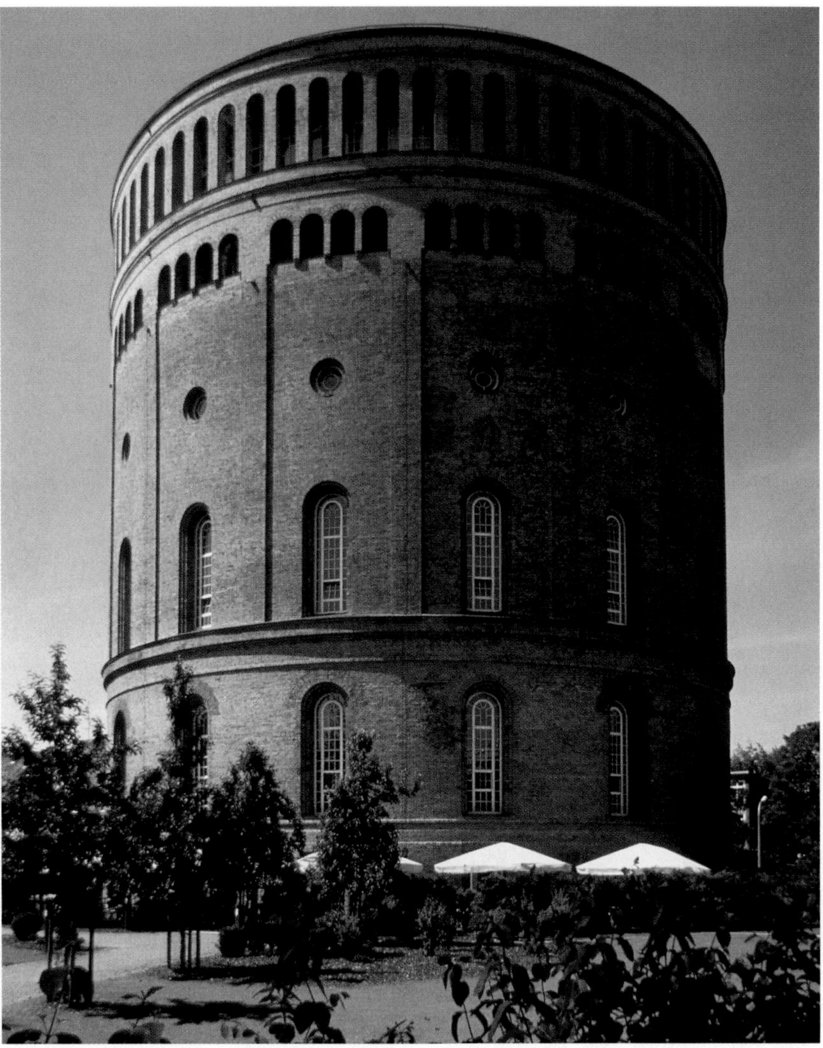

DES IGN HOT ELS

HOTEL IM WASSERTURM

KAYGASSE 2, D-50676, COLOGNE, GERMANY
TEL: 49 221 20080 FAX: 49 221 200 8888

This fascinating hotel, once a water tower which, in 1872, was the highest in Europe, was partially destroyed in the Second World War and rebuilt under the aegis of the Conservation Authorities, Original brickwork was replicated and windows introduced where once blind archways stood. Today the hotel, standing in its own parkland yet close to the city centre, is a landmark in Cologne. The interior reflects the talents of a top French designer who created a modern hotel without diminishing its historical past. The luxurious bedrooms are spacious and the mosaic tiled bathrooms have separate toilets and bidets. There is a fitness centre for sauna and massage. The bar is well stocked, and high up at roof level is the glass domed restaurant, a spectacular and romantic venue for a candle-lit dinner or an american breakfast on a fine summer morning. Cologne offers art galleries, museums, concerts, operas, musicals and theatres. There are river boats down the Rhine, trips round breweries, the casino and night clubs. The Conference and Exhibition complex is quite near. **Directions:** From Nord-Süd-Fahrt take Blaubach into Rothgerberbach, turning right into Poststrasse, then left into Alte Mauer am Bach and Kaygasse. Underground parking. Price guide: Single 320Dm–420Dm; double 390Dm–520Dm; suites 590Dm–2,400Dm.

BÜLOW RESIDENZ

RÄHNITZGASSE 19, 01097 DRESDEN, GERMANY
TEL: 49 351 80030 FAX: 49 351 8003100

A magnificent baroque Saxon mansion, dating back to 1730, the Bülow Residenz has successfully brought together all the gracious attributes of its history and the luxury of today's prestigious hotel. The façade is a welcoming golden yellow and there is an enchanting inner courtyard, cool and green, where guests can relax over a long drink. The glamorous bedrooms have tall windows, hand crafted furniture and lavish bathrooms. The fourth floor is designated non-smoking. Once the coal cellar, the attractive vaulted Caroussel Bar is the perfect place to enjoy a cocktail at the end of the day before adjourning to the elegant Caroussel Restaurant with its team of talented chefs preparing modern interpretations of delicacies from Swabia (a duchy in South West Germany) and classical gourmet meals. Many fine châteaux are included in the extensive wine list. Guests enjoy exploring Dresden, which has a wonderful cathedral and museums dedicated to the famous fine china. There is an excellent theatre and opera house. Alternatively take a boat trip along the Elbe. **Directions:** The railway station and airport are both nearby. By car, cross the Elbe by the Augustbrücke. Rähnitzgasse is reached turning left from the Hauptstrasse. Price guide: Single 290Dm; double/twin 370Dm–390Dm; suites 460Dm.

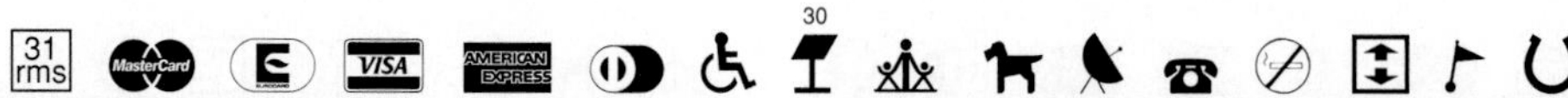

WALD & SCHLOSSHOTEL

D–74639 FRIEDRICHSRUHE / ZWEIFLINGEN, GERMANY
TEL: 49 79 41 60870 FAX: 49 79 41 61468

This graceful hunting lodge, once the summer residence of Prince Johann-Friedrich of Hohenlohe-Oehringen, is now an elegant hotel. It stands in a magnificent park and the adjacent fascinating stable block has been renovated recently to increase the accommodation. Visitors will appreciate the handsome reception rooms, with their high ceilings, traditional furniture, splendid family portraits and gilt mirrors. The guest rooms are decorated in harmonious colours and extremely comfortable. Some are in the second building. A third building is now a beauty farm with a wide range of treatments available. The bar is an ideal meeting place before dining in the 2 Michelin stars restaurant, with candles and chandeliers providing attractive lighting as guests appreciate the sensational international menu and first-class wines. A second, less formal, restaurant with hunting relics on its walls offers regional dishes. There is also an impressive banqueting room for private functions. The terrace is perfect for al fresco refreshments. Leisure facilities include indoor and outdoor pools, tennis, fishing, riding and an 18-hole golf course. **Directions:** Leave the BAB 6 at the Öhringen exit, following signs towards Zweiflingen, finding signs to the Wald & Schlosshotel at Friedrichsruhe. Price guide: Single Dm195–Dm310; double/twin Dm295–Dm420; suite Dm520–Dm700.

In association with MasterCard

REINDL'S PARTENKIRCHNER HOF

BAHNHOFSTRASSE, 15, GARMISCH PARTENKIRCHEN, GERMANY
TEL: 49 88 21 58025 FAX: 49 88 21 73401

Garmisch Partenkirchen, where the Winter Olympics have been held, is a small town standing at the foot of the Zugspitze mountain surrounded by verdant pine forests. The hotel is an attractive building, with flower-bedecked wooden balconies along all sides. Inside there is a feeling of spaciousness, warmth and comfort – the furnishings are traditional. The bedrooms and apartments are delightful, and most have sunny balconies. Not all are in the main building, but close by in the Haus Alpspitz and Haus Wetterstein which are more contemporary without losing their regional charm. The bar is the perfect rendezvous, whether for aperitifs before, or digestifs after, a memorable meal in the handsome Reindl's Gourmet-Restaurant accompanied by the finest wines. There are also an elegant banqueting room and conference facilities. There are no shortage of activities – some may prefer to relax in the large pool and sauna while others may exercise in the gym. Outside in winter ski-ing predominates but in summer there is tennis and magnificent countryside to explore – perhaps in the hotel's horse-drawn carriage. At night the casino is a popular venue. Directions: Entering Partenkirchen, turn right at the main crossroads heading towards station. Hotel is 100m down the road on the left. Price guide: Single Dm135–Dm150, double/twin Dm145– Dm175; suites Dm200–Dm275.

HOTEL KÖNIGSHOF

KARLSPLATZ, 25, D–80335 MUNICH, GERMANY
TEL: 49 89 551 360 FAX: 49 89 5513 6113

One of the most prestigious hotels in Munich, in the centre of the city, overlooking the spectacular fountain in the Stachus plaza, the Königshof is ideal for business people or those exploring the metropolis. This is a modern grand hotel, reflecting the talents of skilled interior decorators. The salons are spacious and the piano bar is stylish. Beautiful fabrics have been used throughout, especially in the luxurious bedrooms. All the rooms are sound-proofed against the noises of the traffic, air conditioned and provided with many amenities. The bathrooms are opulent. Shoes are cleaned and laundry returned within 8 hours! The Königshof Restaurant has twice won accolades as the best hotel restaurant in Germany. The tables stand well apart, – crisp white cloths set with gleaming silver, sparkling crystal and fine porcelain. The menu offers inspired Bavarian dishes prepared by international chefs. The wine list extends world wide. There are private dining rooms. Days can be filled exploring museums, art galleries, museums and historic buildings. Evenings can be filled with theatre, opera and concerts or the city night life of clubs, discos and casinos. **Directions:** Exit A9 at Schwabing exit, left into Leopoldstrasse, meeting Altstadt ring, turn right continuing on to Karlsplatz. Private garage. Price guide: Single 320Dm–395Dm; double/twin 370Dm–520Dm; suites 600Dm–1200Dm.

80

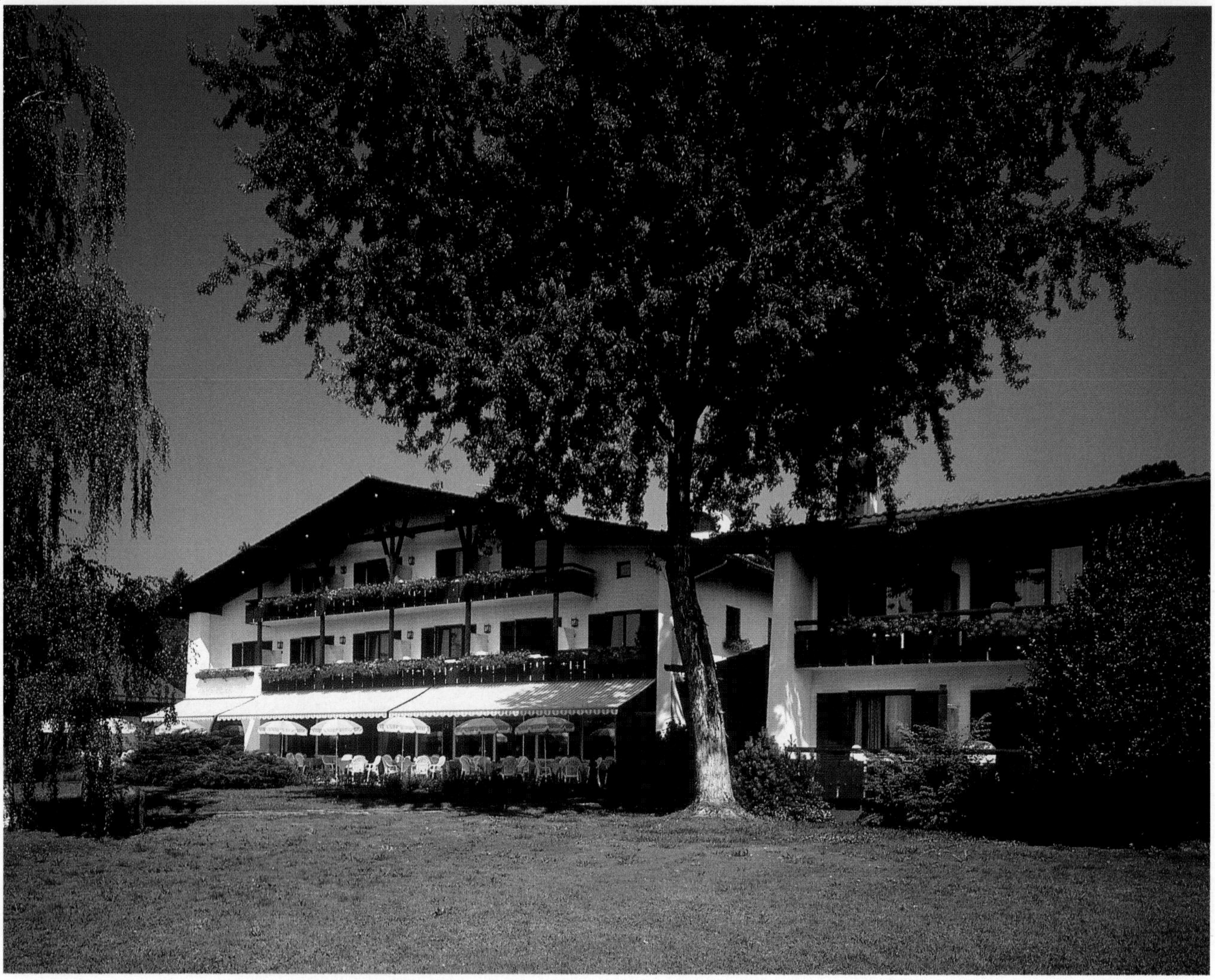

Alpenhof Murnau

RAMSACHSTRASSE 8, D–82418 MURNAU, GERMANY
TEL: 49 8841 4910 FAX: 49 8841 5438

This enchanting traditional Alpine hotel, built in 1967, is in a marvellously peaceful location, outside the village of Murnau, looking across to the Bavarian Alps. On arrival guests are immediately conscious of the warm ambience. They are greeted by staff in national costume, flowers are everywhere, the ceilings have beams, the floor has colourful rugs and the rustic furniture looks inviting. The pretty bedrooms are delightful, all having balconies looking out to the snow-topped mountains, the forests and meadows filled with wild flowers. The bathrooms have been carefully designed and equipped with many luxuries. Drinks are enjoyed on the terrace on warm days or later on in the attractive bar before entering the spacious dining room with picture windows overlooking the garden. Meals are of the highest standard, and the well-chosen wines are from France, Italy and Germany. The outdoor pool is heated from May/October, surrounded by sunbeds. Bikes are available. Some guests enjoy going on wonderful walks, others ride on the horse-wagon. Bavaria has magnificent castles, spas and casinos. **Directions:** Leave A95 from Munich towards GarmischPartenkirchen, then exit for Murnau. Drive through the village, watching for signs to the hotel. Price guide: Single 115DM–195DM; double/twin 190DM–395DM; suites 460DM–495DM.

40 rms

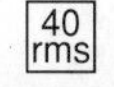

SCHLOSSHOTEL OBERSTOTZINGEN

STETTENER STRASSE 35–37, 89168 NIEDERSTOTZINGEN, GERMANY
TEL: 49 7325 1030 FAX: 49 7325 10370

An elegant small castle built in the 17th century, surrounded by private parkland, has been carefully restored and today it is the exclusive Schlosshotel Oberstotzingen. Guests mounting the steps to enter the baroque front door appreciate the historic ambience and warm welcome. The reception rooms are charming, in restful colour schemes, and extremely comfortable, looking out over the peaceful gardens and leading onto the attractive terrace. The bedrooms are enchanting, with pretty fabrics, gilt mirrors and small chandeliers. Several of these are in an adjacent annex. It should be noted that some of the bathrooms only have showers. The bar is convivial, and there is a also a small beer garden The sophisticated restaurant has an unusual vaulted ceiling and residents enjoy substantial regional cooking and good local wines are among those listed. Additionally there is a galleried dining hall for use on special occasions, where concerts are held occasionally. The excellent meeting rooms have all topical presentation facilities. There is excellent golf nearby and the hotel offers special packages. It has two tennis courts and riding can be organised. There are castles to explore. **Directions:** Leave A7 at junction with A8 towards Gunzburg, after 5 minutes folow sign to Niederstotzingen. Price guide: Double/twin Dm290; maisonette Dm390.

EUROPEAN CASTLE HOTELS & RESTAURANTS

BURGHOTEL AUF SCHÖNBURG

D-55430 OBERWESEL/RHEIN, GERMANY
TEL: 49 67 44 93 930 FAX: 49 67 44 16 13

High up on the Schönburg, a hill overlooking the Rhine, close to where the Lorelei used to lure sailors onto the rocks, there is a romantic castle, built in the 10th century. Behind its ramparts and towers is an intimate and élite hotel. Many of the original features, the stone walls and pillars, archways and old beams have been carefully restored so that history and luxurious comfort are both in evidence. Outside, vineyards slope down to the river and ivy clings to the castle walls. The bedrooms are enchanting with fairytale drapery over the beds, lovely traditional furniture, and big bowls of fruit and flowers. The bathrooms are modern and quite opulent. In the evenings guests gather for a Bellini in the magnificent salon with stone walls, a handsome fireplace, crossed swords and shelves of leatherbound books before dining on specialities of the Middle Rhine Valley or indulging themselves with the gourmet menu. Dinner is served either in the Knights' Dining Room or on the Rhine terrace with its spectacular view of the river. Prestigious wines are listed. This is a marvellous base for exploring this part of Germany. **Directions:** Take the Oberwesel exit off the A61. Once in the town take a right turn at the Schönberg sign and then follow hotel signs up the hill. Price guide: Single 110–135Dm; double/twin 240–320Dm; suites 340–360Dm.

HOTEL EISENHUT

HERRNGASSE 3-7, D-91541, ROTHENBURG OB DER TAUBER, GERMANY
TEL: 49 9861 7050 FAX: 49 9861 70545

Rothenburg is an unspoilt medieval town standing on the River Tauber. It is surrounded by the original city walls and in the centre stands the Hotel Eisenhut, created from three adjacent 14th century town houses. The hotel has a superb portico entrance and, inside, gleaming suits of armour, relics of the imperial armies. Jewel coloured rugs on the stone floors, superb antiques, salons with open fireplaces, tapestries, splendid carved statues and handsome chairs add to the historic ambience. The bedrooms are luxurious and spacious with delightful flowered bedcovers and big gilt mirrors adding to their charm. Modern bathrooms provide those extra comforts that all travellers expect today. Delicious cocktails are sipped to soft music in the inviting bar. The sophisticated international menu offers local specialities. The cellar holds fine German wines in addition to Burgundies and Bordeaux. Guests relax in the beer garden or on the terrace overlooking the garden with its streams and colourful plants. Tennis and golf are accessible. Exploring the town is fascinating. **Directions:** Leave A7 at Rothenburg exit, and reaching the town centre Marktplatz watch for signs to hotel. Price guide: Single 155Dm–225Dm; double/twin 195Dm–380Dm; suites 520Dm–640Dm.

JAGDSCHLOSS NIEDERWALD

AUF DEM NIEDERWALD 1, D–65385 RÜDESHEIM AM RHEIN
TEL: 49 67 22 1004 FAX: 49 67 22 47970

The philosophy of this enchanting hotel, a former royal hunting lodge surrounded by woodland and well kept gardens, is 'pure enjoyment' created by the informal ambience, while making each arrival feel like an important guest. The decor is not elaborate, and its simplicity combined with rustic furniture encourages guests to relax. The bedrooms are charming and sleepers awake to a generous buffet breakfast. Guests have a choice of eating-places – the Park Restaurant where guests eat under ancient plane trees, the Green Salon which is perfect for private celebrations or the handsome Panorama Restaurant which often enhances its imaginative menu with special items such as a Lobster Festival! The cellar contains many fine wines, most from local vineyards. The hotel has an indoor pool, sauna and solarium, tennis courts, jogging and rambling trails through the woods, while less energetic visitors can visit the local cellars and the Eberbach Monastery where wine courses are held. Historic venues and cultural pursuits are all within reach, and boat trips down the Rhine can be organised. **Directions:** Leave the A6 at Wiesbaden, taking B42 for Rüdesheim then follow signs to Niederwalddenkmal then take road to Jagdschloss. There is a car ferry down the Rhine and a heliport at the hotel. Price guide: Single Dm145–Dm185; double/twin Dm210–Dm280; suite Dm290–Dm360.

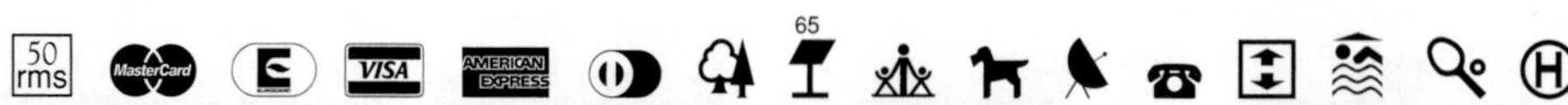

PARKHOTEL SCHLANGENBAD

RHEINGAUER STRASSE 47, D-65388 SCHLANGENBAD, GERMANY
TEL: 49 61 29 420 FAX: 49 61 29 41 420

Schlangenbad is a village on the outskirts of the Rhine-Taunus Nature Park, and the Park Hotel stands in lovely, peaceful countryside. It is a haven for many guests needing revitalisation, and ideal for conferences. The entrance is spacious and impressive, with archways and marble columns. The elegant salon has a long white terrace and below is a large courtyard for alfresco living. The bedrooms are delightful, the curtains and covers in beautiful materials and many lead onto a balcony. In the sophisticated piano bar wonderful cocktails will be concocted by the barman, non-alchoholic drinks for those guests who prefer them. Menus in the glittering Les Therms restaurant are hedonistic yet health-conscious. Many German wines are listed and occasionally a wine seminar is held, followed by a feast. Conference facilities are magnificent, with a big theatre for presentation. State-of-the-art equipment is available in all rooms in this complex. The hotel has a big pool, a gymnasium where exercise classes are organised and a beauty salon. The energetic ride mountain bikes or follow the jogging trail. Golf, tennis, horse riding and shooting are other sports in the neighbourhood. **Directions:** The B260 from Martinsthal leads to Schlangenbad. Price guide: Single Dm180–Dm215; double/twin Dm270–Dm340; suites Dm360–Dm500.

Hotel Burg Wassenberg

KIRCHSTRASSE 17, D–41849 WASSENBERG
TEL: 49 2432 9490 FAX: 49 2432 949100 E-MAIL: burgwassenberg@at-online.de

This delightful small castle, carefully renovated so that modernisation does not intrude into history, is at the top of a little hill, looking down on to the town of Wassenberg, about 20 miles north of Aachen. The interior reflects its past, with coats of armour, mullioned windows, antiques, wrought-iron candelabra and log fires. A sitting room is over the gateway but now there are no invaders to watch for, only new arrivals! These might be delegates coming to use the excellent conference facilities. The bedrooms are delightful, with rustic furniture and modern amenities. There is efficient room service, and one room has easy access for those with mobility problems. This is ideal for guests who appreciate fine food and drink. Exotic cocktails can be prepared before dinner, perhaps enjoyed by the big open fire, before a feast of beautifully presented dishes accompanied by the best wines. In summer barbecues on the balcony are sumptuous. There is a fitness and health centre, and tennis and golf are a short distance away. Crossing the border into Holland is an interesting excursion. **Directions:** Leave the A46 at the Erkelenz-Sud exit,turning left 3 times and yet again in Wassenberg, take the Burgauffahrt im Kreisverkehr, looking for signs to the hotel. Price guide: Single: Dm95–Dm245; double/twin Dm200–Dm295; suite Dm395.

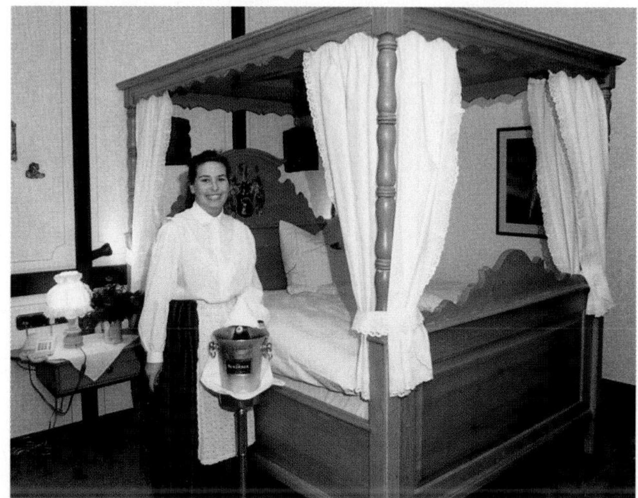

SCHWEIZER STUBEN

D–97877 WERTHEIM – BETTINGEN

TEL: 49 93 42 3070 FAX: 49 93 42 307155 E-MAIL: stuben@relaischateaux.fr

This modern hotel complex, beautifully situated in the Main valley, combines old world charm with contemporary architecture. The bedrooms are in four houses, the Hotel itself, the Villa and the two Landhauses. They are extremely spacious and many have balconies. Pine furniture and floral prints provide a light yet warm ambience. The suites are magnificent. There are two important reasons to visit the Schweizer Stuben, and food is one of them. It is the home of Fritz Schilling, one of Europe's leading chefs specialising in Provençal cuisine. He also ensures that fine wines are available to accompany not only his own brilliant cooking, but also that of the chefs in the Italian and Swiss restaurants found in this gastronomic haven. Sport is the other dominant feature of the hotel, especially tennis as there are six outdoor courts, indoor courts and excellent teaching available. There are golf practice facilities, indoor and outdoor pools and a marvellous beauty salon for total relaxation. Visitors explore the lovely countryside on bicycles or enjoy the flower-filled meadows from the hotel's horse-drawn carriage. The river, castles, lakes and local vineyards are alternative focal points. A member of Relais et Chateaux. **Directions:** From Frankfurt leave A3 at exit "Wertheim-Lengfurt" turning left onto L2310, then right following signs to the Tennis-Hotel. Price guide: Single Dm240–Dm400; double/twin Dm145–Dm225pp; appartment Dm260pp; suite Dm315–Dm625pp.

Greece

The country's enduring attraction is its archaeological sites – those who travel through Greece journey not only through the landscape but also through time, witnessing the legacy of Europe's greatest ages – the Mycenaean, Minoan, classical, Hellenistic and Byzantine.

You cannot wander far in Greece without stumbling across a broken column, a crumbling bastion or a tiny Byzantine church, each perhaps neglected and forgotten but still retaining an aura of former glory.

Greece is much more than beaches and ancient monuments. Its culture is a unique blend of West and East, the latter influence, inherited from the long period of Ottoman rule and apparent in its food, music and traditions. The mountainous countryside is a walker's paradise criss-crossed by age-old donkey tracks leading to stunning vistas.

Most of the country is moutainous. The Pindos Mountains in Epiros are the southern extension of the Dinaric Alps, which run the length of former Yugoslavia. The range continues down through central Greece and the Peloponnese, and re-emerges in the mountains of Crete. Crete like other Greek Islands is heavenly for summer holidays.

The variety of flora is unrivalled in Europe. The wild flowers are spectacular. Today there are fewer animals in the wild. The brown bear, Europe's largest mammal, survives in very small numbers in the Pindos Mountains, as does the grey wolf. Lake Mikri Prespa in Macedonia has the richest colony of fish eating birds in Europe, while the Dadia Forest Reserve in Thrace numbers such majestic birds as the golden eagle and the giant black vulture among its residents.

The magnetism of Greece is also due to less tangible attributes – the dazzling clarity of the light, the floral aromas which permeate the air, the spirit of every place – for there is hardly a grove, mountain or stream which is not sacred to a deity, and the ghosts of the past still linger. And then again, many visitors come to Greece simply to get away from it all and relax in one of Europe's friendliest and safest countries.

ANDROMEDA

22, TIMOLEONTOS VASSOU STR, GR–115 21 ATHENS
TEL: 30 1 64 37302/4 FAX: 30 1 64 66361

Although named after the mythical Andromeda, who married Perseus after he had rescued her from a sea monster, this is an exclusive new world hotel in the heart of modern Athens, close to the business community. The 20th century interior is softened by lovely Persian rugs. Stylish contemporary furniture, unique art pieces commissioned from famous designers and inspired stucco work from Venice together give arrivals a unique yet warm welcome. By contrast, the penthouse suites, an apartment for long–staying business guests and the delightful bedrooms, decorated in restful colours, have handmade traditional furniture. The bathrooms are exciting with crystal and stainless steel abounding. The bar is at one end of The White Elephant restaurant which seats only 35 people for exotic Oriental specialities. Fine wines are listed. Andromeda has excellent meeting and communication facilities. The conventional board room and the larger Oasis room interlink and quickly transform into private dining rooms. The hotel is close to the National Gallery, museums and the new concert hall. Tours of the Acropolis can be arranged. Exploring the port of Piraeus is also fascinating. **Directions:** The hotel is off Vassilisis Sofias Avenue, next to the American Embassy. Price Guide: Single US$190–$310, double US$210–$325; suite US$290–$460

150

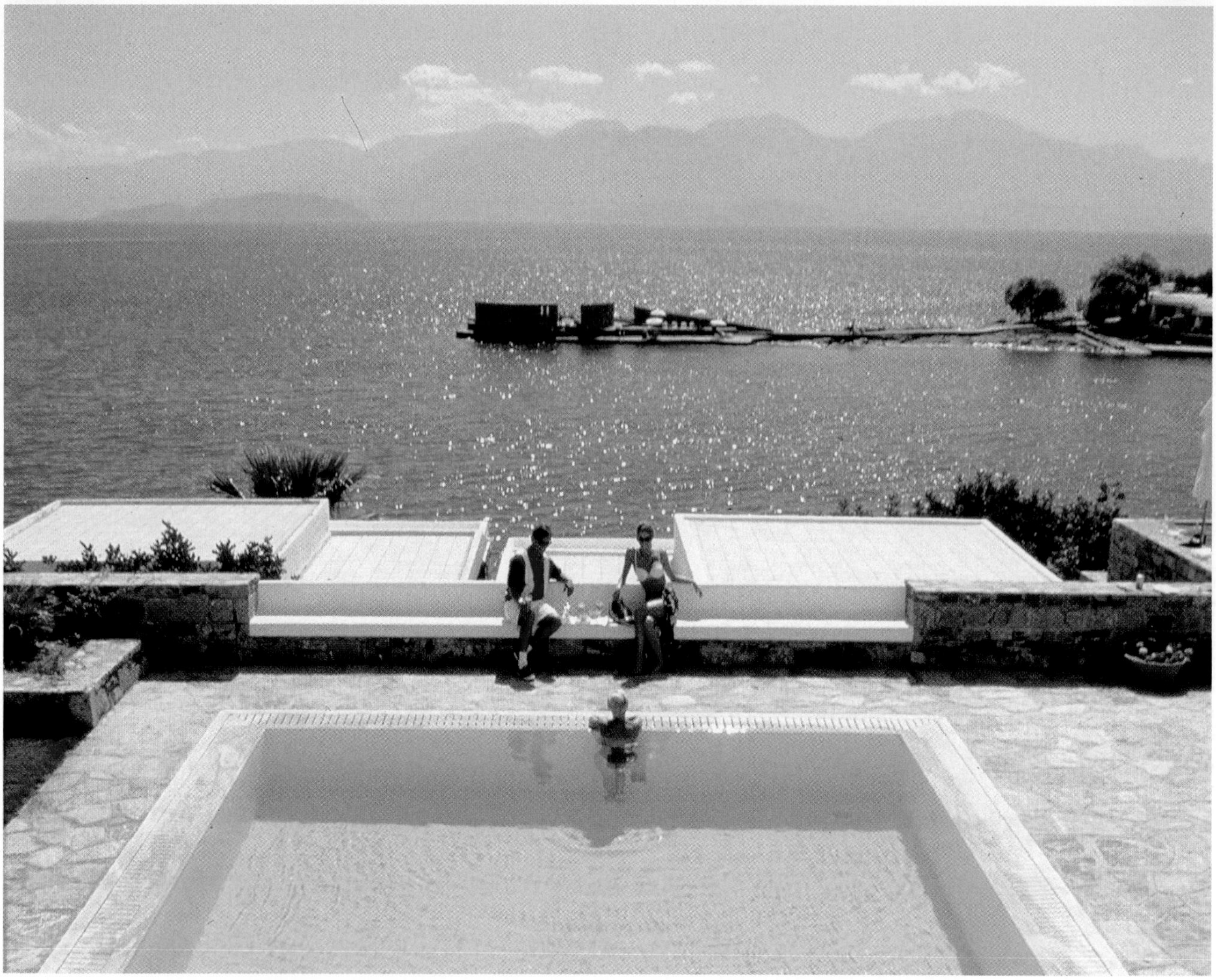

PrimaHotels

ELOUNDA BAY PALACE

721 00 AGHIOS NIKOLAOS, CRETE, GR–72100, GREECE
TEL: 30 841 41502 FAX: 30 841 41783

Crete is an island of legends, and this splendid hotel, its white buildings close to the sparkling blue waters of Mirabello Bay and set against a background of verdant forests, is fast becoming a legend in itself. Guests either stay in the hotel or in bungalows in the extensive gardens. All bedrooms are air-conditioned, have marble bathrooms and gorgeous views. The design and decorations reflect the region – cool tiled floors, colourful fabrics – very inviting! Guests relax in the stylish lounges or on the colourful terraces, watching the shimmering water. Children have their own supervised activities, games rooms and pool. Thirst-quenching drinks are served at the Poseidon poolside bar or the Aeolous beach bar, and exotic cocktails are shaken in the Erato Piano Bar far into the night. Brilliant buffet breakfasts and lunches are offered in the traditional Aretousa Restaurant, also five-course dinners. The joyous sea-front Ariadne restaurant serves local specialities, has barbecues, fish evenings and Greek nights with folk dancing. The Palace has a private beach, several pools, a water sports centre and floodlit tennis courts A schooner makes expeditons to other islands; Crete has to be explored. Golf can be arranged. Directions: The hotel is 45 minutes drive from the airport outside Heraklion, signed from Aghios Nikolaos. Price guide: Single ; double/twin ; suites .

196 rms 450

ELOUNDA BEACH

GR–72100 AGHIOS NIKOLAOS, CRETE, GREECE
TEL: 30 841 41 412/3 FAX: 30 841 41 375

An idyllic modern hotel complex on the North East coast of this beautiful island which is so steeped in history, Elounda Beach is surrounded by its own verdant estate and clear blue water. It is a sophisticated playground, especially for those who enjoy aquatic sports. Apart from the main hotel building, guests can stay in one of the many private villas on the water's edge or the famous bungalow suites with private swimming pool. A variety of restaurants meet every taste – the splendid Artemis restaurant for gourmet meals, the à la carte Restaurant Dionyssos for dinner, the Argonaut Restaurant for light meals and Italian tastes for dinner while the Kafenion offers Cretan specialities. Guests mingle in the piano bar, relax by the pool bar and enjoy the whole day at the unique Veghera bar in the middle of the sea. For early hours entertainment dance in the Olous nightclub. Children have their own activities while their parents enjoy tennis, a fitness centre, mini-golf and the famed water sport centre for Scuba diving, para-sailing, water ski-ing and sailing. Others may enjoy a leisurely cruise on the hotel schooner, or exploring nearby Aghios Nikolaos and local fishing villages. For a free video tape kindly fax number above. **Directions**: Elounda Beach is 45 minutes from Heraklion International Airport. Price guide: Single from 36,000Dr; double/twin from 46,000Dr; suite from 92,000Dr.

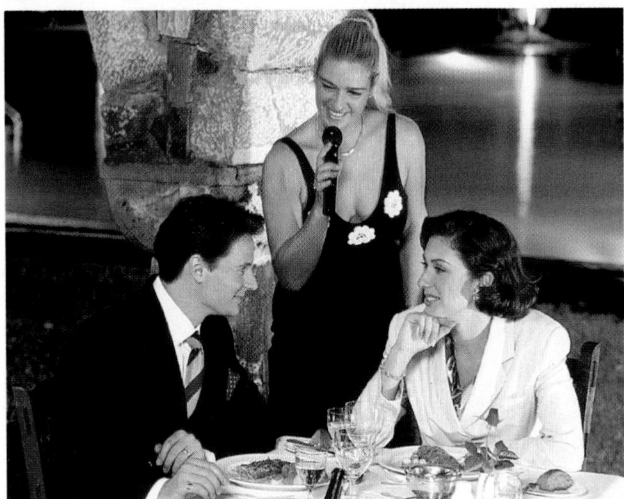

Hungary

What Hungary lacks in size, it makes up for in music, food, architecture, beauty and charm. Western Hungary is dominated by the largest lake in central Europe. Lake Balaton. Its shores are lined with Baroque villages, relaxing spas, magnificent vineyards, and shaded garden restaurants serving the catch of the day, as sailing yachts and ferryboats cut patterns on the surface of the water.

In Eastern Hungary, the Great Plain offers visitors a chance to explore the folklore and customs of the people. It is an area of spicy food, strong wine, and proud horsemen. The unspoilt towns of the provincial areas are rich in history and culture.

Hungarians are known for their hospitality and love of talking to visitors, although their strange Magyar language may be a problem. Today, however, everyone seems to be learning English, especially the young. But what all Hungarians share is a deep love of music from Budapest's famous opera and operetta to its annual spring music festival and the serenades of gypsy violinists during evening meals.

Hungary's capital, Budapest unites the colourful hills of Buda and the wide Parisian boulevards of Pest. It is the cultural, political, intellectual and commercial heart of Hungary – 20% of the country's population live there on the banks of the massive Danube.

Much of the charm of a visit to Budapest lies in unexpected sights of wonderful art nouveau buildings, many of which despite World War II splendidly and defiantly survive.

The city too has many thermal spa baths that attract health-seekers and recreational bathers – locals and tourists alike – wanting to soak in the relaxing waters. You should try some of the many massages and other therapeutic pleasures for yourself. They were started here by the Romans and carried on by the Turks. It's your turn now!

Danubius Hotel Gellért

ST. GELLÉRT TÉR 1, H-1111 BUDAPEST, HUNGARY
TEL: 36 1 185 2200 FAX: 36 1 166 6631

Historically this is one of the 'grand' hotels of Europe and with many businessmen and travellers coming again to Budapest, it is ready to regain this accolade. A founder member of Danubius Hotels, The Gellért is in one of the most beautiful parts of the city, the central district in Buda, with the River Danube on one side and a green hill on the other. The style of the interior is art nouveau, with high glass domed ceilings and ornate ironwork. The furnishings are formal, of traditional Central European design. There are many single bedrooms in addition to double rooms and delightful suites, some overlooking the Danube, others Gellért Hill. The hotel has retained its gastronomic reputation, won by the legendary Gundel, offering Hungarian specialities and international dishes, accompanied in the evening by gypsy music. The wines are mostly local led by the majestic Tokay, beloved by Louis XIV. The Coffee Shop is famous for its patisseries and ice-creams. Below the hill at the rear of the hotel are the renowned and popular Gellért baths, a variety of warm pools fed by natural spings with age-old healing properties. Budapest prides itself on its architecture, music, night-life, art galleries, its Danube and its beautiful women. **Directions:** Take an expensive taxi or the inexpensive minibus from the airport, or the hydrofoil down the Danube from Vienna. Price guide: Single 128Dm–158Dm; double/twin 250DM–326Dm.

Iceland

Once you've seen Iceland, you won't wonder about its popularity. Nowhere on earth are the forces of nature more evident than in Iceland, where glaciers, ice-caps, hot springs, geysers, active volcanoes, tundra, snow-capped peaks, vast lava deserts, waterfalls, craters and even Jules Verne's gateway to the centre of the earth all vie for the visitor's attention. On the high cliffs that characterise much of the coastline, there are some of the most densely populated sea bird colonies in the world and the lakes and marshes are teeming with waterfowl.

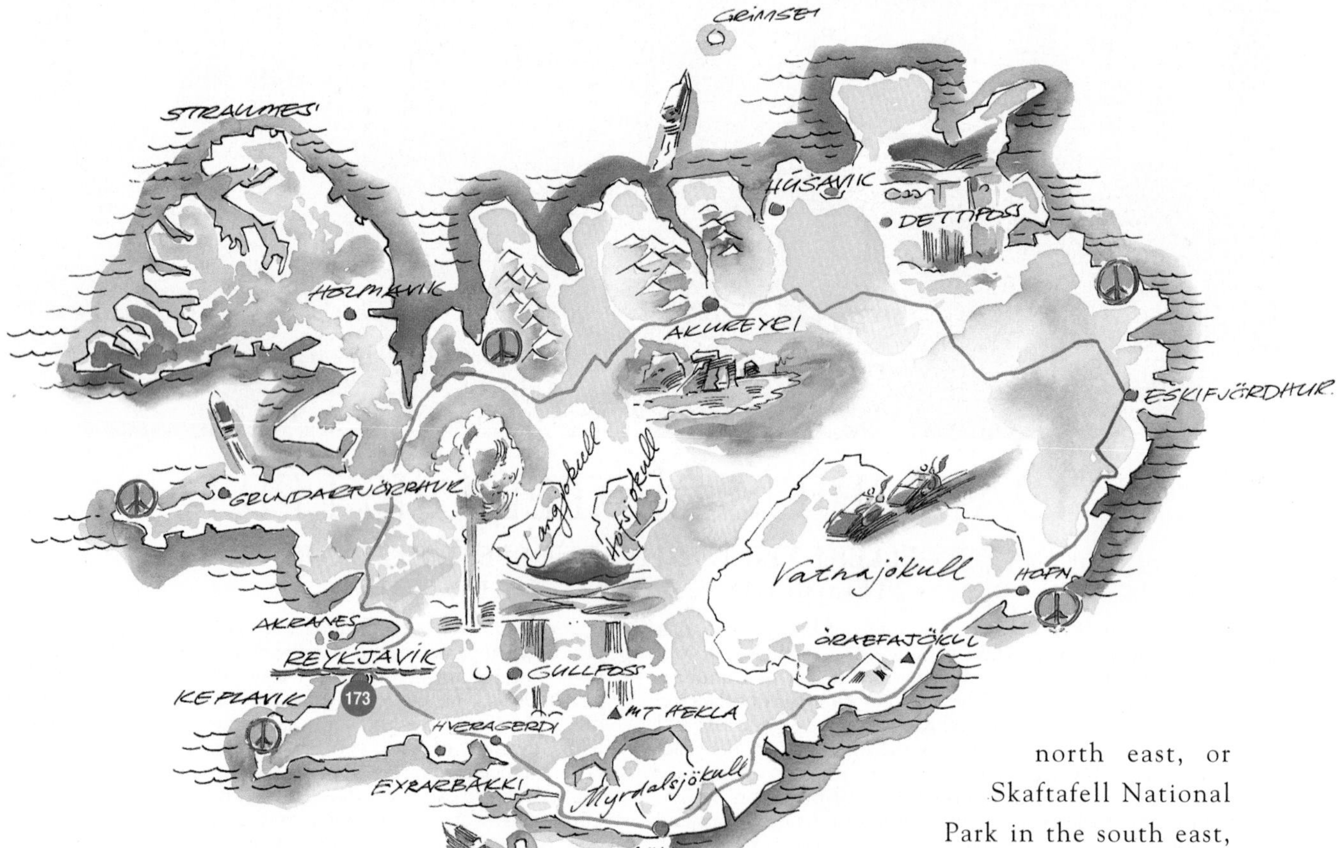

Superimposed on all this wilderness is a tough and independent society, descendants of the farmers and warriors who fled the tyranny of medieval Scandinavia to settle in a new and empty country.

Most visitors to Iceland agree that the best way to see the country is on foot, whether on an afternoon hike or a two week wilderness trek. If you have the proper equipment and maps, you'll find trekking opportunities unlimited. The best months for walking in the highlands are July and August.

Your travel to Iceland would be incomplete without visiting the Myvatn and Krafla in the north east, or Skaftafell National Park in the south east, known for its green moorlands and numerous waterfalls with their backdrop of rugged snowcapped peaks and glaciers, Lakagigar in south east Iceland – the beautiful and eerie crater responsible for the largest and most destructive volcanic eruption in Iceland's history. And the Gullfoss and Geysir in south central Iceland is the country's most visited tourist attraction. The two-tiered waterfall and Geysir contains the country's best examples of hot springs.

HOTEL BORG

PÓSTHÚSSTRŒTI 11,PO BOX 200,121 REYKJAVÍK, ICELAND
TEL: 354 551 14 40 FAX: 354 551 14 20

This exclusive hotel in the centre of Reykjavik, under new ownership in the last decade, has been renovated and discreetly modernised and it is now restored to its original Art Deco splendour. Each bedroom is personalised, some with dramatic colour schemes and clever reproductions of 1920s furniture. The suites are especially luxurious. Twentieth century accessories include CD players, and the reception has a stock of jazz and classical music. The lounges are decorated in warm colours and extremely comfortable. Matisse prints decorate the walls. The bar is an ideal rendezvous before entering the charming Palm Court Restaurant. The reasonably priced menu offers a wide range of dishes, including some Icelandic specialities and a fabulous seafood buffet. The wine list is good. Private rooms are available for corporate hospitality or special occasions, and these can also be used for conferences or meetings with presentation equipment provided. The concierge organises excursions and theatre tickets. The city has a beautiful cathedral and several art galleries. The main shopping street, Laugavegur, is only minutes walk away. **Directions:** Flybuses at the airport deliver guests to all the major hotels. The hotel has no parking facilities. Price guide: Single 11,600kr–12,900kr; double/twin 15,900kr; suites 23,900kr–25,900kr.

Italy

Italy has great art, historic cities, dazzling landscapes, delectable food and wines, and of course the many charms of the Italians themselves. Walk through the twisiting streets of Rome, Venice, or Florence, past ancient palaces and time honoured churches, admiring some of the world's greatest art in sumptuous settings and be seduced by the experience.

The whole of Italy is one vast attraction, but the triangle of its most visited cities – Rome, Florence and Venice – gives a good idea of the great variety to be found here. In Rome and Florence especially, you can feel the uninterrupted flow of the ages, from the classical era of the ancient Romans to the bustle and throb of contemporary life carried on in centuries old settings.

Antiquity is taken for granted in Rome, where successive ages have piled the present on top of the past – building, layering, and overlapping their own particular segments of Rome's 2,500 years of history to form a fascinating landscape. Most of the city's major sights are located in a fairly small area known as the 'centro'. At its heart lies ancient Rome where the Forum and Colosseum stand.

Venice by contrast seems suspended in time, the same today as it was when it held sway over the eastern Mediterranean and the Orient. Each of these cities presents a different aspect of the Italian character: the Baroque exuberance of Rome, Florence's serene stylishness and the sensuality of Venice.

From May through to September, key sights are very busy. Off season travel means there will be fewer people at the major sights, and you will find the experience much more pleasant during the crisp Spring mornings, or afternoons in late Autumn.

Making the most of your time in Italy doesn't mean rushing through it. Do what you really want to do, and if that means skipping a museum to sit at a pretty café, enjoying the sunshine and a cappuccino, you're getting into the Italian spirit. Art and life are to be enjoyed, and the Italians can show you how.

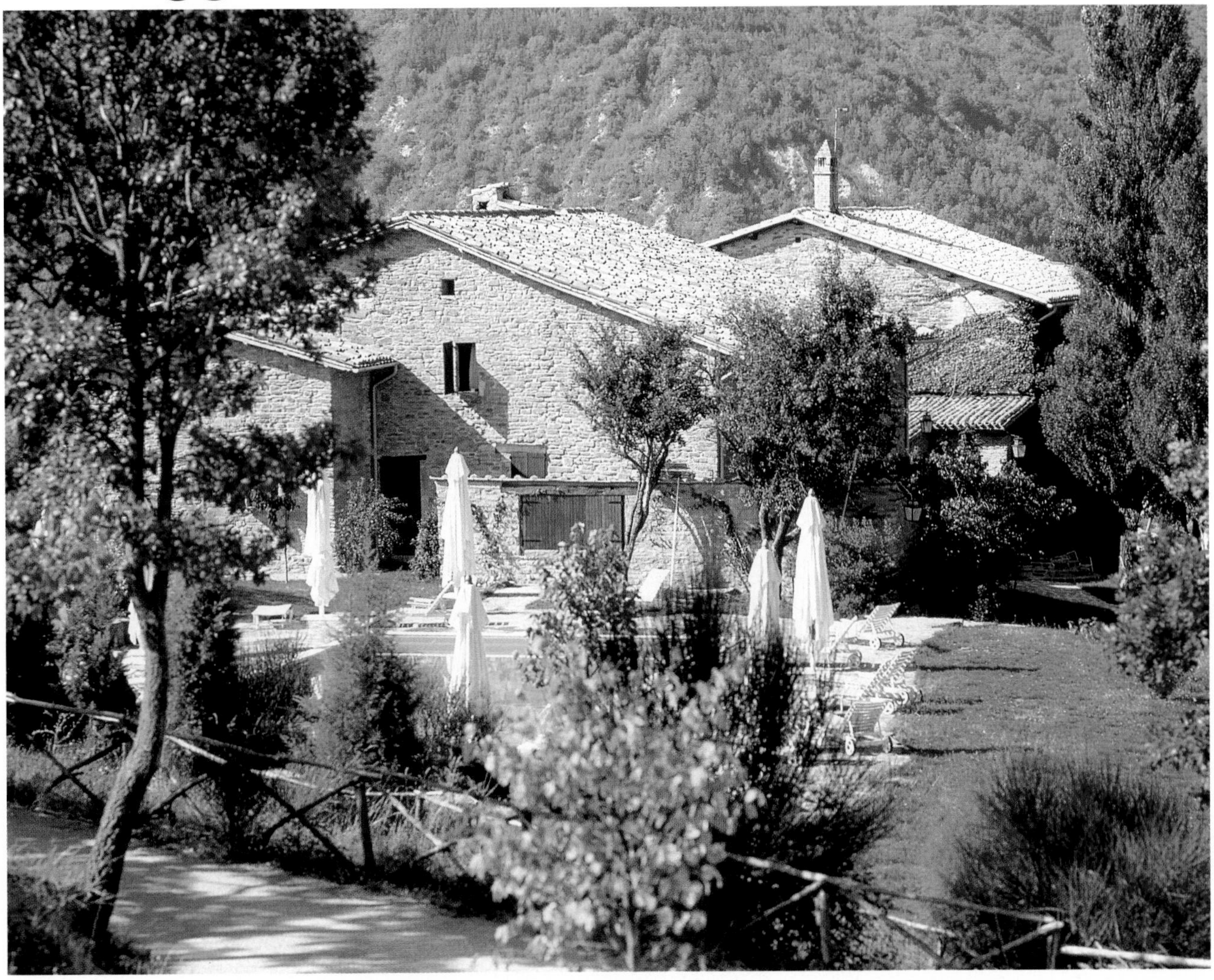

Le Silve Di Armenzano

I–06081 LOC. ARMENZANO, ASSISI (PG), ITALY
TEL: 39 75 801 90 00 FAX: 39 801 90 05

This historic small hotel dates back to before the birth of St Francis of Assisi, and looking across the beautiful Umbrian countryside, with its deer and horses, one understands how he became the patron saint of animals. Le Silva is 700 metres above sea level, built in local stone on a plateau at the foot of the Subasio mountains. The air is scented by olive groves. The charming bedrooms are pristine with country furniture, and there is a choice of bath or shower. The comfortable bar/sitting room looks out over the estate; a pianist plays at weekends. Umbrian cooking is delicious and at Le Silve the bread is baked, traditionally, in the fireplace. Local cheeses are special and wine is from the area. The restaurant is cool and rustic, the ancient beams and walls contributing to its charm. Eating al fresco is encouraged on warm days. The hotel also has four suites in the original farmhouse, and the Basaletto, a little further away, has seven interconnecting flats and its own pool. Activities include riding, swimming, tennis, minigolf and relaxing in the gardens. Excursions can be made to the Basilica of St. Francis in Assisi, Perugia and the wine growers in Orvieto **Directions:** On reaching Assissi from Perugia, take the S.75, turning right after 12 km towards Armenzano. Price guide: Single 140,000 lire; double/twin 280,000 lire. Apartment prices on request.

Hotel Parigi

LUNGOMARE ARGENTINA 18, 18012 BORDIGHERA (IM), ITALY
TEL: 39 184 261405 FAX: 39 184 260421

Bordighera has long been an elite resort, quieter than nearby San Remo, and the Hotel Parigi has attracted distinguished guests since it was built at the turn of the century, close to the beach, and surrounded by verdant countryside. Like many fin de siècle establishments it reflects the Art Nouveau era, with its graceful facade and interior decorations. Some of the bedrooms, all in soft colours, are in the two annexes, either overlooking the sea or the hillside, and there are facilities for disabled visitors. The bathrooms are designed to give pleasure as well as being functional. The salons are cool and restful, looking out onto the gardens, while the traditional bar has leather chairs and marble-topped tables. A full buffet breakfast is served in a light, flower-filled room, and the restaurant, with lovely striped awnings, overlooks the sea. Healthy Mediterranean cooking is the Chef's speciality, and there are wonderful displays of fresh fruit, fish and other produce – also fine Italian wines selected by the Sommelier!. The Parigi also has a Thalassorelax Centre, taking advantage of its proximity to the sea, and its private beach has cabins, umbrellas and waiter service. Visiting local castles, olive groves and vineyards are recommended diversions. **Directions:** A10, exit Bordighera, follow signs for seafront and hotel. Price guide: Single 140,000–190,000 lire; double/twin 120,000–250,000 lire; suites 460,000–550,000 lire.

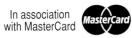

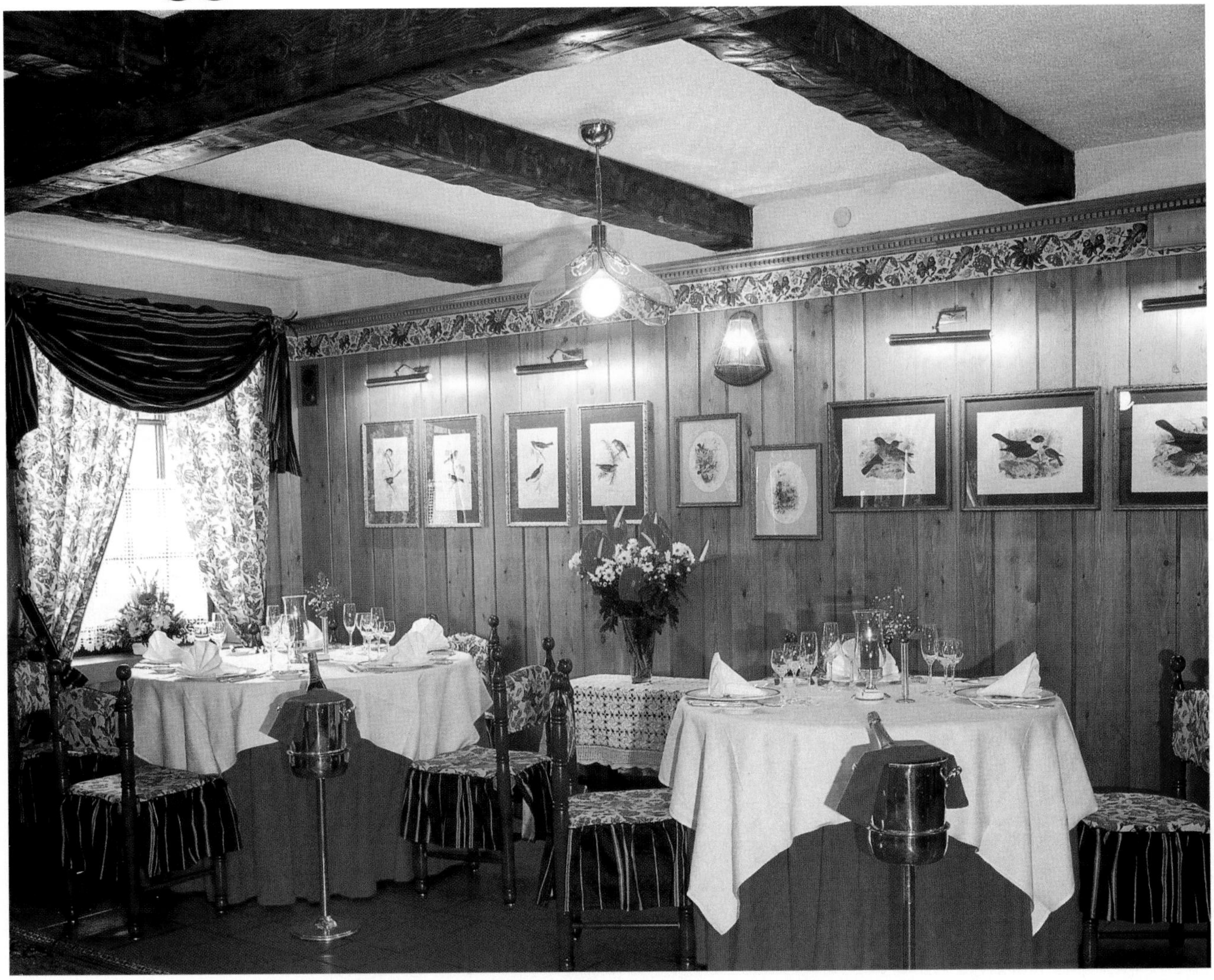

HOTEL BUCANEVE

PIAZZA JUMEAUX 10, 11021 BREUIL-CERVINIA (AO), ITALY
TEL: 39 166 949119/948386 FAX: 39 166 948308

Breuil Cervinia is an enchanting village high up in the Alps, at the foot of the awe-inspiring Matterhorn. It is a spectacular setting for this delightful chalet style hotel, be it summer or winter. Hotel Bucaneve has a warm ambience, created by the friendliness of the owners and their staff, open fires and the joyous colourful upholstery of the large, comfortable chairs in the living room. Big bowls of flowers are everywhere. The bedrooms are charming, with traditional furniture, and have gorgeous views over the mountains. Guests usually mingle in the convivial piano bar, but there is a quiet reading room. The rustic dining room is most attractive. Breakfast is a buffet and dinner is fabulous barbecue food, cooked on the open grill followed by luscious homemade puddings. Some superb wines are listed. Cervinia is a sophisticated winter sports resort and the hotel is close to the many ski-lifts and cable cars. After exhilarating days on the pistes, the sauna and Jacuzzi are welcome. In summer guests play golf on the highest 9-hole course in Europe, swim, play tennis and go hiking into the mountains. Afterwards they enjoy the inns, fondues and local night life. **Directions:** Leave A5 motorway at Saint Vincent/Chatillon, It is 25km to Breuil-Cervinia along a winding mountain road. The hotel has a garage and there is also a car-park. Price guide: Double/twin 120,000 lire–180,000 lire; suites 150,000 lire–230,000 lire. Per person half board.

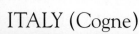

Romantik Hotel Miramonti

AVENUE CAVAGNET 31, 11012 COGNE (AO), ITALY
TEL: 39 165 74030 FAX: 39 165 749378

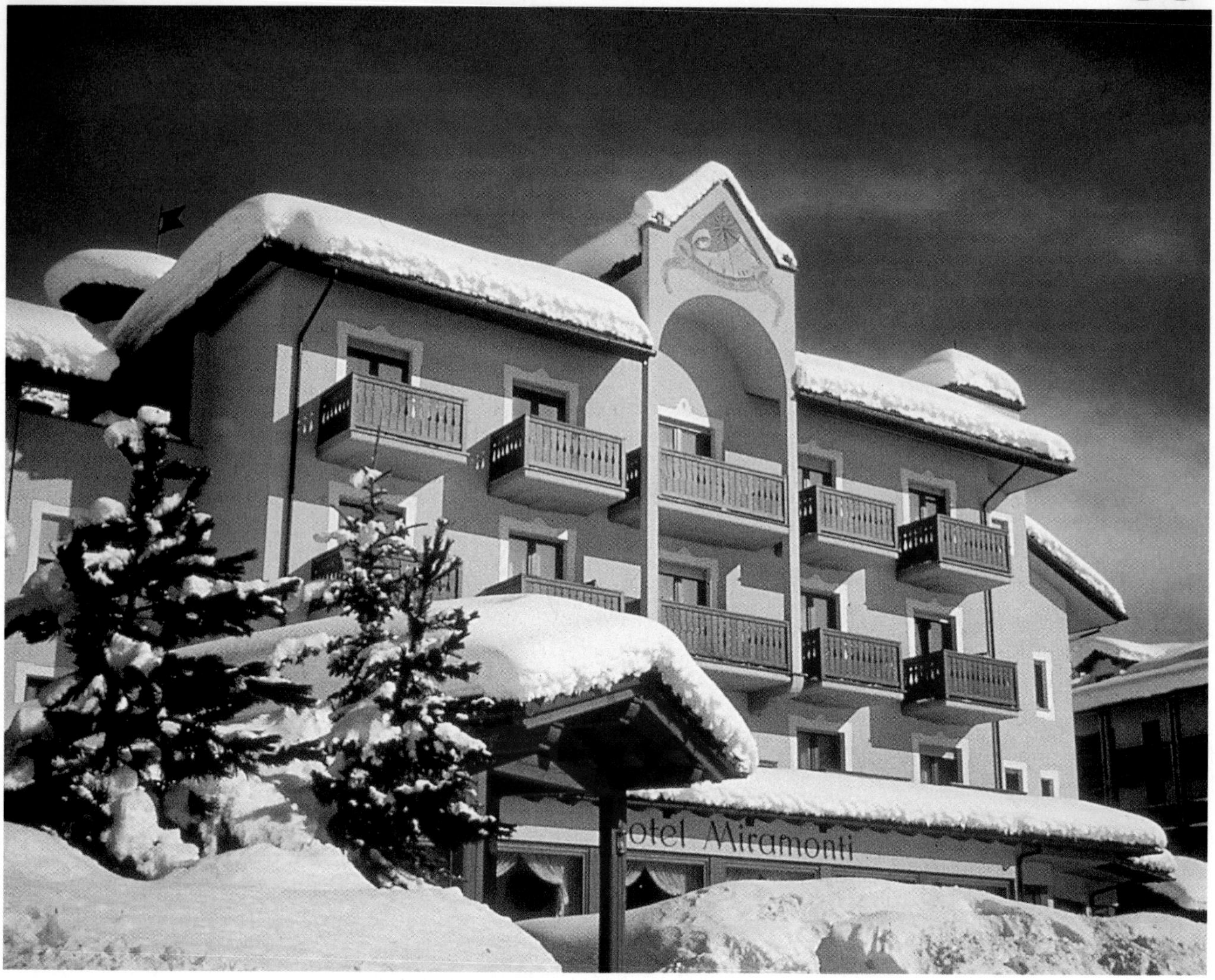

It is wonderful to visit this enchanting hotel at any time of the year. It is picturesque when the snows come and, being in the heart of the magnificent Parc National du Grand Paradis, the views are always spectacular. The ambience reflects the loving care given by three generations of the Gilliavod family to this unique hotel, for it is as if they welcome guests into their home. The interior is decorated in grand style, and visitors admire the wonderful panelling, handpainted with traditional designs. Period furniture and handsome family portraits adorn the salon walls. The bedrooms are delightful, light and airy with pretty fabrics, quite compact, and equipped with all modern necessities. Every room looks out over the glorious park to the soaring mountains, including the attractive bar where visitors mingle before entering the splendid restaurant where guests indulge themselves with appetizing dishes and good wines. The current conference facilities are to be extended to an entire complex, with all the latest technology available. Cross country ski-ing is the main winter sport, and sunbathing in the rooftop solarium or relaxing on the terraces admiring the view is a year-round recreation. Barbecues and tennis are part of the summer programme. **Directions:** Take the Aosta Ouest-St Pierre road in the direction of Aymarilles on SR47 to Cogne.

ALBERGO TERMINUS

LUNGO LARIO TRIESTE, 14–22100 COMO, ITALY
TEL: 39 31 329111 FAX: 39 31 302550

This elegant hotel, a fine example of turn-of-the-century architecture, is close to the Cathedral with a spectacular view across Lake Como. It has an impressive hall with tall pillars and a carved balustrade and all the spacious reception rooms have beautiful ceilings, graceful period furniture, antiques and handsome paintings. The charming, delightfully decorated, bedrooms have soundproof doors and windows and air conditioning. Some are designated non-smoking. The bathrooms are luxurious. The attractive café restaurant "Bar delle Terme" opens on to a lovely garden terrace. The atmosphere is charmingly intimate with places for only 20 guests seated at small tables where they can enjoy dinner, lunch or a snack al fresco while admiring the beautiful lakeside panorama from the very heart of Como. The hotel has its own gymnasium complemented by sauna and massage facilities. Having its own landing stage, boat trips on the Lake can be arranged. Away from the water Como is a fascinating town to explore. **Directions:** From Switzerland on A9 exit at Como Nord, take the Lungo Lario along the lake or from Milan turn off at the Como Sud exit, then Cattaneo Street, joining the Lecco Bergamo road towards the lake. Price guide: Single 180,000lire–210,000lire; double/twin 200,000lire– 300,000lire; suite 400,000lire–550,000lire.

PrimaHotels

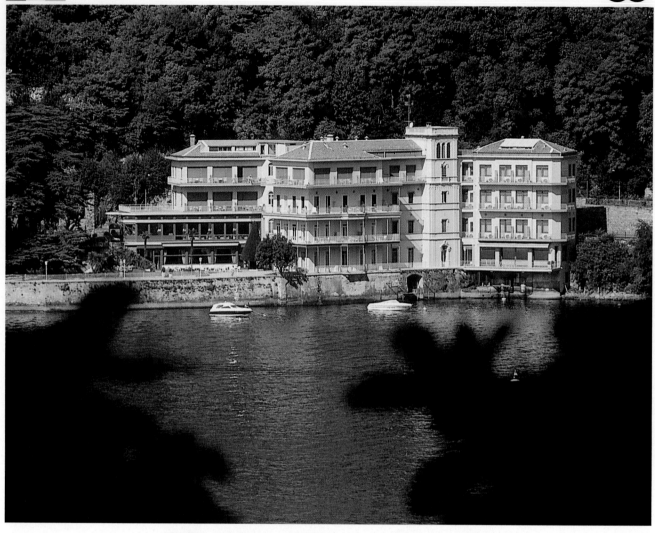

HOTEL VILLA FLORI

VIA CERNOBBIO, I–22100 COMO, ITALY
TEL: 39 31 573105 FAX: 39 31 570379

Built on the spot where General Garibaldi married his Guiseppina this traditional hotel is in a superb position on the edge of Lake Como, set against a background of its own verdant park, fragrant from the orange and lemon trees which thrive in the temperate climate. It has its own landing stage for guests arriving by yacht or motor boats! All the spacious bedrooms have period furniture and balconies overlooking the lake where lapping ripples romantically lull guests to sleep. 18th century splendour is reflected in the salons,with their draped windows, decorated ceilings and chandeliers. Outside, the sunny terraces are ideal for enjoying apéritifs. The Raimondi Restaurant has large picture windows so diners can appreciate the lovely gardens and waterfront. Aromatic Italian dishes are served and a wide selection of fine Italian wines is listed. Villa Flori is only a short drive from Milan and its excellent conference facilities and choice of meeting rooms, which transform into elegant private dining rooms, have made it a popular venue for corporate events. Guests enjoy boat trips on Lake Como and exploring the countryside with its ancient villas and museums. **Directions:** Leave A9 exit Como North direction Como. The hotel has good parking arrangements. Price Guide: Single 170,000Lire–240,000Lire; double 200,000Lire–300,000 Lire; suite 380,000lire–500,000lire.

RELAIS IL FALCONIERE

FRAZIONE SAN MARTINO, 52044 CORTONA (AR)
TEL: 39 575 612679 FAX: 39 575 612927

On a hilltop in the heart of Tuscany there is a a tiny piece of paradise – an exquisite 17th century villa standing in gardens fragrant from olive trees, cypress, herbs and flowers. The view over the countryside is breathtaking. Welcome to the Relais Il Falconiere! The owners, Silvia and Riccardo Baracchi, have lovingly transformed the villa into an elegant small hotel, cherishing the Tuscan traditions. The guest rooms – some in garden cottages – have hand-painted furniture, local lace, gorgeous fabrics and bathrooms with decorated tiles – a few with hydromassage baths. The small salon is a delight, designed with impeccable taste. In the old lemon-house, an inviting bar area adjoins the restaurant – a gorgeous room with an arched ceiling, frescoes on the ceiling, tables set with sparkling crystal and delicate porcelain. Silvia Baracchi is a passionate cook and prepares delicious Tuscan dishes, served with carefully selected wines. They are also splendid hosts, knowledgeable and fun. Sunbathing around the pool, relaxing in the gardens, eating and inbibing well, occasionally stirring to visit the cultural towns of Siena, Perugia and Cortona or exploring the Cells of St Francis – enjoy this idyllic lifestyle! **Directions:** Leave A1 at Valdichiana, following signs for Perugia, then take second exit for Cortona. Price guide: Double/twin 340,000 lire; junior suite 540,000 lire

Hotel Villa Paradiso Dell'Etna

VIA PER VIAGRANDE 37, 95030 SAN GIOVANNI LA PUNTA, ITALY
TEL: 39 95 7512409 FAX: 39 95 7413861

This grand hotel is in a magnificent position at the foot of Mount Etna. It was built in 1927 and immediately had an elite clientele of artists and well known personalitites of the era. Today, having been renovated and discreetly modernised it is a sophisticated and luxurious hotel. The facade is very elegant, with pillars, wrought iron balconies, and tall windows. The surrounding grounds are beautifully kept. and the sight of the volcano from the Roof Garden is breathtaking, The salons are exquisite with inlaid marble floors, trompe l'oeil and lovely plaster mouldings. Fine antiques, traditional comfortable seating, Art Deco stained glass, and cheeky cherubs add to the stylish ambience. The bedrooms are sumptuous, with lovely drapes in strong colours, Sicilian period furniture; the bathrooms are lavish. Some are designed for those with mobility difficulties. The American Bar is a handsome meeting place, a pianist playing at night,and La Pigna restaurant is famous for its superb interpretation of Sicilian and cosmopolitan dishes, with great wines from many Italian regions in the cellar. The villa has a lovely pool; tennis and the 'Riviera' are nearby and golf 40kms away. Excursions to Catania, Etna and Acreale can be arranged. **Directions:** A18, ext San Gregorio, then head for S.G. La Punta, and look for signs to the hotel. Price guide: 180,000 lire; double/twin 240,000 lire; suites 340,000 lire.

RIPAGRANDE HOTEL

VIA RIPAGRANDE 21, I–44100 FERRARA, ITALY
TEL: 39 532 765250 FAX: 39 532 764377 E-MAIL: ripa@mbox.4net.it

Ferrara is the perfect place to stay or to break a journey between Venice and Florence, for it's a lovely university town and the capital of the Dukes of Este. On the the banks of the Po in the old part of the town is this superbly restored XV century palace – the élite Ripagrande Hotel. The Renaissance interior is appropriate to the history of the hotel, and the entrance hall is spectacular with its marble staircase and pillars, wrought iron banisters and beamed ceiling. Cool, elegant salons and terraces encourage guests to relax while upstairs the spacious bedrooms are in excellent contemporary style, some having terraces cut into the slope of the tiled roofs. The furnishings are comfortable, in discreet colours. The attractive Riparestaurant serves many traditional Ferrarese specialities. Superb Italian wines are featured. Two enchanting courtyards make wonderful settings for banquets. The breakfast room offers an excellent buffet to start the day. perhaps before a seminar in the well-equipped meeting room. Bicycles are the popular way to explore this fascinating medieval town, with its castle, cathedral and the Diamond Palace. Sophisticated boutiques offer fine leather and high fashion. Internet: http://www.4net .com/business/ripa **Directions:** Ferrara is off the A13, 112 km from Venice and 150 km to Florence. Price guide: Single 230,000 lire; double/twin 300,000 lire; Junior suites 320,000–360,000 lire.

40 rms · 65

ROMANTIK HOTEL TURM

PIAZZA DELA CHIESA 9, FIÈ ALLO SCILIAR, BOLZANO, ITALY 39050
TEL: 39 471 725014 FAX: 39 471 725474

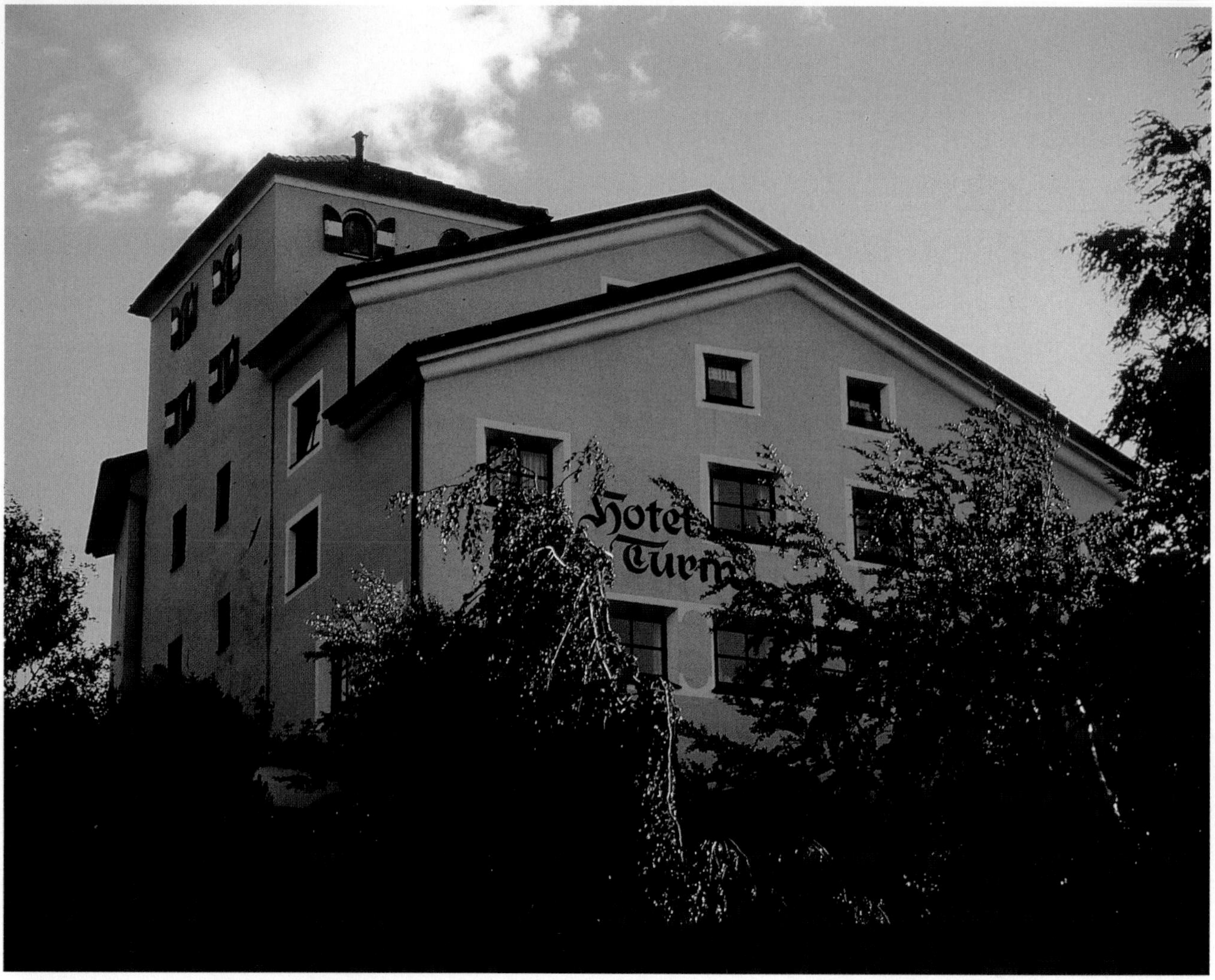

Parts of this splendid tower date back to the 13th century, and at one time it was a dungeon. However all traces of such inhospitality have disappeared, as today it is a delightful hotel offering a warm welcome to its guests. It stands quite high up, in the centre of a wildlife park. The bedrooms, some of them in the nearby Kraiterhaus, are charming, comfortable and pretty, with local fabrics and fine old carved pine furniture. The well-designed bathrooms are efficient. The hall is delightful with a big open stove and fascinating prints on the walls. The lounge is a typical Tyrolean Stube, with pine walls and rustic chairs. The convivial bar is similar. Walter the maitre supervises the handsome restaurant while Stephan, the chef and owner, demonstrates his skills in the kitchen. Aromatic variations of local specialities are served in great style, accompanied by fine wines. The Turm is close to good skiing and other winter sports. In summer it is an ideal centre for hiking, riding, golfing and exploring the nature reserve. Tennis and boating on the lakes can be arranged. The hotel also has a sybaritic indoor pool and spa area. Directions: A22, exit Bolzano North, towards Brennero, take left hand tunnel for Altoplan, finding the hotel near the village church. Price guide (per person): Rooms 90,000–157,000 lire.

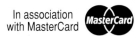

Hotel J&J

VIA MEZZO 20, 50121 FLORENCE, ITALY
TEL: 39 55 234 5005 FAX: 39 55 240 282

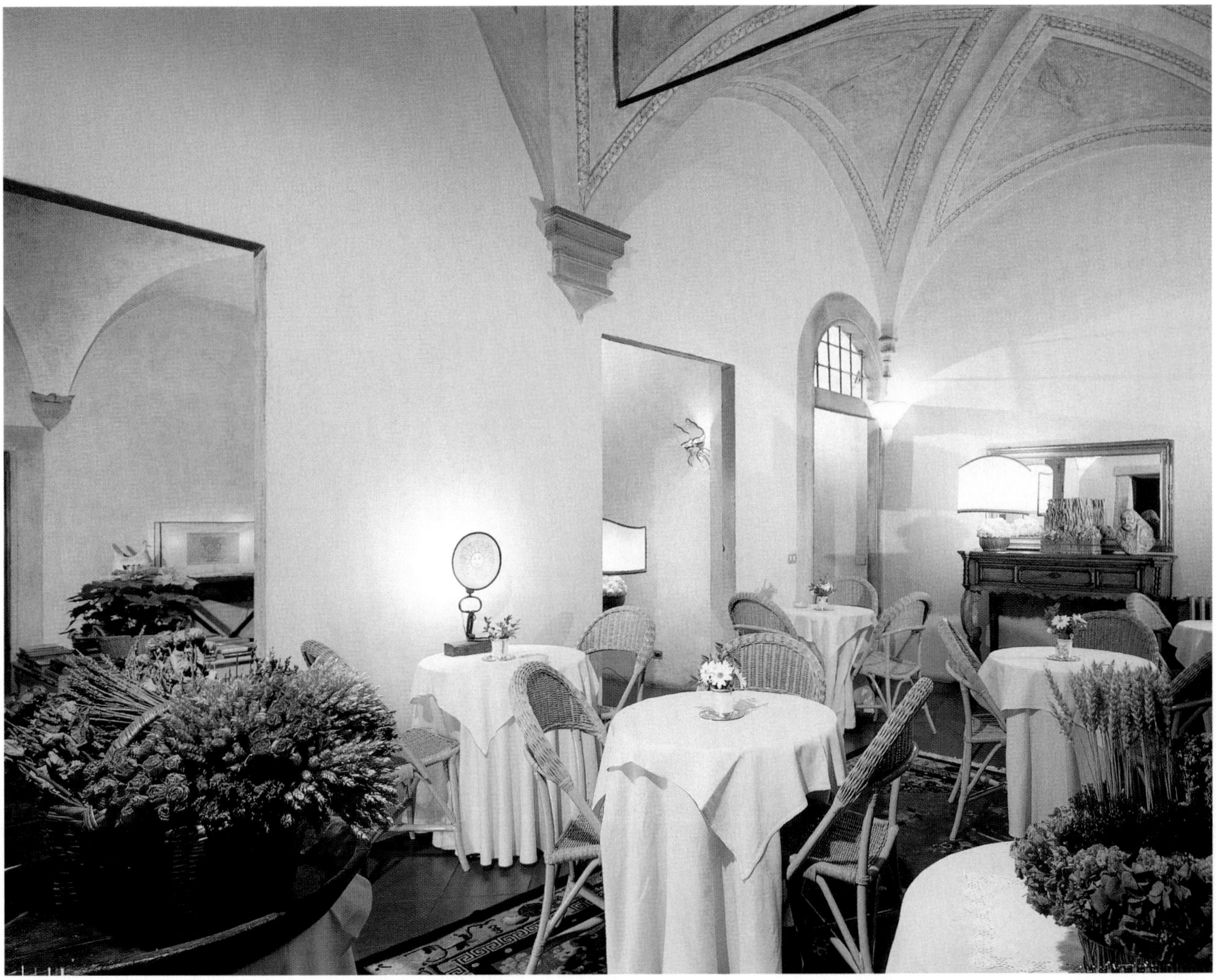

This is a veritable retreat for travellers, a charming transformation from a convent to a delightful small hotel. There is a wonderful tranquillity about Hotel J and J, far from the bustle of the commercial world, despite its location in the very heart of Florence. The bedrooms vary, each one having its individuality; some look out over the roof tops, others look down onto concealed courtyards. They are furnished with antiques and handwoven fabrics, extremely comfortable and the white bathrooms are well equipped. The lounge is very elegant and a small bar leads into a courtyard which is a pleasant spot for drinks in fine weather. There is no restaurant but the hotel staff will direct guests to interesting restaurants nearby. This is an ideal bases for exploring old Florence, the Renaissance Palace with its fine frescoes, graceful cloister and Doric columns being not far away and the Duomo only a short distance from there. The Baptistry, the Uffizi Gallery, the Medici chapels, the Opera House, so many museums and art galleries all make the days and evenings so busy. and the shops are magnificent when seeking a rest from culture. **Directions:** The hotel is located near Borgo Pinti close to the city centre. Car parking is provided. Price guide: Double/twin 350,000 lire–450,000 lire; suite 500,000 lire–600,000 lire.

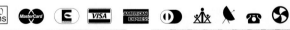

Residence Castello Di Gargonza

52048 MONTE SAN SAVINO – AREZZO, ITALY
TEL: 39 575 847021/22/23 FAX: 39 575 847054 E-MAIL: gargonza@teta.it

Gargonza is unique, a thirteenth century walled village which pays tribute to the principles of Tuscan country living. Today it is a wonderful retreat, up in the hills, offering an unsophisticated life distant from the twentieth century pressures. The Residence is reached up winding roads scented from the cypress trees and olive groves, and entered through the old Siena gate. This is not a traditional hotel, but a delightful array of ancient buildings modernised sufficiently to ensure guests are comfortable but simplicity is the keyword, not luxury. The ambience is magical, the houses built in old brick with tiled roofs, and it is so peaceful. The pristine apartments have contemporary furniture, and the bathrooms are modern. Visitors mingle in the salons, cool with tiled floors, and filled with delightful rustic antiques, or talk over a drink in the colourful gardens. The bar is a small, part of the La Torre di Gargonza restaurant just outside the walls, which serves aromatic Tuscan specialities and good Italian wine. The old olive press is a quiet place in which to read – or enjoy the occasional concert. The Castello has a swimming pool and cycling or walking are gentle pursuits while 'recharging the batteries'. Siena, Florence and Perugia are not far away. **Directions:** A1, exit Monte San Savino, following signs to Gargonza. Price guide: Single 140,000–160,000lire; double/ twin 170,000–190,000lire; suites 240,000–260,000lire.

HELLENIA YACHTING HOTEL

VIA JANNUZZO 41, 90835 GIARDINI NAXOS (ME) ITALY
TEL: 39 942 51737 FAX: 39 942 54310

The Hellenia Yachting Hotel is ideal for a seaside holiday, and new arrivals relax as soon as they see the soft pink, typically Sicilian, building so close to the beach – it has a happy ambience, definitely a place for enjoyment. Many of the cool, white bedrooms open onto a balcony or terrace, Curtains and covers are in vibrant colours and some of the bathrooms are in black marble. Children are very welcome and there is a baby sitting service available. The reception rooms are spacious, well-lit and comfortable; the hotel is particularly proud of its new conference rooms, also available for private celebrations. While much of the eating and drinking is al fresco on the terraces, the piano bar has its own aficianados. It is decorated in 'sea colours'and has friendly, efficient staff. The smart restaurant is spacious, with soft golden overtones. Local fish, wonderful salads and Sicilian specialities feature on the menu and many of the wines listed are Italian. There is also a pool-side bar and the private beach has its bar and restaurant, umbrellas and deck chairs. Wind-surfing, pedalboats and tennis are available. Taormina is fascinating to explore and has an antiques market the last weekend of each month. **Directions:** A18, Giardini Naxos exit, left following signs to Recamati, then hotel is signed. Price guide: Single 135,000–165,000 lire; double/twin 200,000–260,000 lire; suites 260,000–320,000 lire.

LA VILLAROSA

VIA GIACINTO GIGANTE, 5, 80077 PORTO D'ISCHIA (NAPOLI), ITALY
TEL: 39 81 99 13 16 FAX: 39 81 99 24 25

Ischia, 'The Green Island', is where the Phoenicians traded metals in an earlier millennium and mythology transformed volcanic activity into monsters. La Villarosa, an exquisite old farmhouse was converted in the 1950s into an elite and idyllic hotel, surrounded by a luxuriant garden. An ambience of country house living has been created by simple furnishings, lovely antiques and discreet decorations, all in impeccable taste. The salons are dedicated to pleasure. The cosy sitting-rooms are perfect for reading or letter-writing and the Piano-bar, where the barman creates exotic cocktails, leads onto the colourful thermal swimming pool area. The entrancing bedrooms, each uniquely designed, look out to the sea or over the botanical garden, a few having small balconies. Exclusive chalets are hidden among the foliage. The attractive dining rooms lead onto a romantic roof garden, and guests feast on Ischian dishes, fresh fish, pastas and delicious local wines. The thermal pool in the grounds, spa waters and supervised treatments in the clinic are highly recommended. The hotel boat visits the various bays and beache. Excursions can be made to Pompeii, Capri and the Amalfi coast. **Directions:** Ferry (75 mins) or hydrofoil (20 mins) from Naples. Price guide (per person per day): Single 100,000 lire–180,000 lire; double/twin 85,000 lire–165,000 lire.

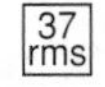

Hotel Villa Ottone

LOCALITÀ OTTONE, 1-57037 PORTOFERRAIO, ISOLA D'ELBA, ITALY
TEL: 39 565 933042 FAX: 39 565 933257

Arriving by ferry is the perfect way to appreciate the setting of this fabulous summer hotel on Elba, the island off Tuscany where Napoleon was first kept in exile. Villa Ottone, built in the 19th century, is a graceful white house on the edge of the blue Bay of Portoferraio. It is surrounded by exotic plants and verdant parkland. The entrance hall and salons are delightful, with cool tiled floors, glistening chandeliers and period furniture. The bar has an exquisite painted ceiling and elegant wrought iron gates lead into the restaurant. Many of the charming bedrooms are in the villa, but there are also bungalows scattered among the trees, and in the new hotel some have Jacuzzis. This is a hotel for out-door living, starting with breakfast on the terrace and ending the day relaxing in the verandah piano bar. Lunch is a gorgeous barbecue by the pool or you may have lunch at the enchanting restaurant. The menu includes aromatic Tuscan specialities and fish from the sea enjoyed with fragrant local wines. Guests appreciate sunbeds, towels, beach unbrellas, pedal-boats and all water sports on the private beach, tennis and a children's playground while golf is 3kms away. **Directions:** The hotel can be reached by ferry or taxi (Livorno 2hrs 50mins), Piombino (1hr). Villa Ottone is 11 km west of Portoferraio. Price guide (per person, half board): Double/twin 120,000 lire–230,000 lire.

GRAND HOTEL FASANO

VIA ZANARDELLI 160, I–25083 GARDONE RIVIERA (LAKE GARDA), ITALY
TEL: 39 365 290220 FAX: 39 365 290221 INTERNET: http://www.grand-hotel-fasano.it

This truly aristocratic hotel on the shores of Lake Garda has an art nouveau facade, flanked by palm trees. It stands in an extensive park filled with exotic foliage and beautiful, flowering plants. The reception area and salons are regal, with elegant period seating vying with fine antiques. Staff with the courtesy of yesteryear enhance the hotel's imperial heritage. All the bedrooms have a balcony overlooking the lake with its spectacular sunrises and sunsets. They are luxuriously furnished and decorated, and the well appointed bathrooms have either shower or bath. The cocktail bar is full of rich colour with dramatic wall hangings and plush chairs. An extravagant breakfast buffet is provided in the soft morning air overlooking the water and later in the day Italian specialities, tempting antipasto and salads and gourmet dishes are served either outside or in the grand restaurant. Romantic evenings under the stars, listening to soft music watching the lights on the waterfront are idyllic. Steamboat and hydrofoil trips, sailing, water-skiing, wind surfing and golf are close at hand. The hotel has its own pool and tennis court, and strolling through its park is very relaxing. **Directions:** Densenzano/Brescia – follow signs for Salò, then Gardona Riviera. Price guide (per person): Single 125,000 lire–280,000 lire; double/twin 95,000 lire–255,000 lire; suites 250,000 lire–350,000 lire.

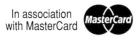

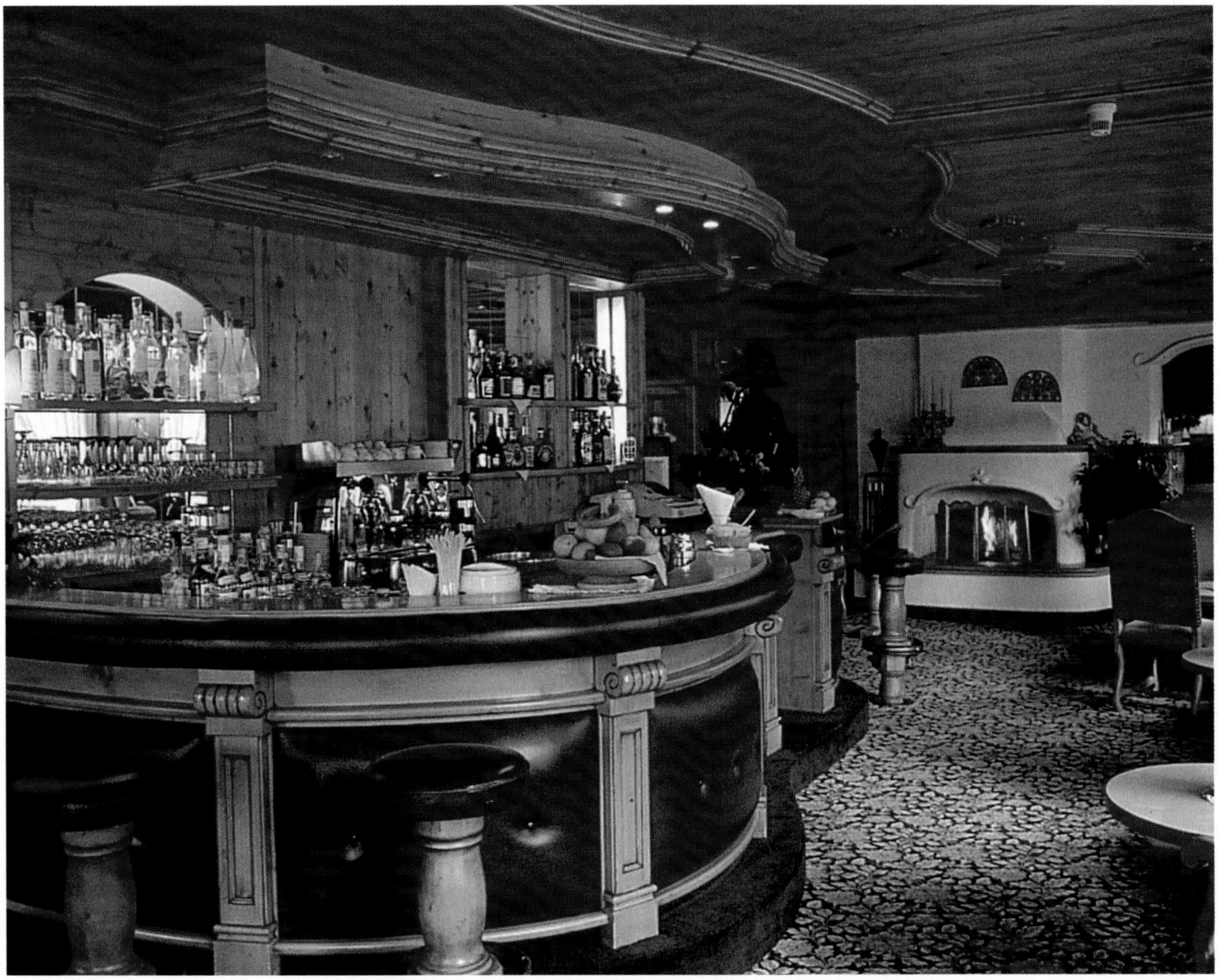

Hotel Lorenzetti

VIA DOLOMITI DI BRENTA, 119, I–38084 MADONNA DI CAMPIGLIO (TN) ITALY

TEL: 39 465 44 14 04 FAX: 39 465 44 06 44

This enchanting chalet-style hotel, with its flower-bedecked balconies, looking across the Brenta Chain, stands apart from the main ski-lifts and village centre, enabling guests to relax in peace! The interior is very elegant. The views over the mountains are spectacular. Three of the pleasant bedrooms have been designed for those with mobility problems. The suites are special, some having hydromassage. All have their own balconies. On sunny days, guests enjoy a drink on terrace and in the evening they congregate in the splendid bar before dining in style in the handsome restaurant which offers both international and delicious local dishes. The reading room is a quiet place to end the day. The hotel can host small conferences, having an ideal meeting room and modern presentation equipment. Winter sports enthusiasts appreciate the fine ski-ing and the ice rink. In summer residents stroll in the lovely gardens, walk in the mountains, play golf, tennis or fish close by while all year the fitness centre and games room are very popular. **Directions:** From Milan after 3 hours leave the motorway at Brescia Est, following signs for Madonna di Campiglio. The hotel has a heated garage for 20, and outside parking for a further 40 cars. Price guide per person (half board): Single 145,000 lire–260,000 lire; double/twin 120,000 lire–290,000 lire; suites 140,000 lire–330,000 lire.

ROMANTIK HOTEL VILLA CHETA ELITE

85041 MARATEA – LOC. ACQUAFREDDA (PZ) – ITALY
TEL: 39 973 878 134 FAX: 39 973 878 135

Many travellers never explore the beautiful southern tip of Italy, but those that do return again, especially if they are fortunate enough to stay at this lovely Liberty-style villa. It has been meticulously restored, and is a glorious sight, painted sienna and cream, with graceful balconies, black shutters and elegant mouldings. Acquafredda di Maratea is a fascinating small village on the coast, and just above it, the hotel looks out to the Mediterrean. The surrounding gardens are exquisite, filled with statues and urns, brilliant flowers, exotic trees and foliage, the air redolent with their perfume. The interior of this romantic villa reflects the Art Nouveau era, with its stained glass panels and Tiffany lamps. The bedrooms are pristine, and most have superb views. The traditional dining room has immaculate white lace tablecloths – but most days the climate is so balmy that guests prefer to take breakfast and dinner on the terrace, sipping good Italian wine under the stars and relishing the aromatic home-cooking. Communication may be a slight problem but big smiles say it all. Visitors enjoy the beach, just minutes away, go out in fishersmen's boats and explore the port, the Pollino National Park, grottos, and historical edifices. **Directions:** Leave A3 exit Lagoniglo Nord – Maratea, and follow signs to Safri – Maratea. Price guide: Double/twin 185,000–220,000 lire.

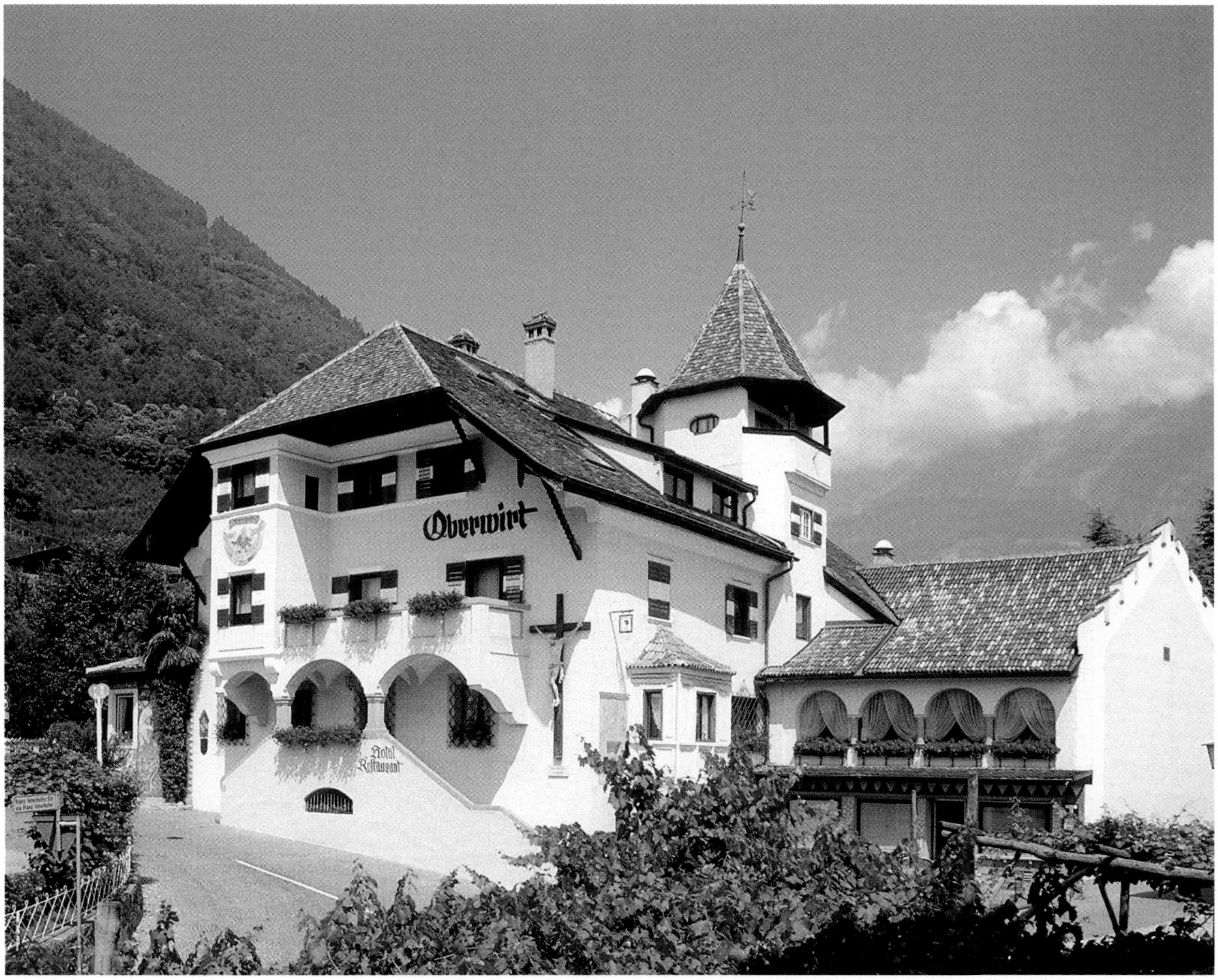

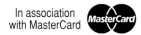

ROMANTIK HOTEL OBERWIRT

ST FELIXWEG 2, I-39020 MARLING/MERAN, ITALY
TEL: 39 473 22 20 20 FAX: 39 473 44 71 30

An inn offering hospitality since the 15th century, this hotel has been owned by the Waldner family since 1749. Part of it has an even longer history, the outdoor pool being built on an original Roman design. The traditional architecture has not been marred by modernisation. Window-boxes and shutters enhance the original tower and white walls set against a background of the majestic Dolomites. There are now 44 bedrooms, luxuriously appointed, with views across the valley to the mountains. The Tyrolean bar is very convivial, although on fine days guests may prefer to sip their apéritif on the flower-bedecked terrace, which is floodlit at night. The Waldners are proud of their elegant restaurant. The meals are exquisite and the carefully selected wines reasonably priced. When sunbathing by the Roman pool is not possible, guests appreciate the fitness centre, with its indoor heated pool, sauna, Jacuzzi and massage facilities. The hotel has a relationship with the Dolomite Golf Club reducing green fees for guests, also with the Riding Club of Meran. Five tennis courts, two indoor, with a coach available are 1km away. **Directions:** Leave the Innsbruck Verona road at Bozen Sud for Meran, then follow signs to Marling (3km). Price guide: Single 110,000 lire–130,000 lire; double/twin 110,000 lire–130,000 lire per person; suites 130,000 lire– 170,000 lire per person.

MUSEO ALBERGO ATELIER SUL MARE

VIA CESARE BATTISTI, CASTEL DI TUSA (ME), SICILY
TEL: 39 921 334 295 FAX: 39 921 334 283

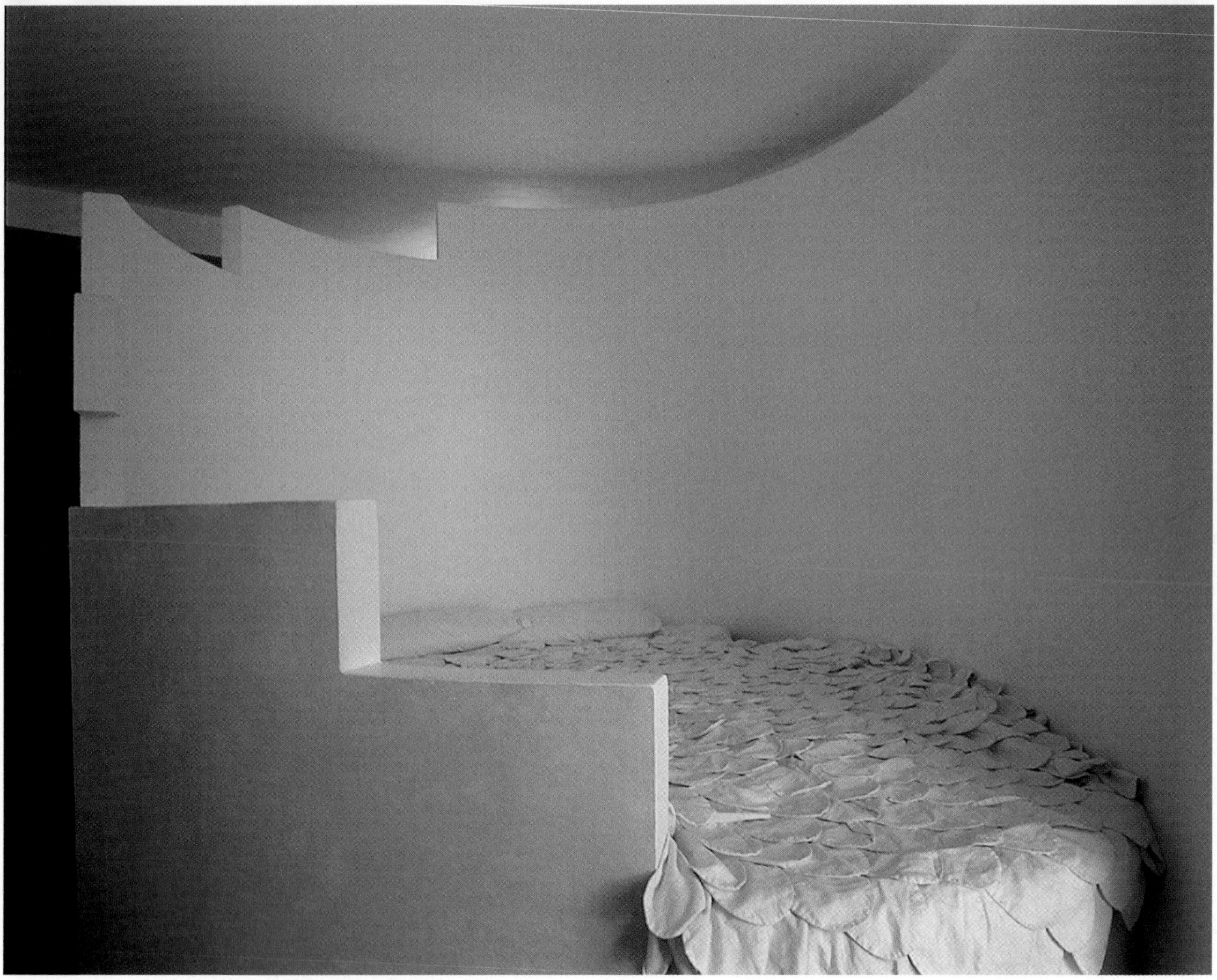

The coastline between Palermo and Messina is magnificent and in one of the many beautiful bays is the small holiday resort of Castel di Tusa. Contrasting with the traditional homes of its fishermen is a dazzling white unique hotel, the Museo Albergo Atelier sul Mare. The interior is exciting, truly avant garde. The reception area is filled with 20th century objets d'art and unusual sculptures and the bar-hall, where guests enjoy exotic cocktails, has videos playing work by the Fiumara d'Arte group. This merges into a relaxing drawing room. Each bedroom has been designed by different contemporary artists, contributing their own interpretation of serenity, some being simplistic, others reflecting imaginative philosophies. The walls of the big, light restaurant are covered in paintings, and here guests can enjoy the finest Sicilian food – marvellous fish, colourful vegetables and fragrant herbs. Delicious local wines are suggested. This is a place for living and breathing contemporary art – imbuing a philosophy that enriches the soul – taking a course in pottery, relaxing in the sun, learning from the artisans of San Stephans di Camastra, going out in the fishing boats. Internet: www.fiumararte.aessenet.com **Directions:** Leave Palermo, driving east, on A20 to Cefalu, then follow the coast road towards Messina. Price guide: Single 80,000 lire–140,000 lire; double/twin 60,000 lire–100,000 lire.

THE REGENCY

112 VIA ARIMONDI, I–20155 MILAN, ITALY
TEL: 39 2 39 21 60 21 FAX: 39 2 39 21 77 34

This 18th century residence has been transformed recently into an elegant hotel, ideal for those attending the Milan Fair and Exhibition Grounds, being just a few minutes' walk away. It is also only a few minutes by taxi from the city centre.The bedrooms – some designated non-smoking – have been very well designed, and clever use of colour plays an important part in their attraction. The marble bathrooms are contemporary, mostly having power showers rather than baths.Vibrant, beautiful fabrics add to the charm of the reception rooms, where the stylish furniture reflects the talents of Italian designers, and the bar has a warm ambience – enhanced by a big fire in the winter months. The hotel has good conference facilities, with well-equipped meeting rooms. Buffet breakfasts are served but other meals are not available. The management will direct guests to excellent restaurants close by. Milan has many historic buildings – its wonderful Opera House, the Duomo, the Brena Art Gallery to name but a few. For those touring Europe, Milan has good motorway access to Venice, Turin, the Italian Lakes and Switzerland.Directions: Leave the A4 at Certosa. Via Arimondi is just off the Piazza Firenza, close to Garibaldi Station. Parking is nearby. Price guide: 188,000 lire–235,000 lire, double/twin 290,000 lire–330,000 lire, suites 390,000 lire.

59 rms       50  

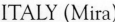

Villa Margherita

VIA NAZIONALE, 416/417, I-30030 MIRA (VENEZIA), ITALY
TEL: 39 41 42 65 800 FAX: 39 41 42 65 838

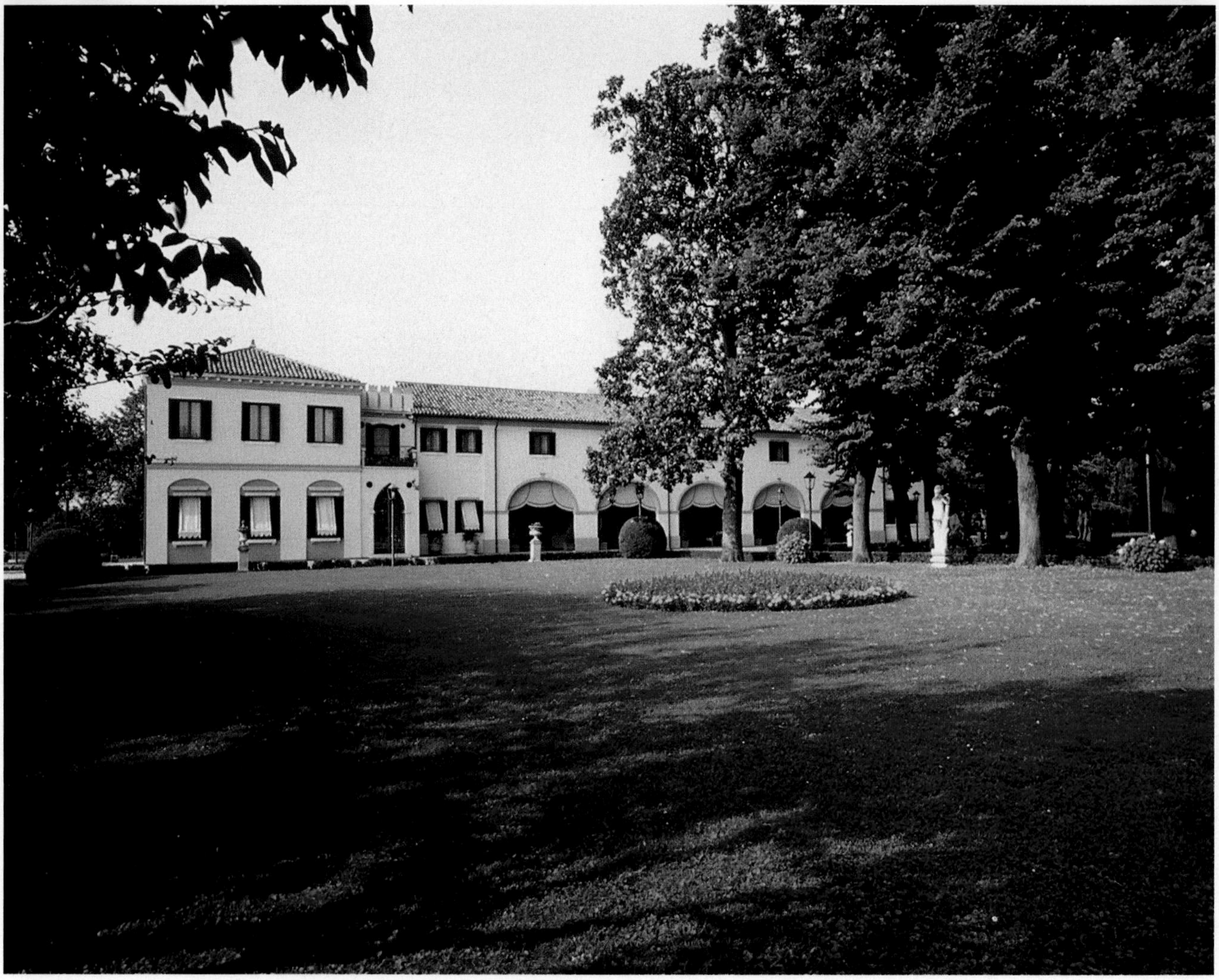

Just outside Venice, the legendary Palladian villas built in the 16th and 17th centuries for noble families are reflected in the waters of River Brenta, and at Mira on a particularly beautiful bend of the river is Villa Margherita. Its approach by land is along an enchanting avenue, lined with lime trees interspersed with statues. This idyllic villa was enlarged in the 19th century by a five arch portico which is wonderfully cool and peaceful. It has a tiled floor, elegant blinds and graceful furniture. The salons are luxurious, with exquisite frescoes and painted ceilings, mirrors and marble pillars and the bedrooms are faultless – traditional, stylish and comfortable with superb views over the surrounding parkland. Breakfast is served in the light, airy and colourful dining hall which leads onto the sunny terrace and gardens. The Ristorante Margherita is just fifty metres away, a delightful 19th century building decorated with captivating wall paintings. Here guests feast on Venetian specialities including delicious fish dishes and appreciate fine Italian wine. Should one leave this magical place, there is the Riviera del Brenta to explore and Venice with its magnificent buildings, glass blowing and lace making on the islands, romantic trips in gondolas and Carnival time. **Directions:** Leave Via A4 at Dolo-Mirano exit,then take S11 towards Mira Porte. Price guide: Single 145,000 –175,000 lire; double/twin 220,000–320,000 lire.

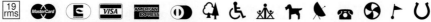

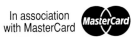

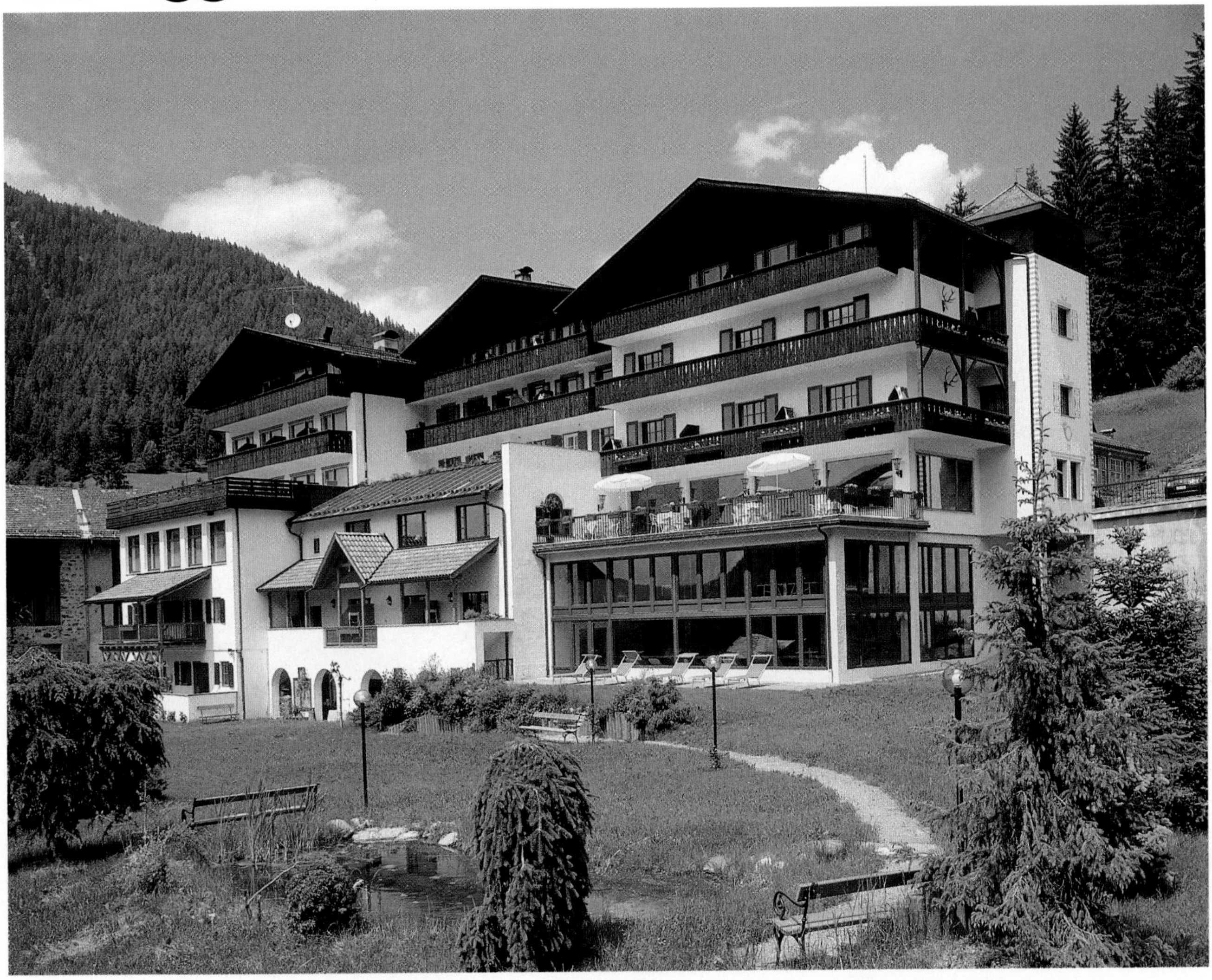

POSTHOTEL WEISSES RÖSSL

VIA CAREZZA 30, I–39056 NOVA LEVANTE (BZ), DOLOMITES, ITALY
TEL: 39 471 613113 FAX: 39 471 613390

Situated at the end of the impressive Val d'Ega in the heart of the magnificent Dolomites stands this former staging post with its frescoed facade and flower bedecked balconies. Since 1865 the Wiedenhofer Family has been welcoming guests, in winter for skiing, in summer for walking, climbing and golf in this alpine wonderland. The lounge with its marble floor and traditional wooden ceiling radiates a peaceful atmosphere overlooking meadows and forests. Guests gather for drinks in the cosy ambience of the bar with its rustic, local-style furniture, adorned with hunting trophies. Lunches are informal, in summertime on the sunny terraces, dinners are fine and delicately elaborate, a delicious range of Tyrolean and Mediterranean dishes, accompanied by selected wines from South-Tyrol and Italy. The sympathetically restored bedrooms are cheerful, all with balcony and a wonderful view of the near mountains. Countless pleasures to choose from: outdoor and indoor swimming pool, tennis, whirl-pool, sauna, steam bath, massage, beauty salon, solarium and billiards. Playroom and outside playground for children with childminder in charge. **Directions:** Autostrada A22, exit Bolzano North, driving south following signs for Val d'Ega – Lago di Carezza, reaching Nova Levante after 18km Price guide (per person, half-board): Double/twin 120,000–200,000 lire

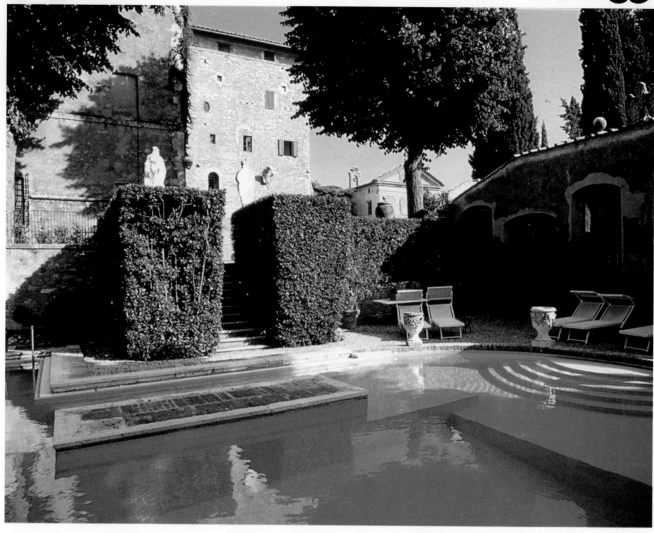

HOTEL RELAIS LA SUVERA

53030 PIEVESCOLA – SIENA, ITALY
TEL: 39 577 960300 FAX: 39 577 960220

The Relais La Suvera has a fascinating history, in 1197 a castle, then a gift in 1507 to the reigning Pope who had it transformed into a Renaissance villa. In 1989 the Marchese Ricci and his wife Principessa Eleonora Massimo created this elite and luxurious hotel – composed of four beautifully restored houses surrounding the courtyard. To have an opportunity to stay in the Marchese's Tuscan home is a unique experience – the elegant Reception has a welcoming ambience, enhanced by a display of wines from their own vineyard. The exquisite salons are filled with the finest antiques and the family art collection, a connoisseur's paradise. The heavenly guest rooms and magnificent suites are scattered between the four main houses, the Papal Villa, the Stables, the Olive Oil House and the Farm. Decorated in rich colours, furnished with lovely antiques, the rooms also have modern amenities. The bathrooms are opulent. The traditional Bar is in the Olive Oil House, as is the classical Oliviera Restaurant. Gorgeous Tuscan dishes accompanied by superb wines from the estate combine to make a feast each night. The residence has tennis and a swimming pool, guests can visit the vineyard, play golf or fish nearby. **Directions:** From Superstrada Siena-Florence, exit Colle Val d'Elsa, head towards Grosseto, followings signs to Relais La Suvera. Price guide: Double/twin 370,000–500,000 lire; suites 470,000–700,000 lire.

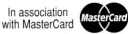

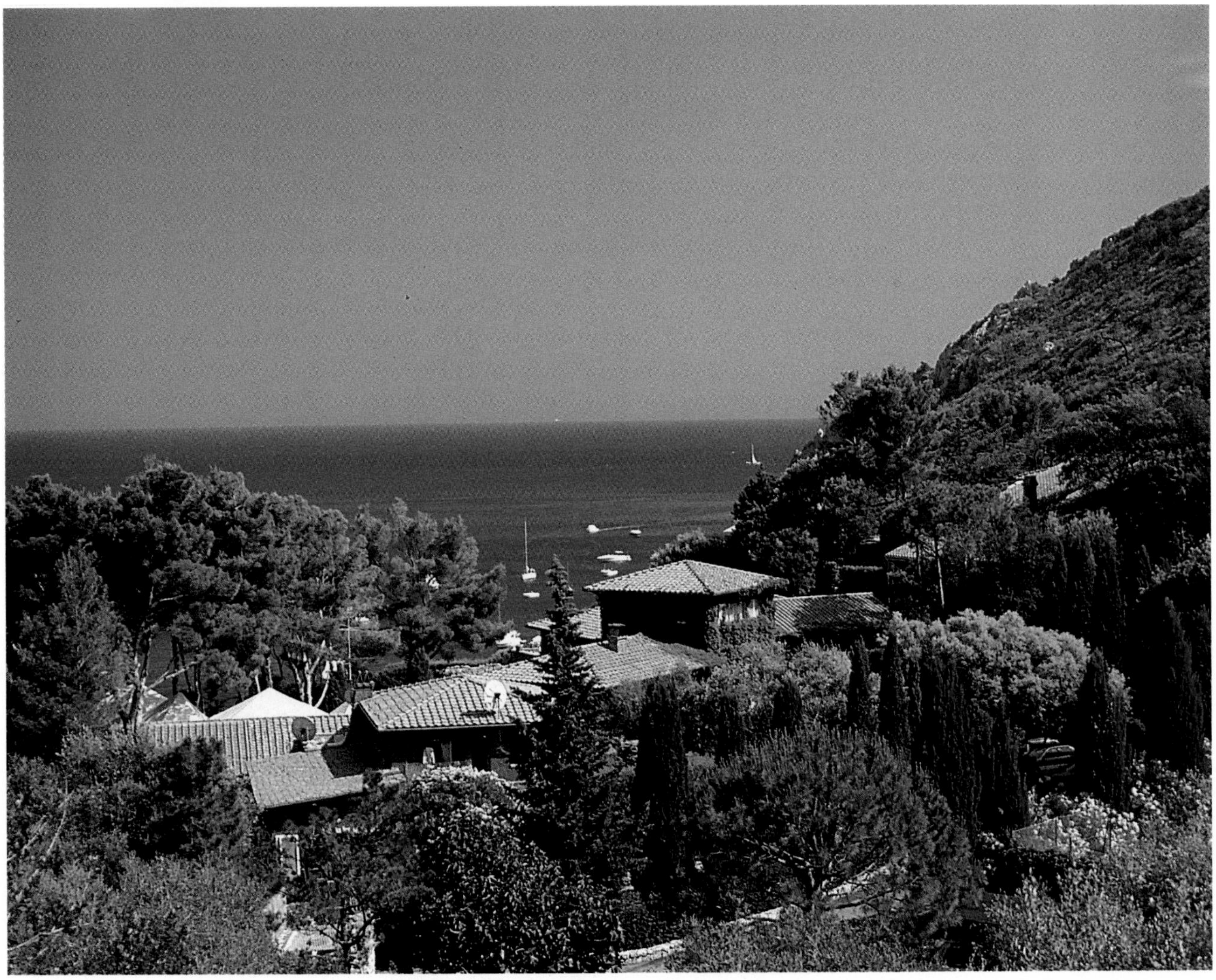

Il Pellicano

HOTEL IN PORTO ERCOLE, I-58018 PORTO ERCOLE (GR), ITALY
TEL: 39 564 833801 FAX: 39 564 833418

What hotel in Italy can compare with the spectacular setting of Il Pellicano? One of the most delightful, intimately-sited hotels in the world (Sunday Telegraph). A cluster of cottages, centred around the main ivy-clad villa, with traditional tiled roofs, ochre walls and flower patios interspersed with tall pine, cypress and olive trees overlooking the breathtaking Argentario Peninsula. The atmosphere of Il Pellicano is like a very private club (Harpers & Queen). The bedrooms and suites are individually furnished and enjoy spectacular views. Guests can choose between the mouth-watering barbecue buffets or romantic candelit dinners in the beautiful restaurant, providing the best in national and international food and wines. Enjoy sports like water-skiing, tennis, cycling, or just relax in the heated swimming pool or on the terraced private beach or in the beauty centre. If it's more activity you crave, then there's plenty going on in the nearby marina and waterfront. Play a game of golf or explore the Roman and Etruscan ruins, within driving distance in the hotel limousine if preferred. On a verdant hillside, overlooking a shimmering sea, you'll find Il Pellicano – a hotel in a class of its own. **Directions.** Take the A12 from Rome towards Civitavecchia, then the Orbetello exit towards Porto Ercole. Double 315,000 lire–920,000 lire; suites 710,000 lire–1,875,000 lire.

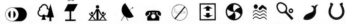

Romantik Hotel Poseidon

VIA PASITEA, 148, I–84017 POSITANO (SALERNO), ITALY
TEL: 39 89 81 11 11 FAX: 39 89 87 58 33 E-MAIL: poseidon@starnet.it

Positano, the 'jewel of the Mediterranean' is situated on the spectacular Amalfi coast, a combination of sea and mountains, with pastel shaded houses clinging to the cliffs. The four star Romantik Hotel Poseidon, owned and run by the Aonzo family, was once their private summer residence and is located in the heart of town. The charming, pristine bedrooms, decorated with rustic furniture, have balconies overlooking the village. The spacious, comfortable living room and bar, are nearby to the sunbathing terrace and swimming pool. The decor and atmosphere of the indoor dining area are in total harmony with the rest of the hotel. In the warmer months the restaurant service takes place on a vast terrace covered with vines. There is a wide varied menu, including fresh fish specialities and the best Italian wines are available. The new Beauty and Fitness Centre, in co-operation with Terme di Saturnia, offers a full range of body treatments, facials, massages, Turkish bath and complete Fitness programme. There is a conference room for up to 50 people. Sea-fishing trips in the Gulf can be arranged.Internet: http://www.starnet.it/poseidon **Directions:** Driving South from Naples on A3, take the exit Castellammare di Stabia, turning off at Meta di Sorrento and follow the signs to Positano. Garage: 35,000lire per day. Price guide: Single 250,000–370,000 lire; double/twin 270,000–390,000 lire; suites 530,000–600,000 lire.

Hotel Farnese

VIA ALESSANDRO FARNESE, 30 (ANGOLO VIALE GIULIO CESARE), I–00192 ROME, ITALY
TEL: 39 6 321 25 53 FAX: 39 6 321 51 29

An aristocratic 19th century villa set in a quiet tree-lined residential area of Rome. You enter through a small, lovely fronted garden, up an impressive stone stairway to the reception desk. Graceful archways and elegant classical Italian furniture, chandeliers from Murano and decorative frescos, antiques and fine colourful rugs together make-up the charming reception areas of the ground floor of the original villa. Downstairs a buffet breakfast is the only meal served in the subterranean dining room – but drinks will be brought to the roof garden overlooking St.Peter's Square or the terrace off the reception lounge. Several interesting restaurants are to be found locally. Raphaël murals, parquet floors and period furniture make the bedrooms very attractive, and they have delightful marble bathrooms, equipped to meet the needs of modern travellers. Most conveniently situated among all the historical buildings to explore in this city, it is particularly close to the Castel St. Angelo, St. Peter's and the Vatican. Those visiting Rome on business appreciate the easy accessibility to the commercial districts. **Directions:** There is private parking space for residents' cars, alternatively the Lepanto Metro station is only 50 metres from the hotel. Price guide: Single 240,000lire–290,000 lire; double/twin 330,000lire–390,000lire; junior suite 450,000lire.

23 rms

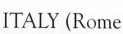

Romantik Hotel Barocco

PIAZZA BARBERINI, 9, I-00187 ROME, ITALY
TEL: 39 6 48 72 001 FAX: 6 48 59 94

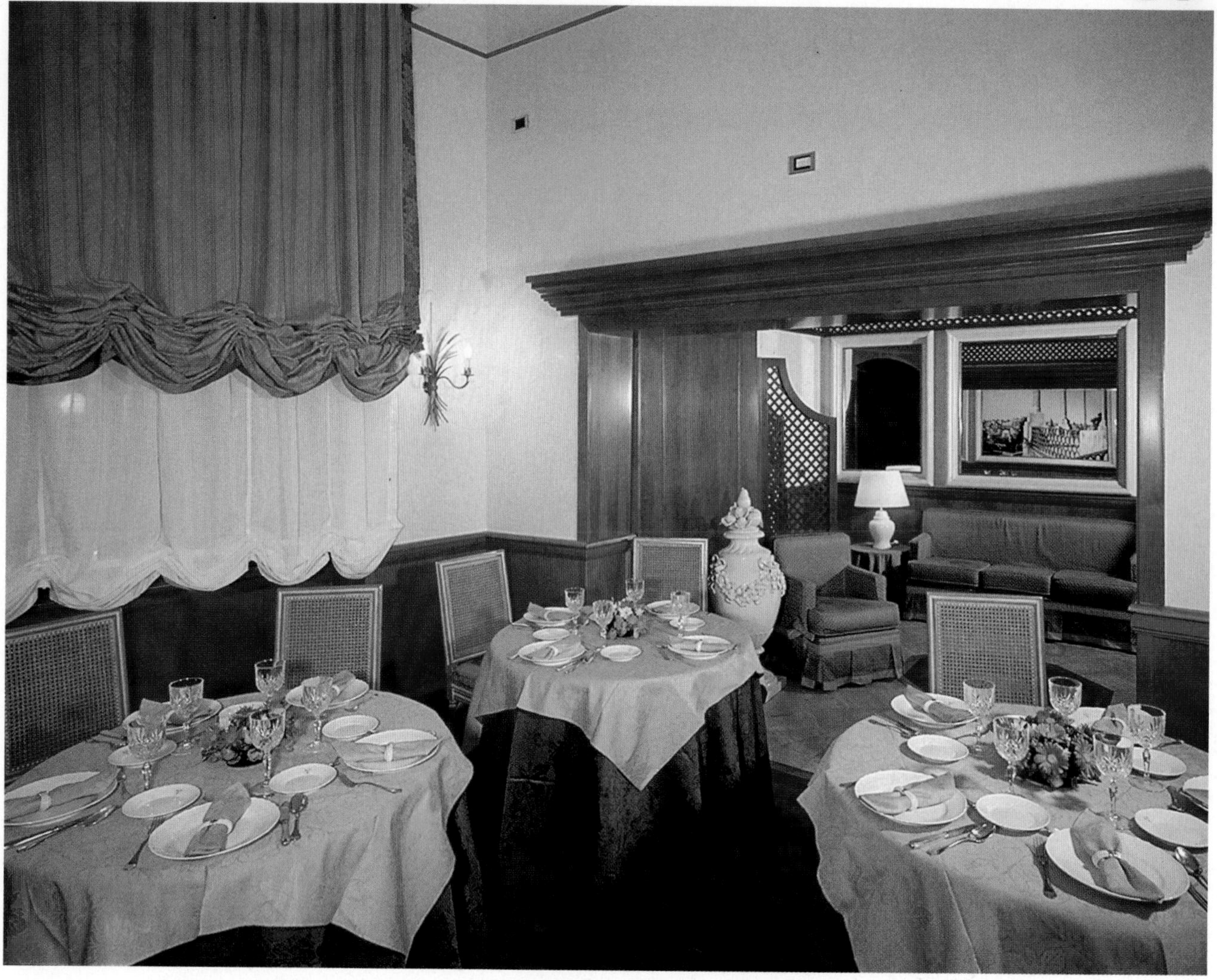

This delightful intimate hotel, its architecture indicating that it was built during the 19th century art deco era, is in the centre of Rome. Local landmarks are the famous Trevi Fountain and the Spanish Steps, yet it is also convenient for the business sector. Lovely warm cherrywood dominates the interior decor – in the fin de siècle entrance hall and in the bedrooms. These are delightful, and thoughtfully designed to ensure guests have all possible modern amenities, including insulation from the noise of the city below. The Junior Suite which has its own terrace, overlooks the Piazza and can be reserved. The bathrooms are contemporary and luxurious, furnished in marble. The hotel has a small bar. There is a breakfast room on the ground floor. Breakfast is also served in bedrooms. There is no hotel restaurant but the staff will always suggest good restaurants that are nearby. Rome is an exciting city to explore, with St Peter's and the Vatican, the Colosseum and Pantheon in the ancient city, world famous museums and art galleries, the exclusive boutiques and luxurious shops. It also offers a sophisticated night life. **Directions:** Piazza Barberini is where Via Barberini meets the Via del Tritone and Via Veneto. Parking is 300m from the hotel. Price guide: Single 320,000 lire; double/twin 420,000 lire. Week-end rates available.

28 rms       

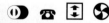

PARKHOTEL SOLE PARADISO

VIA HAUNOLD 8, SAN CANDIDO (BZ), ITALY 39038
TEL: 39 474 913120 FAX: 39 474 913193

San Candido is an enchanting village surrounded by the majestic Dolomites. The Parkhotel Sole Paradiso is well named, for it is a glorious large chalet, the balconies filled with flowers in summer and with spectacular views across the snowfields in winter. The Ortner family greet guests in the pine reception area before showing them to their guest rooms, the beds draped in local lace, the furniture from the region, some leading onto balconies. The bathrooms are modern and efficient. The lounge is cosy and relaxing, with panelled walls, bright upholstery, an amusing old figurehead swinging from the ceiling. The bar is another fascinating room and the elegant diningroom, part Viennese, part Tyrolean, with a 1930's influence, and light from its many windows, is in the talented hands of Chef Hubert Leitgeb and his team. His inspired interpretations of regional dishes will delight the most discerning guest as, indeed, will the fine wine list. This is a wonderful centre for langlauf and downhill skiing, skating, curling and sled excursions, a bus taking visitors to the pistes. Summer sports are tennis, golf and climbing. The Parkhotel also has a superb indoor pool with spa facilities. **Directions:** A22, exit Brixen-Bressanone, driving 60kms along S49, the Val Pusteria, to Innichen San Candido, where the hotel is signed. Parking. Price guide: Single 110,000–160,000 lire; double 260,000–360,000 lire

43 rms · MasterCard · VISA · AMERICAN EXPRESS · 80

Terme Di Saturnia

I–58050 SATURNIA, GROSSETO, ITALY
TEL: 39 564 601 061 FAX: 39 564 601 266

The Terme di Saturnia is the panacea for those wishing to return from their vacation fitter in mind and body as well as having had an enjoyable holiday with interesting people and diverse activities amid beautiful surroundings. The complex combines a spa with modern hospitality. The turn of the century building surrounds a 37C natural thermal spring where it is possible to bathe all year round . The elegant bedrooms are comfortable and the prestigious Villa Montepaldi restaurant has one part reserved for those on special diet regimes. The cellar holds fine wines. Away from the main building is the charming countryhouse Albergo La Stellata, with 14 bedrooms, its own Tuscan restaurant leading onto a pretty terrace and the Saturnia Country Club with additional bedrooms, and the Madre Maremma restaurant featuring typical cusine. Visitors staying at both these houses enjoy the hotel amenities. A medical team advises guests on appropriate treatments at the spa, many based on the properties of the sulphurous waters. A splendid pool, golf driving range, tennis, wonderful countryside to explore on bicycles – so much to do or the opportunity to relax and do nothing. **Directions:** Saturnia is an ancient village in Southern Tuscany between Grosseto and Rome, $1^1/2$ hours by car from Rome Airport. Price guide: Single 275,000 lire – 345,000 lire; double/twin 470,000 lire – 710,000 lire; suites 1,000,000 lire.

HOTEL PALAZZO FIESCHI

PIAZZA DELLA CHIESA 14, SAVIGNONE (GE) 16010 ITALY
TEL: 39 10 9360063 FAX: 39 10 936821

This intriguing Renaissance palazzo stands in the square of the small village of Savignone, near Genoa. It has been lovingly restored and transformed into a unique hotel. Once inside guests find a delightful residence in the style of the 19th century with 20th century comforts. The Palazzo is approached down an attractive cobbled path, under ancient trees. The hall has graceful archways, slate floors; the salons are filled with fine antiques. Flowers are everywhere. The spacious guest rooms have high, beautifully painted ceilings. Period pieces, charming drapes and comfortable beds make the rooms very inviting. The bathrooms are modern, some with hydromassage showers. The handsome, vaulted bar is well stocked, and guests gather here before adjourning to the traditional restaurant which has an unusual slate floor and elaborate frescoes. Genoan specialities and regional wines are offered; many ingredients are from the surrounding gardens, especially the salads, and light diet menus are available. The countryside must be explored, and for those who are not walkers the Palazzo will arrange mountain bikes or horses. A historic tram runs between the village and Genoa. **Directions:** From A7 take Busalla exit and follow signs for Savigione. The hotel has parking. Price guide: Single 130,000 lire; double/twin 180,000 lire; suites 220,000 lire.

24 rms

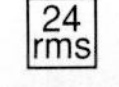

180

Hotel Sochers Resort Club

39048 SELVA VAL GARDENA (BZ), ITALY
TEL: 39 471 792101/02 FAX: 39 471 793537

The dramatic Dolomites are the setting for this sophisticated chalet-style hotel in a skier's paradise. The Sochers Resort Club stands alone in a splendid sunny position outside the village, located at 2000m altitude and is connected with the valley cable railway car running from 9am to 5pm. The hotel is very attractive, with a wide terrace, wonderful views across the slopes to the towering mountain peaks, and direct access to the pistes. The charming bedrooms – many with balconies – are spacious, decorated in soft, restful colours, with smart built-in furniture providing generous storage space. Modern comforts are discreetly present and the marble bathrooms are well designed. The big hall is the heart of the hotel, with the smart bar at one end, leading into the classical restaurant. Here guests talk of their thrills and spills and plan the next day. The meals are excellent, lavish breakfasts, lunch is often on the terrace and delicious Tyrolean or Italian dishes feature on the menu. The wine list is excellent. The ski school has a children's section; there are innumerable ski-lifts and challenging runs for experts, easier ones for beginners. Aching muscles are soon restored in the health club. **Directions:** Leave A22, at Chiusa Klausen North exit, towards Selva Wolken Stein, watching for signs to the hotel. Parking. Price guide (per person): Double/twin 137,000–184,000 lire.

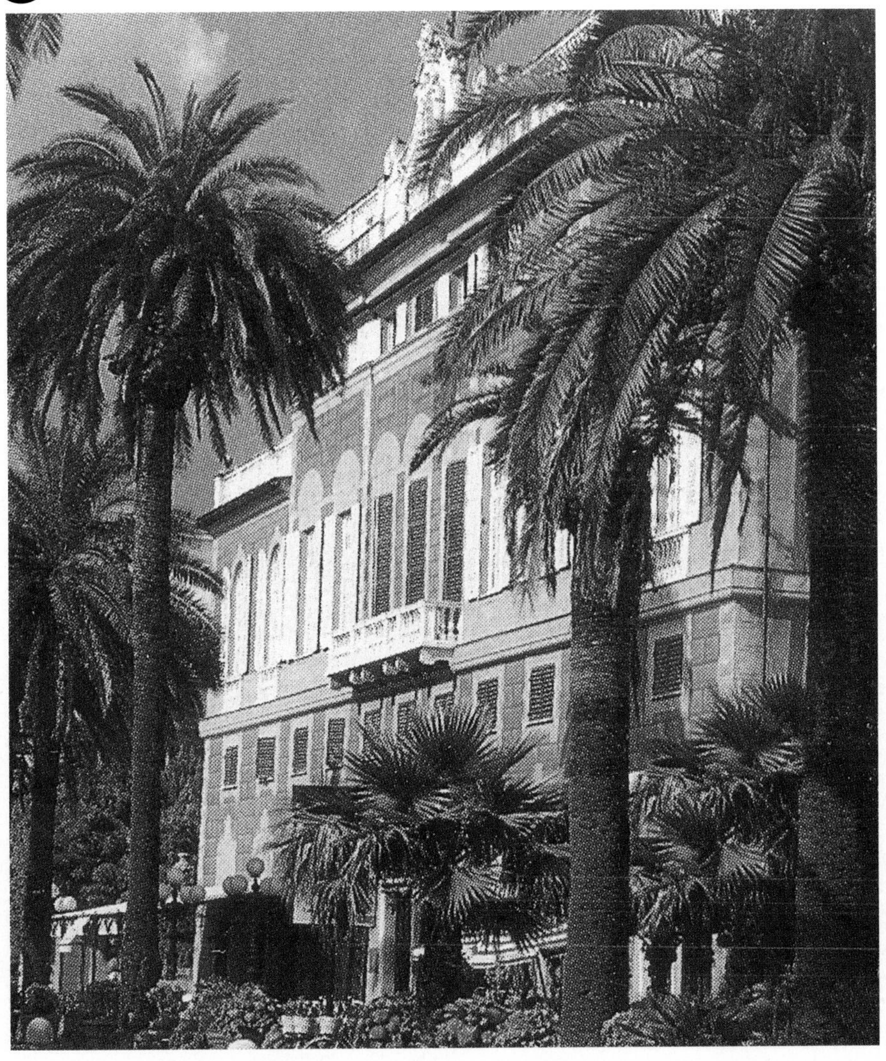

GRAND HOTEL VILLA BALBI

VIALE RIMEMBRANZA 1, 16039 SESTRI LEVANTE (GE), ITALY
TEL: 39 (0)185 42941 FAX: 39 (0)185 482459

Sestri Levante is on the Italian Riviera, south of Portofino, and the Villa Balbi was built as a summer palace in the 17th century. The hotel of today stands in a secluded private park that contains magnificent old trees, overlooking the spectacular Gulf of Tigullio. The Villa has a graceful façade, flanked by tall palm trees and the interior rooms are very elegant – tall pillars and soaring arches reaching up to enchanting frescoed ceilings, brilliant chandeliers, marble floors, antique pieces and comfortable chairs. The charming bedrooms are peaceful, traditionally furnished and decorated in tranquil colours, all having lovely views over the water or the park. Some are designated non-smoking. There is a pleasant bar, but guests often prefer their apéritifs on the splendid terrace overlooking the Mediterranean. Breakfast is also served here. The Il Parco Restaurant specialises in Ligurian dishes and fish straight from the sea. Fine Italian wines are listed. With such peaceful surroundings, marvellous views, the pool and private beach many residents seldom leave the hotel, but golf and tennis are nearby. Boat trips can be organised and excursions made to Portofino and Baia del Silenzio. **Directions:** Leave A12 motorway at Sestri Levante exit, following signs for Centro Citta. Price guide: Single 100,000–200,000 lire; double/twin 250,000–350,000 lire; suites 350,000–450,000 lire.

Romantik Hotels & Restaurants

Romantik Hotel Villa Ducale

VIA LEONARDO DA VINCI, 60, I–98039 TAORMINA, SICILY
TEL: 39 942 28153 FAX: 39 942 28710

Once a coaching inn, then the summer villa of a nobleman – an ancestor of the present owner – on the edge of Taormina, this delightful small hotel with spectacular views of Naxos Bay and Mount Etna is in rural surroundings. The interior is charming, with a déjà-vu ambience, and guests can relax in the small lounge decorated with fine pieces of Sicilian pottery. The bedrooms, all different shapes and sizes, have individual colour schemes, fresh flowers, tiled floors and elegant period furniture. There is no formal restaurant but a leisurely breakfast, with a wide range of sweet and savoury dishes, is served until 11.30am on the terrace, where delicious hot snacks and wines are available all day. From the terrace on clear days you can see across to Catania. There is a good choice of restaurants, pizzerias and cafés in the village round the corner. A cable car descends to a sandy beach at Mazzaro, and buses go to Etna and Agrigento. Golfers will enjoy the superb Il Picciolo Golf Course, some 30 minutes' drive away. **Directions:** Take highway A18 from Catania to Taormina, then take the road to Castelmola. The hotel has a small car park. Price guide: Single 190,000 lire–240,000 lire; double/twin 260,000 lire–340,000 lire; suites 320,000 lire–400,000 lire.

GRAND HOTEL COCUMELLA

VIA COCUMELLA, 7, 80065 SANT'AGNELLO, SORRENTO, ITALY

TEL: 39 81 878 2933 FAX: 39 81 878 3712

La Cocumella has a long tradition of hospitality, its origins dating back to the 16th century, when it was a Jesuit Monastery. It was transformed into a hotel in 1822 when Sorrento became an important stop on the Grand Tour. The hotel is surrounded by parkland stretching down to the coast, culminating in a splendid terrace with spectacular views over the Gulf of Naples to Vesuvius. Traces of the monastery still remain, the elegant hall having been the cloisters and the chapel is still used for weddings and concerts. Many charming guest rooms have magnificent antique furniture and the bridal suite has an exquisite painted ceiling. The Scintilla restaurant is enchanting with art deco lampshades and a romantic terrace overlooking the garden. Guests feast on aromatic Mediterranean dishes and local wines, while in summer light buffet lunches are enjoyed in the Orange Grove by the pool. The hotels' historical tall ship, Vera, is perfect for excursions to Capri and the Amalfi Coast. Pompeii is a fascinating expedition. Staying within the hotel grounds, guests can enjoy tennis, go down by lift to the private beach or relax in the beauty farm. **Directions:** Motorway from Naples to Castellammare di Staba then follow the coast road to Sorrento. Price guide: Single 280,000–340,000 lire; double/twin 450,000 lire–550,000 lire; suites 550,000 lire–850,000 lire.

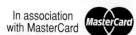

GRAND HOTEL EXCELSIOR VITTORIA

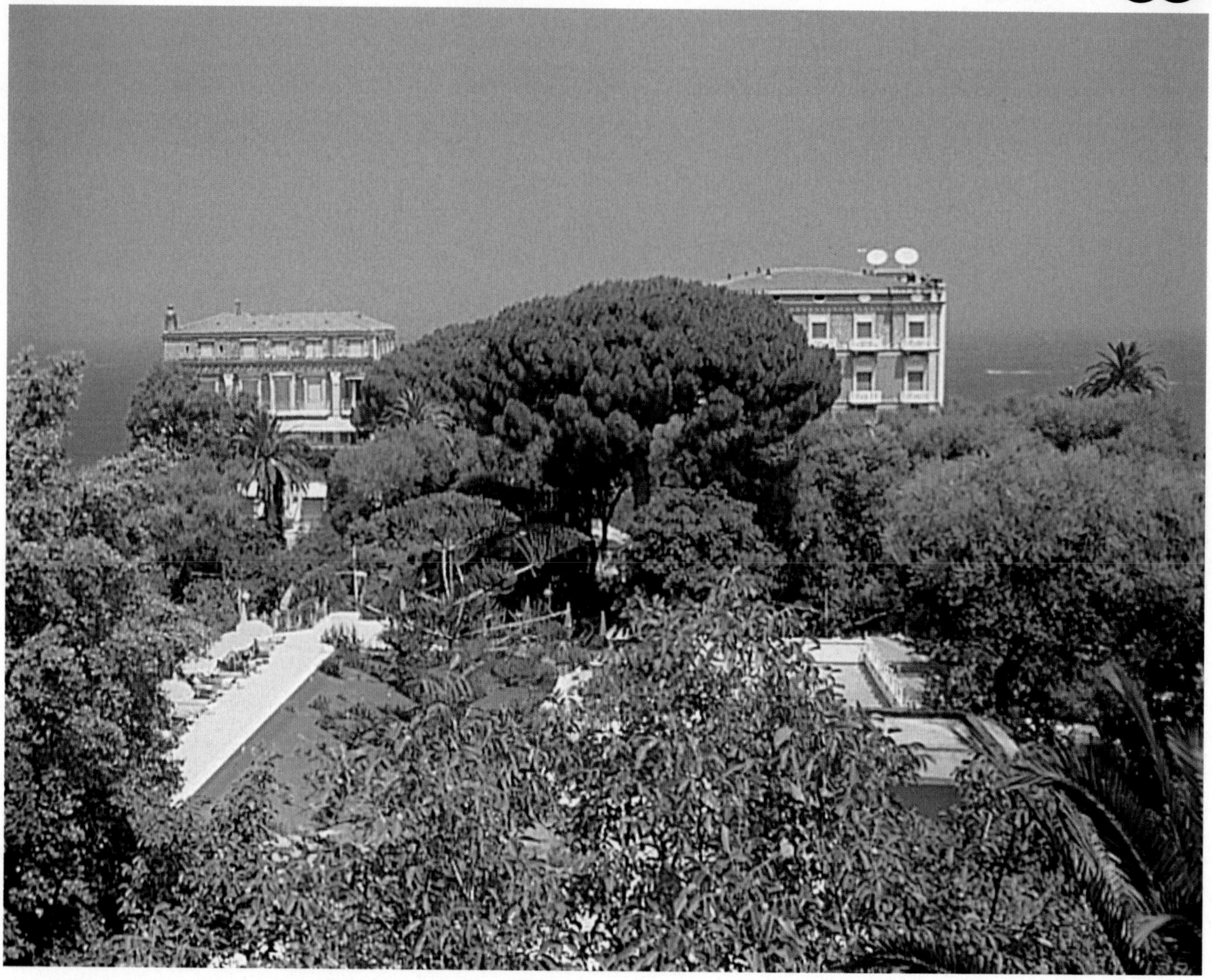

PIAZZA TASSO 34, SORRENTO 80067 (NAPOLI), ITALY
TEL: 39 81 807 1044 FAX: 39 81 877 1206 E-MAIL:exvitt@exvitt.it

The Grand Hotel Excelsior Vittoria was built at the turn of the century, and stands on the Sorrento waterfront, with its own moorings. The architecture is graceful fin de siècle, and the grounds are wondrous, filled with exotic sub-tropical plants and scented from the orange groves and olive trees. This legendary establishment has been in the hands of the same family for four generations, and is immaculately furnished and decorated. The salons are elegant and cool, with Bergère chairs, fine antiques, beautiful rugs on the tiled floors, gilt mirrors, delicate plaster mouldings and palm trees. The meeting rooms are Art Nouveau, with glorious murals and vaulted ceilings (modern technology is available!). The guest rooms, most having balconies or terraces with views over the Bay or gardens, and the suites are magnificent. All have luxurious bathrooms. Eating is "La Cucina Italiana", accompanied by superb wines. The Sala Vittoria Restaurant is very grand, with marble pillars; guests can enjoy al fresco dining in the delightful Restaurant Panoramico; lighter meals are served in the pretty Piscina snack bar. Relaxing by the pool, shopping in Sorrento or expeditions to Capri, Pompeii and Amalfi fill the day. Internet: URL:www.exvitt.it **Directions:** A3, exit Castellamare di Stabia, follow signs to Sorrento. Price guide: Single 355,000 liree; double/twin 390,000–565,000 lire; suites 720,000–1,200,000 lire.

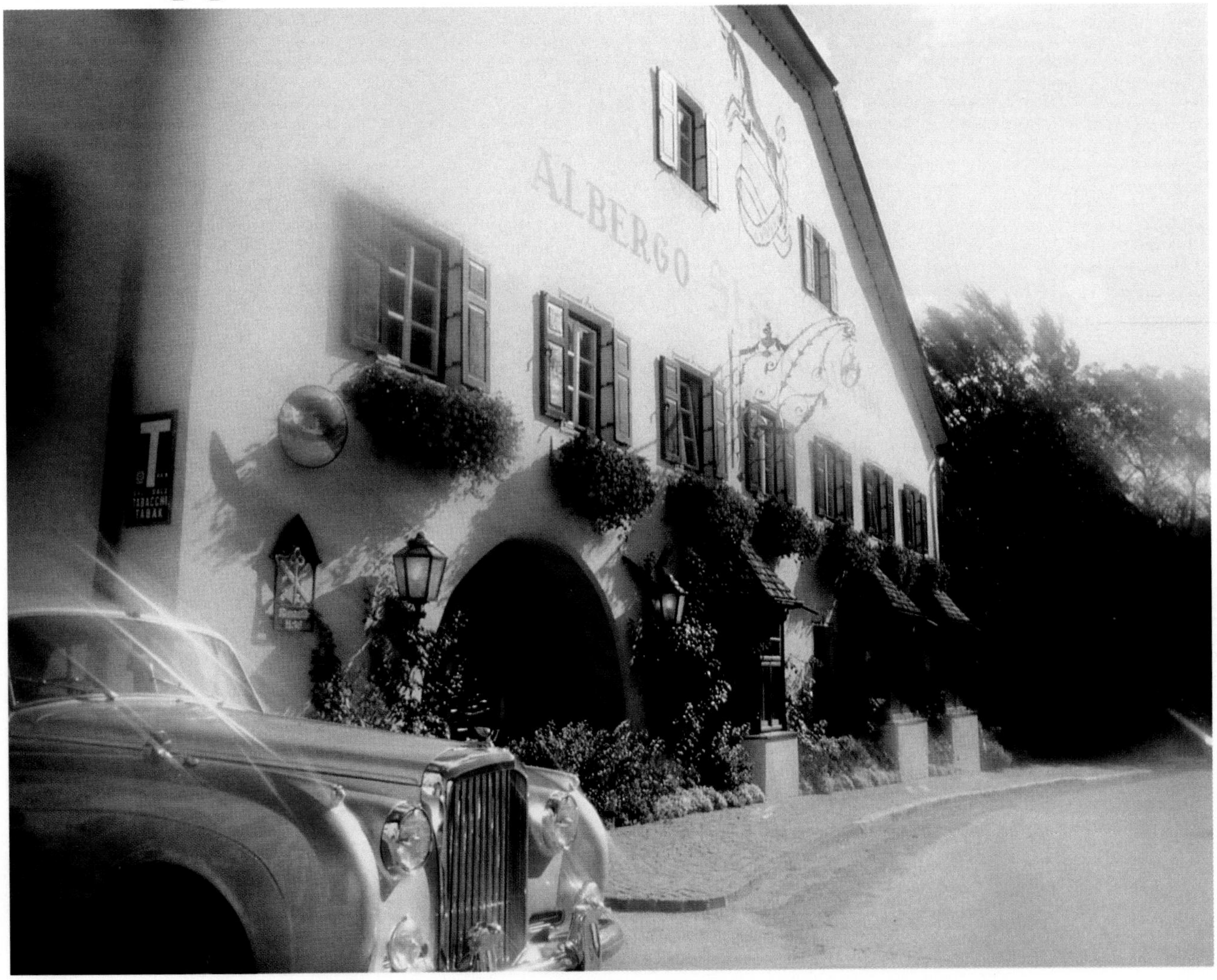

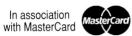

ROMANTIK HOTEL STAFLER

MAULS, 10, 39040 FREIENFELD NR STERTING (BZ), ITALY
TEL: 39 472 77 11 36 FAX: 39 472 77 10 94

This romantic hotel has been offering hospitality to travellers for some 500 years, being one of the oldest inns in the Eisack Valley, just south of the Brenner Pass. It is built in the local style, against an impressive background of pine-clad mountains, the perfect place to stop on a leisurely European tour. The reception area is very handsome, and the salon, with its fine panelled ceiling, is a charming place to relax. Stone walls low archways and lovely antiques are reminders of the inn's history. The bedrooms are light and roomy, comfortably furnished, having soft, harmonious colour schemes and good bathrooms. Some are suitable for those with mobility problems. The intimate bar is very convivial. Eating here is a feast, succulent regional dishes based on local produce are prepared by the talented chef while wines from the area are recommended. This is a marvellous place for families, the big well-kept gardens having room for children to play while their parents relax in the sun or play tennis. The hotel also has an indoor pool. Ski-ing is good in this area; in warmer months tennis is close by and mountain bikes can be hired to explore the countryside and local villages. **Directions:** Autostrade A22, exit for Brixen Bressanone, driving North following signs for Brenner, reaching Mauls after 20 km. Price guide: Single 105,000 lire–130,000 lire; double/twin 170,000 lire–220,000 lire; suites 170,000 lire–220,000 lire.

38 rms      50      

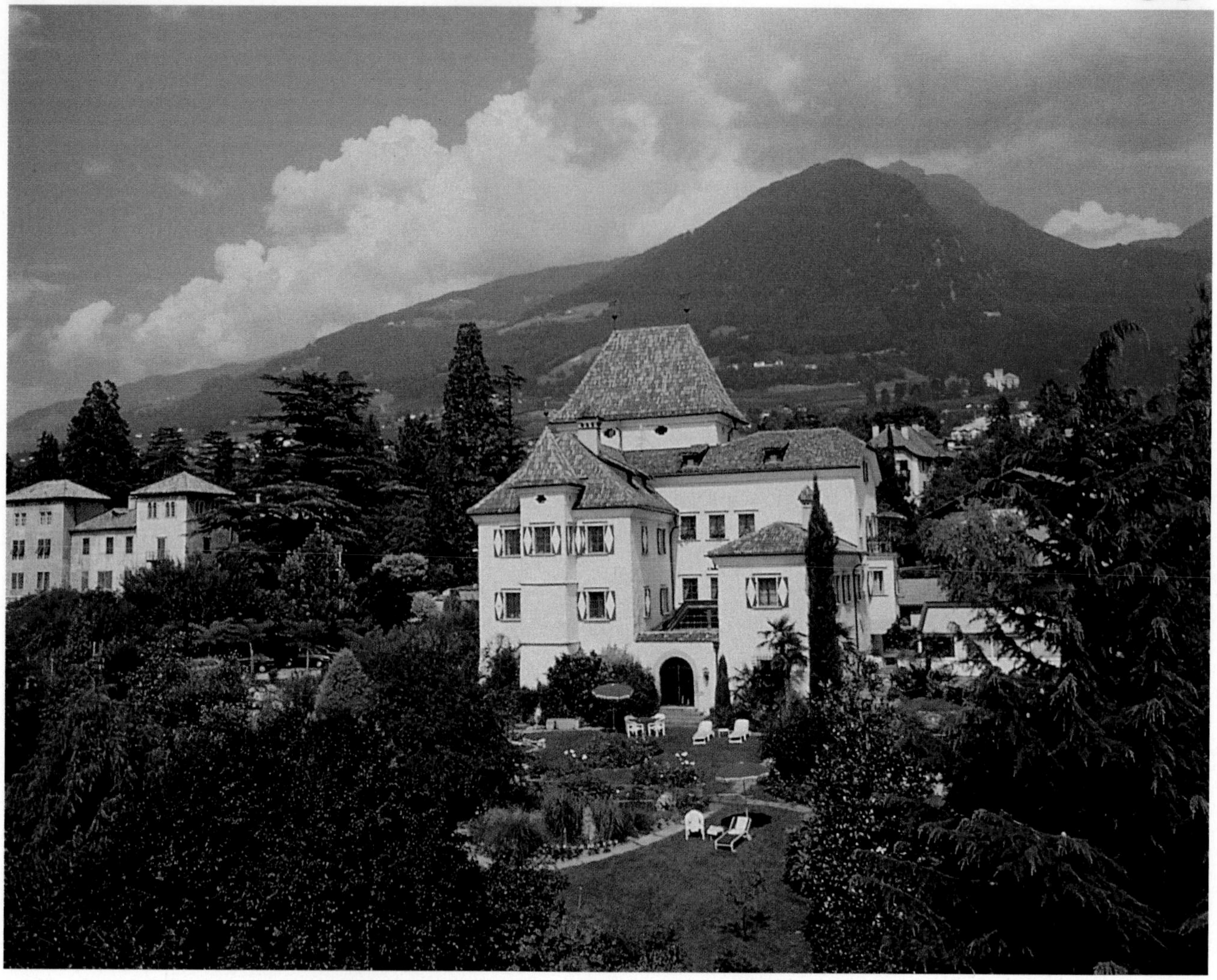

CASTEL RUNDEGG

VIA SCENA, 2–SCHENNASTRASSE 2, I–39020 MERAN (BZ), ITALY
TEL: 39 473 23 41 00 FAX: 39 473 23 72 00

An exquisite small castle in the lovely South Tyrol, Castel Rundegg stands in its own parkland, overlooking Meran, against a backdrop of mountains and pine forests. Careful modernisation has not intruded on its history – and the blend of the past with today's luxury creates a marvellous ambience. The interior is delightful with tiled floors, vaulted ceilings, archways and many fine beams, enhanced by considerate lighting and Persian rugs. The spacious bedrooms are charming and extremely comfortable, all with a view of the town – some being in the new Annex. Guests mingle in the small, friendly bar before choosing local and Mediterranean specialities in the gourmet restaurant, with its beautifully appointed tables or enjoying informal meals on the terrace. Excellent wines are offered. An important aspect of Castel Rundegg is its attention to health and part of its facilities are dedicated to to beauty and fitness. Therapists, fitness and beauty consultants will recommend suitable programmes. Guests enjoy the fine pool, sunbathing and jogging in the park. Golf and tennis can be found locally, in winter good ski-ing is only 1km away. **Directions:** Exit from highway A22 Bolzano Sud to Merano. Follow signs to Passo Giovo until district Maia Alta. Price guide (per person): Single 162,000–179,000 lire; double/twin 135,000–179,000 lire; suites 177,000–248,000 lire.

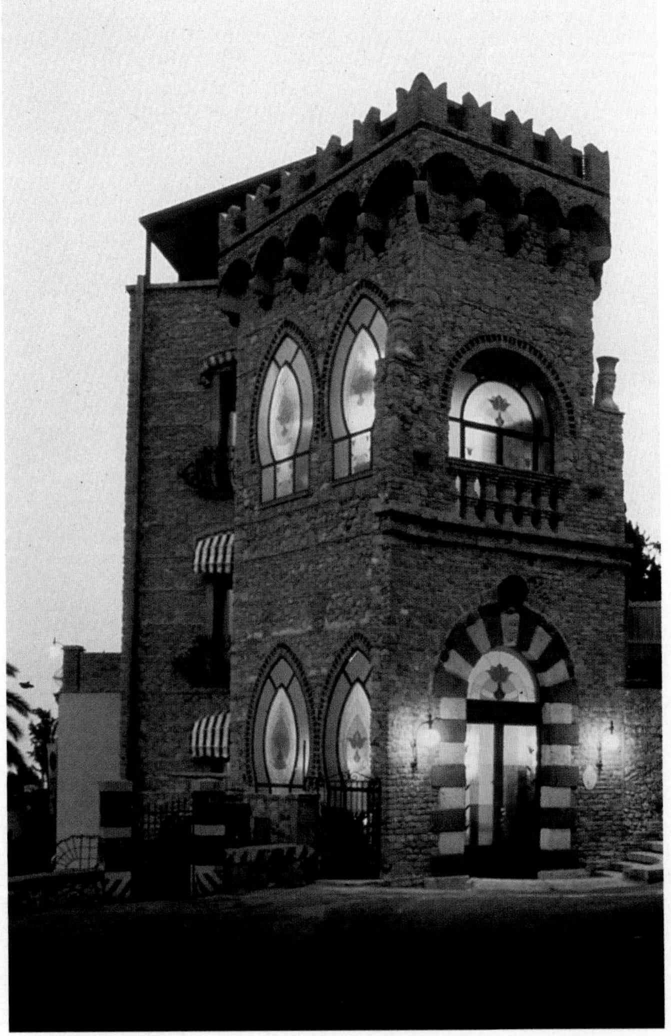

VILLA FABBIANO

VIA PIRANDELLO 81, 98039 TAORMINA (ME), ITALY
TEL: 39 942 626058 FAX: 39 942 23732

This enchanting villa was built in 1896 and had been allowed to fall into disrepair. It has been restored with great love and skill, and today it is an attractive small hotel, on the outskirts of Taormina, set against a background of mountains, looking across to the Ionian Sea and Mount Etna. Surrounded by a pleasant tropical garden, the villa is very peaceful. The guest rooms are charming, light and airy, with pretty wroughtiron balconies or terraces, cool stone floors, open brickwork and soft golden walls. The furniture is in cherrywood. The bathrooms have character, with "Victorian" fittings – some rooms have tubs with legs! The villa's heart is the Panorama Terrace and Winter Garden where guests appreciate the spectacular view while indulging in a superb breakfast or the delicious snacks available 24 hours of the day. There is no restaurant but the town has a variety of places to dine. Babysitting can be arranged. When not relaxing by the hotel pool or playing tennis nearby, visitors can explore ancient monuments and the Greek theatre or go down to the coast. **Directions:** A18, Taormina exit. Follow sign "Mare" to the right and join SS114, towards "Catania" to the right, until hotel "Capotaormina". Turn right following signs to town centre, the hotel is on the left of the main approach. Price guide: Single 180,000–260,000 lire; double/twin 200,000–330,000 lire; suites 350,000–950,000 lire.

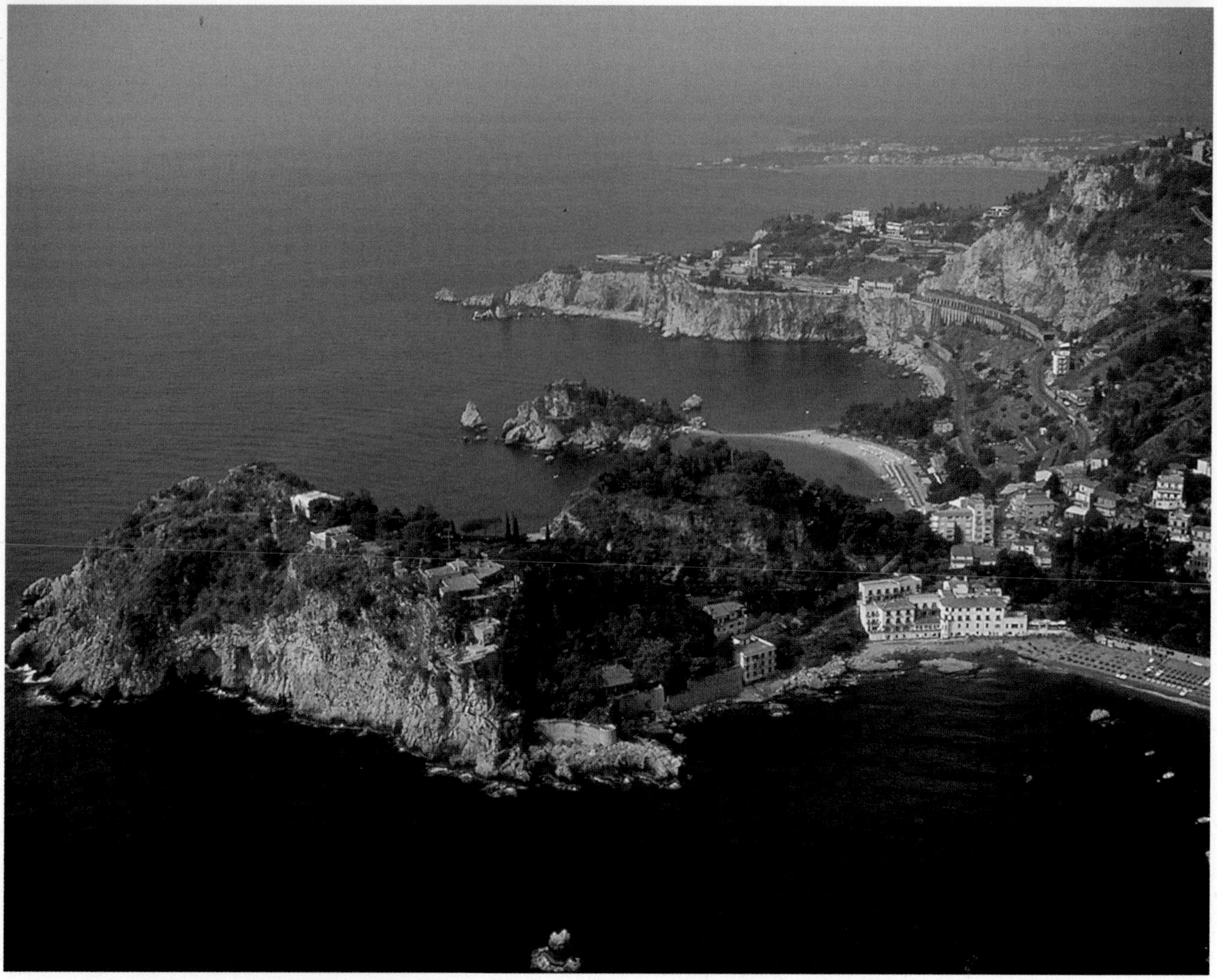

HOTEL VILLA SANT' ANDREA

VIA NAZIONALE 137, 98030 TAORMINA MARE (ME), ITALY
TEL: 39 942 23125 FAX: 39 942 24838

This unique and gorgeous hotel was a private villa built in the 1830s and it has retained its dignified ambience while being transformed into a small part of paradise on the bay of Mazzaro. Set right on the water's edge, the Sant' Andrea is protected by exotic tropical gardens. New arrivals are delighted with the interior, with its graceful archways, cool tiled floors and marvellous collection of fine antiques, handsome paintings and views across the water. The bedrooms are light and airy, many with balconies facing the sea. Some are in the 'dependance' just metres away – all are pretty and comfortable. The elegant salon is peaceful and watching the lights of the fishing fleet from the well stocked piano bar is a pleasant way to spend an evening, perhaps later dancing the night away under the stars. The Olivero Restaurant also extends under the floodlit trees on the terrace, a brilliant scenario at night. Gorgeous Mediterranean food and good Italian wines enhance the ambience. The hotel has its own beach, with sunbeds, windsurfing and other water sports on request. A nearby cablecar will take guests to Taormina, the Roman and Greek theatre and tennis courts. Between Mount Etna and Taormina is situated the "Picciolo Golf Club". **Directions:** Leave Route 18 at Taormina exit, then follow signs to the hotel. Price guide (pr person): Single 205,000–365,000 lire; double/twin 155,000– 265,000 lire; suites 100,000lire supplement.

Hotel Cipriani, Palazzo Vendramin And The Palazzetto

GIUDECCA 10, 30133 VENICE, ITALY

TEL: 39 41 2207745 FAX: 39 41 5203930 E-MAIL: cipriani@gpnet.it

Just a few minutes by private launch from St Mark's, on the Island of Giudecca, the Hotel Cipriani offers secluded privacy, amongst three acres of flowered gardens which are unique for a hotel in Venice. The elegant interiors are reminiscent of the Venetian style while the rooms and bathrooms offer a sober yet elegant atmosphere which conveys the feeling of being in one's own home. Across a flowered courtyard there are now two butler serviced Annexes which offer rooms and suites with breathtaking views over St. Mark's square. The delightful 15th century Palazzo Vendramin has been joined by the Palazzetto which has its own restaurant, "Cip's at the Palazzetto", serving simple, fresh Italian specialities and, of course, fabulous pizzas! Residents can have their breakfast in the lagoon terrace, enjoy al fresco buffets by the pool, sip Bellinis in the chic Piano Bar and linger over delicious gourmet dishes and connoisseurs' wines in the graceful Cipriani restaurant or on the panoramic terrace under the stars. The Cipriani has a superb heated salt-water pool and a clay tennis court, both unique in Venice. Golf is on the Lido, 40 minutes by boat. Venice offers historic buildings, fine art and excellent shopping. **Directions:** Guests are collected from the private jetty off St Mark's Square. Price guide: Single 680,000–950,000 lire; double/twin 950,000–1,400,000 lire; suites 2,100,000–4,300,000 lire.

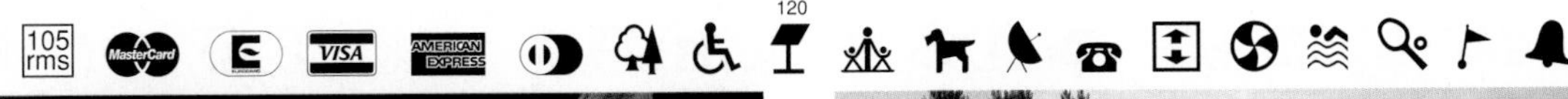

Metropole Hotel

SAN MARCO, RIVA DEGLI SCHIAVONI 4149, 30122 VENICE
TEL: 39 41 5205044 FAX: 39 41 5223679

Do try and arrive at this excellent hotel on a Friday – when the usual doorman's welcome is given by characters from the Commedia dell'Arte – including Harlequin and Brighella. This will confirm that the Metropole is rather special. The architecture is 18th century, and its position is superb, overlooking the canal and the lagoon, just three minutes walk from St Mark's Square. The talented Beggiato family have had great pleasure in restoring this lovely building to its former splendour. Exquisite painted ceilings, lovely panelling, over 2000 antiques – including a beautiful clock embraced by cherubs – rich colours in the decor, and a friendly angel beckoning guests into the Zodiac Bar, which has a special cocktail for each of the twelve signs – combine to make it a joyous place to stay. The charming bedrooms are air-conditioned, and overlook the waterfront or the hotel garden. The Buffet Trattoria is a popular rendezvous for Venetians as well as hotel guests, all enjoying the extensive display of exotic and traditional dishes, and some evenings special dinners are held with romantic musical themes. There is all Venice to explore by day, the casino to enjoy at night, boat trips to Murano to watch the glass blowers at work, the smart Lido beach and a good golf course, Directions Vaporetto to St Marks. Price guide: Single 220,000–400,000 lire; double/twin 300,000–590,000 lire; suites 500,000–750,000 lire.

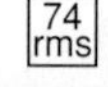

Albergo Quattro Fontane

30126 LIDO DI VENEZIA, ITALY
TEL: 39 41 526 0227 FAX: 39 41 526 0726 E-MAIL: quafonve@tin.it

A distinctive country house set in an idyllic garden on the Lido amongst orchards and productive vineyards on this long island, away from the hustle and bustle of Venice, the Albergo is only ten minutes by water-bus from San Marco square. The outside is more reminicent of a Swiss chalet, while the interior is more traditional, with tiled floors and big stone fireplaces. Signore Bevilacqua, whose family has owned Albergo Quattro Fontane for over forty years, has collected some very unusual antique furniture, art and artefacts from all over the world. A unique ambience greets you when you enter the Barchessa, the attractive annexe adjacent to the Albergo, where the bedrooms maintain the simplistic charm of individually chosen antique furniture. Large windows look out over the extensive terraces, where there is an outdoor dining area for summer meals. The menu is based on Venetian specialities, with the emphasis on traditional country cooking. The wines are from local vineyards. Regular water-buses to Venice. The Lido has its own famous beach and a golf course by day, and the casino at night. **Directions:** Either a private water-taxi from the airport straight to the Albergo with its own canal or a public water-bus every hour from the airport to the Lido via San Marco, then five minutes taxi ride to the Albergo. Price guide: Single 270,000 lire–380,000 lire; double/twin 370,000 lire–480,000 lire.

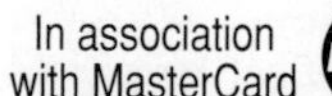

VILLA CONDULMER

31020 ZERMAN DI MOGLIANO VENETO, TREVISO, ITALY
TEL: 39 41 457100 FAX: 39 41 457134

The Villa Condulmer – an immaculate and magnificent 18th century mansion just 18 kilometres from Venice – has an illustrious past. It has been home to a pope, cardinal, famous soldiers, diplomats, men of law and even a saint. Today this patrician house, with its graceful facade, is a prestigious, secluded hotel. surrounded by extensive parkland. A warm greeting awaits arrivals at this grand house, with its glorious hall, fine antiques and Moretti Laresi frescoes. The bedrooms are classically furnished in the Venetian style. Guests enjoy aperitifs in the elegant piano bar while selecting appetizing and aromatic dishes from the menu of the traditional restaurant, the tables set with gleaming crystal and silver. Superb Italian wines are proffered. A meeting room able to seat 100 delegates is available for corporate events. The Villa has its own 27 hole golf course, swimming pool, tennis court and stables. The undulating park provides delightful walks with its lake, bridges and shady trees. Venice must be explored – St Mark's Square, The Doge's Palace, the sophisticated Lido, superb shops and little boats take visitors to the islands to see glass blowing and lace making. **Directions:** Leave A/4 for Mogliano, then follow signs to the Villa. Price guide: Single 180,000–260,000 lire; double/twin 300,000–400,000 lire; suites 400,000–600,000 lire.

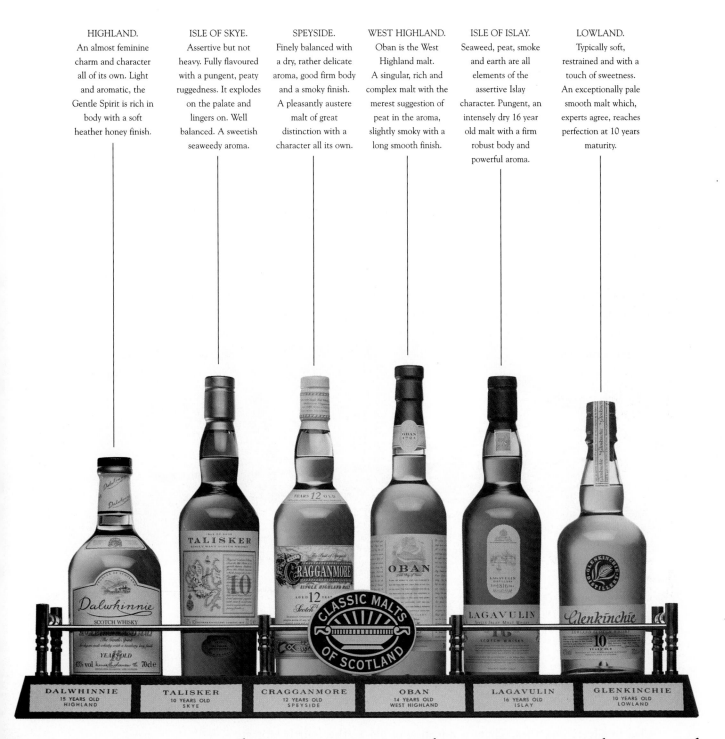

HIGHLAND.
An almost feminine charm and character all of its own. Light and aromatic, the Gentle Spirit is rich in body with a soft heather honey finish.

ISLE OF SKYE.
Assertive but not heavy. Fully flavoured with a pungent, peaty ruggedness. It explodes on the palate and lingers on. Well balanced. A sweetish seaweedy aroma.

SPEYSIDE.
Finely balanced with a dry, rather delicate aroma, good firm body and a smoky finish. A pleasantly austere malt of great distinction with a character all its own.

WEST HIGHLAND.
Oban is the West Highland malt. A singular, rich and complex malt with the merest suggestion of peat in the aroma, slightly smoky with a long smooth finish.

ISLE OF ISLAY.
Seaweed, peat, smoke and earth are all elements of the assertive Islay character. Pungent, an intensely dry 16 year old malt with a firm robust body and powerful aroma.

LOWLAND.
Typically soft, restrained and with a touch of sweetness. An exceptionally pale smooth malt which, experts agree, reaches perfection at 10 years maturity.

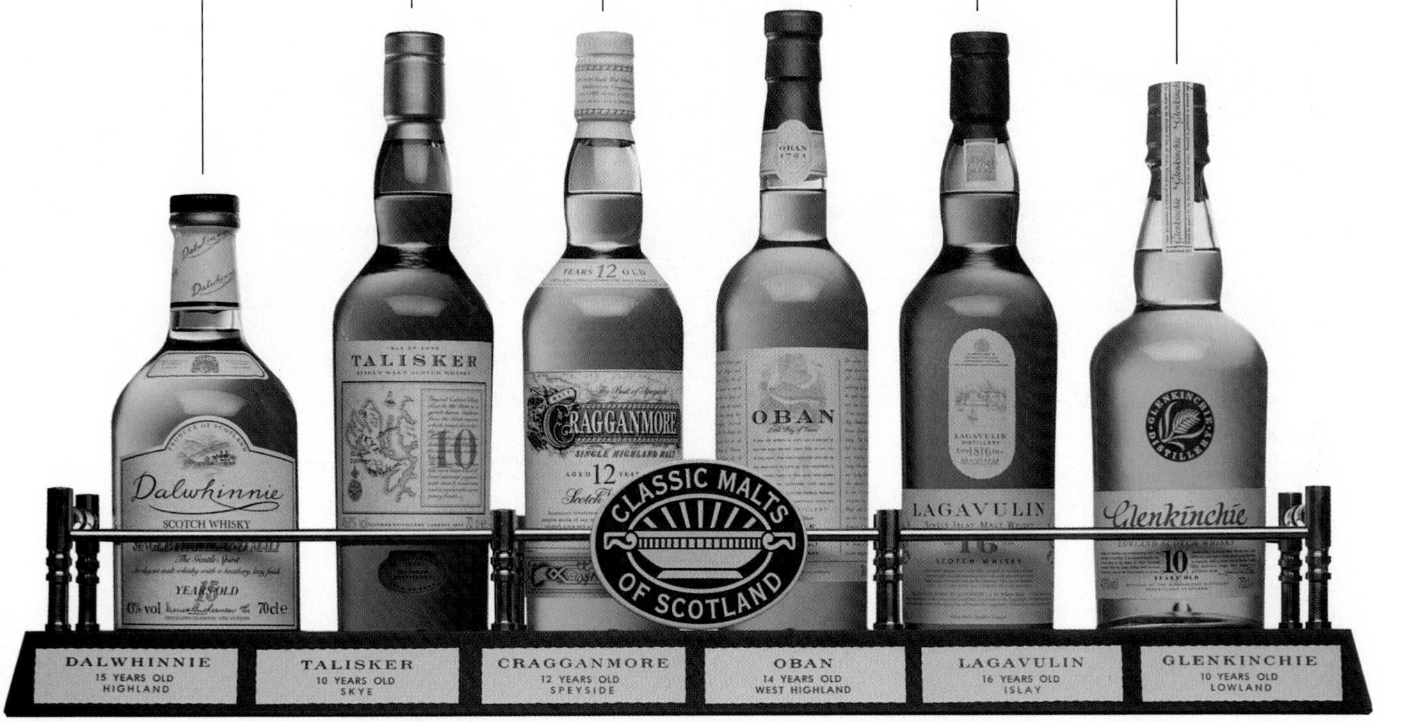

DALWHINNIE
15 YEARS OLD
HIGHLAND

TALISKER
10 YEARS OLD
SKYE

CRAGGANMORE
12 YEARS OLD
SPEYSIDE

OBAN
14 YEARS OLD
WEST HIGHLAND

LAGAVULIN
16 YEARS OLD
ISLAY

GLENKINCHIE
10 YEARS OLD
LOWLAND

Les grands crus de Scotland.

In the great wine-growing regions, there are certain growths from a single estate that are inevitably superior.

For the Scots, there are the single malts. Subtle variations in water, weather, peat and the distilling process itself lend each single malt its singular character.

Each Malt is an authentic, traditional malt with its own identity, inherent in both taste and aroma.

The Classic Malts are the finest examples of the main malt producing regions. To savour them, one by one, is a rare journey of discovery.

SIX OF SCOTLAND'S FINEST MALT WHISKIES

Latvia

The Baltic Republics have a running battle over which is the most beautiful capital, but Latvia's capital, Riga, probably reigns supreme. Riga, is an old Hanseatic city on the banks of the Daugava river, 10 miles inland from the Baltic.

The town was founded in the 13th century by a Bishop Albert from Germany and folklore says he tricked Latvian peasants into allowing his knights to settle here. The city is now a major Baltic port, second only to Leningrad and is dotted with quaint corner cafés, crumbling merchant mansions and bulky churches clad in silvery grey tiles. There is a feeling of old Germany about the place.

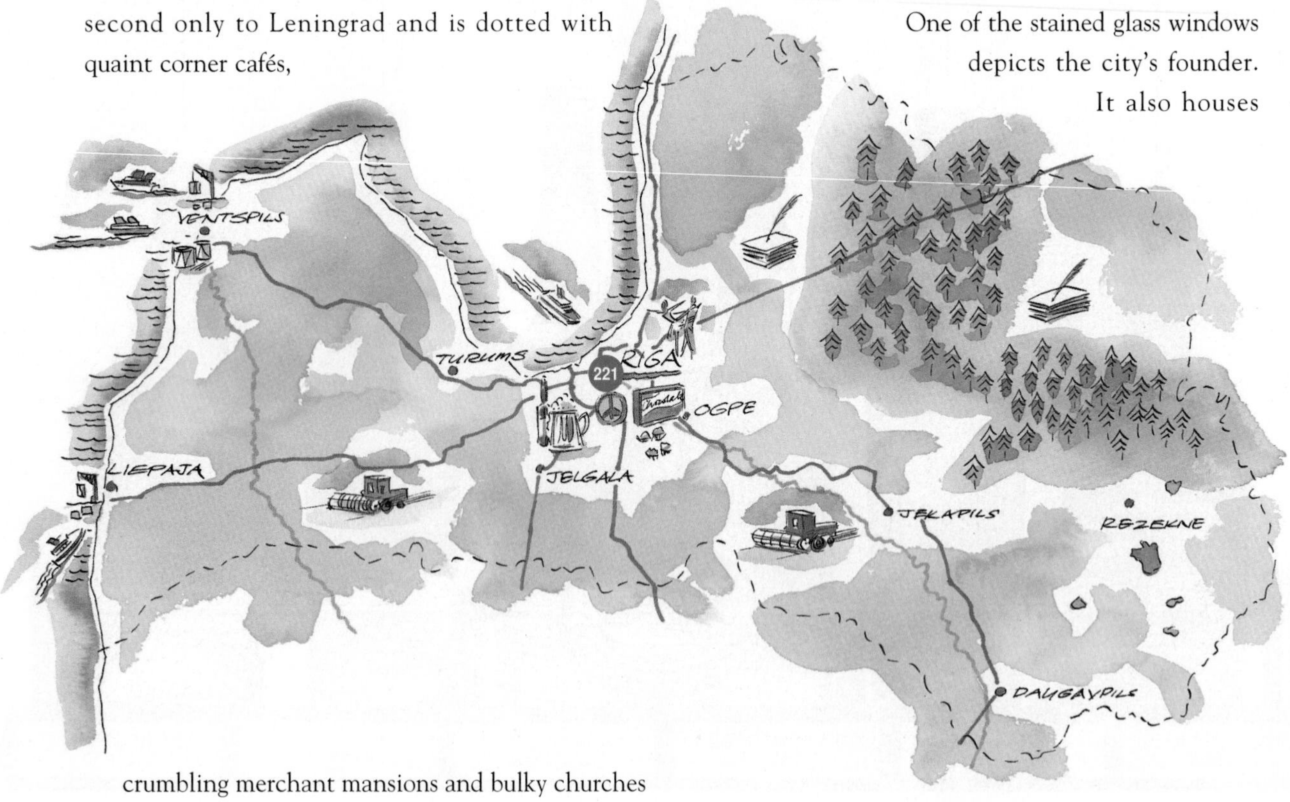

The Daugava river is crossed by three bridges. The principal one leads from Pardaugava into Lenina Iela, Riga's main street. The highest point of Riga is Cuckoo Hill (named due to the abundance of the bird) which is part of Dzeguzhkaha Park on the left bank.

Latvia is one of the few places in this part of the world where the mouth watering descriptions of local specialities are realised. You'll find an excellent choice of restaurants in Riga and you should have fun in discovering some of the more unusual cafés in Europe. Try the Café of Thirteen Chairs (which literally has thirteen chairs and thirteen only). Or the Petercailis at 25 Skarnu Iela, which is open air and not far from the magnificent Dome Cathedral on June Square.

This building took over 500 years to complete and is beautifully decorated with glorious wood carving and portraits of Lutheran worthies on the wall. One of the stained glass windows depicts the city's founder. It also houses the fourth largest organ in the world with a total of 6,768 pipes and each Sunday morning its sound is to be heard through the streets surrounding the building.

For entertainment, the Riga circus has a good reputation but non-circus goers could try the opera and ballet theatre on Padomju Bluvar. Wagner was resident conductor at the opera house until he had to flee his creditors and Schumann gave concerts here. He once wrote home saying that Rigans knew nothing about music and only talked about food! Nowadays there is just as much on the concert programme as there is on the menu.

Hotel De Rome

KALKUIELA 28, LV-1050, RIGA, LATVIA
TEL: 371 7 222 841 FAX: 371 7 228 251

Latvia became independent in 1990 and this delightful hotel, one of the grand establishments in the 1920s and 1930s, reopened in 1991. In an excellent position, ideal for business people, being close to the commercial section of Riga, it overlooks the city gardens and the Freedom Momument. The new Hotel de Rome has a splendid façade, influenced by the Latvian Art Deco era, but the interior is contemporary. The bedrooms are spacious, decorated in harmonious colours, and have comfortable modern furniture. Each floor has a lounge overlooking the Atrium, exhibiting exciting paintings. The smart Aspazijas Bar is a popular rendezvous. The Piano Bar is adjacent to the elegant Restaurant Otto Schwarz, renowned for delicious food and superb wines. Opera music is played daily and nightly in the Cafe "Romas Operas Galerija", famous for its cosy and relaxing atmosphere and used by opera lovers and business people alike. The well-equipped conference rooms have a 'no alcohol' regime. Interpreters and secretarial services available. The hotel is five minutes from the River Daugava, the markets, theatres and Latvian National Opera. The Art Nouveau street and Old Town are fascinating. To the west is Jurmala, a summer resort on the Baltic Sea, and the countryside is glorious. **Directions:** Riga can be reached by ship, plane, train or car. Parking. Price guide: Single LS 91; double/twin LS 100; suites LS 125.

90 rms 100

Liechtenstein

Fall asleep in the train and you might miss Liechtenstein. Its territory measures just under 18 miles across from north to south, and an average of four miles from west to east. In some ways you could be forgiven for mistaking it for a part of Switzerland. There are many international day trips out of Zurich to this charming miniature country..

An independent nation since 1719, Liechtenstein has a customs union with Switzerland, which means they share trains, currency, and diplomats – but not stamps, which is why collectors prize the local releases. It's easiest to get there by car, since Liechtenstein is so small that Swiss trains pass through without stopping.

Green and mountainous, its Rhine shores lined with vineyards, Liechtenstein is lovely. In fairy tale Vaduz, Prince Johannes Adam Pius still lives in Vaduz Castle, a massive 16th century fortress perched high on the cliff over the city. Only honoured guests of the Prince tour the castle's interior, but its exterior and the views from the grounds are worth the climb. In the modern centre of town, head for the tourist information office to have your passport stamped with the Liechtenstein crown. Upstairs, the Prince's Art Gallery and the State Art Collection display Flemish masters and on the same floor, the Postage Stamp Museum attracts philatelists from all over the world to see the three hundred frames of beautifully designed and rare stamps.

Next, move on to the Liechtenstein National Museum, which houses historical artefacts, church carvings, ancient coins and arms from the prince's collection.

In Schaan, just north of Vaduz, visit the Roman excavations and the parish church built on the foundations of a Roman fort.

Or drive up to the chalets of the picturesque Triesenberg for spectacular views of the Rhine Valley. Higher still the Malbun is a sun drenched ski bowl with comfortable slopes and gentle ambience.

Liechtenstein has a cuisine of its own, although there is plenty of French, Swiss and Austrian influence. Try tender home-made Schwartenmagen (pressed pork), and Sauerkäse (sour cheese) and Kaseknopfli (cheese dumplings), – plus lovely meats and the local crusty, chewy bread. The wines are worth sampling too.

PARKHOTEL SONNENHOF

MAREESTRASSE 29, 9490 VADUZ, PRINCIPALITY OF LIECHTENSTEIN
TEL: 4175/232 11 92 FAX: 4175/232 00 53

The microstate of Liechtenstein, just 61 square miles, on the east bank of the Upper Rhine, dating back to 1342, is delightful and easily accessible from the Swiss motorways or international trains heading for Austria. On the fringes of Vaduz, this enchanting hotel is surrounded by verdant countryside and has uninterrupted views across to the mountains. The house is resplendant with ivy, colourful window boxes and bright sunblinds shading the individual balconies and patios. The inviting gardens are well tended and filled with flowers – although this is also a winter sports haven. After a peaceful night's sleep in the enchanting bedrooms, guests enjoy a fabulous breakfast buffet. The reception hall has a rustic charm; the library is a handsome, relaxing room with a chess table set out by the winter fire, and the bar is convivial. Big picture windows add to the attractions of the spacious, elegant restaurant; beautifully presented, original dishes accompanied by good wine ensure every meal is a special occasion. Convenient for businessmen meeting in Vaduz, the hotel is also popular with skiers, the slopes just 15 minutes away. Tennis, cycling, golf and walking fill summer days. The hotel has an indoor pool, other water sports are on Lake Constance. **Directions:** A12 Feldkirch exit, watch for hotel signs on left before reaching Vaduz. Price guide: Single Sfr240–Sfr270; double/twin Sfr300–Sfr360; suites Sfr390–Sfr430.

Luxembourg

Don't be fooled by the size of Luxembourg. This nation, with its cities burnished with age, is seriously wealthy. With the fourth highest standard of living in the world, rivalling Switzerland with more than 120 banks within an area smaller than the size of Greater London, and more gastronomique restaurants per capita than any other place in Europe, it is unsurprising that those who live here find it a very pleasurable place to work and play.

The natives of Luxembourg present a solid front to the outside world, interacting in French, German, or English, but maintaining a private world in their own native Letzebuergesch – Luxembourgish. They have survived centuries of conquest and occupation, not to mention from the European Union 'Eurocrats' and more than a hundred international banks – and still retain their own identity.

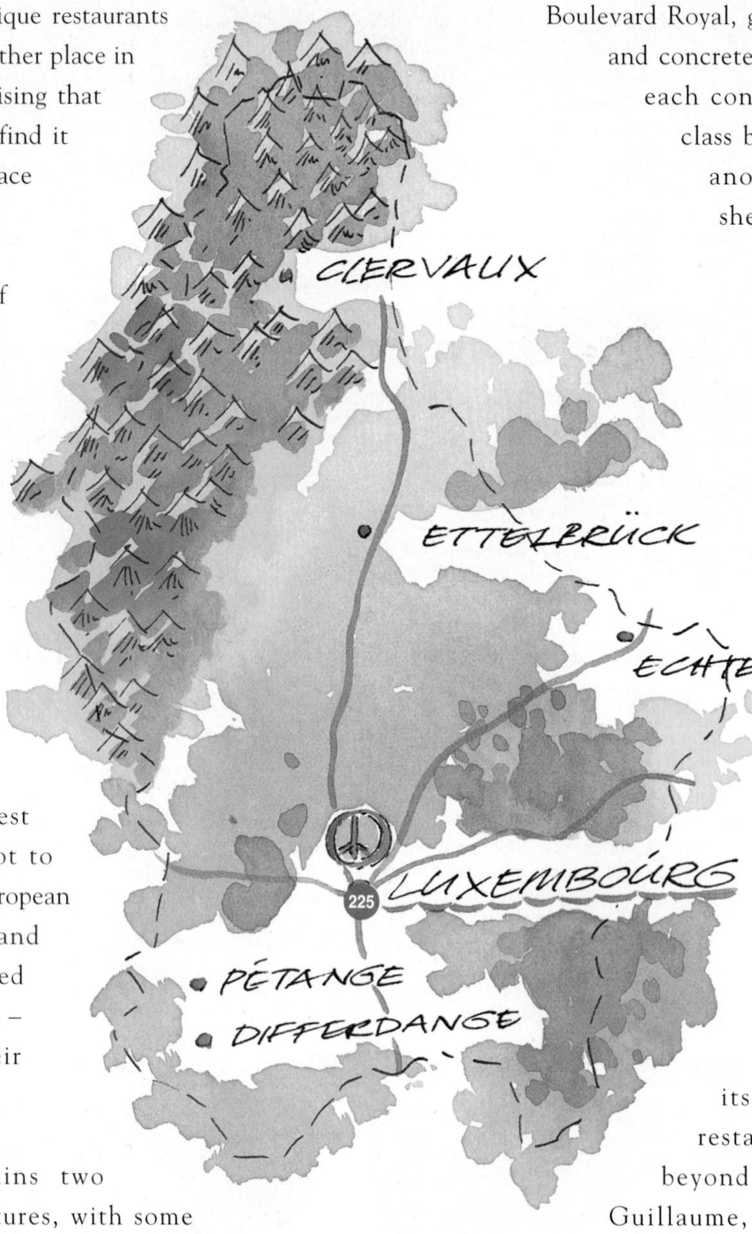

Luxembourg sustains two parallel eating cultures, with some establishments catering for international tastes while others reserved for the loden coated locals may greet a lost visitor with stunned silence as thick as the cigarette smoke which fills the air.

Entering the eponymous capital of tiny Luxembourg across the Grande Duchesse Charlotte Bridge, first time visitors are greeted by an awe inspiring view – a panorama of medieval stonework, jutting fortification walls, slit windowed towers, ancient church spires, massive gates straight out of a 17th century engraving.

Turn left and enter the 20th century as the Boulevard Royal, glitters with glass and concrete office buildings, each containing a world class bank and untold, anonymous, well sheltered fortunes. The lively Place d'Armes, with its cafés and restaurants lies just beyond the Place Guillaume, and open air concerts are held here every evening during the Summer months.

Luxembourg's most famous product is Villeroy and Boch porcelain, available in most gift shops in Luxembourg City.

PARC HOTEL

16 RUE DE GRUNDHOF, L-6550 BERDORF, LUXEMBOURG
TEL: 352 790 195 FAX: 352 790 223

This charming hotel on the outskirts of the village of Berdorf built on the forest edge was founded some sixty years ago. It is a peaceful retreat away from the commercial activity of Luxembourg, standing in its own parkland, the well tended gardens having romantic pools with bulrushes and waterlilies as well as rare, exotic trees. The bedrooms retain their original charm, but have been modernised to suit today's traveller. Many have balconies looking across the verdant countryside. The panelled salon is handsome, the ideal spot for a digestif after enjoying dinner in the spacious restaurant, with its unusual circular serving area in the centre of the room. The chefs are very creative, the menu cosmopolitan and the dishes beautifully presented. The wine list is extensive and reasonably priced. On fine days guests take their apéritifs and eat alfresco on the cool terrace, with green vines winding up the pillars and across the ceiling. Relaxing on comfortable garden chairs in the park is a popular pastime while more energetic guests walk in 'Little Switzerland' or use the hotel open-air pool. Tennis and mini-golf are nearby. **Directions:** Leave the E44 from Luxembourg City, taking the E29 to Echternach, following signs to Berdorf. There is parking at the hotel. Price guide: Single Bf2200–Bf3800; double/twin Bf3000–Bf4900.

20 rms

Monaco

Whether you go there for pleasure or on business Monaco has everything you want or need. The calendar of events held in this small principality is second to none in Europe and being so compact, the events are usually within walking distance of your hotel. Indeed, you may be able to watch the Monaco Grand Prix without leaving your bedroom balcony. This is truly a place where the climate is excellent and you can – if you so wish – work hard and play hard.

The Sporting Club, perched out on its own peninsula juts into the Meditteranean and you will quickly discover that it is the place to dine, dance and "celebrity spot". The fireworks on warm Summer Saturday evenings are quite spectacular. This Club hosts many prestigious events during the year – one being the World Music Awards which consequently attracts a host of the good, the great and the notorious.

For those in need of serious relaxation, the excellent Thalassotherapy centre, where you can pamper and preen yourself in the ultimate luxury, adjoins the Hermitage, and guests of the Hermitage benefit from a reduced entry fee and treatments.

If you have time for sightseeing, visit the Grimaldi Palace in the heart of Monaco Ville – the cobbled, characterful part of town, or the Aquarium – regarded as the best in Europe or the Jardin Exotique, with its unusual and varied range of cacti, most growing to the size of a baby elephant.

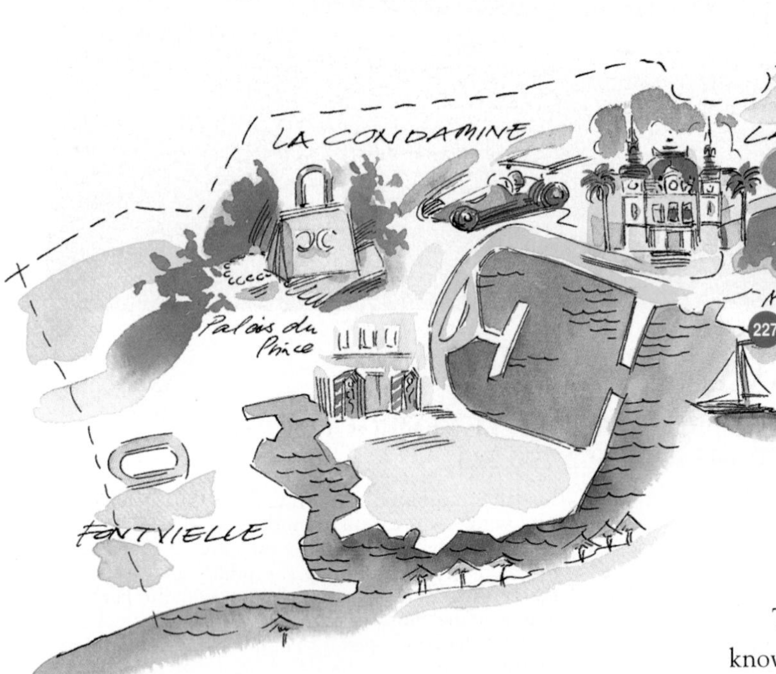

There is, of course, the casino – but less well known are the superb tennis club and golf club – the latter is situated high up into the hills overlooking Monaco Ville. Both clubs host pro-celebrity tennis and golf tournaments respectively – and Seve Ballesteros (who is a resident) and Boris Becker (who is not) are regular visitors to the principality. The views are without exception wonderful. "People watching" is entertaining and why pay for entry to a fashion show when you can view the latest haute couture on these smartest of streets?

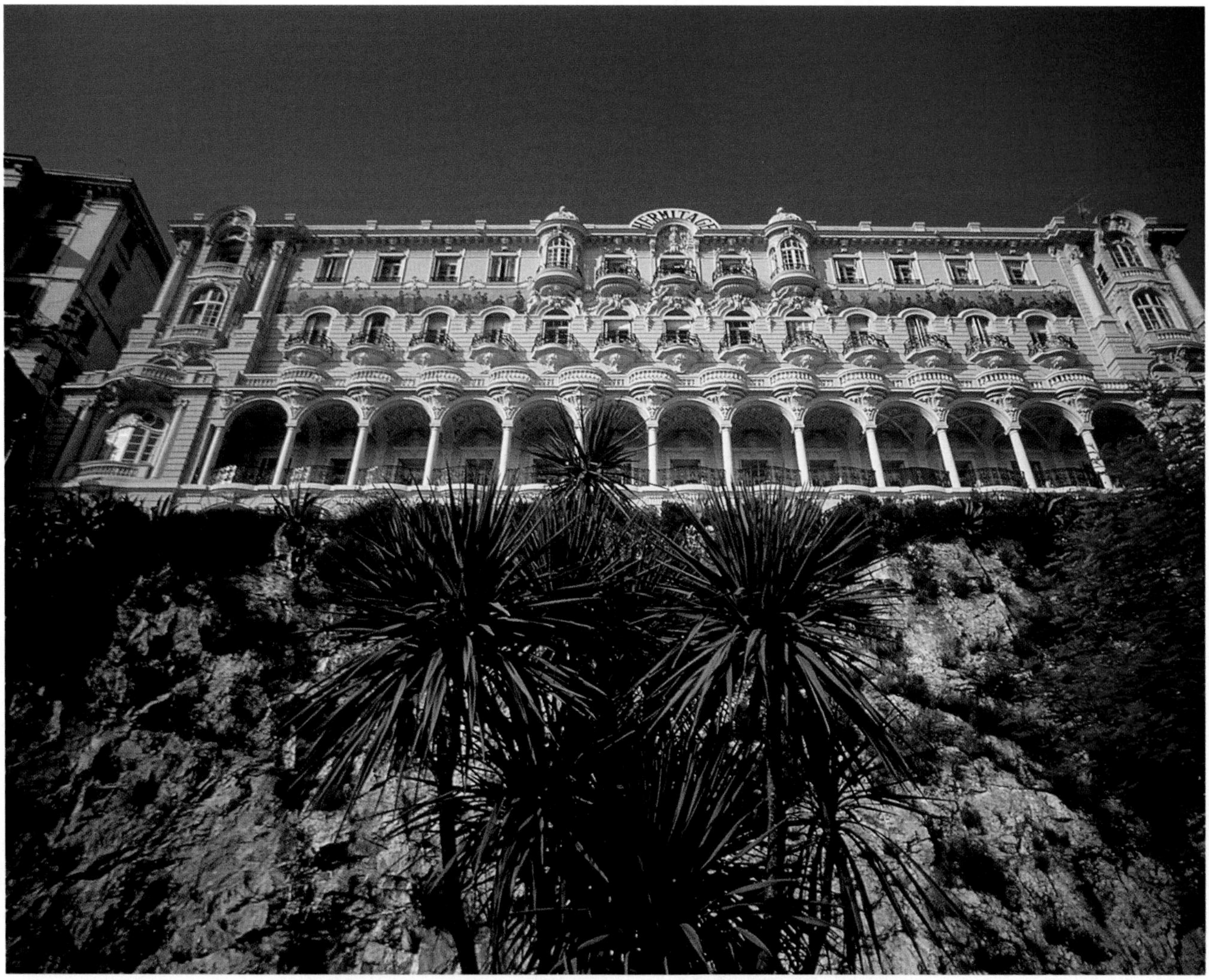

HÔTEL HERMITAGE

SQUARE BEAUMARCHAIS, BP277, MC 98005 MONACO CEDEX, MONACO
TEL: 377 92 16 40 00 FAX: 377 92 16 38 52

One of the great hotels of the Belle Époque, the Hôtel Hermitage has maintained its high standards and today it is still elite and prestigious. The approach is impressive, with its grand facade and entrance, and once inside guests are enchanted by the exquisite Winter Garden with its Art Nouveau stained glass domed roof, the spectacular floral chandelier, the graceful balconies, pillars and elegant furnishings. The bedrooms are luxurious, extremely comfortable, peaceful and decorated in delightful harmonious colours. Many have balconies overlooking the coast line. The Belle Époque restaurant, with its marble pillars, glistening chandeliers and elaborate ceilings, is well named. In summer it extends onto a waterside terrace, for romantic dining under the stars. Talented chefs prepare sumptuous dishes, the sommelier presides over a magnificent cellar. The Terrace Bar, surrounded by exotic plants, and the graceful Salon Excelsior are attractive rendezvous, perhaps before going to the fabled casino. Championship golf course and major tennis tournaments. Les Thermes Marins de Monte Carlo, with direct access from the hotel, has a fabulous salt-water pool, a brilliant gymnasium and full spa facilities. **Directions:** The hotel is easy to find, set back from the seafront. Price guide: Single Ff1300–Ff2500; double/twin Ff1600–Ff2750; suites Ff4300–Ff10000.

The Netherlands

Holland, more correctly The Netherlands, is one of Europe's smallest countries. Tourist posters feature windmills, tulips, canals, and girls wearing lacy caps and clogs – and these picturesque images are still to be found. But there is far more to this country than these clichés portray. Remember too, that this is the land of such creative men of genius as the painters Rembrandt, Hals, and Vermeer.

Amsterdam's medieval Nieuwe Kerk, both a church and cultural centre is a sign of Amsterdam's cultural prominence. This city is now as famous for its jazz, modern art and ballet as it is for its Rembrandts and van Goghs. Small and densely packed with fine buildings, many dating from the 17th century or earlier, it is easily explored by foot or by bike. The old heart of the city consists of canals, with narrow streets radiating out from a central hub of the central station – a building dating from 1885, and an excellent example of Dutch architecture at its most flamboyant.

The Hague, sedate and refined, presents a striking contrast to Amsterdam's vitality and eccentricity. This is the national seat of government and home to the International Court of Justice, where diplomacy and ceremony colour the lives of all residents, from Queen Beatrix, ambassadors and parliamentarians downwards.

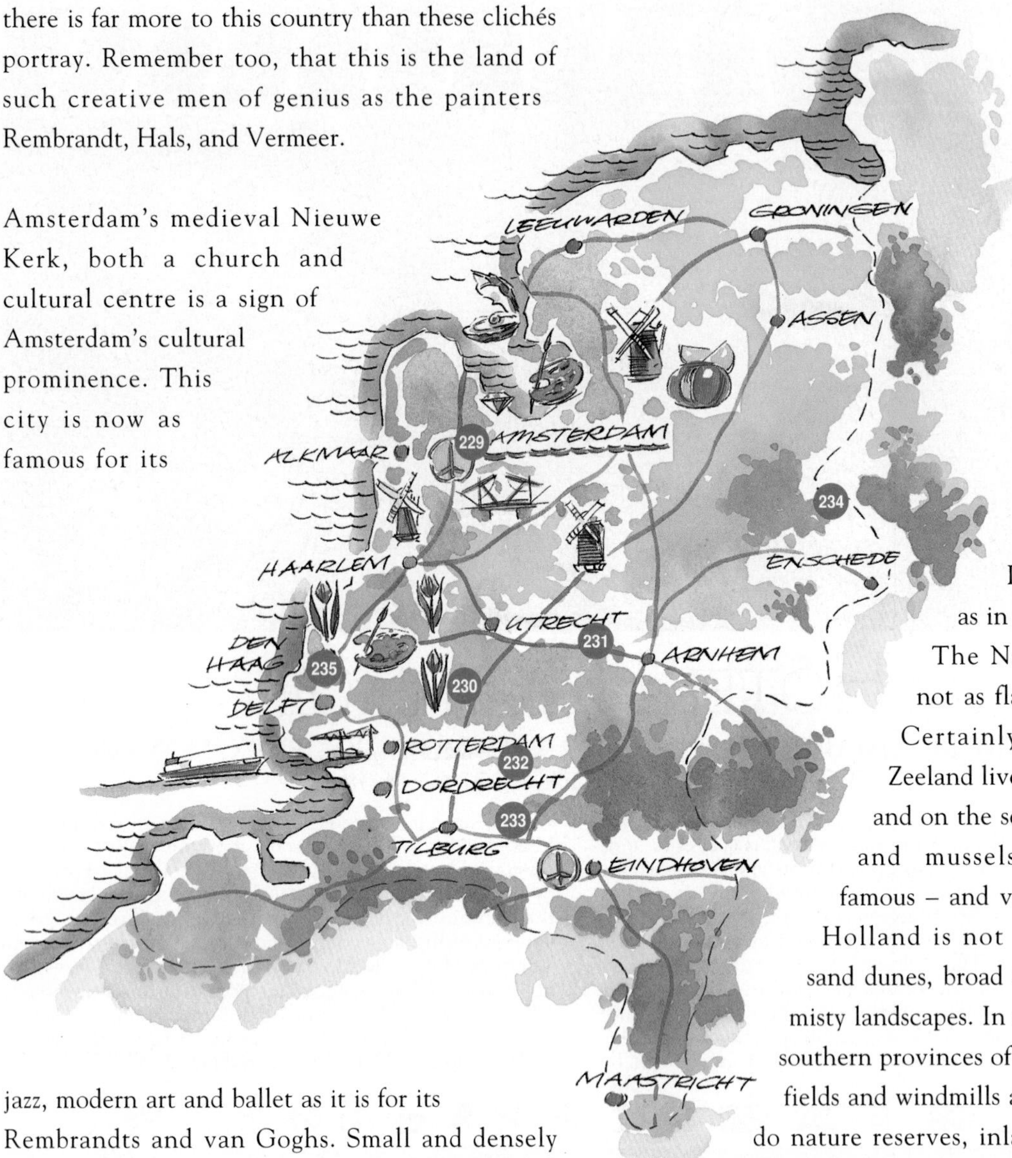

In landscape as in food however, The Netherlands is not as flat as it seems. Certainly, low-lying Zeeland lives with the sea and on the sea – its oysters and mussels are world famous – and versatile North Holland is not restricted to sand dunes, broad seascapes, and misty landscapes. In and across the southern provinces of Holland, bulb fields and windmills abound, but so do nature reserves, inland lakes and lush valleys.

The prime tourist season in Holland runs from April through to October and it peaks during Easter and the Summer. Dutch bulb fields bloom from early April to the end of May and June is an ideal time to catch the warm weather and miss the crowds, but who cares about the weather when the museums house half the best paintings in Europe?

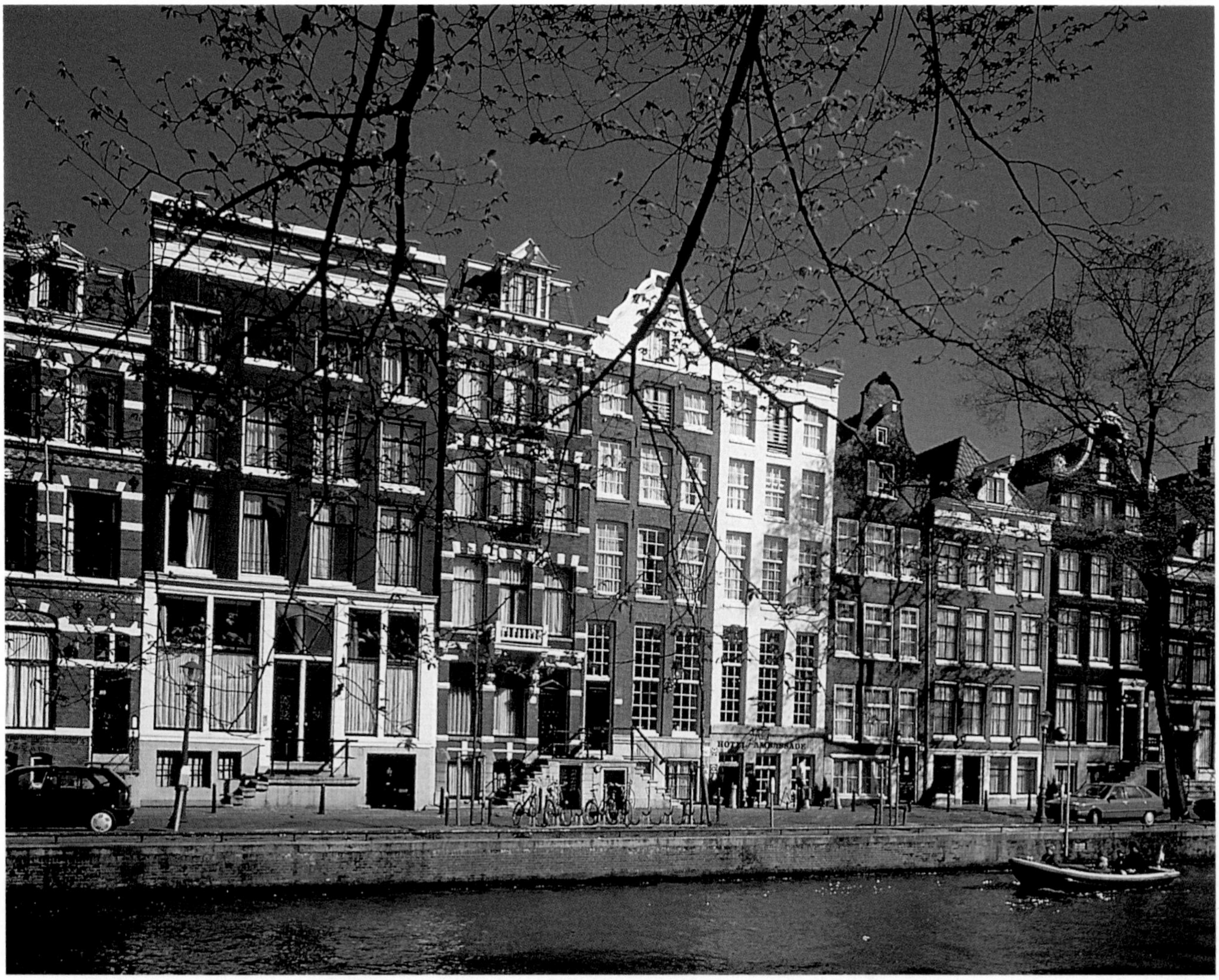

HOTEL AMBASSADE

HERENGRACHT 341, 1016 AZ AMSTERDAM, THE NETHERLANDS
TEL: 31 20 62 62 333 FAX: 31 20 62 45 321

The Ambassade is a most attractive hotel in the heart of Amsterdam. Originally ten separate houses, each the home of a wealthy merchant on the Herengracht (The Gentlemen's Canal), the hotel has been converted into one building which retains all the erstwhile interior architecture and the external façades. No two bedrooms are alike, and each has its own colour scheme in accordance with its style. The graceful furniture complements the history of the building. The five suites are superb and the apartments luxurious. Overlooking the canal are two elegant and spacious lounges, with tall windows, splendid oil paintings on the walls and fine Amsterdam grandfather clocks. Breakfast is served in the traditional dining room, or guests can take advantage of the efficient room service available. There is no restaurant in the Ambassade, but there is a wide choice of places to eat in the city, among them the historic Vijff Vlieghen, and many small bistros along the canal-sides. Amsterdam has wonderful museums and art galleries to visit – the famous Rijksmuseum, Rembrandt's House and the Van Gogh Museum. Anne Franks' House is very special. After seeing the flower market and fantastic shops, visitors can sample the lively nightlife. **Directions:** Parking is not easy. 20 minutes by taxi from Schiphol Airport. Price guide: Single Fl 240–250; double/twin Fl 295–315; suites Fl 395–495.

HOTEL DE ARENDSHOEVE

MOLENLAAN 14, 2861 LB, BERGAMBACHT, NETHERLANDS
TEL: 31 182 35 1000 FAX: 31 182 35 1155 E-MAIL: juwo@euronet.nl

This elite hotel, just a pleasant drive from Rotterdam, has achieved a timeless ambience with its graceful lines, ornamental garden and a traditional windmill as its landmark. Under this windmill is "Onder de Molen" serving Dutch cuisine, one of the hotel's two restaurants. The hotel is a long, low building and the interior is entrancing – all Europe is reflected in the decorations and furnishings, each fireplace, piece of carved panelling or fine antique having its own history, be it from a castle or private mansion. The bedrooms have a character of their own – a melange of the past and present, with many hospitable extras. The lounge is a perfect rendezvous and the sociable Scarlatti Bar is ideal for drinks at the end of the day. The pièce de résistance is Restaurant Puccini, with its exquisite Italian renaissance decor, in the octagonal pavilion overlooking the gardens. Guests feast on imaginative, appetizing dishes and superb wines. There is a dramatic Roman-style indoor pool with adjacent spa facilities and Uithalgo Health Spa Centre, or tennis and a putting green for those needing fresh air. Ample meeting facilities. Cycling through the countryside is another diversion. **Directions:** From Rotterdam head for Capelle, then follow N210 to Bergambacht. finding the hotel close to the windmill. Price guide: Single Fl 215,00–Fl 275,00; double/twin Fl 265,00–Fl 325,00; suites Fl 375,00–FL 425,00.

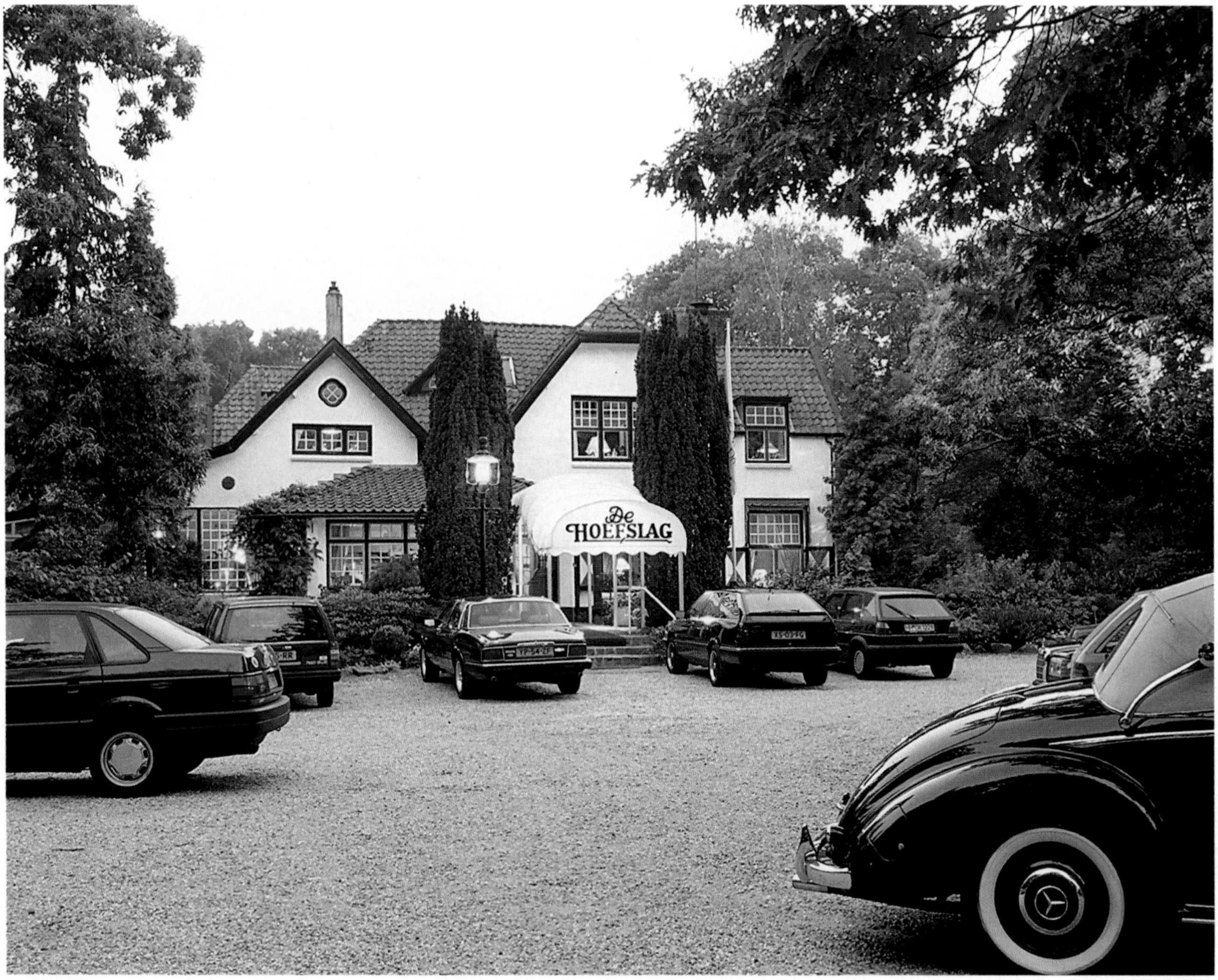

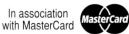

DE HOEFSLAG

VOSSENLAAN 28, 3735 KN BOSCH EN DUIN
TEL: 31 30 225 1051 FAX: 31 30 228 5821

Just twenty minutes from Amsterdam, on the outskirts of Utrecht, in a peaceful residential area, the joy of serendipity awaits those escaping city pressures – a delightful fin-de-siècle manor house surrounded by fragrant flowers. De Hoefslag is cosmopolitan – it has the ambience of an English country house, the architecture has attractive Mediterranean features and the cooking is French! The comfortable bedrooms are decorated in soft colours and have nice extras like bathrobes. The Senior Suites have balconies and whirlpools, one of the Junior Suites is designed for those with mobility problems. The hotel has a charming sitting room and small bar where guests mingle while deciding whether to dine in the smart restaurant, a member of the exclusive Alliance Gastronomique Néerlandaise, or try the Carte Créative in the informal bistro. There are excellent arrangements for seminars and corporate entertaining. Leisure facilities in the region include golf, tennis, exploring the countryside on cycles, riding or visiting the interesting galleries and museums in the neighbourhood. Internet: http://www.hoefslag.nl **Directions:** From Utrecht take highway A28 towards Amersfoort, exit Zeist–Oost/Den Dolder. Pass McDonalds, then second left Den Dolder/Bosch en Duin/Bilthoven turn left again and follow this road until hotel in sight. Car parking. Price guide: Double/twin Fl 230–300; suites Fl 300–525.

HOTEL DE DUINRAND

STEERGERF 2, 5151 RB DRUNEN, NETHERLANDS
TEL: 31 416 372498 FAX: 31 416 374919

The top twelve restaurants in Holland belong to an exclusive club, "Les Patrons Cuisiniers", and Restaurant "De Duinrand" is one of these elite dozen, while also having superb residential facilities. It stands in woodlands, yet is easily accessible from the motorway. Peace and privacy are ensured as the hotel is surrounded by extensive well-kept gardens. The suites and bedrooms are very stylish, with exciting contemporary furniture and every imaginable extra, including double basins and bathrobes. The suites have Jacuzzis and patios, while the VIP-Suite is on two floors with its own champagne bar! Disabled guests have been remembered. Before dining, guests can order cocktails in the lounge or on the terrace, while deciding which exquisite dishes to order from the menus, with wine suggestions for each course. The handsome restaurant is sophisticated, with pristine linen, sparkling crystal and intriguing flower arrangements. Breakfast is al fresco on fine mornings. There are also excellent meeting rooms. Smoking is discouraged. Those needing exercise cycle through the countryside or play tennis nearby Golf is further away. Others relax in the gardens, take a boat down the canal or explore Heusden and 's-Hertogenbosch, historic cities in the region. **Directions:** From A2 take A59, on reaching Drunen follow signs to the restaurant. Price guide: Single Fl 195; double/twin Fl 225; suites Fl 325–Fl 600

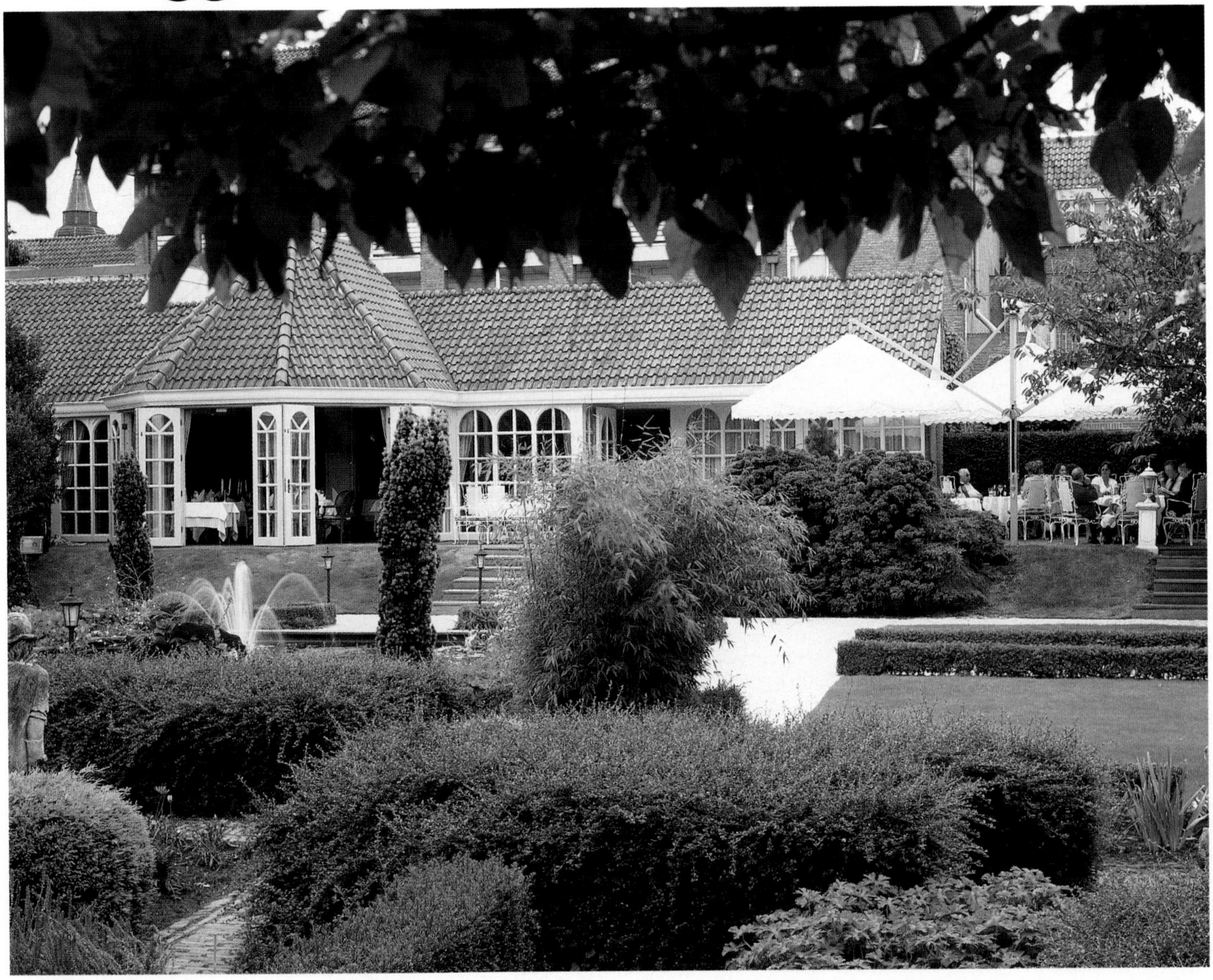

HOTEL RESTAURANT DE SWAEN

DE LIND 47, 5061 HT OISTERWISK, NETHERLANDS
TEL: 31 135 23 3233 FAX: 31 135 28 5860

To stay at De Swaen is an epicurean experience, for this enchanting hotel, overlooking the town square and English Garden, has a proprietor who is an enthusiastic chef and sets himself the highest standards of hospitality. De Swaen dates back to 1628, then a brewing house. Today, having maintained its historic charm, it is an elegant building with a decorative balcony along its facade and attractive terraces for al fresco refreshments. The lounge is richly decorated, full of colour and comfort, an ideal meeting place. The guest rooms, each unique, are luxurious and air conditioned, and gorgeous antiques blend happily with fax machines and other contemporary needs. Disabled visitors have been remembered. Delicious appetizers in the intimate bar titillate the palate; the most exacting bon viveur will appreciate the fabulous dishes exquisitely presented in the magnificent restaurant – bergère chairs, big gilt mirrors, gleaming silver and immaculate napery. The wines are sublime. Less formal is the attractive Auberge De Jonge Swaen, a sophisticated bistro serving delicious, reasonably priced dishes. Hosting corporate events, seminars and banquets is effortless at this exclusive hotel. Golf, cycling, tennis and riding are all within easy reach. **Directions:** From Einhoven E38, then A58, Moergestel exit, finding De Swaen in centre of Oisterwijk. Valet parking. Price guide: Single Fl 285; double/twin Fl 325–395; suites Fl 495–795.

24 rms 150

HOTEL DE WIEMSEL

WINHOFFLAAN 2, F–7631 HX OOTMARSUM, NETHERLANDS
TEL: 31 541 292 155 FAX: 31 541 293 295

An enchanting medieval village and a thriving farm form the background of this excellent and attractive hotel located some 80 miles east of Amsterdam. The architecture is typical of the region and the surroundings are rural. There is a marvellous feeling of space, with wide arches dividing the reception rooms and big windows overlooking the terrace or verdant countryside. The furnishings are contemporary and colourful. There are also smart, well-equipped meeting rooms. There are more suites than bedrooms, all are spacious and have been decorated in relaxing colour schemes, while the bathrooms are luxurious, marble with gold taps. Outdoor living is encouraged, with bright garden furniture set out on the terrace round the outdoor pool – perfect for al fresco breakfast or apéritifs. Both the Restaurant de Wanne as well as the Restaurant de Gouden Korenaar are very elegant, an appropriate setting for superb cosmopolitan dishes accompanied by fine wines. Marvellous picnic hampers can be arranged for those borrowing bicycles to explore the countryside. The hotel offers tennis and a superb health/beauty complex with a pool. Hot air balloon trips start from the garden. **Directions:** A1 towards Hengelo, exit Oldenzaal/Ootmarsum, after 12 km, in Ootmarsum, take the road to Denekamp. Price guide: Single Fl 250; double/twin Fl 310; suites Fl 275–Fl 425.

RESTAURANT HOTEL SAVELBERG

OOSTEINDE 14, 2271 EH VOORBURG, NETHERLANDS
TEL: 31 70 3872081 FAX: 31 70 3877715

This enchanting hotel with its second name, 'Vreugd & Rust', which means 'Pleasure and Peace', the name of the lovely 17th mansion and its park, can be found in the old village of Voorburg, not far from The Hague. It has been restored with great care and is now a listed historical building. Guests are immediately aware of the grace evocative of its past combined with the luxury of today. The bedrooms and suites are spacious and light, overlooking the estate, and have every modern comfort. The elegant lounge is a quiet rendezvous, alternatively the big terrace is ideal for an aperitif in the sun. The excellent meeting rooms, with full office support and presentation equipment available, quickly transform into impressive private dining rooms suitable for corporate entertaining or special celebrations. The handsome restaurant is a very important part of this hotel, having won many accolades for its inspired use of seasonal fare and absolutely superb wine list. It offers both gourmet à la carte and delicious set menus. Strolling round the lake enjoying the country air is a peaceful way to end a busy day. **Directions:** From Amsterdam A4 towards Rotterdam/Delft, the A12 to Voorburg, finding the entrace to the hotel in Oosteinde 14. Price guide: Double/twin Fl 250,00–Fl 300,00; suites Fl 450,00–Fl 495,00.

Norway

Norway boasts some of the most remote and romantic scenery in Europe. Along the west coast, deep fjords knife into steep mountain ranges. Inland, cross-country ski trails follow frozen trout streams and downhill paths idle through forests whose floors teem with wildflowers and berries during the summer. This is also the land of the midnight sun.

The best way to get around the capital Oslo is to use the Oslo Card which offers unlimited travel for one, two or three days on all Oslo's public transport – which includes bus, T-bane (the underground), tram and even local ferries. You can buy the Oslo Card at Oslo tourist offices, from hotels, travel agents in Oslo, and large department stores.

Oslo is a small, wonderfully compact capital and excellent to explore on foot. The main street, Karl Johans Gate, runs right through the centre of town, from Oslo Central station uphill to the Royal Palace. Half its length is closed to traffic, and it is in this section you will find many of the city's colourful shops and vibrant outdoor cafes.

Start at the Royal Palace, the King's residence, where the surrounding park is open to the public. Time your visit to coincide with the changing of the guard – daily at 1.30pm. When the king is in residence – the red flag flies and the Royal Guard strikes up the band.

Then walk down Karl Johans Gate to the old university where each year on December 10, the Nobel Peace prize is presented in the main hall.

The other major city in Norway – Bergen, is also best seen when travelling on foot. Despite disastrous fires in the past, much of medieval Bergen has remained intact and seven surrounding mountains pose a magnificent backdrop to the weathered wooden houses, cobbled streets, and warehouses of the harbour.

Bergen is the start of the Fjord cruises of all descriptions. Crossing fjords is a necessary as well as a scenic way to travel in Norway and Hardangerfjord, Sognefjord, and Nordfjord are three of the most popular and deepest.

KVIKNE'S HOTEL

N – 5850 BALESTRAND, NORWAY

TEL: 47 57 69 11 01 FAX: 47 57 69 15 02 E-MAIL: booking@kviknes.no

Hospitality at Balholm, the site of this impressive residence, has been a tradition since 1752. The Kvikne family, who own the hotel, made this imaginative purchase in 1877, and now, over a century later, it is one of Norway's largest prestigious hotels. Its situation is magnificent, on the shores of the fjord at Balestrand, and the register records many eminent names over the decades. The interior of Kvikne's is an antique collector's dream, so many beautiful pieces, together with fine objets d'art and handsome paintings. The Hoiviksalen is a magnificent example of handcarving in the Dragon style: the chairs, tables, ornaments are all unique – and comfortable! The bedrooms are charming, and such is the popularity of this hotel that a new wing has been added to accommodate the influx of guests. Most have balconies overlooking the fjord, and all have modern amenities. Drinks are enjoyed in the bars or on the terraces, and enjoying superb Norwegian specialities, including a fabulous Smorgasbord, in the spacious, restaurant is a great pleasure. Boat trips down the fjord, helicopter rides over the mountains, are exciting; fishing and exploring the region are more leisurely occupations. Internet: http://www.kviknes.no **Directions:** From the airport, take the main road for Balestrand, finding Kvikne's Hotel in the centre. Parking for residents. Price guide (per person): Single 600–785NOK; double/twin 400–735NOK; suites 885NOK.

190 rms         200      

First Hotel Bastion

SKIPPERGATEN 7, 0152 OSLO, NORWAY
TEL: 47 22 47 77 00 FAX: 47 22 33 11 80

Old Oslo is fascinating – dating aback to the Middle Ages and now re-emerging with fine old buildings being renovated,and the vibrant Stock Exchange located there. In the midst of this stimulating ambience, at the foot of the Akershus Fortress there is a new hotel, The First Bastion. It is a modern hotel with contemporary fabrics, fireplace and lighting in the Library/Bar, yet it has lovely polished old wooden floors enhancing the ambience. The bedrooms, decorated in warm colours and with comfort an important criterion, meet various needs – non-smoking, smoking, adapted for those with mobility problems or suitable for guests with special business needs such as fax or cordless telephones so they can be accessed throughout the hotel. The hotel does not have a restaurant, however there is a marvellous 'Oslo Breakfast' served in the attractive dining room. A lunch buffet is served Monday to Friday, and at night the concierge will recommend good places to dine. The Bastion has a small fitness centre and spa, popular with delegates participating in seminars in the self-contained conference area at the top of the hotel. The hotel is ideally situated for the ferries, trains and buses. It is close to shops, restaurants, museums and the commercial centre. **Directions:** In the centre of old Oslo. There is parking. Price guide: Single 545–1175NOK; double/twin 695–1275NOK.

FLEISCHER'S HOTEL

N–5700 VOSS, NORWAY

TEL: 47 56 51 11 55 FAX: 47 56 51 22 89

This grand and favourite hotel is in a superb position, overlooking the lake and not far from the station, one hour from Bergen. The facade with its towers and pointed dormer windows is reminiscent of Switzerland. The surrounding countryside is spectacular, Voss being between two large fjords. Built in 1889 and still run by the same family, Fleischer's has been discreetly modernised, without losing its original charm. There is a warm ambience in the foyer with its convivial coffee shop, and the elegant salons lead onto the attractive terrace which, with its magnificent views over the water, is popular for alfresco refreshments. The pretty bedrooms are light and comfortable, some having balconies. All have modern amenities and the bathrooms are efficient. The panelled and well stocked bar has a pianist in the evenings. Delicious food, including local fish and Norwegian specialities, is served in the restaurant – with its big windows and warm colour scheme. Leisure facilities include a pool with spa, tennis, riding, fishing, bikes to explore the fascinating countryside, canoeing and white water rafting on the river. Boats and bikes can be hired. It is a good base for winter sports too. Directions: From Bergen take E16 towards Voss, finding the hotel on the lakeside. Price guide: Single NOK895; double/twin NOK1190.

150

Portugal

The Portuguese like the British. The affection is mutual. They are the only nation within the European continent with whom the British have not fought at one time or another.

Portugal is divided into six historic provinces.

Most visitors head for the low lying plains of the southern Algarve or the region around Lisbon – the Estoril coast, but as traditional tourist destinations become more crowded, Johansens travellers are trekking in all directions.

The capital, Lisbon, is a mass of steep inclines which are best traversed by tram or by the excellent funicular railway. The majestic city centre elevator makes walking tours fun even on the hottest summer day.

One of the best ways to appreciate the delights of the Minho, the mountains, Coimbra and the Gold Coast, Oporto and Tras-os-Montes is to take the train. The rail network is fast, efficient and provides an excellent way to interact with the locals if you want to give the car a rest.

One of the most picturesque lines is that from Lisbon to Guarda via Abrantes. Shortly after passing the romantic castle of Almourol on an island in the Tagus, the train follows the river for some 40 miles on a single track line cut out of the side of the hills. There is no road along the track – so you can't see the sights if you go by car. The slopes are sparsely cultivated and olive trees perch on what look like inaccessibly steep bluffs. Rare birds swoop and dive and the colour of the water below is constantly clear due to the springs from which it feeds.

If you are journeying to neighbouring Madeira be prepared for the landing. It is unexpectedly dramatic and spectacular at the same time. Passengers regularly applaud the pilot on achieving what appears to be an impossible manoeuvre. But don't let this knowledge deter you from travelling to this wonderful island which has immense character and charm, and an excellent climate throughout the year. Madeira has so much more to offer than its celebrated eponymous wine.

Hotel Palacio Agueda

QUINTA DA BORRALHA, 3750 AGUEDA, PORTUGAL

TEL: 351 34 60 1977 FAX: 351 34 60 1978

This magnificent 17th century mansion, with its traditional tiled roof, elegant windows and balconies, is reflected in the lake in front of the hotel. The surrounding verdant gardens add to its charm, and there is a delightful chapel where weddings take place. Portugal's reputation for hospitality is evident here – the ambience is most welcoming. The cool salons have handsome oil paintings on the walls, antiques from the region and wonderfully comfortable chairs. The suites are luxurious, with four poster beds and private balconies; the bedrooms charming with harmonious colour schemes. The classical bar is a popular rendezvous before dining in the spacious restaurant. The menu includes local specialities and internationally favourite dishes - the wine list is predominantly Portuguese. An al fresco lifestyle is encouraged, but local business people also appreciate the excellent conference facilities available. The Palacio has its own pool and tennis court; other diversions include golf, archery, canoeing, fishing, riding, folk dancing and boat trips around Aveiro harbour. Visits can be arranged to famous port cellars in Oporto, to the mountains or Roman ruins at Conimbriga. Directions: IP1 motorway from Lisbon North towards Oporto, taking the Agueda exit. Price guide: Single 15,000–16,500esc; double/twin 18,000–19,500esc; suites 24,000esc. Extra Bed 4,000esc.

Hotel Quinta Das Lagrimas

SANTA CLARA, P–3040 COIMBRA, PORTUGAL
TEL: 351 39 44 1615 FAX: 351 39 44 1695

Quinta das Lagrimas was the country Estate of the Tears – but the only sadness staying in this exquisite hotel will be leaving it. Here centuries ago Dona Ines de Castro, beloved by the Prince Dom Pedro, wept as she died. Coimbra is the home of the Fado, tragic poems sung by the students of Portugal's oldest university in the medieval quarter of the town. The hotel is quintessentially Portuguese, a palatial 18th century villa with terraces, a graceful facade, balustrades and ornate mouldings, surrounded by extensive, immaculate gardens. The salons have graceful chairs and stylish terracotta colour schemes. The bedrooms are prettily designed and have cool wooden floors and modern amenities. The suites have four posters. Guests relax in the bar over canapés and aperitifs, then enter the lovely restaurant, with its romantic terrace, to linger over superb Portuguese dishes and fine wines. Residents wander among the exotic trees and fountains in the grounds, swim (pool bar) or play tennis, There are endless treasures and ancient buildings to explore while in Coimbra and opportunities to sample port in cellar restaurants. Directions: From Lisbon Motorway A1-IP1 towards Porto, take Coimbra exit, following signs to Santa Clara Convent, finding hotel signed on the right. Price guide: Single 15,000–22,000esc; double/twin 18,500–27,000esc; suites 50,000–60,000esc.

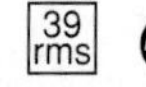

100

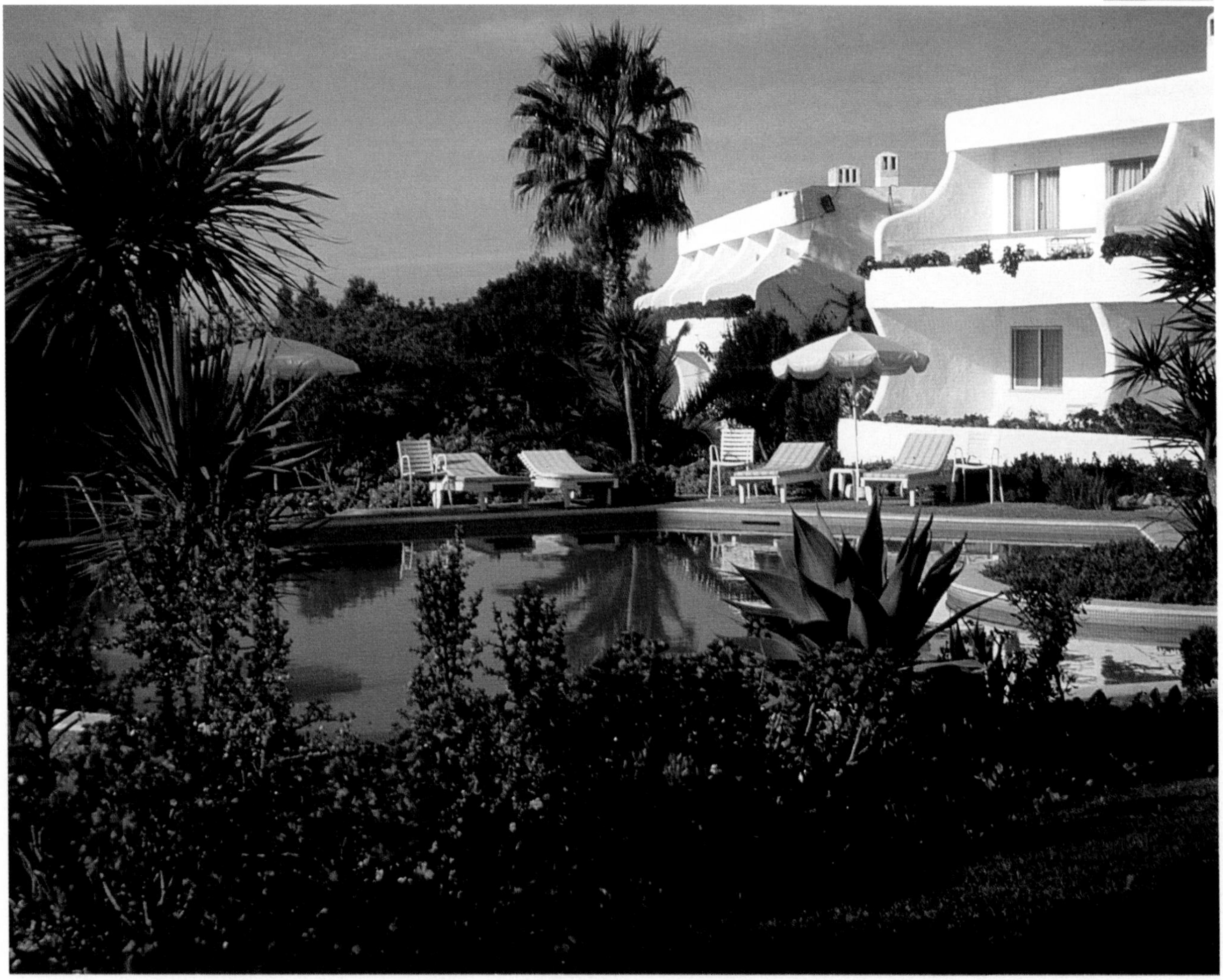

LA RÉSERVE

SANTA BARBARA DE NEXE, P–8000 FARO, ALGARVE, PORTUGAL
TEL: 351 89 9904 74 FAX: 351 89 9904 02

An élite small hotel that is a magnificent example of the best of modern Portuguese architecture which stands in its own well-tended estate in air scented by the eucalyptus, with almond and olive trees on the surrounding hills. The interior is of imaginative traditional furniture in sophisticated surroundings. The suites are superb, each with its own terrace looking out to the distant sea and luxurious bathrooms with big robes and designer toiletries. The spacious, marble-floored foyer with decorative wrought-iron work, bowls of flowers and colourful seating is a pleasant meeting place en route to the bar before entering the brilliant La Réserve restaurant for a gourmet meal prepared by the chef-patron who will also suggest which of the fine local wines would be appropriate for lunch. Informal meals are served at the poolside snack bar. Apart from swimming, guests play tennis or wander through the lovely gardens. Several good courses in the vicinity will challenge golfers. Those seeking a change of scenery can enjoy the coast with its golden beaches or drive through the countryside exploring the old towns and villages. The hotel is conveniently located 10 kms from Faro airport and Faro centre.It is important to note that credit cards are not accepted here. **Directions**: From Faro N125 to Patacão, then follow signs to Santa Bárbara de Nexe. Price guide: Single 18,000esc–30,000esc, double/twin 28,000esc–40,000esc, suites 30,000esc–44,000esc.

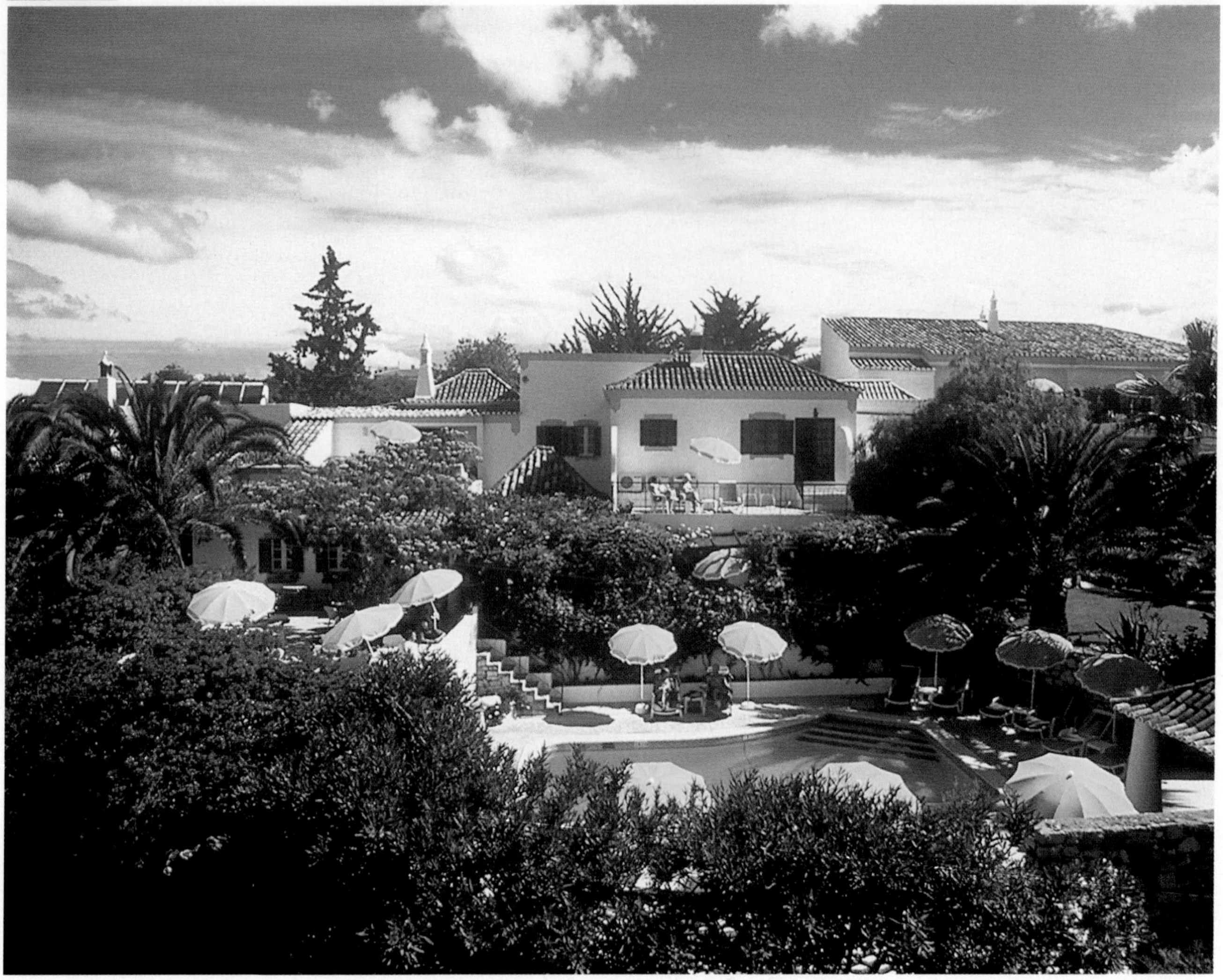

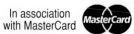

MONTE DO CASAL

CERRO DO LOBO ESTOI, P–8000 FARO, ALGARVE
TEL: 351 89 991503 FAX: 351 89 991341

This elegant Algarve country house, built in the 18th century, is wonderfully peaceful, surrounded by almond, olive and fruit trees, with Bougainvillaea climbing up the terraces and a view across the countryside to the coast. Several of the cool, spacious bedrooms are on the ground floor with direct access to the pool and sun terraces, while the rooms higher up have their own terraces and lounge areas. Breakfasts of squeezed orange juice and fresh bread from the village bakery are the perfect start to the day! The bar and restaurant are in the converted coach house. The bar is inviting, with doors leading onto the terrace. While light lunches are available, dining is an important part of the programme – magnificent International dishes, superb Portuguese specialities, including the regional smoked swordfish, and fine wines from the extensive cellar. Strolling in the gardens and swimming in the floodlit pool are evening diversions. Unspoilt beaches, famous golf courses, Loule market on Saturdays, boat trips to the islands of Olhao and exploring Faro add to guests' enjoyment. **Directions:** Follow the blue signs marked IP1 to motorway, then take exit 5 for Faro, turn left into Estoi and follow yellow signs for 3kms towards Moncarapacho. Price guide: Single £41.25–£79.50; double/twin £55–£106; Deluxe £60–£120; Suite £72–£147.

13 rms 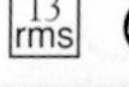     16    

Romantik Hotels & Restaurants

ROMANTIK HOTEL VIVENDA MIRANDA

PORTO DE MOS, P-8600 LAGOS, ALGARVE, PORTUGAL

TEL: 351 82 763 222 FAX: 351 82 760 342 E-MAIL: romantik-hotel-viv.miranda@ip.pt

Vivenda Miranda is a delightful small hotel, with Moorish influence evident in its architecture, built high up on the cliffs of Western Algarve. Its secluded position is enhanced by the exotic gardens around the terraces – which have spectacular views across to the Atlantic Ocean as well as looking down on the Porto de Mos beach. The cool bedrooms are pleasantly furnished and extremely comfortable, guests should enjoy many a peaceful night's sleep. A few rooms, equally charming, are in the nearby annexe. Some bathrooms have showers only. Both the lounge and diningroom – drinks are served in the former from a most attractive bar – have spectacular views over the water at night. Breakfast is on the terrace, and the lunch menu is brief but good. Dinner at night is more of an occasion – gourmet dishes with organic ingredients accompanied by the best of Portuguese wines. There are restaurants on the beach, and tennis nearby, mountain bikes available, sailing and wind surfing at the Marina. Local golf courses offer hotel guests discounted green fees. Weekly inclusive packages for golfers are a feature of Vivenda Miranda – which has its own pool and spa offering therapeutic treatments and massages. **Directions:** From Faro follow the EN 125 to Lagos, then watch for signs to Praia de Porto de Mos. Price guide: Single £42–£70; double/twin £47–£75; suites £52–£80.

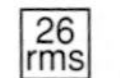

As Janelas Verdes

RUA DAS JANELAS VERDES 47, P–1200 LISBON

TEL: 351 1 39 68 143 FAX: 351 1 39 68 144 E-MAIL: plaza.hotels@mail.telepac.pr

Once the home of the famous Portuguese writer, Eca de Queiros, this classical 18th century townhouse in the old part of Lisbon, close to the River Tagus, is now an exquisite small hotel. Graceful archways, a wide staircase with ornate banisters, mahogany woodwork, alcoves filled with pedestals of flowers and warm yellow walls are an appropriate setting for the elegant period furniture, antiques and paintings in the charming salons. The bedrooms are peaceful, all double-glazed and air-conditioned, traditionally furnished and very comfortable. The back of the house is clad in ivy, and there is a delightful patio where guests enjoy breakfast in the summer, and refreshments are served later in the day. In cooler months they retreat to the reading room. The hotel staff will suggest restaurants with national and cosmopolitan menus for dinner at night. Lisbon is a fascinating city to explore, starting at the Museum of Ancient Art right next to the hotel, and there are so many beautiful buildings – cathedrals and palaces – botanical gardens and the castle to visit. Tramcars are in walking distance, and golfers have a choice of good courses near Estoril. **Directions:** Rua das Janelas Verdes is just off the Avenida Vinte de Quatro de Julho. Price guide: Single 18,500esc–45,000esc; double/twin 19,500esc–45,000esc. American buffet breakfast and taxes included.

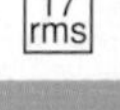

QUINTA DA BELA VISTA

CAMINHO DO AVISTA NAVIOS, 4, P–9000 FUNCHAL, MADEIRA, PORTUGAL
TEL: 351 91 764144 FAX: 351 91 765090

This is the perfect hotel for those seeking country-house living in peaceful surroundings – it is a joy to stay in this traditional house, with its tall windows and green shutters, overlooking Funchal Bay and surrounded by exotic gardens. The interiors are a blend of sophistication and rich, classical furnishings – lovely antiques, fine paintings and great comfort. The suites are all in the original building, having period furniture and luxurious bathrooms, while the bedrooms are in the new, adjacent annex and therefore rather more contemporary. Most have twin beds and many have balconies overlooking the Bay. Guests enjoy their apéritifs in the cheerful bar or on the sunny terraces before choosing between the elegant restaurant serving fine food and the best wines or the more informal diningroom with its à la carte menu, which is also open at lunchtime. Afterwards they probably relax over a glass of Madeira wine in the charming salon or the library. Leisure facilities abound, there is a freshwater pool with its own snack bar, tennis, billiards, a gymnasium with a sauna and Jacuzzi. A regular minibus service is available for those wishing to visit the shops or explore the town. Excellent golf is nearby. Directions: Needed from Inspector – 3 miles from centre of Funchal but which way? car parking available. Price guide: Single 17,700esc–30,000esc; double/twin 23,600esc–38,000esc; suite 49,800esc–56,000esc.

HOTEL PÁLACIO DE SETEAIS

RUA BARBOSA DE BOCAGE, 10, SETEAIS, P–2710 SINTRA, PORTUGAL
TEL: 351 1 923 32 00 FAX: 351 1 923 42 77

This magnificent eighteenth century neo-classical palace, with its dramatic triumphal arch added in 1802 in honour of visiting royalty, was transformed into a hotel during the 1950's – great care being taken to preserve its aristocratic elegance. Its location is spectacular, on the Sintra mountain and the hotel has extensive grounds filled with fragrant flowers, exotic shrubs and shady trees. The interior is exemplary – very light, with attractive rugs on polished floors, an ornate staircase and balustrades in pale wood. The salons are flawless, one having exquisite mythological frescoes, The chairs are graceful, the chandeliers brilliant and the drapes are in soft harmony with the paintings. The guest rooms match the era of the Palace; lovely antiques and pieces of local furniture, muted colours, blissfully cool and quiet – television sets can be installed on request! The stylish bar has amusing murals; the attractive terrace is ideal for sipping cocktails. The enchanting Oval Dining Room and grand Restaurant offer a sophisticated menu and great wines. A traditional meeting room is available. The Palace has its own attractive pool, tennis courts and riding school; golf is nearby. Lord Byron praised the Old Town and the Serra de Sintra is paradisiacal. The beaches are good and local vineyards must be visited. **Directions:** Sintra Mountain and Seteais are signed from Sintra. Price guide: Single 40,000esc; double/twin 44,000esc.

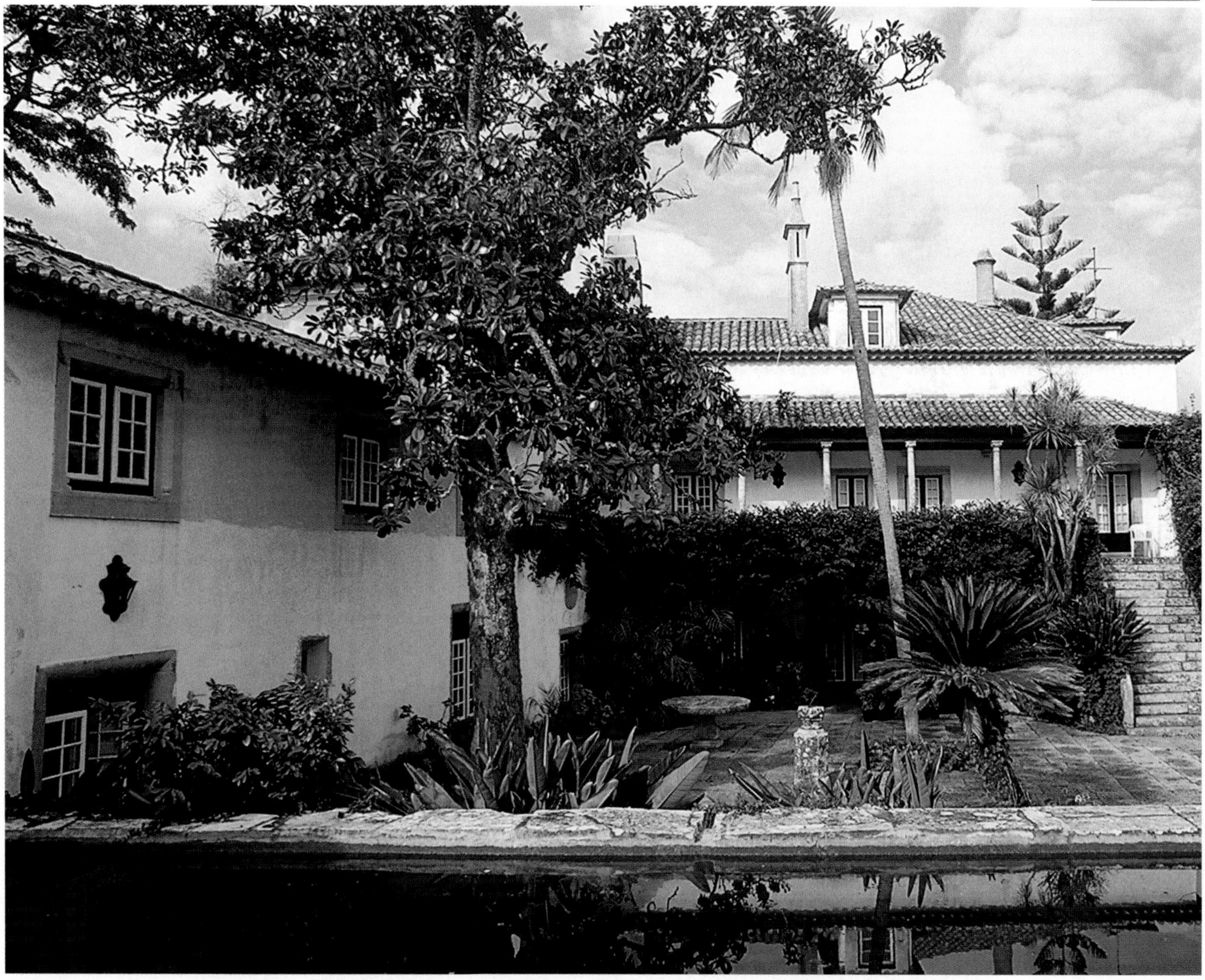

Quinta De São Thiago

SINTRA 2710, PORTUGAL

TEL: 351 1 923 29 23 FAX: 351 1 923 43 29

Sintra is fascinating – it has been the summer home of Portuguese royalty, celebrated by Lord Byron in his poem "Childe Harold", and has two palaces and a Moorish castle. With spectacular views across the forest and countryside, the Quinta de São Thiago – a monastery in the 16th century – is now the enchanting home of Mrs Bradell, who welcomes guests as friends. This immaculate house, with its pink tiled roof, is surrounded by beautifully kept gardens, steps leading down to an attractive pool. The charming bedrooms are furnished with classic period furniture. The Drawing Room, where residents gather for pre-dinner drinks, white port perhaps, has the original tiled floor, beamed, arched ceiling and fine Portuguese antiques; the Library shelves are full and the Music Room abounds with records. On special evenings, delicious candlelit dinners in Mrs Bradell's Dining Room or barbecues on the patio end the day. House pursuits are swimming, tennis and sunbathing. Golf, riding and the beach are nearby, Sintra and the hills deserve exploring and the casino at Estoril is an evening diversion. Directions: Leave Lisbon on Sintra road, take S. Pedro road at Mobil garage, head for Seteais, one mile after palace find sign on right to the Quinta, drive 900 metres – green wooden gate. Price guide: Single 17,000esc; double/twin 19,000esc; suites 24,000–28,000esc.

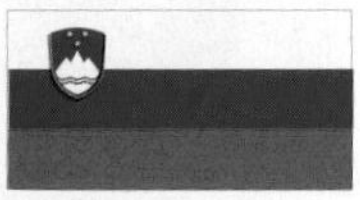

Slovenia

Slovenia lies between Austria and Croatia, with much shorter borders with Italy and Hungary. The smallest country in Eastern Europe, about the size of Wales, Slovenia is like a Europe in miniature such is its variety and charm.

The scenery is breath taking. Fairy tale architecture, glorious cities, a network of caves and one of the most romantic lakes in Europe - Lake Bled with its emerald water and ancient castle.

As elsewhere around the Mediterranean, April to September are the best months to visit as the days are long and the weather is warm. Snow lingers in the mountains as late as June, but spring is a good time to visit as everything is fresh and in blossom in the lowlands.

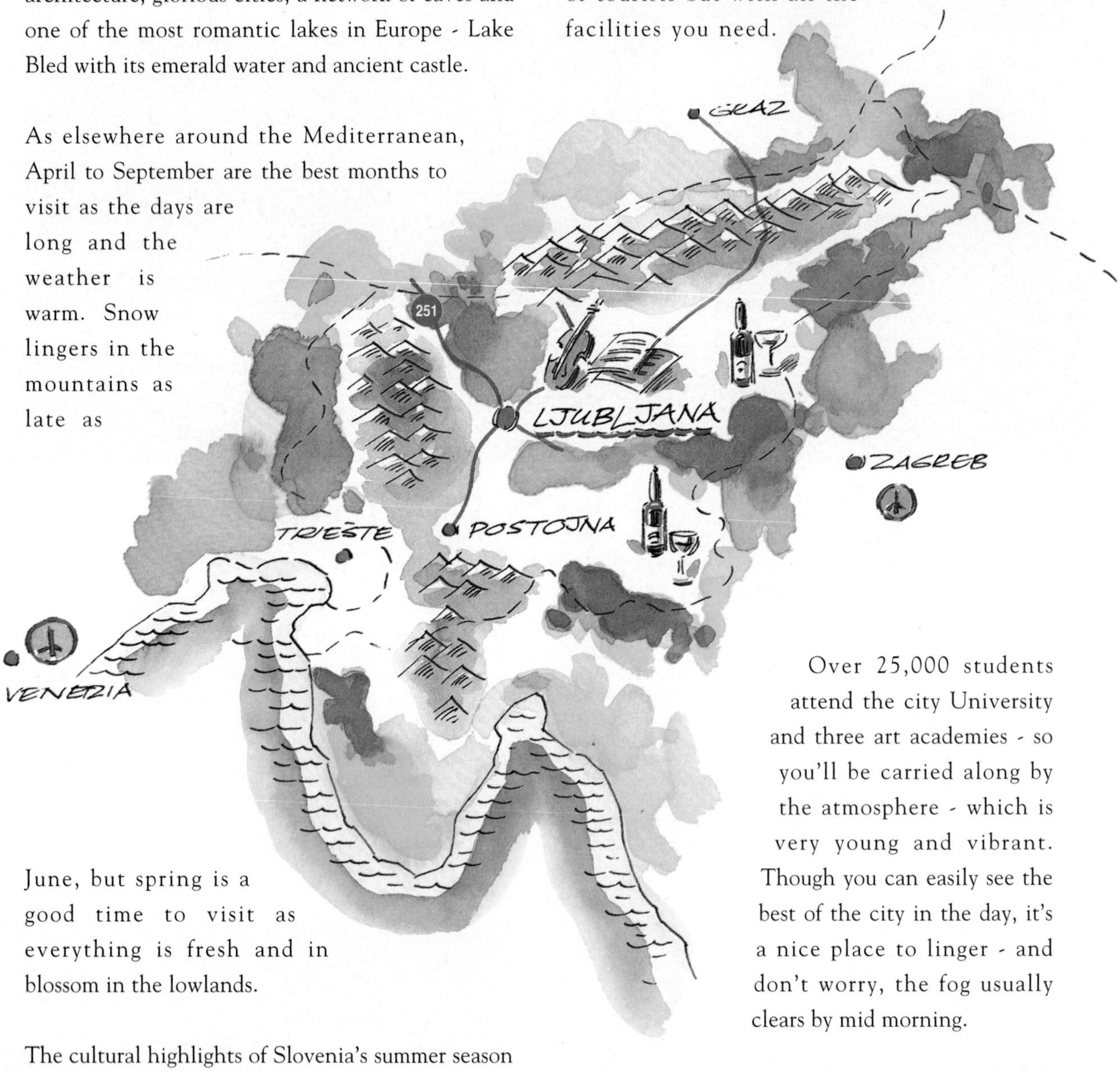

The cultural highlights of Slovenia's summer season are the International Summer Festival in the capital, Ljubljana and the Piran Musical Evenings held in the lovely cities of Piran and Portoroz, both in July and August. Many events in old Ljubljana accompany the colourful International Wine Fair in August or early September.

Ljubljana is a pleasant, small city and renowned for being foggy in the mornings. This adds to the mystery of the place and fails to detract from the natural splendour of the graceful architecture and surrounding countryside. The most beautiful part is along the Ljubljanica River below the castle. Ljubljana is like a little Prague without the hordes of tourists but with all the facilities you need.

Over 25,000 students attend the city University and three art academies - so you'll be carried along by the atmosphere - which is very young and vibrant. Though you can easily see the best of the city in the day, it's a nice place to linger - and don't worry, the fog usually clears by mid morning.

Slovenia is an excellent place for those who enjoy to be active on holiday. The tiny country boasts many well equipped ski resorts in the Julian Alps, especially Vogel above Bohinj, and Kransjka Gora where the Winter Olympics will be held in 2002.

HOTEL VILA BLED

CESTA SVOBODE 26, SI-4260 BLED, SLOVENIA
TEL: 386 64 79 15 FAX: 386 64 74 13 20

This villa has an illustrious past, having been the summer home of the Yugoslavian royal family between the two World Wars. In the late 1940s Tito played host to many world leaders here. Bled is in the Southern Alps, and this lovely now predominantly 1950s style hotel stands in secluded flower-filled parkland overlooking Lake Bled with awe-inspiring mountains on the horizon. The region is famous for its long warm summer, pure air and exhilarating spa waters. Many of the delightful bedrooms and suites have balconies with magical views over the lake at night. The salons reflect the 50s era. Marble and glass are much in evidence in the reception hall and stylish bar where guests gather while deciding which of the exquisite dishes to eat, either on the romantic terrace watching the lights on the water, or in the traditional restaurant. The wines are Slovenian, the whites from Styria while the reds include the famous 'black' varieties. Relaxation includes rowing, visiting the old castle, enjoying the private beach and strolling in the lovely grounds. Energetic visitors use the hotel tennis court, indulge in water-sports or play golf 2km away. After dark Bled offers discotheques, clubs and its Casino. **Directions:** E55 from Salzburg and at the Karawankentunnel on the Austrian border follow the E61/A1. Price guide: Single £66–£90; double/twin £91–£114; suites £100–£251.

PREFERRED PARTNERS

Preferred partners are those organisations specifically chosen and exclusively recommended by Johansens for the quality and excellence of their products and services for the mutal benefit of Johansens members, readers and independent travellers.

MasterCard International

Knight Frank International

Dunhill Tobacco of London Ltd

Halliday Meecham

Hildon Ltd

Moët & Chandon Champagne

Honda UK Ltd

Classic Malts of Scotland

Lakesure Ltd in association with Charter Insurance Ltd

Pacific Direct

NPI

Spain

Independent travellers take completely different routes from those taken by package tourists when they visit Spain. Package tours, thankfully, tend to limit themselves to specific seaside areas and leave much of the real charm, grace and colour of this glorious country untouched.

In continental Spain and in the islands too there are treasures inland. Villages, Moorish legacies and an exotic capital, Madrid, which as well as being one of the highest in Europe, is also one of the most youthful and energetic.

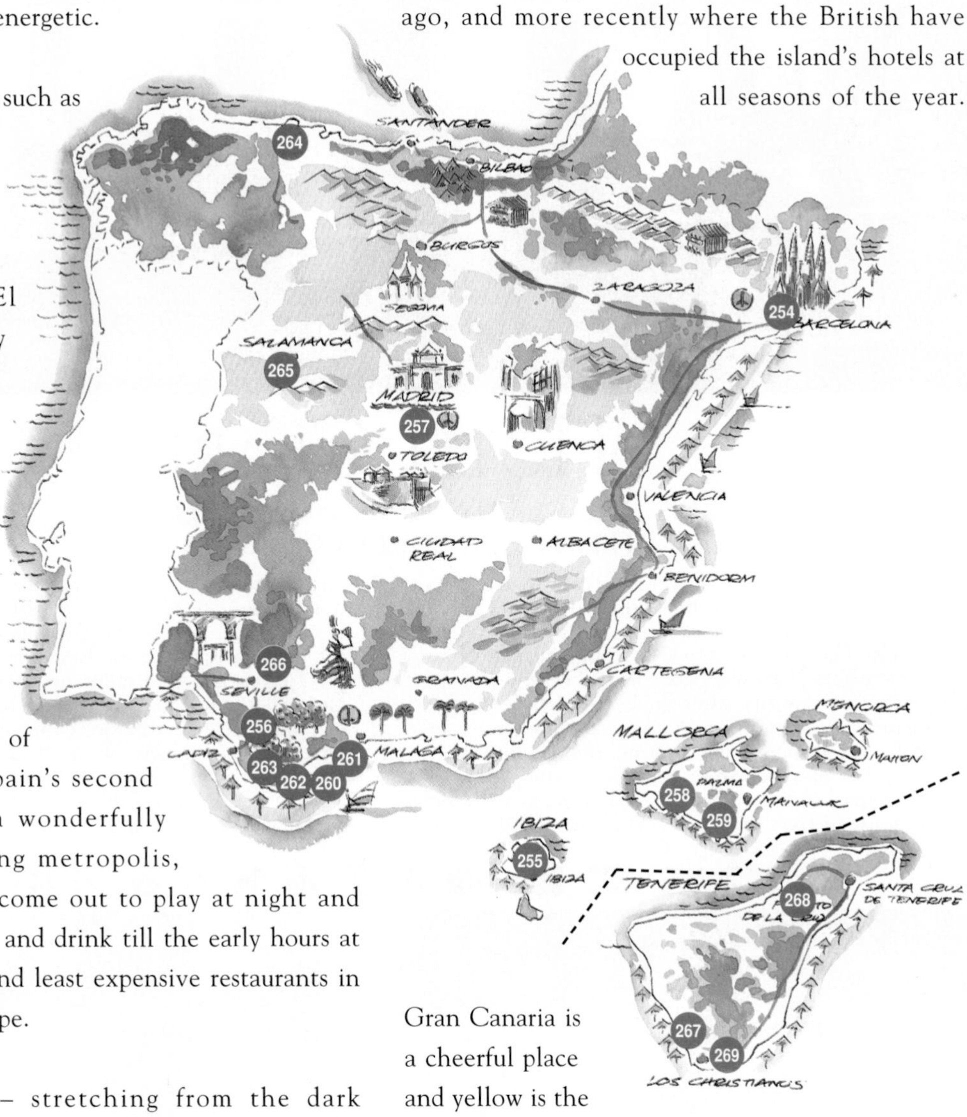

Visit historic cities such as ancient Toledo, where you'll discover the great palace monastery of El Escorial, the sturdy medieval walls of Avila, and the magnificent old university city of Salamanca, all comfortably reached by car or train from Madrid.

Barcelona, capital of Catalonia and Spain's second largest city, is a wonderfully vibrant and young metropolis, where the youth come out to play at night and where you can eat and drink till the early hours at some of the best and least expensive restaurants in any capital in Europe.

Moorish Spain – stretching from the dark mountains of the Sierra Morena in the north to white snow capped Sierra Nevada and Andalucia in the south. This region and its people will enchant with their magic. They are unlike any other within the country.

There are three principal Balearic isles. Mallorca, greater in nature and in name than Menorca, has been loved at different times by Chopin, Picasso and Winston Churchill – what better referees could one muster? Menorca has beautiful scenery and beaches. It is delightfully insular. The third island, Ibiza, hosts a cosmopolitan life style.

There are five Canary Islands, the most popular and populous being Gran Canaria and Tenerife, the latter being where Nelson lost his arm 200 years ago, and more recently where the British have occupied the island's hotels at all seasons of the year.

Gran Canaria is a cheerful place and yellow is the "in" colour. First the little birds, then the bananas and now the yellow bottles of sun tan oil. The Canary Islands are fun. Lots of sport and lots of sunshine.

DES IGN HOT ELS

HOTEL CLARIS

PAU CLARIS 150, 08009 BARCELONA
TEL: 34 3 487 62 62 FAX: 34 3 215 79 70

This unique hotel introduces new arrivals to the lovely architecture of the 19th century, still retaining its graceful Renaissance facade from the era when it was the Palace of the Vedruna family. The interiors are extravagant examples of avant garde design – metres of marble, glass, rare timbers and cast stone. The spacious foyer is dramatic while the lounge beyond is softened by colourful rugs, 5th century Roman mosaics and the gentle sound of a waterfall. The bedrooms are exciting, eclectic in style with antique objets d'art and modern furnishings cleverly blended, and opulent bathrooms, some with Jacuzzis. They are sound-proofed against the noise of the city. The cocktail bar and the rooftop terrace, with its pool, are perfect places to relax before indulging in the luxuries offered in the Caviar Caspio. Ampurdan cuisine can be sampled in the gourmet restaurant, matched by local wines. Informal meals are in the Restaurant Barbecoe. The state-of-the-art conference and meeting rooms transform into elegant banqueting and private dining rooms. The hotel's Museum demands attention before exploring the City and Cathedral. **Directions:** In centre of city in a narrow road, Pau Claris, on north-east side of Paseo de Gracia, where it crosses Calle de Valencia. Parking available. Price guide: Single 22,000–27,300pts; double/twin 22,000–34,100pts; suite from 40,000pts.

PIKES

SAN ANTONIO DE PORTMANY, 07820 ISLA DE IBIZA, BALEARIC ISLANDS, SPAIN
TEL: 34 71 34 22 22 FAX: 34 71 34 23 12

Hotel Pikes is an old 15th century finca beautifully converted into an idyllic hotel. Built in natural stone, it blends easily into the countryside and the surrounding olive groves. beautiful gardens and flower-filled terraces add colour to this lovely hotel, situated within easy reach of beaches and Ibiza Town, just some 10 minutes away by car. The rooms and suites are of different shapes and sizes, tastefully furnished with a mix of antiques and modern sculptures. The ambience is relaxing – breakfast is served until noon, no need to get up early. The intimate restaurant is renowned throughout the island for its fine cooking and wines. The hotel's special atmosphere is maintained by the friendly and discreet staff. There are numerous sun terraces for relaxing around the swimming pool, a floodlit tennis court, sauna, Jacuzzi and a gymnasium. Hotel staff will organize riding, sailing, scuba diving and other activities. Golfers can use the practice nets before playing on Ibiza's championship course. The hotel's Privilege Card gives guests VIP treatment at most disco clubs and the popular Casino as well as food discounts in many first class boutiques. In the summertime special events such as Barbecue nights, Flamenco evenings etc are arranged by the pool side. Internet: http://ibiza-online.com/Pikes **Directions:** Pikes is signed off the Camino de sa Vorera. Price guide (per person): double/twin 10,000–13,500pse; suites 12,000–48,000pse.

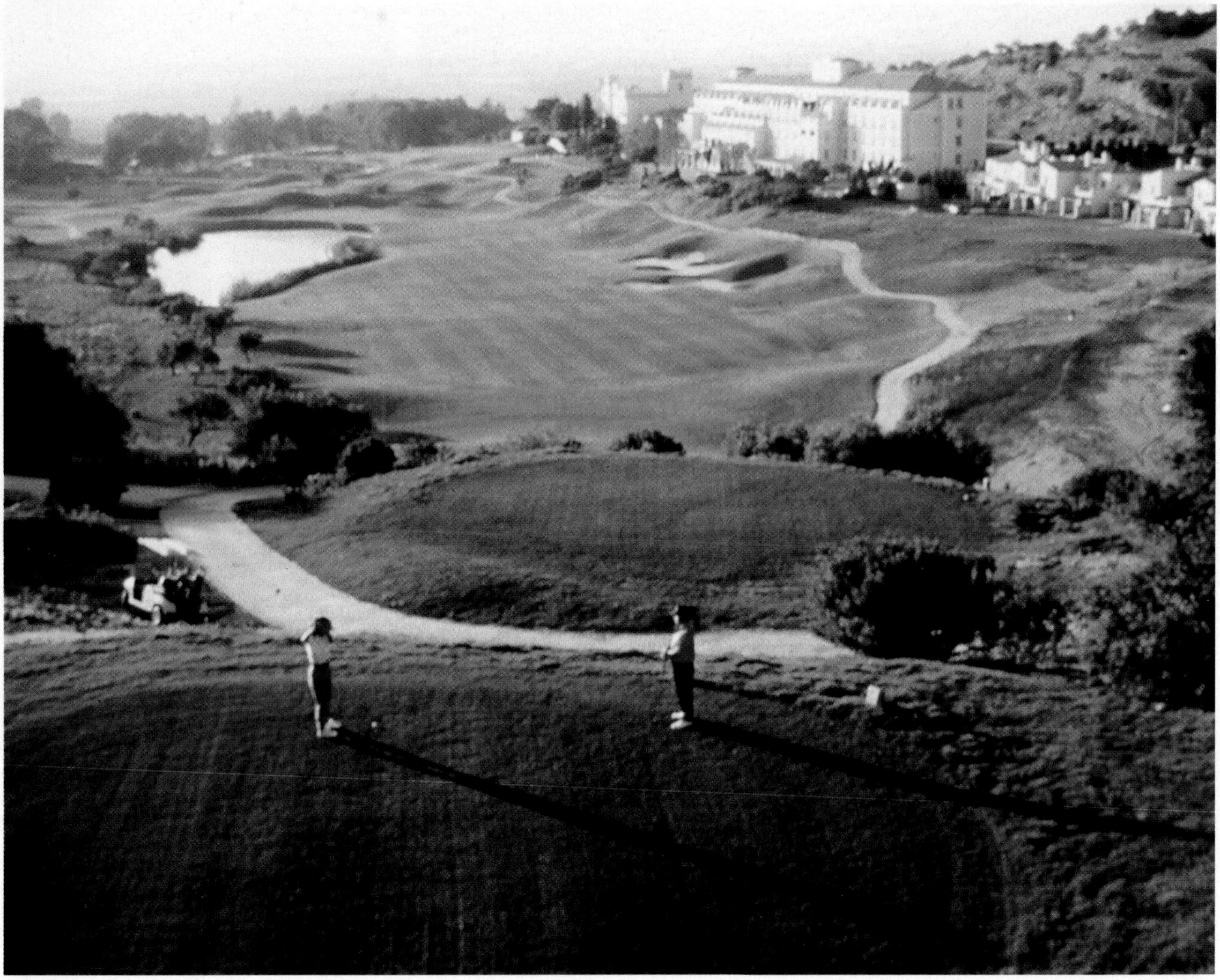

MONTECASTILLO HOTEL & GOLF CLUB

CTRA. DE ARCOS, 11406 JEREZ, CADIZ, SPAIN
TEL: 34 56 15 1200 FAX: 34 56 15 12 09

Andalusia is one of the most beautiful parts of Spain, and on the outskirts of Jerez de la Frontera – the capital of sherry – the magnificent Montecastillo Hotel dominates the skyline. Next to it is the lovely old castle, today, after skilled renovation, the clubhouse for an 18-hole course designed by Jack Nicklaus. The entrance hall, leading into the salon, is superb – cool, uncluttered, classic modern rattan furniture. The spacious bedrooms (marble bathrooms) reflect the locality with traditional, comfortable furnishings. Guests relax while enjoying quiet drinks and light meals in the delightful El Almijar Bar which overlooks the course, or sample Andalusian dishes in the attractive El Lagar restaurant. The Club House also has a convivial bar and a big terrace for al fresco dining. Wonderful Spanish wines are listed. Apart from golf, there are two pools and paddle tennis courts. Most water sports including sailing can be found at Cadiz, thirty minutes away. The Headquarters of the Spanish Riding School is in Jerez. Wine and sherry tastings can be arranged. Dance the flamenco at night. **Directions:** Leave Jerez on Arcos road. After about 5 miles the Montecastillo is signed on the right. The hotel has hire cars available. Price guide: Single 14,500–25,600pts; double/twin 18,500–32,000pts; suites 24,000–120,000pts.

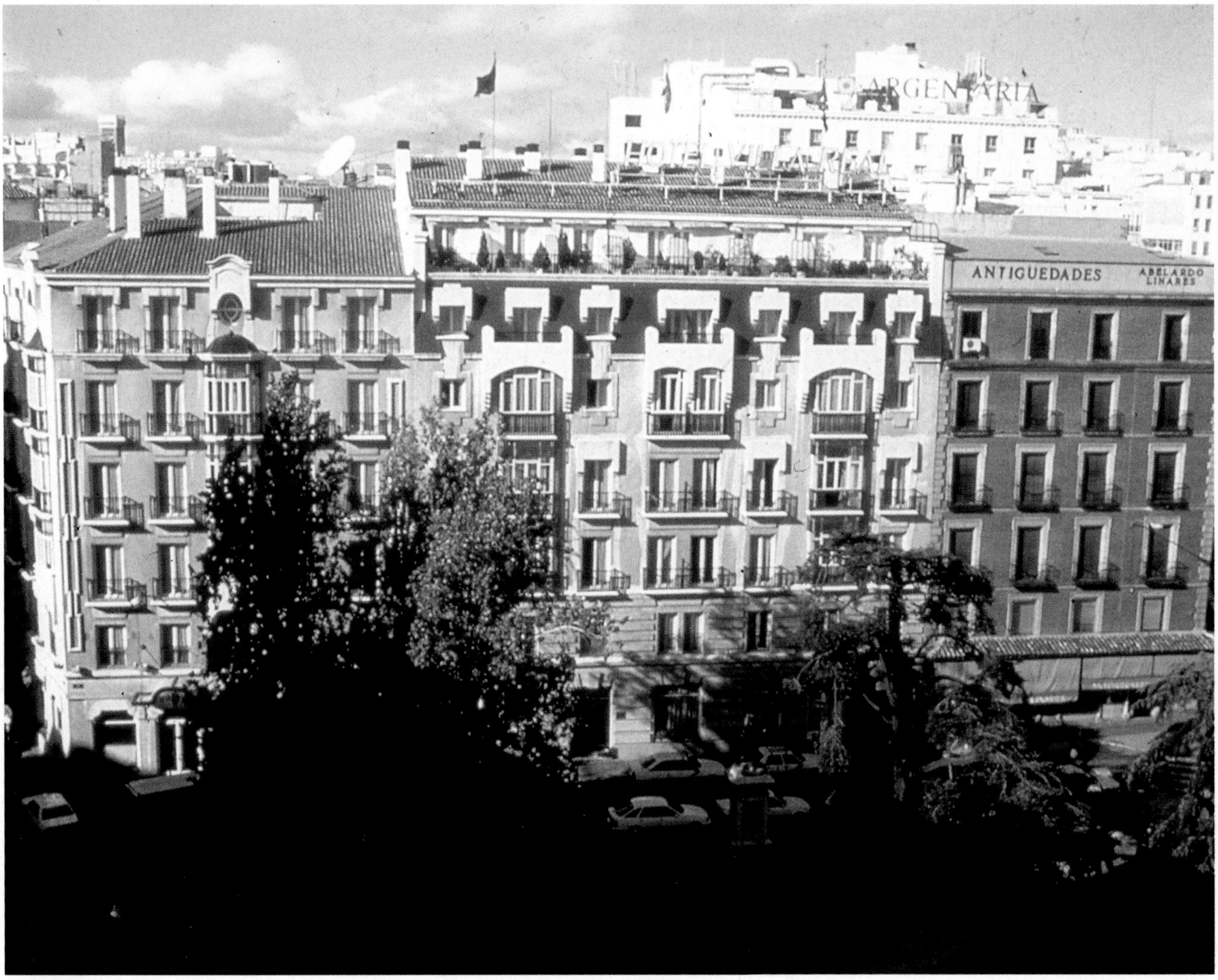

VILLA REAL

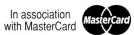

PLAZA DE LAS CORTES, 10, MADRID E–28014, SPAIN
TEL: 34 1 420 37 67 FAX: 34 1 420 25 47

To stay at this elite and prestigious hotel in the heart of Madrid is a memorable experience. The position is superb, the service impeccable and the interior is palatial – spacious salons with wonderful antiques and mirrors, handsome rugs on marble floors, period furniture, fine panelling hung with tapestries and inspired lighting. All the luxurious bedrooms are suites, with elegant sitting areas, soundproofed from the noises of the city, opulent bathrooms, some with terraces for al fresco breakfasts looking out over Madrid, others with Jacuzzis and saunas. The sophisticated bar is a popular meeting place and the charming Principe de Asturias restaurant offers a choice of quick, light meals or full gourmet meals, accompanied by fine Spanish wines. The elegant Salón Principe de Asturias is also marvellous for banquets and can be transformed into a superb conference room together with the Salón Cibeles, popular for presentations. The hotel is located nearby the commerial centre, the Prado Museum, the National theatres Le Comedia and La Zarzuela, art galleries, antique shops and good restaurants. Directions: Private parking available. Find the hotel in the centre of Madrid near the Puerta del Sol, Gran Via and Retiro Park, just ten minutes from the airport. Price guide: Single 19,500–26,500pts; double/twin 19,500–34,100pts; suite from 35,000pts.

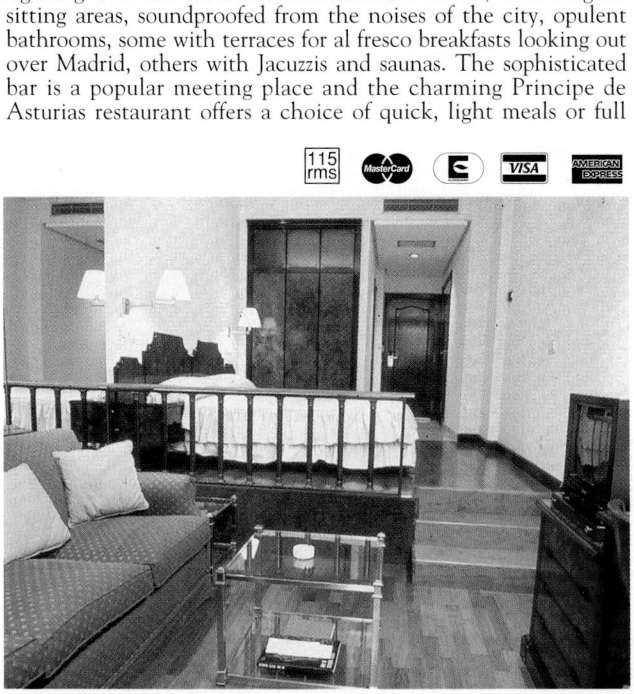

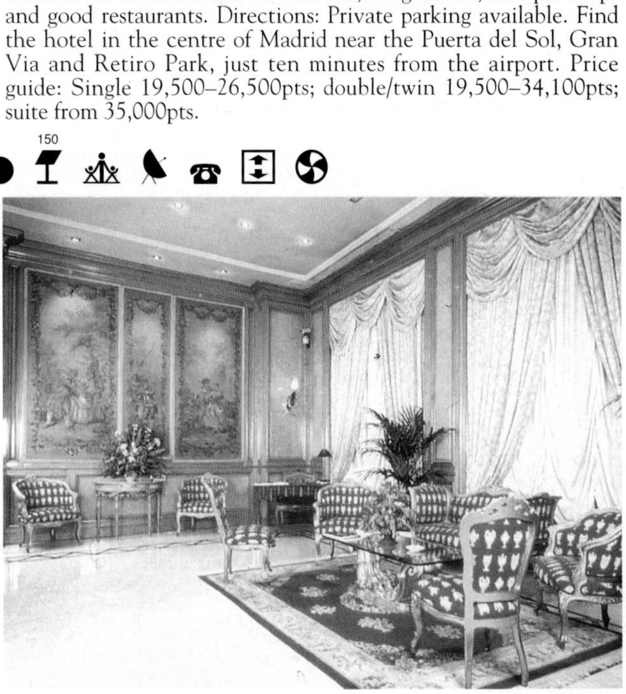

HOTEL VISTAMAR DE VALLDEMOSA

CTRA VALLDEMOSA, ANDRATX, KM. 2, 07170 VALLDEMOSA, MALLORCA, SPAIN
TEL: 34 71 61 23 00 FAX: 34 71 61 25 83 E-MAIL: vistamarhotel@redestb.es

This lovely house, recently transformed into an elite and peaceful hotel, is at the top of a beautiful valley, surrounded by pine and olive trees which scent the air, and overlooking a fascinating small fishing port on the edge of the Mediterranean. Guests relax immediately on entering the cool pebbled courtyard and are enchanted with the elegant reception rooms, filled with Majorcan antiques and traditional fabrics woven by craftsmen on the island. A picture gallery of fine 19th Spanish century paintings overflows on to walls throughout the house. The bedrooms are delightful, some in the main building and others in the adjacent annex. All are beautifully furnished with local period pieces and many have balconies. The new bathrooms are well designed and equipped. Guests appreciate delicious cocktails in the bar before entering the excellent restaurant with its big terrace for al fresco dining. Mediterranean cooking at its best and good Spanish wines from the extensive cellar make meals here memorable. Vistamar has its own pool. The beach of Port Valldemosa, with clear water, is perfect for swimming and sunbathing. Boat trips can be arranged. Valldemosa has a fine art centre where artists gather. Internet: http://www.VISTAMARhotel.es **Directions:** 2km outside of Valldemosa. Price guide: Single 17,000Pts–19,000Pts; double/twin 25,000Pts –30,000Pts. Breakfast 1500pts/person. VAT 7% not included.

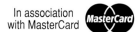

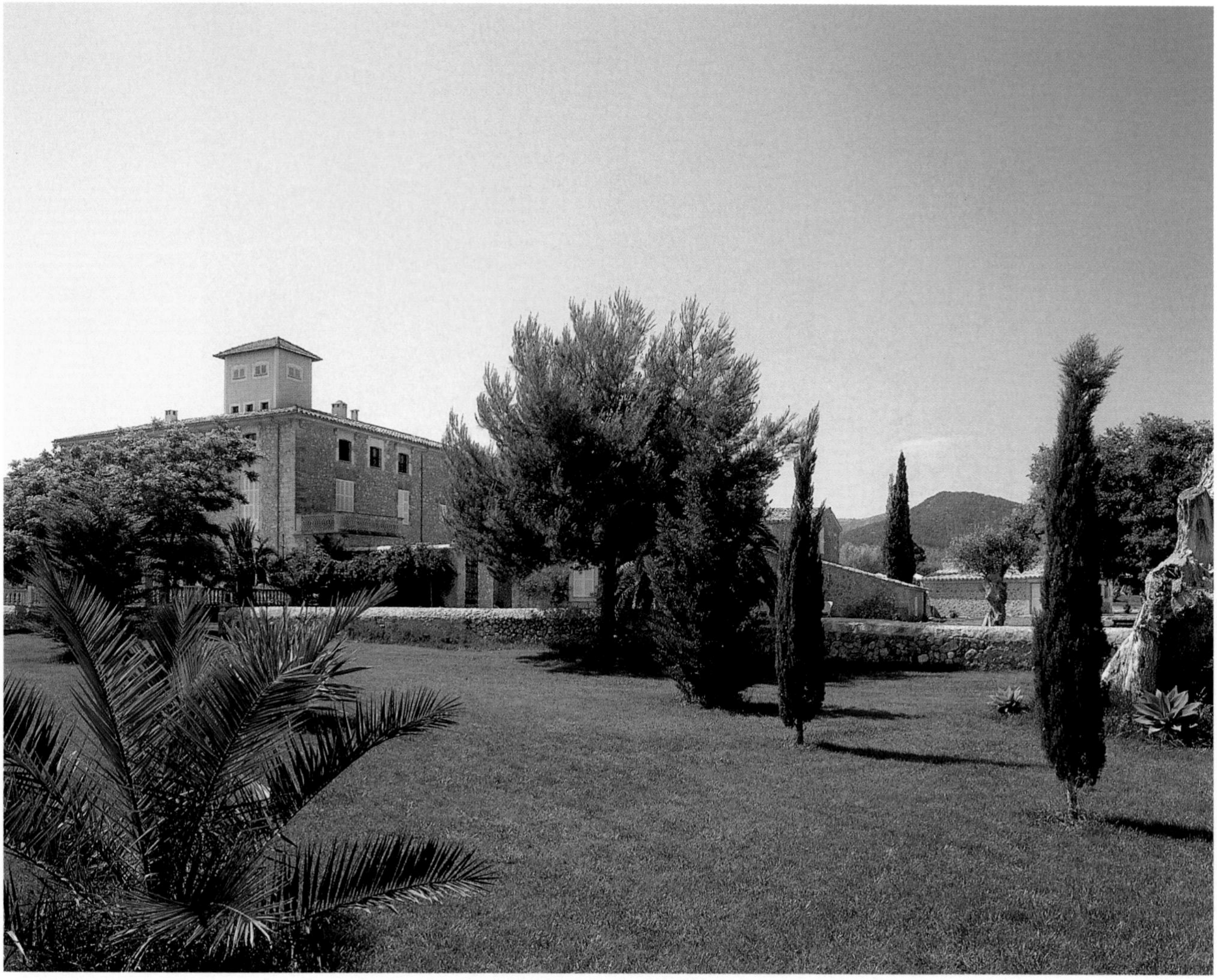

READ'S

CA'N MORAGUES, SANTA MARIA, MALLORCA, SPAIN

TEL: 34 71 140 261 FAX: 34 71 140 762

This idyllic 16th century mansion, surrounded by verdant gardens, is now a unique country hotel. Built in the traditional local stone it is set against a backdrop of mountains and breathtaking scenery, yet is only 15 minutes from Palma. Once inside, guests find they are in an exotic treasure trove, the pastel walls making a perfect setting for fine antiques, delicate porcelain, paintings and objets d'art found throughout the hotel. An elegant grand piano stands at the foot of the impressive staircase leading to the bedrooms, each of which is spacious and individually designed. One of the salons is an elegant drawing room and the other the olive pressing room with its original fittings. The bar is unique, the walls a mural of the sky – visitors sense they are in a magical place. The restaurant, one of the best in the Island, with its 10 metre high arches and exquisitely executed murals, is a perfect setting for the excellent cuisine. In summer the terraces overlooking the mountains offer a delightful alternative. The hotel has a large pool surrounded by sweeping lawns and a tennis court with golf courses only twenty minutes away. From Read's you are perfectly situated for exploring the beauty that is Majorca. **Directions:** Take motorway north towards Inca, then exit to Sta. Maria. Hotel is signposted between Sta. Maria and Alaró. Price guide: Double/twin 21,000–34,500pse; suites 32,000–44,000pse.

Hotel Puente Romano

P.O. BOX 204, 29600 MARBELLA, SPAIN
TEL: 34 5 282 09 00 FAX: 34 5 277 57 66

A sophisticated hotel in a wonderful position on the Spanish coast, between Marbella and Puerto Banús. It has low-rise white buildings built in the local Andalusian style with terraces facing the sun, overlooking the verdant gardens interspersed with little waterfalls. The salon is delightful, in golden tones, one wall being all windows and this harmonious colour scheme is reflected in the reception areas with the use of soft wood panelling and tiled floors. The guest rooms and many luxurious suites, all having private terraces, are in the maisonettes stretching the width of the garden with the talents of top designers evident throughout. There are four restaurants, ranging from al fresco meals by the pool, superb buffets and the opportunity to sample local specialities – particular fish – in the gourmet La Plaza. Excellent Spanish wines are listed. Apéritifs are enjoyed in the La Cascada piano bar, perhaps before dining in the courtyard, and later in the evening dancing the night away in The Club discotheque Régine's. This hotel is paradise for sporting guests – two fresh water pools, the beach and a championship tennis club/school, with facilities including paddle tennis and a fitness centre. There are a selection of golf courses, polo, riding and watersports nearby. **Directions:** Between Marbella and Puerto Banús on the Golden Mile. Price guide: Single 20,500–34,400pts; double/twin 26,000–47,000pts; suites 33,000–150,000pts.

226 rms

160

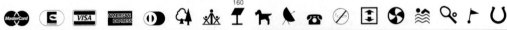

The Leading Hotels of the World®

MARBELLA CLUB HOTEL

BOULEVARD PRINCIPE ALFONSO VON HOHENLOHE, S/N, 29600 MARBELLA, SPAIN
TEL: 34 5 282 22 11 FAX: 34 5 282 98 84

This elite hotel was the inspiration of Prince Alfonso von Hohenlohe, who in 1954 extended and transformed his family home, so founding The Marbella Club. It immediately acquired a sophisticated clientele and has retained its exclusive reputation. The hotel is an elegant traditional Andalusian residence, standing in a vast expanse of sub-tropical gardens and olive groves, reaching down to the sea. Apart from the luxurious bedrooms and suites with their opulent bathrooms and private terraces, there are clusters of cottages and bungalows, each with private gardens and some with their own pools. Discreet staff provide room service The salons are charming and cool, and there are delightful courtyards and patios in which to relax. In summer guests sip aperitifs to live music in the Summer Bar, sample the superb seafood buffet by the pool and dine under the stars in the terrace restaurant. During cooler months the chef demonstrates his skills on the open Grill Restaurant. The hotel has two pools, while the Beach Club offers water sports. Many fine golf courses are close by, as is good tennis. At night the casino, discos and clubs are vibrant. **Directions:** The Marbella Club Hotel is on the Golden Mile beachroad between Marbella and Puerto Banús. Price guide: Single 22,500–37,500pts; double/twin 26,000– 61,000pts; suites 42,500–105,000pts.

HOTEL RINCON ANDALUZ

CRTA. DE CADIZ, K.M. 173, 29600 MARBELLA, SPAIN
TEL: 34 5 281 1517 FAX: 34 5 281 41 80

This smart hotel complex, built in the style of an Andalusian village, is surrounded by its own extensive parkland yet only 1 kilometre from the high life of Puerto Banus, favoured by the rich and famous. It is a mecca for top sportsmen, close to famous golf courses and other facilities, yet offering some privacy. The air-conditioned bedrooms are in villas and small houses off the 'streets, squares and gardens' of the village – which even has its own chapel. There are large suites especially suitable for families, accommodating up to six people. No building is more than three stories high. Guests are offered a choice of bars and restaurants – Sir Francis Drake with its large lounge, by the first pool, the Tropical Restaurant in the exotic gardens and the Crocodile Bar & Restaurant by the second pool. Additionally there is the sophisticated Beach Club, with further pools, children's area, beauty salon. Meals are usually buffet-style. Marbella is famous for its magnificent golf courses, all offering special arrangements for the hotel's guests,and the tennis club has 11 courts. The Golden Mile has splendid beaches, with wind surfing and water ski-ing off shore, and a jet-set night life, with discos and casinos. **Directions:** The hotel is signed from the Ctra Nacional 340, east of Marbella.Price guide: Single double/twin 15,500–26,000pts; suites 21,500–48,500pts.

LAS DUNAS SUITES

CRTA. DE CADIZ, KM163.5, 29689 MARBELLA/ESTEPONA (MALAGA)
TEL: 34 5 279 4345 FAX: 34 5 279 4825 E-MAIL: lasdunas@senda.ari.es

This exciting complex is almost an annex to the luxurious Las Dunas Beach Hotel & Spa (illustrated above), as residents in the suites have the benefit of the many fine facilities of the hotel and yet they can enjoy the freedom of an apartment. The stylish residences feature "Designers Guild" furnishings and vary from one to three bedrooms – including one duplex, each having fully equipped modern kitchen, bathrooms, air conditioning, private terrace or balcony, daily cleaning – and access to the pool (heated) and beach. Entrée to the luxurious hotel opens the doors of one of the best cuisines in the locality – the Lido restaurant, supervised by Michelin star chef Heinz Winkler – featuring his "Cuisine Vitale Mediterranéenne". More informal meals are served in "La Terraza" and the smart "Piano Bar Félix" has live music and is open until 3am. Room service is also available. The Spa has a Jacuzzi, sauna, gym, therapist and beautician. This is a golfer's heaven, with reduced green fees for Las Dunas guests and resident golf-pro. A variety of watersports can be arranged. Sunbathing on the beach, exploring inland villages, visiting Granada and Seville are pleasant pastimes. Marbella offers a jet-set night life! **Directions:** Las Dunas is between Marbella and Estepona, on the coast road (Crta de Cadiz). Parking facilities. Price guide(+VAT): Garden level suites 22,000–110,000pts.

Hotel De La Reconquista

GIL DE JAZ, 16, 33004 OVIEDO, PRINCIPADO DE ASTURIAS
TEL: 34 8 524 11 00 FAX: 34 8 524 11 66

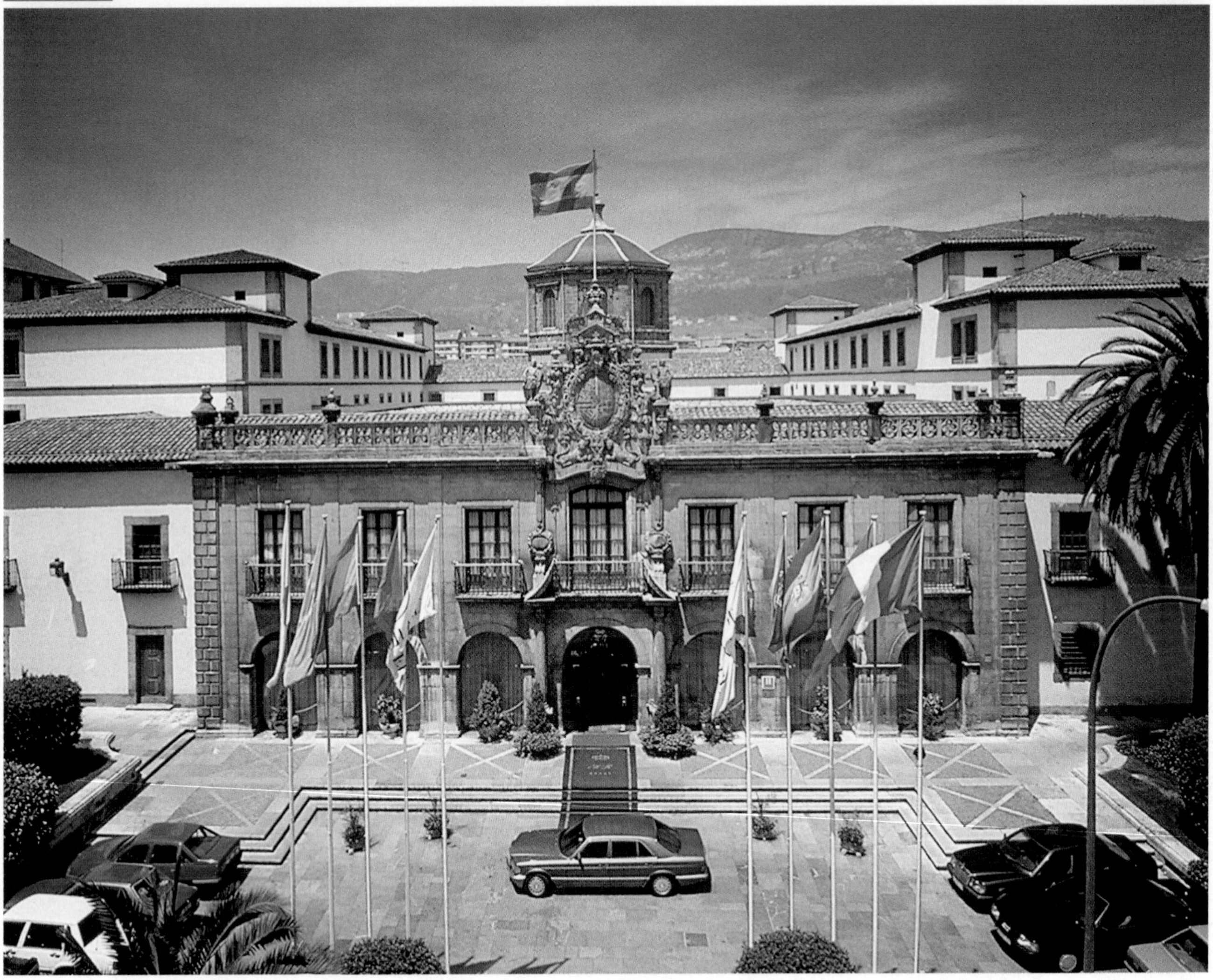

Oviedo in the Principado de Asturias is one of the few parts of Spain which the Moors failed to conquer and influence. The Hotel de la Reconquista is a delightful blend of history and sophistication. An archway in the baroque facade leads to the dramatic Patio de la Reina. The galleried Hall is impressive – with the famous Comida Campestre painting a focal point – indeed a fine collection of art is displayed throughout the hotel. Ornate period furniture adds interest to the spacious and comfortable bedrooms, all with grand marble bathrooms. The graceful salons have an aura of tranquility – guests relax listening to the pianist most evenings. In the cafeteria light meals and tapas are served all day in an informal atmosphere. The Bar Americano is ideal for a drink before or after dinner. The Florencia Restaurant offers superb regional and cosmopolitan dishes accompanied by the finest Spanish wines. Visiting industrialists appreciate the efficient services of the excellent Business Club, eight well equipped meeting rooms, and the Ancient Chapel, suitable for conferences or special occasions. Golf, sailing, tennis, winter sports, salmon fishing, riding and mountaineering are all accessible. **Directions:** In the heart of Oviedo, close to the Parque de San Francisco, with private car parking. Price guide: Single 18,750–23,200pta; double/twin 23,500–29,000pta; suites 42,500–67,000pta. (Ex. VAT)

Residencia Rector

RECTOR ESPERABÉ, 10-APARTADO 399, 37008 SALAMANCA, SPAIN
TEL: 34 23 21 84 82 FAX: 34 23 21 40 08

This exclusive hotel, with its elegant façade, stands by the walls of the citadel, looking up to the Cathedral – a magnificent golden vision at night when floodlit. Indeed this is a golden city, much of Salamanca being built in a soft yellow stone. The interior looks cool and elegant, with archways between the spacious reception hall and the welcoming bar. Unique features in the main salon, with its big leather furniture and tapestries on the walls, are two exquisite modern stained glass windows. Beyond these there is a courtyard garden. There are just 13 bedrooms, of ample size, all air-conditioned and double-glazed. The furnishings are delightful and facilities in the marble bathrooms include a telephone. The hotel only serves breakfast, but is easy to find restaurants serving traditional Spanish dishes or gastronomic experiences. It is possible to communicate in English in the hotel. There are many wonderful historical buildings in this city, including the Cathedral and the university and the city guide has two recommended routes and the firsts of these starts close to the hotel. **Directions:** Arriving on the main road from Madrid, drive up Avenida De Los Reyes Espana and turn left onto Pa de Rector Esperabe, finding the hotel approximately 300 metres on the left. Price guide: Single 12,000pse; double/twin 17,000pse; suites 21,000pse.

13 rms

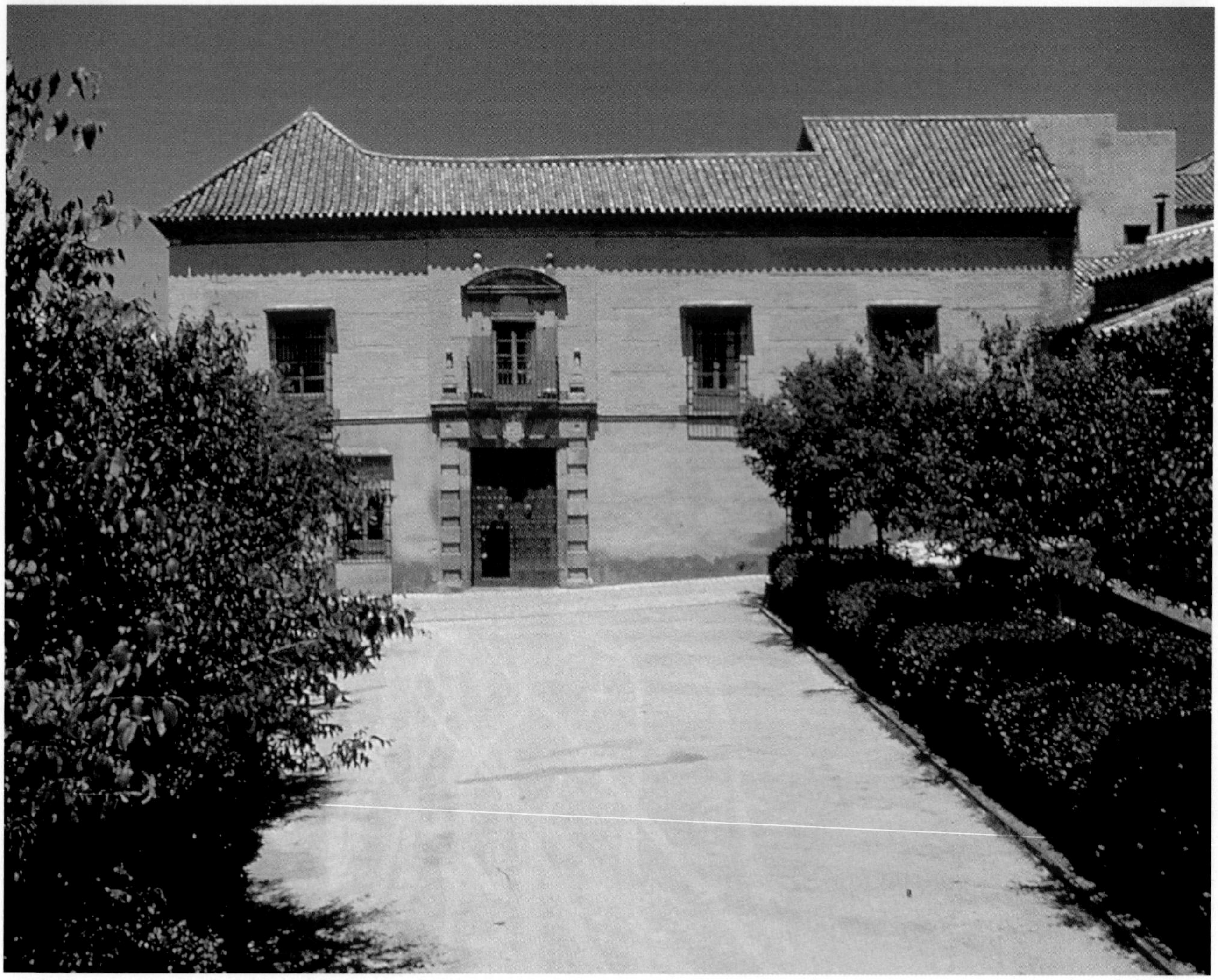

CASA DE CARMONA

PLAZA DE LASSO 1, E-41410 CARMONA, SEVILLE, SPAIN
TEL: 34 54 19 10 00 FAX: 34 54 19 01 89

Brilliant restoration of the 16th century Lasso de la Vega palace has ensured that today guests, upon entering, feel impressed that they may actually stay in such a fine palace. It is very exclusive, in that it is only open to residents and their friends, not to the casual passer-by. The staff are wonderful, the concierge conducts arrivals to their rooms, explaining how everything works, and the chambermaids will unpack bags and take away laundry. Then it is time to explore the Casa. The exterior is in warm golden stone and the venerable door leads into spacious terracotta-tinted courtyards, the loggia terrace, an Arabian garden and an exchanting pool, surrounded by exotic plants. The salons are very regal, in wonderful harmonising colours and containing many fine antiques. The cool traditional bedrooms are delightful, with pristine linen, and the suites are luxurious. The wines and delicious dishes served in the handsome restaurant are Spanish. Conferences and seminars take place in four meeting rooms, furnished with the latest presentation equipment. Archeologists appreciate Italica, other guests explore Seville, visit Andalucia, taste sherry in Jerez, enjoy the beaches at Cadiz or play golf nearby. **Directions:** From Seville NIV towards Cordoba, take the exit signed Carmona and follow signs to the hotel. Price guide: Single 17,000pse–29.000; double/twin 18,000pse–39,000pse; grand suite 80,000pse–120,000pse.

30 rms · MasterCard · VISA · AMERICAN EXPRESS · 150

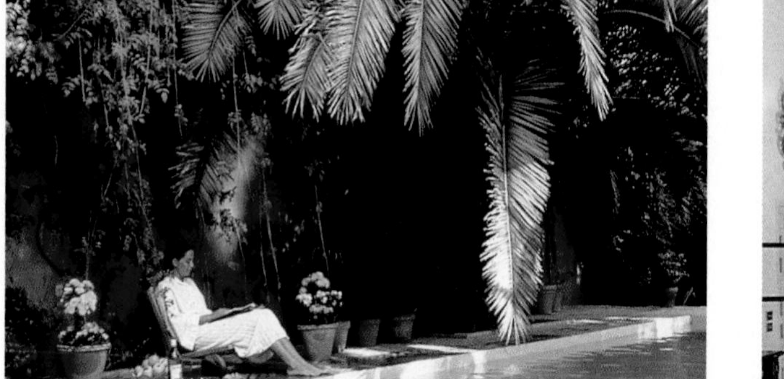

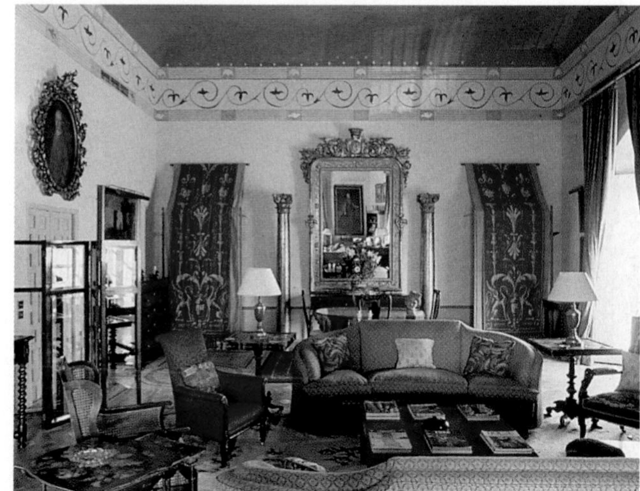

Gran Hotel Bahia Del Duque

38660 ADEJE, COSTA ADEJE, TENERIFE SOUTH, CANARY ISLANDS
TEL: 34 22 74 69 00 FAX: 34 22 74 69 25

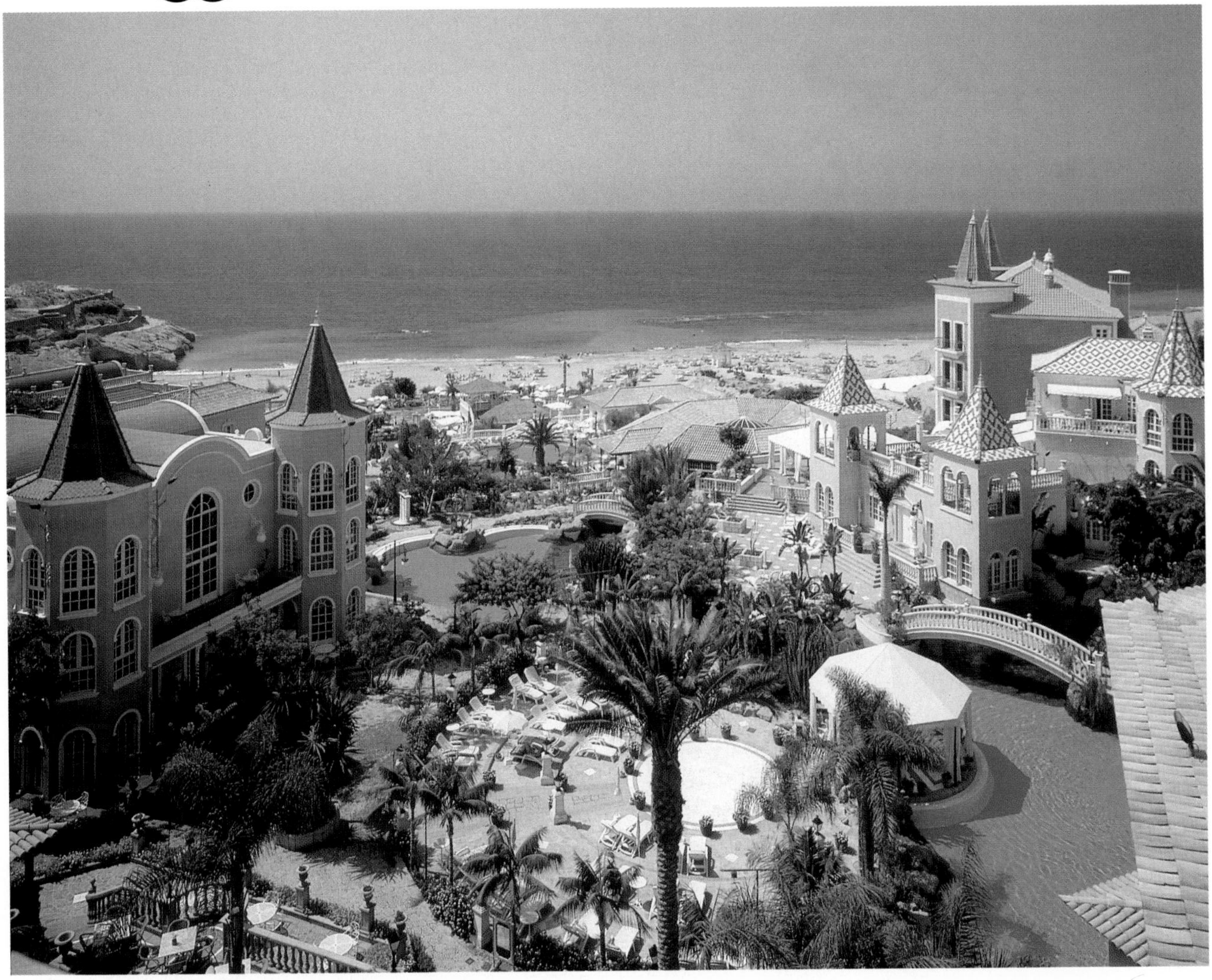

Gran Hotel Bahia Del Duque is a private romantic village created on a gentle hill sloping down to the sea. Nineteen houses in turn-of-the-century Canarian architecture form this prestigious complex in a large estate with sculptured terraces and pools. Corinthian columns flank the entrance, staff in period costume greet guests.There is a well-equipped conference and exhibition area. The bedrooms are in low colour-washed buildings, many with terraces facing the sea. The furniture has been specially designed, the floors are cool Spanish tiles, the bathrooms are luxurious. The Casas Ducales – Manor houses – have a separate reception area, breakfast room and butler service. Descending towards the coast guests find a fountain-filled patio surrounded by several restaurants – French, Spanish, Italian and the à la carte restaurant "El Duque".Two bars and a reading room. Below are four swimming pools, further bars and restaurants. Floodlighting makes these even more spectacular. Leisure activities include strolling among the tropical trees, a beach club, tennis, putting and a fully equiped gym. Golf, windsurfing and diving are nearby. Visiting La Gomera by ferry or the Tenerife National Park is a fascinating experience. **Directions:** The hotel will meet guests at Reina Sofia Airport – there is parking for those hiring a car. Price guide: Single 31,500pse–45,000pse; double/twin 42,000pse–52,600pse; suites 72,000pse–200,000pse. (Plus 4.5% IGIC)

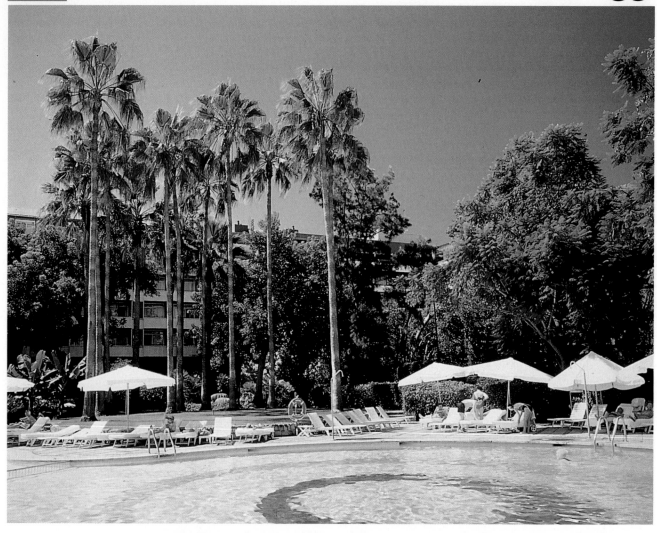

HOTEL BOTÁNICO

AVDA. RICHARD J. YEOWARD, URB. BOTANICO, E 38400 PUERTO DE LA CRUZ, TENERIFE, CANARY ISLANDS
TEL: 34 22 38 14 00 FAX: 34 22 38 15 04

The Botánico stands in extensive gardens filled with tropical plants, lush green foliage, bridges over lakes with fountains playing and shady places for those wishing to escape the sun. This is an opulent 21st century hotel, with marble much in evidence. The dramatic foyer is filled with light and colour. There are ten luxurious penthouse suites in addition to many lavish bedrooms, provided with every 'extra' imaginable, and glamorous bathrooms. Twenty-four hour room service is available. The Botánico has spectacular views of the Atlantic, Mount Teide and the Orotava Valley. Guests often meet in the arcade, at one of the pool bars by day or at night in the piano bar. They can choose between three delightful restaurants offering grills, Thai or Italian dishes. The wine list is superb. Tennis (floodlit), two pools, a driving range (good golf nearby also an 18 hole putting-green which is free to guests is adjacent to the hotel) and going out on the hotel launch occupy the day; alternatives are being pampered in the beauty centre or exploring old towns and villages up in the cool mountains. The Botánico also has a shuttle bus to the town centre which has intriguing shops and a vibrant night-life. **Directions:** The hotel will meet guests at the airport on request. Parking for those with a car. Price guide: Single 19,600–33,600pts; double/twin 27,800–52,700pts; suites 66,000–95,600pts.

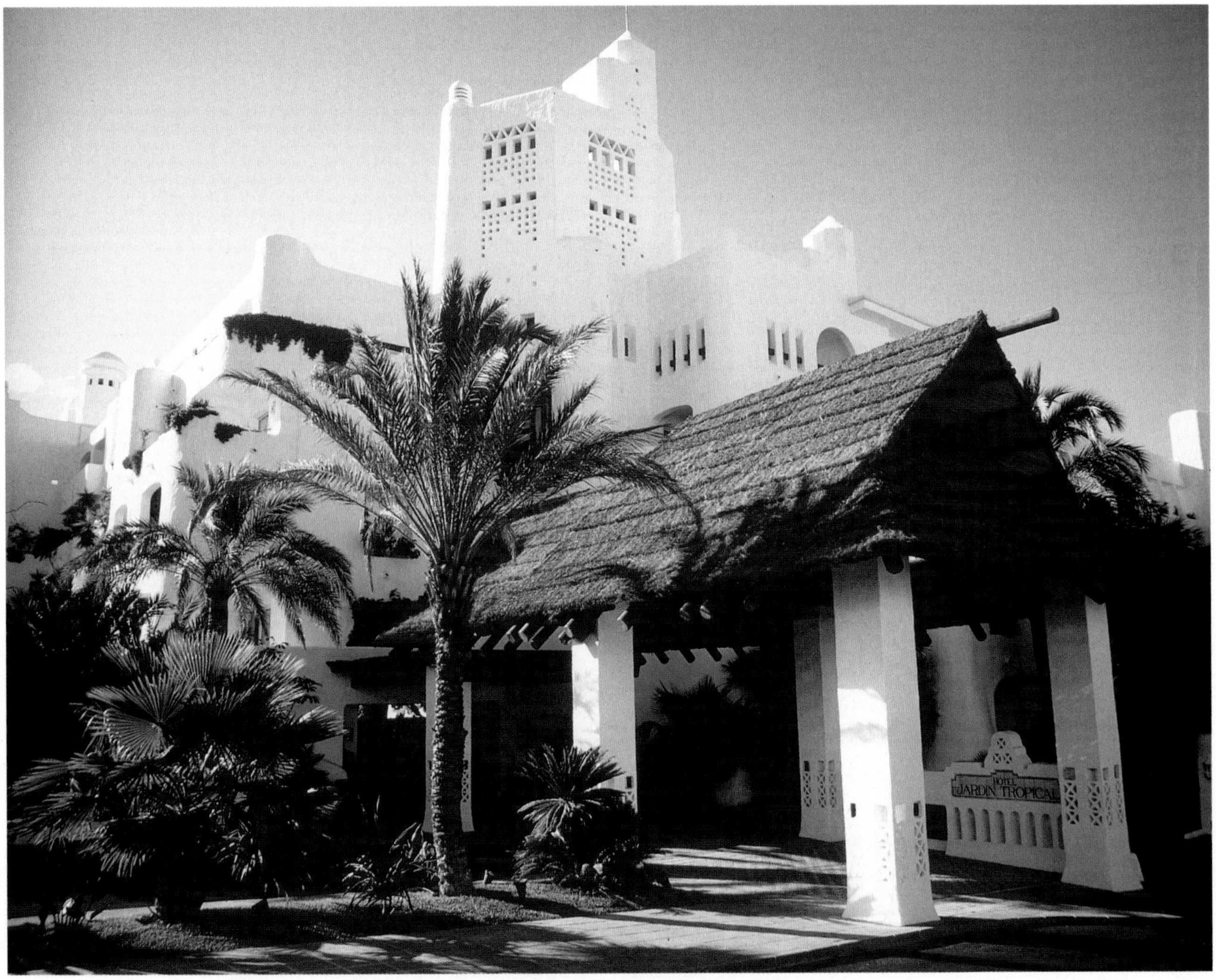

HOTEL JARDIN TROPICAL

CALLE GRAN BRETAÑA, 38670 COSTA ADEJE, TENERIFE, CANARY ISLANDS
TEL: 34 22 75 01 00 FAX: 34 22 75 28 44

This sensational hotel was built just ten years ago, a magnificent Moorish palace embellished with domed towers, its white walls contrasting brilliantly with its setting of exotic green foliage – there are 300 types of trees and 16,000 plants in the tropical garden after which it is named – interspersed with blue pools and colourful flowers. The interior rooms are cool luxury, tiled floors, big windows, attractive fabrics, every bedroom having a terrace, and the exclusive Las Adelfas Suites are phenomenal, spacious and furnished in great style. Guests have a choice of five restaurants: Las Mimosas with its splendid buffets, Los Cucurucho poolside snack bar and Las Cuevas à la carte restaurant, Las Rocas specialising in seafood and El Patio for gourmet feasts. There is a piano in the Lobby Bar,dancing in the Café de Paris and a champagne room for sybarites. This part of Tenerife has no beach, but Las Rochas Beach Club adjacent to the hotel offers a seawater pool and sunbathing terraces with bar service, a health spa and fabulous restaurant. Golfers will appreciate special fees arranged with two local golf clubs. Deep sea fishing and exploring the island are other popular activities. **Directions:** Drivers follow signs to San Eugenio. Price guide: Single 23,500pts; double/twin 34,500pts; suites 59,000pts.

Sweden

Sweden requires the visitor to travel far, in terms of both distance and attitude. Approximately the size of California, Sweden reaches as far north as the Arctic fringes of Europe, where glacier-topped mountains and thousands of acres of pine, spruce, and birch forests are broken here and there by wild rivers, countless pristine lakes and desolate moor land.

In the more populated south, roads meander through mile after mile of softly undulating countryside, skirting lakes and passing small villages with their requisite sharp pointed church spires. Here, the lush forests which dominate Sweden's northern landscape have largely fallen to the plough.

Sweden possesses stunning natural assets. In the forest, moose, deer, bears and lynx roam. Fish abound in sparkling lakes and tumbling rivers, sea eagles and ospreys soar over myriad pine-clad islands in the archipelagos off the east and west coasts.

A country of contrasts, streamlined ultra modern cities give way to the forests and may-poles around which villagers still dance at midsummer in traditional costume evoking pagan early history and more recent agrarian culture.

Stockholm, one of Europe's most beautiful and clean capitals, skyscraper lined boulevards are a short walk from twisting medieval streets in this modern yet pastoral city. Because Stockholm's main attractions are concentrated in a relatively small area, it can be fully explored in a few days.

Built on 14 small islands among open bays and narrow channels, the city has been dubbed the 'Venice of the North'. The city is an ideal place to find items that reflect the very best in Swedish design and elegance, particularly glass, porcelain, furs, handicrafts, home furnishings and leather goods. The quality is uniformly high, and you can take advantage of the tax free shopping service in most stores.

Dalarna, the central region of Sweden, is considered to the be most typically Swedish of all the country's 24 provinces – capturing the very best of the country's finest qualities. A place of forests, mountains, and red painted wooden farm houses and cottages to be found by the shores of sun dappled lakes. Bliss.

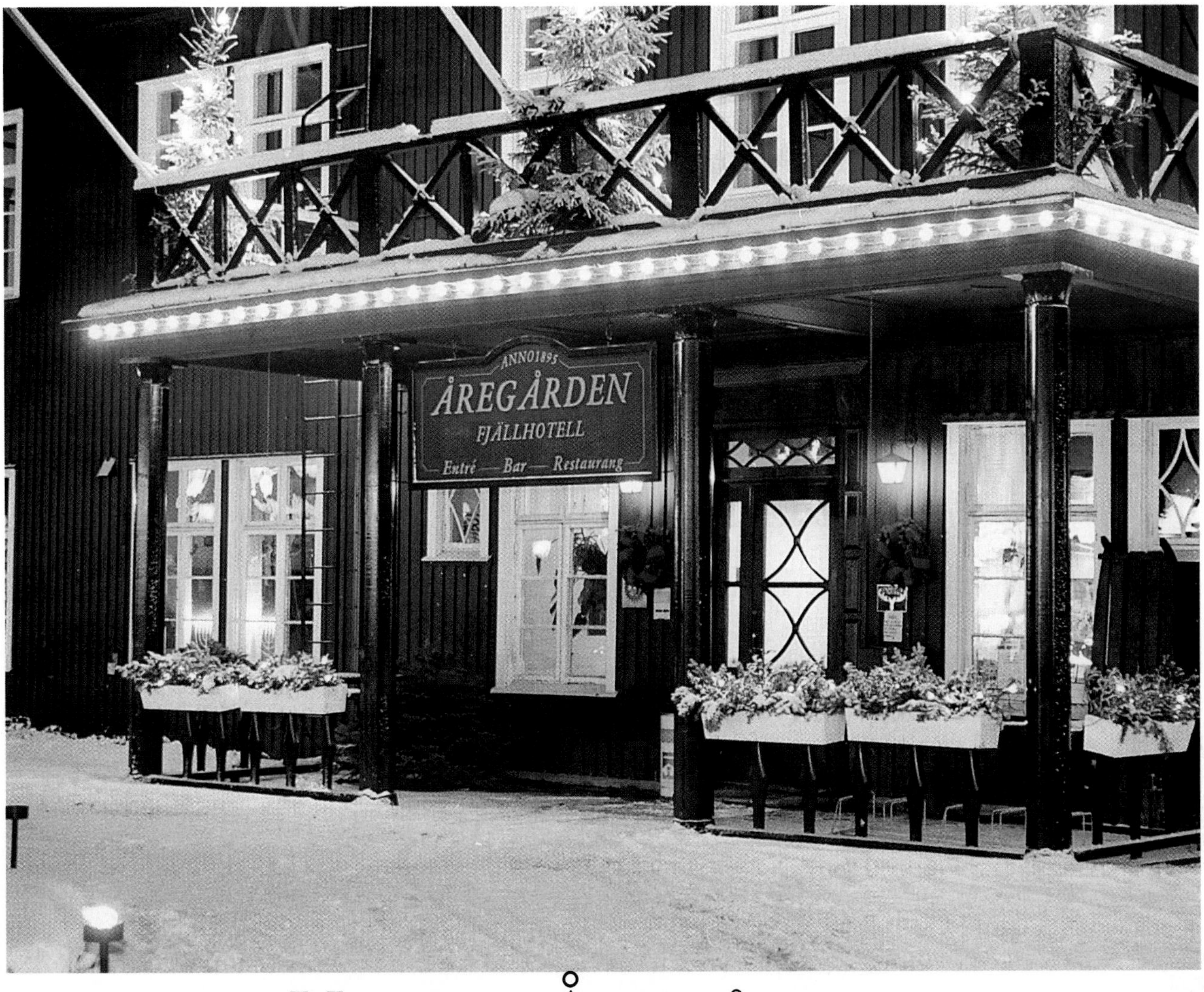

HOTELL ÅREGÅRDEN

BOX 6, S–83013 ÅRE, SWEDEN

TEL: 46 647 178 00 FAX: 46 647 17960

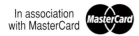

This lovely fin-de-siècle century house has been a hotel for some 100 years. Standing in the centre of Åre, it has a fantastic position, close to the ski-lifts, shops and other local attractions, with a background of snowclad mountains. The interior is traditional, with fine pine panelling much in evidence, and the friendly staff contribute to the warm ambience of this excellently-run hotel. The charming bedrooms are light and colourful, the furnishings comfortable. There are pleasant apartments for 4-8 people in adjacent small houses. Hotell Åregården has a convivial bar, and two excellent restaurants where delicious Swedish specialities are served. Guests also enjoy themselves in its popular Country Club, with famous live bands perfmorming. A recent addition is a conference complex of seven meeting rooms, all having the latest communication and presentation equipment. Visitors relax in the splendid pool, saunas and sunbeds, ideal after a long winter day's ski-ing (the discounts on ski rental are appreciated) In summer guests explore the countryside on bikes, walk among the mountains, or fish, play golf. Internet: www.diplomat-hotel.se. **Directions:** Årefjällen is off the E14 between Trondheim and Östersund. Price Guide: Single SEK595–SEK895; double/twin SEK495–SEK795 pp; suite SEK795–SEK995 pp.

Aspa Herrgård

S–69693, ASPA BRUK, ASKERSUND, SWEDEN
TEL: 46 583 50210 FAX: 46 583 50150

Aspa Bruk is a very special place in Sweden, much admired by the 1916 Nobel Prize winning poet, Verner von Heidenstam, and he used to stay at Aspa Herrgård, an enchanting 18th century manor house on the shores of Lake Vättern, by the verdant Tiveden National Park. The hotel has a marvellous tranquil ambience, created by the decorations in muted colours, the graceful period furniture, the bowls of flowers, beautiful objets d'art and memorabilia, fine paintings, views over the lake and park and, of course, the immaculate staff. The bedrooms are charming, comfortable and peaceful – some for non-smokers. The salons and library are traditional, and there is a pleasant bar. The elegant dining room, with its exquisite table-settings, is the pièce de résistance, having won many accolades including that of the unique Relais Gourmand, while superb wines can be found in the 15th century cellar. The former stables are a museum to the Swedish poet, Bellman, and the Manor hosts various cultural events, including art exhibitions and musical soirées, throughout the year. There are facilities for boules, croquet, golf and canoeing at hand. **Directions:** From Stockholm drive E20 towards Örebro, then take road 50 towards Akersund. Take right road 49 towards Skövde/Karlsborg. Price guide: Single SEK990–SEK1290; double/twin SEK1380–SEK2090; suite SEK2340.

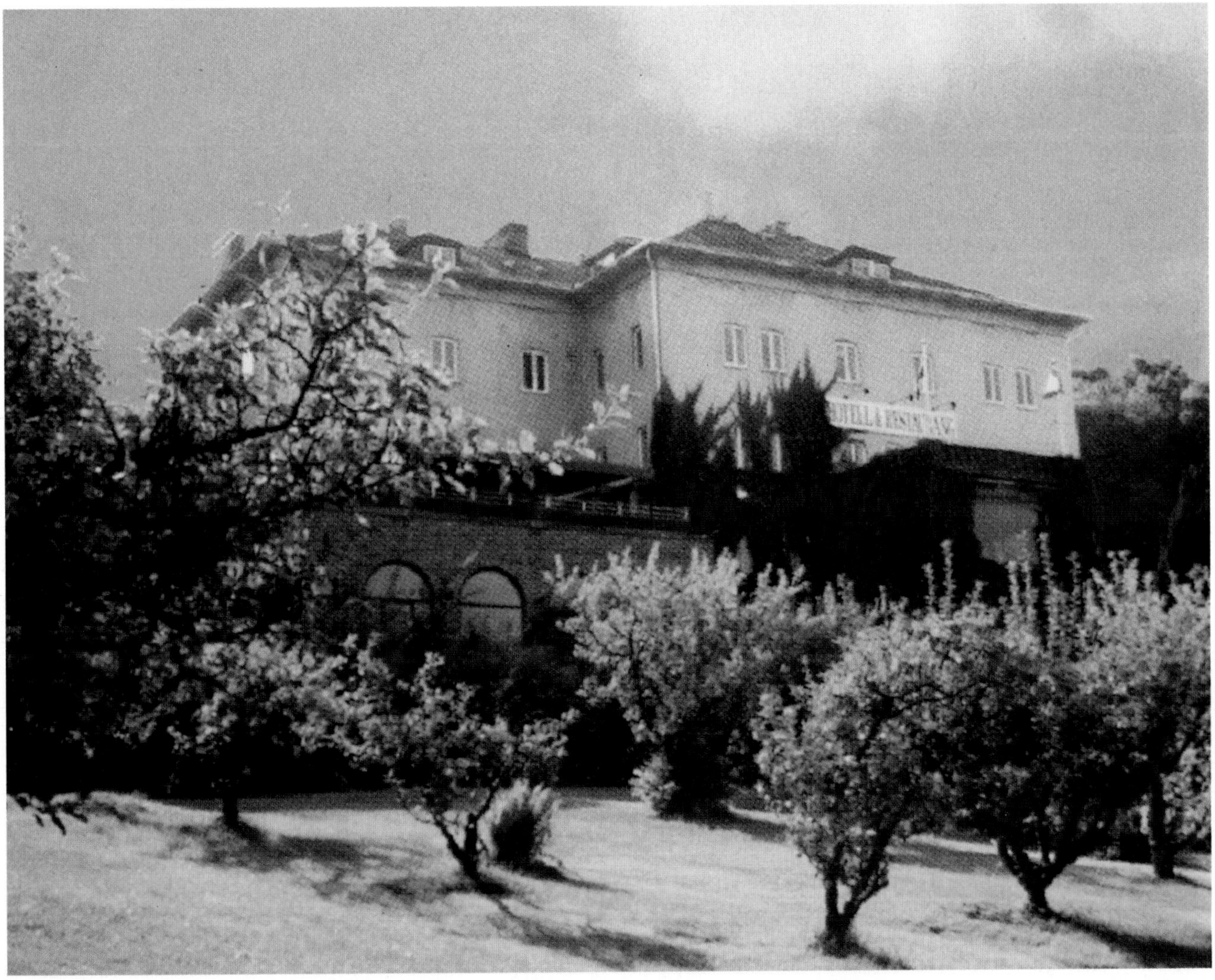

HOTEL BUENA VISTA

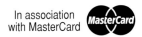

TARRAVÄGEN 5, 26935 BÅSTAD, SWEDEN
TEL: 46 431 760 00 FAX: 46 431 791 00

This is an unusual hotel to find on the coast of Southern Sweden – built at the last fin de siècle, Buena Vista is in the style of a grand Spanish villa It stands in the centre of Båstad, sufficiently elevated to have spectacular views of Laholm's Bay. The hotel is surrounded by pleasant gardens. The decor is immaculate, the ambience welcoming. The Hall at the bottom of the impressive galleried staircase is the heart of the villa – here guests rendezvous to have a drink and discuss their day. The bedrooms are charming and have well designed bathrooms. There are several elegant dining rooms – small and romantic or somewhat bigger, with views over the waterfront – all serving beautifully presented regional and seasonal dishes. The wine list is splendid. In fine weather the spacious open-air restaurant is popular. Buena Vista enjoys catering for meetings, seminars and special celebrations. It has a pristine chapel, enchanting for weddings or christenings. This is a mecca for golfers, with five good courses nearby. Excellent tennis facilities are nearby. The coast is 200m away, for strolls along the beach and sea swimming is fantastic. **Directions:** From Malmö or Gothenburg take the E6 motorway to picturesque Båstad, finding the hotel in the town centre. The nearest airports are Halmstad and Angelholm. Parking. Price guide: Single SEK660–750; double/twin SEK850–990; suites SEK1295.

HALLTORPS GÄSTGIVERI

S–38792, BORGHOLM, SWEDEN
TEL: 46 485 85000 FAX: 46 485 85001

The Halltorps Inn is one of the oldest manors recorded on the Viking island of Öland – and it was only in 1975, following major reconstruction, that it became a hotel. In 1991 the extensive annex was completed, blending carefully with the original house. The position is superb, overlooking the spectacular Kalmar Sound. The eleven guestrooms in the original mansion are romantic and traditional, but the hotel is also very proud of its twenty-five rooms in the extension, each personalised by designers from different Swedish provinces. The spacious bathrooms have hightec showers. The welcoming reception rooms have comfortable leather furniture and guests enjoy sampling the house speciality, spiced Aquavit, in the friendly bar! This is a hotel for gourmets, the inspired menu incorporating many local delicacies such as fish from the Baltic, and wine-lovers will appreciate the selection available. Guests relax on the sun terrace, play boules or croquet on the lawn, use the saunas or 'springcool' and in winter appreciate the three open fires, perhaps after cross-country skiing. Golf is just 1km distant.The hotel arranges bird-watching safaris, wild-flower excursions, wine tasting, and fishing tours. **Directions:** From the mainland E22, then the country road 136. Price guide: Single SEK795–SEK830; double/twin SEK990–SEK1090; suite SEK1300–SEK1520.

Hotel Sundbyholms Slott

S–63508 ESKILSTUNA, SWEDEN
TEL: 46 16 96500 FAX: 46 16 96578

Not all buildings called "castles" have battlements. This graceful dwelling, built in 1640, is reminiscent of a château. It stands in its own extensive parkland, leading down to the shores of lovely Lake Malaren. There is a famous painting of Sundbyholm, by Prince Eugen, who had a studio on the second floor. The enchanting castle has undergone sympathetic restoration. The bedroom accommodation is however in other various areas, most having views of the lake. All rooms have modern showers. The superior suites are outstanding. The restaurant is in the castle, in the Knights Hall, which is famed for its brilliant cuisine and fine wines. Sparkling crystal, gleaming silver, beautiful flowers and brilliant chandeliers enhance the ambience. The Old Bailiff's House has been transformed into a modern conference complex. Another important feature is the Sundbyholm Country Club, with its magnificent championship golf course. Additionally it has teaching and practice grounds. Residents enjoy the local harbour – some even arrive by boat – and beautiful beaches on the lakeside. Others stroll through the beech groves, seeking the famous Sigurd runic rock. **Directions:** From Stockholm leave the E20 at Eskilstuna, follow signs. Sundbyholm is situated 12km north of Eskilstuna. Price guide: Single SEK600–SEK1100; double/twin SEK850–SEK1520.

120

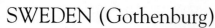

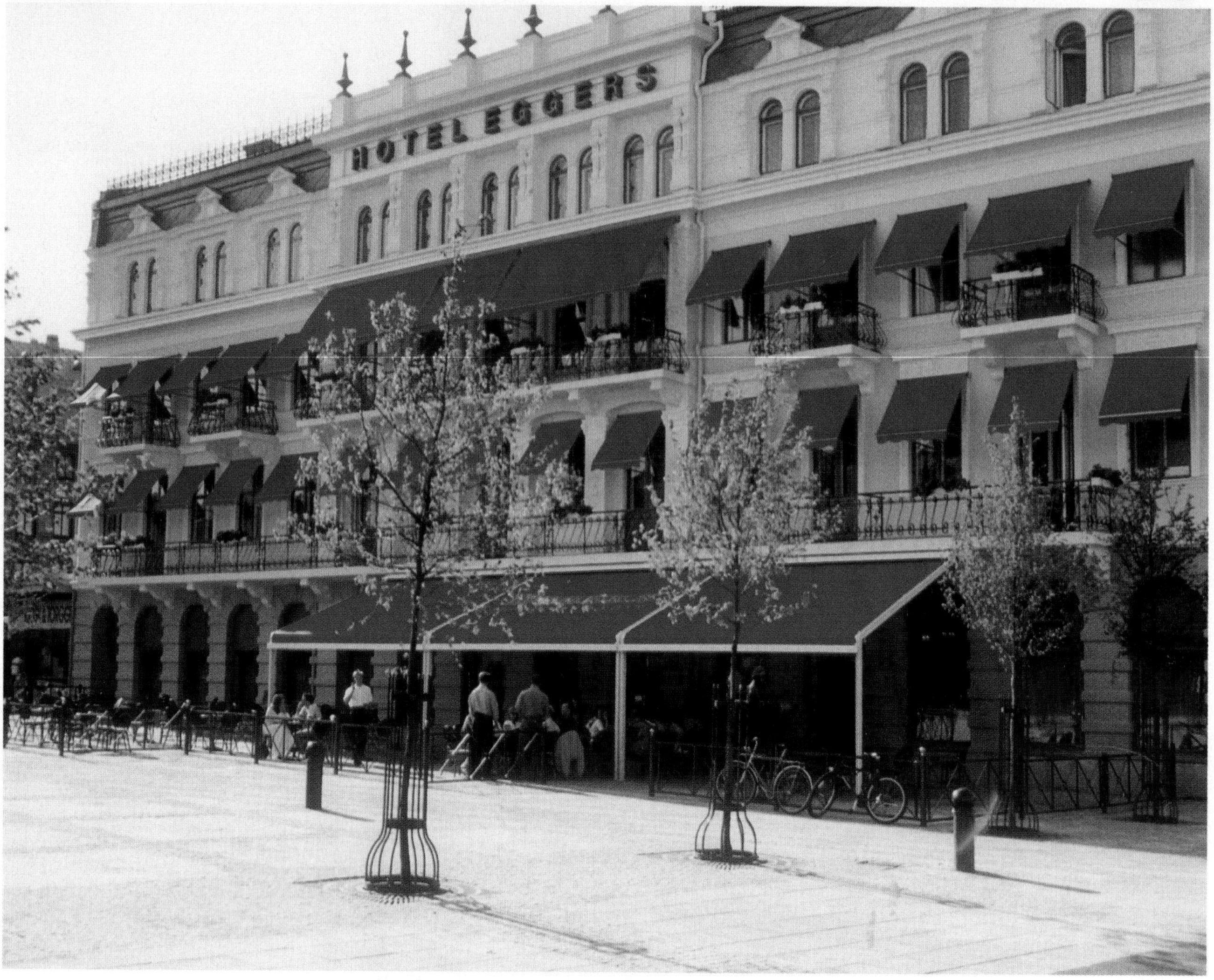

HOTEL EGGERS

DROTTINGTORGET, BOX 323, 40125 GOTHENBURG, SWEDEN
TEL: 46 31 80 60 70 FAX: 46 31 15 42 43

Gothenburg is a delightful city to visit, and it can be reached by air, rail or sea, for it is an important port, playing a significant part in the Scandinavian shipping industry as well as having cruise ships calling in. The Eggers is a fine traditional hotel, the second oldest in Sweden. It has a big foyer which has tall pillars, a graceful staircase and is pleasantly furnished. It is popular with the nearby business community because it has excellent meeting facilities with audio visual and other communication equipment available. Each bedroom differs from the next in style or colour, but all are extremely comfortable, thoughtfully equipped with modern amenities and have efficient bathrooms. The bar is an ideal rendezvous, decorated in warm colours and leading into the elegant "Eggers Restaurant", which has lovely wall coverings and brilliant chandeliers. While Swedish specialities are served, especially at the splendid breakfast buffet, the menu includes cosmopolitan favourites. It is also possible to hold receptions or small banquets here during conventions. Cruises round the islands are enjoyable; Gothenburg also has ten excellent golf courses. Additionally it is an ideal base for touring. The pedestrian shopping area is splendid and the maritime museum is fascinating. At night visitors enjoy the opera. **Directions:** The hotel is next to the station. It has parking. Price guide: Single SEK595–1085; double/twin SEK840–1325

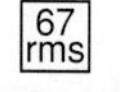

TOFTAHOLM HERRGÅRD

TOFTAHOLM PA, S-34014 LAGAN, SWEDEN
TEL: 46 370 440 55 FAX: 46 370 440 45

This splendid manor house, with a history dating back over 600 years and a secret tunnel through which a king escaped from marauders in the sixteenth century, is in a magnificent position right on the shores of Lake Vidostern yet sheltered by forests of fragrant pine trees. This elegant hotel is timeless, old fashioned courtesies prevail, yet it meets the demands of today's travellers, who share it with a gentle ghost. The salons are elegant, peaceful and beautifully decorated and the traditional meeting room has plenty of natural light from the many windows. The quiet bedrooms, each individually styled, are charming, with delicate colour schemes and they look out over the countryside. Powerful hot showers are a feature of the bathrooms. Aperitifs are served on the terrace on warm evenings; otherwise there is a convivial corner next to Reception. Swedish cooking at its best is offered in the attractive restaurant, a wonderful array of tempting dishes. Hidden in the gardens is an authentic old inn serving tankards of frothy lager! Energetic guests appreciate the lakeside beach, the proximity of two superb golf courses, fishing, cycling, rowing, canoeing, cycling, jogging trails and skiing – and afterwards the sauna. Others relax on the lawn watching the boats. **Directions:** From Stockholm follow E4 to sign to Toftaholm. Price guide: Single SEK790–940; double/twin SEK1140–1180; suites SEK1490.

49 rms

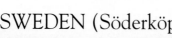

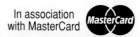

Romantik Hotel Söderköpings Brunn

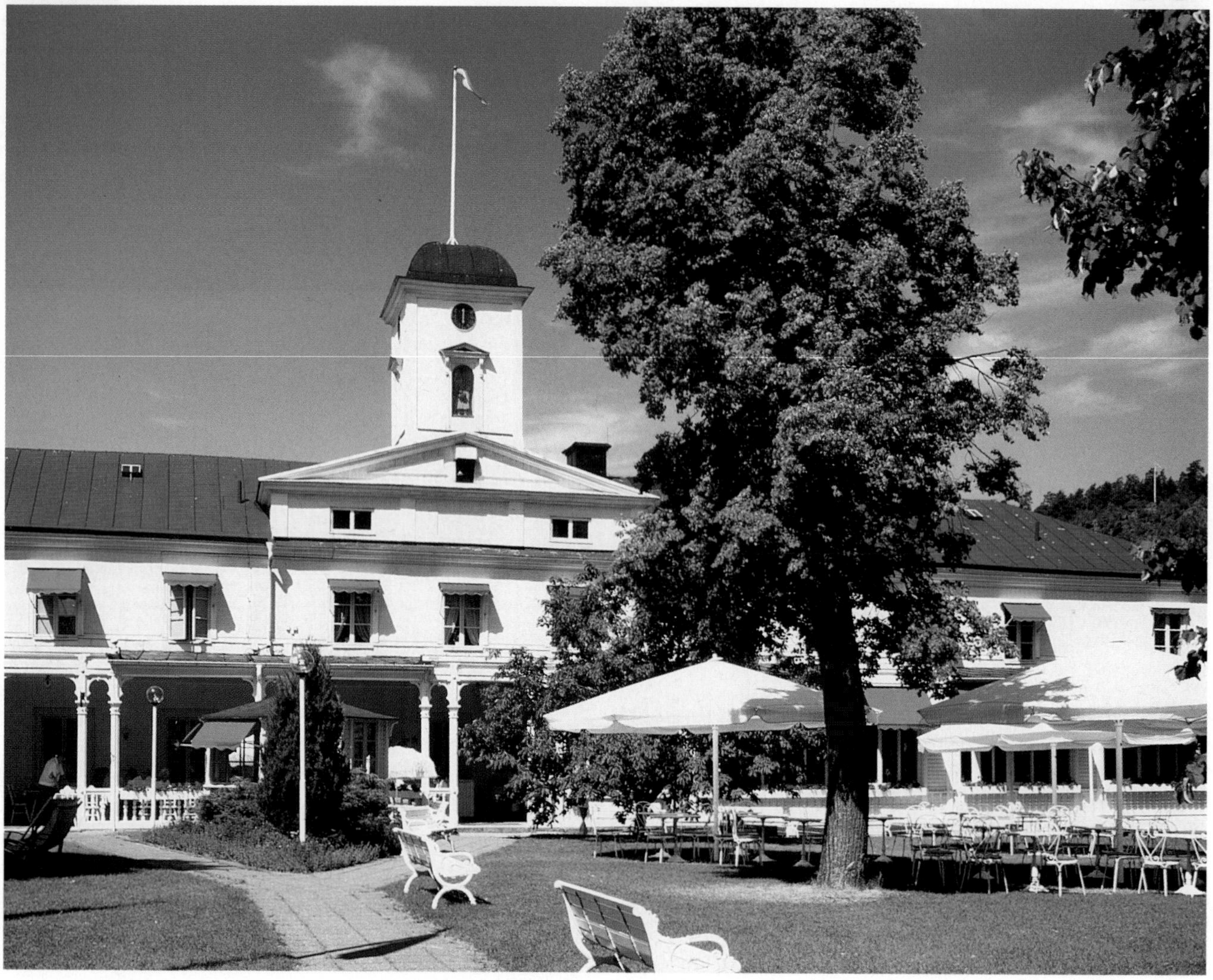

SKÖNBERGAGATAN 35, BOX 44, S–61421 SÖDERKÖPING
TEL: 46 121 10900 FAX: 46 121 13941

In 1719 it was discovered that the water from S:t Ragnhilds had medicinal properties and the Söderköping spa was built. It became a famous health resort in the 19th century and it is still possible to 'take the water' from a spring in Reception. Following considerate restoration, which has not disturbed the style of the original buildings – an important feature of the town – Söderköpings Brunn is now an impeccable modern hotel. The light and airy bedrooms are delightful, overlooking the gardens. Some are designated non-smoking and four are suitable for those with mobility problems. The bedrooms are divided between two houses. Guests gather in the lounge and bar before enjoying good food and good wine, perhaps on the verandah in summer, otherwise in the spacious restaurant. Outside is a small bandstand with an open-air dance floor. The recent extensions included topical conference facilities and corporate entertaining can take place in the legendary 'Society Parlour'. The hotel has its own boats for trips along the Göta Canal and the River Storån or guests can take out a canoe. Active visitors can climb the Ramunder mountain, play tennis or enjoy golf alongside Lake Asplången, cycle, fish or explore the old town. **Directions:** Söderköping is near the E22, 15km south of Norrköping with its airport and railway station. Price guide: Single SEK600–SEK975; double/twin SEK850–SEK1175.

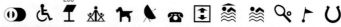

HOTELL DIPLOMAT

STRANDVÄGEN 7 C, BOX 14059, S–104 40, STOCKHOLM, SWEDEN
TEL: 46 8 663 58 00 FAX: 46 8 783 66 34

It is always a joy to stay at a hotel overlooking a harbour, and The Diplomat is magnificently positioned on the water's edge yet close to centre of Stockholm. Both the exterior and interior are fine examples of the Art Nouveau era, from the little tower and style of the windows to the spectacular bronze lift and delightful stained glass windows. Nonetheless it is a sophisticated and modern hotel. It has been beautifully decorated, even the corridors having brilliant harmonious colour schemes and fine period furniture. These lead to attractive, spacious and well-equipped bedrooms. The elegant lounge is an ideal meeting place, an alternative rendezvous being the stylish bar, with its leather chairs and old prints on the walls. Buffet breakfasts, appetising lunches and dinners are served in the Diplomat Tea House. Private dining can be arranged in the smart Board Room. If not attending meetings in the nearby commercial centre, guests explore the fascinating Old Town, visit the museums or shopping centre. Boat trips round the harbour. Golf and tennis are not far away. Internet: www.diplomat-hotel.se **Directions:** The hotel is on Strandvägen, close to the Nybroviken Ferry terminal. Parking facilites can be arranged. Price guide: Single SEK1465–SEK1995; double/twin SEK1995–SEK2195; suite SEK3295–SEK5690.

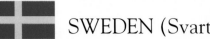

Svartå Herrgård

693 93 SVARTÅ, SWEDEN
TEL: 46 585 500 03 FAX: 46 585 503 03

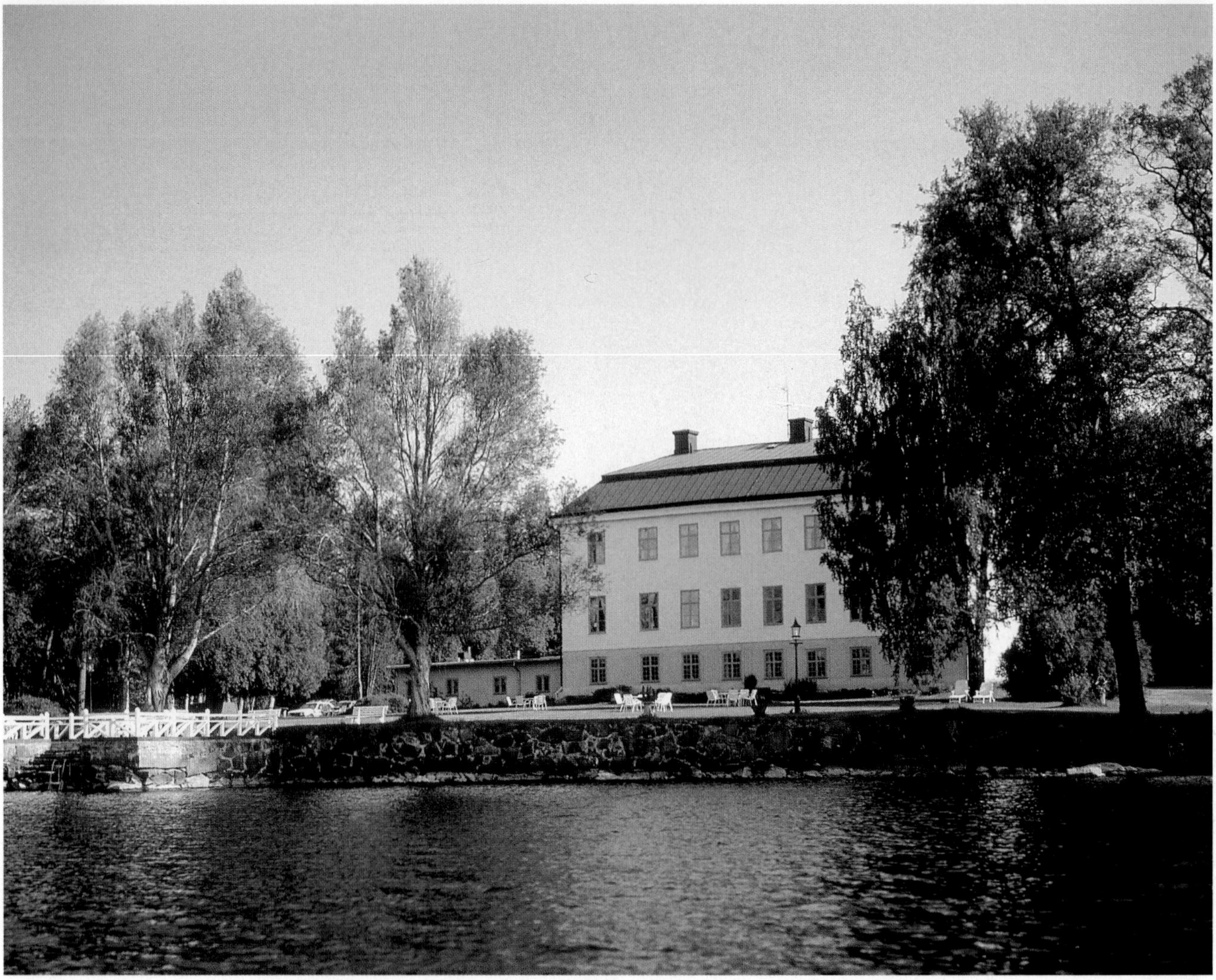

In the centre of Sweden, east of Stockholm, in the glorious wooded countryside surrounding Svartå, there is a magnificent manor house built in 1782. It has been lovingly restored and discreetly modernised and today it is an immaculate, romantic hotel standing in well-kept gardens stretching down to a sparkling lake. The fascinating history of the Svartå Herrgard is reflected in the elegant decorations,fine antiques, graceful chairs, brilliant chandeliers and handsome portraits. The wonderfully peaceful guest rooms are exquisite, with delicate colour schemes, period furniture and views over the countryside. The bathrooms are modern. The lounge bar has a splendid vaulted ceiling and grand snooker table; the breakfast room is refreshing in blue and white. Dining in the handsome restaurant, with its lovely frescoes, is memorable – inspired interpretations of Swedish specialities and cosmopolitan favourites are offered, and the wine list is excellent. The adjacent Villa Lugnsbo is a self contained conference centre, with various sized meeting rooms, excellent equipment and its own cafeteria. Boating on the lake, exploring Svartå, playing golf and tennis nearby are summer sports; in winter good ski-ing is accessible. **Directions:** E18 from Stockholm, then Road 204 to Svartå, watching for signs to the hotel. Price guide: Single SEK 800; double/twin SEK 1000–1600.

Romantik Hotels & Restaurants

ROMANTIK HOTEL ÅKERBLADS

S–79370 TÄLLBERG, SWEDEN
TEL: 46 247 50800 FAX: 46 247 50652

This charming traditional farmhouse, now extended and modernised without detracting from the original buildings, has been the home of the Åkerblad family since the 16th century. It is on a hillside in the village of Tällberg, and has spectacular views over the Siljan Lake. Today most of the bedrooms are separate from the main building, being in three adjacent houses. They are wonderfully light, with big windows, pine furnishings and soft harmonising colour schemes. The bathrooms are more inclined to have showers than baths. There is a spacious Skänrummet, with lovely stone walls, which is very convivial – sometimes enlivened further by folk-dancing – and a cosy, colourful, small bar. The traditional dining room offers a wonderful array of Smörgåsbord in addition to a delicious evening menu based on grandmother's cooking! The cellar holds many splendid wines. A larger salon transforms into a superb banqueting hall. Excellent conference facilites are also available. In winter ski-ing and sleigh-rides are on the programme, in summer there are boat trips on the lake, museums and crafts shops and even gold washing at nearby Orsa. Nightlife can be found in most of the neighbouring villages. **Directions:** From Stockholm the E70 leads all the way to Tällberg. Price guide: Single SEK350–SEK600; double/twin SEK500–SEK1200.

Hotel Tänndalen

S–84098 TÄNNDALEN, SWEDEN
TEL: 46 684 220 20 FAX: 46 684 224 24

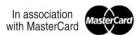

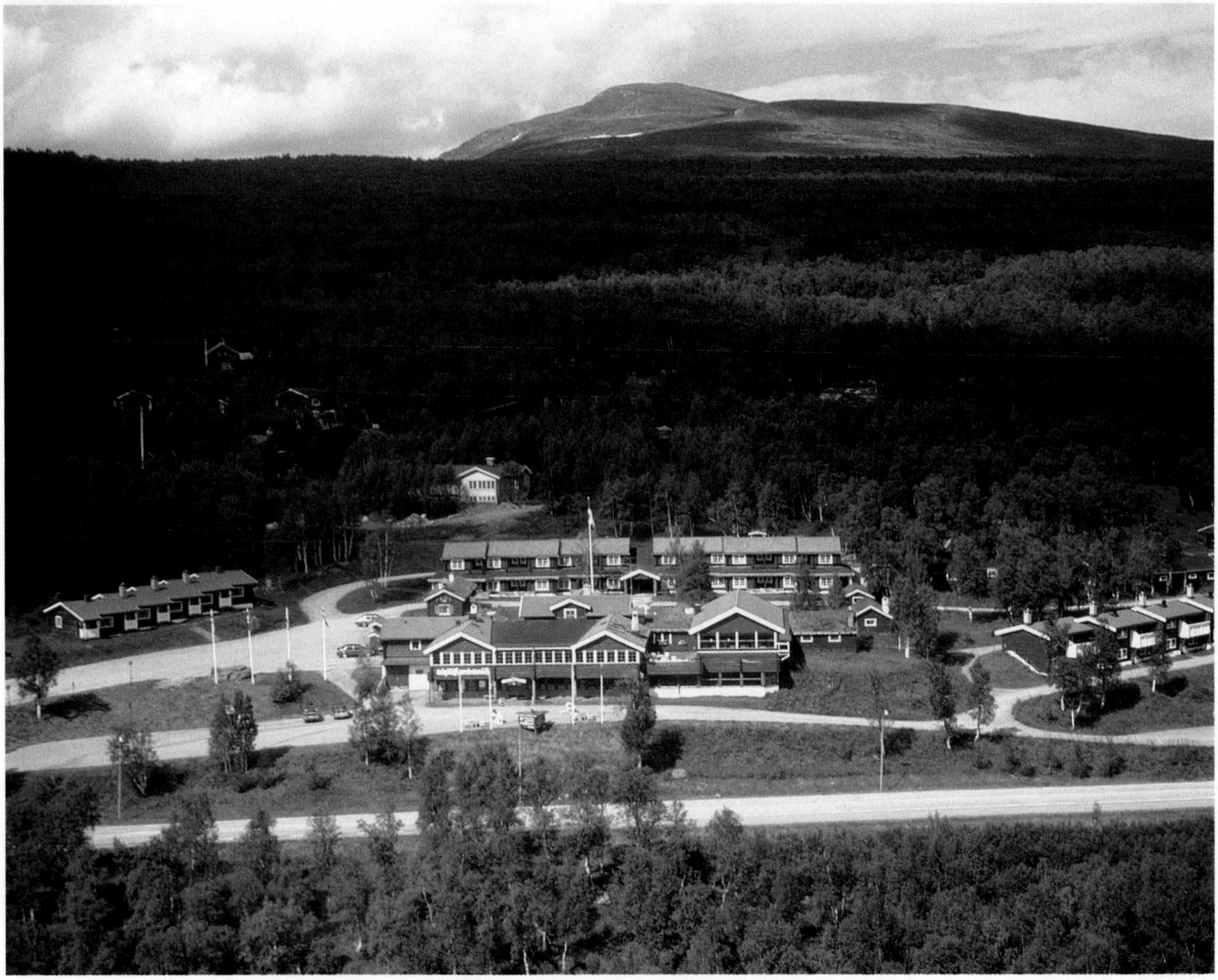

To reach Tänndalen you fly to Norway, for it is close to the border, high up in the Swedish mountains. In reality this is much more than a hotel, it is almost a village in itself – a complex of attractive wooden buildings set against magnificent scenery. Created by the hospitable Mortberg family, its reputation is for fine living and good sport! Many of the comfortable bedrooms and self-catering apartments (with paintings and ornaments by local artists) are in charming rustic chalets and houses just minutes walk from the hotel itself, where guests relax in the congenial halls before open fires, investigate the shop stocked by nearby craftsmen, fraternise in the coffee shop and bar or dive into the swimming pool. The restaurant has a reputation for delicious food – including regional specialities such as reindeer, trout and cloudberries – and for excellent wines. There are also superb conference facilities. In winter there is fantastic skiing, both down hill and cross country. The Mortbergs organise dog sledging and snowmobile safaris. Summer brings alpine flora and fauna – reindeers, elks and bears! Activities are hiking, climbing, tennis, golf, fishing and canoeing. Local markets are fascinating. The Tänndalen arranges evening entertainments. **Directions:** Road 84: 12 miles west of Funasdalen, 18km from the border. Roras is the nearest airport. Parking. Price guide: Single SEK 695–995; double/twin SEK 990–1209; suites SEK 1200–1600.

TANUMS GESTGIFVERI

S – 457 00, TANUMSHEDE, SWEDEN
TEL: 46 525 290 10 FAX: 46 525 295 71

There has been an inn at Tanumshede for over 300 years, for its was on 6th July 1663 that Bjørn of Hee received the right to become an inn-keeper, on condition he built a stable for travellers' horses. Offering fine hospitality has therefore been a long tradition at this unique small hotel. The current owners, Regine and Steiner Oster, after considerable research and restoration work, have resurrected the 17th century spirit of the Inn, especially in the Butler's Pantry and the dining rooms. Guests stay in the Old Doctor's Villa, where gorgeous suites and bedrooms, each differing form the next, have flowery or velvet upholstery, period furniture and all modern comforts, including splendid bathrooms. Visitors with mobility problems have not been overlooked. The rustic bar serves snacks, and the restaurant menu features fresh fish from the nearby coast and Bohuslan archipeligo, game and berries from the hinterland. The ancient cellars hold fine wines. The Gestgifveri has a sauna, and residents enjoy a game of billiards in the evening. The balmy climate is perfect for exploring the unspoilt countryside. The region is known for ancient rock paintings, Viking graves and ancient churches. The fishing ports are fascinating. Golf and sailing are in the vicinity. **Directions:** Route E6, Grebbestad exit, take Route 163 to Tanunshede. Price guide: Single SEK 650; double/twin SEK 910; suites SEK 1410–1910.

27 rms 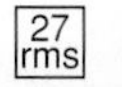       35    

KARLABY KRO

272 93 TOMMARP, SWEDEN
TEL: 46 414 203 00 FAX: 46 414 204 73

Skåne is in the South, the peninsular across the sea from Denmark. The region is unspoilt, magnificent countryside. In its midst the Fridlund family have created enchanting Karlaby Kro. Originally a farmhouse, today it is an attractive small hotel, open all the year round. It is a delightful building, long, low and white, and new arrivals are delighted by the warm greetings, lovely interior rooms and relaxing ambience. The peaceful guest rooms, many on the ground floor opening onto the gardens, are generously sized. They are comfortable, decorated in rich colours, have period furniture, big chairs and well-equipped bathrooms. Guests mingle in the inviting, well stocked bar, which has a the traditional tiled floor, an open fireplace and leather seating. The unexpectedly sophisticated gourmet restaurant has an exemplary wine list. There is also a large rustic dining room, ideal for celebrations or meetings. In summer refreshments are served on the terrace. The hotel has an indoor pool, sauna, gym, a darts board and a boules pitch outside. Three excellent golf courses are nearby. The fishing port of Simrishhamn is fascinating and interesting expeditons can be made to burial sites and prehistoric stones. **Directions:** From Everöd airport take Road 10. The hotel is 7 km west of Simrishhamn. Guest car parking. Price guide (per person): Single SEK 695–1050; double/twin SEK 495–680

21 rms 40

MAURITZBERGS SLOTT

S-61031 VIKBOLANDET, SWEDEN
TEL: 46 125 501 00 FAX: 46 125 501 04

This enchanting manor house, built over 400 years ago, stands on a hill overlooking Braviken Bay. Liisa Lipsanen, now Lady of the Manor, acquired it in 1990 and skillfully converted Mauritzbergs Slott into a modern hotel without detracting from its history. The bedrooms have individual styles and vary in size. The decorations are charming and restful. The bars and lounges have comfortable traditional furniture and the fine library serves as the billiard room. Many of the rooms are ideal for meetings and the old stable has been converted into a gallery, suitable for exhibitions and other events. The menu in the Jagarsal restaurant reflects the abundance of fresh fish and produce available. Alternatively there is Café Kvarnen, once the old mill and laundry cottage and now a delightful summer café. There are diverse activities offered in the extensive grounds – saunas, tennis, boules, hunting, clay pigeon shooting, fishing and boating, Golf is 20 km distant. Expeditions can be made to Kolmrden's Animal Park, the Gota Canal and St Anna's Archipeligo. Braviken Bay offers other excitements and concert visits can be arranged. **Directions:** From Stockholm take E4, then the Vagverket ferry (every half hour) across Braviken Bay; alternatively from Norrköping take the 209, turning to the coast at Ostra Husby. Price guide: Single 900Skr–1300Skr; double/twin 1300Skr–2100Skr; suites 2600Skr.

Switzerland

Those intriguing Swiss bank accounts may be numbered and hidden, but the nation's visible marvels are countless. And priceless. Everything is squeezed into some 16,000 square miles; three Switzerlands would fit neatly into the area of England. And yet, for a country so small, the variety is astonishing.

The climate ranges from the subpolar of some of Europe's loftiest mountains to the near-Mediterranean in southernmost Ticino.

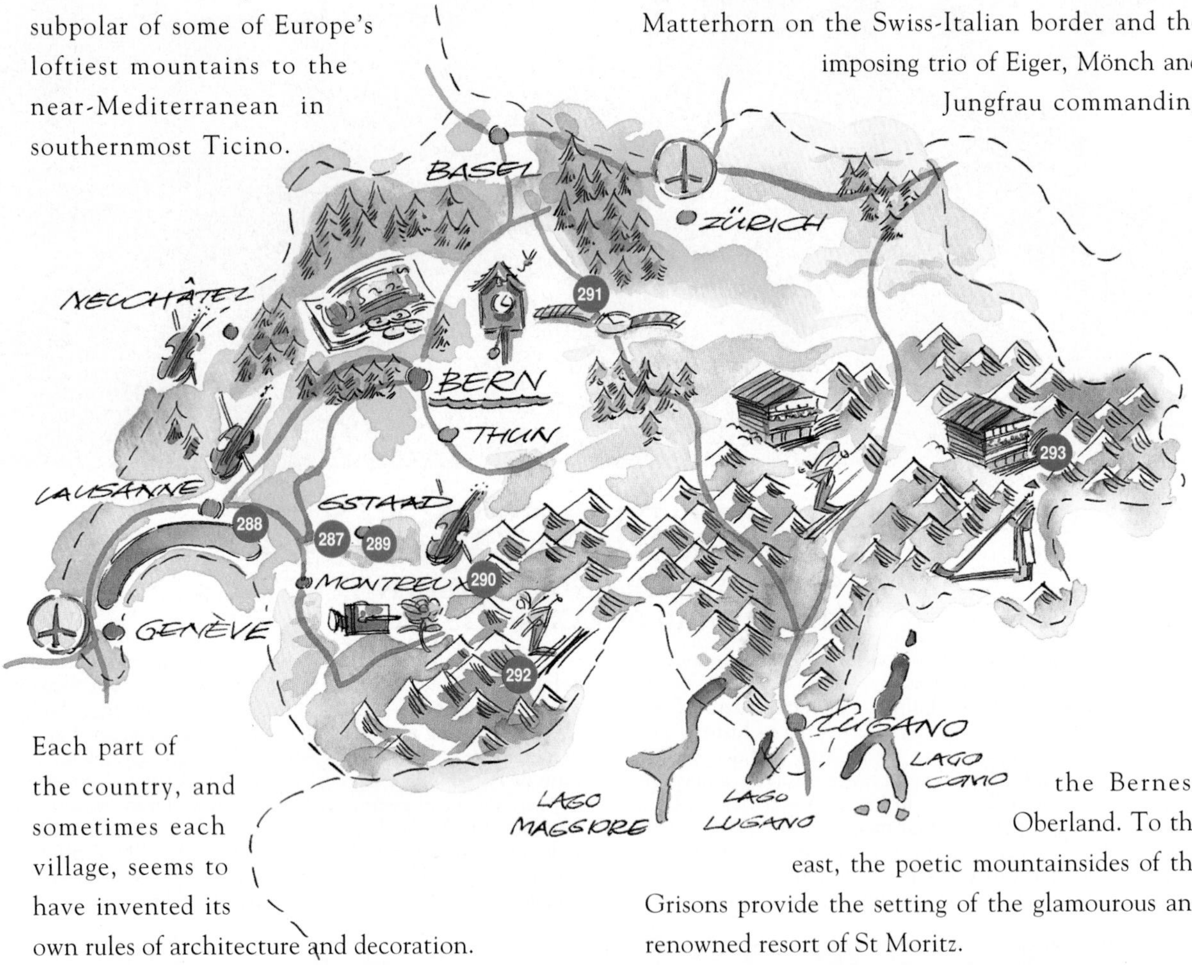

Each part of the country, and sometimes each village, seems to have invented its own rules of architecture and decoration.

Attention to detail and a sense of order carry over into just about every aspect of life. Notice how the pedestrians wait interminably for the traffic light to change rather than dart across an empty street. Even in French speaking, and hence more relaxed, Lausanne, the metro trains depart every seven and a half minutes, measured in seconds. From any café table or park bench you can observe a cross section of Swiss society: old ladies in hats with overfed dogs, conservatively dressed businessmen, well-mannered children, neatly uniformed street-cleaners shining the pavements with mechanical scrubbers.

Standard two-dimensional maps of Switzerland don't convey the country's geographical realites, which are based much more on altitude than latitude or longitude. About two thirds of the land is mountainous and some peaks rise up to 15,000 feet. Among the jagged highlights are the mystical Matterhorn on the Swiss-Italian border and the imposing trio of Eiger, Mönch and Jungfrau commanding the Bernese Oberland. To the east, the poetic mountainsides of the Grisons provide the setting of the glamourous and renowned resort of St Moritz.

All the cities and towns of Switzerland share a tidy allure, yet each is distinctive in its atmosphere and accent, traditions and interests. It's no more than a morning's drive from the covered bridges of Lucerne to the orange trees of Lugano in the heart of the Italian-speaking region, but the change of language, culture and climate is as dramatic as the Alps that separate them. Switzerland's villages are also well worth exploring.

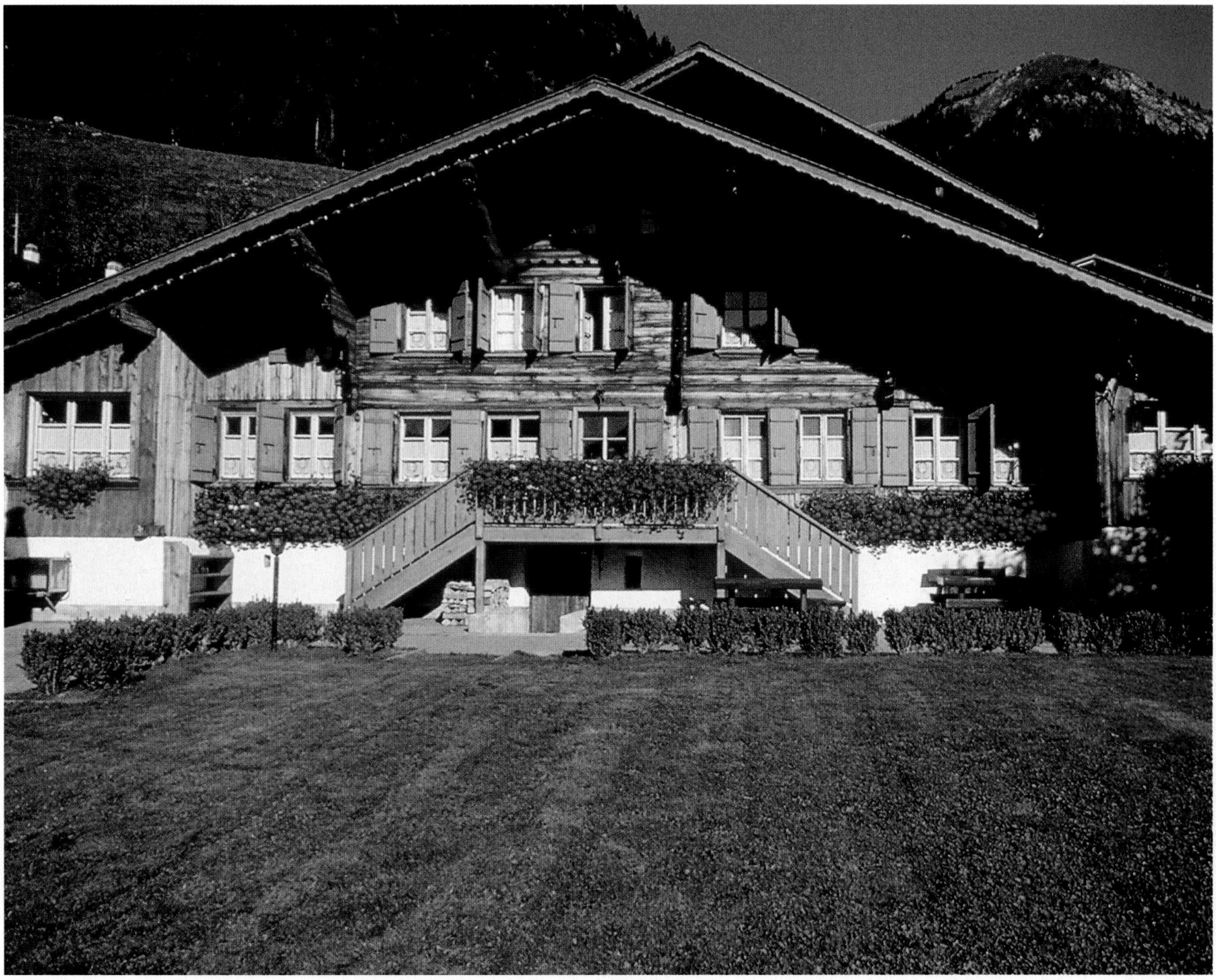

HOSTELLERIE BON ACCUEIL

1837 CHÂTEAU D'OEX, SWITZERLAND
TEL: 41 26 924 6320 FAX: 41 26 924 5126

In the region known as Pays d'Enhaut, 1000m above sea level, there is a 18th century chalet, cleverly and discreetly transformed into the pretty Hostellerie Bon Accueil, on the outskirts of Château d'Oex, famed for its cheese making. The hotel is in a sunny position, surrounded by mountains, forests and meadows. The reception rooms are traditionally furnished, and have big windows looking out across to the peaks. The bedrooms are delightful and decorated in pretty floral fabrics. A few are in the new annex, adjacent to the hotel. Happy evenings can be spent in the rustic Cellar-Bar, with its big fire and old stone walls. The cuisine is of the highest standards, with a French influence, enjoyed in the romantic candle-lit diningroom or, in summer, on the splendid terrace with its spectacular views. This is serious winter-sports territory, with runs for all standards, being close to the Gstaad Super Ski Region. In summer walkers appreciate the wild flowers and mountain streams. Others participate in river rafting, golf, tennis, canoeing and hot air ballooning. **Directions:** Leave E27 at Bulle or Aigle. Follow signs to Chateau d'Oex, turn left, crossing the railway track, watching for signs for the hotel. Price guide: Single Sf90–Sf120; double/twin Sf140–S210.

Hotel Victoria

CG–1823 GLION, SWITZERLAND
TEL: 41 21 963 3131 FAX: 41 21 963 1351

Glion owes its early recognition as a renowned holiday resort to Lord Byron and Jean-Jacques Rousseau, both of whom praised its unique blend of spectacular scenery and tranquillity. Above Montreux, overlooking Lake Geneva, with magnificent views of the mountains, the Hotel Victoria is the epitome of old fashioned charm and standards. It is surrounded by landscaped gardens and the south facing facade is embellished with decorative wrought iron balconies where guests can relax in the sun. Inside it is a tribute to the Belle Epoque – handsome paintings on the walls, beautiful antiques, elegant chandeliers, ormolu clocks and memorabilia; the immense salon is a joy and the conservatory with its stained glass windows and rattan furniture is enchanting. The spacious guest rooms have individual colour schemes, period furnishings and wonderful views. The roomy bathrooms are excellent, containing all the luxuries. Aperitifs can be sipped in the traditional bar and the splendid restaurant, extending onto the terrace in summer, offers superb menus, including fish from the lake, and great wines. Sporting residents ski, sail, climb,play tennis, swim, practise their golf swing – others sunbathe, or enjoy boat trips on the lake. **Directions:** Head for Montreux, near town centre follow signs to Caux Glion. Price guide: Single Sf130–Sf240; double/twin Sf220–Sf340; suites Sf420–Sf570.

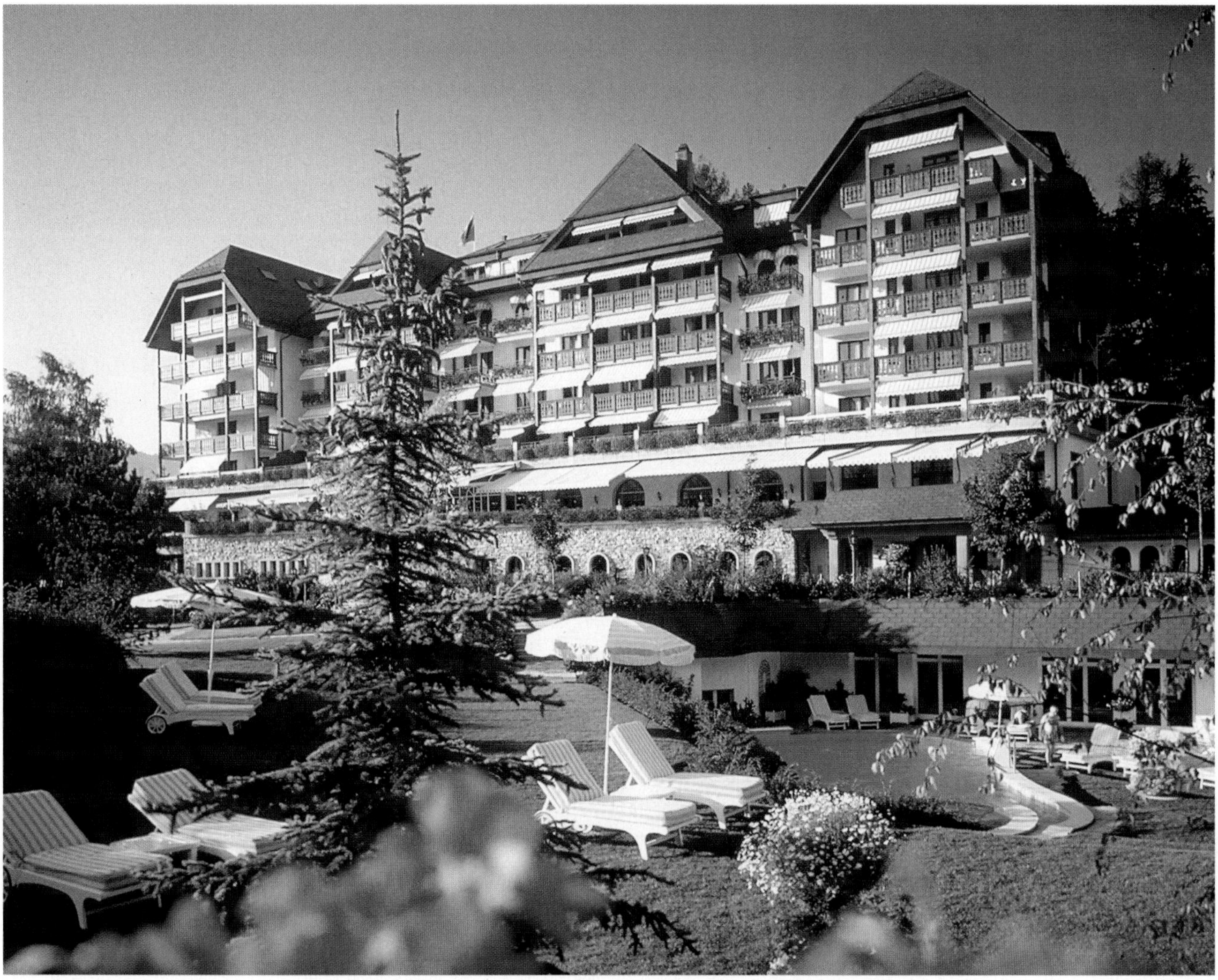

PrimaHotels

GRAND HOTEL PARK

CH–3780 GSTAAD, SWITZERLAND
TEL: 41 3374 89800 FAX: 41 3374 89808

Gstaad – in winter the ski resort favoured by the famous, and in summer host to a prestigious music festival and international tennis tournament. What better location for this impressive chalet hotel, surrounded by lovely gardens, with a backdrop of dramatic mountains and pine forests. The interior has a stylish ambience, with elegant carved ceilings and panelled walls, a superb tapestry dominating the lobby. The guest rooms have decorative wallhangings, antique furniture from the region, spectacular views and lavish marble bathrooms. Guests start the day with magnificent breakfasts in the Greenhouse, enjoy après-ski activities in the Kaminbar – or in summer relax by the poolside bar and lunch on the flowery Terrace – dine well in the rustic Grill or the sophisticated Belle Epoque Grand Restaurant and linger over digestifs in the Piano Bar. Fondue parties take place in the romantic Waldhaus and other festivities are held in the wine cellar. Every winter sport is possible, and when the snow goes, golf, tennis, climbing and exploring the Bernese Oberland are popular. The Aqua & Fitness Club offers a splendid pool, spa facilities, pampering, bridge and snooker. **Directions:** Leave A9 at Aigle, follow signs to Les Diablerets, to Gstaad and then hotel. Price guide: Single Sf335–580; double/twin Sf490–840; suites Sf840–1650.

ROYAL HOTEL BELLEVUE

CH–3718 KANDERSTEG, SWITZERLAND
TEL: 41 33 675 88 88 FAX: 41 33 675 88 80

This distinguished country house hotel, one of the Leading Hotels of the World, lies in a small unspoiled village resort in the middle of the Bernese Oberland. Surrounded by its own spacious gardens and lawns (12,000 square meters), the hotel offers an exceptional variety of leisure activities, summer and winter sports: easy alpine skiing and cross country skiing, open-air and indoor pools, fitness, beauty parlour, tennis and riding (both with instructors), golf practice areas, golf Interlaken 38km, yacht sailing and a 350HP motorboat, waterskiing, mountain-bikes and superb walking. In the classic restaurant, candlelight dinners are served in impeccable style with piano music. The Taverna rustic restaurant is ideal for meals in informal or sport dress. Light lunch is served near the poolside, overlooking the private park with magnificent views of mountains and glaciers. The bright and cheerful interior, furnished in antiques with elegantly fashionable soft colours, creates an atmosphere of comfort and refinement. All rooms and suites are luxuriously decorated in individual styles, all with bathrooms providing the highest comfort. A member of Relais et Châteaux. **Directions:** N6 Bern to Interlaken, take Spiez exit, 20km to Kandersteg. Direct trains from Zurich Airport. From Bern Airport trains every hour, Limousine at Kandersteg station. Price guide: Single Sf200–Sf350; double/twin Sf300–Sf440; suites Sf450–Sf700

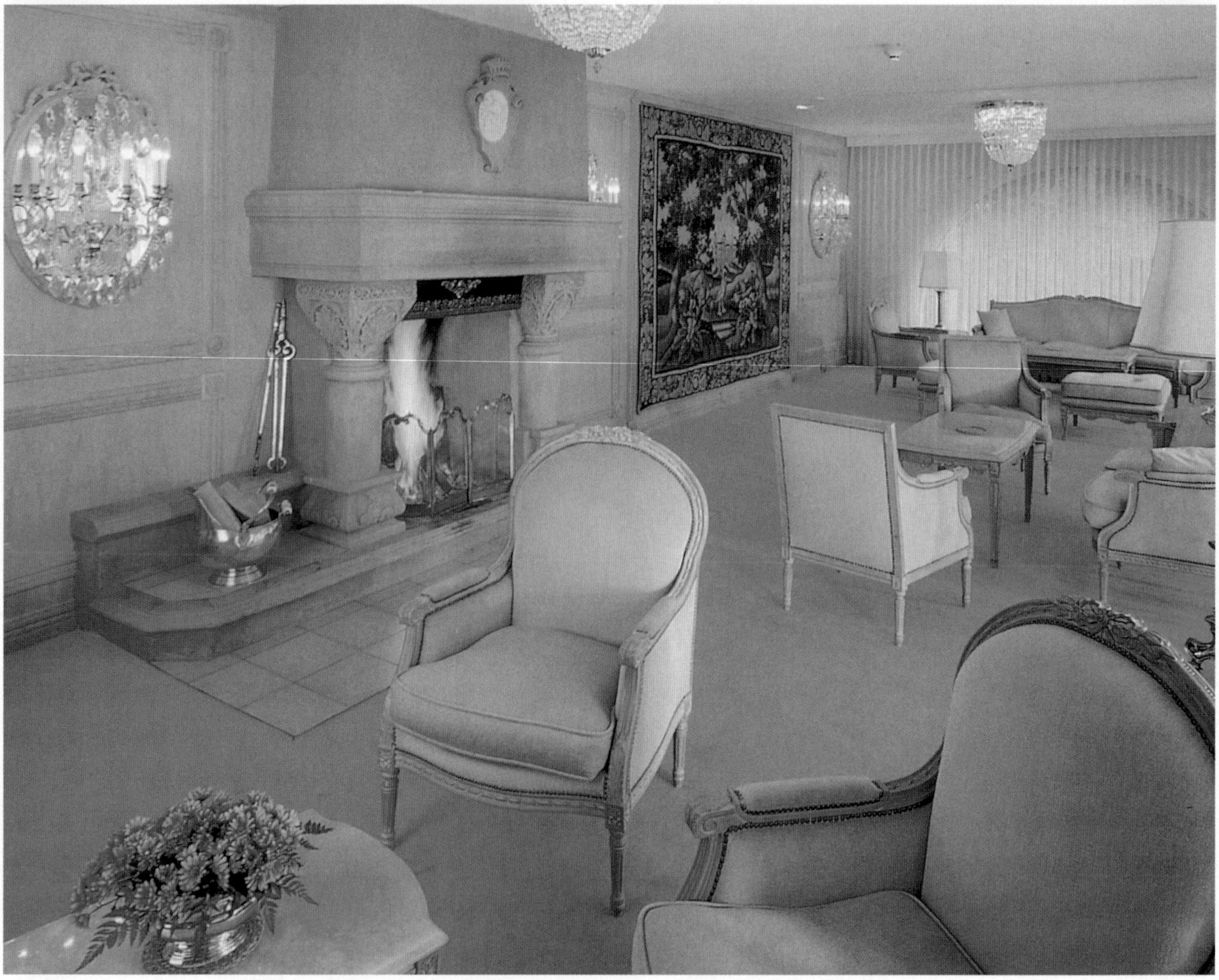

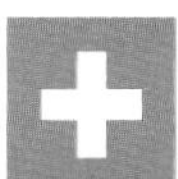

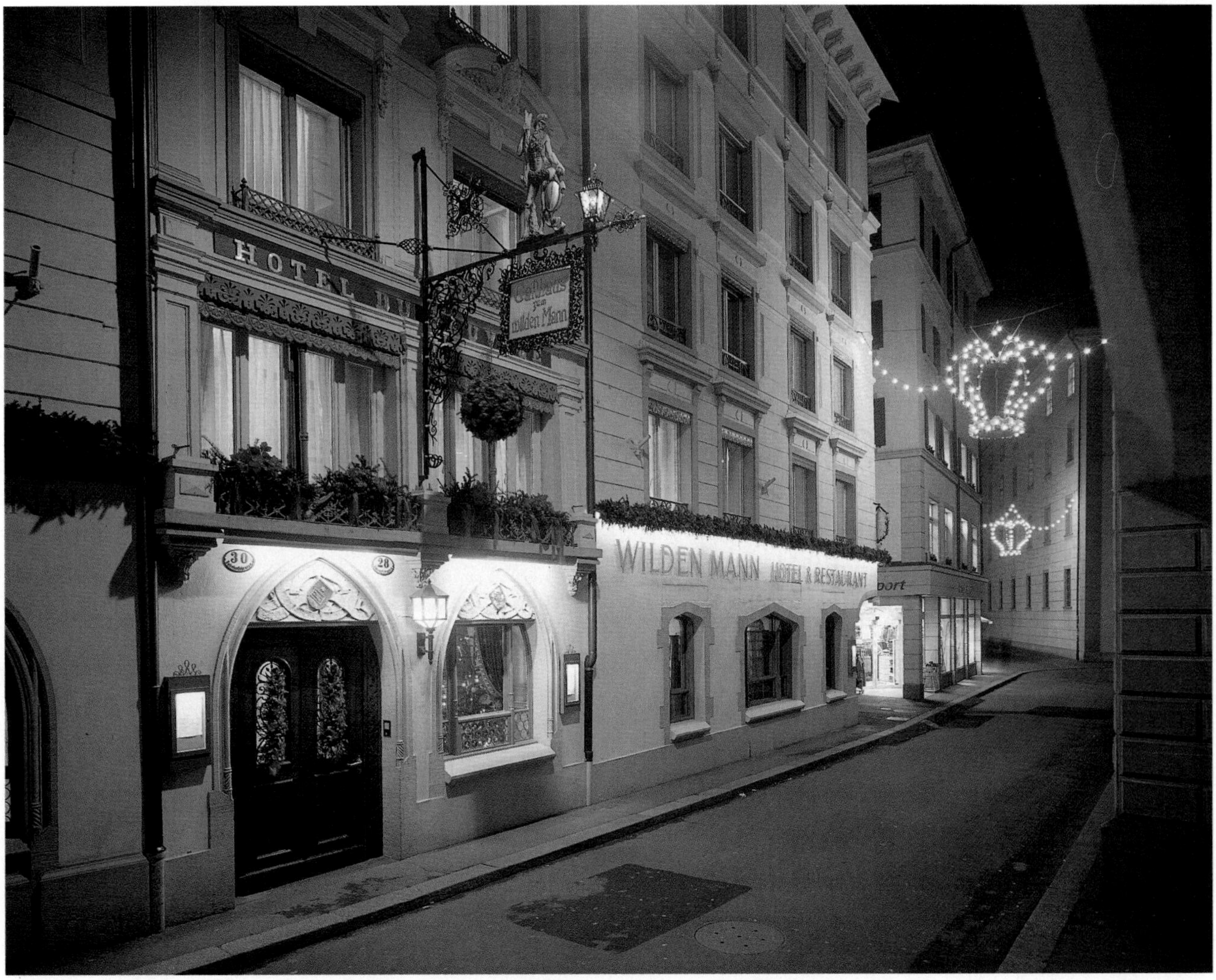

ROMANTIK HOTELS & RESTAURANTS

ROMANTIK HOTEL WILDEN MANN

BAHNHOFSTRASSE 30, CH-6000 LUCERNE 7, SWITZERLAND
TEL: 41 41 210 16 66 FAX: 41 41 210 16 29

This elegant hotel, whose history dates as far back as 1517, is a small jewel possessing incomparable charm of a medieval townhouse in the fascinating Old Town of Lucerne, with its beautiful lake and woodland scenery immortalised in the story of William Tell. The hotel's façade with its arched doorway, bright window boxes, pretty blinds and balconies immediately tells arrivals that the Wilden Mann is special – the lobby is a joy with fine antiques and comfortable welcoming furniture. Each bedroom and junior suite is individually decorated and offers modern comfort. The salon is a delightful place for apéritifs before trying one of the three well-known restaurants. The "Wilden Mann Stube" is the connoisseurs' meeting point for French and International cuisine and fine wines. The light, airy "Geranium Terrace", where grill specialities are served, is perfect in summer weather, while the rustic "Burgerstube" is cosy and casual, serving local specialities. There are also handsome private dining rooms which can be used for meetings. The Wilden Mann is a "home from home" for the discerning traveller looking for small scale refinement and charm. **Directions:** In the heart of Lucerne, 200m to Chapel Bridge. 500m to railway station and lake. Parking 50m around the corner. Price guide: Single Sf155–Sf240; double/twin Sf240–Sf350; suites Sf310–Sf420.

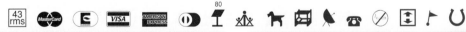

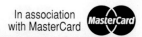

Romantik Hotel Beau-Site

3906 SAAS-FEE, SWITZERLAND
TEL: 41 27 958 1560 FAX: 41 27 958 1565

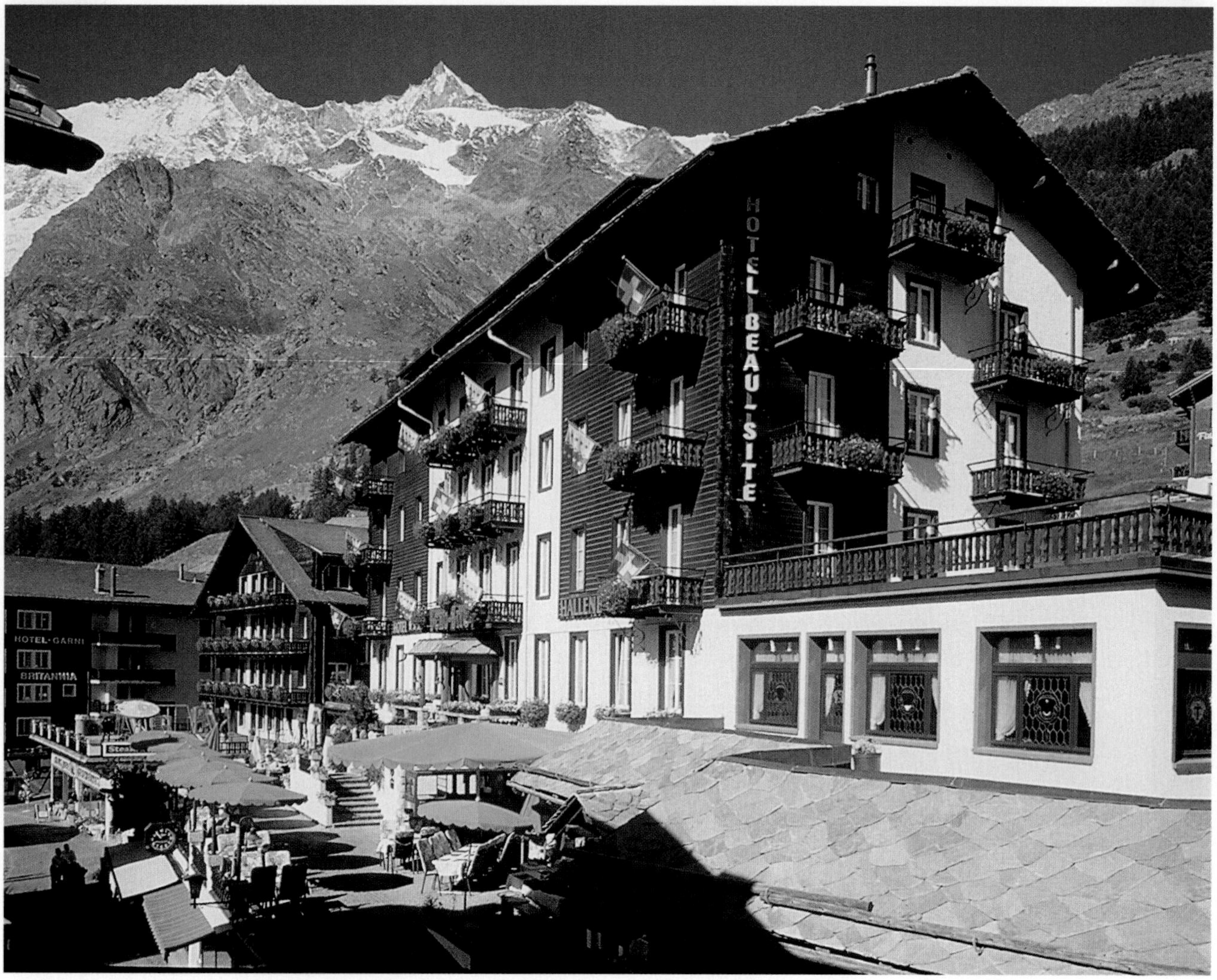

Saas-Fee is high up in the Alps, truly at the end of the road, for no cars are allowed into the village. The Hotel Beau-Site has a large car park just outside from which the hotel collects new arrivals. The hotel is aptly named for it is in a glorious position, surrounded by the snowclad mountains, pine forests and glaciers. Stone walls and carved pine create a relaxing ambience. Guests read by the log fire, or talk over a glass of wine in the bar. Comfort is the important criterion of the bedrooms, many of which have balconies with spectacular views of the Alps. There are family apartments available. One special feature of the dining room is the handsome hand carved regional furniture, the other is the superb food and wine. The diverse menu includes imaginative cosmopolitan dishes and substantial Swiss meals. The hotel has a sophisticated leisure area, with a pool, spa and many treatments available. In winter Saas-Fee is a thriving ski resort;in summer the glaciers and mountains are tackled by expert climbers. Others explore the countryside or sunbathe on the terrace. Tennis and golf are nearby. **Directions:** From Bern take the Milan road, taking the Sion/Gent exit. At Visp follow the signs for Saas Fee and watch for the car park near the hotel. Price guide: Single Sf144–Sf194; double/twin Sf117–Sf179; suites Sf177–Sf227. Prices include half board.

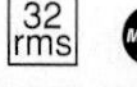

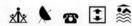

POSTHOTEL ENGIADINA

VIA MAISTRA, ZUOZ, SWITZERLAND
TEL 41 81 85 41 021 FAX: 41 81 85 43 303

This traditional Swiss manor house, for over 120 years an immaculate hotel, is in Zuoz, a village that has kept much of its 16th century architectural charm. In winter the snow-covered Engadine provides superb ski-ing, and in summer it offers wonderful walks among the flower-filled meadows, lakes and forests of the Swiss National Park. The Posthotel reception hall is spacious with graceful vaulted ceilings. The attractive lounges have lovely tiled fireplaces, period furniture and a peaceful ambience. The bedrooms all look across to the Alps. Energetic visitors start the day with a breakfast from the extensive buffets in the colourful Sela Verda and Sela Melna dining rooms, to which they return later in the day for the table d'hôte dinner. Two other handsome restaurants, La Posta Veglia and La Prüveda offer haute cuisine and marvellous Swiss, French and Italian wines. Evenings often end in the La Chamanna bar. In summer the hotel pool, tennis court and bicycles are popular. Europe's highest golf course is nearby, trout fishing can be arranged, and surf boarders go to the Engadine lakes. Winter sports enthusiasts appreciate the sauna to relax their weary muscles. **Directions:** By road or rail, through Chur. Zuoz is signed from St. Moritz, just 15km away. Price guide: Single Sf124–Sf154; double/twin Sf168–Sf288.

Turkey

The legacy of the Greeks, Romans, Ottomans, and numerous other civilisations has made the country a vast outdoor museum. The most spectacular of the reconstructed classical sites are to be found along the western Aegean and the southwest Mediterranean coast, both of which are lined with magnificent sandy beaches and little fishing villages.

The countryside landscape along the Aegean is for the most part one of gently rolling hills and fertile valleys covered in olive groves, vineyards, cypresses and pine trees.

Turkey's Aegean shore is endlessly indented with bays and inlets, the result of earth movements over the millennia. This makes the coastline tremendously long and means that although a few pockets are now developed, you need never go very far to find empty beaches and unspoilt fishing villages.

Most people think of Istanbul when they think of Turkey. Any first time visitor immediately becomes aware of the sense of ancient culture, a legacy of this mystical city's distinguished history as capital to three empires, the Roman, the Byzantine and the Ottoman. For nearly a thousand years this was one of the dominant cities of the western and near eastern worlds.

Besides the staggering wealth of its historical monuments, contemporary Istanbul is also memorable for its vibrant atmosphere, alive with movement and bustle. The city is set astride the Bosphorus straits so that its humming activity is transfered from land to water and back again, as cars and lorries, carts and vans cross bridges reflected in the Golden Horn and ferries ply their way to virtually every quarter. The best way to get around all the magnificent monuments in Sultanahmet in Old Istanbul is to walk. They're all within easy distance of each other, along streets filled with peddlars, shoeshine boys, children playing and craftsmen working.

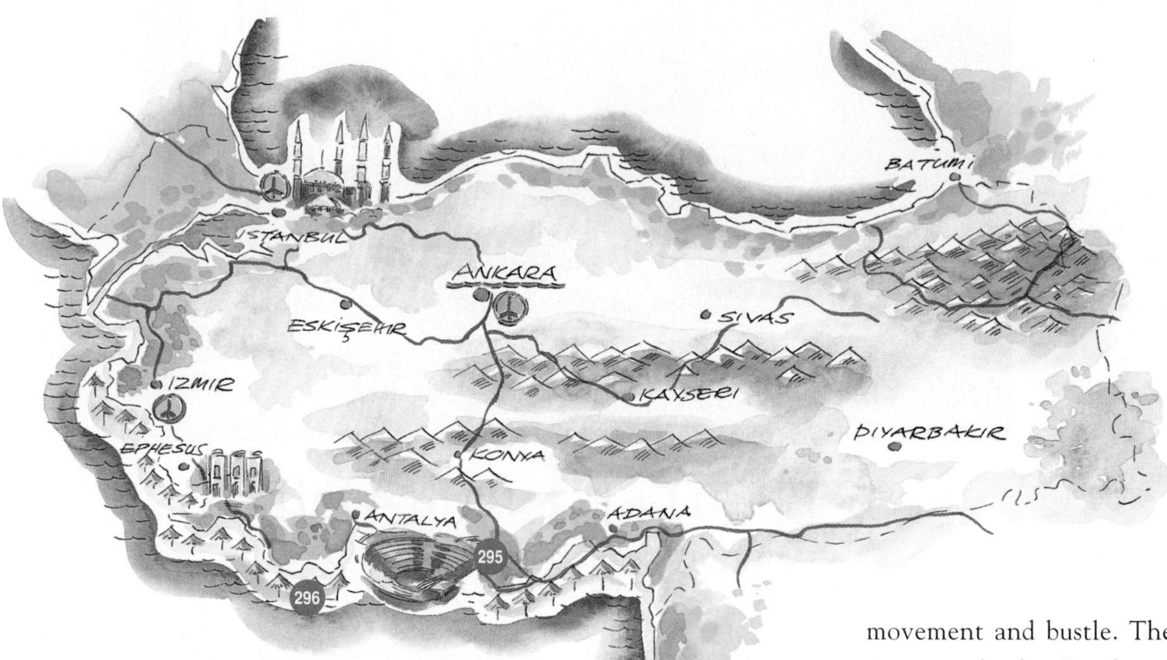

Turkish cooking is one of the best in the world and the old cliché about it being hard to find a bad meal in Paris aptly applies to Istanbul, where the tiniest little hole in the wall serves delicious food and turns the concept of the simple kebab into a wonderful eating experience.

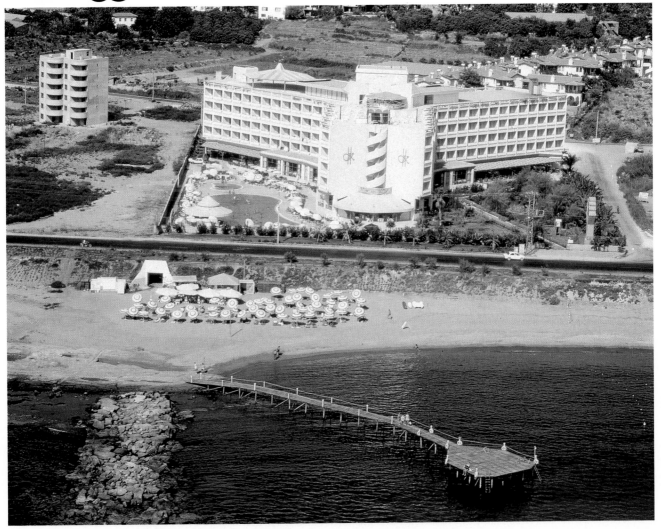

HOTEL GRAND KAPTAN

OBA, GÖL MEVKII, 07400 ALANYA, TURKEY
TEL: 90 242 514 0101 FAX: 90 242 514 0092

This large, modern hotel offers so many amenities that it is virtually a self-contained complex which guests need never leave throughout their stay. Its position is marvellous, right on the Mediterranean shore. Many of the bright, air-conditioned bedrooms have terraces with wonderful views of the sun setting over the water, a spectacular alternative to international TV channels. The bathrooms have all today's extras. Children are well catered for, with their own play areas while adults can sample the Lobby Bar, the romantic Terrace Bar overlooking the sea, the Beach Bar, Vitamin Bar and the unique Pool Bar with its seats actually in the water. The Kaptan specialises in extensive buffets for breakfast and again later in the day when the range of dishes offered is very cosmopolitan. There is an à la carte menu available, and a good wine list. The café offers lighter dishes. Most meals are enjoyed out of doors and there are occasional barbecues. Dress is extremely informal. Sporting activities include a freshwater pool, floodlit tennis, and many water sports including the Seabike. The hotel has an extensive private beach, a fitness room, sauna, billiards and table tennis and at night a casino and cabarets to entertain guests. There is also a shopping arcade. **Directions:** From Antalya airport take the coast road,following signs to Alanya. Price guide: Single US$50–US$103; double/twin US$55–US$138.

Hotel Villa Mahal

P,K. 4 KALKAN, 07960 ANTALYA, TURKEY
TEL: 90 242 844 32 68 FAX: 90 242 844 21 22

This intimate hotel stands on a hillside, overlooking the spectacular Bay of Kalkan. It is surrounded by olive trees and is perfect for a secluded holiday away from the stresses of the twentieth century. However, because of its position, there are a number of steps to climb and it is not recommended for those with any mobility problems. The villa is built round a delightful courtyard, and with a maximum of 17 guests, the ambience is more like that of a private house than a hotel. The bedrooms are bright and airy, cooled by ceiling fans, and have roof terraces. The bathrooms have showers. Breakfast is a delicious buffet and light lunches are served at the beach bar – the villa having its private beach 100 steps below the hotel. Evening apéritifs are enjoyed on the terrace before dining under the stars, feasting on succulent Turkish specialities. Sometimes there are barbecues. The hotel's boat takes guests across the bay to Kalkan, a fascinating small town with its harbour, market, tavernas and cafés – an opportunity to meet the locals! Tennis is nearby. Water sports and cruises can be arranged. Exploring ancient ruins at Xanthos or other historic sites and going up into the mountains are also recommended expeditions. Closed 1 November to 30 April. **Directions:** Taking main road from the airport towards Kas, turn left 700m after the Kalkan sign, driving towards the beach. Price guide: Single 90Dm–105Dm; double/twin 120Dm–140Dm; suites 160Dm–180Dm.

1998 Johansens Recommended Hotels in Europe listed alphabetically by Country

Alphabetical lists of Johansens recommendations in Great Britain and Ireland, and also North America, published in full in other Johansens guides. **See the back cover and p304 for more details and how to order all these publications.**

Hotels

London

Mayfair	The Ascott Mayfair	0171 499 6868
Knightsbridge	Basil Street Hotel	0171 581 3311
Knightsbridge	The Beaufort	0171 584 5252
Knightsbridge	Beaufort House Apartments	0171 584 2600
South Kensington	Blakes Hotel	0171 370 6701
Knightsbridge	The Cadogan	0171 235 7141
Wimbledon Common	Cannizaro House	0181 879 1464
Knightsbridge	The Cliveden Town House	0171 730 6466
Mayfair	The Dorchester	0171 629 8888
Chelsea	Draycott House Apartments	0171 584 4659
Holland Park	The Halcyon	0171 727 7288
Kensington	Harrington Hall	0171 396 9696
Lancaster Gate	The Hempel	0171 298 9000
Portman Square	The Leonard	0171 935 2010
Knightsbridge	The London Outpost of the Carnegie Club	0171 589 7333
Kensington	The Milestone	0171 917 1000
Knightsbridge	Number Eleven Cadogan Gardens	0171 730 7000
South Kensington	Number Sixteen	0171 589 5232
Chelsea	Park Consul Hotel	0171 225 7500
Kensington	Pembridge Court Hotel	0171 229 9977
St James'	The Ritz	0171 493 8181

England

Abberley	The Elms	01299 896666
Aldeburgh	Wentworth Hotel	01728 452312
Alderley Edge	The Alderley Edge Hotel	01625 583033
Alfriston	White Lodge Country House Hotel	01323 870265
Altrincham	Woodland Park Hotel	0161 928 8631
Amberley	Amberley Castle	01798 831992
Ambleside	Holbeck Ghyll Country House Hotel	015394 32375
Ambleside	Rothay Manor	015394 33605
Ambleside	Nanny Brow Country House Hotel	015394 32036
Ambleside	Langdale Hotel & Country Club	015394 37302
Andover	Esseborne Manor	01264 736444
Appleby-in-Westmorland	Appleby Manor Country House Hotel	017683 51571
Appleby-In-Westmorland	Tufton Arms Hotel	017683 51593
Arundel	Bailiffscourt	01903 723511
Ascot	Royal Berkshire	01344 23322
Ashbourne	Callow Hall	01335 343403
Ashburton	Holne Chase Hotel	01364 631471
Ashford	Eastwell Manor	01233 219955
Ashford-In-The-Water	Riverside Country House Hotel	01629 814275
Axminster	Tytherleigh Cot Hotel	01460 221170
Aylesbury	Hartwell House	01296 747444
Aylesbury	The Priory Hotel	01296 641239
Bagshot	Pennyhill Park Hotel And Country Club	01276 471774
Bakewell	Hassop Hall	01629 640488
Banbury	Hellidon Lakes Hotel & Country Club	01327 262550
Banbury	Wroxton House Hotel	01295 730777
Basingstoke	Tylney Hall	01256 764881
Baslow	The Cavendish Hotel	01246 582311
Baslow	Fischer's	01246 583259
Bath	The Bath Spa	01225 444424
Bath	Combe Grove Manor & Country Club	01225 834644
Bath	The Priory	01225 331922
Bath	The Queensberry	01225 447928
Bath	The Royal Crescent	01225 823333
Bath	Lucknam Park	01225 742777
Bath	Homewood Park	01225 723731
Bath	Hunstrete House	01761 490490
Bath	Ston Easton Park	01761 241631
Battle	Netherfield Place	01424 774455
Battle	Powdermills Hotel	01424 775511
Beaminster	Bridge House Hotel	01308 862200
Beaulieu	The Montagu Arms Hotel	01590 612324
Bedford	Woodlands Manor	01234 363281
Berwick-Upon-Tweed	Marshall Meadow Country House Hotel	01289 331133
Berwick-Upon-Tweed	Tillmouth Park	01890 882255
Bibury	The Swan Hotel At Bibury	01285 740695
Birmingham	The Burlington Hotel	0121 643 9191
Birmingham	The Swallow Hotel	0121 452 1144
Birmingham	The Mill House Hotel & Lombard Room	0121 459 5800
Birmingham	New Hall	0121 378 2442
Bishop's Stortford	Down Hall Country House Hotel	01279 731441
Bolton Abbey	The Devonshire Arms Country House Hotel	01756 710441
Bournemouth	The Norfolk Royale Hotel	01202 551521
Bovey Tracey	The Edgemoor	01626 832466
Bradford	The Victoria Hotel	01274 728706
Bradford-On-Avon	Woolley Grange	01225 864705
Brampton	Farlam Hall Hotel	016977 46234
Bray-on-Thames	Chauntry House Hotel & Restaurant	01628 73991
Bray-on-Thames	Monkey Island Hotel	01628 23400
Brighton	Topps Hotel	01273 729334
Bristol	Swallow Royal Hotel	0117 9255200
Bristol South	Daneswood House Hotel	01934 843145
Broadway	Dormy House	01386 852711
Broadway	The Lygon Arms	01386 852255
Brockenhurst	Careys Manor Hotel	01590 623551
Brockenhurst	New Park Manor	01590 623467
Brockenhurst	Rhinefield House Hotel	01590 622922
Bromsgrove	Grafton Manor Country House Hotel	01527 579007
Burford	The Bay Tree Hotel & Restaurant	01993 822791
Burton upon Trent	The Brookhouse	01283 814188
Bury St Edmunds	The Angel Hotel	01284 753926
Bury St Edmunds	Ravenwood Hall	01359 270345
Buxted, near Uckfield	Buxted Park Country House Hotel	01825 732711
Canterbury	Howfield Manor	01227 738294
Castle Combe	The Manor House	01249 782206
Castle Donington	The Priest House On the River	01332 810649
Chaddesley Corbett	Brockencote Hall	01562 777876
Chagford	Gidleigh Park	01647 432367
Chelmsford	Pontlands Park Country Hotel	01245 476444
Cheltenham	Hotel On The Park	01242 518898
Cheltenham	The Cheltenham Park Hotel	01242 222021
Cheltenham	The Greenway	01242 862352
Chester	The Chester Grosvenor	01244 324024
Chester	Crabwall Manor	01244 851666
Chester	Broxton Hall Country House Hotel	01829 782321
Chester	Nunsmere Hall	01606 889100
Chester	Rowton Hall Hotel	01244 335262
Chichester	The Millstream Hotel	01243 573234
Chipping Campden	Charingworth Manor	01386 593555
Chipping Campden	The Cotswold House	01386 840330
Clanfield	The Plough at Clanfield	01367 810222
Cobham	Woodlands Park Hotel	01372 843933
Colchester	Five Lakes Hotel Golf & Country Club	01621 868888
Colchester	The White Hart Hotel & Restaurant	01376 561654
Coventry	Nailcote Hall	01203 466174
Coventry	Coombe Abbey	01203 450450
Crathorne	Crathorne Hall Hotel	01642 700398
Croydon	Coulsdon Manor Hotel	0181 668 0414
Cuckfield	Ockenden Manor	01444 416111
Darlington	Headlam Hall	01325 730238
Dartford	Rowhill Grange	01322 615136
Dedham	Maison Talbooth	01206 322367
Derby	Mickleover Court	01332 521234
Derby	Makeney Hall Country House Hotel	01332 842999
Diss	Cornwallis Arms	01379 870326
Durham	Lumley Castle Hotel	0191 389 1111
Egham	Great Fosters	01784 433822
Evershot	Summer Lodge	01935 83424
Evesham	The Evesham Hotel	01386 765566
Evesham	Wood Norton Hall	01386 420007
Falmouth	Penmere Manor	01326 211411
Falmouth	Nansidwell Country House	01326 250340
Falmouth	Budock Vean Golf & Country Club	01326 250288
Falmouth	Meudon Hotel	01326 250541
Fawkham	Brandshatch Place Hotel	01474 872239
Flitwick	Flitwick Manor	01525 712242
Forest Row	Ashdown Park Hotel	01342 824988
Gatwick	Langshott Manor	01293 786680
Gatwick	Alexander House	01342 714914
Gittisham	Combe House Hotel	01404 42756
Glossop	The Wind In The Willows	01457 868001
Gloucester	Hatton Court Hotel	01452 617412
Grange-Over-Sands	Graythwaite Manor	015395 32001
Grantham	Belton Woods	01476 593200
Grasmere	Michaels Nook	015394 35496
Grasmere	The Wordsworth Hotel	015394 35592
Grayshott	Grayshott Hall Health Fitness Retreat	01428 604331
Guildford	The Angel Posting House And Livery	01483 564555
Hadley Wood	West Lodge Park	0181 440 8311
Halifax	Holdsworth House	01422 240024
Harlow	The Manor of Groves Hotel	01279 600777
Harrogate	The Balmoral Hotel	01423 508208
Harrogate	Grants Hotel	01423 560666
Harrogate	Rudding Park House & Hotel	01423 871350
Harrogate	Hob Green Hotel & Restaurant	01423 770031
Harrogate	The Boar's Head Hotel	01423 771888
Haslemere	Lythe Hill Hotel	01428 651251
Hathersage	George Hotel	01433 650436
Haytor	Bel Alp House	01364 661217
Hazlewood	Hazlewood Castle	01937 530530
Hebden Bridge	The Carlton Hotel	01422 844400
Helmsley	The Pheasant	01439 771241 /770416
Hemel Hempstead	Stocks Hotel Golf & Country Club	01442 851341
Henley-On-Thames	Phyllis Court Club	01491 574366 / 570528
Hockley Heath	Nuthurst Grange	01564 783972
Horsham	South Lodge Hotel	01403 891711
Hovingham	The Worsley Arms Hotel	01653 628234
Huddersfield	Bagden Hall Hotel & Golf Course	01484 865330
Huntingdon	The Old Bridge Hotel	01480 452681
Hythe	Hythe Imperial Hotel	01303 267441
Ilkley	Rombalds Hotel	01943 603201
Ilsington	Ilsington Country Hotel	01364 661452
Ipswich	Belstead Brook Manor Hotel	01473 684241
Ipswich	Hintlesham Hall	01473 652268
Keswick	The Borrowdale Gates Hotel	017687 77204
King's Lynn	Congham Hall	01485 600250
Kingham	Mill House Hotel	01608 658188
Kington	Penrhos Court	01544 230720
Lacock	Beechfield House	01225 703700
Lake Ullswater	Sharrow Bay Country House Hotel	017684 86301
Lake Ullswater	Rampsbeck Country House Hotel	017684 86442
Launceston	Percy's at Coombeshead	01409 211236
Leamington Spa	Mallory Court	01926 330214
Ledbury	Hope End Hotel	01531 633613
Leeds	Haley's Hotel and Restaurant	0113 278 4446
Leeds	Oulton Hall	0113 282 1000
Leeds	42 The Calls	0113 244 0099
Leeds	Monk Fryston	01977 682369
Leicester	Quorn Country Hotel	01509 415050
Lewdown	Lewtrenchard Manor	01566 783 256
Lichfield	Swinfen Hall	01543 481494
Lichfield	Hoar Cross Hall Health Spa Resort	01283 575671
Lifton	The Arundell Arms	01566 784666
Liverpool	The Woolton Redbourne Hotel	0151 421 1500/428 2152
Lower Slaughter	Lower Slaughter Manor	01451 820456
Lower Slaughter	Washbourne Court Hotel	01451 822143
Ludlow	Dinham Hall	01584 876464
Lymington	Passford House Hotel	01590 682398
Lymington	Stanwell House	01590 677123
Lyndhurst	Parkhill Hotel	01703 282944
Maidenhead	Fredrick's Hotel & Restaurant	01628 635934
Maidenhead	Cliveden	01628 668561
Maidstone	Chilston Park	01622 859803
Malmesbury	The Old Bell	01666 822344
Malmesbury	Whatley Manor	01666 822888
Malmesbury	Crudwell Court Hotel	01666 577194
Malvern	The Colwall Park Hotel	01684 540206
Malvern Wells	The Cottage In The Wood	01684 575859
Manchester Airport	Etrop Grange	0161 499 0500
Manchester	The Stanneylands Hotel	01625 525225
Marlborough	Ivy House Hotel	01672 515333
Marlow-On-Thames	Danesfield House	01628 891010
Matlock	Riber Hall	01629 582795
Middle Wallop	Fifehead Manor	01264 781565
Middlecombe	Periton Park Hotel	01643 706885
Midhurst	The Angel Hotel	01730 812421
Midhurst	The Spread Eagle Hotel	01730 816911
Milton Keynes	Moore Place Hotel	01908 282000
Moreton-In-Marsh	The Manor House Hotel	01608 650501
Nantwich	Rookery Hall	01270 610016
New Milton	Chewton Glen	01425 275341
Newbury	Donnington Valley Hotel & Golf Course	01635 551199
Newbury	Hollington House Hotel	01635 255100
Newbury	Elcot Park Hotel & Country Club	01488 658100
Newcastle-Upon-Tyne	Slaley Hall Hotel Golf Resort & Spa	01434 673350
Newcastle-Upon-Tyne	Linden Hall Hotel	01670 516611
Newmarket	Swynford Paddocks Hotel & Restaurant	01638 570234
Newton Abbot	Passage House Hotel	01626 55515
Newton Aycliffe	Redworth Hall Hotel & Country Club	01388 772442
North Huish	Brookdale House Restaurant & Hotel	01548 821661
Norwich	Sprowston Manor Hotel	01603 410871
Norwich	Park Farm Hotel & Leisure	01603 810264
Norwich	Petersfield House Hotel	01692 630741
Nottingham	Langar Hall	01949 860559
Oakham	Hambleton Hall	01572 756991
Otley	Chevin Lodge Country Park Hotel	01943 467818
Oxford	Le Manoir Aux Quat' Saisons	01844 278881
Oxford	Studley Priory	01865 351203
Oxford	Weston Manor	01869 350621
Painswick	The Painswick Hotel	01452 812160
Penrith	Temple Sowerby House Hotel	017683 61578
Peterborough	The Haycock	01780 782223
Plymouth	Kitley	01752 881555
Poole	The Mansion House Hotel and Dining Club	01202 685666
Poole	The Haven Hotel	01202 707333
Portloe	The Lugger Hotel	01872 501322
Prestbury	The Bridge Hotel	01625 829326
Preston	The Gibbon Bridge Country House Hotel	01995 61456
Redhill	Nutfield Priory	01737 822066
Richmond-Upon-Thames	The Richmond Gate Hotel And Restaurant	0181 940 0061
Rochester	Bridgewood Manor Hotel	01634 201333
Ross-On-Wye	The Chase Hotel	01989 763161

Location	Hotel	Telephone
Ross-On-Wye	Pengethley Manor	01989 730211
Rutland Water	Barnsdale Lodge	01572 724678
Rutland Water	Normanton Park Hotel	01780 720315
Rye	Broomhill Lodge	01797 280421
Salcombe	Bolt Head Hotel	01548 843751
Salcombe	Soar Mill Cove Hotel	01548 561566
Scarborough	Hackness Grange	01723 882345
Scarborough	Wrea Head Country Hotel	01723 378211
Sheffield	Charnwood Hotel	0114 258 9411
Sheffield	Whitley Hall Hotel	0114 245 4444
Shepton Mallet	Charlton House	01749 342008
Shrewsbury	Rowton Castle Hotel & Restaurant	01743 884044
Shrewsbury	Albrighton Hall Hotel & Restaurant	01939 291000
Shrewsbury	Hawkstone Park Hotel	01939 200611
Sidmouth	Hotel Riviera	01395 515201
Slough	Stoke Park	01753 717171
Sonning-On-Thames	The French Horn	01734 692204
South Molton	Whitechapel Manor	01769 573377
South Molton	Northcote Manor	01769 560501
Southwold	The Swan Hotel	01502 722186
St Agnes	Rose-in-Vale Country House Hotel	01872 552202
St Albans	Sopwell House Hotel & Country Club	01727 864477
St Ives	The Garrack Hotel	01736 796199
St Keyne	The Well House	01579 342001
Stamford	The George Of Stamford	01780 755171
Stansted	Whitehall	01279 850603
Stapleford	Stapleford Park, An Outpost of The Carnegie Club	01572 787522
Stonehouse	Stonehouse Court	01453 825155
Storrington	Little Thakeham	01903 744416
Stow-On-The-Wold	The Grapevine Hotel	01451 830344
Stow-On-The-Wold	Wyck Hill House	01451 831936
Stratford-Upon-Avon	Billesley Manor	01789 279955
Stratford-Upon-Avon	Ettington Park Hotel	01789 450123
Stratford-Upon-Avon	Salford Hall Hotel	01386 871300
Streatley-On-Thames	Swan Diplomat	01491 873737
Sturminster Newton	Plumber Manor	01258 472507
Swindon	The Pear Tree at Purton	01793 772100
Talland-By-Looe	Talland Bay Hotel	01503 272667
Taunton	Bindon Country House Hotel & Restaurant	01823 400070
Taunton	The Castle At Taunton	01823 272671
Taunton	The Mount Somerset Country House Hotel	01823 442500
Taunton	Rumwell Manor Hotel	01823 461902
Tavistock	The Horn Of Plenty	01822 832528
Telford	Madeley Court	01952 680068
Tetbury	Calcot Manor	01666 890391
Tetbury	The Close Hotel	01666 502272
Tetbury	The Snooty Fox	01666 502436
Tewkesbury	Corse Lawn House Hotel	01452 780479 / 771
Ticehurst	Dale Hill Hotel And Golf Club	01580 200112
Torquay	Orestone Manor Hotel & Restaurant	01803 328098
Torquay	The Palace Hotel	01803 200200
Torquay	The Osborne Hotel & Langtry's Restaurant	01803 213311
Tring	Pendley Manor Hotel	01442 891891
Truro	Alverton Manor	01872 276633
Tunbridge Wells	Hotel Du Vin & Bistro	01892 526455
Tunbridge Wells	The Spa Hotel	01892 520331
Uckfield	Horsted Place Sporting Estate And Hotel	01825 750581
Upper Slaughter	Lords Of The Manor Hotel	01451 820243
Uppingham	The Lake Isle	01572 822951
Veryan	The Nare Hotel	01872 501279
Wallingford	The Springs Hotel	01491 836687
Ware	Hanbury Manor	01920 487722
Wareham	The Priory	01929 551666
Warminster	Bishopstrow House	01985 212312
Warwick	The Glebe At Barford	01926 624218
Wetherby	Linton Springs	01937 585353
Wetherby	Wood Hall	01937 587271
Weybridge	Oatlands Park Hotel	01932 847242
Weymouth	Moonfleet Manor	01305 786948
Willington	Willington Hall Hotel	01829 752321
Winchester	Hotel Du Vin & Bistro	01962 841414
Winchester	Lainston House Hotel	01962 863588
Windermere	Gilpin Lodge	015394 88818
Windermere	Langdale Chase	015394 32201
Windermere	Linthwaite House Hotel	015394 88600
Windermere	Lakeside Hotel On Lake Windermere	015395 31207
Windsor	Oakley Court	01753 609988
Witherslack	The Old Vicarage Country House Hotel	015395 52381
Wiveliscombe	Langley House Hotel	01984 623318
Wolverhampton	The Old Vicarage Hotel	01746 716497
Woodbridge	Seckford Hall	01394 385678
Woodstock	The Feathers Hotel	01993 812291
Woolacombe	Woolacombe Bay Hotel	01271 870388
Woolacombe	Watersmeet Hotel	01271 870333
Yarmouth	The George Hotel	01983 760331
York	The Grange Hotel	01904 644744
York	Middlethorpe Hall	01904 641241
York	Mount Royale Hotel	01904 628856
York	York Pavilion Hotel	01904 622099

Wales

Location	Hotel	Telephone
Abergavenny	Llansantffraed Court Hotel	01873 840678
Abergavenny	Allt-Yr-Ynys Hotel	01873 890307
Abersoch	Porth Tocyn Country House Hotel	01758 713303
Aberystwyth	Conrah Country House Hotel	01970 617941
Anglesey	Trearddur Bay Hotel	01407 860301
Bala	Palé Hall	01678 530285
Barmouth	Bontddu Hall	01341 430661
Brecon	Peterstone Court	01874 665387
Brecon	Llangoed Hall	01874 754525
Bridgend	Coed-Y-Mwstwr Hotel	01656 860621
Caernarfon	Gwesty Seiont Manor Hotel	01286 673366
Cardiff	Miskin Manor	01443 224204
Cardiff	Egerton Grey Country House Hotel	01446 711666
Chester	Soughton Hall Country House Hotel	01352 840811
Corwen	Tyddyn Llan Country House Hotel	01490 440264
Criccieth	Bron Eifion Country House Hotel	01766 522385
Crickhowell	Gliffaes Country House Hotel	01874 730371
Dolgellau	Penmaenuchaf Hall	01341 422129
Harlech	Hotel Maes-Y-Neuadd	01766 780200
Lake Vyrnwy	Lake Vyrnwy Hotel	01691 870 692
Llandegla	Bodidris Hall	01978 790434
Llandudno	Bodysgallen Hall	01492 584466
Llandudno	St Tudno Hotel	01492 874411
Llangammarch Wells	The Lake Country House	01591 620202
Llangollen	Bryn Howel Hotel & Restaurant	01978 860331
Machynlleth	Ynyshir Hall	01654 781209
Monmouth	The Crown At Whitebrook	01600 860254
Newport	The Celtic Manor Hotel & Golf Club	01633 413000
Pembroke	The Court Hotel & Restaurant	01646 672273
Portmeirion Village	The Hotel Portmeirion	01766 770228
St David's	Warpool Court Hotel	01437 720300
Swansea	Norton House Hotel & Restaurant	01792 404891
Tenby	Penally Abbey	01834 843033
Tywyn	Tynycornel Hotel	01654 782282
Usk	The Cwrt Bleddyn Hotel	01633 450521

Scotland

Location	Hotel	Telephone
Aberdeen	Ardoe House Hotel & Restaurant	01224 867355
Aberdeen	Thainstone House Hotel & Country Club	01467 621643
Aberfeldy	Farleyer House Hotel	01887 820332
Alloa	The Gean House	01259 219275
Appin	Invercreran Country House Hotel	01631 730 414
Auchencairn	Balcary Bay Hotel	01556 640217
Ballater	Darroch Learg Hotel	013397 55443
Beasdale By Arisaig	Arisaig House	01687 450622
Biggar	Shieldhill	01899 220035
Blairgowrie	Kinloch House Hotel	01250 884237
Callander	Roman Camp Hotel	01877 330003
Craigellachie	Craigellachie Hotel	01340 881204
Dalbeattie	Baron's Craig Hotel	01556 630 225
Dunoon	Enmore Hotel	01369 702230
Edinburgh	The Albany Townhouse Hotel	0131 556 0397
Edinburgh	Channings	0131 315 2226
Edinburgh	The Howard	0131 557 3500
Edinburgh	Dalhousie Castle Hotel & Restaurant	01875 820153
Edinburgh	Borthwick Castle	01875 820514
Edinburgh	Johnstounburn House	01875 833696
Edinburgh	The Norton House Hotel	0131 333 1275
Elgin	Mansion House Hotel & Country Club	01343 548811
Elgin	Rothes Glen	01340 831254
Fort Augustus	Knockie Lodge Hotel	01456 486276
Fort William	Allt-nan-Ros Hotel	01855 821210
Gatehouse Of Fleet	Cally Palace Hotel	01557 814341
Glasgow	The Beardmore Hotel	0141 951 6000
Glasgow	Gleddoch House	01475 540711
Glenshee	Dalmunzie House	01250 885224
Gullane	Greywalls	01620 842144
Inverness	Bunchrew House Hotel	01463 234917
Inverness	Kingsmills Hotel	01463 237166
Inverness	Culloden House Hotel	01463 790461
Irvine	Montgreenan Mansion House Hotel	01294 557733
Isle Of Eriska, by Oban	Isle Of Eriska	01631 720371
Isle Of Mull	Western Isles Hotel	01688 302012
Kelso	Ednam House Hotel	01573 224168
Kelso	Sunlaws House Hotel and Golf Course	01573 450331
Kilchrenan by Taynuilt	Ardanaiseig	01866 833333
Kildrummy	Kildrummy Castle Hotel	019755 71288
Kinbuck nr Stirling	Cromlix House	01786 822125
Loch Lomond	Cameron House	01389 755565
Loch Ness	Craigdarroch House Hotel	01456 486 400
Lochinver	Inver Lodge Hotel	01571 844496
Newton Stewart	Kirroughtree House	01671 402141
Oban	Knipoch Hotel	01852 316251
Peebles	Cringletie House Hotel	01721 730233
Perth	Kinfauns Castle	01738 620777
Perth	Parklands Hotel & Restaurant	01738 622451
Perth	Huntingtower Hotel	01738 583771
Perth	Ballathie House Hotel	01250 883268
Portpatrick	Knockinaam Lodge	01776 810471
Scone	Murrayshall House Hotel & Golf Course	01738 551171
St Andrews	Rufflets Country House	01334 472594
St. Andrews	St. Andrews Golf Hotel	01334 472611
Stranraer	Corsewall Lighthouse Hotel	01776 853220
Strathpeffer	Coul House Hotel	01997 421487
Torridon	Loch Torridon Hotel	01445 791242
Troon	Piersland House Hotel	01292 314747
Uphall	Houstoun House	01506 853831

Ireland

Location	Hotel	Telephone
Ballymena, N. Ireland	Galgorm Manor	01266 881001
Belfast, N. Ireland	Culloden Hotel	01232 425223
Carrickmacross	Nuremore Hotel & Country Club	00 353 42 61438
Cong	Ashford Castle	00353 92 46003
Connemara	Renvyle House Hotel	00 353 95 43511
Dublin	The Hibernian	00 353 1 668 7666
Dublin	The Merrion Hotel	00 353 1 603 0600
Dublin	Portmarnock Hotel & Golf Links	00 353 1 846 0611
Dublin	Barberstown Castle	00 353 1 6288157
Dublin	Kildare Hotel & Country Club	00 353 1 601 7200
Gorey	Marlfield House	00 353 55 21124
Kenmare	Sheen Falls Lodge	00 353 64 41600
Killarney	Aghadoe Heights Hotel	00 353 64 31766
Killarney	Hotel Dunloe Castle	00 353 64 44111
Killarney	Muckross Park Hotel	00 353 64 31938
Limavady, N. Ireland	Radisson Roe Park Hotel &Golf Resort	015047 22222
Newmarket-On-Fergus	Dromoland Castle	00 353 61 368144
Parknasilla	Parknasilla Hotel	00 353 64 45122
Rathnew	Hunter's Hotel	00 353 404 40106
Rosslare	Kelly's Resort Hotel	00 353 53 32114
Wicklow	Tinakilly Country House Hotel	00 353 40469274

Channel Islands

Location	Hotel	Telephone
Jersey	Château La Chaire	01534 863354
Jersey	The Atlantic Hotel	01534 44101
Jersey	Hotel L'Horizon	01534 43101
Jersey	Longueville Manor	01534 25501

Inns with Restaurants

England

Amberley,Near Arundel	The Boathouse Brasserie	01798 831059
Ambleside	The New Dungeon Ghyll Hotel	015394 37213
Appleby-In-Westmorland	The Royal Oak Inn	017683 51463
Ashbourne	Red Lion Inn	01335 370396
Askrigg	The Kings Arms Hotel And Restaurant	01969 650258
Badby nr Daventry	The Windmill At Badby	01327 702363
Bassenthwaite Lake	The Pheasant Inn	017687 76234
Beckington nr Bath	The Woolpack Inn	01373 831244
Belford	The Blue Bell Hotel	01668 213543
Blakeney	White Horse Hotel	01263 740574
Boroughbridge	The Crown Hotel	01423 322328
Bourton-On-The-Water	The Old Manse	01451 820082
Bridport	The Manor Hotel	01308 897616
Brixham	Ye Olde Churston Court Inn	01803 842186
Broadway	The Broadway Hotel	01386 852401
Burford	Cotswold Gateway Hotel	01993 822695
Burford	The Lamb Inn	01993 823155
Burnham Market	The Hoste Arms Hotel	01328 738777
Burnley	Fence Gate Inn	01282 618101
Burnsall	The Red Lion	01756 720204
Burton Upon Trent	The Old Vicarage Restaurant	01283 533222
Burton Upon Trent	Boar's Head Hotel	01283 820344
Calver, nr Bakewell	The Chequers Inn	01433 630231
Camborne	Tyacks Hotel	01209 612424
Cambridge	Panos Hotel & Restaurant	01223 212958
Carlisle	The Tarn End House Hotel	016977 2340
Castle Ashby	The Falcon Hotel	01604 696200
Castle Combe	The Castle Inn	01249 783030
Castle Donington	Donington Manor Hotel	01332 810253
Cheltenham	Kingshead House Restaurant	01452 862299
Chester	The Swan Hotel	01829 733838
Chester	Wild Boar Hotel & Restaurant	01829 260309
Chipping Campden	The Noel Arms	01386 840317
Cirencester	The New Inn	01285 750651
Cirencester	The Masons Arms	01285 850164
Clavering	The Cricketers	01799 550442
Cleobury Mortimer	Crown At Hopton	01299 270372
Cleobury Mortimer	The Redfern Hotel	01299 270 395
Clovelly	New Inn Hotel	01237 431303
Colchester	The Red Lion Hotel	01206 577986
Crowborough	Winston Manor	01892 652772
Dartmouth	The Victoria Hotel	01803 832572
Dorchester-On-Thames	The George Hotel	01865 340404
Dulverton	The Anchor Country Inn & Hotel	01398 323433
East Grinstead	The Woodcock Inn & Restaurant	01342 325859
East Witton	The Blue Lion	01969 624273
Eccleshall	The George Hotel	01785 850300
Egton	The Wheatsheaf Inn	01947 895271
Eton/Windsor	The Christopher Hotel	01753 811677 / 852359

Evesham	Riverside Restaurant And Hotel	01386 446200
Exmoor	The Royal Oak Inn	01643 831506/7
Eyam	The Bulls Head Inn	01433 630873
Falmouth	Trengilly Wartha Country Inn & Restaurant	01326 340332
Fordingbridge	The Woodfalls Inn	01725 513222
Fulbeck	Hare & Hounds	01400 272090
Goathland	Mallyan Spout Hotel	01947 896486
Godalming	Inn On The Lake	01483 415575
Goring-On-Thames	The Leatherne Bottel Riverside Inn	01491 872667
Grimsthorpe	The Black Horse Inn	01778 591247
Grindleford	The Maynard Arms	01433 630321
Halifax/Huddersfield	The Rock Inn Hotel	01422 379721
Handcross	The Chequers At Slaugham	01444 400239/400996
Harrogate	The Low Hall Hotel	01423 508598
Harrogate	The Boar's Head Hotel	01423 771888
Hatherleigh	The George Hotel	01837 810454
Hathersage	The Plough Inn	01433 650319
Haworth	Old White Lion Hotel	01535 642313
Hay-On-Wye	Rhydspence Inn	01497 831262
Hayfield	The Waltzing Weasel	01663 743402
Helmsley	The Feathers Hotel	01439 770275
Helmsley	The Feversham Arms Hotel	01439 770766
Henley	The Fox Country Hotel	01491 638289
Hinkley	Barnacles Restaurant	01455 633220
Honiton	Home Farm Hotel	01404 831278
Kirkby Lonsdale	Whoop Hall Inn	015242 71284
Knutsford	Longview Hotel And Restaurant	01565 632119
Ledbury	Feathers Hotel	01531 635266
Leek	The Three Horseshoes Inn & Restaurant	01538 300296
Leominster	Wheelbarrow Castle	01568 612219
Long Melford	The Countrymen	01787 312356
Ludlow	The Roebuck	01584 711230
Lynmouth	The Rising Sun	01598 753223
Maidenhead	Boulters Lock Hotel	01628 21291
Maidstone	Ringlestone Inn	01622 859900
Maidstone	The Harrow At Warren Street	01622 858727
Malmesbury	The Horse And Groom Inn	01666 823904
Mells nr Bath	The Talbot Inn at Mells	01373 812254
Milton Keynes	The Different Drummer	01908 564733
Minchinhampton	The Ragged Cot	01453 884643/731333
Montacute	The King's Arms Inn & Restaurant	01935 822513
Moretonhampstead	The White Hart Hotel	01647 440406
Newark	The Willow Tree	01636 626613
Newbury	The Swan Hotel	01635 298314
Newby Bridge	The Swan Hotel	015395 31681
Norwich	The Garden House Hotel	01603 720007
Nottingham	Hotel Des Clos	01159 866566
Oakham	The Whipper-In Hotel	01572 756971
Onneley	The Wheatsheaf Inn At Onneley	01782 751581
Oxford	Holcombe Hotel	01869 338274
Oxford	The Jersey Arms	01869 343234
Oxford	The Mill & Old Swan	01993 774441
Oxford	The Talkhouse	01865 351648
Padstow	The Old Custom House Hotel	01841 532359
Pelynt,nr Looe	Jubilee Inn	01503 220312
Petworth	Badgers	01798 342651
Petworth	White Horse Inn	01798 869 221
Pickering	The White Swan	01751 472288
Port Gaverne	The Port Gaverne Hotel	01208 880244
Porthleven	The Harbour Inn	01326 573876
Preston	Ye Horn's Inn	01772 865230
Reepham	The Old Brewery House Hotel	01603 870881
Rugby	The Golden Lion Inn of Easenhall	01788 832265
Saddleworth	The Old Bell Inn Hotel	01457 870130
Settle	The New Inn Hotel	015242 51203
Sevenoaks	The Royal Oak	01732 451109
Shaftesbury	The Coppleridge Inn	01747 851980
Sherborne	Walnut Tree	01935 851292
Shipton Under Wychwood	The Shaven Crown Hotel	01993 830330
Shipton-Under-Wychwood	The Lamb Inn	01993 830465
Shrewsbury	The Nesscliffe	01743 741430
Southport	Tree Tops Country House Restaurant	01704 879651
St Mawes	The Rising Sun	01326 270233
Stafford	The Dower House	01889 270707
Stow-On-The-Wold	The Royalist Hotel	01451 830670
Stow-On-The-Wold	The Kings Head Inn & Restaurant	01608 658365
Stow-on-the-Wold	The Horse and Groom	01451 830584
Stratford-upon-Avon	The Coach House Hotel	01789 204109 / 299468
Telford	The Hundred House Hotel	01952 730353
Thelbridge	Thelbridge Cross Inn	01884 860316
Thornham	The Lifeboat Inn	01485 512236
Thorpe Market	Green Farm Restaurant And Hotel	01263 833602
Tintagel	The Port William	01840 770230
Torbryan Nr Totnes	The Old Church House Inn	01803 812372
Torquay	The Barn Owl Inn	01803 872130
Totnes	The Sea Trout Inn	01803 762274
Troutbeck	The Mortal Man Hotel	015394 33193
Tunbridge Wells	The Royal Wells Inn	01892 511188
Upton-Upon-Severn	The White Lion Hotel	01684 592551
Weobley	Ye Olde Salutation Inn	01544 318443
West Witton	The Wensleydale Heifer Inn	01969 622322
Whitewell	The Inn At Whitewell	01200 448222
Worcester	The Talbot	01886 821235
Worcester	The Old Schoolhouse	01905 371368
Worthing	The Old Tollgate Restaurant And Hotel	01903 879494
Wroxham	The Barton Angler Country Inn	01692 630740
Yattendon	The Royal Oak Hotel	01635 201325
York	The George at Easingwold	01347 821698
York	The Jefferson Arms	01904 448316

Wales

Chepstow	The Castle View Hotel	01291 620349
Llanarmon Dyffryn Ceiriog	The West Arms Hotel	01691 600665
Llandeilo	The Plough Inn	01558 823431
Ruthin	Ye Olde Anchor Inn	01824 702813
Welshpool	The Royal Oak Hotel & Restaurant	01938 552217
Welshpool	The Lion Hotel And Restaurant	01686 640452

Scotland

Banchory	Potarch Hotel	013398 84339
Blair Atholl	The Loft Restaurant	01796 481377
Blairgowrie	The Glenisla Hotel	01575 582223
Isle Of Skye	Hotel Eilean Iarmain or Isle Ornsay Hotel	01471 833332
Isle Of Skye	Uig Hotel	01470 542205
Moffatt	Annandale Arms Hotel	01683 220013
Pitlochry	The Moulin Hotel	01796 472196
Powmill	Whinsmuir Country Inn	01577 840595

Ireland

Crawfordsburn, N. Ireland	The Old Inn, Crawfordsburn	01247 853255

Channel Islands

Jersey	The Moorings Hotel	01534 853633
Jersey	Sea Crest Hotel And Restaurant	01534 46353

Country Houses & Small Hotels

England

Alcester	Arrow Mill Hotel And Restaurant	01789 762419
Alston	Lovelady Shield Country House Hotel	01434 381203
Appleton-Le-Moors	Appleton Hall	01751 417227
Arundel	Burpham Country House Hotel	01903 882160
Ashbourne	The Beeches Farmhouse	01889 590288
Ashbourne	Porch Farmhouse	01538 304545
Ashwater	Blagdon Manor Country Hotel	01409 211224
Atherstone	Chapel House	01827 718949
Bakewell	East Lodge Country House Hotel	01629 734474
Bakewell	The Peacock Hotel at Rowsley	01629 733518
Bamburgh	Waren House Hotel	01668 214581
Barwick Village	Little Barwick House	01935 423902
Bath	Apsley House	01225 336966
Bath	Bloomfield House	01225 420105
Bath	Eagle House	01225 859946
Bath	Oldfields	01225 317984
Bath	Paradise House	01225 317723
Bath	Widbrook Grange	01225 864750 / 863173
Bath	Bath Lodge Hotel	01225 723040
Bath	Woolverton House	01373 830415
Belper	Dannah Farm Country Guest House	01773 550273 / 630
Bibury	Bibury Court	01285 740337
Bideford	Yeoldon House Hotel	01237 474400
Biggin-By-Hartington	Biggin Hall	01298 84451
Blackpool	Mains Hall Hotel & Brasserie	01253 885130
Blockley	Lower Brook House	01386 700286
Bolton	Quarlton Manor Farm	01204 852277
Bonchurch	Peacock Vane Hotel	01983 852019
Bournemouth	Langtry Manor	01202 553887
Bourton-On-The-Water	Dial House Hotel	01451 822244
Bridgnorth	Cross Lane House Hotel	01746 764887
Bristol	Chelwood House	01761 490730
Broadway	The Old Rectory	01386 853729
Brockenhurst	Thatched Cottage Hotel & Restaurant	01590 623090
Brockenhurst	Whitley Ridge & Country House Hotel	01590 622354
Cambridge	Melbourn Bury	01763 261151
Canterbury	The Garden Hotel	01227 751411
Carlisle	Number Thirty One	01228 597080
Carlisle	Crosby Lodge Country House Hotel	01228 573618
Cartmel	Aynsome Manor Hotel	015395 36653
Chagford	Easton Court Hotel	01647 433469
Cheddar	The Oak House Hotel	01934 732444
Cheltenham	Charlton Kings Hotel	01242 231061
Cheltenham	Halewell	01242 890238
Chichester	Crouchers Bottom	01243 784995
Chichester	Crouchers Bottom	01243 784995
Chichester	Woodstock House Hotel	01243 811666
Chippenham	Stanton Manor	01666 837552
Chipping Campden	The Malt House	01386 840295
Clearwell	Tudor Farmhouse Hotel & Restaurant	01594 833046
Coalville	Abbots Oak	01530 832 328
Colchester	Hockley Place	01206 251703
Combe Martin	Ashelford	01271 850469
Crediton	Coombe House Country Hotel	01363 84487
Dartmoor	Prince Hall Hotel	01822 890403
Dedham Vale	Gladwins Farm	01206 262261
Diss	Salisbury House	01379 644738
Dorchester	Yalbury Cottage Hotel	01305 262382
Dover	The Woodville Hall	01304 825256
Dover	Wallett's Court	01304 852424
Dronfield	Manor House Hotel & Restaurant	01246 413971
Dulverton	Ashwick Country House Hotel	01398 323868
Dunster	The Exmoor House Hotel	01643 821268
Enfield	Oak Lodge Hotel	0181 360 7082
Evesham	The Mill At Harvington	01386 870688
Exeter	The Lord Haldon Hotel	01392 832483
Exford	The Crown Hotel	01643 831554/5
Fakenham	Vere Lodge	01328 838261
Falmouth	Trelawne Hotel-The Hutches Restaurant	01326 250226
Fenny Drayton	White Wings	01827 716100
Fressingfield	Chippenhall Hall	01379 588180 / 586733
Gatwick	Stanhill Court Hotel	01293 862166
Glossop	The Wind In The Willows	01457 868001
Golant by Fowey	The Cormorant Hotel	01726 833426
Grasmere	White Moss House	015394 35295
Great Snoring	The Old Rectory	01328 820597
Hadleigh	The Old Rectory	01449 740745
Hampton Court	Chase Lodge	0181 943 1862
Hamsterley Forest	Grove House	01388 488203
Harrogate	The White House	01423 501388
Hawes	Simonstone Hall	01969 667255
Hawes	Rookhurst Georgian Country House Hotel	01969 667454
Haytor	Bel Alp House	01364 661217
Helford River	Tregildry Hotel	01326 231378
Helston	Nansloe Manor	01326 574691
Hereford	The Bowens Country House	01432 860430
Hereford	The Steppes	01432 820424
Honiton	The Belfry Country Hotel	01404 861234
Hope	Underleigh House	01433 621372
Keswick	Dale Head Hall Lakeside Hotel	017687 72478
Keswick	Swinside Lodge Hotel	017687 72948
Keswick-On-Derwentwater	Grange Country House Hotel	017687 72500
Kingsbridge	The White House	01548 580580
Kirkby Lonsdale	Hipping Hall	015242 71187
Lavenham	Lavenham Priory	01787 247404
Leominster	Lower Bache	01568 750304
Lifton	The Thatched Cottage Country Hotel	01566 784224
Lincoln	D'Isney Place Hotel	01522 538881
Lincoln	Washingborough Hall	01522 790340
Looe	Allhays Country House	01503 272434
Looe	Coombe Farm	01503 240223
Ludlow	Delbury Hall	01584 841267
Ludlow	Overton Grange Hotel	01584 873500
Luton	Little Offley	01462 768243
Lydford	Moor View House	01822 820220
Lyme Regis	Thatch Lodge Hotel	01297 560407
Lymington	The Gordleton Mill Hotel	01590 682219
Lynton	Hewitt's Hotel	01598 752293
Maidstone	Tanyard	01622 744705
Malton	Newstead Grange	01653 692502
Matlock	The Manor Farmhouse	01609 534246
Middlecombe	Periton Park Hotel	01643 706885
Middleham	Millers House Hotel	01969 622630
Midsomer Norton	The Old Priory	01761 416784
Minchinhampton	Burleigh Court	01453 883804
Minehead	Channel House Hotel	01643 703229
Minehead	The Beacon Country House Hotel	01643 703476
Morchard Bishop	Wigham	01363 877350
New Romney	Romney Bay House	01797 364747
North Walsham	Beechwood Hotel	01692 403231
North Walsham	Elderton Lodge Hotel & Restaurant	01263 833547
Norwich	The Beeches Hotel & Victorian Gardens	01603 621167
Norwich	Norfolk Mead Hotel	01603 737531
Norwich	The Stower Grange	01603 860210
Norwich	The Moat House	01508 570149
Norwich	Catton Old Hall	01603 419379
Norwich	The Old Rectory	01603 700772
Nottingham	The Cottage Country House Hotel	01159 846882
Oswestry	Pen-y-Dyffryn Country Hotel	01691 653700
Oulton Broad	Ivy House Farm	01502 501353
Owlpen	Owlpen Manor	01453 860261
Oxford	Fallowfields	01865 820416
Peterborough	Midstone House	01780 740136
Porlock Weir	The Cottage Hotel	01643 863300
Porthleven	Tye Rock Hotel	01326 572695
Portsmouth	The Beaufort Hotel	01705 823707
Pulborough	Chequers Hotel	01798 872486
Redditch	The Old Rectory	01527 523000
Ross-On-Wye	Glewstone Court	01989 770367
Rye	White Vine House	01797 224748
Saham Toney	Broom Hall	01953 882125
Saunton	Preston House Hotel	01271 890472
Seavington St Mary	The Pheasant Hotel	01460 240502

Location	Hotel	Telephone
Sedgeford	The Sedgeford Estate	01485 572855
Sheffield	Staindrop Lodge	0114 284 6727
Sherborne	The Eastbury Hotel	01935 813131
Shipton Under Wychwood	The Shaven Crown Hotel	01993 830330
Simonsbath	Simonsbath House Hotel	01643 831259
South Molton	Marsh Hall Country House Hotel	01769 572666
St. Ives	Olivers Lodge Hotel & Restaurant	01480 463252
St Ives	The Countryman At Trink Hotel	01736 797571
St Mawes	The Hundred House Hotel	01872 501336
Stamford	The Priory	01780 720215
Stamford	The Old Mill	01780 740815
Staverton	Kingston House	01803 762 235
Stevenage	Redcoats Farmhouse Hotel & Restaurant	01438 729500
Stonor	The Stonor Arms	01491 638345
Stow-On-The-Wold	Conygree Gate Hotel	01608 658389
Stratford-upon-Avon	Glebe Farm House	01789 842501
Sudbury	Tarantella Hotel & Restaurant	01787 378879
Sutton Coldfield	Marston Farm Country Hotel	01827 872133
Taunton	Langford Manor	01460 281674
Taunton	Higher Vexford House	01984 656267
Tewkesbury	Upper Court	01386 725351
Tintagel	Trebrea Lodge	01840 770410
Titchwell	Titchwell Manor Hotel	01485 210221
Truro	The Royal Hotel	01872 270345
Uckfield	Hooke Hall	01825 761578
Venn Ottery	Venn Ottery Barton	01404 812733
Wareham	Kemps Country House Hotel & Restaurant	01929 462563
Warwick	The Ardencote Manor Hotel	01926 843111
Wells	Beryl	01749 678738
Wells	Glencot House	01749 677160
Whitby	Dunsley Hall	01947 893437
Wimborne Minster	Beechleas	01202 841684
Wincanton	Holbrook House Hotel	01963 32377
Winchelsea	The Country House At Winchelsea	01797 226669
Windermere	Braemount House Hotel	015394 45967
Windermere	Quarry Garth Country House Hotel	015394 88282
Windermere	Fayrer Garden House Hotel	015394 88195
Woodbridge	Wood Hall Hotel & Country Club	01394 411283
York	The Parsonage Country House Hotel	01904 728111
Yoxford	Hope House	01728 668281

Wales

Location	Hotel	Telephone
Aberdovey	Plas Penhelig Country House Hotel	01654 767676
Abergavenny	Glangrwyney Court	01873 811288
Abergavenny	Llanwenarth House	01873 830289
Abergavenny	Penyclawdd Court	01873 890719
Betws-y-Coed	Tan-y-Foel	01690 710507
Brecon	Old Gwernyfed Country Manor	01497 847376
Caernarfon	Ty'n Rhos Country House	01248 670489
Cardigan	The Pembrokeshire Retreat	01239 841387
Conwy	Berthlwyd Hall Hotel	01492 592409
Conwy	The Old Rectory	01492 580611
Dolgellau	Dolmelynllyn Hall	01341 440273
Harlech	Aber Artro Hall	01341 241374
Tenby	Waterwynch House Hotel	01834 842464
Tintern	Parva Farmhouse and Restaurant	01291 689411

Scotland

Location	Hotel	Telephone
Ballater, Royal Deeside	Balgonie Country House	013397 55482
Blairlogie	Blairlogie House	01259 761441
Dalbeattie	Auchenskeoch Lodge	01387 780277
Dalbeattie	Broomlands House	01556 611463
Dingwall	Kinkell House	01349 861270
Drumnadrochit	Polmaily House Hotel	01456 450343
Edinburgh	No 22 Murrayfield Gardens	0131 337 3569
Fife	Chapel House	01337 831790
Fintry	Culcreuch Castle Hotel	01360 860555
Fort William	Ashburn House	01397 706000
Glasgow	Chapeltoun House	015604 82696
Grantown-on-Spey	Ardconnel House	01479 872104
Huntly	The Old Manse of Marnoch	01466 780873
Inverness	Culduthel Lodge	01463 240089
Isle Of Harris	Ardvourlie Castle	01859 502307
Isle Of Mull	Killiechronan	01680 300403
Kentallen Of Appin	Ardsheal House	01631 740227
Killiecrankie, By Pitlochry	The Killiecrankie Hotel	01796 473220
Kinlochbervie	The Kinlochbervie Hotel	01971 521275
Kinross	Nivingston House	01577 850216
Moffat	Well View Hotel	01683 220184
Nairn	Boath House	01667 454896
Oban	Dungallen House Hotel	01631 563799
Oban	The Manor House Hotel	01631 562087
Old Meldrum	Meldrum House	01651 872294
Perth	Dupplin Castle	01738 623224
Perth	Newmiln Country House	01738 552364
Pitlochry	Dunfallandy House	01796 472648
Port Appin	Druimneil	01631 730228
Port Of Menteith	The Lake Hotel	01877 385258
Strathtummel	Queen's View Hotel	01796 473291
Tongue	Borgie Lodge Hotel	01641 521332

Ireland

Location	Hotel	Telephone
Annalong	Glassdrumman Lodge Country House	013967 68451
Caragh Lake	Caragh Lodge	00 353 66 69115
Carragh Lake	Ard na Sihde	00 353 66 69105
Cashel	Cashel Palace Hotel	00 353 62 62707
Dublin	Aberdeen Lodge	00 353 1 2838155
Kilkee	Halpins Hotel & Vittles Restaurant	00 353 65 56032
Killarney	Earls Court House	00 353 64 34009
Letterkenny	Castle Grove Country House	010 353 745 1118
Portaferry, N. Ireland	Portaferry Hotel	012477 28231
Riverstown	Coopershill House	00 353 71 65108
Skibbereen	Liss Ard Lake Lodge	00 353 28 22365
Sligo	Markree Castle	00 353 71 67800
Wicklow	The Old Rectory	00 353 404 67048

Channel Islands

Location	Hotel	Telephone
Guernsey	Hotel Hougue Du Pommier	01481 56531
Guernsey	La Favorita Hotel	01481 35666
Guernsey	Bella Luce Hotel & Restaurant	01481 38764
Jersey	Hotel La Tour	01534 43770

Hotels & Inns North America

Canada

Location	Hotel	Telephone
British Columbia (Victoria)	Dashwood Manor	1 250 383 1763
Ontario (Jackson's Point)	The Briars	1 905 722 3271

Carribbean

Location	Hotel	Telephone
Caribbean (Antigua)	Star Clippers	01473 292200
Caribbean (Bermuda)	Lantana	1 441 234 0141
Caribbean (Bermuda)	The Newstead Hotel	1 441 236 6060
Caribbean (Bermuda)	Surf Side Beach Club	1 441 236 7100
Carribean (St Vincent)	Petit St Vincent Resort	1 809 458 8801

United States of America

Location	Hotel	Telephone
Arizona (Sedona)	Canyon Villa Inn	1 520 284 1226
Arizona (Tucson)	Tanque Verde Ranch	1 520 296 6275
California (Eureka)	Carter House	1 800 404 1390
California (Healdsburg)	Madrona Manor	1 707 433 4231
California (Hollywood)	Château Marmont	1 213 656 1010
California (Hopland)	Thatcher Inn	1 707 744 1890
California (Mill Valley)	Mountain Home Inn	1 415 381 9000
California (Muir Beach)	Pelican Inn	1 415 383 6000
California (Nevada City)	Red Castle Inn Historic Lodging	1 916 265 5135
California (Pacific Grove)	The Martine Inn	1 408 373 3388
California (Sacramento)	The Sterling Hotel	1 916 448 1300
California (San Francisco)	Nob Hill Lambourne	1 415 433 2287
California (Yosemite National Park)	Château du Sureau	1 209 683 6860
Connecticut (Mystic)	Steamboat Inn	1 860 536 8300
Connecticut (New Preston)	The Boulders	1 860 868 0541
Connecticut (Old Saybrook)	Saybrook Point Inn & Spa	1 860 395 2000
Connecticut (Washington)	The Mayflower Inn	1 860 868 9466
Florida (Key West)	The Marquesa	1 305 292 1919
Florida (Lake Wales)	Chalet Suzanne	1 941 676 6011
Florida (Miami Beach)	The Richmond	1 305 538 2331
Georgia (Macon)	1842 Inn	1 912 741 1842
Georgia (Savannah)	Foley House Inn	1 912 232 6622
Georgia (Savannah)	The Gastonian	1 912 232 2869
Georgia (Savannah)	The Jesse Mount House	1 912 236 1774
Georgia (St. Simons Island)	Little St Simons Island	1 912 638 7472
Illinois (Chicago)	The Whitehall Hotel	1 312 944 6300
Indiana (Indianapolis)	Canterbury Hotel	1 317 634 3000
Louisiana (Napoleonville)	Madewood Plantation House	1 504 369 7151
Maine (Bar Harbor)	Breakwater 1904	1 207 288 2313
Maine (Cape Elizabeth)	Inn By The Sea	1 207 799 3134
Maine (Greenville)	The Lodge at Moosehead Lake	1 207 695 4400
Maine (Kennebunkport)	Old Fort Inn	1 207 967 5353
Maine (Prouts Neck)	Black Point Inn Resort	1 207 883 4126
Maryland (St Michaels)	The Inn at Perry Cabin	1 410 745 2200
Maryland (Taneytown)	Antrim 1844	1 410 756 6812
Massachusetts (Boston)	The Eliot	1 617 267 1607
Massachusetts (Cambridge)	A Cambridge House	1 617 491 6300
Massachusetts (Cape Cod)	Wedgewood Inn	1 508 362 5157
Massachusetts (Chatham)	The Captain's House Inn	1 508 945 0127
Massachusetts (Chatham)	Pleasant Bay Village Resort	1 508 945 1133
Massachusetts (Deerfield)	Deerfield Inn	1 413 774 5587
Massachusetts (Eastham)	The Whalewalk Inn	1 508 255 0617
Massachusetts (Lenox)	Wheatleigh	1 413 637 0610
Massachusetts (Stockbridge)	The Inn At Stockbridge	1 413 298 3337
Michigan (Petoskey)	Staffords Perry Hotel	1 616 347 4000
Mississippi (Natchez)	Monmouth Plantation	1 601 442 5852
New Hampshire (Jackson)	Inn at Thorn Hill	1 603 383 4243
New York (Dover Plains)	Old Drovers Inn	1 914 832 9311
New York (Ithaca)	The Rose Inn	1 607 533 7905
New York (New York)	The Kitano New York	1 212 885 7000
New York (New York)	The Lowell	1 212 838 1400
New York (New York)	The Peninsula New York	1 212 247 2200
North Carolina (Lake Toxaway)	The Greystone Inn	1 704 966 4700
North Carolina (Pittsboro)	The Fearrington House	1 919 542 2121
North Carolina (Waynesville)	The Swag Country Inn	1 704 926 0430
Pennsylvania (Farmington)	Nemacolin Woodlands Resort & Spa	1 412 329 6195
Pennsylvania (South Sterling)	The French Manor	1 717 676 3311
Rhode Island (Newport)	Cliffside Inn	1 401 847 1811
South Carolina (Summerville)	Woodlands Resort & Inn	1 803 875 2600
Vermont (Barnard)	Twin Farms	1 802 234 9999
Vermont (Chittenden)	Mountain Top Inn & Resort	1 802 483 2311
Vermont (Goshen)	Blueberry Hill	1 802 247 6735
Vermont (Manchester Village)	1811 House	1 802 362 1811
Vermont (Shelburne)	The Inn at Shelburne Farms	1 802 985 8498
Vermont (Stowe)	The Mountain Road Resort	1 802 253 4566
Vermont (West Townshend)	Windham Hill Inn	1 802 874 4080
Virginia (Alexandria)	Morrison House	1 703 838 8000
Virginia (Keswick)	Keswick Hall	1 804 979 3440
Virginia (Paris)	The Ashby Inn & Restaurant	1 540 592 3900
Virginia (White Post)	L'Auberge Provençale	1 540 837 1375
Washington (Orcas Island)	Turtleback Farm Inn	1 360 376 4914
Washington (Seattle)	Inn at the Market	1 206 443 3600
Washington (Seattle)	Sorrento Hotel	1 206 622 6400
Washington (Winthrop)	Sun Mountain Lodge	1 509 996 2211
Wyoming (Jackson Hole)	The Alpenhof Lodge	1 307 733 3242

Hotels in Europe accepting Johansens Privilege Card

Guest Survey Report

Your own Johansens 'inspection' gives reliability to our guides and assists in the selection of Award Nominations

Name/location of hotel: ______________________ Page No: __________

Date of visit: ______________________

Name & address of guest: ______________________

______________________ Postcode: __________

Please tick one box in each category below:	Excellent	Good	Disappointing	Poor
Bedrooms				
Public Rooms				
Restaurant/Cuisine				
Service				
Welcome/Friendliness				
Value For Money				

PLEASE return your Guest Survey Report form!

Occasionally we may allow other reputable organisations to write with offers which may be of interest.
If you prefer not to here from them, tick this box ☐

To: Johansens, FREEPOST (CB264), 175-179 St John Street, London EC1B 1JQ

Guest Survey Report

Your own Johansens 'inspection' gives reliability to our guides and assists in the selection of Award Nominations

Name/location of hotel: ______________________ Page No: __________

Date of visit: ______________________

Name & address of guest: ______________________

______________________ Postcode: __________

Please tick one box in each category below:	Excellent	Good	Disappointing	Poor
Bedrooms				
Public Rooms				
Restaurant/Cuisine				
Service				
Welcome/Friendliness				
Value For Money				

PLEASE return your Guest Survey Report form!

Occasionally we may allow other reputable organisations to write with offers which may be of interest.
If you prefer not to here from them, tick this box ☐

To: Johansens, FREEPOST (CB264), 175-179 St John Street, London EC1B 1JQ

Order Coupon

To order Johansens guides, simply indicate which publications you require by putting the quantity(ies) in the boxes provided. Choose you preferred method of payment and return this coupon (NO STAMP REQUIRED). You may also place your order using FREEPHONE +44 990 269397 or by fax on +44 171 251 6113.

❏ I enclose a cheque for £______________ payable to Johansens.

❏ I enclose my order on company letterheading, please invoice me. (UK companies only)

❏ Please debit my credit/charge card account (please tick)

❏ MASTERCARD ❏ VISA ❏ DINERS ❏ AMEX ❏ SWITCH

Switch Issue Number

Card No

Signature ______________________ Expiry Date ________________

Name (Mr/Mrs/Miss) ______________________________

Address ______________________________

______________________ Postcode ________________

(We aim to despatch your order within 10 days, but please allow 28 days for delivery)

Post free to: Johansens, FREEPOST (CB264), 43Millharbour, London E14 9BR

Occasionally we may allow reputable organisations to write to you with offers which may interest you. If you prefer not to hear from them, tick this box ❏

save £10

	PRICE	QTY	TOTAL
The Collection of 4 Johansens Guides *+ Recommended Hotels & Inns – North America FREE* ~~£53.80~~	£43.80		
The Collection in a Presentation Boxed Set ~~£58.80~~ *+ Recommended Hotels & Inns – N. America FREE*	£48.80		
The 2 CD ROMS ~~£49.90~~	£39.00		
Recommended Hotels – Great Britain & Ireland 1998	£18.95		
Recommended Country Houses and Small Hotels – GB & Ireland 1998	£10.95		
Recommended Inns with Restaurants – GB & Ireland 1998	£9.95		
Recommended Hotels – Europe 1998	£13.95		
Recommended Hotels – North America 1998	£9.95		
Historic Houses Castles & Gardens, Published and mailed to you in March 1998	£6.95		
CD ROM – Hotels, Country Houses & Inns Great Britain & Ireland 1998 with Historic Houses Castles & Gardens	£29.95		
CD ROM – Recommended Hotels & Inns N. America and Recommended Hotels Europe 1998	£19.95		
1998 Privilege Card – *10% discount, room upgrade when available. VIP Service at participating establishments*			FREE
The Independent Traveller – *Johansens newsletter including many special offers*			FREE
Postage & Packing *UK: £4 – or £2 for single orders and CD-Roms Outside UK: Add £5 – or £3 for single orders and CD-Roms*			
	TOTAL	**£**	

CALL THE JOHANSENS CREDIT CARD ORDER SERVICE FREE ☎+44 990 269397

PRICES VALID UNTIL 31/08/98 **2J5**

Order Coupon

To order Johansens guides, simply indicate which publications you require by putting the quantity(ies) in the boxes provided. Choose you preferred method of payment and return this coupon (NO STAMP REQUIRED). You may also place your order using FREEPHONE +44 990 269397 or by fax on +44 171 251 6113.

❏ I enclose a cheque for £______________ payable to Johansens.

❏ I enclose my order on company letterheading, please invoice me. (UK companies only)

❏ Please debit my credit/charge card account (please tick)

❏ MASTERCARD ❏ VISA ❏ DINERS ❏ AMEX ❏ SWITCH

Switch Issue Number

Card No

Signature ______________________ Expiry Date ________________

Name (Mr/Mrs/Miss) ______________________________

Address ______________________________

______________________ Postcode ________________

(We aim to despatch your order within 10 days, but please allow 28 days for delivery)

Post free to: Johansens, FREEPOST (CB264), 43Millharbour, London E14 9BR

Occasionally we may allow reputable organisations to write to you with offers which may interest you. If you prefer not to hear from them, tick this box ❏

save £10

	PRICE	QTY	TOTAL
The Collection of 4 Johansens Guides *+ Recommended Hotels & Inns – North America FREE* ~~£53.80~~	£43.80		
The Collection in a Presentation Boxed Set ~~£58.80~~ *+ Recommended Hotels & Inns – N. America FREE*	£48.80		
The 2 CD ROMS ~~£49.90~~	£39.00		
Recommended Hotels – Great Britain & Ireland 1998	£18.95		
Recommended Country Houses and Small Hotels – GB & Ireland 1998	£10.95		
Recommended Inns with Restaurants – GB & Ireland 1998	£9.95		
Recommended Hotels – Europe 1998	£13.95		
Recommended Hotels – North America 1998	£9.95		
Historic Houses Castles & Gardens, Published and mailed to you in March 1998	£6.95		
CD ROM – Hotels, Country Houses & Inns Great Britain & Ireland 1998 with Historic Houses Castles & Gardens	£29.95		
CD ROM – Recommended Hotels & Inns N. America and Recommended Hotels Europe 1998	£19.95		
1998 Privilege Card – *10% discount, room upgrade when available. VIP Service at participating establishments*			FREE
The Independent Traveller – *Johansens newsletter including many special offers*			FREE
Postage & Packing *UK: £4 – or £2 for single orders and CD-Roms Outside UK: Add £5 – or £3 for single orders and CD-Roms*			
	TOTAL	**£**	

CALL THE JOHANSENS CREDIT CARD ORDER SERVICE FREE ☎+44 990 269397

PRICES VALID UNTIL 31/08/98 **2J5**